The One God, the Father, One Man Messiah Translation

New Testament with Commentary

SECOND EDITION

Sir Anthony F. Buzzard, MA (Oxon.), MATh, A.R.C.M., Hon. PhD

Restoration Fellowship
www.restorationfellowship.org
www.onegodtranslation.com

First edition published 2015. Second edition 2020.
ISBN: 978-0-578-71607-7

Table of Contents

On the cover: A scene from our garden. Cover design by Alexander Dávila.

Introduction

"The deity of Jesus is *inherently* unJewish. The witness of Jewish texts is unvarying: belief that a second being is God involves departure from the Jewish community."[1]

"According to the New Testament witnesses, in the teaching of Jesus and the Apostles, relative to the monotheism of the Old Testament and Judaism, there had been no element of change whatsoever. Mark 12:29 recorded the confirmation by Jesus himself, without any reservation, of the supreme monotheistic confession of faith of Israelite religion in its complete form."[2]

Born and bred as a member of the Church of England (Anglican), I attended church with family, and at boarding school, dutifully every Sunday. The hymns were beautiful, the buildings many centuries old, the list of clergy dating back for half a millennium. The ten-minute homily on Sunday came very far short of giving us a biblical education. At 20 years old, I went to Oxford to gain a suitable qualification in modern languages (German and French). It was at that time that I was invited to attend an evangelical "get saved" meeting. I was curious to know what that "acceptance of Jesus in my heart" meant. This event brought me to my first serious investigation of Scripture, where I found in Jesus' Gospel of the Kingdom the irrepressible hope and promise that Jesus, in addition to having died for the sins of the world, will, at his spectacular return, bring about the worldwide peace which has so obviously not been produced by current political effort.

Some 60 years after my first engagement with the Bible, after a degree in theology, and a career as teacher of the Bible and its languages in a small Bible college, I have gained the strong impression (as have many others) that the Jesus of history and his impassioned proclaiming of the Gospel of the Kingdom were unknown to us in those Church of

[1]Maurice Casey, *From Jewish Prophet to Gentile God*, Westminster/John Knox Press, 1992, p. 176.
[2]Dr. Martin Werner, *Formation of Christian Dogma*, Harper and Brothers, 1957, p. 241.

England days. The biblical plot and story had been drastically distorted. Perhaps not surprisingly, church-going is now reduced to a tiny handful of my fellow Englishmen. It appears that what we got of "Bible" was heavily filtered through a mass of alien tradition. We were allowed only a severely censored version of Scripture.

Concluding that Jesus was a Jew and a claimant to Messiahship, and believing that his claims were and will be entirely vindicated, I have attempted to read the New Testament in its very Jewish, Messianic context. I soon noted, by reading widely, that scholars of all stripes fully admit that the Jesus of actual history and of "Church" are often poles apart. In some cases those experts are less than accessible or straightforward enough to register a clear complaint, much less an urgent call for reform and restoration. As watchdogs their bark has been tragically feeble. The consequences of "bucking the system" may be costly.

Dr. J.A.T. Robinson of Cambridge was fearlessly correct when he stated that "heaven is never in fact used in the Bible for the destination of the dying."[3] This powerful observation should point to the dire need for a careful examination of what we learned, uncritically, in church. The future of our blighted earth, and the promise of a state of international peace, when nations will "never again learn war" (Isa. 2:2-4), when the Sandhursts and West Points of today's system will become curio museums, at the time when the Messiah makes his spectacular return to this earth as the royal Davidic king who alone can produce peace — this is rather obviously the compelling goal of the biblical story from Genesis to Revelation. It is also the core of the Christian Gospel of the Kingdom which was preached in advance to Abraham (Gal. 3:8), who has never yet inherited the land promised to him personally, as well as to his "seed" (Acts 7:5; Heb. 11:13, 39). But he will, along with all the faithful.

The land promise, Kingdom of God promise, is the theme which drove Jesus and all the biblical writers. The vision of nations at peace I found rivetingly interesting as soon as I was exposed to Scripture. The claims of the monotheistic Jew Jesus to be the Son of Man, Son of God and the long-promised lord Messiah (Luke 2:11), the one who will eventually bring order to our chaotic world, I have found irresistible for

---

[3]J.A.T. Robinson, *In the End God*, Fontana Books, 1968, p. 104.

the past 60 years. I fear only that the appalling complications which Greek philosophically influenced Gentile church leaders imposed, from the second century onwards, on the essentially simple teachings of the Bible, have rendered intelligent reading of Scripture in its own original context almost impossible.

This translation, then, has as its premise the conviction that the Church today, in its preaching, teaching and tradition, generally gives you a strongly Greek philosophically-influenced version of the New Testament. This unfortunate departure from the original faith of Jesus and the Apostles dates from the second century AD, that is, after the canon of the New Testament closed with the book of Revelation. A full reformation and return to the beliefs of the New Testament Church did not occur in the 16th-century Reformation under Luther and Calvin.

The tragic lapse from apostolic truth leads you away from the original New Testament community's essentially simple account of the faith — "the faith handed down once for all time to the saints" (Jude 3). Voices of protest and alarm, among many, may be cited in support of our thesis:

Eberhard Griesebach wrote: "In its encounter with Greek philosophy Christianity became theology. That was the fall of Christianity."[4] Anglican Canon Goudge said: "When the Greek and Roman mind instead of the Hebrew mind came to dominate the Church, there occurred a disaster in doctrine and practice from which we have never recovered."[5] Anglican Dean Farrar was frank enough to concede that the Church has constantly made a mess of its attempt to interpret the Bible. He notes that "Holy Scripture contains everything necessary for salvation" (6th Article of the Church of England) and that "the plain teachings of Christ are the sole infallible guide." He then laments the evident failure of expositors to agree on what the Bible says. "Truly, if over the whole extent of what we call 'religion' men have an infallible guide, they have — and that to all appearance inevitably — rendered it worse than useless by fallible expositions."[6]

Then this marvelous insight from E.F. Scott, D.D.: "Christianity, in the course of the Gentile mission, had changed into another religion. The

[4]*Lecture on Christianity and Humanism*, 1938.

[5] "The Calling of the Jews," in the collected essays *Judaism and Christianity*, 1939.

[6]*The Bible, Its Meaning and Supremacy*, Longmans, Green, and Co., 1897, p. 144-145.

Church…had forgotten or refused to know what Jesus had actually taught."[7]

William Winwood Reade, British historian and philosopher, reinforces our point:

> The church diverged in discipline and dogma more and more widely from its ancient form, till in the second century the Christians of Judea, who had faithfully followed the customs and tenets of the twelve apostles, were informed that they were heretics. During that interval a new religion had arisen. Christianity had conquered paganism, and paganism had corrupted Christianity. The legends which belonged to Osiris and Apollo had been applied to the life of Jesus. The single Deity of the Jews had been exchanged for the Trinity, which the Egyptians had invented, and which Plato had idealized into a philosophic system. The man who had said, "Why do you call me good? There is none good but one, that is God" had now himself been made a god, or the third part of one.[8]

If the Bible is taken at face value within its brilliant, Jewish apocalyptic setting, "sooner or later the time will come when the simple and natural will be recognized as the true."[9]

Dr. Martin Werner's summary of the early chaos which overcame the Messianic Jesus and his teaching deserves the widest possible hearing:

> The cause of the Trinitarian-Christological problem, which so perplexed post-Apostolic Christianity, lay in the transition from the apocalyptic Messiah-Son of Man concept of the primitive Christian eschatological faith, with its sense of imminence, to the new dogma of the Divinity of Jesus. There was certainly no need nor justification…to substitute for the original concept of the Messiah, simply a Hellenistic analogy, such as that of a redeeming Divine Being…Indeed it was wholly invalid. It was a myth behind which the historical Jesus completely disappeared.[10]

---

[7]*The Kingdom of God in the New Testament*, Macmillan Co. 1931, p. 156.

[8]*The Martyrdom of Man*, 1892, p. 230.

[9]Albert Schweitzer, *Geschichte der Leben-Jesu-Forschung*, cited by Martin Werner, p.17.

[10]*The Formation of Christian Dogma*, p. 298.

J. Christiaan Beker in *Paul's Apocalyptic Gospel* points out that the shift from Jesus' and Paul's apocalyptic Gospel of the Kingdom "does indeed constitute something like a fall of Christendom." He calls this rightly "a fall from the apocalyptic world of early Christianity to Platonic categories of thought…The *surrender* of Paul's apocalyptic had indeed a tremendous impact on the history of Christian thought," producing "an alienation of Christianity from its original Jewish matrix."[11]

Translations, particularly some modern ones like the NIV (New International Version), "help" the reader to see things in the New Testament which reinforce his or her impression that later "orthodoxy" is solidly biblical. But this involves "pushing" the Greek text beyond what it actually says. This unfair process is an attempt to justify the later *departure* from the original faith. It smooths over the embarrassing difference between the original Greek Scripture of the original community of faith and what from the second century developed as a tragic departure from the biblical orthodoxy of Jesus and Paul.

The most striking example of this embarrassing difference between Jesus and the beliefs of those claiming to follow him is the unitarian creed affirmed with maximum emphasis by Jesus in discussion with a colleague Jew (Mark 12:28-34). On this critical passage of Scripture the Church has adopted an alarming posture of silence! (Often it is what we do *not* say which gives away a flaw in our thinking.)

In that marvelously instructive passage of Scripture a Jewish scholar had asked Jesus about what is the *most critically important command of all.* Jesus replied by endorsing the monumentally significant creed of Israel's heritage, the core of all true religion: "The Lord our God is one Lord" (as read from the New Testament Greek, citing the LXX, Greek version of the OT). This is a unitary monotheistic and certainly not a Trinitarian creed. "One" is a quantifier, a simple, mathematical numeral, and God is defined here, as innumerable times in the Hebrew Bible and the New Testament, as one *single* divine Lord, one Person, one divine Self, one Yahweh. He is so described by thousands of singular personal pronouns, which as we all know designate a single person. Malachi 2:10 encapsulates with delightful simplicity the totality of the Bible's view of

---

[11]J. Christiaan Beker, *Paul's Apocalyptic Gospel: The Coming Triumph of God,* Fortress Press, 1982, pp. 107-8.

God as one Person: "Do we not all have one Father? Has not one God created us?"

The importance of this point needs to be repeated: The clash between the original teachings of Jesus and what later emerged as Christianity is most starkly demonstrated by the failure of Bible readers to take with utmost seriousness Jesus' own unitarian, i.e. unitary monotheistic definition of God in Mark 12:29. In that classic passage Jesus is seen to be in total harmony with a friendly Jewish Bible scholar. In John 17:3 Jesus proposed as the key to the Life of the Age to Come (inadequately rendered in most versions as "eternal life") that we come to recognize and know the Father as "the only one who is true God" (cp. John 5:44). In John's writings the Father is equated with God nearly 150 times and in the New Testament it is obvious that "God" (often "*the* God" in the original Greek) means the Father and not Jesus. "God" means the Father about 1300 times in our New Testament.

The creed of Israel was never Trinitarian. Thus the fact that Jesus affirms and endorses the unitarian creed of Judaism ought to provide a provocative and life-changing embarrassment to today's Church, which has ceased to quote and believe the creed of Jesus. It has departed from Jesus at the most crucial level of all theological and spiritual endeavor. Thus Christianity is distinguished by the remarkable characteristic that it is the only world religion which begins by discarding its own founder's creed. Mark 12:29, and Jesus as our rabbi-teacher, not just one who provided forgiveness by dying for us, must be reinstated, if Bible study and preaching are to be honest with the Christian documents.

There are places in some modern translations which plainly depart from the Greek in order to give the impression that the later "orthodoxy" is biblically based. A classic example is in Philippians 2:5 where the Son of God is described in the NIV as "being in very nature God." But this is a horrible imposition on the text, which says not a word about Jesus *being* God. The word "nature" here is meant to encourage the notion of a "God the Son" who is of the same "essence" as the Father. But "essence" and "hypostasis" belong to a theological vocabulary of post-biblical times, when the simplicity of the pristine belief in God the Father as "the only one who is true God" (John 17:3) had been lost.

We note too that in a very subtle way the NIV does not want you to see that the Gospel (of the Kingdom) was preached equally by Jesus and

Paul. Introducing the ministry of Jesus, the NIV reports him as preaching "the Good News," while Paul is said to be preaching "the Gospel." But that distinction is absent from the original Greek and encourages a discontinuity between Jesus and Paul. Both Jesus and Paul, who followed Jesus faithfully, preached the same saving Gospel of the Kingdom. It is misleading to translate *evangelion* for Jesus' preaching as "good news" and the same word for Paul's preaching as "gospel." It points to a dangerous systematic error — that Jesus' teaching has been discarded in favor of a misunderstood "Gospel of Paul." We have failed to call Jesus "rabbi and lord" (John 13:13) when he everywhere urged us never to fall short of grasping and obeying his saving words (John 3:36; 12:44-48; cp. Heb. 5:9).

My hope is to bring into clear focus the very uncomplicated New Testament definition of God as the Father of Jesus and certainly not as triune. We want to emphasize constantly the definition of the saving Gospel as the Gospel **about the Kingdom of God**, of which Jesus was the original and authoritative preacher (Heb. 2:3; Luke 4:43; Acts 10:36). I have of course gained immensely from all of some 60 modern translations, in various languages, available on the standard software used by scholars. These translations mostly convey the sense of the Greek in varied but entirely acceptable ways. However in certain key passages they misrepresent the Greek text, in an effort to portray Jesus as God the Son, second member of an eternal Trinity.

This major objective, to define the saving Gospel as Jesus defined it, means restoring the voice and mind of Jesus to our Bible reading. At present the public never gets a clear concept of what Jesus preached as the saving Gospel. Our observation is that the "Gospel about the Kingdom," with which Jesus laid the foundation of all sound belief (Mark 1:14-15), is virtually absent from contemporary tracts, books and websites and blogs offering "salvation." The voice of Jesus, at the most fundamental level of defining the Gospel, has been silenced and censored.

In place of the Gospel as Jesus preached it to the public, we hear offered a very "washed out" version of the Gospel, geared largely to psychological self-improvement, or as Dallas Willard calls it, "gospels of sin management."[12] Popular evangelicalism has been emptied of its vivid, apocalyptic flavor, announcing the future of human society and warning of the future return of Jesus in judgment and to rule on a renewed earth. The Gospel announces God's future revolutionary government which will put an end to all war!

Without grasping the proper starting point, following Jesus himself, Bible readers are left with a hazy conception as to the definition and content of the saving Gospel. Paul is then often twisted by a selection of a few verses taken without regard to context. Romans 10:9-10 is typical, and Jesus' version of the Gospel is bypassed in the process. Paul did not contradict Jesus' insistence on the necessity of believing the Gospel of the Kingdom (Mark 1:14-15). Paul concludes Romans 10 by saying that faith comes by hearing and believing the "word [Gospel] of the Messiah" (v. 17), that is, the Gospel **the Messiah himself preached**. Paul is misunderstood (with the NIV, not the more accurate NASB) when he is made to say that one needs only to "hear *of*" Jesus, i.e. about him, when in fact one must "hear Jesus," that is, hear and respond intelligently to his own Gospel of the Kingdom message.

In 1 Corinthians 15:1-3 Paul should not be pitted against Jesus! Paul did not say there that the all-important death and resurrection of Jesus comprise the *whole* Gospel. Those facts were items "among matters of first importance" (v. 3). After all Jesus had preached the Gospel for years without, at that stage, so much as a mention of his death and resurrection, introduced first in Matthew 16:21.

My conviction about the absence of the center of the saving Gospel from popular preaching, as the Kingdom, is trenchantly stated by a professor of missiology. Dr. Mortimer Arias observed:

> We seem to be faced with what can be called **an eclipse of the reign [Kingdom] of God lasting from the apostolic age to the present**, particularly in our theology for evangelization...The reign of God is God's own dream, his project for his world and for humanity! He made us dreamers, and he wants us to be seduced by his dream and to dream with him...It is not we who dream but God who dreams in us...**When I left the seminary the first time, I had no clear idea of the Kingdom of God and**

---

[12]*The Divine Conspiracy,* Harper One, 1998, p. 57.

> **I had no place in my theology for the second coming or parousia...**
>
> Thousands of books are printed and circulated every year on evangelization; most of these fall into the category of methodology, the "how-to" manuals for Christians and churches. Not all of this activity or activism, however, is a sign of health and creativity...It is obvious that our traditional mini-theologies of evangelization (the "plan of salvation" or "four spiritual laws" type) do not do justice to the *whole* Gospel..."The good news of the kingdom" is not the usual way we describe the Gospel and evangelization...The kingdom-of-God theme has practically disappeared from evangelistic preaching and has been ignored by traditional "evangelism." The evangelistic message has been centered in personal salvation, individual conversion, and incorporation into the church. The kingdom of God as a parameter or perspective or as content of the proclamation has been virtually absent...Those interested in evangelization have not as yet been interested in the kingdom theme...Why not try Jesus' own definition of his mission — and ours? For Jesus, evangelization was no more and no less than announcing the reign of God![13]

This translation attempts to restore to the Gospel of the Kingdom the central prominence it always enjoys throughout the New Testament.

It is clear that Jesus was a Jew as the descendant of David. On no account should any reader of the New Testament in its own context imagine that Jesus believed in the Trinity of post-biblical councils! In this translation I make a concerted effort to remind readers of the unitary monotheistic faith of the New Testament, the definition of the Son of God as the lord Messiah, who was born (Luke 2:11), and not a second

---

[13]*Announcing the Reign of God*, Fortress Press, 1984, pp. 55, 115-116, 85, xii-xviii. For further quotations from leading authorities about the almost total absence of the Kingdom of God from church Gospel teaching, see my *The Coming Kingdom of the Messiah* (free at our website, **restorationfellowship.org**) and my "Kingdom of God in the Twentieth-Century Discussion and the Light of Scripture" (*Evangelical Quarterly*, 64:2, 1992, pp. 99-115). For an excellent treatment of the NT Gospel of the Kingdom, see *The Gospel of the Kingdom* by Wiley Jones, 1879, available free at archive.org

Person of a Triune Godhead. God cannot be born and the immortal God cannot die.

A great deal of refreshing simplicity and peace of mind results from reading the writings of the New Testament community in their Jewish, first-century context. We are touching base with the original roots of the faith, and the New Testament comes alive in a brilliant way. Ignorance of the Bible produces a disastrous alienation from God (Eph. 4:18). Evidently a lot of my fellow countrymen have abandoned the Bible entirely, since they go to church regularly in the UK only at the rate of about 5%, and the rest only to be "hatched, matched and dispatched."

The confusion caused by the later (from the early second century) fall from the original faith is gargantuan in its effects. It will take time to clear the air and defog our minds. We have been drinking toxic theology and the church needs to be decontaminated. But the effort is well worth it, although revolutions are never without pain.

Religion from the second century developed its own "improved version" of the biblical drama presented in Scripture. The Bible itself is a gripping drama, portraying the great Plan of God to bestow on human persons the gift of indestructible life, immortality. There will be peace on earth when the nations are required to beat swords into plowshares, and learning to make war will never again be permitted. No one will be permitted to take a gun and shoot his neighbor. This sounds like good sense and Good News to me!

From the second century, the emerging Catholic Church created its own embroidered version of the Bible's original plot and thus lost the plot for itself and its billions of followers. At the same time the "improved version" created a powerful and wealthy hierarchy designed to suppress the ignorant and guarantee a huge prestige to its priest leaders. They capped this effort finally by declaring the chief leader, the Pope, to be infallible when speaking officially.

The spectacular drama of the *origin* of the unique Son of God, Jesus Messiah (*genesis*, Matt. 1:18), provided in the birth narratives of Matthew and Luke, was given an additional tabloid twist when Mary, a teenage virgin, was said to be herself always sinless (the doctrine of "the immaculate conception") and permanently a virgin, without sexual experience for her whole married life. Jesus' half-brothers had then to be denied that status and turned into cousins (or children of Joseph by a previous marriage). Mary was said to have been assumed to heaven bodily without dying.

The Roman Catholic Church assumed power over the secular state as the Kingdom of God coming in advance of Jesus at his future Second Coming. In Scripture the nations of this present world system are never the Kingdom of God. The saints are *not* ruling at present (though they will), and Jesus is the only ultimately legitimate King and world ruler. The system of faith promoted by the "new improved version" of the biblical drama elevated priests as the only ones educated to minister the mysteries of the new faith. The laity were put under guardians.[14] The control of millions of minds was ensured and theological education was denied to all but leadership. The permanence of this massively powerful tradition was thus guaranteed. Harnack, as a master historian of the Christian faith, records the astonishing facts about the early "history of the suppression[15] of the historical Christ by the pre-existent Christ, of the Christ of reality by the imagined Christ in dogmatics, finally the victorious attempt to substitute the mystery of Christ for the person himself."

The Protestant reformation in the 16th century was provoked by the obvious abuses of the inherited system, to call for change, but its reform was partial. The same mysterious triune God continued to replace the single God of the Bible, the Father of Jesus. Jesus' unitarian heritage and definition of God, long suppressed by tradition, was not permitted in general to resurface from under the rubble of tradition which held the minds of the masses under its sway.

Heaven (or eternal hell) at death for "immortal souls" continued to replace the biblical vision of resurrection into the Kingdom of God on a renewed earth, which was the heart of the Hebrew dream of peace on earth, as well as the heart of the saving Gospel of the Kingdom announced by Jesus and the New Testament community.

---

[14]See Harnack, *History of Dogma*, Vol. 3, p. 10, translated by Neil Buchanan, Dover Publications, 1961. The original German of *Lehrbuch der Dogmengeschichte* is found in the 1883, 4th ed., pub. Wissenschaftliche Buchgesellschaft, p. 704.

[15]Note that the standard English translation "softens" the German "Verdrängung" (suppression) to "replacement" and the German "gedacht" (imaginary or imagined) to the vague "of thought."

A smaller, more radical wing of the Reformation was cruelly suppressed when it challenged the theology of the major Reformation led by Luther and Calvin. Englishman John Biddle, a school-master who exposed the error of the Trinity, had the "honor" of having an act of the British parliament passed against him and he died in prison. His crime was merely to have pointed to the unvarnished simplicity of Jesus' own definition of God in the Shema, the "Hear, O Israel" of Deuteronomy 6:4 and Mark 12:29. The brilliant Spanish scholar Michael Servetus was burned at the stake at the instigation of Protestant reformer John Calvin, in an act of unrepented brutality. Servetus' "crime" was having shown that the Trinity is not a biblical doctrine. Does the public know of this atrocity in the name of religion?

The emerging Church achieved an enormous success by adding a number of show-stopping features to its version of the biblical drama. However the casualty in this unfortunate development was the original divine drama of Scripture in two acts, offering to suffering mankind the hope of immortality and a place of responsibility in the future Kingdom of God on earth, when Jesus returns to take up his position on the restored throne of David. The original storyline and plot of the divine drama in the pages of Scripture was replaced with a dazzling but perverted story, a mixture of paganism and Scripture. Once we lose the plot of the astonishing drama, Scripture becomes confusing, Church tradition takes over and intelligent Bible reading is obstructed.

Professor J. Harold Ellens makes our point, based on the clear testimony to what the Church has done with its central figure:

> It is time therefore for the Christian Church to acknowledge that it has a very special type of material which constitutes its creedal tradition. **It is not a creedal tradition of biblical theology**. It is not a unique, inspired and authoritative word from God. It is, rather, a special kind of Greek religio-philosophical mythology…It should be candidly admitted by the Church, then, that **its roots are not in Jesus of Nazareth**…not in the central tradition of biblical theology…Its roots are in Philonic Hellenistic Judaism and in the Christianized **Neo-Platonism** of the second through the fifth century. Since this is so, the Church should acknowledge to the world of humans seeking truth and to the world of alternate religions, that the Christian Church speaks only

> with its own historical and philosophical authority and appeal and with neither a divine nor a unique revelation from Jesus Christ nor from God.[16]

The "complication" of God through the addition of two other Persons to the God known to Jesus led inevitably to the complication of the Messianic personality of Jesus. Once he became God, true monotheism was violated. The result:

> Jesus Christ was now no longer a man of flesh and blood like ourselves, but a [preexisting] heavenly being of supernatural origin in human form. With the help of a metaphysical system taken over from Greek philosophy, christological dogma came into being, and an attempt was made to describe the person of Jesus Christ in the form of the so-called "Doctrine of two natures." "Jesus Christ, true man and true God." So men said...From the very beginning right until the present day the Church has been tempted to stress the "divinity" of Christ so one-sidedly that his "manhood" threatened to become a mere semblance. In this way Jesus Christ was made an historical abnormality...What happened to this Christ was no longer the fate of a man, but the fate of a remarkable, shadowy, fairy-tale figure, half man and half God...[People have] woven a golden veil of pious adoration, love and superstition and spread it over the rugged contours of God's action in history.[17]

Theologians lost themselves in a maze of obfuscating language, and indignation at this lamentable exercise was well expressed by Harvard Professor Andrews Norton in 1833, in his *Statement of Reasons for Not Believing the Doctrines of Trinitarians*. He begins with a scathing attack on the complex issue of how Jesus can be 100% God and 100% man at the same time:

> The doctrine of the Communication of Properties, says Le Clerc, "is as intelligible as if one were to say that there is a circle which is so united with a triangle, that the circle has the properties of the triangle, and the triangle those of the circle." It is discussed at length by Petavius, with his usual redundance of learning. The

---

[16]*The Ancient Library of Alexandria and Early Christian Theological Development*.
[17]Heinz Zahrnt, *The Historical Jesus,* Harper and Row, 1963, p. 29.

> vast folio of that writer containing the history of the Incarnation [and Trinity] **is one of the most striking and most melancholy monuments of human folly which the world has to exhibit**. In the history of other departments of science, we find abundant errors and extravagances; but orthodox theology seems to have been the peculiar region of words without meaning; of doctrines confessedly false in their proper sense, and explained in no other; of the most portentous absurdities put forward as truths of the highest import; and of contradictory propositions thrown together without an attempt to reconcile them. A main error running through the whole system, as well as other systems of false philosophy, is that words possess an intrinsic meaning, not derived from the usage of men; that they are not mere signs of human ideas, but a sort of real entities, capable of signifying what transcends our conceptions; and that when they express **to human reason only an absurdity**, they may still be significant of a high mystery or a hidden truth, and are to be believed without being understood (p. 78).

From Cambridge in recent years comes an impressive analysis of the disaster that occurred when the Jewish Jesus was replaced by a pre-existing eternal Son. The consequences of the process of reinterpretation by which the Son of God became identified with "God the Son" are far-reaching indeed. Professor Lampe points out that when the Son was projected back on to an eternally existing pre-human Son, and when the holy spirit was turned into a third "hypostasis":

> The Christian concept of God then becomes inescapably **tritheistic**; for three "persons" in anything like the modern sense of the word "person" mean in fact **three Gods**...The effects, especially in popular piety, have been even more far-reaching than this. The Nicene Creed speaks of "Jesus Christ" in person, not the Logos, as pre-existent...It is thus the Jesus of the Gospels whom the imagination of the worshipper pictures as pre-existing in heaven and descending to earth...[There is] the absurdity of the picture of Jesus reflected in much traditional devotion which is essentially that of a superman[18] who voluntarily descends into

[18]Very much like a Hindu avatar.

> the world of ordinary mortals, choosing, by a deliberate act of will, to be born as man...God the Son is conceptualized as Jesus, Son of God; the obedience of Jesus, the Servant of God and Son of God, the true Adam indwelt and inspired by God's spirit, is attributed to God the Son; God the Son becomes eternally the subject of Jesus' self-dedication to his Father's will, and eternally the object of the Father's love...This means in effect the **abandonment of monotheism**, for such a relation between God the Son and God the Father is incompatible with the requirement of monotheism that we predicate of God one mind, one will and one single operation.

Professor Lampe was a specialist in the post-biblical development of the Trinity and observed also that "the interpretation of Jesus as pre-existent Son and of the Son as a pre-existent Jesus causes inconsistency and confusion...This doctrine, which follows from the identification of Jesus with a pre-existent personal divine being, is ultimately **incompatible with the unity of God**."

Equally problematic for a true monotheism and a genuinely human Messiah is the Trinitarian concept of the Son as "assuming human nature." Professor Lampe reminds us that "a person is created by his relationships with other people, and especially by his interaction with his parents and family." What happened then to the first-century Galilean Jew Jesus? He was lost and replaced by a philosophical abstraction whose identity as the son of David, and thus the true and only Messiah, became irrelevant.

> The Christological concept of the pre-existent divine Son...reduces the real, socially and culturally conditioned personality of Jesus to the metaphysical abstraction "human nature." It is this universal humanity which the Son assumed and made his own...According to this Christology, the eternal Son assumes a timeless human nature, or makes it timeless by making it his own; it is a human nature which owes nothing essential to geographical circumstances; it corresponds to nothing in the actual concrete world; Jesus Christ has not, after all, really "come in the flesh."[19]

---

[19]Lampe, *God as Spirit*, Trinity Press International, 1983, pp. 132, 136-138, 140-144.

The observant reader will note that the professor rather obviously assigns to the orthodox doctrine of Jesus the label of antichrist. It was the Apostle John who late in the New Testament period warned that any reduction of the human individual Jesus Christ to a personality not essentially human is a menace to true faith (1 John 4:2-3). The Jesus to be confessed, as distinct from other Jesuses, is the one who has truly "come in the flesh," as a fully human person. Luther set the pattern for reading into John's "theological test" the post-biblical definition of Jesus. Luther mistranslates 1 John 4:2 as "Jesus Christ coming *into* the flesh." The doctrine of the Incarnation was thus imposed on John.

Christianity is defined by God's purpose. The divine Plan is discovered in the purpose statement of Jesus in Luke 4:43. There he stated that the One God had commissioned him for the express purpose of announcing the good news or Gospel about the coming Kingdom of God. The purpose could have a frightful negative outcome. Jesus expressed this in Luke 13:28. He warned his fellow countrymen that they ran the risk of a colossal failure: "There will be weeping and grinding of teeth when you see Abraham, Isaac, Jacob and all the prophets in the Kingdom of God but yourselves being thrown out." To avoid this catastrophic negative outcome Jesus exhorted the people, and us all, to pay the closest attention to his teachings, which provide the only route to rescue and salvation — living forever.

Jesus' first and last words are critically important. He begins by issuing a first and fundamental command, that we are to repent and *believe the Gospel about the Kingdom of God* (Mark 1:14-15). Jesus' last words summarize and reemphasize the all-important matter of obedience to his teachings. These are found for example at the conclusion of his public ministry in John 12:44-50. The words/Gospel of Jesus are the criterion for our future judgment. We neglect them at our peril, since the words of Jesus are the words of God who commissioned and inspired him:

> Then Jesus **called out**, "The person who believes in me does not believe in me, but in the One who commissioned me. And the one who sees and undertstands me sees and understands Him who commissioned me. I was born into the world as a light, so that everyone who believes in me would not remain in darkness. **If someone hears my words and does not obey them**, I do not

> judge him. For I did not come to judge the world, but to save the world. The person who **rejects me and refuses to accept my teachings** has this as his judge: the Gospel-word I have spoken will judge him on the last day of this age. For I have not spoken on my own initiative, but the Father Himself who commissioned me has given me a command as to what I should say and what I should speak. And I know that His command means Life in the Coming Age. So the things I speak, I speak just as the Father instructed me" (John 12:44-50).

Christianity is based on our making a choice between two different ways. The principle is beautifully encapsulated by John 3:36, where belief in Jesus is equivalent to obedience, and unbelief is refusal to obey. These stark alternatives are laid out for us in the introductory Psalm 1. Two contrasted lifestyles are depicted here, the one leading to disaster, an extinction of life, and the other to indestructible life, immortality in the future Kingdom of God on a renewed earth. We all have to choose. (In Calvinism the word "choose" has been emptied of intelligible content.)

As early as the second century, would-be followers of Jesus began to lose the central storyline of God's great unfolding drama, embodied in the Gospel of the Kingdom and the work of the Messiah Jesus. The influence of alien Greek philosophy confused the drama of salvation. The person of Jesus was replaced gradually by an abstract "God the Son," who by definition really could not be a true human being, since his origin was antedated prior to his actual origin as Son of God in the womb of his mother (Luke 1:35). Once this new form of belief, affecting the central creed of the Bible, had been worked out over a period of centuries, it was enforced on pain of death and excommunication. At the Council of Nicea in 325 anathemas were attached to any who might question the Church's central dogma.

Readers of English versions of Scripture sometimes express their desire to have a "literal translation" of the original. What they really need is one that conveys the sense of the original (in this case Greek) faithfully into the target language. There are occasions when a "literal," "word for word" translation is the least desirable. In fact it can lead to nonsense! What if I render the English "I am pulling your leg" literally, or "I have a frog in my throat" word for word? The misunderstanding will be obvious. "I am mad about my flat" can well mean in British English that "I am excited about my apartment." In the USA it pictures a person angry about changing a flat tire. "Jane and John have broken up" means in the UK that their school term is ended. In the USA quite a different sense would be conveyed. The list could be multiplied. "Bouncing off the wall" does not need to be translated literally into another language. It will mislead.

More seriously, a literal word for word translation in John 17:5 is misleading. Jesus' words translated word for word, "glorify me with the glory I had with you" lead or mislead the reader to think that Jesus was with the Father before he came into existence, was born! The Hebrew idiom "to have something with someone" means to have a reward promised and stored up in advance. Jesus warned that ostentatious performance of "good works" will mean that we "have" (present tense) "no reward with the Father" (Matt. 6:1). This means of course that if we do well we now have a reward stored up for the future, a reward to be given at the return of Jesus. Jesus in the very same discourse in John 17 spoke of *having given* glory to Christians who were not even born when he made that promise! (v. 22). It was the same glory which had been promised to Jesus by the Father. It is glory prepared and planned in heaven with the Father ready to be bestowed in the future. Jesus asked in John 17:5 to be rewarded with the glory promised to him at the completion of his ministry. It was a glory stored up and promised by God from the beginning. It was not a glory to be "restored" to him, since he had never yet had it.

This issue is parallel exactly to the misleading idea conveyed by the NIV in some places. In John it takes liberties with the text in the interests of inherited dogma. It makes Jesus say what he did not say. The NIV renders John 16:28, 13:3 and 20:17 as "going back," or "returning" to the Father. But the historical Jesus had not been there yet! There is a world of difference between "going," which is what John wrote, and "going back."

Another example of misleading translation is found in many versions in Luke 23:43. It is a matter of punctuation. Since Jesus had not yet been to the Father on the Sunday of his resurrection (John 20:17), he could not have promised the thief a place in his presence that day, the day of his death. Jesus was abandoned to the grave, the world of the dead, until his resurrection on Sunday (Acts 2:27, 31, 32). The thief had asked to be remembered when Jesus comes back in the future, inaugurating his Kingdom. Jesus' promise goes beyond the request and assures him on that very day, that he would indeed be with Jesus in that future Kingdom of God, the paradise restored (Rev. 2:7). "I say to you today [you don't have to wait until the future for this assurance], that you will be with me in the future paradise of the Kingdom" (cp. Acts 20:26). In this way one verse will not be made to contradict Luke in 14:14 and 20:35, where rewards are not given until the resurrection. Nor will that one verse be made to contradict and confuse the rest of Scripture.

There are of course verses which in their sublime simplicity and clarity ought to be definitive. Most striking of these is Luke 1:35 where the words of the angel define with precision the meaning of the title "the Son of God." Very few verses come with their own "built-in" definition, but Luke 1:35 does. No footnotes are needed, no special glossary. Luke 1:35 includes its own lucid explanation. Gabriel defined how, why and where Jesus is to be Son of God. Son of God is who he is "because of," "precisely because of" (*dio kai*) the miracle worked by God in the womb of Mary. It is "for that reason" and no other that Jesus is the Son of God. This defining statement rules out at once any possibility of an "eternally begotten" Son. Luke and Gabriel could not have been Trinitarians, and nor was Jesus (Mark 12:29; John 17:3).

The celebrated commentary on Luke by Godet got it right when he stated:

> By the word "therefore" the angel alludes to his preceding words: he will be called the Son of the Highest. We might paraphrase it: "And it is precisely for this reason that I said to you…" We have then here, from the mouth of the angel himself, an authentic explanation of the term Son of God, in the former part of his message. After this explanation Mary could only understand the title in this sense: a human being of whose existence God Himself is the immediate author. It does not convey the idea of preexistence.[20]

Alas, the Church disregarded the explicit theology of Gabriel. Alas, too, Godet did not, as he should have, provoke a complete rethinking of

---

[20]*Commentary on Luke*, Funk and Co., 1881, p. 58.

Christology. Instead there has occurred a flurry of plain contradictions of the text, to uphold beloved conciliar "orthodoxy." A striking example of these is the statement of Dr. John MacArthur: "I do not believe that the virgin birth alone proves that Jesus is the Son of God. In other words, *Jesus is not the Son of God because He was born of a virgin*. He was born of a virgin because He was the Son of God. Jesus existed long before Mary."[21] Note that MacArthur is in direct opposition to Scripture and Gabriel. J.P. Mackey rightly criticizes J.G. Davies when he says that "this creative act did not bring into being a new person." Mackey says, "With this kind of cobbling any theological conclusion could be 'proved from Scripture.'"[22]

So brain-breakingly complicated and abstract were the terms of what became the official creed that unitarian scholar and poet John Milton was moved to lament the appallingly confused language in which it was presented as dogma:

> Christ himself therefore, the Son of God, teaches us nothing in the Gospel respecting the one God but what the Law had before taught and everywhere clearly asserts Him to be, his Father. John 17:3: "This is eternal life: that they might know You, the only true God, and Jesus Christ whom You have sent." 20:17: "I ascend to my Father and your Father; to my God and your God." If therefore the Father is the God of Christ and the same one is our God, and if there is no God but one, there can be no God beside the Father...Though all this *is so self-evident* as to require no explanation — namely that the Father alone is a self-existent God, that a being which is not self-existent cannot be God — it is wonderful with what futile subtleties, or rather with what juggling artifices, certain individuals have endeavored to elude or obscure the plain meaning of these passages; leaving no stone unturned, recurring to every shift, attempting every means, as if their object were not to preach the pure and unadulterated Truth of the Gospel to the poor and the simple, but rather by dint of vehemence and obstinacy to sustain some absurd paradox from

---

[21]"Unleashing God's Word One Word at a Time," Issue 3.

[22]*The Christian Experience of God as Trinity*, SCM Press, 1983, p. 277.

> falling, by the aid of sophisms and verbal distinctions, borrowed from the barbarous ignorance of the schools.[23]

Sir Isaac Newton was no less scathing about the very non-Jewish definition of God as Trinity:

> Newton became almost obsessed with the desire to purge Christianity of its mythical doctrines. He became convinced that the a-rational dogmas of the Trinity and the Incarnation were the result of conspiracy, forgery and chicanery…[Newton maintained] that the spurious doctrines of the Incarnation and the Trinity had been added to the creed by unscrupulous theologians in the fourth century. Indeed, the Book of Revelation had prophesied the rise of Trinitarianism — "this strange religion of ye west, the cult of three equal Gods" — as the abomination of desolation.[24]

Bible readers need a fresh reading of the New Testament, with some of the encumbrance of later "orthodoxy" which now blocks a clear understanding, removed. No translation is final, of course. There is no perfect translation. There are scores of different ways of conveying the same propositions. Most of the New Testament is perfectly intelligible in many of the different versions. Readers of the Bible should avail themselves of various translations. No one translation conveys all of the truth. Some do much better than others.

Some contemporary commentary on the traditional doctrine of the Incarnation of "God the Son" becoming a man ought, we suggest, to shock readers into the realization that something has gone terribly wrong. Dr. Jim Packer is well known for his evangelical writings. In his widely read *Knowing God*, in a chapter on "God Incarnate," he says of the doctrine of the Trinity and the Incarnation:

> Here are two mysteries for the price of one — the plurality of the persons within the unity of God, and the union of Godhead and manhood in the person of Jesus. It is here, in the thing that happened at the first Christmas, that the profoundest and the most unfathomable depths of the Christian revelation lie. "The Word was made flesh" (John 1:14); God became man; the divine Son

---

[23]John Milton, *On the Son of God and the Holy Spirit*, British and Foreign Unitarian Association, pp. 15, 16, 20.

[24]Karen Armstrong, *The Battle for God*, Ballantine Books, p. 69.

> became a Jew; the Almighty appeared on earth as a helpless baby, unable to do more than lie and stare and wriggle and make noises, needing to be fed and changed and taught to talk like any other child. And there was no illusion or deception in this: the babyhood of the Son of God was a reality. The more you think about it, the more staggering it gets. *Nothing in fiction is so fantastic as is this truth of the Incarnation*. This is the real stumbling block in Christianity. It is here that the Jews, Muslims, Unitarians, Jehovah's Witnesses…have come to grief…If he was truly God the Son, it is much more startling that he should die than that he should rise again. "'Tis mystery all! The immortal dies," wrote [Charles] Wesley…and if the immortal Son of God really did submit to taste death, it is not strange that such a death should have saving significance for a doomed race. Once we grant that Jesus was divine, it becomes unreasonable to find difficulty in any of this; it is all of a piece and hangs together completely. The Incarnation is in itself an unfathomable mystery, but it makes sense of everything else that the New Testament contains.[25]

Had the lucidly simple description of the Son of God proposed by Luke been allowed to stand as the official doctrine of the Son of God, the course of the Christian faith and of church history would have been vastly different: "the holy thing begotten in you will be called the Son of God" (Luke 1:35) was easy enough. But when evangelicals rewrite the biblical story and read into it an eternal Son of God, this is the result. Charles Swindoll, chancellor of Dallas Theological Seminary, writes:

> On December 25th shops shut their doors, families gather together and people all over the world remember the birth of Jesus of Nazareth…Many people assume that Jesus' existence began like ours, in the womb of his mother. But is that true? Did life begin for him with that first breath of Judean air? Can a day in December truly mark the beginning of the Son of God? Unlike us, Jesus existed before his birth, long before there was air to breathe…long before the world was born.

Swindoll goes on to explain:

---

[25] J.I. Packer, *Knowing God*, Intervarsity Press, 1998, p. 46-47, emphasis added.

> John the Baptist came into being at his birth — he had a birthday. *Jesus never came into being*; at his earthly birth he merely took on human form...Here's an amazing thought: the baby that Mary held in her arms was holding the universe in place! The little newborn lips that cooed and cried once formed the dynamic words of creation. Those tiny clutching fists once flung stars into space and planets into orbit. That infant flesh so fair once housed the Almighty God...As an ordinary baby, God had come to earth...Do you see the child *and* the glory of the infant-God? What you are seeing is the Incarnation — God dressed in diapers...See the baby as John describes him "in the beginning" "with God." Imagine him in the misty pre-creation past, thinking of you and planning your redemption. Visualize this same Jesus, who wove your body's intricate patterns, *knitting a human garment for himself*...Long ago the Son of God dove headfirst into time and floated along with us for about 33 years...Imagine the Creator-God tightly wrapped in swaddling clothes.[26]

Dr. Swindoll then quotes Max Lucado who says of Jesus, "He left his home and entered the womb of a teenage girl...Angels watched as Mary changed God's diaper. The universe watched with wonder as the Almighty learned to walk. Children played in the street with him."[27]

No one opening a New Testament and reading the matchless story of the origin of Jesus will be misled into thinking that "God was born," or that as a Roman Catholic priest said on television, "God came to Mary and said, 'Will you please be My mother?'"

We offer this version of the New Testament with a view to restoring the truth that God is one Person, that Jesus is the Messiah, Son of God by miracle and that the saving Gospel is about the Kingdom of God, as Jesus preached it, and about all that Jesus said and did to instruct in the way that leads to indestructible life in the future Kingdom of God. Jesus of course spoke in Paul too and the other writers of New Testament Scripture. And none of these writers discarded the precious writings of the Hebrew Bible, but developed the truths of the New Covenant,

---

[26]*Jesus: When God Became a Man*, W Publishing Group, 1993, p. 1-8, emphasis added.
[27]Ibid., p. 10, quoting Max Lucado, *God Came Near*, Thomas Nelson, 2004.

working from a base in the Hebrew Scriptures which Jesus had endorsed as inspired canon in Luke 24:44.

If we are seeking the mind of Christ the obvious place to start is with Mark 1:14-15, Jesus' opening first command to us all. "Jesus came announcing God's Gospel. He said, 'The time predicted has come. The Kingdom of God is coming soon. Repent and believe that Gospel about the Kingdom.'" God's Gospel is the Gospel of salvation which originates in God. God's saving Gospel **about the Kingdom** was preached by all the New Testament writers and of course first by Jesus himself (Heb. 2:3). God issues the ultimate statement about the Kingdom, and His great immortality program is modeled in the man Jesus and taught by him as saving Gospel in addition of course to his substitutionary death and resurrection. The "testimony of Jesus" in Revelation means Jesus' own Gospel preaching which one must hear to be saved (Rom. 10:14-17; Luke 8:12); "the Gospel of the age to come" (Rev. 14:6); the Kingdom about to begin (Luke 21:31; Rev. 11:15-18, cp. Luke 19:11ff).

Repentance means a complete reorientation in thinking and understanding, and in lifestyle. The first command of Jesus is thus to believe the Gospel about the Kingdom of God, which is the empire of the Messiah, certainly not just a figurative kingdom "in the heart." Some translations such as Ferrar Fenton's correctly render Daniel 2:44, "In the days of those kings the God of heaven will establish an everlasting **empire**, which is indestructible, whose sovereignty will not be transferred to another people." Thus also in Daniel 7:17, 18, 22, 27:

> Those four great beasts which you have seen are four **great empires** which will be established on the earth. The saints of the Most High will afterwards take the **empire** and possess it forever and ever…The time came for the saints to possess **the empire**…**The empire** and dominion and grandeur of the **empire under the whole heavens** will be given to the Holy People of the Most High. All nations will serve and obey them.

Hence the reward of the faithful in the New Testament is nowhere said to be to "go to heaven," but to have the governorship of ten towns or five towns (Luke 19:17, 19). Jesus echoed this same Gospel promise when he said to the apostles: "You who have followed me, when the world is reborn and the Son of Man will sit on his throne of glory, you too will sit on twelve thrones, governing the twelve tribes of Israel"

(Matt. 19:28). Paul was surprised that his converts had forgotten the elementary truth that the saints "are going to govern the world" (1 Cor. 6:2). Jesus will be Head of State in the coming Kingdom and the saints will be his assistants, associate rulers, princes (see Dan. 2:44; 7:14, 18, 22, 27; Isa. 32:1). "In Revelation the eternal messianic Kingdom is placed *on a renovated earth* so that Christ comes to his people on earth rather than gathering them to a heavenly abode."[28]

In order to get off to the right start with Bible reading, it is essential that Jesus' saving Gospel of the Kingdom be understood. What better place to define the Kingdom than with the gospel of Matthew? The analysis of Matthew's phrase "Kingdom of God"[29] offered by Professor W.C. Allen of Oxford is lucidly clear. And since the Kingdom is the key term for understanding all New Testament preaching, we offer the professor's following fine statement. To misunderstand "Kingdom" is to misunderstand the whole New Testament teaching about the Gospel which saves us, and leads to immortality.

> The Kingdom — **the central subject** of Christ's doctrine...With this **he began** his ministry (4:17), and wherever he went he taught this as good news [**Gospel**] (4:23). The Kingdom, he taught, was coming, **but not in his lifetime**. After his ascension he would come as Son of Man on the clouds of heaven (16:27; 19:28; 24:30; 25:31)...and would sit on the throne of his glory...Then the twelve Apostles would sit on twelve thrones judging the twelve tribes of Israel (19:28). In the meantime he himself must suffer and die, and be raised from the dead. How else could he come on the clouds of heaven? And his disciples were to **preach the Good News [Gospel] of the coming Kingdom** (10:7; 24:14) among all nations, making disciples by [water] **baptism** (28:18). The body of disciples thus gained would naturally form a society bound by common aims...Hence the disciples of the Kingdom would form a new spiritual Israel (21:43) [cp. Gal. 6:16; Phil. 3:3]...
>
> In view of the needs of this new Israel of Christ's disciples...who were to await his coming on the clouds of

---

[28]David Aune, *Word Biblical Commentary*, Rev. 17-22, Thomas Nelson, 1998, p. 1069.
[29]Or its exact synonym "Kingdom of Heaven."

> heaven, it is natural that a large part of the teaching recorded in the Gospel should concern **the qualifications required in those who hoped to enter the Kingdom when it came**...[Thus the parables] convey some lesson about the nature of the Kingdom and **the period of preparation for it [sowing before harvest]**...[The parables] taught lessons about the Kingdom of the heavens **in the sense in which that phrase is used everywhere else in his Gospel, of the Kingdom which was to come when the Son of Man came upon the clouds of heaven**. Thus the parable of the Sower illustrates the varying **reception met with by the good news [Gospel] of the Kingdom as it is preached amongst men**. That of the Tares also deals not with the Kingdom itself, but with **the period of preparation for it**. At the **end of the age** the Son of Man will come **to inaugurate his Kingdom**...There is nothing here or elsewhere in this Gospel to suggest that **the scene of the Kingdom is other than the present world renewed**, restored and purified.[30]

The last sentence of our quotation makes the excellent point that Matthew (and the whole New Testament, indeed the whole Bible) does not expect believers to "go to heaven," but that Jesus will **come back to the earth** to rule with them on a renewed earth (Rev. 5:9-10; Matt. 5:5; Dan. 7:14, 18, 22, 27). The perceptive reader of the New Testament will note the striking difference between the biblical view of the Kingdom, and thus of the Gospel of salvation, and what in post-biblical times was substituted for it: a departure of the faithful at death to a realm removed from the earth. (Bishop Tom Wright tries to have both systems when he speaks of "Life *after life* after death." Better to shed the philosophically based life before **resurrection**, which **always** means coming not from life, but from death!) There can be no resurrection from the dead, if a person is not really dead!

The popular idea that the Kingdom is mainly a "spiritual" state of mind or lifestyle *now*, or social ethics expecting to bring the Kingdom in *now*, is false to the New Testament. Joseph of Arimathea, a Christian,

---

[30]W.C. Allen, MA, *The Dictionary of Christ and the Gospels*, Vol. II, p. 144-45, emphasis added. The same view of the Kingdom is expressed by Allen in his commentary on Matthew (*The International Critical Commentary, St. Matthew,* T & T Clark, 1907, pp. lxvii-lxxi).

was "waiting for the Kingdom" after the ministry of Jesus (Mark 15:43). Luke 19:11-27 teaches us to connect the arrival of the Kingdom with the **future return of Jesus** (cp. above: "The Kingdom, he taught, was coming, but not in his lifetime"). So say leading analysts of the Gospel records.

Luke 21:31 presents the Kingdom of God as the event to **be introduced at the Second Coming**. This is exactly Revelation 11:15-18 — the Kingdom of God beginning at the future, seventh, resurrection trumpet (=last trumpet, 1 Cor. 15:23, 52-55).

We may add a further statement from a recognized authority on Luke:

> It cannot really be disputed that Luke means by the Kingdom **a future** entity. The spiritualizing interpretation according to which the Kingdom is present in the Spirit and in the Church is completely misleading…It is *the message* of the Kingdom that is present, which in Luke is distinguished from the Kingdom itself. He knows nothing of an immanent [i.e., already present] development on the basis of the preaching of the Kingdom.[31]

The *International Standard Bible Encyclopedia* gets the emphasis on the future right, and thus clarifies the Christian Gospel, and thus the Christian faith:

> "The Kingdom of God is at hand" had the inseparable connotation "judgment is at hand," and in this context, "repent" in Mark 1:14-15 must mean "lest you be judged."[32] Hence our Lord's teaching about salvation **had primarily a future content: positively admission into [entrance into] the Kingdom of God and negatively, deliverance from the preceding judgment [fire]**. So the Kingdom of God is the highest good of Christ's teaching…Man's nature is to be perfectly adapted to his spiritual environment and man is to be with Christ (Luke 22:30) and with the patriarchs (Matt. 8:11). Whatever the Kingdom is,[?!] it is

---

[31]Hans Conzelmann, *The Theology of St. Luke,* Harper and Row, 1961, p. 122.

[32]The popular notion of an unending, torturous hell-fire for the wicked is utterly unbiblical. The fate of the incorrigibly wicked, after full exposure to the Gospel, is annihilation, ceasing to exist. See Fudge, *The Fire That Consumes*, Providential Press, 1982 (foreword by F.F. Bruce).

> most certainly not exhausted by a mere reformation of the present order of material things.[33]

Equally clear is Eduard Schweizer:

> Mark 1:14-15: Mark gives a brief summary of the preaching of Jesus. Preaching and Good News (Gospel) are Mark's favorite expressions. **The Gospel call of Jesus is accurately summed up** in 1:15, where the association of repentance and faith reveals the language of the church (Acts 5:31; 11:18; 20:21). Mark's concern is to make clear that in this preaching Jesus continues to go forth into the world and this call, therefore, is being directed also to the one who reads this Gospel today. Consequently this section serves as **a caption** to the whole Gospel (cp. the epilogue).
>
> **The Kingdom of God**. When Jesus proclaims that the Kingdom of God is near, he is adopting a concept which was coined in the OT. Although it denotes God's sovereignty over creation (Ps. 103:19; 145:11ff), it **refers primarily to God's unchallenged sovereignty in the end time (Isa 52:7)**...Judaism spoke of the reign of God which comes after the annihilation of every foe [Isa. 24:6] and the end of all suffering...In the New Testament the **Kingdom of God** is conceived **first of all as something in the future** (Mark 9:1, 47; 14:25; Matt. 13:41-43; 20:21; Luke 22:16, 18; 1 Cor. 15:50; Luke 21:31*, et al*) which comes from God (Mark 9:1; Matt. 6:10; Luke 17:20; 19:11). Therefore it is something man can only **wait for** (Mark 15:43), seek (Matt. 6:33), receive (Mark 10:15; cp. Luke 12:32) and inherit (1 Cor. 6:9ff; Gal. 5:21; James 2:5), but is not able to create it by himself...In the acts and words of Jesus the future Kingdom has come upon him already. It is decided at that very moment whether or not he will ever be in the Kingdom...**Repentance is nothing less than a whole-hearted commitment to the Good News [of the Kingdom]**.[34]

Ernest Scott, D.D., Professor of New Testament at Union Theological Seminary, on the other hand reveals the hopeless confusion into which the Church has fallen in regard to Jesus' Gospel and thus the

---

[33]*International Standard Bible Encyclopedia*, Eerdmans, 1929, Vol. 4, p. 2667.

[34]*The Good News According to Mark,* John Knox Press, 1970, p. 45-47.

Christian faith. He seems uncertain about the Gospel, but gives us a good sense of what it meant to Jesus and his followers:

> It seems almost impossible to define the Christian "Gospel." Sometimes it is identified with our religion as a whole, sometimes with some element in it which is regarded as central. To accept the Gospel is to believe in the atonement or the love of God, or the revelation in Christ or the fact of human brotherhood [!]. Yet it is well to remember that the word which is now used so **loosely** had at the outset a meaning which was **clearly understood**. "Jesus came into Galilee, preaching the Gospel of the Kingdom of God and saying, 'The time is fulfilled and the Kingdom of God is at hand.'" The Gospel underwent a marvelous development…but the Good News has always been essentially what it was at the first — **the announcement of the Kingdom**. It is evident from the manner in which Jesus made the announcement that he took up an idea which was already familiar. He did not explain what he meant by the Kingdom, **for he could assume that all his hearers were looking forward to it**. Their hope for it had been newly stimulated by John the Baptist…They had long been thinking of the Kingdom and wondering when it would come, and a prophet had now arisen who declared that it was close at hand…**In the religion of Israel we must seek for the immediate origin of the Kingdom idea of Jesus**…The idea persisted long after the royal house was firmly established that the reigning king was only the vice-regent of the invisible King…Israel had been chosen by a unique God who was known as yet only by His own people, but was nonetheless King of the whole earth. **The day was coming when all nations would own His sovereignty**…On the higher levels of prophecy the purified Israel of the future is conceived as attracting all nations by its high example, to the service of the One God. More often it is assumed that Israel when fully disciplined will be restored to God's favor and advanced by Him to the sovereign place (Acts 1:6). As King of this preeminent people God will reign at last over the world…On the one hand God is already King. On the other hand it is recognized that the Kingship lies in the future…They look for **a coming day** when He will overcome

> all usurping powers and assert Himself as King. So the prophets keep before them **the vision of a new age when the Kingdom of God will be fully manifested**. In that happy time Israel will be exalted, the cause of justice will be established, the earth full of the glory of the Lord. Nature in that day will be restored to its pristine glory, and the wolf will lie down with the lamb, and cattle will feed in large pastures. The light of the moon will be as the light of the sun. He [and His Messiah] will reign from Mount Zion and all nations will serve Him. King over a righteous nation, He will extend His dominion over the whole earth.[35]

The admission of one of today's leading evangelical scholars, N.T. Wright, confirms the chaos into which the Gospel had fallen:

> In one sense, I have been working on this book on and off for most of my life. Serious thought began, however, when I was invited in 1978 to give a lecture in Cambridge on "The Gospel in the Gospels." The topic was not just impossibly vast; **I did not understand it. I had no real answer**, then, to the question of how Jesus' whole life, *not just his death* on the cross in isolation, was somehow "gospel." Fifteen subsequent years of teaching in Cambridge, Montreal and Oxford have convinced me that this question…is worth asking.[36]

But the question is just as mystifying to millions of Bible readers. This ought not to be so.

Further authorities point us in the right direction: "In the Book of Acts the Kingdom of God was still the general formula for the substance of Christian teaching."[37] This formula is absent from evangelical tracts promoting salvation.

On the lips of Jesus the term Kingdom of God unquestionably summarized the very heart of his Message. "The Kingdom of God is the central theme of the teaching of Jesus, and it involves his **whole understanding** of his own **person and work**."[38] Luke 4:43 is repeated

---

[35]*The Kingdom of God in the New Testament*, Macmillan Co., 1931, pp. 11-21.

[36]*Jesus and the Victory of God*, Fortress Press, 1996, Vol. 2, p. xiv.

[37]*Hastings Dictionary of the Bible*, Vol. II, p. 855.

[38]Alan Richardson, *Theological Word Book of the Bible*, SCM Press, 1950, p. 119. "Golf tournament" and "tennis tournament" would be meaningless if "golf" and "tennis" are not understood.

by Paul in Acts 20:24-25 where Paul defines his own ministry as the Gospel of the grace of God = the **preaching of the Gospel of the Kingdom**.

"The Kingdom announced by the Messiah who is the Son of Man is possible only through his death and will be finally and fully realized **on earth only at his glorious return**. **This is indeed the heart of the Gospel**."[39]

The essential understanding conveyed by Jesus' teaching is captured by these propositions about Messiah: "The Son of God came to give us an **understanding** so that we might know God" (1 John 5:20). "By his knowledge My servant will make many righteous" (Isa. 53:11).

The New Testament is based on the Old. Jesus came to:

1) Proclaim the **Gospel about the Kingdom of God** (Luke 4:43; John announced the same Gospel of the Kingdom, Matt. 3:1). This is the whole reason for Christianity, including, of course, the death and resurrection of Jesus. Jesus commands believers to continue announcing the same Gospel of the Kingdom (Matt. 28:19-20).

2) Confirm the Abrahamic and Davidic promises made to the fathers (Rom. 15:8; Gal. 3:8).

3) Give us an understanding that we might know God (1 John 5:20).

4) Make people righteous, right before God, not only by his death but by his knowledge (Isa. 53:11; Dan. 12:3).

5) Invite whoever will believe in God's plan for themselves and the world to prepare now to rule the world with Jesus when he returns. "Don't you know the saints are going to manage the world?" (1 Cor. 6:2, Moffat; see also Dan. 7:14, 18, 22, 27; Rev 3:21; 2:26; 5:10; 20:1-6; Matt. 5:5; 19:28; Isa. 16:5; 32:1).

6) Sow the seed message of the Gospel of the Kingdom. In Luke 8:12 and Mark 4:11-12, an intelligent reception of the Kingdom Gospel is the necessary condition for repentance and forgiveness. Without a clear statement about the Kingdom how can anyone repent and believe Jesus?

In post-biblical times the original faith in the Gospel of the Kingdom suffered massive alteration, turning the Gospel into something quite different. Greeks rather than Jews became leaders in the church, and they imported alien Greek philosophy into the church's teachings. Galatians

---

[39]Donald Hagner, *Word Biblical Commentary, Matthew 1-13,* 1993, p. 214.

3:8, which defines the Christian Gospel as the content of the promises **made to Abraham**, about land, progeny and blessing, is missing from contemporary versions of the "Gospel."

Billy Graham was mistaken when he claimed that "Jesus came to do three days' work, to die, to be buried and to rise."[40] This dictum would render the Gospel preaching of Jesus virtually unnecessary. A fatal "dispensationalism" underlies much popular preaching. 1 Timothy 6:3, 2 John 7-9, Hebrews 2:3, and John 3:36 are fair warning.

Perhaps the most profoundly disturbing saying of Jesus is the one in Matthew 7:21-23: "Not everyone who says to me 'lord, lord' will enter the Kingdom of heaven [Kingdom of God]; rather it is those who do the will of my Father in heaven. There will be many who say to me on the day of judgment, 'lord, lord, did we not preach for you and drive out demons in your name, and perform many miracles with your authority?' Then I will declare to them, 'I never recognized you. Depart from me, you who practice wickedness.'"

This statement is made in the closest connection with Matthew 7:13-14, where Jesus warns: "Enter [the Kingdom] through the narrow entrance, because wide is the entrance and broad the way which leads to destruction, and many go that way. But small is the entrance and narrow is the way which leads to Life [in the Kingdom], and only a few find it." And then in the very same breath, Jesus said, "**Beware false prophets**, who come in sheep's clothing, but inside are vicious wolves. You will recognize them by their fruits" (7:15-16). (Compare the parable of the sower to see what seed is necessary to produce true fruit: Matt. 13:19: "the word about the Kingdom," Mark 4, Luke 8).

Now connect this to Jesus' other reference to people saying, "lord, lord": "Why do you call me 'lord, lord,' when **you refuse to do what I say**? Let me give you an illustration of someone who comes to me, listens to my words, and does them. He is like a man who built a house..." (Luke 6:46-48). The one *hearing the words/teaching of Jesus but not doing them* is building his house without a foundation. Only the ones hearing and obeying the words of Jesus are the true Christians.

---

[40]"What is the Gospel?" Roy Gustafson, Billy Graham Association, 1980. Equally unbiblical is Billy Graham's notion of the prospect for believers of "polishing rainbows in heaven" and "preparing heavenly dishes" (*Hope for the Troubled Heart*, Harper Collins, 1993, p. 214).

So then, the strong and alarming warning of Jesus is simply this: It is fatal to address Jesus as "lord," if we do not also lay the foundation of believing his Gospel-teaching and teachings, the Gospel of the Kingdom. In other words Jesus without his Gospel of the Kingdom word and words is a false, counterfeit Jesus. Calling Jesus "lord" and not believing his teachings and words is the fatal trap into which we must not fall. False prophets are those who speak of Jesus, but not of his Gospel-teachings/words. When the phrase "Gospel of the Kingdom" is absent, beware! Be alarmed!

This central and dramatic warning was so essential that it was repeated by both the Apostles Paul and John. In 1 Timothy 6:3, Paul said, "If anyone **does not bring the teachings of Jesus**," be alarmed and beware. You are being scammed!

John repeated exactly the same apostolic warning in 2 John 7-10: "Many deceivers have gone out into the world, who do not confess Jesus Messiah as coming as a fully human being. This is a deceiver and an antichrist...Everyone who in the name of 'progress' **does not remain in the teaching of the Messiah**, does not have God. The person who remains in **his teaching** has both the Father and the Son. If anyone comes to you and does not bring **that teaching**, do not welcome him into your house or greet him as a fellow believer." We are to distance ourselves from anyone who does not stress, emphasize and insist on the **Gospel teaching and teachings of Messiah Jesus**.

Now please listen to these statements from recent times. Dr. James Kennedy of Coral Ridge Ministries (he died in 2007):

> **Many people today think that the essence of Christianity is the teachings of Jesus. That isn't so.** The teachings of Jesus are somewhat secondary to Christianity. If you read the epistles of the apostle Paul, which make up about half of the New Testament, you'll see almost nothing whatsoever said about the teachings of Jesus. Not one of his parables is mentioned. In fact, throughout the rest of the New Testament there's little reference to the teachings of Jesus. In the Apostles' creed, the most universally held Christian creed, there is no reference to the teachings of Jesus or to the example of Jesus. In fact, in recounting Christ's earthly life, the creed states simply that He was "born of the virgin Mary, suffered under Pontius Pilate, was

> crucified, dead and was buried." It mentions only two days in Jesus's life — that of His birth and that of His death. **Christianity centers not in the teachings of Jesus but in the person of Jesus as the incarnate God who came into the world to take upon himself our guilt and to die in our place.**[41]

Also from Kennedy:

> But Jesus says, "I am the way." **It is not the teachings of Jesus, it is not the preaching of Jesus**, it is not the example of Jesus, it is not the Sermon on the Mount, it is not the Beatitudes, or anything else that He taught or said that is the way. The way is Christ Himself, the divine second Person of the Trinity, the Creator of the galaxies that came into this world.[42]

This is a huge and glaring falsehood, since Paul preached the same Gospel of the Kingdom as did Jesus, to all, Jews and Gentiles alike, in Acts (14:22; 19:8; 20:24-25: 28:23, 31).

Now this equally astonishing and alarming statement from another top evangelical scholar, Dr. Harold O.J. Brown:

> Christianity takes its name from its founder, or rather from what he was called, the Christ. Buddhism is also named for its founder. And non-Muslims often call Islam Mohammedanism. But while Buddhism and Islam are based primarily on the *teaching* of the Buddha and Mohammed, respectively, **Christianity is based primarily on the person of Christ**. **The Christian faith is *not* belief in his teaching**, but in what is taught **about him**. The appeal of Protestant liberals to "believe as Jesus believed," rather than to believe in Jesus, is a dramatic transformation of the fundamental nature of Christianity.[43]

That is a colossal lie. You cannot believe in Jesus and not believe his teaching!

Then also C.S. Lewis. Lewis denies Jesus while claiming to follow him! He wrote: "The **Gospels are not 'the gospel**,' the statement of the Christian belief."[44] So then the words of Jesus are not the Gospel! This

---

[41] D. James Kennedy and Jerry Newcombe, *The Presence of a Hidden God*, 2008, chapter "How I Know Jesus Is God," p. 82, emphasis added.

[42] *"The Only Way," Daily Truth* devotional, emphasis added.

[43] *Heresies*, 1984, p. 13, emphasis added.

[44] Introduction to J.B. Phillips' *Letters to Young Churches*, p. 9-10, emphasis added.

must be the ultimate falsehood, the ultimate deception. So Jesus has to be rescued from "church"!

Dr. James Dunn:

> Hurtado does not think it **necessary for Jesus to have thought and spoken of himself in the same terms as his followers thought and spoke of him** in the decades subsequent to his crucifixion, in order for the convictions of those followers to be treated as valid by Christians today; though he also notes that most Christians probably think that there was "some degree of continuity" between what Jesus thought of himself and subsequent Christology.[45]

Has he read the New Testament?!

Professor Richard Hiers made this amazing admission: "Interpreters of Christian **persuasion have ordinarily not been especially interested in what Jesus intended and did in his own time**."[46]

Note this carefully from Dr. H.A. Wolfson, leading authority on what the post-biblical "church fathers" did:

> The Church Fathers' conception of the Trinity was a combination of Jewish monotheism and pagan polytheism, except that to them this combination was a good combination. In fact, it was to them an **ideal combination of what is best in Jewish monotheism and of what is best in pagan polytheism**, and consequently they gloried in it and pointed to it as evidence of their belief. We have on this the testimony of Gregory of Nyssa, one of the great figures in the history of the philosophic formulation of the doctrine of the Trinity. His words are repeated by John of Damascus, the last of the Church Fathers. The Christian conception of God, argues Gregory of Nyssa, is neither the polytheism of the Greeks nor the monotheism of the Jews, and consequently it must be true. "For the truth passes in the mean [middle] between these two conceptions, destroying each heresy, and yet accepting what is useful to it from each. **The Jewish dogma is destroyed** by the acceptance of the Word and by belief in the Spirit, while the polytheistic error of the Greek school is

---

[45] *Did the First Christians Worship Jesus?* p. 93, fn. 2.

[46] *Jesus and the Future*, 1981, p. 1, emphasis added.

made to vanish by the unity of the nature abrogating this imagination of plurality" (*Oration Catechetica*, 13).[47]

The church fathers admitted that they were rejecting the Jewish (and Jesus') understanding of God. They worked out the later fearfully complicated definitions of God, and Jesus in relation to God, and found themselves caught in a web of impossibly difficult arguments, trying to explain how God can be one and at the same time three.

But the easy truth is this: "There is no indication that Jesus would have understood the 'Father,' from whom he felt himself to have been sent and to whom he probably felt himself to be related in a special way, differently from the monotheistic God of Judaism."[48]

"The Shema was the prayer which all pious Jews were expected to recite three times daily…It occupied a similar special position in late Judaism to the Lord's prayer in Christianity." That is very true, but then Dr. Anderson speaks of "the Church that did not any longer recite the shema. But here at least in his statement of the first commandment, Jesus stands foursquare within the orbit of Jewish piety."[49]

But on what authority was this fundamental teaching of Jesus defining the one true God discarded? The Church did not abandon the lord's prayer! Why abandon his creed?

The process of restoration is furthered when people earnestly **seek the original meaning of the Kingdom of God as preached by the original (human) Jesus**. The Gospel itself is all about the Kingdom of God, as well as the death and resurrection of Jesus, and "Gospel" should never be divorced from the Kingdom. The pagan notion of "heaven" for "souls" at death has replaced the hope of the Kingdom coming on earth. That paganism must be banished from the Christian vocabulary if the Bible is to be understood.

This necessary return to "the faith handed down once for all time to the saints" (Jude 3) can be facilitated by the constant use of what might be called "comprehensive summary verses," which encapsulate the basic, non-negotiable truths of Scripture. These would be a new set of "John 3:16's." For example, brilliant summaries are supplied by John 3:36;

---

[47] Wolfson, *The Philosophy of the Church Fathers*, p. 361-363.

[48] Karl-Heinz Ohlig, *One or Three? From the Father of Jesus to the Trinity*, Lang, 2000, p. 31.

[49] Hugh Anderson, *New Century Bible Commentary on Mark*, p. 280.

Hebrews 5:9; Acts 8:12; Luke 8:12; Mark 1:14-15; Matthew 28:18-20, and many others. These verses, which are strikingly absent from contemporary preaching, will provide a framework within which the complete biblical story of man's destiny will become clear to Bible readers.

Harper Collins' Bible Dictionary states: "The Gospel is the proclamation of the Kingdom announced by Jesus (Mark 1:14-15) and now proclaimed by the church." But is it? Do churches preach the Gospel of the Kingdom of God?

One might say that the churches are playing golf with the club held upside down. A complete restructuring is needed. No cosmetic alterations will solve the problem. There is a fatal flaw in the foundation of what we know as the faith. The Kingdom Gospel is missing in current preaching, or at best hopelessly vague.

Gary Burge says in the *NIV Application Commentary*, "Stanley Grenz has reviewed the failed attempts of evangelical theology to fire the imagination of the modern world. He argues for 'the kingdom of God' as **the new organizing center** of what we say and do."[50] It ought to be, and must be if Jesus in Luke 4:43 is really heard. And Paul in Acts 20:24-25; 19:8; 28:23, 31 (cp. Acts 8:12).

Do seminaries understand the Gospel?

> Over the course of the past year, faculty from each of Fuller's three schools have met together to discuss the question: What is the Gospel? A dozen years ago, the late Robert Guelich made the question the topic of his inaugural address, noting that years of professional work had returned him again and again to this fundamental subject. Guelich told the story of an encounter with the founder Charles Fuller after a seminary forum, with the "inspiration of Scripture" as its topic. Fuller commented that he longed for the day **when the seminary would host a forum on the question: "What is the Gospel?"**[51]

This is an amazing and instructive admission. The fact is that they really are not sure what the Gospel is, and yet they say they are saving people by preaching "it." The plain fact is that the Gospel of the

[50]Gary Burge, *Letters of John*, NIV Application Commentary, p. 62.
[51]*Theology, News and Notes*, Fuller Theological Seminary, spring 2004.

Kingdom, including of course the covenant-ratifying and atoning blood of Jesus and his resurrection, is the Gospel. Until the "heaven" at death teaching, which is Plato's and not Jesus', is dropped, how can progress be made? And how can we be sure that anyone is saved by believing the teaching of Plato and calling it the teaching of Jesus? Is God as sloppy as we are with our thinking?! Is He so indulgent that He really does not care as long as we are sincere, although ignorant — of the nature of man, his destiny, the identity of God as the one God of Israel (Mark 12:29) and Jesus as the Messiah lord, not God (Luke 2:11)? And Jesus' own definition of the Gospel?

Shailer Matthews, D.D., Professor of Theology, Chicago Seminary, saw how essential a part is played in the teaching of Jesus, by the Kingdom:

> It is a serious error to hold that **the Kingdom of God** plays no important role in apostolic Christianity. Such a view both lacks historical perspective and is at variance with the entire thought of the literature of apostolic Christianity. The very name of the new movement, *Christ*ianity, would suggest the contrary opinion. So far from the eschatological Kingdom of God being a secondary element in the early church, **it is its great conditioning belief**. The preaching of the first evangelists was not a call to ethical ideals or an argument as to certain truths. Rather it was the proclamation of a message [about the Kingdom]...As regards the person of the Messiah, there is of course no question that the early church believed that Jesus was the Christ who had gone to heaven, whence he would come to introduce the new age and the new Kingdom. **This was the very core of the entire Christian movement...To think of Jesus as deliberately using a term [Kingdom of God] with a meaning different from what it would have been for others is not only to raise a question as to his morals, but as to his capacity as a teacher.**[52]

How very *much unlike* popular evangelism the New Testament data on the Gospel of the Kingdom sounds!

---

[52]*The Messianic Hope in the New Testament,* University of Chicago Press, 1905, pp. 144, 155.

I make no apology for repetition. Churchill said: "If you have an important point to make, don't try to be subtle or clever. Use a pile driver. Hit the point once. Then come back and hit it again. Then hit it a third time — a tremendous whack."

I have adopted in this translation what I admit is a somewhat shocking practice of placing a lower-case "l" on "lord" when the reference is to Jesus. The point is to remind readers of the fundamental distinction between the Lord God (YHVH) and the lord Messiah (Luke 2:11). This is based on the Bible's favorite umbrella text in Psalm 110:1 where YHVH, the one GOD, addresses an oracle to the predicted Messiah, who is David's son and also his lord (*adoni*, "my lord," not Lord). In 1 Corinthians 8:4-6 Paul echoes the unitarian creed of Jesus in Mark 12:29. He defines God as the Father from whom all originates, and then adds his definition of Jesus as the one "lord Messiah." Psalm 110:1 and its very easy distinction between the one Lord YHVH and the non-Deity lord (*adoni*, "my lord," all 195 times not Deity!) lies behind Paul's thinking, as it does behind all the thinking of Jesus (Mark 12:28-37). On no account should the two lords of Psalm 110:1 be muddled, resulting in two who are "Lord God," an obvious violation of monotheism. *Adoni*, my lord, is the deliberate and unambiguous non-Deity title for Jesus, the man Messiah (1 Tim. 2:5, etc.).

Sometimes the New Testament text does not make it clear whether the Lord God or the lord Messiah is intended. This affects nothing of vital importance, since Jesus and God are working in harmony (John 10:30), Jesus being the supreme agent of God his Father, who is also Jesus' God (Heb. 1:9). The point of using lower case for the lord Jesus is to remind readers over and over again of the central truth provided by the oracle of YHVH in Psalm 110:1. The relationship between God and Jesus is firmly established by the contrast between YHVH, the One God of the Bible, and the non-Deity figure now appointed to sit at the right hand of YHVH, pending his return to the earth to rule in the future Kingdom. Jesus is the *adoni,* "my lord" of Psalm 110:1 and his relation to the Father is repeated continually in the New Testament, summarized by Paul's un-complex creed in 1 Timothy 2:4-5: God "wants all people to be saved and come to the knowledge of the truth, namely that there is one God and one mediator between that one God and humanity, Messiah

Jesus, who is himself **human**." This is the task of a Church desiring to be faithful to Jesus and Scripture.

For those readers of this translation who might be skeptical that the long-held, cherished traditions of Christianity could be radically mistaken, the words of the leading Christologist, Dr. James Dunn, are suggestive:

> There is of course always the possibility that "popular pagan superstition" became popular *Christian* superstition, by a gradual assimilation and spread of belief at the level of popular piety (we must beware of assuming that all developments in Christian thought stem from the Pauls and Johns of Christianity).[53]

It may well be that "orthodoxy's" massive dependence on John and Paul ought to raise our suspicions that the Bible is being used selectively and thus misleadingly to bolster the status quo. The reader is invited to assess this issue with a Berean attitude (Acts 17:11). Luke in that verse commends a searching, noble-minded approach suitable to all those invited to rule the world with Jesus in the coming Kingdom on earth.

Finally, I suggest that the popular definition of God as "three in one" tends to keep millions of Jews and Muslims at arm's length from the real, historical, now risen Jesus of Nazareth, for whom unitary monotheism was the basis of true faith (Mark 12:29; John 17:3). Is it not time for intelligent worshipers of God in church to make clear to themselves the meaning of their public confession of belief in Jesus as "begotten, not made," lest that confession run the risk of being mere tradition learned by rote, and words without meaning?

I leave the reader to consider again and take to heart the astonishing admission of missiologist Mortimer Arias quoted previously: "Why not try Jesus' own definition of his mission — and ours? For Jesus, evangelization was no more and no less than announcing the kingdom of God!" I suggest that the Gospel of the Kingdom be given its actual biblical meaning as the Kingdom of David to be restored, that is by the greater son of David, Jesus Messiah (1 Chron. 18:14; 28:5; 2 Chron. 13:8; 21:7; Isa. 1:26; Mark 11:10).

---

[53] *Christology in the Making*, SCM Press, second edition, 1989, p. 251.

The unique value of this translation lies in its introduction and accompanying notes, designed to correct widespread misunderstandings caused by post-biblical, unexamined tradition. Some modern translations use other translations as a base text. I have translated some of the New Testament books directly from the Greek text (ed. Aland, Metzger, et al, 1983). For other books, I have used and heavily modified public domain Bible translations, including the Wikipedia Bible (aka Free Bible Version).

Other Publications

The Amazing Aims and Claims of Jesus (2006)
The Coming Kingdom of the Messiah (2002)
The God of Jesus in Light of Christian Dogma by Kegan Chandler (2016)
Jesus Was Not a Trinitarian (2007)
The Law, the Sabbath and New Testament Christianity (2005)
Our Fathers Who Aren't in Heaven: The Forgotten Christianity of Jesus, the Jew (1999)
They Never Told Me This in Church! by Greg Deuble (2010)
What Happens When We Die? (booklet)
Who Is Jesus? (booklet)
Focus on the Kingdom (free monthly magazine)

Also *The Doctrine of the Trinity: Christianity's Self-Inflicted Wound*
by Anthony Buzzard and Charles Hunting (1998)

www.restorationfellowship.org
www.thehumanjesus.org

Matthew

1 1This is the origin[1] of Jesus the Messiah, the son of David, and the son
of Abraham, beginning with the genealogical record: 2Abraham
fathered[2] Isaac; and Isaac fathered Jacob; and Jacob fathered Judah and
his brothers; 3and Judah fathered Perez and Zerah (their mother was

---

[1]Matthew has deliberately used the powerful Greek word *genesis*, origin, to ensure that readers understand that the Son of God, the promised Messiah whom he presents is a real human being, though supernaturally "begotten in Mary" (1:20). His words are a direct allusion to Gen. 5:1 which speaks of the "genesis, the origin and birth record of Adam." On no account are we to think of the much later, post-biblical concept of an "eternally begotten" Son, who had no beginning in time, to whom Greek philosophically minded church fathers attributed the nonsense phrase "beginningless beginning." CEB translates, "A record of the ancestors of Jesus Christ." Holman: "A historical record of Jesus Christ." Matthew intended to rule out and block the very confusing and complicated idea that the Son was older than his ancestors! This excellent statement makes our point, and Matthew's, very well: "Not only was the Gospel of Matthew referred to among Greek-speaking Jews as **Genesis,** but also his phrase 'the book of the genesis of Jesus Christ' is strongly reminiscent of the Greek version of Gen. 5.1, 'the book of the genesis of human beings' and Gen. 2.4, 'the book of the genesis of heaven and earth' [the account of God working with preexisting material to fashion the world for Adam]. In Jesus Christ, God had made a new beginning. To borrow from the language of Hollywood, the first Gospel could be billed as 'Genesis II, the Sequel'" (Douglas R.A. Hare, *Matthew*). The major importance of Matt. 1:1 is that it defines who Jesus is. John and Paul should not be twisted to contradict this primary, "umbrella" definition of Jesus, meant to identify the true Son of God, the Messiah. Jesus is the visible image of the invisible one God. In Jesus we see the visible glory of God (John 1:18), and Jesus is the visible stamp or impress of his Father, who alone is God (Heb. 1:2). Man is "the image and glory of God" (1 Cor. 11:7), and in Jesus that ideal image is restored. He does what Adam failed to do. Jesus is the "man Messiah" of 1 Tim. 2:5 and certainly not "GOD," which would make two who are GOD — and this breaks the first command and the creed of Jesus and Israel (Mk. 12:29; John 17:3).

[2]"begat" = to cause to come into existence, to procreate, to father. Equally true of the Son of God who was begotten, brought into existence by miracle by God in 1:18, 20. The begetting of the Messiah by God was predicted in Isa. 9:6: "A child/Son will be begotten [by God, a divine passive]"; Isa. 7:14: "The virgin will conceive," implying a divine paternity. See 2 Sam. 7:14 and 1 Chron. 17:13, where God *will become* the Father of the Messianic son of David (Heb. 1:5). Also Ps. 2:7 and Ps. 110:3 (LXX). Lk. 1:35 and Mt. 1:18, 20 take up the prophecies of divine begetting and show how they were fulfilled in history. John 1:13 (see Jerusalem Bible) speaks of the virginal begetting in the case of the Son of God, Jesus. Heb. 1:5 and 5:5 see the fulfillment of

Tamar); and Perez fathered Hezron; and Hezron fathered Ram; 4and Ram
fathered Amminadab; and Amminadab fathered Nahshon; and Nahshon
fathered Salmon; 5and Salmon fathered Boaz (his mother was Rahab);
and Boaz fathered Obed (his mother was Ruth); and Obed fathered Jesse;
6and Jesse fathered King David.

David fathered Solomon (his mother had been Uriah's wife); 7and
Solomon fathered Rehoboam; and Rehoboam fathered Abijah; and
Abijah fathered Asa; 8and Asa fathered Jehoshaphat; and Jehoshaphat
fathered Joram; and Joram fathered Uzziah; 9and Uzziah fathered
Jotham; and Jotham fathered Ahaz; and Ahaz fathered Hezekiah; 10and
Hezekiah fathered Manasseh; and Manasseh fathered Amon; and Amon
fathered Josiah; 11and Josiah fathered Jeconiah[3] and his brothers, at the
time of the exile to Babylon.

12After the exile to Babylon, Jeconiah fathered[4] Shealtiel; and
Shealtiel fathered[5] Zerubbabel; 13and Zerubbabel fathered Abiud; and

---

Ps. 2:7 at the birth of Jesus, as does Acts 13:33 (not KJV, which mistranslates here) where the "raising up" is fulfilled when Jesus is *begotten.* Acts 13:34 speaks in contrast of the later resurrection of Jesus *from the dead.* 1 John 5:1 speaks of God as the begetter and 1 John 5:18 (not KJV, corrupted in this verse) of the coming into existence, begetting of the Son, who now protects believers. The begetting of the Son in 1 John 5:18 defines a time when this happened. To dissolve the easy word "beget" into timelessness destroys both the unitary monotheism (God is a single divine Person) and the human Messiah, who in order to be a real human, must begin in the womb of his mother (cp. Isa. 49:1, 5). Jesus is the second Adam, and everyone knows that Adam was a human person. Creedal Trinitarianism led to the impossible claim that Jesus is "*man* but not *a* man"!

[3]Known also as Jehoiachin. It is important to know that the royal line from Solomon expired in Jehoiachin (Jer. 22:28-30). The royal successor was "borrowed" from the Nathan line found in Luke 3:27. Shealtiel (Salathiel) is found in both lists. Jeconiah (Jehoiachin) was considered the legal father of Shealtiel (Salathiel). Thus the blood line came through Nathan when the line expired in the list from Solomon. Shealtiel was the uncle of Zerubbabel. Joseph and Mary would both then be of the seed of David. Mary of course had to be, since Jesus, in order to qualify as Messiah (Mt. 1:1), must be related by blood to David (Acts 2:30; Ps. 132:11). Jesus is Son of God by miraculous intervention from God, creating the second Adam, the head of the new creation, and son of Mary and of David, as well as being the promised seed of Eve (Gen. 3:15. For further info. see my *Who Is Jesus?* at restorationfellowship.org)

[4]That is, legally, to supply a successor for Jeconiah who was not allowed to have a son on the throne of David.

[5]Actually the uncle of Zerubbabel.

Abiud fathered Eliakim; and Eliakim fathered Azor; 14and Azor fathered
Zadok; and Zadok fathered Achim; and Achim fathered Eliud; 15and
Eliud fathered Eleazar; and Eleazar fathered Matthan;[6] and Matthan
fathered Jacob; 16and Jacob fathered Joseph, who was the husband of
Mary, from whom Jesus was born,[7] the one who is called the Messiah.

17So all the generations from Abraham to David total fourteen; from
David to the Babylonian exile total fourteen; and from the Babylonian
exile to the Messiah total fourteen.

18The origin[8] of Jesus Messiah was like this: His mother, Mary, was
engaged to be married to Joseph, but before they came together she
became pregnant through holy spirit. 19Joseph, her husband-to-be, was a
good man, and since he did not want to shame her publicly, he decided to
break the engagement quietly. 20As he was thinking about these things,

---

[6]Probably the grandfather of Mary and Joseph, Matthat in Luke 3:24. Mary and Joseph would be first cousins, both descendants of the royal house of David. See Lord Hervey's fine work on the *Genealogies of Jesus Christ*, also in *Smith's Bible Dictionary*. Both lists would be Joseph's line, i.e. from Solomon, whose line expired, and from Nathan, another son of David.

[7]The careful reader of Scripture will notice the string of verses which speak of the "begetting" = coming into existence of the Son of God. Thus in Isa. 7:14, the virginal begetting of the Messiah is predicted. In Isa. 9:6 the child/Son (in parallel) is said to be "begotten," that is, by God, a divine passive. Here in the genealogy of the Son of God, he is "begotten" in and from Mary; the implied Father is God. In the list preceding, fathers begat their sons, but in the case of Mary, the fathering, begetting was authored by GOD. 1 John 5:18 speaks of the Son of God, Jesus, as "the one who was begotten" (aorist pointing to a moment in time). The impossible idea of an "eternal generation," a phrase with no intelligible meaning, is entirely foreign to the Bible, unknown to any Bible writer.

[8]The word is *genesis* = origin (as in 1:1), not just birth, but the point of time at which the Son of God came into existence. A variant *gennesis* was attempted by some manuscripts because "origin" for Jesus was highly embarrassing, as it still ought to be, to the much later notion that the Son was begotten *not in time*, but eternity! The later concept of "eternal generation" is foreign to the Bible and has no intelligible meaning. Any reader who is not in the grip of later tradition will have no difficulty at all with Matthew's Son of God, Jesus, who came into existence some 2000 years ago. Luke's account of the coming into existence of the Son is no less pointedly explicit (Lk. 1:35). Jesus is called the Son of the Father, and God called the Father of Jesus hundreds of times. This text can create the revolution necessary for returning to Scripture to identify who Jesus, the Son of God, is. And in this way the pure monotheism of Jesus, which he stated was the most important of all teachings, can be restored (Mk. 12:29; 10:18; Jn. 17:3; 5:44).

an angel of the Lord appeared to him in a dream and said, "Joseph, son
of David, do not be afraid to take Mary to be your wife, because the
child who has been fathered[9] in her is from holy spirit. 21 She will give
birth to a son and you will name him Jesus, because he will save his
people from their sins." 22 All this happened to fulfill what the Lord said
through the prophet: 23 "Look: the virgin will become pregnant, and will
give birth to a son, and they will call him Immanuel," which means "God
is with us."[10] 24 Joseph woke up and did what the angel of the Lord had
told him to do. He married Mary, 25 but did not have marital relations with
her until she gave birth to a son,[11] whom he named Jesus.

---

[9]The verb is *gennao* which means "to cause to come into existence," "to beget," since this is the activity *in* Mary, not the later birth of the Son, and it describes the activity of the Father (that is, God, working through His creative operational power, the holy spirit, to effect a miracle). The *origin* of the Son of God, the Messiah is thus based firmly in history, and the Son of God is a real human being supernaturally conceived and begotten, having his origin in Mary. In later post-biblical theology under the influence of pagan ideas, the Messiah's origin was antedated to a time before Genesis and later to eternity. This made Jesus essentially non-human, since he was said to be pre-human. The birth, origin, narratives of Matthew and Luke were thus perverted and essential truth about Jesus was lost. Matthew's and Luke's accounts of the origin of Jesus were specifically written to counteract and block the notion of a pre-human Son of God. But tradition and dogma later overwhelmed these accounts. The gospel of John was later used or misused, wrongly, to contradict the very straightforward accounts of the origin of the Son of God. Readers of Scripture would do well to ground themselves in the historical narrative of the origin of the Son of God, who is the head of the new creation, the second Adam. The whole history of dogma turns out to have been a rejection of Scripture at a fundamental level. It is highly significant and instructive to know that people holding to the "orthodox" definition of the Son of God are taught to believe that Jesus was "man, but not a man." This is incomprehensible and defeats the biblical insistence on the Son of God being "the man Messiah Jesus" (1 Tim. 2:5, and very often). For an account of the human Jesus, see Daniel Kirk, *A Man Attested by God*.

[10]This title does not of course mean that the Son of God *is* God, making two GODS! It describes the function of Jesus as God's unique agent and revealer of God's will for humankind. "God was in Christ reconciling the world to Himself" (2 Cor. 5:19). "God was *in* Christ," not "God *was* Christ." A lady in Proverbs 30:1 named her son Ithiel, which is Hebrew for "God is with me." No one imagined the child was actually God! It was descriptive of the mother's conviction that God had given her a son. No one in NT times imagined that God could be born, much less that He could die or be tempted!

[11]After the birth of Jesus, Joseph and Mary had a normal sexual relationship, producing half brothers and sisters of Jesus named in Mark 6:3. The Roman Catholic notion that

2 1After Jesus was born in Bethlehem in Judea during the reign of King
Herod, magi came from the east to Jerusalem. 2"Where is he who was
born king of the Jews?" they asked. "We saw his star in the east, and we
came to kneel in honor[12] before him." 3When King Herod heard about
this he was very disturbed, as was the whole of Jerusalem. 4Herod
summoned all the chief priests and religious teachers of the people, and
asked them where the Messiah was supposed to be born. 5"Bethlehem in
Judea," they said to him, "because that is what the prophet wrote: 6'You,
Bethlehem in the land of Judea, you are certainly not the least important
of Judah's leaders, because a ruler will come from you who will
shepherd My people Israel.'" 7Then Herod secretly called the magi and
established from them when the star had appeared. 8He sent them on to
Bethlehem, saying, "When you get there, search for the child, and when
you find him let me know so that I can go and kneel before him too."

9After listening to the king they went on their way, and the star which
they had seen in the east led them onwards until it stopped above the
place where the child was. 10When they saw the star they were

---

Mary never had a sexual relationship with Joseph, the doctrine that she was *perpetually* a virgin, is completely false. Equally false is the idea that Mary was sinless (called the doctrine of the immaculate conception, not to be confused with the virginal birth), and that she was assumed to heaven bodily at death. Mary is currently dead, sleeping the sleep of death (Ps. 13:3; Ecc. 9:5, 10; John 11:11, 14). She will be raised to life in the future resurrection. Mary was turned into a pagan goddess, along with "saints," who are in fact now dead. Praying to the dead is strictly forbidden in the Bible as it encourages contact with the demonic world. It was from the second century that paganism entered the church camouflaged, and this is in need of reform in our time. Justin Martyr, a church father of the second century, was deceived to the point of thinking that the holy spirit which overshadowed Mary was actually a preexisting Son effecting his own conception! (see Fitzmyer, *Anchor Bible,* on Luke 1:35).

[12]To translate this in our time as "worship" is inevitably confusing since worship in contemporary English is due only to God. The wise men certainly did not imagine the Messiah to be GOD! They were perhaps relying on earlier Bible passages including Daniel (especially 9:24-27) who as a Jew worked in Babylon. The planetary sign for this unique historical event was provided by a conjunction of the king star Jupiter alongside Regulus in connection with Virgo (cp. Rev. 12:1). The stopping of the star over the place where Jesus was born could refer to the retrograde movement of Jupiter, which changes direction.

overwhelmed with joy. 11They went into the house and saw the child[13]
with Mary his mother. They bowed and knelt before[14] him. Then they
opened their treasures and presented him with gifts of gold, frankincense,
and myrrh. 12Warned by God in a dream not to go back to Herod, the
magi left for their own country by a different road.

13After they had left, an angel of the Lord appeared to Joseph in a
dream and said, "Get up and take the child and his mother and flee to
Egypt, and stay there until I tell you, because Herod is going to look for
the child to kill him." 14So Joseph got up and took the boy and his
mother, and left during the night for Egypt, 15and stayed there until
Herod's death, fulfilling what the Lord had said through the prophet: "I
called My son out of Egypt."[15]

16When Herod realized he had been tricked by the magi, he was
extremely angry.[16] He sent men to kill all the young boys two years old

---

[13]By this time not a tiny babe but a young child, a toddler, under 2 years old. The place was the house and not a guestroom with a manger. The popular traditions confuse the accounts of Matthew and Luke.

[14]The word "worship" in Scripture is used of reverence to God and kneeling in honor before distinguished persons. It is very misleading to think that "worship," as used in the Bible, is offered exclusively to God. The words for worship are "flexible" terms and describe reverence for, kneeling in honor, doing homage before both God and superior human persons (see for example 2 Chron. 29:20; Rev. 3:9; 1 Kings 1:16, 23; 1 Sam. 25:23).

[15]The original reference in Hosea 11:1 was to Israel, but since Jesus represents the "ideal Israel," this prophecy is true of him too, and in all its fullness of meaning. Jesus is what Israel was intended to be, but failed to be. Jesus as Son of God perfectly reflected the One God and His will, and thus Jesus was called by a name which described the unique work of the One God in Jesus, i.e. Immanuel, "With us is God." Jesus was the ideal Son, obedient always to the Father, learning the "trade" of the Father and representing the Father as perfect agent.

[16]Opposition to God in any form is likely to provoke an irrational reaction. The demonic world headed by Satan opposes truth at every point. The Devil was from the beginning the master liar, and he has not changed in this respect. His lies are murderous since they deprive people of the life-giving power of God transmitted by the words of God, spoken by Jesus and the Apostles, and Scripture. All falsehood and false belief is thus a poison to be avoided at all costs. The Devil trades on the colossal lie that "doctrine" does not matter! All teaching is doctrine and we need true teaching, not false. The Gospel of the Kingdom (Lk. 4:43) truly taught and believed imparts energy and eventually immortality (1 Thess. 2:13). Those who "love the truth" will be saved (2 Thess. 2:10), and those who despise it or treat it lightly will not. Ignorance is culpable in 2 Pet. 3:5; Mt 13:10-17; Acts 28:23-27.

and under in Bethlehem and its surrounding areas, according to the time
period he had learned from the magi. 17This then fulfilled the prophecy
spoken through Jeremiah: 18"In Ramah a cry was heard, much weeping
and mourning, Rachel crying for her children. And she refused to be
comforted, because they are no more."
19When Herod died an angel of the Lord appeared in a dream to
Joseph in Egypt, and said, 20"Get up and take the child and his mother,
and go to the land of Israel, because those who were trying to kill the
child are dead." 21So Joseph got up and took the boy and his mother, and
went back to the land of Israel. 22But when he heard that Archelaus had
succeeded his father Herod as king of Judea, Joseph was afraid to go
there. Warned by God in a dream, he went to the region of Galilee, 23and
settled down in a village called Nazareth, to fulfill what was said through
the prophets: "He will be called a Nazarene."[17]

3 1In those days John the Baptist came on the scene. He was in the
Judean desert, proclaiming the Gospel: 2"Repent, because the
Kingdom of Heaven has drawn near."[18] 3This is the one Isaiah the
prophet spoke about when he said, "A voice cries out in the desert,
'Prepare the way of the Lord; make the road straight for Him.'"[19] 4John
was wearing camel-hair clothes tied with a leather belt around his waist.
His food was locusts and wild honey. 5People were going out to him from

---

[17]Perhaps a play on words, the Hebrew "*nezer*," branch, i.e. of David, being a Messianic title (Isa. 4:2; 11:1; 53:2; Jer. 23:5; 33:15; Zech. 3:8; 6:12; see Ps. 72, 89; 1 Chron. 17; 2 Chron. 13:8).

[18]This does not mean that the Kingdom had come! The whole presentation of Matthew is that the Kingdom of God was approaching, but not yet revealed in its true Messianic sense. This is to be expected only at the future return of Jesus at his Parousia (Lk. 21:35; 2 Tim. 4:1). The Gospel of the Kingdom, the Christian Gospel, is the Gospel about the Kingdom of David to be restored by Jesus (1 Chron. 17; 2 Chron. 13:8). The Kingdom of Heaven is not remotely to do with going to heaven at death, or at any time! It is the Kingdom coming to earth when God sends it (Dan. 2:44; 7:27; Mic. 4:1-8).

[19]Jesus as the unique agent of YHVH, the God of Israel, represents the Lord God. Jesus is of course not the Lord GOD (which would make two GODS!) but the special and unique agent (*shaliach* in Hebrew) of the One God of monotheism. Jesus was a unitarian in the biblical sense, agreeing with complete conviction to the creed of his Jewish, biblical heritage (Mk. 12:29ff; Jn. 17:3; Mal. 2:10; Ps. 110:1: "my lord" not "my Lord," *adoni* not *Adonai*).

Jerusalem, all over Judea, and all the region around the Jordan, 6and they
were being baptized[20] by him in the Jordan River, confessing their sins.
7But when John saw many Pharisees and Sadducees coming to be
baptized, he said to them, "You brood of vipers, who warned you to flee
from the coming wrath? 8Produce fruit which corresponds to repentance,
9and do not imagine telling yourselves, 'Abraham is our father.' I tell you
that God could make children of Abraham out of these stones. 10Right
now the axe is ready to chop down the trees. Every tree which does not
produce good fruit[21] will be cut down and thrown into the fire.
11"As for me, I baptize you in water for repentance, but the one who
is coming after me is more powerful than I am. I am not worthy to carry
his sandals. He will baptize you in holy spirit[22] and fire. 12His winnowing
tool is in his hand and he will clear his threshing floor. The wheat he will
gather into the storehouse, but the chaff he will burn up[23] with fire which
cannot be put out."[24]
13Then Jesus came from Galilee to the Jordan River to be baptized by
John. 14But John tried to dissuade him. "I need to be baptized by you, and
you are coming to me to be baptized?" he said. 15"Let it be done now,
because it is appropriate for us to fulfill all that is right,"[25] Jesus said to

---

[20]Baptism in water is fundamental to the Christian faith, and to deny it or refuse it puts one in the dangerous position of resisting Jesus and the Apostles (see Lk. 7:30). It is disobedience (see John 3:36; Heb. 5:9; 1 Tim. 6:3) and without obedience there can be no salvation.

[21]Reminiscent of the famous Ps. 1, which depicts the two possible ways of life for all human beings. Bearing fruit in the NT is based on the seed of the Kingdom of God Gospel (Mt. 13; Mk. 4; Lk. 8). Repentance and forgiveness depend on believing and obeying the Gospel of the Kingdom (Mk. 4:11-12; Mt. 13:19; Lk. 8:12).

[22]Not of course to the exclusion of baptism in water, which is commanded everywhere and in the Great Commission until the end of the age, the return of Jesus (28:19-20).

[23]The concept is of a consuming and destructive fire, not a fire inflicting eternal torture. The concept of unending conscious punishment is foreign to Scripture. Jude 7 refers to the "eternal fire" which consumed Sodom and Gomorrah. It is the "fire of the age to come."

[24]The idea is that it will not be extinguished until it has completed its work of consuming its victims. There is no hint of an "eternal torment" here.

[25]Baptism in water is an essential Christian teaching, based on the command and practice of Jesus and contained in the Great Commission which is the marching order for the Church until the end of the age (28:19-20; for "end of the age" see 13:39, 40, 49; 24:3). To remove water baptism from the Christian scheme is to confront Jesus head

him. So John agreed. 16After he was baptized, Jesus immediately got out
of the water, and heaven opened before him, and he saw God's spirit like
a dove descending and landing on him. 17A voice out of the heavens said,
"This is My Son,[26] the one I love, who pleases Me."

4 1Then Jesus was led by the spirit into the desert to be tempted by the
Devil.[27] 2After fasting forty days and forty nights, he was hungry.

---

on! It is fatal disobedience to the Messiah. No salvation is possible for those who disobey (Heb. 5:9).

[26]Jesus was of course Son of God from the moment of his begetting, coming into existence in Mary (Mt. 1:18, 20; Lk. 1:35; 1 John 5:18, not KJV: the Son was begotten from God). He did not begin to be the Son of God at baptism. Rom. 1:1-3 recognizes him in the same way as Son of God because he is of the Messianic lineage of David, and declared to be Son of God, *with power*, by his resurrection and ascension. Acts 13:33 applied the begetting event "You are my Son, today I have begotten you" (Ps. 2:7) to the beginning of the life of Jesus, his coming on the scene of history (mistranslated in the KJV which misleadingly adds "again") and v. 34 refers to the resurrection, raising up *again.* 2 Sam. 7:14 similarly applies the promise that God will be the Father of the Messiah to the beginning of the life of the Son, and Isa. 9:6 had predicted the same event: "To us a child will be begotten [by GOD, a divine passive]; to us a Son will be given." The typical parallelism of the two statements make both statements about the Messiah apply to the same moment. The truth of Isa. 9:6 was developed by Luke in 1:32-35. And the same begetting, beginning of the Son is described in Heb. 1. The NT speaks with a united voice on the time of the origin of the Son of God. Later Greek philosophically influenced theology turned all this into a complex nightmare, and the Son was no longer allowed to have a beginning, as every human being must, in history and time, from the womb of his/her mother.

[27]*The* Devil or *the* Satan is certainly not just "a satan, an adversary," much less is he just a name for the sinful tendency in man! "The Satan" is the external, supernatural enemy of God and man, a liar and murderer from the beginning, as Jesus said. The Devil approached, "came up to Jesus" in v. 3, thus proving that he did not originate in the mind of Jesus! The Devil "fell into condemnation" (1 Tim. 3:6) for his rebellion against God. He was not created evil! The demons (Lk. 4:41; James 2:19) are under his control and in the narrative accounts the demons are separate, intelligent personalities, never confused with their human victims, who are called "the demonized," "demon-influenced" or "demoniacs." To alter the meaning of "demon" to mean a demoniac is a tragic assault on the integrity and truth of Holy Scripture, and an affront to the meaning of easy words. God's revelation must never be suppressed to conform to some imagined "scientific" theory. We all know about the dangers of altering the meaning of easy words — like "marriage." The Trinitarian idea of GOD likewise involved a change in meaning of the biblical words for GOD. God in the Bible in some 11,000 instances (YHVH, *Elohim*, *Adonai*, *Theos*) never once means a triune God.

3The Tempter came up to him and said to him, “If you are the Son of
God, then tell these stones to become bread.” 4Jesus replied, “It is
written,[28] ‘People do not live just by eating bread, but by every word
which comes from the mouth of God.’” 5Then the Devil took him to the
holy city and had him stand on a high point of the Temple. 6“If you are
the Son of God, then throw yourself off,” he said to Jesus, “because it is
written, ‘He will command His angels to take care of you,’ and ‘They
will catch you in their hands so that you will not fall down when you trip
over a stone.’” 7Jesus said, “On the other hand, it is written, ‘You must
not put the Lord your God to the test.’” 8Then the Devil took Jesus to a
very high mountain and showed him all the kingdoms of the world in all
their majesty, and said to him, “I will give you all these if you bow down
and worship me.” 10Jesus said to him, “Go away, Satan! It is written,
‘Worship the Lord your God, and serve Him[29] alone.’” 11Then the Devil
departed from him, and angels came[30] and took care of him.

12When Jesus learned that John had been arrested, he went back to
Galilee. 13Leaving Nazareth, he went and lived in Capernaum, which is
beside the lake in the region of Zebulun and Naphtali. 14This was to
fulfill what Isaiah the prophet had said: 15“The land of Zebulun and the
land of Naphtali, on the road to the sea, beyond the Jordan, Galilee of the
Gentiles: 16The people sitting in the dark saw a great light, and to those
sitting in the country of death and shadow, on them a light dawned.”
17From then on Jesus began to preach the Gospel, saying, “Repent,
because the Kingdom of Heaven[31] is near.”

---

[28]Unlike many today, Jesus was a convinced believer in the integrity and authority of holy Scripture. God had spoken to man in Scripture, and it is our wisdom to heed this fundamental fact (see Lk. 24:44; 2 Tim. 3:16; 2 Pet. 3:16).

[29]This is one of thousands of verses in the Bible proving that God is a single Person, a single Self. The later post-biblical definition of God as Triune is false to Scripture and puts a barrier between us and the pure teaching of Jesus, our rabbi and master. The one and only Lord God is the One God of the central unitarian creed of Israel in Deut. 6:4, fully endorsed as “the most important command of all,” in agreement with a Jewish professional teacher of religion, in Mark 12:28ff. Jesus claimed to be the lord Messiah of Ps. 110:1, where *adoni*, my lord, refers, as it always does all 195 times, to a superior figure who is *not* Deity.

[30]Precisely the same word as is used earlier in v. 3 of the Devil approaching Jesus (from outside, certainly not an internal temptation, certainly not Jesus talking to himself!).

[31]The Kingdom of Heaven is of course an exact synonym for the Kingdom of God and is based on Dan. 2:44; 7:14, 18, 22, 27, and the whole vision of the prophets for peace

18As he was walking by the Sea of Galilee Jesus saw two brothers.
Simon, called Peter, and his brother Andrew were casting a net into the
sea, because they were fishermen. 19He said to them, "Come and follow
me, and I will make you fishermen to catch people." 20Immediately they
left their nets and followed him. 21Going further on, he saw two other
brothers, James the son of Zebedee, and John his brother. They were in a
boat with their father Zebedee, mending their nets. He called them. 22And
immediately they left the boat and their father, and followed him.

23Jesus was traveling throughout Galilee, teaching in their
synagogues and proclaiming the Gospel about the Kingdom,[32] and
healing people of every kind of disease and illness. 24News about him
spread all over Syria, and they brought to him everyone who was sick,
suffering from various diseases and pains, demon-influenced, epileptic,
paralyzed, and he healed them. 25Large crowds followed him from
Galilee, the Decapolis, Jerusalem, Judea, and the region beyond the
Jordan.

5 1When Jesus saw the crowds he went up the mountain.[33] He sat down
and his disciples joined him. 2He started to teach them, saying:
3"Blessed are the poor in spirit, because the Kingdom of Heaven is theirs.
4Blessed are the grieving, because they will be comforted. 5Blessed are
the gentle, because they will inherit the whole earth.[34] 6Blessed are those

---

on earth when the Messiah reigns on earth at his future return. The Kingdom of God is the core and center of the Christian Gospel (Acts 8:12; 19:8; 20:24-25; 28:23, 31).

[32]The central non-negotiable heart and core of the Christian faith as announced by Jesus and the whole NT. Repentance is not just "being forgiven" but it demands a firm, clear understanding of the Gospel of the Kingdom, which is the seed (Lk. 8:11) of immortality. The Devil, knowing this, concentrates his efforts on suppressing, hiding, removing the Gospel about the Kingdom of God. To define the Kingdom we recommend this excellent statement: It is primarily and overwhelmingly the new order and government to be introduced on earth when Jesus comes back and in which Christians are destined, as immortalized, to manage the world with Jesus (Dan. 2:44; 7:14, 18, 22, 27; Lk. 19:11-27; 21:31; Rev. 2:26-27; 11:15-18, etc).

[33]As the new Moses, giving a new Law from a mountain. Verse 2 is literally "He opened his mouth," an idiom for speaking in a somewhat formal way, by a teacher or one in authority (see Matt. 13:35; Acts 8:35; 10:34; Eph. 6:19; Rev. 13:5-6).

[34]This is the ultimate fulfillment of the great land promise made to Abraham and Israel, and thus to the Messiah who offers the same destiny to his true followers. The reward is very different from what became a tradition of the church that the faithful go to heaven

who are hungry and thirsty for what is right, because they will be filled.
7Blessed are the merciful, because they will be shown mercy. 8Blessed
are those who have clean[35] hearts, because they will see God. 9Blessed
are those who make peace, because they will be called children of God.
10Blessed are those who have been persecuted for what is right, because
the Kingdom of Heaven is theirs. 11Blessed are you when people insult
you and persecute you, and tell all kinds of evil lies against you because
of me. 12Be happy and full of joy, because your reward in heaven[36] is
great, because they persecuted the prophets who were before you in the
same way.

13"You are the salt of the earth, but if the salt becomes tasteless, how
can it be made salty again? It is useless, and it is tossed out and trampled
underfoot. 14You are the light of the world. A city built on a hill cannot
be hidden. 15People do not light a lamp and put it under a bucket. Instead
they put it on a lampstand and it gives light to everyone in the house. 16In
the same way, let your light shine in front of people, so that they can see
the good things you do and praise your heavenly Father.

17"Do not imagine that I came to abolish the Law or the prophets'
writings. I did not come to abolish them, but to fulfill them.[37] 18I tell you,

---

when they die! In fact they will inherit the land/earth when Jesus comes back (Ps. 37:9, 11, 18, 22, 29, 34). Cp. Ps. 25:13; 115:16; Isa. 65:9; 62:4; 57:13; 49:8; Dan. 7:18, 22, 27; Rom. 4:13. Why would anyone want to go to heaven when Jesus won't be there?! He is coming back to the earth.

[35]Cleansing occurs when people obey the words of the Gospel as Jesus preached it (Jn. 15:3).

[36]Rewards in the Bible are stored up as treasure "with God" and will be conferred on the faithful at the return of Jesus to rule in the worldwide Kingdom of God on earth. Thus Christians "have" a reward "with God," although it is possessed only in promise and prospect. In exactly the same sense, in John 17:5 Jesus prayed at the conclusion of his ministry to received the reward of glory which he "had with God," promised by God before the world began. Such is the certainty and guarantee of God's promises. Christians "have been glorified" (Rom. 8:30) and this is likewise expressed in the past tense, although it is only in promise and prospect since believers will be glorified only when Jesus returns to the earth to reward the faithful with "the reward of the inheritance" of the Kingdom (Col. 3:24). Nowhere did Jesus ever ask for the restoration of glory he had had already, just as he nowhere (despite mistranslations in NIV at Jn. 13:3; 16:28; 20:17) said he was going *back* to GOD!

[37]The fulfillment brought by Jesus meant teaching the spiritual intention of the Law, not just the letter of the Law of Moses.

until heaven and earth pass away, not the smallest letter or stroke will
pass from the Law until everything is fulfilled. 19Whoever invalidates one
of the least important commandments, and teaches others to do so, will
be called the least in the Kingdom of Heaven; but whoever practices and
teaches them will be called great in the Kingdom of Heaven. 20I tell you
this: unless your righteousness exceeds that of the religious teachers and
the Pharisees, you will not enter the Kingdom of Heaven.[38]

21"You have heard what was said to the people of long ago: 'You
shall not murder, and anyone who commits murder will be judged as
guilty.' 22But I tell you, anyone who is angry with his brother will be
judged as guilty. Whoever curses his brother with insults will be liable to
the court, and whoever calls his brother a fool is liable to hell-fire. 23So if
you are at the altar making an offering, and remember that your brother
has something against you, 24leave your offering on the altar and go and
make peace with him first, and afterwards come back and make your
offering. 25Agree with your opponent quickly while you are with him on
the way to court, so that he does not hand you over to the judge, and the
judge hand you over to officer, and you are thrown into jail. 26I tell you
the truth: you will not get out of there until you have paid the last penny.

27"You have heard that it was said, 'Do not commit adultery.' 28But I
tell you that everyone who looks at a woman lustfully has already
committed adultery with her in his heart. 29If your right eye leads you to
sin, then tear it out and throw it away, because it is better to lose one part
of your body than to have your whole body thrown into hell-fire. 30If

---

[38]It is obvious that Jesus was not teaching the Law of Moses *in the letter*. If Jesus were advocating Moses *in the letter of the law*, Paul was a great false teacher, when he insisted, against the clear instructions of Gen. 17, that circumcision in the flesh was not required of anyone (1 Cor. 7:19; Gal. 5:2, 3, 11). Circumcision in the flesh was *essential* for anyone, Jew or Gentile, to be part of the covenant people in Gen. 17. Jesus brought in the *spiritual intention* of the law, its "filling full," and in Mark 7:19 it is clear that the church understood him to have abolished the food laws of Lev. 11, as did Paul obviously in Rom. 14:14, 20. Paul considered foods clean (*katharos*) which were in Lev. 11 listed as unclean (*akathartos*). Jesus very wisely pointed out that even in OT times the priests were not guilty for breaking the sabbath, in the course of their duty (Mt. 12:5). Jesus has "abolished the law of commandments in ordinances" (Eph. 2:14-15), those requirements like observing the Jewish calendar and food laws (see the parallel in Col. 2:16-17). The wearing of tassels is not required under the new covenant, nor is physical circumcision for anyone, Jew and Gentile believer (see Gen. 17; Gal. 5:3, 11).

your right hand leads you to sin, then cut it off and throw it away,
because it is better for you to lose one of your limbs than for your whole
body to go into hell-fire.

31"It was said, 'Whoever divorces his wife, let him give her a
certificate of divorce.' 32But I tell you that everyone who divorces[39] his
wife, except for sexual immorality, causes her to commit adultery, and
whoever marries a divorced woman commits adultery.

33"And again, you have heard what was said to the people of long
ago, 'You shall not make false vows; instead keep the oaths you swear to
the Lord.' 34But I tell you, do not swear at all, not by heaven, because it
is the throne of God, 35 nor by the earth, because it is God's footstool, nor
by Jerusalem, because it is the city of the great King. 36Do not even
swear by your head, because you are not able to make one hair white or
black. 37Simply say yes or no. Any more than this is from the Evil One.

38"You have heard that it was said, 'An eye for an eye, and a tooth for
a tooth.' 39But I say to you, do not resist an evil person. If someone slaps
you on the right cheek, turn the other cheek to them as well. 40If someone
wants to get a judgment against you and take your shirt, give him your
coat as well. 41If someone forces you to go one mile, go with him two.
42Give to those who ask you, and do not turn away from those who want
to borrow from you.

43"You have heard that it was said, 'Love your neighbor and hate
your enemy.' 44But I say to you, love your enemies and pray for those
who persecute you, 45so that you may be children of your heavenly
Father. He makes His sun rise on the evil and the good, and He makes
rain fall on the righteous and the unrighteous. 46For if you love those who
love you, what reward do you have? Do not even the tax-collectors do
that? 47If you only speak kindly to your family, are you doing more than
anyone else? Do not even the Gentiles do that? 48So be perfect, as your
heavenly Father is perfect."

---

[39]It should not be necessary to add that divorce on legal grounds given by Jesus means the end of a marriage. Jesus was not asked about and is not talking about *separation* but about divorce. People who are divorced within the scope of Jesus' teaching are not married and are free to marry, within the faith of course.

6 1"Be careful not to do your good deeds in front of people, in order to
be noticed. Otherwise you have no reward[40] with your Father who is
in heaven. 2When you give to the poor, do not trumpet this before others
like the hypocrites do in the synagogues and in the streets, so that they
will be praised by people. I tell you the truth: they have already received
their reward. 3When you give to the poor, do not let your left hand know
what your right hand is doing, 4so that your charitable giving may be in
secret, and your Father who sees what happens in secret will reward you.

5"When you pray, do not be like the hypocrites, because they love to
stand up and pray in the synagogues and on the street corners so that
people can see them. I promise you, they have already received their
reward. 6But you, when you pray, go indoors and close the door, and
pray to your Father in private, and your Father who sees what happens in
private will reward you. 7And when you are praying, do not use
meaningless repetition as the Gentiles do, who think they will be heard
because of all the words they speak. 8Do not be like them, because your
Father knows what you need before you ask Him. 9So pray like this: 'Our
Father in heaven, may Your name[41] be held in honor. 10May Your
Kingdom come.[42] May Your will be carried out on earth as it is in
heaven. 11Please give to us today the bread we need to live each day.
12Forgive us our sins, as we have forgiven those who sinned against us.
13Do not bring us into temptation, but rescue us from the Evil One.' 14For
if you forgive those who sin against you, your heavenly Father will also
forgive you. 15But if you do not forgive those who sin against you, then
your heavenly Father will not forgive your sins.

---

[40]See note 36 above on rewards promised.

[41]"Name" in the Bible stands for the whole agenda, character and purpose of a person — certainly not how to pronounce a name in Hebrew! (see Jn. 17:6, parallel to word). Note that in John 14:14 Jesus said, "If you ask **me** anything in my name [i.e. a believer understanding the faith] **I** will do it." It is not wrong to speak to Jesus and note that Paul thanked Jesus for putting him in ministry (1 Tim. 1:12). See also Acts 7:59, mistranslated in the KJV.

[42]Note the very obvious parallel in the Judaism of the day. Jesus would have heard this Kaddish ("holy") prayer from childhood in the synagogue. It was the national prayer of Judaism, rather like the "oath of allegiance" in the USA: "Exalted and hallowed be His great name in the world which he created according to His will. May He let His Kingdom rule in your lifetime and in your days and in the lifetime of the whole house of Israel, speedily and soon, and to this say Amen" (cp. 1 Chron. 29:11; Rev. 22:20.)

16“When you fast, do not be like the hypocrites who put on gloomy
faces and make themselves look bad so it is obvious to people they are
fasting. I tell you, they have their reward in full. 17But you, when you
fast, wash your face and take care of your appearance, 18so that people
will not see that you are fasting, and your Father who sees what happens
in secret will reward you.

19“Do not store up wealth for yourselves on earth where moths and
rust ruin it, and where thieves break in and steal. 20Instead, store up
wealth for yourselves in heaven, where moths and rust do not ruin it, and
where thieves do not break in and steal. 21For wherever your wealth is
stored up, that is where your heart[43] will be too.

22“The eye is the body’s lamp. So if your eye[44] is clear, then your
whole body will be lit up. 23But if your eye is bad, then your whole body
will be in the dark. Then if the light in you is darkness, how dark is that!

24“No one can serve two masters. Either you will hate one and love
the other, or you will be devoted to one and despise the other. You
cannot serve God and money. 25That is why I am telling you not to worry
about your life, about what to eat, or what to drink, or what clothes to put
on. Is not life more than food, and the body more than clothes? 26Look at
the wild birds. They do not sow or reap or store food in barns, and yet
your heavenly Father feeds them. Are you not worth more than they are?
27And which of you by worrying can add a minute to your life? 28And
why are you worried about clothes? Look at the beautiful wildflowers in
the field, how they grow. They do not work hard, nor do they spin
thread. 29But I tell you that not even Solomon in all his majesty was
dressed like one of these flowers. 30So if God decorates the grass in the
fields like this, which is here today and tomorrow is thrown into the fire,
will He not do much more for you, you people of little faith? 31So do not
worry, thinking, ‘What will we eat?’ or ‘What will we drink?’ or ‘What
will we wear?’ 32All these things are what the pagans seek after, but your
heavenly Father knows everything you need. 33Seek His Kingdom first,
and His way of being and doing right,[45] and everything else will be given

---

43“Heart” in the Bible is certainly not the seat just of emotions as opposed to intellect. Heart is the center of the entire personality, especially the source of thought and planning.

44The spiritual eye of spiritual understanding and character.

45The obedience of faith (Rom. 1:5; 16:26; Jn. 3:36; Heb. 5:9; 1 Tim. 6:3).

to you. 34So do not worry about tomorrow, because tomorrow can worry
about itself. Each day has enough problems of its own."

7 1"Do not judge others, and you will not be judged. 2For whatever
standard you use to judge others will be used to judge you, and
whatever measurement you use to measure others will be used to
measure you. 3Why do you look at the speck in your brother's eye and do
not notice the plank in your own eye? 4How can you say to your brother,
'Let me take the speck out of your eye' when you have a plank in your
own eye? 5You hypocrite, first get rid of the plank in your own eye, and
then you will see clearly to take the speck out of your brother's eye. 6Do
not give what is holy to dogs,[46] and do not throw your pearls to pigs, so
that they do not trample them under foot, and then turn and tear you to
pieces.

7"Keep asking, and it will be given to you; keep seeking, and you
will find; keep knocking, and the door will be opened for you. 8Everyone
who goes on asking, receives; and whoever keeps seeking, finds; and
whoever keeps knocking has the door opened for them. 9Is there any one
of you who when your son asks for bread, would give him a stone? 10Or
if he asks for fish, would you give him a snake? 11If even you who are
evil know how to give good things to your children, how much more will
your heavenly Father give good things to those who ask Him?
12Whatever you want people to do to you, do to them too. This sums up
the Law and the prophets.

13"Enter through the narrow entrance, because wide is the entrance
and broad the way which leads to destruction, and many go that way.
14But small is the entrance and narrow is the way which leads to Life,[47]
and only a few find it.

15"Beware false prophets who come in sheep's clothing, but inside
are vicious wolves. 16You will recognize them by their fruits. Do people
harvest grapes from thorn bushes, or figs from thistles? 17In the same way

---

[46]Jesus' admonition not to judge obviously does not mean that Christians are not to be discerning about others. If we are not to cast pearls before "dogs" or "pigs," this implies that we are able to discern who is in that category. This is an exercise of judgment and discernment.

[47]The only life which is really life, the Life of the Age to Come in the Kingdom, based on Dan. 12:2; see 1 Cor. 15:23.

every good tree produces good fruit, but a bad tree produces bad fruit.
18A good tree cannot produce bad fruit, nor can a bad tree produce good
fruit. 19Every tree that does not produce good fruit is chopped down and
thrown into the fire. 20So by their fruits you will recognize them.[48]

21"Not everyone who says to me 'lord, lord' will enter the Kingdom
of Heaven;[49] rather it is those who do the will of my Father in heaven.
22There will be many who say to me in the day of judgment, 'lord, lord,
did we not preach for you and drive out demons in your name, and
perform many miracles with your authority?' 23Then I will declare to
them, 'I never recognized you. Depart from me, you who practice
wickedness.'[50]

24"Therefore everyone who hears these words of mine, and obeys[51]
them, is like a wise man who built his house on solid rock. 25The rain
poured down, and the floods rose, and the winds blew hard against the
house, but it did not fall down, because its foundations were on solid
rock. 26Everyone who hears my words, and does not obey them, is like a
moron who built his house on the sand. 27The rain poured down, and the
floods rose, and the winds blew hard against the house, and it fell down
— it totally collapsed."

---

[48]The test of right understanding is presented by 1 John 4:1ff, where the correct definition of who Jesus is is critically important. "All flesh" there means every human being. Only a fully human Jesus qualifies as the true Messiah. Luke 1:35 defines the Son of God, Messiah, simply and beautifully (also Mt. 1:20: "begotten, brought into existence in her").

[49]That is, be saved. Obedience to Jesus is required for salvation (Heb. 5:9).

[50]While imagining that they were true believers, they will find out that they had accepted falsehoods uncritically. Tradition learned by heart was a major threat to true belief, Jesus said. A passion for truth in order to be saved is the first prerequisite for true discipleship and avoiding the grave danger of being deceived. (2 Thess. 2:10).

[51]Obviously adherence to the teaching of Jesus is the central point of the Christian faith. This core message of the NT is neatly summed up by Heb. 5:9: "Salvation is granted to those who obey the Son." Paul reflected exactly this same idea with the phrase which frames the book of Romans, the "obedience of faith" (Rom. 1:5; 16:26, and 2:8, citing the principle of obedience from Prov. 5:7, 13; 7:24; 8:6, 32, 33; 12:15; 19:20; 23:22). Faith without obedience is false faith. Obedience implies works of course, and so James was right to warn, "You see, brothers and sisters, that salvation is by works and not by faith alone" (2:24; i.e. a false faith without obedience). Obedience begins with our intelligent response to Jesus' opening command in Mark 1:14-15 to "believe the Gospel of the Kingdom," and also to pay close attention to Jesus' primary command, that we hear and believe that "the Lord our God is one single Lord" (Mk. 12:29).

28When Jesus had finished these words,[52] the crowds were amazed at his teaching, 29because he was teaching like someone with authority, and not like their religious teachers.

8 1Large crowds followed Jesus after he came down from the mountain. 2A leper approached him, bowed down before him, and said, "lord, if you are willing, you can heal me." 3Jesus reached out and touched him with his hand. "I am willing," he said. "Be healed!" Immediately his leprosy was healed. 4"Make sure you do not tell anyone," Jesus said to him. "Go and show yourself to the priest and make the offering which Moses commanded, as a testimony to them."

5When Jesus entered Capernaum, a centurion came to him, pleading with him, 6"lord, my servant is at home lying down, unable to walk, and in terrible agony." 7Jesus said to him, "I will come and heal him." 8The centurion answered, "lord, I do not deserve that you should come to my home. Just say the word, and my servant will be healed. 9For I too am a man under authority, with soldiers under my command. I tell one 'Go!' and he goes, and another, 'Come!' and he comes, and to my servant I say 'Do this!' and he does it." 10When Jesus heard what he said, he was amazed and said to those who were following him, "I am telling you the truth: I have not found such faith in Israel. 11I assure you that many will come from the east and the west and sit down at the banquet with Abraham and Isaac and Jacob in the Kingdom of Heaven, 12but the heirs of the Kingdom[53] will be thrown out into the outer darkness, where there will be weeping and grinding of teeth." 13And Jesus said to the centurion, "Go home. Let it be done for you as you have believed." The servant was healed that very moment.

14When Jesus arrived at Peter's house, he saw that Peter's mother-in-law was sick in bed with a fever. 15He touched her hand and the fever left

---

[52]This is the first of five parallel phrases (11:1; 13:53; 19:1; 26:1) dividing the teachings presented by Matthew into five blocks, no doubt instructing us that Jesus is the final Moses, whose teachings appeared in the Torah, five books. Matthew echoes the phrases in Ex. 34:27-28; Num. 16:31; Deut. 31:1; 31:24-30; 32:45-47.

[53]That is, those who *ought* to be heirs. The royal family ought to be Israelites, but many of them were disqualified by refusing to accept their Messiah. Royal privilege is now extended to whoever will believe the Gospel of the Kingdom as Jesus preached it and obey Jesus (Heb. 5:9; Mt. 13:19; Mk. 1:14-15; 4:11-12).

her. She got up and began making them a meal. 16When evening came
they brought to him many who were demon-oppressed, and he ordered
the evil spirits to leave, and he healed all those who were sick. 17This
fulfilled what was said through the prophet Isaiah: "He removed our
diseases, and took away our illnesses."

18When Jesus saw the crowds around him, he gave orders to go to the
other side of the lake. 19One of the religious teachers came to him and
said, "Teacher, I will follow you wherever you go!" 20Jesus said to him,
"Foxes have their dens, and wild birds their nests, but the Son of Man
has nowhere to lie down and rest." 21Another disciple said to Jesus, "lord,
let me first go and bury my father." 22Jesus replied, "Follow me, and let
the dead bury their own dead."

23Jesus got into a boat and his disciples followed him. 24A great storm
arose and waves crashed over the boat, but Jesus was asleep. 25The
disciples went over to him and woke him up. "Save us, lord! We are
going to drown!" they said. 26"Why are you so afraid, you people of little
faith?" he asked them. Then he got up and commanded the winds and the
sea, and it became completely calm. 27The disciples were astonished and
said, "What kind of a man is this, that even the winds and the sea obey
him?"

28When he got to the other side of the lake, in the region of the
Gadarenes, two demon-influenced men met him, coming out of the
graveyard. They were so violent that nobody could pass by that way.
29They shouted out, "What business have you with us, you Son of God?
Have you come to torture us before the appointed time?" 30Some way off
there was a large herd of pigs feeding. 31The demons[54] pleaded with him,
"If you are going to drive us out, send us into the herd of pigs." 32"Go!"
Jesus said. The demons left the men and went into the pigs, and the
whole herd ran down the steep hillside into the sea and drowned. 33The
pig herders ran away and went to the town. There they reported

[54]The demons in the NT are supernatural, non-human intelligent evil personalities. It is a serious assault on Scripture to try to explain them away in the interests of (false) "science." Jesus spoke to the demons, who recognized him as the Messiah (the public generally did not). The demons spoke to Jesus (Lk. 4:41). *Daimonia* in Greek is an easy word and never describes a human person, much less a mental disease. Some of the demons, products of angel-human female marriage, in Gen. 6 are in Tartarus, and Jesus' triumph was announced to them as "spirits in prison" of 1 Pet. 3:19.

everything that had taken place, and what had happened to the
demonized men. 34The whole town came out to meet Jesus and when
they found him, they begged him to leave their region.

9 1Jesus got into a boat and went back across the lake to his home town.
2There some people brought to him a paralyzed man lying on a mat.
Jesus saw their faith and said to the paralyzed man, "Son, do not be
afraid. Your sins are forgiven." 3Some of the religious teachers said to
themselves, "He is speaking blasphemy!" 4But Jesus knew what they
were thinking and asked them, "Why are you thinking evil thoughts in
your hearts? 5Which is easier to say: 'Your sins are forgiven,' or 'Get up
and walk'? 6But in order that you can be sure that the Son of Man does
have the authority on earth to forgive sins," he said to the paralyzed man,
"Get up, pick up your mat, and go home!" 7The man got up and went
home. 8But when the crowds saw what had happened, they were
awestruck, and they praised God that He had given such authority to
human beings.[55]

9As Jesus left there he saw a man called Matthew sitting in the tax
collector's booth. Jesus said to him, "Follow me!" He got up and
followed Jesus. 10As Jesus was eating at Matthew's home, many tax
collectors and sinners came and ate with Jesus and his disciples. 11When
the Pharisees saw this they asked Jesus' disciples, "Why is your teacher
eating with tax collectors and sinners?" 12When Jesus heard this, he
replied, "People who are well do not need a doctor, but those who are
sick do. 13But go and learn what this means: 'I want mercy, and not
sacrifice,' because I did not come to call those who are right with God,
but sinners."[56]

14Then the disciples of John came and asked, "Why do we and the
Pharisees fast frequently, but your disciples do not fast?" 15Jesus replied,
"Do the groomsmen mourn while the bridegroom is with them? But the

---

[55]Their spiritual intelligence was far superior to much modern thinking. Today it is customary to hear people say that "Jesus must be God, because only God can forgive sins." The real point is that God had conferred on the sinless man Jesus the right to forgive.

[56]That is, invite them to prepare now to gain immortality in the coming Kingdom on earth. This is certainly not an invitation to a disembodied, post-mortem life in heaven, as is popularly taught and believed.

time is coming when the bridegroom will be taken away from them, and
then they will fast. 16And no one puts a new patch on old clothes;
otherwise it will shrink and make a worse tear. 17People do not put new
wine[57] into old wineskins either; otherwise the wineskins burst, and the
wine spills and the wineskins are ruined. No, people put new wine into
new wineskins, and both are kept safe and sound."

18While he was saying these things, one of the leading officials came
and bowed before him. "My daughter has just died, but if you come and
place your hand on her, I know she will come back to life," he said.
19Jesus and his disciples got up and followed him. 20A woman who had
been sick with bleeding for twelve years came up behind him and
touched the edge of his clothes. 21She said to herself, "If I can just touch
his clothes, I will be healed." 22But Jesus turned and saw her and said,
"Daughter, take heart. Your faith has healed you." And the woman was
healed from that moment on. 23Jesus arrived at the official's house and
saw the flute players and the crowd mourning loudly. 24"Please leave," he
said to them, "because the girl is not dead but asleep."[58] And they
laughed at him. 25But when the crowd had been sent out, he went in and
took the girl by the hand, and she got up. 26News of what happened
spread throughout that region.

27As Jesus went on from there, two blind men followed him,
shouting, "Son of David,[59] have mercy on us!" 28When Jesus got to the
house, the blind men went in too. "Do you believe that I am able to do
this?" he asked them. "Yes, lord," they replied. 29Then Jesus touched
their eyes and said, "It will be done for you according to your faith."
30And they could see. Then Jesus gave them strict instructions, telling

---

[57]Wine in the Bible is not grape juice! This is a simple lexical fact. Paul did not say, "Do not get drunk on grape juice" (Eph. 5:18). In many societies an enforced abstinence from moderate use of alcohol creates the wrong impression, since even non-Bible readers know that Jesus at the wedding turned 120 gallons of water into alcohol. It is a mistake to try to be more righteous than Jesus. Drunkenness is of course always forbidden.

[58]She was, of course, in fact dead, but "asleep" was an appropriate word to use because he was intending to raise her from the sleep of death.

[59]What commends people in the New Testament is their belief that Jesus was the Messiah, descended from David, certainly not that he was God, violating the first, great commandment (Mk. 12:29; Jn. 17:3).

them, "Make sure nobody knows about this." 31But they went out and
spread the word about Jesus everywhere.

32As Jesus and his disciples were going out, a mute, demon-oppressed
man was brought to him. 33After the demon was expelled, the mute man
spoke, and the crowds were amazed. "Nothing ever happened like this
before in Israel," they said. 34But the Pharisees were saying, "He expels
demons by the power of the leader of the demons."

35Jesus was going through all the towns and villages, teaching in their
synagogues, preaching the Gospel about the Kingdom,[60] and healing all
kinds of sicknesses and diseases. 36Seeing the crowds, he was deeply
moved with compassion for them, because they were troubled and
dejected, like sheep without a shepherd. 37He said to his disciples, "It is a
large harvest, but there are only a few workers. 38So ask the Lord of the
harvest to send out workers into His harvest."

10 1Jesus called in his twelve disciples and gave them authority over
evil spirits, to cast them out, and to heal every kind of sickness
and disease. 2Now the names of the twelve Apostles are these: first,
Simon, who is called Peter, and Andrew his brother; James the son of
Zebedee, and John his brother; 3Philip and Bartholomew; Thomas and
Matthew the tax collector; James the son of Alphaeus, and Thaddaeus;
4Simon the Zealot, and Judas Iscariot, who betrayed him.

5These twelve Jesus sent out, instructing them, "Do not go to the
Gentiles, and do not enter any Samaritan town, 6but go instead to the lost
sheep of the house of Israel. 7Wherever you go, preach the Gospel,
saying, 'The Kingdom of Heaven is near.'[61] 8Heal the sick, raise the

---

[60]A reminder at a significant juncture in the narrative, recalling Matt. 4:17, 23 and Luke 4:43, that the saving Christian Gospel is about the Kingdom of God as first preached by Jesus (Heb. 2:3). Paul preached the same Gospel of the Kingdom as is clearly seen in Acts 19:8; 20:24-25; 28:23, 30, 31. Cp. Acts 8:12 for an essential early creed. Thus Paul carried out Jesus' orders given in the Great Commission which is binding on believers to the end of the age, when Jesus returns (Mt. 28:19-20). Water baptism is a non-negotiable command of Jesus.

[61]Kingdom of Heaven is of course the exact synonym of Kingdom of God. Only Matthew uses the term Kingdom of Heaven based on Dan. 2:44. The Jews avoided the name God and replaced it sometimes by Heaven. The Kingdom has God as its author and the Christian Gospel is all about the Kingdom and how to enter it by obedience to Jesus (Mk. 1:14-15; Lk. 4:43).

dead, cleanse the lepers, cast out demons. Freely you have received, so freely give. 9Take no gold, nor silver, nor copper in your money belts, 10no bag for your journey, nor even two coats, or sandals, or a staff; for a worker is worthy of his support. 11Whatever town or village you enter, inquire who in it is worthy, and stay at his house until you leave that town. 12As you enter a house, give it your blessing. 13If the house is worthy, give it your blessing of peace, but if it is not worthy, take back your blessing of peace. 14Whoever will not receive you or pay attention to your words, when you leave that house or that town, shake the dust off your feet. 15I am telling you the truth: it will be more tolerable for Sodom and Gomorrah on the Day of Judgment than for that town.

16"Look, I am sending you out as sheep among wolves. Therefore be as wise as serpents, and as innocent as doves. 17Beware of people who will hand you over to the courts and flog you in their synagogues. 18You will even be brought before governors and kings for my sake, as a witness to them and to the Gentiles. 19But when they deliver you up, do not be anxious about how or what you should speak, because it will be given to you in that hour what you should say. 20For it is not you who will speak, but the spirit of your Father will speak in you.

21"Brother will deliver up a brother to death, and a father his child. And children will rise up against parents and condemn them to death. 22You will be hated by all people because of me, but the one who endures to the end will be saved. 23But when they persecute you in one town, flee to the next. I am telling you the truth: you will not have finished going through the towns of Israel before the Son of Man comes.[62]

---

[62]Referring to an end-time missionary campaign in Israel. As frequently the "you" incorporates and includes the successors of the disciples. The Great Commission (Mt. 28:19-20) was given until the end of the age, the Second Coming. Jesus accused the Pharisees of his day of having been responsible for the death of Abel and Zechariah (Mt. 23:34-35, from the beginning to the end of Jesus' Bible, in order from Genesis to 2 Chronicles) and he spoke of the temple existing in his day as of a temple which would be there at the time of the final great tribulation (Mt. 24:15), close to the arrival of Jesus in power at his Second Coming. This is a non-western, but very Hebrew way of thinking. When he spoke of "this generation" he meant the whole of society which is evil right up to the time of the arrival of the future Kingdom of God on earth. He did not mean a period of 40 or 70 years. Thus "save yourself from this generation" (Acts 2:40) means separate yourself from society which is chronically evil during the present evil age (Gal. 1:4), dominated by Satan who is the prince and ruler of current society

24“A disciple is not above his teacher, nor a servant above his master.
25It is enough for the student that he becomes like his teacher, and the
servant like his master. If they have called the head of the house
Beelzebul, how much more the members of his household!

26“So do not fear them, because there is nothing covered which will
not be revealed, and nothing hidden which will not be known. 27What I
tell you in the darkness, speak in the light, and what you hear whispered
in your ear, shout from the rooftops. 28Do not be afraid of those who can
kill the body, but cannot kill the soul.[63] Rather fear Him who can destroy
both soul and body in the Gehenna fire of destruction. 29Are not two
sparrows sold for a penny? But not one of them falls to the ground
without your Father knowing. 30Even the hairs of your head are all
numbered. 31So do not fear; you are more valuable than many sparrows.

32“Therefore everyone who confesses me before people, I will also
confess him before my Father who is in heaven. 33But whoever denies me
before people, I will also deny him before my Father who is in heaven.

34“Do not think that I came to bring peace on the earth. I came not to
bring peace, but a sword. 35I came to divide a man against his father, and
a daughter against her mother, and a daughter-in-law against her mother-in-law. 36And a man’s enemies will be the members of his own
household.

37“He who loves father or mother above me is not worthy of me, and
he who loves son or daughter above me is not worthy of me.[64] 38And he
who does not take up his cross and follow me is not worthy of me. 39He
who finds his life will lose it, and he who loses his life for my sake will
find it.

40“He who receives you receives me, and he who receives me
receives Him who commissioned me. 41He who receives a prophet in the

---

across the whole world (Rev. 12:9). “Generation” is contrasted with the future society which will begin at the Second Coming (Mk. 8:38). See also *genea*, type of person, “kind” in Luke 16:8.

[63]The inner man and character cannot be destroyed, because God intends to resurrect the faithful from death at the future resurrection when Jesus returns (1 Cor. 15:23).The dead are not presently conscious, but God has perfect memory of them and can restore them to life by resurrection (Dan. 12:2; 1 Cor. 15:23). Resurrection is the only way out of death. There is no survival of an immortal soul anywhere in the Bible.

[64]This is typical of Jesus’ uncompromising demands for undivided allegiance to himself. Even family relationships must take second place to loyalty to the Messiah.

name of a prophet will receive a prophet's reward, and he who receives a righteous person in the name of a righteous person will receive a righteous person's reward. 42And whoever in the name of a disciple gives one of these humble ones even a cup of cold water to drink, I am telling you the truth: he will not lose his reward."

11 1When Jesus had finished giving these instructions[65] to his twelve disciples, he left there to teach and preach the Gospel in the towns.

2Now when John heard in prison of the works of the Messiah, he sent his disciples 3to ask him, "Are you the coming one, or should we look for someone else?" 4Jesus answered them, "Go and report to John the things which you hear and see: 5Blind people receive sight and lame people walk, lepers are healed and deaf people hear, dead people are resurrected and poor people have the Gospel preached to them. 6And blessed is he who will not be offended by me."

7As these men were leaving, Jesus began to say to the crowds about John, "What did you go out to the desert to see? A reed shaken by the wind? 8But what did you go out to see? A man wearing delicate clothes? Those who wear such clothes are in kings' palaces. 9So then what did you go out to see? A prophet? Yes, I say to you, and one who is more than a prophet. 10This is the one about whom it is written: 'Look, I send My messenger ahead of you, who will prepare your way before you.' 11I am telling you the truth: among those born of women there has not arisen a greater one than John the Baptist. Yet the one who is least in the Kingdom of Heaven is greater than John. 12From the days of John the Baptist until now the Kingdom of Heaven suffers violence, and violent people are trying to seize it for themselves. 13For all the prophets and the Law prophesied until John. 14And if you are willing to accept it, he is Elijah who was to come. 15He who has ears to hear, listen!

16"To what can I compare this generation?[66] It is like children sitting in the market places calling to their companions, 17'We played the flute

---

[65]The close of the second of the five blocks of teaching arranged by Matthew to remind us that Jesus is the second and ultimate Moses, bringing the Torah to its full and intended meaning.

[66]*Genea* ("generation") means wicked society which will prevail during the "present evil age," to be ended when Jesus returns (Mk. 8:38). At the seventh, the last, trumpet (Rev. 11:15-18) the kingdoms of this evil system will become the Kingdom of God, but

for you, and you did not dance. We sang mournful songs for you, and
you did not weep.' 18For John came neither feasting nor drinking, and
they say, 'He has a demon!' 19But the Son of Man came feasting and
drinking normally, and they say, 'Look, a glutton and a drunk, a friend of
tax collectors and sinners!' Yet Wisdom[67] is proven to be right by what
she does."

20Then he began to denounce the towns where most of his miracles
were done, because they did not repent. 21"Alas for you, Chorazin; alas
for you, Bethsaida! If the miracles which were done in you had been
done in Tyre and Sidon, they would have repented long ago in sackcloth
and ashes. 22But I say to you that it will be more tolerable for Tyre and
Sidon on the Day of Judgment than for you. 23And you, Capernaum, will
not be exalted to heaven, will you? No, you will be brought down to
Hades, because if the miracles which were done in you had been done in
Sodom, it would have remained until this day. 24 But I say to you that it
will be more tolerable for the land of Sodom on the Day of Judgment
than for you."

25At that time Jesus said, "I praise You, Father, Lord of heaven and
earth, that You have hidden these things from the wise and intelligent,
and have revealed them to children. 26Yes, Father, because this was
pleasing in your sight. 27All things have been delivered to me by my
Father, and no one knows the Son except the Father, nor does anyone
know the Father except the Son, and anyone to whom the Son wills to
reveal Him. 28Come to me, all you who labor and are burdened, and I will
give you rest. 29Take my yoke on you, and learn from me, because I am
gentle and humble in heart, and you will find rest for your selves. 30For
my yoke is easy, and my burden is light."

---

not until then. Until then Christians are called to be resident aliens in a foreign country. Satan is currently the governor of the sublunar space (Eph. 2:2; 6:12: "world forces of this darkness"), granted a large degree of influence as the god of this age (2 Cor. 4:4; Rev. 12:9; 1 John 5:19).

[67]Jesus is the very expression of the wisdom and word of God. He is the embodiment of God's wise plan, but certainly not the Incarnation of a previously existing God the Son, making two GODs! John 1:1 reads, "In the beginning was the word [not Word] and that word belonged to God, was God Himself, and was fully expressive of the One God."

12 1At that time Jesus went through the grain fields on the Sabbath
day, and his disciples were hungry and began to pick the heads of
grain and eat. 2But when the Pharisees saw this, they said to him, “Look!
Your disciples are doing what is not lawful to do on the Sabbath.” 3But
he said to them, “Have you not read what David did when he and his
companions were hungry, 4how he entered the house of God and they ate
the consecrated bread, which was not lawful for them to eat, but only for
the priests? 5Or have you not read in the Law that on the Sabbath day the
priests in the temple break the Sabbath, and are innocent?[68] 6But I say to
you that one greater than the temple is here. 7But if you had understood
this: ‘I want mercy, and not sacrifice,’ you would not have condemned
the innocent. 8For the Son of Man is lord of the Sabbath.”[69]

9Departing from there, he went into their synagogue. 10A man who
had a withered hand was there. Looking for a reason to accuse Jesus,
they asked him, “Is it lawful to heal on the Sabbath?” 11He replied,
“Which of you who has a sheep, and if it falls into a pit on the Sabbath,
will not take hold of it and pull it out? 12How much more valuable is a
person than a sheep! So then it is lawful to do good on the Sabbath.”
13Then he said to the man, “Stretch out your hand.” He stretched it out,
and it was restored to normal, just like the other hand. 14But the Pharisees
went out and conspired together as to how they might destroy him.

15But Jesus, aware of this, left there. Large crowds followed him and
he healed them all. 16He ordered them not to make him known, 17so that
what was spoken by Isaiah the prophet would be fulfilled: 18“Look, My
servant whom I have chosen, My beloved with whom I am pleased. I
will put My spirit on him, and he will proclaim justice to the nations.
19He will not struggle or cry out, nor will anyone hear his voice in the
streets. 20A bruised reed he will not break, and a smoldering wick he will

---

[68]Anticipating here the later clearer teaching (Col. 2:16-17) that the weekly Sabbath, a part of the trio of Jewish OT calendar observances, is not binding in the New Covenant headed by Jesus and his followers. Col. 2:16-17 includes, of course, the weekly Sabbath.

[69]How the Sabbath is dealt with in the teaching of Jesus emerges as further truth unfolded, i.e. in the writings of Paul (esp. Col. 2:16-17 where the entire calendar is a single shadow now replaced by the living power and operational presence of the risen Christ). If one teaches people obligatory observance of the calendar, one is moving away from Christ back into the shadows, going back under the letter of the Law (Gal. 3:19-29).

not put out, until he leads justice to victory.[70] 21And in his name the
nations will hope."

22Then there was brought to him a demonized[71] man who was blind
and mute. Jesus healed him so that the mute man was able to both speak
and see. 23All the crowds were amazed and were saying, "Could this man
be the son of David?" 24But when the Pharisees heard this they said,
"This man only casts out demons by Beelzebul, the prince of the
demons." 25Jesus knew their thoughts and said to them, "Every kingdom
divided against itself is ruined, and every city or house divided against
itself will not stand. 26If Satan casts out Satan, he is divided against
himself. How then will his kingdom stand? 27And if I cast out demons by
Beelzebul, by whom do your people cast them out? Therefore they will
be your judges. 28But if I cast out demons by the spirit of God, then the
Kingdom of God has come upon you.[72] 29How can anyone enter a strong
man's house and take his belongings unless he first ties up the strong
man? If you tie him up first, then you can take away all his belongings.
30He who is not with me is against me, and he who does not gather with
me scatters. 31Because of this I say to you: every sin and blasphemy will
be forgiven people, but blasphemy against the spirit will not be forgiven.
32Whoever speaks a word against the Son of Man[73] will be forgiven. But
whoever speaks against the holy spirit will not be forgiven, either in this
present age or in the Age to Come.[74]

33"Either make the tree good and its fruit good, or make the tree bad
and its fruit bad, because the tree is known by its fruit. 34You brood of
vipers, how can you, being evil, speak good things? For the mouth

---

[70]By subduing his enemies and introducing the first successful world government, the Kingdom of God, at his return in glory.

[71]The human being who is demonized is carefully distinguished in the synoptic narratives from the demons, who are evil supernatural personalities.

[72]Meaning, of course, that the power and authority of God's Kingdom had dramatically affected that individual's life — not that the Messianic Kingdom had been established on earth, which will happen only when Jesus comes back.

[73]The supreme human being, introduced in Daniel.

[74]The unpardonable sin means attributing to the Devil what is the demonstrable activity of God. See also Heb. 10:26ff which speaks of the fate of those who have truly been enlightened and come to the knowledge of the truth and then turn back to the world (cp. 2 Pet. 2:21-22). There remains for them no further sacrifice for sin. It would have been better for them never to have known the truth.

speaks from what fills the heart.[75] 35The good person from his good treasure brings out good things, and the evil person from his evil treasure brings out evil things. 36I say to you that every useless word that people say, they will give an account of it on the Day of Judgment. 37For by your words you will be justified, and by your words you will be condemned."

38Then some of the religious teachers and Pharisees said to him, "Teacher, we want to see a miraculous sign from you." 39But he answered them, "An evil and unfaithful people craves a miraculous sign, and no sign will be given to them except the sign of the prophet Jonah: 40Just as Jonah was in the belly of the great fish for three days and three nights, so will the Son of Man be in the heart of the earth for three days and three nights.[76] 41The people of Nineveh will stand up in the judgment and will condemn this evil society, because they repented at the preaching of Jonah, and look: someone greater than Jonah is here! 42The Queen of the South will be resurrected in the judgment and condemn this evil society, because she came from the ends of the earth to hear the wisdom of Solomon, and look: someone greater than Solomon is here!

43"Now when an evil spirit goes out of a person, it passes through waterless places looking for rest, and does not find it. 44Then it says, 'I will go back to my house which I came from.' When it goes back it finds the house empty, swept, and put in order. 45Then it goes and brings along seven other spirits more evil than itself, and they all go in and live there. And the last state of that person is worse than the first. So it will be for this evil society also."

---

[75]"As a man thinks, so is he" (Prov. 23:7).

[76]It is a mistake to read this time idiom in a western fashion, requiring a full 72 hours. This throws the major, repeated evidence into confusion. Jesus was crucified on the Jewish preparation day, which is Friday, and he rose on the third day, Sunday. Luke's inclusive reckoning is more than clear (Lk. 24:21). See notes on Luke relative to the predicted "third day" for the resurrection. "Sabbath was approaching…They prepared spices…and rested on the sabbath" (Lk. 23:54, 56). It would be a completely confusing account if Luke wanted his readers to understand two different days by "sabbath." Sabbath in the NT means Saturday and the Saturday sabbath as *falling in the Passover week* was a special sabbath (Jn. 19:31, NIV). It was still Saturday, the Saturday of Passover week. John uses "Passover" to mean the entire festival, not just the meal eaten on the 15th Nisan. Jesus, as the synoptics say unmistakably, ate the Passover meal at the same time as the nation. He died the next day, Friday and rose on the third day which counting inclusively was Sunday (Lk. 24:21 is decisive). See Luke 13:32-33 for inclusive reckoning.

46While he was still speaking to the crowds, his mother and his
brothers stood outside, wanting to talk with him. 47Someone said to him,
"Look, your mother and your brothers are standing outside, wanting to
talk with you." 48But Jesus replied to that person, "Who is my mother,
and who are my brothers?" 49Gesturing toward his disciples, he said,
"Look — my mother and my brothers! 50For whoever does the will of my
Father who is in heaven is my brother and sister and mother."

13 1Later that day Jesus left the house, and sat down by the lake. 2So
many people came to him that he got into a boat and sat down to
teach, while all the crowds stood on the beach. 3He taught them many
things using parables:[77] "The sower went out sowing seed. 4As he was
sowing, some of the seeds fell on the road, and the birds came and ate
them up. 5Other seeds fell on stony ground where there was not much
dirt. There they sprouted at once. 6But then the sun came up and
scorched them because they had no roots, and they withered. 7Other
seeds fell among thorns, and the thorns grew up and choked them. 8Still
other seeds fell on good soil, and produced a harvest — some one
hundred, some sixty, and some thirty. 9Anyone who has ears to hear,
listen!"

10The disciples came to Jesus and asked, "Why do you speak to them
using parables?" 11He replied, "You are privileged to know the revealed
mysteries[78] of the Kingdom of Heaven, but they are not given such
insights. 12For whoever already has understanding, to them more will be
given, and they will have an abundance. But whoever does not have
understanding, whatever they have will be taken away from them. 13That
is why I speak to them in parables. Seeing, they do not actually see; and
hearing, they do not really hear, nor do they understand. 14In their case
the prophecy of Isaiah is being fulfilled: 'Even though you hear, you will
not understand, and even though you see, you will not comprehend.
15These people have a stubborn attitude. They do not want to listen, and
they have closed their eyes.[79] Otherwise they would see with their eyes,

---

[77]Comparisons, illustrations.

[78]Not mystifications, but the revealed and spiritually discerned information about God's immortality program through Jesus and his Gospel of the Kingdom teaching.

[79]Showing that blindness is *self-induced* by a choice not to listen carefully and intelligently to the saving words of Jesus (cp. Acts 28:23-27; 2 Thess. 2:10; 2 Pet. 3:5).

hear with their ears, and understand in their minds, and return and repent, and I would heal them.' 16Blessed are your eyes, because they see, and your ears, because they hear. 17I am telling you the truth: many prophets and good people longed to see what you are seeing, but did not see it, and longed to hear what you are hearing, but did not hear it.

18"So listen to the parable of the sower.[80] 19When someone hears the Gospel-word about the Kingdom, and does not understand it, then the Evil One comes and snatches away what was sown in his mind. This is what happens to the seeds sown on the road. 20The seeds sown on stony ground are people who hear the Gospel-word and immediately accept it with joy. 21They last for a while, but because they do not have roots, when problems and trouble come because of the Gospel-word, they immediately fall away. 22The seeds sown among thorns are people who hear the Gospel-word, but then the worries of this age and the temptation of wealth choke the Gospel-word and it bears no fruit. 23The seeds sown on good soil are people who hear the Gospel-word and understand it, and who produce a good harvest — some one hundred, some sixty, and some thirty."

24Jesus presented another parable to them: "The Kingdom of Heaven is like a man who sowed good seed in his field. 25But while his workers were sleeping, his enemy came and sowed false wheat[81] on top of the wheat, and left. 26So when the wheat grew and produced grain, the false wheat also appeared. 27The farmer's workers came to him and asked, 'Sir, did you not sow good seed in your field? So where has the false

---

Tradition uncritically accepted and often learned in church is very often the greatest barrier against grasping the truth as taught by Jesus. Or the opinions of others often count more than the approval of Jesus and God. The Bereans were commended in Acts 17:11 for being noble-minded truth-seekers, and Jesus spoke in Luke 8:15 of the Gospel word falling on some "good and honest" hearts. We must choose to embrace the Gospel message of salvation, the Gospel of the Kingdom, offered to us all by God.

[80]In which Jesus provided his theology of salvation. This is much neglected by evangelicals who reduce the Gospel to the death and resurrection of Jesus and have not made the Kingdom the heart of the Gospel, too. Jesus' first command to us all is: "Repent and believe God's Gospel about the Kingdom of God" (Mk. 1:14-15). 1 Cor. 15:1-3 lists "matters of first importance," not the whole Gospel.

[81]A clever counterfeit. Until fully ripe, tares or darnel look like genuine wheat. False teaching appears to be true but is poisonously false. A pseudo-wheat is hard to detect. We must be relentlessly discerning.

wheat come from?' 28'This is the work of an enemy,' he replied. 'Do you
want us to go and pull them up then?' they asked him. 29'No,' he
answered, 'in case while you are pulling up the false wheat, you uproot
the wheat too. 30Let them grow together until harvest, and at harvest-time
I will tell the reapers, "First gather the false wheat and tie them up in
bundles to burn them up. Then gather the wheat into my barn."'"

31He presented another parable to them: "The Kingdom of Heaven is
like a mustard seed, which a man sowed in his field. 32Even though it is
the smallest of all the seeds, when it is grown it is bigger than other
plants. It grows into a tree and birds come and nest in its branches."[82]

33He told them another parable: "The Kingdom of Heaven is like
yeast, which a woman took and mixed with three measures of flour, until
all the dough was raised."

34Jesus taught the crowds all these things using parables, and did not
speak to them without using parables. 35This was to fulfill the prophet's
words: "I will open my mouth in parables, and I will reveal things hidden
from the foundation of the world."

36Then he left the crowds and went inside a house. His disciples came
to him and asked, "Please explain to us the parable about the false wheat
in the field." 37Jesus explained, "The one who sows the good seed is the
Son of Man.[83] 38The field represents the world. The good seed represents
the children of the Kingdom.[84] The false wheat represents the children of
the Evil One. 39The enemy who sowed the false wheat is the Devil. The
harvest is the end of the age,[85] and the reapers are angels. 40Just as the
false wheat is gathered up and burned up, so it will be at the end of the
age. 41The Son of Man will send out his angels, and they will gather out

---

[82]The worldwide Kingdom of God foreseen in Daniel, to be inaugurated at the return of Jesus.

[83]The Human Being, Jesus' favorite self-designation based on Dan. 7. Jesus is the second Adam, the head of the new creation of human persons destined for immortality in the Kingdom.

[84]The children of the Kingdom are the royal family in training now to rule and govern as kings in the future Kingdom (Dan. 7:14, 18, 22, 27; 1 Cor. 6:2; Rev. 2:26-27; 5:10).

[85]We are living in the "present evil age" (Gal. 1:4), dominated and deceived by Satan (Rev 12:9). At the end of the age (Matt. 13:39, 40, 49; 24:3; 28:20), the present evil nation-states will be replaced by the Kingdom of God when Jesus returns to inaugurate the age to come, a new society on a renewed earth. This is the core of the Christian Gospel.

of his Kingdom every sinful thing and everyone who does evil, 42and will
throw them into the burning furnace, where there will be weeping and
grinding of teeth.[86] 43Then the righteous will shine like the sun[87] in the
Kingdom of their Father. Whoever has ears, listen!

44"The Kingdom of Heaven is like treasure hidden in a field. A man
found it, reburied it, and happily went and sold everything he owned and
bought that field.

45"Again, the Kingdom of Heaven is like a trader looking for fine
pearls. 46When he found the most expensive pearl of all, he went and sold
everything he owned and bought it.

47"Again, the Kingdom of Heaven is like a fishing net thrown into the
sea, which caught all kinds of fish. 48When the net was full the fishermen
dragged it up on the beach, and they sat down and put the good fish in
baskets, but the bad they threw away. 49That is how it will be at the end
of the age.[88] The angels will go out and separate the evil people from
among the good, 50and will throw them into the burning furnace where
there will be weeping and grinding of teeth.

51"Have you understood everything?" he asked. "Yes," they replied.
52And Jesus said to them, "So then every religious teacher who becomes
a disciple of the Kingdom of Heaven is like a homeowner who brings out
from his storehouse both the new and the old."

53When Jesus had finished giving these parables,[89] he departed from
there. 54He returned to his hometown and began teaching them in their
synagogue. People were astonished and asked, "Where does this man get
his wisdom and miraculous powers from? 55Is he not the carpenter's son?
Is not his mother Mary, and his brothers[90] James, Joseph, Simon, and
Judas? 56Are not his sisters living here among us? So where does this
man get all this from?" 57And they took offense at him. "A prophet has

---

[86]The fate of the wicked is annihilation, being consumed in fire, not an "eternal torture," about which the Bible says nothing. See Mal. 4:3; Ps. 37:20; Rev. 18:8.

[87]Citing, as Jesus often does, the book of Daniel (12:3; cp. Rev. 1:16). The event is the resurrection (Dan. 12:2; Isa. 26:19).

[88]The end of the age is the moment when Jesus returns to establish the Kingdom of God worldwide, bind the Devil and grant immortality to the faithful of all ages.

[89] The end of the third of the five blocks of Jesus' teachings, showing him to be the ultimate Moses whose law is written in five books (cp. Deut. 18:18-19; John 12:44-50; Acts 3:22; 7:37).

[90]Half-brothers, the children of Mary and Joseph.

respect, but not in his hometown nor in his family," Jesus said to them.
58And because of their unbelief he did not do many miracles there.

14 1At that time Herod the tetrarch heard the news about Jesus, 2and
he said to his servants, "This is John the Baptist, resurrected from
the dead, and that is why such miraculous powers are at work in him!"
3For Herod had arrested John, and had him bound and imprisoned on
account of Herodias, the wife of Philip, Herod's brother. 4For John had
been saying to him, "It is not lawful for you to marry her." 5Herod
wanted to kill John, but he was afraid of the people's reaction, because
they considered John to be a prophet. 6However, on Herod's birthday the
daughter of Herodias danced for the party, and Herod was very pleased
with her. 7As a result he promised with an oath to give her whatever she
wanted. 8Prompted by her mother, she said, "Give me here and now the
head of John the Baptist on a plate." 9The king was upset, but because of
the oaths he had made and his dinner guests, he ordered it to be done.
10He sent word and had John beheaded in the prison. 11John's head was
then brought on a plate and given to the girl, who took it to her mother.
12John's disciples came and took the body and buried him. Then they
went and told Jesus.

13When Jesus heard the news he went away by boat to a quiet place to
be alone, but when the crowds found out where he was, they followed
him from the towns by land. 14When he went ashore he saw the large
crowd, and felt compassion for them and healed their sick. 15As evening
was approaching the disciples came to him and said, "This is an empty
place, and it is getting late. Send the crowds away so they can go to the
villages and buy themselves food." 16But Jesus said to them, "They do
not need to leave. You give them something to eat." 17They replied, "All
we have here are five loaves and a couple of fish." 18Jesus said, "Bring
them to me." 19He told the crowds to sit down on the grass. Then he took
the five loaves and the two fish, looked up to heaven and blessed them.
He broke the loaves into pieces and gave them to the disciples, and the
disciples gave them to the crowds. 20Everybody ate until they were full,
and then they collected the leftovers, which filled twelve baskets. 21Those
eating numbered about 5,000 men, not counting women and children.

22Immediately he told the disciples to get into the boat and go back to
the other side of the lake while he dismissed the crowds. 23After he had

sent the crowds on their way, he went up into the mountains to pray. Evening had come and he was there all alone. 24By then the boat was a long way out from land, being buffeted by the waves because the wind was blowing against it. 25About three a.m. Jesus caught up with them, walking on the sea. 26When the disciples saw him walking on the sea, they were terrified, screaming in fear, "It is a ghost!" 27Jesus spoke to them immediately, "Do not worry; it is me. Do not be afraid!" 28Peter replied, "lord, if it is really you, command me to walk to you on the water." 29"Come!" said Jesus. Peter got out of the boat and walked on the water toward Jesus. 30But when he looked around at the stormy wind, he was frightened and started to sink. He cried out, "lord, save me!" 31Immediately Jesus reached out and took hold of him, and said, "You have such little faith! Why did you doubt?" 32And when they got into the boat, the wind died down. 33All of them in the boat worshipped[91] him and said, "You really are the Son of God!"

34When they had crossed the lake they arrived at Gennesaret. 35When the people there realized it was Jesus, they sent word around the whole region and brought everyone who was sick to him. 36They pleaded with him that they might just touch the edge of his clothes. Everyone who touched it was healed.

15 1Then some Pharisees and religious teachers from Jerusalem came to Jesus and asked him, 2"Why do your disciples break the tradition of our forefathers and do not wash their hands before they eat a meal?" 3He replied, "And why do you break God's commandment because of your tradition? 4For God said, 'Honor your father and mother,' and 'Anyone who speaks evil of their father or mother should be put to death.' 5But you say that if someone says to their father or mother, 'Whatever you might have expected to get from me is now a gift

---

[91]It is important to remember that the word for "worship" in Hebrew and Greek does not imply an activity directed only to Deity. David was "worshiped" in the OT (1 Chron. 29:20) as were others of importance. Jesus was worshiped as the Son of God, certainly not GOD, which would make two Gods and violate the first commandment and the fundamental creed of the Bible in both Testaments — the Shema of Mark 12:29 which defines God as one single LORD. Paul defined the One God as "the Father and no one else but HE" (see 1 Cor. 8:4-6). This is exactly in line with Mal. 2:10 and the whole OT. God is strictly one single Person, never three in one.

to God,' 6then they do not have to honor their father or mother. In this
way you have annulled the word of God because of your tradition. 7You
hypocrites, Isaiah prophesied rightly about you: 8'These people honor
Me with their lips, but their hearts are far from Me. 9Their worship of Me
is pointless, because they are teaching as doctrines just human rules.'"[92]

10Jesus called the crowd over to him and said to them, "Listen and
understand: 11it is not what goes in through the mouth that defiles you,
but what comes out of the mouth — that is what defiles you." 12Then the
disciples came to him and said, "Do you know that the Pharisees were
offended by what you said?" 13He replied, "Every plant which my
heavenly Father did not plant will be uprooted. 14Leave them alone. They
are blind guides of the blind. If a blind person leads a blind person, then
they will both fall into a pit." 15Then Peter asked, "Please explain this
parable to us." 16Jesus replied, "Do you not understand yet? 17Do you not
see that whatever goes in through the mouth passes through the stomach,
and then leaves as waste? 18But whatever comes out through the mouth
comes from the heart, and that is what defiles you. 19For out of the heart
come evil thoughts, murder, adultery, sexual immorality, theft, lies, and
slander, 20and these are what defile you. To eat with unwashed hands
does not defile you."

21Jesus left there and went to the region of Tyre and Sidon. 22A
Canaanite woman from that region came and cried out, "lord,[93] son of
David, please have mercy on me, because my daughter is suffering
severely from a demon." 23But Jesus did not reply at all. His disciples
came to him and begged him, "Send her away. She is really bothering us
with her shouting!" 24Jesus said to the woman, "I was commissioned only
to the lost sheep of the house of Israel." 25But she came and bowed down
before him and said, "lord, please help me!" 26He said, "It is not right to
take the children's food and throw it to the dogs." 27She replied, "Yes,
lord, but even the dogs can eat the crumbs that fall from their master's

---

[92]The threatening possibility of being rejected by Jesus, despite one's "sincerity," is shown by Jesus' powerful warning in 7:21-29.

[93]An obvious use of the Messianic title "lord" (*adoni*, my lord) based on the key text in Ps. 110:1, where the second lord is never the designation of Deity. Cp. Lk. 2:11: "Messiah lord" as distinct from "the Lord's [Yahweh's] Messiah" (Lk. 2:26).

table." 28Jesus answered, "O woman, your faith is great! May it be as you wish." And her daughter was healed at that very moment.[94]

29Jesus left there and went towards the Lake of Galilee. He went into the mountains and sat down there. 30Great crowds came to him, bringing people who were lame, blind, crippled, mute, and many others. They laid them on the ground at his feet, and he healed them. 31The crowd was astounded at what they saw: the deaf speaking, the crippled healed, the lame walking, and the blind seeing. They praised the God of Israel.[95]

32Jesus called his disciples over and said to them, "I feel compassion for all these people, because they have been with me now for three days and have not had anything to eat. I do not want to send them away hungry, in case they faint on their way home." 33The disciples responded, "Where could we find enough bread in this empty place to feed such a huge crowd?" 34Jesus asked them, "How many loaves of bread do you have?" They replied, "Seven, and a few small fish." 35Jesus told the crowd to sit down on the ground. 36He took the seven loaves and the fish, and after giving thanks he broke them into pieces and gave them to the disciples, and the disciples gave them to the crowd. 37Everybody ate until they were full, and then they collected the left-overs, filling seven baskets. 38Those eating numbered 4,000 men, not counting women and children. 39Then he sent the crowds away, got into a boat, and went to the Magadan region.

16 1The Pharisees and Sadducees came up to Jesus to test him, demanding that he show them a miraculous sign from heaven. 2He answered, "When it is evening you say, 'It will be a fine day tomorrow, because the sky is red,' 3while in the morning you say, 'It will be bad weather today, because the sky is red and threatening.' You know how to

---

[94]This beautiful episode gives us the story of an argument which Jesus did not win! The lady's faith overcame all obstacles. So should ours.

[95]The One God of the unitary monotheism of the creed of Israel and of Jesus in Mark 12:28ff. The Trinity was unknown to Jesus and the Apostles. It was a later attempt to explain God in the alien terms of Greek philosophy. The later attempts to base it on the NT were to justify what became embedded in creeds as tradition. The fruits of that misdevelopment have been horrifying in terms of contention, argumentation and division. Many have been martyred, notably Servetus murdered with the approval of John Calvin, for their loyalty to the creed of Jesus in Mark 12:29 and John 17:3. John Milton and Sir Isaac Newton were strong anti-Trinitarians.

predict the weather, but you cannot recognize the signs of the times. 4An
evil and unfaithful society wants a miraculous sign, and no sign will be
given to it but the sign of Jonah." He left them and went away.
5Going to the other side of the lake, the disciples forgot to bring
bread. 6"Watch out and be careful of the yeast of the Pharisees and
Sadducees," Jesus said to them. 7"It is because we did not bring any
bread," the disciples said to each other, discussing it. 8Knowing what
they were saying, Jesus said to them, "You who have so little faith, why
are you discussing among yourselves about not having any bread? 9Do
you not understand yet? Do you not remember the five loaves that fed
5,000, and how many baskets of left-overs you collected? 10Or the seven
loaves that fed the 4,000, and how many baskets of left-overs you
collected? 11How is it that you have not understood yet that I was not
talking to you about bread? Watch out for the yeast of the Pharisees and
Sadducees!" 12Then they realized that he was not warning them about
yeast for bread, but about the teachings[96] of the Pharisees and Sadducees.
13When Jesus arrived in the region of Caesarea Philippi, he asked his
disciples, "Who do people say that the Son of Man is?" 14They replied,
"Some say John the Baptist, others Elijah, and still others Jeremiah or
another one of the prophets." 15He asked them, "But what about you —
who do you say I am?" 16Simon Peter answered, "You are the Messiah,
the Son of the living God."[97] 17Jesus said to him, "You arc blessed,
Simon son of Jonah, because human flesh and blood did not reveal this
to you, but my Father who is in heaven. 18I also tell you, you are Peter,
and on this rock[98] I intend to build my church, and the gates of Hades will
not overpower it. 19I will give you the keys of the Kingdom of Heaven,
and whatever you ban on earth will have been banned in heaven, and
whatever you allow on earth will have been allowed in heaven." 20Then
he warned his disciples not to tell anyone that he was the Messiah.
21From then on Jesus began to explain to his disciples that he must go
to Jerusalem, and suffer greatly at the hands of the elders, chief priests,

---

[96]False teachings of all sorts are to be avoided as toxic and contaminating to the spiritual life. "A love of the truth" is required for salvation (2 Thess. 2:10).

[97]The phrase is from Hosea 1:10 and describes the ideal Israelite. The Messiah was of course perfectly obedient to God, and fully representative of the One God of Israel.

[98]That is, the rock confession of Jesus as the Messiah of Israel and uniquely the Son of God (Lk 1:35), certainly not a second member of a triune God! See also 1 John 5:1, 10.

and religious teachers; and be killed, and be raised up on the third day.[99]
22Peter took Jesus aside and started to reprimand him, saying, "God
forbid, lord![100] This will never happen to you!" 23Jesus turned to Peter
and said, "Get away from me, Satan! You are a stumbling block to me,
because you are thinking not about God's interests, but man's!" 24Then
Jesus said to his disciples, "If anyone wants to be my follower, they must
deny themselves, and pick up their cross and follow me. 25For whoever
wants to save their life will lose it, and whoever loses their life for my
sake will find it. 26What does it benefit anyone to gain the whole world,
and lose their life? What would anyone give in exchange for their life?
27For the Son of Man is going to come in the glory of his Father with his
angels. Then he will give to everyone what they deserve for what they
have done. 28I am telling you the truth: there are some people standing
here who will not die until they see the Son of Man coming in his
Kingdom."

17 1Six days after saying this,[101] Jesus took with him Peter, James and
his brother John and led them up a high mountain by themselves.
2Before their eyes his appearance changed: his face shone like the sun,
and his clothes became as bright as light. 3Right then Moses and Elijah
appeared to them, talking with Jesus. 4Peter spoke up and said to Jesus,
"lord, it is so good for us to be here. If you like, I will make three
shelters — one for you, one for Moses, and one for Elijah." 5While he
was still speaking, a bright cloud came over them and a voice came from

---

[99]This verse is a critically important juncture in the history of Jesus. For the first time, late in his ministry, he speaks of his death and resurrection. But he had been preaching the saving Gospel of the Kingdom (Mk. 1:14-15), and so had the disciples, for the whole of his ministry up to this point. The Kingdom remained the basis of the Gospel of course, and Paul always preached the Kingdom of God as Gospel (Acts 19:8; 20:24-25; 28:23, 30, 31). Contemporary evangelical preaching has subtracted the Kingdom from the Gospel, leaving only the facts about his death and resurrection, which Paul preached as "among things of first importance" (1 Cor. 15:3), not as the whole Gospel. A return to Jesus will be under way when the Kingdom of God is restored to the Gospel, and in this way Jesus will be believed and obeyed.

[100]Reminding us that Jesus is not the Lord God, but the second lord (my lord, *adoni*) of Ps. 110:1. *Adoni* ("my lord") is never a reference to Deity.

[101]Showing that the prediction of the Kingdom of God was fulfilled in the vision (17:9) of the Kingdom which followed.

the cloud: “This is My Son whom I love, who pleases Me. Listen to
him!” 6On hearing this, the disciples were absolutely terrified and fell
face down. 7Jesus went over to them and touched them. “Get up, and do
not be afraid,” he said. 8When they looked up, they saw nobody there
except Jesus by himself.

9As they descended the mountain Jesus gave them strict instructions:
“Do not tell anybody about the vision[102] until the Son of Man has been
raised from the dead.” 10The disciples asked, “So why then do the
religious teachers say that Elijah has to come first?” 11Jesus answered, “It
is right to expect Elijah to come and restore everything, 12and I tell you
that Elijah already came and people did not recognize him. They
mistreated him in whatever way they wanted. In the same way the Son of
Man will suffer at their hands.” 13Then the disciples realized that Jesus
was speaking to them about John the Baptist.

14When they came towards the crowd, a man came up to Jesus and
knelt before him. 15He pleaded, “lord, please have mercy on my son. He
is demonically influenced and suffers terribly because he often falls into
the fire or into water. 16I brought him to your disciples but they could not
heal him.” 17Jesus responded, “You faithless and perverted society! How
long do I have to remain with you? How long do I have to put up with
you? Bring him here to me!” 18Jesus commanded the demon and it left
the boy, and he was healed right away. 19Then the disciples came to Jesus
in private and asked, “Why could we not cast it out?” 20He said to them,
“It is because you have so little faith. I am telling you the truth: if you
have faith even as small as a mustard seed, you will say to this mountain,
‘Go from here to over there,’ and it will do it, and nothing will be
impossible for you. [21But this kind does not go out except by prayer and
fasting.”][103]

---

[102]This was a vision of the future Kingdom as Peter explained in 2 Pet. 1:16-18. They saw the Parousia (2 Pet. 1:16), the spectacular arrival of Jesus in glory to set up the Kingdom. The idea that the Kingdom came invisibly in 1914 is one of the most astonishing false teachings ever to be imposed on the NT writings. Other failed dates are equally to be regretted as causing unnecessary disturbance and disappointment (for example in 1844).

[103]Early manuscripts do not contain verse 21.

22When they were together in Galilee, Jesus said to them, “The Son
of Man will be betrayed into human hands. 23They will kill him, but on
the third day he will be raised.” And they were terribly sad.

24When they got to Capernaum, those who were in charge of
collecting the half-shekel temple tax came to Peter and asked him, “Does
your teacher not pay the half-shekel tax?” 25He replied, “Yes.” When
Peter came into the house, Jesus spoke first. “What do you think,
Simon?” Jesus asked him. “The kings of this world, who do they collect
their taxes or customs from? From their sons or from strangers?” 26When
Peter said, “From strangers,” Jesus replied, “In that case the sons are
exempt. 27But to avoid causing offense to anyone, go to the lake and
throw out a line with a hook. Pull in the first fish you catch, and when
you open its mouth you will find a shekel coin. Take it and give it to
them for both me and you.”

18 1At that time the disciples came to Jesus asking, “So who is the
greatest in the Kingdom of Heaven?” 2Jesus called over a small
child and placed him before them. 3He said, “I am telling you the truth:
unless you are converted and become like children, you will not enter the
Kingdom of Heaven. 4But whoever humbles themselves and becomes
like this little child is greatest in the Kingdom of Heaven. 5Whoever
accepts a little child like this in my name[104] accepts me.

6“But anyone who causes one of these little ones who believe in me
to stumble, it would be better for them to have a huge millstone hung
around their necks and be drowned in the depths of the sea. 7Shame on
the world because it causes people to stumble! Stumbling blocks will
surely come, but shame on the person through whom the temptation
comes! 8If your hand or your foot causes you to sin, cut it off and throw
it away. It is better for you to enter Life[105] crippled or lame rather than to
have two hands or two feet and be thrown into the fire[106] of the Age to
Come. 9If your eye causes you to sin, pluck it out and throw it away. It is

---

[104]That is, as representing me and my religion, all that I stand for.

[105]That is, the Life of the Age to Come, in the future Kingdom of God to be established on earth at the return of Jesus (Dan. 7:18, 22, 27).

[106]The destructive, consuming fire which will burn up the wicked, putting them out of existence.

better for you to enter Life with one eye than to have two eyes and be
thrown into the fire of Gehenna.

10"Make sure you do not look down on one of these little ones. I tell
you that their angels in heaven always see the face of my Father who is
in heaven. [11For the Son of Man has come to save that which was
lost.][107] 12What do you think? If a man has a hundred sheep, and one of
them gets lost, will he not leave the ninety-nine on the hills and go
looking for the one that is lost? 13And if he finds it, I tell you he rejoices
over that sheep more than the ninety-nine which did not get lost. 14In the
same way it is not the will of your Father in heaven that any of these
little ones perish.

15"If your brother sins against you, go to him privately and point out
his fault. If he listens to you, you have won your brother over. 16But if he
does not listen, then take one or two more people with you, so that with
two or three witnesses the truth can be established. 17And if he refuses to
listen to them, then tell the church. If he refuses to listen to the church as
well, then consider him as a Gentile and a tax collector.

18"I am telling you the truth: whatever you ban on earth will have
been banned in heaven, and whatever you allow on earth will have been
allowed in heaven. 19I also tell you that if two of you agree on earth about
something you are asking for, it will be done for you by my Father who
is in heaven. 20For where two or three gather together in my name, I am
there with them."

21Then Peter came to Jesus and asked him, "lord, how many times
should I forgive my brother for sinning against me? Seven times?"
22Jesus said to him, "I am not telling you seven times, but seventy times
seven!

23"That is why the Kingdom of Heaven can be compared to a king
who wanted to settle accounts with those servants who owed him money.
24When he began to settle accounts, one servant was brought to him who
owed him 10,000 talents. 25But since he did not have the money to pay,
his lord ordered him to be sold, together with his wife and children and
all his possessions, so that the debt could be paid. 26The servant fell to his
knees and begged, 'Please be patient with me and I will pay everything
back.' 27The servant's lord felt compassion, released him, and forgave

---

[107]Early manuscripts do not contain verse 11.

him the debt. 28But that servant went out and found one of his fellow
servants who owed him just a hundred denarii. He seized him by the
neck and began to choke him, saying, 'Pay me back what you owe me!'
29So his fellow servant fell down and begged him, 'Be patient with me
and I will pay you back.' 30But the man refused, and went and threw his
fellow servant into prison until he paid off what he owed. 31When the
other servants saw what he had done they were very upset and went and
told the lord what had happened. 32Then the lord called the man back and
said to him, 'You evil servant! I forgave you all your debt because you
pleaded with me. 33Should you not have had mercy on your fellow
servant, just as I had mercy on you?' 34His lord became angry and
handed him over to the prison guards until he repaid all the debt. 35My
heavenly Father will do the same to you unless you forgive your brothers
from the heart."

19 1When Jesus had finished these words,[108] he left Galilee and went
to the region of Judea beyond the Jordan. 2Large crowds followed
him, and he healed them there.

3Some Pharisees came to put him to the test. They asked, "Is it lawful
for a man to divorce his wife for any reason?" 4Jesus replied, "Have you
not read that He who created man[109] at the beginning made them male
and female? 5God said, 'This is the reason why a man will leave his
father and mother and be joined to his wife, and the two become one
flesh.' 6So they are no longer two, but one flesh. What God has joined
together let no one separate." 7They asked, "Then why did Moses
command to give her a written certificate of divorce and send her away?"
8Jesus responded, "Because of your hard-hearted attitude Moses
permitted you to divorce your wives, but it was not like that from the
beginning. 9I tell you, whoever divorces his wife, except for sexual
immorality,[110] and marries another commits adultery." 10His disciples
said to him, "If that is the case in marital matters, it is better not to

---

[108]The end of the fourth of the five blocks of Jesus' teachings, showing him to be the ultimate Moses whose law is written in five books.

[109]Jesus certainly never claimed to be involved in the Genesis creation! It was God who rested on the seventh day (Heb. 4:4) and the creation was the work of God, the Father of Jesus, alone. God was alone at creation (Isa. 44:24).

[110]A person thus divorced is no longer married and may marry again, within the faith.

marry!" 11Jesus said to them, "Not everyone can accept this statement;
only those it is given to. 12Some are born as eunuchs, some are made
eunuchs by people, and some choose to be eunuchs for the sake of the
Kingdom of Heaven. Whoever can accept this, let them accept it."[111]

13Then people brought little children to him so that he could bless
them and pray for them, but the disciples scolded the people. 14But Jesus
said, "Let the little children come to me; do not stop them. The Kingdom
of Heaven belongs to those like them." 15He placed his hands on them to
bless them, and then he left.

16A man came to Jesus and asked him, "Teacher, what good do I need
to do to get the Life of the Age to Come?" 17Jesus replied, "Why do you
ask me about what is good? There is only one Person who is good.[112] But
if you want to enter that Life, then keep the commandments." 18The man
asked, "Which ones?" Jesus replied, "Do not murder, do not commit
adultery, do not steal, do not lie, 19honor your father and mother, and love
your neighbor as yourself." 20The young man said, "I have kept all these
commandments. What else do I need to do?" 21Jesus said to him, "If you
want to be complete, then go and sell your possessions and give to the
poor, and you will have treasure stored up in heaven. Then come and
follow me." 22When the young man heard Jesus' answer he went away
very sad, because he was very rich.

23Jesus said to his disciples, "I am telling you the truth: it is hard for
rich people to enter the Kingdom of Heaven. 24I also tell you this: It is
easier for a camel to pass through the eye of a needle than for a rich
person to enter the Kingdom of God." 25When the disciples heard this,
they were shocked and asked, "Then who can be saved?" 26Jesus looked
at them and said, "Humanly speaking it is impossible, but all things are
possible with God." 27Then Peter said to him, "Look, we have left
everything and followed you. What reward will we get?" 28Jesus replied,
"I am telling you the truth: you who have followed me, when the world

---

[111]A compulsory celibacy for all ordained ministers, as taught by Roman Catholics, is far outside the mind of Christ and not recommended anywhere in Scripture. The results have been disastrous. A warning is given against this practice in 1 Tim. 4:3.

[112]One of the constant references to the Bible's definition of God not as triune, but as One Person, the Father. This was the belief and creed of Jesus as shown by Mark 12:28-34; John 5:44; 17:3.

is reborn and the Son of Man will sit on his throne of glory,[113] you too
will sit on twelve thrones, governing[114] the twelve tribes of Israel. 29And
everyone who has left their homes, brothers, sisters, father, mother,
children, or properties, because of me, will receive back a hundred times
more, and will inherit the life of the age to come. But many will be last
who are now first, and first who are now last."

20 1"For the Kingdom of Heaven[115] is like this: a landowner went out
early in the morning to hire workers for his vineyard. 2After
agreeing with the workers to pay them one denarius for the day, he sent
them off to work in his vineyard. 3Around nine a.m. he went out and saw
other people standing idle in the marketplace. 4'You go and work in the
vineyard too, and I will pay you what is right,' he said to them. So they
went. 5Around noon and three p.m. he went out and did the same thing.
6About five p.m. he went out and found more people standing idle. 'Why
have you been standing around all day doing nothing?' he asked them.
7'Because nobody hired us,' they answered. 'You go and work in my
vineyard too,' he said to them. 8When evening came, the vineyard owner
said to his manager, 'Call the workers in and pay them their wages,
starting with the last workers up to the first.' 9When those who were
hired at five p.m. came in, they each received one denarius. 10So when
those who were hired first came, they thought they would get more, but
they also received one denarius. 11When they received their pay, they
complained to the owner, 12'Those who were hired last only worked for
an hour, and you have paid them the same as us who worked the whole
day in the burning heat.' 13The owner answered one of them, 'My friend,
I have not treated you unfairly. Did you not agree with me to work for
one denarius? 14Take your pay and leave. I choose to give to the last

---

[113]In the age to come, in his future Kingdom to be inaugurated on earth at his Second Coming, Parousia (Rev. 11:15-18).

[114]"The verb 'judge' in Hebrew means more than administering justice. The meaning of the phrase is close to 'he will govern among the nations' in Ps. 110:6" (*New Jerome Biblical Commentary*). For the royal destiny of the saints, see Ps.111:6; 113:7-8; 1 Sam. 2:8; Dan. 7:18, 22, 27.

[115]It is important to keep in mind always that this is not remotely connected with "going to heaven at death" about which Scripture says nothing. The Kingdom of Heaven is the Kingdom originating with God who is in heaven. It will be on this earth renewed when Jesus comes back.

workers the same as I gave to you. 15Is it wrong for me to do what I want
with my own money? Are you envious because I want to be generous?'
16So the last will be first and the first will be last."
17On his way up to Jerusalem, Jesus took the twelve disciples aside
and said to them, 18"Look, we are going up to Jerusalem, and the Son of
Man will be betrayed to the chief priests and religious teachers, and they
will condemn him to death. 19They will hand him over to the Gentiles to
mock and flog and crucify him.[116] But on the third day[117] he will be raised
from the dead."
20Then the mother of the sons of Zebedee came with her sons to Jesus
and knelt down before him to make a request. 21Jesus said to her, "What
is it that you want?" She asked, "Command that in your Kingdom my
two sons may sit one on your right and the other on your left." 22Jesus
answered, "You do not know what you are asking for. Can you drink the
cup I am about to drink?" They responded, "Yes, we can." 23He said to
them, "You certainly will drink my cup, but to sit on my right or on my
left is not mine to give. These places are prepared for those my Father
chooses."
24When the other ten disciples heard what they had asked, they were
upset with the two brothers. 25But Jesus called them over and said to
them, "You know that the rulers of the Gentiles dominate their people,
and those in power tyrannize them. 26It should not be like that with you.
Whoever wants to become great among you must be your servant, 27and
whoever wants to be first among you must be your slave; 28just as the
Son of Man did not come to be served, but to serve, and to give his life
as a ransom in place of many."
29As they were leaving Jericho, a huge crowd followed Jesus. 30Two
blind men were sitting at the side of the road. When they heard that Jesus
was passing by, they shouted out, "Please have mercy on us, lord,[118] son

---

[116]The third and final announcement of the impending death of the Messiah. The first was in 16:21, the second in 17:22-23.

[117]The crucifixion was on a Friday, the 15th Nisan and the resurrection on Sunday, the first day of the week (Lk. 24:21, the third day since Friday, using Luke's and Jesus' inclusive reckoning).

[118]I have deliberately not capitalized lord to remind readers that Jesus is not the Lord God, but the human lord, as defined by the all-important Ps. 110:1 where the One God Yahweh gave a prophetic utterance in regard to "my lord," the Messiah (*adoni,* not *Adonai*). This verse is cited in the NT more times by far than any other verse. It is the

of David!" 31The crowd sternly told them to be quiet, but they shouted
even more, "Please have mercy on us, lord, son of David!" 32Jesus
stopped and called them. "What do you want me to do for you?" he
asked. 33They replied, "lord, we want to be able to see." 34Jesus felt
compassion for them and touched their eyes. Immediately they were able
to see, and they followed him.

21 1Jesus and his disciples came close to Jerusalem, entering
Bethphage beside the Mount of Olives. Jesus sent two disciples,
2telling them, "Go into the village up ahead and you will immediately
find a donkey tied there with a colt. Untie them and bring them to me. 3If
anyone says anything to you, just say, 'The lord needs them,' and he will
send them immediately." 4This happened to fulfill what was said through
the prophet: 5"Tell the daughter of Zion, 'Look, your king is coming to
you, gentle, and riding on a donkey — on a colt, the offspring of a
donkey.'" 6The disciples went and did as Jesus had told them. 7They
brought back the donkey and the colt. They spread their coats on them,
and Jesus sat on the coats. 8Most of the crowd laid their coats on the
road, while others cut branches from the trees and laid them on the road.
9The crowds who went in front of him, and those following, were all
shouting, "Hosanna[119] to the son of David! Blessed is he who comes in
the name of the Lord! Hosanna in the highest!" 10When Jesus arrived in
Jerusalem, the whole city was in turmoil, with people asking, "Who is
this?" 11The crowds replied, "This is the prophet Jesus, from Nazareth in
Galilee."

12Jesus went into the Temple and threw out all the people trading
there. He overturned the money-changers' tables and the dove-sellers'
seats, 13and said to them, "It is written, 'My house will be called a house
of prayer,' but you are turning it into a robbers' den."

---

key to the relationship of God to Jesus, "the one God and the man Messiah Jesus" in the creed of Paul (1 Tim. 2:5). It is a fundamental fact about NT faith, exemplified by these blind men, that we recognize Jesus as who he really is, the descendant of David, Messiah as well as David's lord. No one in the Bible thought Jesus was God the Son, which would violate the fundamental monotheism of Jesus and Israel.

[119]"Rescue us!" Mk. 11:10 speaks of "the coming Kingdom of our father David." The Gospel of the Kingdom of God is equally the coming Kingdom of our father David. See my *Our Fathers Who Aren't in Heaven*.

14The blind and the lame came to Jesus in the Temple, and he healed
them. 15But when the chief priests and religious teachers saw the
wonderful things he had done, and the children shouting in the Temple,
“Hosanna to the son of David,” they became angry. 16“Do you hear what
these children are saying?” they asked him. “Yes,” Jesus replied. “Did
you not ever read the Scripture: ‘From the mouths of infants and babies
You have prepared praise for Yourself’?” 17And he left them and went
out of the city to Bethany, where he stayed the night.

18The next morning as he walked back into the city, he became
hungry. 19He saw a fig tree by the side of the road, so he went over to it,
but did not find any fruit, just leaves. He said to the fig tree, “You will
never produce fruit from now on!” Immediately the fig tree withered.
20When the disciples saw this, they were astonished. “How did the fig
tree wither so suddenly?” they asked. 21Jesus answered, “I am telling you
the truth: if you have faith and do not doubt, you will do not only what
was done to the fig tree, but even if you say to this mountain, ‘Be lifted
up and thrown into the sea,’ it will happen. 22You will receive everything
you ask for in prayer, if you believe.”

23When Jesus went into the temple, the chief priests and the ruling
elders of the people came to him while he was teaching and asked, “By
what authority are you doing these things, and who gave you this
authority?” 24Jesus replied, “I will ask you a question too. If you answer
me, I will also tell you by what authority I do these things. 25The baptism
of John — where was that from? From heaven, or from people?” They
discussed this among themselves. “If we say ‘From heaven,’ he will ask
us why we did not believe him. 26But if we say, ‘From people,’ we are
afraid of what the people will do, because they all consider John to be a
prophet.” 27So they answered Jesus, “We do not know.” Then he said to
them, “So I am not telling you by what authority I do these things.

28“But what do you think about this? There was a man who had two
sons. He went to the first son and said, ‘Son, go to work today in the
vineyard.’ 29The son answered, ‘I will not,’ but afterwards he was sorry,
and he changed his mind and went. 30The father went to the second son
and said the same thing. He replied, ‘I will go,’ but he did not. 31So

which of the two sons did what his father wanted?"[120] They answered,
"The first." Jesus said to them, "I am telling you the truth: tax collectors
and prostitutes will go ahead of you into the Kingdom of God. 32John
came to tell you the right way and you did not believe him, but the tax
collectors and prostitutes did believe him. Even when you saw this, you
did not change your minds and believe him.

33"Listen to another parable. There was a landowner who planted a
vineyard. He put up a wall around it and dug out a winepress, and built a
watchtower. He rented it to some tenant farmers and then went on a
journey.[121] 34When it was harvest-time, he sent his servants to the farmers
to get his share of the crop. 35The farmers seized his servants, beat one,
killed another, and stoned the third. 36So he sent more servants, and the
farmers treated them the same way. 37So then he sent his son, saying to
himself, 'They will respect my son.' 38But the farmers, when they saw
the son, said to each other, 'Here is the heir. Come on, let us kill him so
that we can take his inheritance!' 39They took him, threw him out of the
vineyard, and killed him. 40So when the vineyard owner comes, what will
he do to those farmers?" 41They said to Jesus, "He will destroy those
terrible men in a terrible way, and rent out the vineyard to other farmers
who will give him his share of the crops at harvest-time."

42"Have you not read the Scriptures?" Jesus asked them. "'The stone
which the builders rejected has become the main cornerstone. This was
from the Lord, and it is wonderful in our eyes.' 43That is why I am telling
you that the Kingdom of God will be taken away from you, and will be
given to a people who produce its fruit.[122] 44Whoever falls on this stone

---

[120]The essence of being a son in the Bible is to obey one's father, to learn the trade from one's father, and to represent the father's interests, acting on his behalf. All these are Christian ideals modeled perfectly by Jesus, the ideal Son of God.

[121]The similar parable in Luke 19:11ff is an excellent place to start when presenting the Gospel of the Kingdom, which will begin in power at the future coming of Jesus, and teaches the requirement of believers to develop their talents now, in the service of the Great Commission. Jesus' proximity to Jerusalem rightly signaled the possibility that the Kingdom of God was going to begin then.

[122]The true people of God, the international "Israel of God" (Gal. 6:16), the true circumcision (Phil. 3:3), as distinct from now natural, national Israel, the Israel of the flesh (1 Cor. 10:18), receive the Kingdom and must show forth the fruit of love (Gal. 6:16). A final repentance after much suffering is expected for a collective whole of now blinded Israel (see Rom. 9-11).

will be broken to pieces, but on whomever it falls it will crush them to
dust."[123] 45When the chief priests and the Pharisees heard his parables,
they realized he was speaking about them. 46They tried to arrest him, but
they were afraid of the crowd, because the people believed he was a
prophet.

22 1Jesus spoke to them using parables again. 2"The Kingdom of
Heaven is like a king who arranged a wedding reception for his
son," Jesus explained. 3"He sent out his servants to call everyone who
was invited to the wedding reception, but they refused to come. 4So he
sent out other servants, with the instructions, 'Tell those who are invited,
"I have arranged everything for the wedding banquet. The bulls and
fattened calves have been killed. Everything is ready, so come to the
banquet!"' 5But they paid no attention and went off to do whatever they
wanted — one to his fields, another to his business, 6and the rest seized
his servants, mistreated them, and killed them. 7The king became very
angry, and sent his soldiers to kill those murderers and burn down their
town. 8Then the king said to his servants, 'The wedding banquet is ready,
but those who were invited were not worthy to come.[124] 9So go out in the
streets and invite everyone you find to come to the wedding banquet.'
10So the servants went out into the streets and brought back everyone
they could find, both good and bad, and the wedding hall was full. 11But
when the king came in to see the guests, he noticed a man who did not
have wedding clothes on. 12He asked him, 'My friend, how did you get in
here without wedding clothes?' The man was speechless. 13Then the king
said to his servants, 'Tie his hands and feet, and throw him outside into
the darkest place, where there will be weeping and grinding of teeth.'
14For many are invited, but few choose to respond."

---

[123] A reference to Dan. 2:44 which predicts the worldwide Kingdom to be established on earth by the Messiah when he returns, putting to an end all present ungodly human nations (cp. Rev 12:9; 11:15-18; Dan. 7:14, 18, 22, 27; Lk. 19:11ff).

[124] The NT makes it clear that Christians must "walk worthy of the Kingdom" to which they are invited to rule with Jesus on the renewed earth (1 Thess. 2:12; Rev. 2:26-27; Dan. 7:18, 22, 27). The idea of "once saved always saved" is a fatal trap. We must persist to the end and bear fruit. Those who refuse the invitation to salvation in the Kingdom are disqualified (Acts 13:46, where "the life of the age to come" is the synonym for the Kingdom, as often). Some people "believe only for a while" and then fall away (Lk. 8:13).

15Then the Pharisees went and plotted how they could trap him by
what he said. 16They sent to him their disciples together with
representatives of Herod's party. "Teacher, we know that you are a
truthful man, and you teach God's way in truth," they began. "You do
not worry what people think of you, and you are impartial. 17So please
tell us what you think. Is it right to pay taxes to Caesar, or not?" 18Jesus
sensed their evil intentions, and asked them, "Why are you testing me,
you hypocrites? 19Show me the coin used to pay the tax." They brought a
denarius coin to him. 20"Whose image and whose inscription is this?" he
asked them. 21"Caesar's," they replied. "Then give to Caesar what is
Caesar's, and to God what is God's," he said to them. 22When they heard
this they were astonished, and they left him and went away.

23The same day some Sadducees came to him. They say there is no
resurrection. 24They asked him, "Teacher, Moses said that if a man dies
childless, his brother should marry his widow and raise up children on
behalf of his brother. 25Once there were seven brothers among us. The
first married, and died, and being childless left his widow to his brother.
26The same thing happened to the second and third husband, right up to
the seventh. 27Later the woman died too. 28So then, when the resurrection
comes, which of the seven brothers will she be married to?" 29Jesus
replied, "You are much mistaken! You do not know the Scriptures, or the
power of God.[125] 30For in the resurrection people do not marry, and they
are not given in marriage. They are like the angels in heaven. 31And
about the resurrection of the dead, have you not read what was said to
you by God: 32'I am the God of Abraham, and the God of Isaac, and the
God of Jacob'? He is not the God of the dead, but of the living." 33When
the crowds heard what he said, they were astonished at his teaching.

34When the Pharisees heard that he had silenced the Sadducees, they
gathered themselves together. 35One of them, an expert in the Law, asked
him a question to test him: 36"Teacher, which is the greatest
commandment in the Law?" 37Jesus replied, "'Love the Lord your God
with your whole heart, your whole being, and your whole mind.' 38This is
the greatest and first commandment. 39The second is like it: 'Love your

---

[125]The real cause of all error, disagreement and fragmentation among would-be believers.

neighbor as yourself.' 40The whole Law and the prophets hang on these
two commandments."
41While the Pharisees were gathered there, Jesus asked them a
question. 42"What do you think about the Messiah?" he asked. "Whose
son is he?" They replied, "The son of David." 43He said to them, "So how
is it that David by inspiration of the spirit calls him 'lord'? David says,
44'The Lord said to my lord:[126] Sit at My right hand until I put your
enemies under your feet.' 45If David called him lord, how is he his son?"
46Nobody could give him any answer, and nobody from that time on
dared to ask him any more questions.

23 1Then Jesus spoke to the crowds and to his disciples: 2"The
religious teachers and the Pharisees have seated themselves in the
chair of Moses, 3so do what they tell you. But do not do as they do,
because they do not practice what they preach. 4They tie up heavy
burdens and put these burdens on people's shoulders, but they
themselves will not lift a finger to carry them. 5Everything they do is so
that people will notice them. They make themselves extra wide prayer
boxes to wear and extra long tassels on their clothes. 6They love places
of honor at banquets and the chief seats in the synagogues. 7They love
respectful greetings in the market places, and being addressed as 'Rabbi.'
8But do not be called 'Rabbi.' Only one is your master-teacher, and you
are all brothers. 9Do not give anyone on earth the title 'Father.' Only one
Person is your Father, who is in heaven. 10Do not be called 'Leader.'
Only one person is your leader, the Messiah. 11Whoever is the greatest
among you will be your servant. 12Anyone who exalts himself will be
humbled, and anyone who humbles himself will be exalted.
13"But shame on you, religious teachers and Pharisees, you
hypocrites! You slam the door of the Kingdom of Heaven shut in
people's faces. You do not go in yourselves, nor do you allow those
entering to go in. [14Shame on you, religious teachers and Pharisees, you

---

[126]The second lord is not a title of Deity but always a title to designate a non-Deity superior. The Hebrew word is *adoni*, not ADONAI and in all 195 occasions where it appears in the Hebrew Bible it designates someone *other than* God. The idea of God speaking to God is utterly foreign to the unitarianism of the Bible.

hypocrites! You devour widows' houses, and make a show of long prayers; therefore you will receive greater condemnation.][127]

15"Shame on you, religious teachers and Pharisees, you hypocrites! You travel over sea and land to make just one convert, and when you do, you make him twice a candidate for Gehenna-fire[128] as yourselves.

16"Shame on you, blind guides who say, 'If you swear by the Temple, that is nothing, but if you swear by the gold of the Temple, then you are bound to keep your oath.' Blind idiots! 17What is more important — the gold, or the Temple that makes the gold holy? 18You say, 'If you swear by the altar, that is nothing, but if you swear by the sacrifice on the altar, then you are bound to keep your oath.' 19You are so blind! What is more important — the sacrifice, or the altar that makes the sacrifice holy? 20Anyone who swears by the altar swears by it and by everything on it. 21Anyone who swears by the Temple swears by it and by Him who lives in it. 22Anyone who swears by heaven swears by the throne of God and by Him who sits on it.

23"Shame on you, religious teachers and Pharisees, you hypocrites! You pay a tithe of mint, dill, and cumin, but you neglect the weightier matters of the Law — justice, mercy, and faith. These are the things you should have done without neglecting the others. 24You blind guides — filtering out a gnat and swallowing a camel!

25"Shame on you, religious teachers and Pharisees, you hypocrites! You clean the outside of the cup and the plate, but inside you are full of greed and self-indulgence. 26You blind Pharisee, first clean the inside of the cup and the plate, so that the outside may become clean too.

27"Shame on you, religious teachers and Pharisees, you hypocrites! You are like white-washed tombs, which look good on the outside but inside are full of skeletons and all kinds of unclean things. 28In the same way, on the outside you appear to others to be good people, but on the inside you are full of hypocrisy and law-breaking.

---

[127] Verse 14 is not found in early manuscripts.

[128] "Son of Gehenna" means one who is destined to be destroyed in the consuming fire of hell. Gehenna, hell-fire, is to be carefully distinguished from Hades (*sheol* in Hebrew), the place of all the dead, good and bad, until resurrection. Gehenna begins only at the second coming (Rev. 19:20; cp. Isa. 31:6-9). At present all the dead are asleep, unconscious in the realm of the dead, Hades (Dan. 12:2; Isa. 38:18; Ps. 104:29; 146:4).

29“Shame on you, religious teachers and Pharisees, you hypocrites! You build memorial tombs for the prophets, and decorate the tombs of the righteous, 30and you say, ‘If we had lived in our forefathers’ times we would not have joined them in shedding the blood of the prophets.’ 31By saying this you testify against yourselves that you belong to those who murdered the prophets. 32Go on and finish off what your forefathers started! 33You snakes, you brood of vipers, how can you escape the judgment of Gehenna-fire?

34“Look, that is why I am sending you prophets, wise men, and scholars.[129] Some of them you will kill, some of them you will crucify, and some of them you will flog in your synagogues and chase from town to town. 35As a result, you will be held accountable for all the righteous blood shed on earth, from the blood of righteous Abel to the blood of Zechariah son of Berechiah,[130] whom you killed between the temple and the altar. 36I am telling you the truth: the consequences of all this will come down on this evil society.

37“Jerusalem, Jerusalem, who kills the prophets and stones those who are sent to her! So often I wanted to gather your children as a mother hen gathers her chicks under her wings — but you were unwilling.[131] 38Now look — your house is left abandoned, deserted. 39I tell you, you will not see me again until you say, ‘Blessed is the one who comes in the name of the Lord.’”[132]

---

[129]That is, genuine Christian scholars who teach the truth.

[130]This murder is described in 2 Chronicles. Jesus’ remark refers to the fact that from Genesis to 2 Chronicles, the faithful had been mistreated. 2 Chronicles is the last book in the Hebrew Bible which has the same books exactly as our Old Testament but in a different order (see Lk. 24:44).

[131]Jesus was no Calvinist in his view of predetermination! Jesus shows here that human beings can resist the will of God and that they are responsible for making the right choice. Cp. Luke 7:30: “the Pharisees resisted the will of God for themselves” and Acts 13:46, where potential converts judged themselves “unworthy of the life of the age to come.”

[132]A remnant of Jews, the descendants of the ones Jesus addressed, will finally accept Jesus as the Messiah when he returns to establish the Kingdom of God on earth at his Second Coming (see Rom. 9-11). It is then that Jesus will sit on David’s throne (Lk. 1:32; Rev. 3:21).

24 1As Jesus was leaving the Temple his disciples came to him,
pointing out the Temple buildings. 2He said to them, "Do you not
see all these buildings? I am telling you the truth: there will not be one
stone left on another. All will be torn down."

3As Jesus sat on the Mount of Olives, the disciples came to him in
private and asked, "Please explain to us when this will happen, and what
will be the sign of your coming[133] and end of the age?"[134]

4"Be careful no one misleads you," Jesus replied. 5"Many will come
claiming to speak on my authority,[135] saying, 'I am the Messiah,' and will
deceive many people. 6You will be hearing about wars and rumors of
wars, but do not be afraid. These things have to happen, but that is not
yet the end.[136] 7Nations will rise up to fight against other nations, and
kingdoms will fight against kingdoms; there will be famines and
earthquakes in various places, 8but all these things are just the first of the
coming birth pains.[137]

9"Then they will arrest you, persecute you, and kill you. You will be
hated by all nations because of my name. 10At that time many believers
will fall away, betray one another, and hate one another. 11Many false
prophets will come and deceive many people. 12The increasing evil will
make the love of many grow cold, 13but whoever holds out to the end will
be saved.

14"This Gospel of the Kingdom[138] will be preached around the whole
world as a testimony to all the nations, and then the end will come. 15So
when you see standing in the holy place the 'Abomination of Desolation'

---

[133]The Greek *Parousia* means the one splendid and visible arrival of the Messiah, certainly not an invisible coming which has already happened, or will happen prior to the Parousia. The notion that the Kingdom of God came in 1878 or 1914 or 1918 is entirely false to Scripture.

[134]The Second Coming and the end of the age are synonymous and they lie in the future. AD 70 was absolutely not the second coming of Jesus, nor was 1914! The end of the age appears in 13:39, 40, 49; 24:3; 28:20 and refers always to the return of Jesus in the future. The end of the age was definitely not AD 70.

[135]Or represent me, if not actually claiming to be the Messiah.

[136]That is, "the end of the age," the subject of the question to be answered in v. 3.

[137]Birth pains precede the final rebirth of the world which will happen when Jesus comes back to set up his Kingdom (see Mt. 19:28). At present the world has become degenerate.

[138]The one and only saving Christian Gospel preached by Jesus first and then by all the Apostles. This one Gospel is to be preached until the end of the age, the return of Jesus.

predicted by the prophet Daniel[139] (whoever reads this should think about
it carefully), 16then those living in Judea should run away to the
mountains. 17Whoever is on the housetop should not go down and get
what is in the house. 18Whoever is out in the fields should not go back to
get their coat. 19How hard for those who are pregnant, and those who are
nursing babies at that time! 20Pray that you do not have to run away in
winter, or on the Sabbath day.[140] 21For then there will be a great
tribulation[141] such as never was before, from the beginning of the world
up till now, and will never be again. 22Unless those days are cut short,
nobody would be saved, but for the sake of the chosen[142] those days will
be cut short. 23If anyone says to you at that time, 'Look, the Messiah is
here — or there,' do not believe it. 24For false messiahs and false
prophets will come along, and they will perform amazing signs and
miracles in order to deceive even the chosen, if possible. 25"Look, I have
told you this before it happens. 26So if they tell you, 'Look, he is in the
desert,' do not go looking; or 'Look, he is here inside,' do not believe it.
27For the coming of the Son of Man will be like lightning flashing
brightly from east to west. 28'Vultures gather where the carcass is.'

29"Immediately[143] after the tribulation of those days, the sun will be
darkened and the moon will not shine, and the stars will fall from

---

[139]Jesus is citing the verses from Daniel 9:27, 11:31 and 12:11, where the Abomination is predicted to appear at the very close of this age, 1290 days before the resurrection in Dan. 12:2.

[140]Because the sabbath day would continue to be observed by non-Christian Jews. Mark and Luke do not mention this. Paul was against any obligation for New Covenant Christians to observe the Jewish calendar, which he described as a shadow replaced by the substance, the reality which is Christ (Col. 2:16-17).

[141]"The great tribulation" which is a still future time of terrible suffering and distress. It certainly is not a reference to AD 70 because Jesus did not return "immediately after" (v. 29) that time of tribulation in AD 70. Tribulation in general is to be expected by all believers (Acts 14:22), but "the Great Tribulation" is a final short, agonizing time (cp. Zech. 13:8; 14:2), based on Dan. 12:1 and thus just before the resurrection of the faithful in Dan. 12:2. This is what the NT calls the first resurrection (Rev. 20:5-6) and is described too in 1 Cor. 15:23.

[142]The elect or chosen are the true believers of all nations.

[143]The word "immediately" here is *crucially important* for an understanding of the Olivet Discourse, since it proves that Jesus' prophecy was not fulfilled in AD 70. The Second Coming evidently did not occur immediately after the destruction of Jerusalem in AD 70! The Great Tribulation is a brief time of intense distress (3 ½ years from the

heaven, and the powers of the heavens will be shaken. 30Then the sign of the Son of Man will appear in heaven, and all the peoples of the earth will mourn. They will see the Son of Man coming on the clouds of heaven with power and brilliant majesty.[144] 31With a trumpet blast he will send out his angels, and they will gather together his chosen from every direction, from one end of heaven and earth to the other.

32"Learn a parable from the fig tree. When its branches become tender and leaves sprout, you know that summer is near. 33In the same way when you see all these things happening, know that his coming is near, right at the door. 34I am telling you the truth: this present evil society[145] will not pass away until all these things happen. 35Heaven and earth will pass away, but my words will not pass away.

36"Yet no one knows the day or hour when this will be, not even the angels in heaven, nor the Son.[146] Only the Father knows. 37The coming of the Son of Man will be just as in the time of Noah. 38Just as in those days before the flood, they were eating and drinking, marrying and giving in marriage, right up until the day that Noah went into the Ark, 39and they did not realize until the flood came and swept them all away — so the coming of the Son of Man will be. 40Two men will be in the fields. One will be taken; the other left. 41Two women will be grinding grain at the mill. One will be taken; the other left.

42"So stay alert, because you do not know which day your lord is coming. 43But think about this: if a homeowner knew what time a thief was coming, he would keep watch, and would not allow his house to be

---

midpoint of the final "week" of Dan. 9:24-27), as Jesus said, and it makes nonsense of Jesus' description of the Great Tribulation to claim that it refers to a period which began in AD 70 and has now lasted for nearly two millennia! For the Great Tribulation see Dan. 12:1-3, the key to Bible prophecy.

[144]The totally false idea that the Second Coming of Jesus was in 1914 has been rejected by all intelligent Bible study.

[145]The word *genea* here refers to society in all its forms characteristic of the period right up to the future Second Coming. It certainly does not mean a period of 40 years. If it did Jesus would have been a false prophet! Much less could it refer to a period centuries later than Jesus. In that case "*this* genea" would be quite inappropriate. Acts 1:7 proves that Jesus had never set a chronological date, and so *genea* in this passage refers to evil society as constituted by the world systems which will continue to exist in that form until the Kingdom of God at the future Second Coming replaces them all with sound government under the Messiah and the saints.

[146]Proving beyond all argument that the Son of God cannot be GOD.

broken into. 44You too need to be ready, because the Son of Man is
coming when you do not expect him.

45"Who then is the faithful and thoughtful servant — the one his lord
puts in charge of his household, to provide them with food at the right
time? 46Blessed is that servant to be found doing just that when his lord
returns. 47I am telling you the truth: he will put that servant in charge
over everything he has. 48But if he was evil, that servant would say to
himself, 'My lord is taking a long time,' 49and would start to beat his
fellow servants, to feast and drink with the drunks. 50Then the lord of that
servant will return when he is not expecting, and at a time he does not
know. 51He will cut him to pieces and assign him a place with the
hypocrites, where there will be weeping and grinding of teeth."

25 1"Then the Kingdom of Heaven will be like ten bridesmaids, who
took their lamps[147] to go out and meet the bridegroom. 2Five were
foolish and five were wise. 3The foolish girls took their lamps, but did
not take any oil, 4while the wise took containers of oil with them as well
as their lamps. 5The bridegroom took a long time coming, and all the
bridesmaids became drowsy and fell asleep. 6At midnight came the
shout, 'Look, here is the bridegroom! Go out to meet him!'[148] 7All the
bridesmaids got up and trimmed the wicks of their lamps. The foolish
girls said to the wise ones, 8'Give us some of your oil, because our lamps
are going out.' But the wise girls replied, 9'No, because otherwise there
will not be enough for both you and us. Go to the shops and buy some
for yourselves.' 10While they were going to buy oil, the bridegroom
came, and those who were ready went in with him to the wedding feast,
and the door was closed. 11The other bridesmaids came later and said,
'lord, lord, open the door for us.' 12But he answered, 'I tell you the truth:
I do not know you.' 13So stay alert, because you do not know the day or
the hour.

---

[147]Lamp connotes the light of the truth of the Gospel. The oil needed to fuel the light is like the holy spirit.

[148]This is exactly the picture of the Second Coming at which all the saints, those resurrected and those alive at the second coming, will go up to meet the lord Jesus as he comes back to the earth. The royal visitor is to be welcomed and escorted to the earth, the direction in which he is going to take up his position on the royal throne of David in Jerusalem (Lk. 1:32).

14“It is like a man about to leave on a trip who called in his servants
and entrusted them with what he owned. 15To one of them he gave five
talents, to another he gave two, and to another one talent, according to
their abilities.[149] Then he left. 16Immediately the one with five talents put
them to work in business trading and made another five talents. 17In the
same way the one with two talents made another two. 18But the man who
had received the one talent went and dug a hole in the ground and hid his
master’s money.

19“After a long time the master of those servants returned, and settled
accounts with them. 20The one with five talents came and presented the
other five talents. He said, ‘Master, you gave me five talents. Look, I
have made a profit of five talents.’ 21His master said to him, ‘You have
done well, good and faithful servant. You have proven faithful in a few
things, so now I am placing you in charge of many things. Enter into the
joy of your master!’

22“The one with two talents also came. He said, ‘Master, you gave me
two talents. Look, I have made a profit of two talents.’ 23His master said
to him, ‘You have done well, good and faithful servant. You have proven
faithful in a few things, so now I am placing you in charge of many
things. Enter into the joy of your master!’

24“The man with one talent also came. He said, ‘Master, I know that
you are a hard man. You reap where you did not sow, and you harvest
crops you did not plant. 25Because I was afraid I went and buried your
talent in the ground. Look, you can have back what belongs to you.’

26“But his master answered him, ‘You wicked and lazy servant! You
think I reap where I do not sow, and harvest crops I did not plant. 27Then
you should have put my money in the bank so that when I returned I
could have had my money plus interest. 28So take the talent away from
him and give it to the one with ten talents.

29“For everyone who has will be given more, and he will have more
than enough; but everyone who does not have anything, even what they
have will be taken away from them. 30And throw this useless servant out
into the darkness, where there will be weeping and grinding of teeth.’

---

[149]The same centrally important truth is taught in the Lukan parable about the nobleman who went to obtain his Kingdom and then returned and rejected those believers who had failed to develop their talents in the cause of the Great Commission (Lk. 19:11ff).

31“When the Son of Man comes in his glory, and all the angels with
him, then he will sit on his throne of glory.[150] 32All the nations will be
brought before him, and he will separate individuals[151] from one another,
just as a shepherd separates the sheep from the goats. 33He will put the
sheep on his right hand and the goats on his left.

34“Then the king will say to those on his right, ‘Come, you who are
blessed by my Father, and inherit the Kingdom which has been prepared
for you from the foundation of the world. 35For I was hungry, and you
gave me food to eat; I was thirsty, and you gave me a drink; I was a
stranger and you invited me in; 36I was naked and you clothed me; I was
sick and you looked after me; I was in prison and you visited me.’ 37Then
those who did right will answer, ‘lord, when did we see you hungry and
feed you, or thirsty and give you a drink? 38When did we see you as a
stranger and invite you in, or naked and clothe you? 39When did we see
you sick, or in prison, and visit you?’ 40The king will say to them, ‘I am
telling you the truth: whatever you did for one of these least important
brothers and sisters of mine,[152] you did for me.’

41“He will also say to those on his left, ‘Go away from me, you who
are doomed, into the fire of the Age to Come prepared for the Devil and
his angels! 42For I was hungry and you did not give me anything to eat; I
was thirsty and you did not give me a drink; 43I was a stranger and you
did not invite me in; I was naked and you did not clothe me; sick and in
prison and you did not visit me.’ 44Then they too will answer, ‘lord, when

---

[150]“Glory” being the NT synonym for the future Kingdom of God on earth (Mt. 20:21; Mk. 10:37) at the return of Jesus to inaugurate the Messianic government on a renewed earth (Mt. 19:28).

[151]This is not a separation of nations, but individuals selected from the various nations. The judgment is based on their favorable or unfavorable treatment of other Christian believers, the brothers and sisters of Jesus (12:48-50). The individuals selected are permitted to obtain entrance into the life of the age to come, the future Kingdom (v. 46). Those who fail the test are consigned to the punishment of the age to come, the lake of fire, which is annihilation, not conscious torture. This appears to be the third of three parables with a similar point (v. 1, 14, 31).

[152]These of course are the spiritual brothers and sisters of Jesus (12:48-50), not natural Israelites (Jews, as referred to today). The true Israel of God is the international body of true believers (Gal. 6:16; Phil. 3:3; cp. 1 Cor. 10:18: “Israel of the flesh”). Romans 9-11 of course holds out the hope of a *future*, collective conversion of now blinded Israel, at which point they become part of the true Israel of God. Paul refers to presently unconverted Jews as “Israelites” (Rom. 9:4; 11:1; 2 Cor. 11:22).

did we see you hungry, or thirsty, or a stranger, or naked, or sick, or in
prison, and did not look after you?' 45Then he will say to them, 'I am
telling you the truth: whatever you did not do for these least important
brothers and sisters of mine, you did not do for me.' 46They will go away
into the punishment of the Age to Come, but those who are right will
enter the Life of the Age to Come."

26 1When Jesus had finished all these words,[153] he said to his
disciples, 2"You know that the Passover will be in two days' time,
and the Son of Man is to be handed over to be crucified."

3Then the chief priests and the elders of the people assembled in the
courtyard of the high priest, Caiaphas. 4They plotted to seize Jesus on
some pretext and kill him. 5But they were saying, "Let us not do this
during the festival, or the people might riot."

6While Jesus was in Bethany, at Simon the leper's house, 7a woman
came over to him with an alabaster jar of very expensive perfume. She
poured it on Jesus' head while he was sitting eating. But when the
disciples saw what she did, they were indignant. 8"What is all this waste
for?" they questioned. 9"This perfume could have been sold at a high
price and the money given to the poor." 10Aware of what they were
thinking, Jesus said to them, "Why are you upset at this woman? She has
done something good for me. 11You will always have the poor with you,
but you will not always have me. 12In pouring this perfume on my body
she has prepared me for burial. 13I am telling you the truth: wherever this
Gospel[154] is preached in the whole world, what this woman has done will
also be reported, in memory of her."

14Then Judas Iscariot, one of the twelve, went to the chief priests
15and asked them, "What will you give me for handing Jesus over to

---

[153]This is the fifth occurrence of the expression "when Jesus had finished these words." Matthew helps us to think of Jesus as the second Moses, whose words were recorded in the five books of the Law (cp. Deut. 31:1). Jesus' saving Gospel (Heb. 2:3), "the word about the Kingdom" (Mt. 13:19) consists of his many words.

[154]"This Gospel" is understood by the original Christian community as "this Gospel about the Kingdom" (Mt. 24:14). No one had the slightest confusion about the meaning, but today churchgoers do not use the phrase "Gospel of the Kingdom" and would be hard-pressed to define it properly.

you?" They paid him thirty silver coins. 16From then on he looked for an
opportunity to betray Jesus.
17On the first day of the festival of unleavened bread,[155] the disciples
came to Jesus and asked him, "Where do you want us to prepare the
Passover meal for you?"[156] 18Jesus said, "Go into the city and find this
particular man, and say to him, 'The teacher says, "My time is near. I am
coming to keep the Passover at your house with my disciples."'" 19The
disciples did as Jesus had told them, and they prepared the Passover
meal.
20When evening came he sat down to eat with the twelve disciples.
21While they were eating he said to them, "I am telling you the truth: one
of you is going to betray me." 22Terribly upset, each one of them began
asking him, "lord, it is not me, is it?" 23Jesus replied, "The one who
dipped his hand into the dish with me is the one who will betray me.
24The Son of Man will go just as it is written about him, but shame on the
man by whom the Son of Man is betrayed! It would be better for that
man if he had never been born." 25Judas, the one who betrayed Jesus,
asked, "It is not me, is it, rabbi?" Jesus replied, "You said it."
26While they were eating, Jesus took some bread and blessed it. Then
he broke it and gave it to the disciples. "Take and eat this. It is my
body," Jesus said. 27Then he took a cup, gave thanks, and gave it to them.
"Drink from it, all of you," he said to them. 28"This is my blood which
ratifies the covenant,[157] poured out for many for the forgiveness of sins.[158]
29But I tell you, I will not drink this fruit of the vine[159] from now on until

---

[155]"The synoptic Gospels present the last supper as a Passover meal that took place at the normal time, i.e. on 15 Nisan, which began at sundown on Thursday" (*Word Biblical Commentary* on Matthew 14-28, p. 763). The lamb was slain on the afternoon towards the end of the 14th Nisan (Thursday afternoon). The point is perfectly clear and is stated in many commentaries. John can be harmonized with this dating. There is no disagreement.

[156]This was obviously on the same day and at the same time as the nation. The Passover was celebrated at the beginning (evening) of the 15th Nisan, the lamb being slain on the afternoon of the 14th just before.

[157]That is, the blood necessary for ratifying, bringing into force, the New Covenant, based on all Jesus' words. In Lk. 22:29 Jesus "covenanted" the Kingdom to his followers. The parallel with the Old Covenant made in the time of Moses is obvious (Ex. 24:8; Zech. 9:11; cp. Heb. 9:20).

[158]The suffering servant and his death is the basis for this teaching, Isa. 53:12.

[159]This is wine, of course, as the symbol of celebration and joy, appropriate for a feast.

that day when I drink it new with you in the Kingdom[160] of my Father."
30After they had sung a song, they went to the Mount of Olives.
31"All of you will fall away because of me tonight," Jesus said to
them. "It is written, 'I will strike the shepherd, and the flock of sheep
will be scattered.' 32But after I have been raised, I will go ahead of you to
Galilee." 33But Peter objected, "Even if everyone else falls away because
of you, I will never fall away." 34Jesus said to him, "I am telling you the
truth: this very night, before a rooster crows, you will deny me three
times." 35Peter insisted, "Even if I have to die with you, I will never deny
you." All the disciples said the same thing.
36Then Jesus went with his disciples to a place called Gethsemane
and said to them, "Sit down here while I go over there and pray." 37He
took Peter and the two sons of Zebedee with him, and he began to suffer
sorrow and distress. 38Then he said to them, "I am deeply grieved to the
point of death. Wait here and stay awake with me."
39He went a little further, fell face down, and prayed, "My Father, if
possible, let this cup of suffering pass from me, yet not as I will but as
You will." 40He returned to the disciples and found them asleep. He said
to Peter, "You could not stay awake with me for one hour? 41Stay awake
and pray, so that you do not fall into temptation. The spirit is willing, but
the flesh is weak."
42He went away a second time and prayed, "My Father, if this cannot
pass away unless I drink it, then may Your will be done." 43He went back
and found them sleeping; they could not stay awake. 44Then he left them
once more, went off and prayed a third time, saying the same things.
45Then he returned to the disciples and said to them, "Are you still
sleeping and resting? Look, the time has come, and the Son of Man is
being betrayed into the hands of sinners. 46Get up; let us go! Look, the
one who is betraying me is here."
47While he was still speaking, Judas, one of the twelve, arrived with a
large crowd armed with swords and clubs. They had been sent by the
chief priests and elders of the people. 48The betrayer had given them a
signal: "The one I kiss, that is him — arrest him." 49Immediately Judas
came up to Jesus and said, "Hello, rabbi," and kissed him. 50"My friend,

---

[160]Belief in that coming Kingdom of Messiah on a renewed earth is the basis of the saving Gospel (Mk. 1:14-15).

do what you came to do," Jesus said to Judas. So they came and seized
Jesus and arrested him.

51One of those with Jesus reached for his sword and pulled it out, and
struck the high priest's servant, cutting off his ear. 52Then Jesus said to
him, "Put your sword away. Everyone who picks up the sword will
perish by the sword.[161] 53Do you think I cannot ask my Father, and He
would send me at once more than twelve legions of angels? 54Then how
will the Scriptures be fulfilled which say that it must happen like this?"

55Then Jesus said to the crowds, "Have you come with swords and
clubs to arrest me as if I was a criminal?[162] Every day I used to sit in the
temple teaching and you did not arrest me. 56But all this has happened to
fulfill the Scriptures of the prophets." Then all the disciples deserted him
and ran away.

57Those who had arrested Jesus took him to Caiaphas, the high priest,
where the religious teachers and elders were gathered. 58Peter followed
him at a distance as far as the courtyard of the high priest. He sat there
with the guards to see the outcome.

59The chief priests and the whole council were trying to find some
false evidence against Jesus, so that they could kill him. 60But they could
not find anything, even though many false witnesses came forward.
Eventually two came forward 61and reported, "This man said, 'I can
destroy God's temple and rebuild it in three days.'" 62The high priest
stood up and asked Jesus, "Are you not going to say anything in reply?
What is it that these men are testifying against you?" 63But Jesus
remained silent. The high priest said to him, "I place you under oath by
the living God. Tell us whether you are the Messiah, the Son of God."
64Jesus replied, "You have said so.[163] And I tell you that in the future you
will see the Son of Man sitting at the right hand of the One with power,[164]
and coming on the clouds of heaven."[165]

---

[161]One of the very striking non-violence, love your enemies statements of Jesus. This radical teaching indicts the use of violence even against enemies. Christian participation in violence is condemned by this saying of Jesus.

[162]That is, an insurrectionist.

[163]Implying, "you have spoken the truth."

[164]A reference to the key Psalm 110:1 where the second lord is *adoni*, my lord, never a title of Deity. Jesus rightly defines the one at the right hand of God as "son of man," human being, not God. Jesus never claimed to be GOD, i.e. Yahweh, which would have meant that there were two who are God, thus two Gods! The later councils attempted to

65Then the high priest tore his clothes and said, "He has blasphemed!
Why do we need any further witness? Look, you have now heard the
blasphemy! 66What is your decision?" They answered, "He deserves to
die!"

67Then they spat in his face and beat him with their fists. Some of
them slapped him 68and said, "Prophesy to us, you 'Messiah' — who just
hit you?"

69Meanwhile Peter was sitting outside in the courtyard, and a servant
girl came up to him and said, "You were with Jesus the Galilean too."
70But he denied it in front of everyone. "I do not know what you are
talking about," he said. 71He went out into the entrance way where
someone else saw him and said to the people there, "This man was with
Jesus of Nazareth." 72Once again he denied it with an oath, "I do not
know this man." 73A little while later the people standing there came up
to Peter and said, "You really are one of them. Your accent gives you
away." 74Then he started to curse and swear, "I do not know the man!"
And immediately a rooster crowed. 75Then Peter remembered what Jesus
had said to him: "Before a rooster crows, you will deny me three times."
He went out and wept bitterly.

27 1When morning came all the chief priests and the elders of the
people consulted together and decided to have Jesus condemned to
death. 2They tied him up, led him away, and handed him over to Pilate,
the governor.

3When Judas, the one who had betrayed Jesus, saw that Jesus had
been condemned to death, he regretted what he had done and returned
the thirty silver coins to the chief priests and the elders. 4"I have sinned
by betraying innocent blood!" he said to them. "Why does that matter to
us?" they replied. "That is your problem!" 5Judas threw the silver coins

---

follow this rather obvious departure into polytheism by creating a philosophical, non-biblical concept of abstract "oneness." For Jews and Jesus God was one Person, the Father (Mal. 2:10). "God" means the Father 1300 times in the NT and thousands of occurrences of the various words for "God" in the Bible never mean a triune God.

[165]Having received the right to the Kingdom, and coming at his Parousia to rule the world from Jerusalem. Luke 19:11ff describes the same outline of future history. Jesus sits currently at the right hand of God in heaven awaiting the moment when he will subdue his enemies (Ps. 2) at his coming in glory (Heb. 10:13).

into the temple sanctuary and left. He went off and hanged himself. 6The
chief priests took the silver coins and said, “It would not be lawful to put
this in the temple treasury, as it is blood money.” 7So they met together
and decided to buy the potter’s field as a place to bury foreigners. 8That
is why that field is still called today “the Field of Blood.” 9This fulfilled
the prophecy spoken through the prophet Jeremiah: “They took thirty
silver coins, the price of the one whose price had been set by the children
of Israel, 10and they used them to pay for the potter’s field, just as the
Lord ordered me to do.”

11Jesus was brought before the governor, and he asked him, “Are you
the King of the Jews?” Jesus replied, “It is as you say.” 12The chief
priests and elders brought charges against him, but Jesus did not answer
them. 13“Do you not hear how many charges they are bringing against
you?” Pilate asked him. 14But Jesus did not say anything, not a single
word, which greatly surprised the governor.

15During the festival it was the custom of the governor to release to
the crowd whichever prisoner they wanted. 16At that time a notorious
prisoner called Barabbas was being held. 17So when he went to see the
crowd, Pilate asked them, “Whom do you want me to release to you?
Barabbas, or Jesus, called the Messiah?” 18He knew it was because of
envy that they had handed Jesus over to him.

19While he was sitting on the judgment seat, his wife sent a message
to him: “Have nothing to do with this good man, because last night I
suffered terribly because of a dream about him.” 20But the chief priests
and the elders convinced the crowds to ask for Barabbas, and to put Jesus
to death. 21When the governor asked them, “So which of the two do you
want me to release to you?” they said, “Barabbas.” 22Pilate asked them,
“Then what should I do with Jesus, called the Messiah?” They all
shouted out, “Crucify him!” 23Pilate asked, “Why? What wrong has he
done?” But they shouted out even louder, “Crucify him!”

24When Pilate saw it was a lost cause, and that a riot was developing,
he took some water and washed his hands in front of the crowd. “I am
innocent of this man’s blood. It is up to you!” he said. 25All the people
answered, “May his blood be on us and on our children!” 26Then he
released Barabbas to them, but he had Jesus flogged and sent to be
crucified.

27The governor's soldiers took Jesus into the Praetorium and the whole Roman cohort surrounded him. 28They stripped him and put a scarlet robe on him. 29They made a crown of thorns and put it on his head, and put a stick in his right hand, and they knelt down in front of him and mocked him, saying, "We salute you, King of the Jews!" 30They spat on him, and took the stick and hit him on the head with it. 31When they had finished mocking him, they took off the robe and put his own clothes back on him, and led him away to crucify him.

32On the way they found a man called Simon, from Cyrene, and they made him carry Jesus' cross. 33They arrived at a place called Golgotha, meaning "Place of a Skull," 34and they gave him wine mixed with a bitter herb. But after tasting it, he refused to drink it.

35When they had crucified him, they cast lots to divide up his clothes among themselves. 36They sat down and kept watch over him there. 37They placed a sign with the charge against him over his head which read, "This is Jesus, the King of the Jews."

38They crucified two criminals[166] with him, one on the right and one on the left. 39Those who passed by shouted insults at him, shaking their heads 40and saying, "You who promised to destroy the temple and rebuild it in three days, save yourself! If you really are the Son of God, then come down from the cross." 41The chief priests mocked him in the same way, along with the religious teachers and elders. 42"He saved other people, but he cannot save himself!" they said. "If he is the King of Israel, let him come down from the cross, and then we will believe in him! 43He trusts God, so let God rescue him now if He takes pleasure in him, because he claimed 'I am the Son of God.'" 44The criminals crucified with him also insulted him in the same way.

45From noon until three p.m. darkness covered the whole country. 46At about three p.m. Jesus cried out with a loud voice, "Eli, Eli, lama sabachthani?"[167] which means, "My God, my God, why have You abandoned me?" 47When some of those standing there heard this, they said, "This man is calling for Elijah." 48Immediately one of them ran and took a sponge, soaked it in vinegar, put it on a stick, and gave it to Jesus to drink. 49But the others said, "Let us see if Elijah will come to save

[166]Perhaps insurrectionists, freedom fighters.

[167]Aramaic, the native language of Jesus.

him.” 50And Jesus cried out again with a loud voice and breathed his
last.[168] 51Right then the veil of the temple was torn in two from top to
bottom. The ground shook, the rocks split apart, 52and the graves were
opened. Many of the saints who had fallen asleep[169] were raised. 53After
the resurrection of Jesus they left the graveyard and went into the holy
city, where many people saw them. 54When the centurion and those with
him guarding Jesus saw the earthquake and the things that were
happening, they were extremely afraid and said, “This surely was the
Son of God!”[170]

55There were also many women watching from a distance, the ones
who had followed Jesus from Galilee, supporting him. 56These included
Mary Magdalene, Mary the mother of James and Joseph, and the mother
of the sons of Zebedee.[171]

57When evening came, a rich man named Joseph, from Arimathea,
who had become a disciple of Jesus, 58went to Pilate and asked for the
body of Jesus. Pilate ordered it to be handed over to him. 59Joseph took
the body and wrapped it in a clean linen cloth, 60and placed it in his own
new tomb, which he had cut out of the rock. He rolled a large stone
across the entrance to the tomb and left. 61Mary Magdalene and the other
Mary were there, sitting opposite the tomb.

62The next day, the day after Preparation day,[172] the chief priests and
the Pharisees went together to see Pilate, 63and said, “Sir, we recall that
this deceiver said while he was still alive, ‘After three days, I will rise
again.’ 64Give the order to secure the tomb until the third day, so that his
disciples do not come and steal his body and tell people that he has been
raised from the dead, and the last deception would be worse than the
first.” 65Pilate said to them, “I will give you a guard of soldiers. Now go
and make it as secure as you know how.” 66So they went and secured the
tomb, sealing the entrance stone, with the soldiers posted as guards.

---

[168]The death of the person Jesus, the Son of God, should put an end to the impossible idea that he *was* God. The biblical God cannot die, by definition. He alone has immortality inherently (1 Tim. 6:16).

[169]And were then sleeping the sleep of death (Ps. 13:3). “The dead know nothing at all” (Ecc. 9:5, 10).

[170]The Greek could also mean “a son of God.”

[171]James and John.

[172]“Preparation day” is the standard term at that time for Friday. So the day after Preparation day is clearly Saturday, the weekly Sabbath.

28 1After the Sabbath,[173] as dawn broke on Sunday morning, Mary
Magdalene and the other Mary came to look at the tomb. 2There
was a tremendous earthquake, and an angel of the Lord came down from
heaven and rolled away the stone and sat on it. 3His face blazed like
lightning, and his clothes were as white as snow. 4The guards shook with
fear, stunned as if they were dead. 5The angel said to the women, "Do not
be afraid! I know you are looking for Jesus who was crucified. 6He is not
here, because he has been raised,[174] just as he said. Come and see where
he was lying. 7Now go quickly and tell his disciples that he has been
raised from the dead and he is going on ahead of you to Galilee. You will
see him there, I assure you."

8They left the tomb quickly, with fear and great joy, running to tell
his disciples. 9Suddenly Jesus met them and greeted them. They went
over to him, took hold of his feet and bowed before him. 10Then Jesus
said to them, "Do not be afraid! Go and tell my brothers to leave for
Galilee, and they will see me there."

11As they left, some of the guards came into the city and reported to
the chief priests everything that had happened. 12After the chief priests
had met with the elders and worked out a plan, they gave a lot of money
to the soldiers. 13"Tell people, 'His disciples came during the night and
stole him while we were sleeping,'" they said to them. 14"And if the
governor hears this, we will talk to him and you will not have to worry."
15So they took the money and did what they were told, and this story was
widely spread among the Jewish people right up to this day.

16The eleven disciples went to Galilee, to the mountain Jesus had told
them. 17When they saw him they bowed down, though some doubted.
18Jesus came up to them and said to them, "All authority in heaven and

---

[173]The word in Greek is singular in meaning, though plural in form. The singular meaning with plural form is found often in Scripture and is easily explained on the basis of an Aramaic form *sabbata*.

[174]The Greek word means "he has been woken up" (by God) reminding us of the common biblical idea that death is like an unconscious sleep, hence the term "sleep of the dead" in Ps. 13:3 (see Ecc. 9:5, 10; Dan. 12:2; Jn. 11:11, 14). The term "soul sleep" has no identifiable meaning in terms of Scripture, since "soul" in the Bible means "person." Persons sleep in death. Soul never means an immortal part of man which cannot die. The only way out of death for any human person is via resurrection of the whole person. Dan. 12:2 is one of many definitive and decisive verses on this point.

on earth has been given to me. 19So go and make disciples of people of
all nations, baptizing[175] them into the agenda and character[176] of the
Father and the Son and the holy spirit. 20Teach them to follow all the
commands I have given you.[177] Remember, I am always with you, to the
end of the age."[178]

---

[175]Water baptism is commanded throughout the NT (Jn. 4:1-2; Acts 2:38; 8:12; 10:47-48; 16:33; 19:5). It is the non-negotiable public declaration of one's intention to become a member of the Church.

[176]The equivalent in our English of "name." This is not a fixed verbal formula and is therefore not in any way a contradiction of the practice in Acts of baptizing "in the name of Jesus." Only when the phrase is woodenly forced into being a precise "formula of words" is a contradiction unnecessarily created. The linking of Father, Son and holy spirit in no way implies a triune God. 2 Cor. 13:14 links God, Jesus and holy spirit in the same way.

[177]The chief of all commands is "Listen, Israel, the Lord our God is one Lord" (Mk. 12:29), in total agreement with Deut. 6:4, the Shema, and with a Jewish scribe. Trinitarianism is a post-biblical alteration of Jesus' creed and redefines God.

[178]That is, until the return of Christ at his future one Second Coming, the Parousia, which will follow the cosmic signs which immediately follow (24:29) the future Great Tribulation (Dan. 12:1; Mt. 24:21). The Great Commission, the essence of Christianity, involves "the obedience of faith" (Rom. 1:5; 16:26; Heb. 5:9), that is, obedience to all the words of Jesus (Jn. 12:44-50; and the subsequent words revealed to Paul and other Apostles). Included in obedience to Jesus is of course his command that we "Listen…the Lord our God is one Lord" (Mk. 12:29), and that we respond intelligently and with repentance to his opening command that we "believe the Gospel of the Kingdom" (Mk. 1:14-15). When Jesus comes, the saints of all the ages will be caught up to meet Jesus in the air and from there escort him to the earth to which he is returning to rule on the throne of David in Jerusalem. There is no such event as a so-called *pre*-Tribulation coming of Jesus. There is only one single future Second Coming of the Messiah. By one single process, all true believers will be enabled to be "with the lord" (1 Thess. 4:17) — "thus," and by no other means. Until the Second Coming at the end of the age, the Church is to be urgently occupied with the Great Commission. The "end of the age" in Matthew occurs five times (13:39, 40, 49; 24:3 and here). It is positively never a reference to AD 70! It marks the same future event, the return of Jesus to rule on earth in his Kingdom, in each case.

Mark

1 1The beginning of the Gospel of Jesus Messiah,[1] the Son of God.[2] 2As
it is written in Isaiah the prophet: "Look, I am sending My messenger
before you who will prepare your way; 3a voice of one crying out in the
wilderness, 'Make ready the way of the Lord; make His paths straight.'"
4John the Baptist[3] appeared in the wilderness, preaching a baptism of
repentance for forgiveness of sins. 5Everybody from the country of Judea
and from Jerusalem was going out to him to be baptized in the Jordan
River, confessing their sins. 6John wore clothes made of camel hair, with
a leather belt around his waist. He ate locusts and wild honey. 7He was
preaching, "After me will come someone more powerful than I am,

---

[1]Firstly the Gospel of the Kingdom which Jesus preached for salvation (Heb. 2:3), as well as the Gospel *about* him. Many Bible readers do not think, as they should, of Jesus as the original preacher of the Gospel of salvation (Heb. 2:3; 5:9; Lk. 4:43; 8:12; Jn. 12:44ff; Acts 8:12; 28:23, 31, etc). Without Mark 1:1, 14-15 in place as a rock foundation for defining the Gospel, the bottom falls out of the NT. The Kingdom of God must also be defined from its Hebrew OT background (esp. Dan. 2 and 7). The Gospel must never be divorced from its descriptive phrase "about the Kingdom." Otherwise how can one repent and accept the Gospel? If the Gospel is unclear, repentance becomes unclear. Luke 19:11-27 is an excellent parable for defining the Kingdom, its place in the salvation program, and the absolute need for believers to develop their talents in support of the proclamation of the Kingdom Gospel.

[2]It is essential for intelligent Bible study to define and explain the title "Son of God" for Jesus, according to the explicit and simple definition given to Mary by the angel Gabriel in Luke 1:35 and confirmed in Matt. 1:1, 18, 20 ("begotten, fathered in her"). Jesus is the Son of God "precisely because of" (*dio kai*) the biological miracle worked in Mary by God (Lk. 1:35). Jesus is unique as having no human father, and he was thus directly the Son of God, the second Adam (Lk. 3:38) and the head of the new creation of human persons. Matt. 1:18 speaks of the origin, beginning of the Son of God and provides the right understanding of who Jesus is. The concept of a "God the Son," coequal with the Father, is a post-biblical development of "church fathers" and church councils and is not found in Scripture.

[3]The immerser in water. Water baptism is commanded throughout the NT and is a non-negotiable, essential part of the Great Commission (Mt. 28:19-20). To deny water baptism is to put oneself in a position of clear disobedience to the command of Jesus and the Apostles. Baptism was performed when candidates had a clear idea of the Gospel of the Kingdom and who Jesus is (Acts 8:12).

whose sandals I am not fit to bend down and undo. 8I baptized you with water, but he will be baptizing you in holy spirit."[4]

9Then Jesus arrived from Nazareth in Galilee and was baptized in the Jordan by John. 10Immediately coming up from the water, he saw the heavens split apart and the spirit like a dove which came down on him. 11A voice came from the heavens, "You are My beloved Son. I am delighted with you."

12Immediately the spirit sent him out into the desert 13where he was tempted[5] by Satan for forty days. He was there with the wild animals, with angels taking care of him.

14After John was put in prison, Jesus went to Galilee, preaching God's Gospel.[6] 15"The time is fulfilled," he said. "The Kingdom of God is near. Repent and believe in that Gospel."[7]

---

[4]Not only from Pentecost onwards! Everything which Jesus did as ministry imparted holy spirit. See especially his words which were "spirit and life" (Jn. 6:63), and of course still are! The holy spirit was given in a special public demonstration for the first time from *the risen Messiah* in Acts. But that does not mean that the holy spirit was not *very* active before that. Special people were filled with spirit (Lk. 1:41, 67), and John the baptizer had the spirit even in the womb of his mother Elizabeth. The spirit is the creative operational presence and power of God working in various ways. The spirit is identified also with the "comforter" and in 1 John 2:1 Jesus is that Comforter, returning to his people in spirit power and presence to assist them after he went to heaven at the Ascension.

[5]God cannot be tempted (James 1:13) and so the whole episode here would be a farce if Jesus were God!

[6]God's Gospel — the Gospel of salvation which originates in God. God's saving Gospel **about the Kingdom** preached and announced by all the NT writers and evangelists and of course by God's unique Son (Lk. 1:35), Jesus himself (Lk. 4:43; Heb. 2:3). God issues the ultimate statement and challenge to belief in the Kingdom, and His great immortality program is modeled in the man Jesus and taught by him as saving Gospel, in addition of course to his substitutionary death and his resurrection to immortality. The Gospel of the Kingdom is the Good News that man, by obeying Jesus in faith, can attain to immortality. Jesus was the pioneer preacher of this saving Gospel of the Kingdom now directed to the whole world (Mt. 24:14). "God's Gospel" is found 7 other times in the NT: Rom. 1:1; 15:16 (framing the book of Romans); 2 Cor. 11:7; 1 Thess. 2:2, 8, 9; 1 Pet. 4:17. This label for the Gospel beautifully unites the whole NT in one saving Kingdom of God Gospel, originating with Jesus. (E.W. Bullinger with his five differing gospel messages [App. to *Companion Bible*] did untold damage to good Bible study. The NT is torn in shreds by that system.) Paul (Rom. 1:1) and Jesus (Mk. 1:14-15) preached God's Gospel. The Gospel of the grace of God is identical to the

16As Jesus was walking by the Sea of Galilee, he saw Simon and his
brother Andrew. They were fishermen, and were busy in the sea casting
a net. 17"Come, follow me," he said to them, "and I will make you fishers
of people."[8] 18Immediately they left their nets and followed him.
19Walking further, Jesus saw James and his brother John, the sons of
Zebedee. They were in a boat repairing their nets. 20Immediately he
called them. They left their father Zebedee in the boat with the hired
hands, and followed Jesus.[9]

---

proclaiming of the Kingdom (Acts 20:24-25). Only Matthew uses the term "Kingdom of Heaven," which is the exact synonym of "Kingdom of God."

[7]Repentance means a complete reorientation in thinking and understanding, and in lifestyle. The first command of Jesus is thus *first* to believe the Gospel about the Kingdom of God (Acts 8:12), which is the empire of the Messiah, certainly not a figurative kingdom "in the heart." Some translations such as Ferrar Fenton's correctly render Dan. 2:44, "In the days of those kings the God of heaven will establish an everlasting **empire**, which is indestructible, whose sovereignty will not be transferred to another people." Thus also in Dan. 7:17-27, "Those four great beasts which you have seen are four **great empires** which will be established on the earth. The saints of the Most High will afterwards take the **Empire** and possess it for ever, and for ever and ever...The time came for the saints to possess **the empire**...**The empire** and dominion and grandeur of the **empire under the whole heavens** will be given to the Holy People of the Most High." Hence the reward of the faithful in the NT is nowhere described as "going to heaven," but "You shall have the governorship of ten towns" (Lk. 19:17; cp. Mt. 5:5: "inherit the earth"). Jesus echoed this same Gospel promise when he said to the Apostles, "You who followed me, when the world is reborn, when the Son of Man will sit on his throne of glory [Mt. 25:31], you will sit on 12 thrones governing the 12 tribes of Israel" (Mt. 19:28). Paul was surprised that his converts had forgotten the elementary truth that the saints "are going to govern the world" (1 Cor. 6:2). See Rev. 5:9-10; 3:21; 2:26; 20:1-6. If the word "empire" has the wrong connotations, we should understand that this is a benign empire, with Jesus as its emperor-king. We may know of "politics" as "dirty politics," but the Kingdom of God will be the first system, as a theocracy, which will be completely benevolent politics. The point is that Kingdom in the NT is a real world government, whose spirit can be tasted in advance of its real beginning in Rev. 11:15-18, where, at the last trumpet, God and His Messiah "*begin* to reign." Luke 19:11-27 is a key passage to define the "Kingdom" as the coming Messianic rule on a renewed earth, with its capital in Jerusalem. Without this fact established, the NT becomes an empty shell. (See my *The Coming Kingdom of the Messiah* and *Our Fathers Who Aren't in Heaven*.)

[8]NT Christian evangelism is an enterprise of persuasion, persuading others to believe Jesus, i.e. what he taught, and believe in him. The two involve each other. Acts 19:8 is a good text for showing Paul at work in evangelism. To be persuaded is to believe.

[9]Becoming his disciples or students and learning the true faith from the master-rabbi.

21They went to Capernaum, and on the Sabbath Jesus entered the
synagogue and taught there. 22The people were astonished at his
teaching, because he taught with authority, unlike the religious
teachers.[10] 23There in the synagogue was a man with an evil spirit.[11]
24"Jesus of Nazareth, what have we got to do with you?" he shouted out.
"Have you come to destroy us? I know who you are. You are the holy
one of God!"[12] 25Jesus reprimanded the evil spirit, "Be quiet, and come
out of him." 26The evil spirit screamed and came out of him, forcing the
man into convulsions. 27Everybody was amazed. They discussed among
themselves, "What is this new teaching with authority? He gives orders
even to evil spirits and they obey him!" 28Immediately news about him
spread all through Galilee.

29They left the synagogue and went to the home of Simon and
Andrew, along with James and John. 30Simon's mother-in-law was sick
in bed with a fever, so immediately they told Jesus about her. 31He went
to her and helped her up with his hand. The fever left her, and she served
them a meal.

32After sundown, people brought to Jesus all the sick and demon-
oppressed. 33All the people of the town gathered outside the door. 34He
healed many people who had various diseases, and drove out many
demons. He would not permit the demons[13] to speak, because they knew
who he was.

---

[10]The professional scholars and teachers of the people (scribes).

[11]A demon. Demons are supernatural non-human personalities, certainly not human beings nor mental sicknesses. They are the cause of mental and other damage. Jesus speaks to them and they speak to him (Lk. 4:41). It is a very dangerous assault on the integrity of the historical narrative to say they do not exist! The reality of supernatural evil, under the charge of Satan, is a fundamentally important dimension of truth as revealed in Scripture. Our struggle is, as Paul said in Eph. 6:12, not essentially against human beings but against "*kosmocrats*" = Satanic forces in the invisible world. Satan is governor of sublunar space (Eph. 2:2) and god of this age (2 Cor. 4:4). His deceptive influence will be totally removed during the millennium. Jesus, after his resurrection, announced his triumph and supremacy over the fallen angels of Gen. 6 (1 Pet. 3:19).

[12]The Messiah predicted to come from the family of David (Ps. 132:11), and the prophet announced by Moses in Deut. 18:15-18. Certainly not "God the Son," a concept completely alien to Jesus and the NT community of believers.

[13]Demons (*daimonia*) is a clear word and an important part of the historical narrative. It is a serious attack on the text of Scripture to try to explain them away. They knew that

35Early in the morning, while it was still dark, Jesus got up and went
by himself to a secluded place to pray. 36Simon and the other disciples
went in search of him, 37and when they found him they said, "Everybody
is looking for you." 38Jesus said to them, "We need to go to the
surrounding towns so that I can preach the Gospel[14] there also, because
that is why I came." 39So he went into their synagogues throughout
Galilee, preaching the Gospel[15] and casting out the demons.

40A leper approached him, asking for help. He kneeled down before
him and said, "If you are willing, you can heal me." 41Moved with
compassion, Jesus reached out to touch the man and said, "I am willing;
be healed." 42Immediately the leprosy left him and he was healed. 43Jesus
gave him clear orders and sent him away. 44"Do not tell anyone about
this," he said. "Just go to a priest and show yourself to him. Take the
offering which Moses required for cleansing, as a testimony to them."
45But the leper who had been healed went away and announced it to
many people, spreading the news around. As a result Jesus could not
travel openly into the cities, but had to stay out in the country where
people came to him from all around.

2 1Several days later Jesus returned to Capernaum, and word spread
that he was there. 2So many people crowded inside the house that
there was no room, even outside the door, as Jesus was preaching the
Gospel-Word[16] to them. 3Four men brought a man who was paralyzed,
4but they could not get close to Jesus because of the crowd. So they took
the roof apart and through the opening lowered the mat down with the
paralyzed man lying on it. 5Seeing their faith, Jesus said to the paralyzed

---

Jesus was the Messiah (Lk. 4:41) and James says that "the demons believe in the One God and tremble" (2:19).

[14]All Gospel preaching in the NT is "preaching the Gospel of the Kingdom." Jesus stated that this preaching of the Gospel of the Kingdom was the basis of his entire mission (Lk. 4:43). Lk. 4:43 is Jesus' mission statement. It remains then the task of his body which is the Church. Otherwise the Church does not sound like Jesus and is in danger of promoting another Jesus.

[15]Gospel about the Kingdom of God, the one saving Gospel preached throughout the NT. The right definition of the Gospel provided by Mark 1:14-15 must be retained throughout one's reading of the NT.

[16]The "word" is the NT shorthand for the Gospel of the Kingdom, the saving message always announced by Jesus (Lk. 8:12) and all his followers (Acts 8:4, 5, 12).

man, “Son, your sins are forgiven.” 6But some of the religious teachers sitting there were thinking to themselves, 7“Why is this man speaking like this? He is blaspheming! Who can forgive sins except God alone?”[17] 8Jesus immediately knew in his spirit what they were thinking, and asked them, “Why are you thinking like this? 9Which is easier: to say to the paralyzed man, ‘Your sins are forgiven,’ or to say, ‘Get up, pick up your mat, and walk’? 10But so that you may be convinced that the Son of Man[18] has the authority on earth to forgive sins,” he said to the paralyzed man, 11“Get up, pick up your mat, and go home.” 12He got up, immediately picked up his mat, and walked out in front of everyone. They were all astonished and praised God, saying, “We have never seen anything like this before!”

13Jesus returned to the sea shore, and was teaching the whole crowd that was coming to him. 14As he walked by, he saw Levi son of Alphaeus sitting at the tax booth. “Follow me,” Jesus said to him. Levi got up and followed him. 15That evening Jesus ate dinner at Levi’s house. Many tax collectors and “sinners”[19] joined Jesus and his disciples for the meal, because there were many of these “sinners” who were following Jesus. 16When the religious leaders of the Pharisees saw that Jesus was eating with such people, they asked Jesus’ disciples, “Why is he eating and drinking with tax collectors and sinners?” 17When Jesus heard this, he said to them, “Healthy people do not need a doctor, but people who are sick do. I did not come to call upright people, but sinners.”

18John’s disciples and the Pharisees were keeping a religious fast. They came to Jesus and asked him, “Why do John’s disciples and the Pharisees’ disciples fast, but your disciples do not?” 19Jesus said to them, “How can the groomsmen fast while the bridegroom is with them? As long as they have the bridegroom with them, they cannot fast. 20But the

---

[17]They suffered from the same spiritual deficiency as “orthodox” people today. They could not believe the amazing power and authority which the One God, the Father of Jesus, had conferred on the man Messiah.

[18]The Human Being, based on Daniel 7. This was Jesus’ favorite way of defining himself. Later theology from philosophically-minded “church fathers” turned him into God and thus complicated and ruined the simple unitary monotheism of Jesus in John 17:3 and Mark 12:29. Paul corrects all that complication and confusion in I Tim. 2:5.

[19]“Sinners” here refers to those who were not seen as strict in their keeping of the religious law, as the religious teachers and the Pharisees required.

days are coming when the bridegroom will be taken away from them,
and then they will fast.

21“No one sews a new patch on old clothes. Otherwise the new piece
will shrink away from the old, and make a worse tear. 22No one puts new
wine in old wineskins. Otherwise the wine bursts the skins, and both the
wine and skins are ruined. No, you put new wine in new wineskins.”

23Jesus was walking through the grain fields on the Sabbath,[20] and his
disciples started picking grain as they walked along. 24The Pharisees
asked Jesus, “Look, why are they doing what is not lawful on the
Sabbath?” 25Jesus replied, “Have you never read what David did when he
and his men were hungry — 26how he went into the house of God in the
time of Abiathar the high priest, and ate the consecrated bread which is
not lawful for anyone to eat except the priests, and gave it to his men to
eat as well? 27The Sabbath was made for people, not people for the
Sabbath. 28So the Son of Man is lord even of the Sabbath.”

3 1Jesus went to a synagogue again, and a man was there with a
crippled hand. 2Some were watching Jesus to see if he would heal the
man on the Sabbath, because they wanted to accuse him. 3Jesus said to
the man with the crippled hand, “Come here and stand in front of
everyone.” He asked them, 4“Is it lawful to do good or to do harm on the
Sabbath? To save a life or to kill?” But they kept silent. 5After looking
around at them with anger, saddened by their hard hearts, he said to the
man, “Stretch out your hand.” The man stretched out his hand, and it was
healed. 6The Pharisees left and immediately began to plot with the
Herodians as to how they might kill Jesus.

7Jesus returned to the sea with his disciples, and a large crowd
followed him. They were from Galilee, Judea, 8Jerusalem, Idumea,
beyond the Jordan, and Tyre and Sidon. This large crowd came to him
because they heard about everything he was doing. 9Jesus told his
disciples to have a small boat ready in case the crowd crushed him,
10because he had healed so many people that all the sick were pressing
towards him so they could touch him. 11Whenever the evil spirits saw

---

[20]“Sabbath” in the NT is Saturday, and Friday is the preparation day. In John 19:31 the Sabbath was special as the Saturday falling in Passover week.

him they would fall down in front of him and shout, “You are the Son of
God!” 12But he sternly warned them not to reveal who he was.
13Jesus went up a mountain and called those he wanted, and they
came to him. 14He chose twelve to be with him, and to send them out to
preach the Gospel, 15and to have authority to cast out demons. 16These are
the twelve he chose: Simon, whom he called Peter; 17James the son of
Zebedee and his brother John, whom he called Boanerges, meaning
“sons of thunder”; 18Andrew, Philip, Bartholomew, Matthew, Thomas,
James the son of Alphaeus, Thaddaeus, Simon the Zealot; 19and Judas
Iscariot, who betrayed him.
20Jesus went into a house, but such a large crowd gathered again that
he and his disciples could not even eat a meal. 21When his family heard
about it, they went to take charge of him, saying, “He has lost his mind.”
22But the religious leaders who had come from Jerusalem were saying,
“He is possessed by Beelzebul. By the authority of the ruler of the
demons, he is expelling demons.” 23But Jesus called them over to him,
and in parables he said to them, “How can Satan cast out Satan? 24A
kingdom divided against itself cannot stand. 25A household divided
against itself cannot stand. 26If Satan attacks himself and is divided, he
cannot stand; he will not last long! 27But if someone tries to break into
the house of a strong man and take his things, he will not get far in his
theft unless he first ties up the strong man.
28“I am telling you the truth: sins and blasphemies can be forgiven,
29but if someone blasphemes against the holy spirit they can never be
forgiven, because they are guilty of a sin against the Age to Come.”[21]
30Jesus said this because they were accusing him of having an evil spirit.[22]

---

[21]Not “an eternal sin,” but a sin against the obvious activity of God through His spirit. That kind of sin would result in being excluded from salvation in the coming age of the Kingdom of God on earth.

[22]A similar editorial comment by Mark occurs in 7:19 where Mark adds that “Jesus said this, thus making all foods clean.” (Paul said the same thing in Rom. 14:14, 20.) The Levitical food laws of Lev. 11 are not part of New Covenant obedience. No one is to interfere with this Christian freedom, in matters of eating and drinking and in regard to the Jewish calendar — annual feasts, new moons and weekly sabbath, which are a shadow of the Messiah who has come (Col. 2:16-17). “Circumcision” is no longer “made with hands.” And circumcision implies “the whole law,” in the letter (see Gal. 4 and 5 where Paul works hard to prevent believers from falling for what today might be called the “Jewish roots” movement, a denial of the freedom of the New Covenant).

31 Then Jesus' mother and brothers arrived and waited outside. They
sent a message to him, asking him to come out. 32 The crowd sitting
around him said to him, "Your mother and brothers are outside, asking
for you." 33 Jesus answered, "Who are my mother and my brothers?"
34 Looking around at everybody sitting there, he said, "These are my
mother and my brothers. 35 Whoever does the will of God[23] is my brother,
and sister, and mother."

4 1 Jesus began teaching again by the sea. So many people came to hear
him that he got into a boat and sat there offshore while the crowd
listened from land. 2 He was teaching them using many parables.[24]
3 "Listen!"[25] he said. "A sower went out to sow. 4 As he was sowing, some
seeds fell on the path. The wild birds came and ate them. 5 Other seeds
fell on rocky ground where there was not much soil. Immediately they
sprouted, but because the soil was not deep, 6 when the sun came up they
dried out because they did not have roots, and they withered. 7 Other
seeds fell among thorns. The thorns grew up fast and choked out the
sprouting seeds so that they produced nothing. 8 Other seeds fell on good
ground where they sprouted and grew, producing a harvest of thirty,
sixty, and a hundred times what was planted. 9 Whoever has ears, listen[26]
to what I am saying."

Paul preached against physical circumcision for all believers, Jewish and Gentile alike (Gal. 5:2-11).

[23]Doing God's will is not a vague "doing good" but a commitment to obedience to the Gospel of the Kingdom as Jesus preached it (see Heb. 5:9; Rom. 1:5; 16:26; Jn. 3:36 for the NT summaries of the faith which leads to salvation).

[24]Comparisons.

[25]Reminding us of the Shema: "Listen, Israel, the Lord our God is one Lord" (Mk. 12:29; Jn. 17:3). Hearing and understanding the parable of the sower is the key to penetrating the mind of Jesus and following him in obedience. The Gospel of the Kingdom is explained in the parable of the sower (cp. Mt. 13:19).

[26]The ultimate issue of immortality is involved in our attention to the parable of the sower and all of Jesus' teachings. The words of Jesus are, so to speak, "supersize" words, compared with which all other considerations are minor and peripheral. Only one issue really matters: whether we gain immortality in the coming Kingdom or whether we perish as unbelievers (cp. Jn. 3:36; 3:16). Paul, of course, and the other writers of Scripture authored inspired words, no less authoritative than the words of Jesus (2 Tim. 3:16; 2 Pet. 3:16).

10When he was alone, his twelve disciples and the others with him
asked him about the parables. 11"The revealed secret of the Kingdom of
God[27] has been given to you to understand," he said to them. "All those
on the outside get everything in parables, 12so that even though they see,
they do not perceive, and even though they hear, they do not understand;
otherwise they would repent and be forgiven."[28]

13He said to them, "Do you not understand this parable? If you do
not, how are you going to understand all the other parables?[29] 14The
sower sows the Gospel-word.[30] 15Those on the path where the Gospel-
word is sown hear it, but immediately Satan comes and takes away the
word which has been sown in them. 16Those on the rocky ground hear the
Gospel-word, and immediately they accept it with joy. 17But because
they have no roots, they survive for a while until trouble or persecution
comes because of the Gospel-word, and then they quickly fall away.[31]
18Others sown among the thorns hear the Gospel-word, 19but the concerns
of this age,[32] the temptation of wealth, and other desires choke the
growth of the word, and it becomes unproductive. 20But those sown on
good soil hear the Gospel-word, accept it, and bear fruit — producing
thirty, sixty, and a hundred times what was first sown."

21And he was saying to them, "No one puts a lamp under a bucket or
beneath a bed, do they? No, they put a lamp up on a lampstand. 22All that
is hidden will be revealed, and all that is secret will come to light.

---

[27]And how to acquire immortality in that Kingdom and a position of rulership with Jesus when he comes back. This is all part of the Gospel about the Kingdom (Dan. 7:14, 18, 22, 27; 1 Cor. 6:2; 2 Tim. 2:12; Mt. 19:28; Rev. 2:26; 3:21; 5:10; 20:1-6, etc.) Repentance is conditioned in the teaching of the NT on grasping and believing the Gospel of the Kingdom.

[28]Note the highly significant fact that no repentance and forgiveness is possible in the absence of a clear understanding of the Kingdom of God Gospel as preached by Jesus and the rest of the NT. Salvation is based on an intelligent grasp of the Kingdom Gospel as preached by Jesus. The Kingdom Gospel is a summary statement of his whole ministry and purpose (Mk. 1:14-15; Lk. 4:43; 8:11-12; Acts 8:12).

[29]This shows that believing the Gospel of the Kingdom as Jesus preached it is the foundation and core of biblical Christianity.

[30]About the Kingdom (Mt. 13:19), the saving Gospel.

[31]Showing that the doctrine of "once saved always saved" is false to the Bible.

[32]The present evil age (Gal. 1:4) which will last until the coming of Jesus, when it will be replaced by the millennium, which introduces the age of the worldwide Kingdom of God.

23Whoever has ears to hear, listen!" 24He said to them, "Pay attention to
what you listen to. What you use to measure will be used to measure to
you, and more. 25To whoever already has, more will be given, but
whoever does not have will have what little they have taken away from
them."

26"The Kingdom of God is like a man who sows seed on the soil,"
Jesus explained. 27"He goes to bed and gets up, day after day, and the
seeds sprout and grow, although he does not know how. 28The soil
produces a harvest automatically. First there is a shoot, then the heads of
grain, and then the heads of grain ripen. 29When the grain is ripe, he
immediately reaps it with a sickle, because the harvest[33] has come."

30"What shall we compare the Kingdom of God to? What parable
shall we use?" he asked. 31"It is like a mustard seed, the tiniest of seeds.
32But when planted it grows larger than other plants. It has big branches
so that birds can nest in its shade."[34]

33Jesus used many parables like this when he spoke the Gospel-word
to them, as much as they were able to understand. 34He always used
parables when he spoke publicly, but in private he explained everything
to his own disciples.

35In the evening of that same day, he said to his disciples, "Let us
cross over to the other side of the lake." 36Leaving the crowds behind, the
disciples got into the boat in which Jesus was sitting. Other boats went
with them too. 37A fierce gale began to blow, and the waves crashed over
the boat, filling it with water. 38Jesus was asleep in the stern, his head on
a pillow. The disciples woke him up and said, "Teacher, do you not care
that we are going to drown?" 39Jesus woke up and commanded the wind
to be calm and said to the sea, "Be peaceful and still." The wind stopped
and the water became completely calm. 40"Why are you afraid? Do you
still have no faith?" he asked them. 41They were terrified and asked each
other, "So who is this that even the wind and the sea obey him?"

---

[33]The harvest in the NT will occur at the future Second Coming of Jesus (Rev. 14:14-16; 19:11-16), the end of the age, to establish his Kingdom on earth (Mt. 13:39, 40, 49; 24:3).

[34]Jesus quotes here from a prophecy of the future Kingdom in Ezek. 17:22-24. Dan. 4:12 gives a similar prophecy of a kingdom in which people shelter and live.

5 1They arrived on the other side of the lake in the region of the
Gerasenes. 2When Jesus stepped out of the boat immediately a man
with an evil spirit came from the graveyard toward him. 3This man lived
in the tombs, and nobody had been able to tie him up, even with a chain.
4He had often been tied with shackles and chains, but he tore the chains
apart and broke the shackles into pieces. Nobody was strong enough to
control him. 5He used to scream all day and all night among the tombs
and in the hills, cutting himself with sharp stones. 6When he saw Jesus at
a distance, he ran over and bowed down before him. He shouted out,
"What do we have to do with each other, Jesus, Son of the Most High
God? I beg you by God, do not torture me!" 8He said this because Jesus
had been saying to him, "You evil spirit, come out of the man." 9Jesus
asked him, "What is your name?" He replied, "My name is Legion,
because we are many."[35] 10He pleaded with Jesus not to send them out of
the region. 11Nearby a large herd of pigs was feeding on the hillside.
12The evil spirits pleaded with him, "Send us into the pigs so we can
enter them." 13Jesus gave them permission, and the evil spirits came out
of the man and went into the pigs. The herd of 2,000 rushed down the
steep bank into the lake and drowned.

14The ones looking after the pigs ran away and reported what had
happened in the town and the surrounding countryside, so people came
to see for themselves. 15They came to Jesus and saw the man who had
had the "legion" sitting down, clothed and in his right mind, and they
were afraid. 16Those who had seen it told the people what had happened
to the demon-influenced man and the pigs. 17They began pleading with
Jesus to leave their region. 18As Jesus was getting into the boat, the man
who had had the demons was begging to go with him. 19But Jesus
refused, and said to him, "Go home to your people, and tell them the
great things the Lord has done for you and how He showed you mercy."
20So the man went off and began to proclaim to the people of Decapolis
everything Jesus had done for him, and they were all amazed.

21Jesus returned again by boat to the other side of the lake. A large
crowd gathered around him, so he stayed by the shore. 22A synagogue
leader named Jairus came up. When he saw Jesus, he fell at his feet 23and
pleaded earnestly, "My little daughter is at the point of death. Please

[35] A strange mixture of singular and plural, "my" and "we."

come and lay your hands on her so that she may be healed and live."
24Jesus went with him, and a large crowd followed, pushing up against
him.

25A woman was there who had been ill from bleeding for twelve
years. 26She had suffered at the hands of many doctors, and had spent all
she had, but she had not been helped at all — in fact she had become
worse. 27She had heard about Jesus, so she came through the crowd
behind him and touched his clothes. 28She had said to herself, "If I can
just touch his clothes, I will be healed." 29The bleeding stopped
immediately, and she felt in her body that she had been healed from her
suffering. 30Jesus realized immediately that power had gone out from
him, turned around in the crowd and asked, "Who touched my clothes?"
31The disciples replied, "Look at the crowd jostling you. Why are you
asking, 'Who touched me?'" 32But Jesus continued looking to see who
had touched him. 33Knowing what had happened to her, the woman,
afraid and trembling, came and fell down before him and told him the
whole truth. 34Jesus said to her, "My daughter, your faith has healed you.
Go in peace, completely healed from the disease that made you suffer."

35While he was still speaking, people came from the synagogue
leader's home. "Your daughter has died," they said. "Why bother the
teacher any more?" 36Jesus overheard what they said, and said to the
synagogue leader, "Do not be afraid; just continue believing." 37He did
not let anyone follow him except Peter, James, and James' brother John.
38When they got to the synagogue leader's house, Jesus saw all the
commotion, with people loudly crying and wailing. 39He went in and
asked them, "Why all this commotion and weeping? The little girl is not
dead; she is sleeping." 40They laughed at him. But Jesus made everybody
leave. Then he went into the room where the little girl was, taking along
the child's father and mother and his three disciples. 41He took the little
girl by the hand and said, "*Talitha koum*!"[36] which translated means,
"Little girl, I tell you, get up!" 42Immediately the little girl got up and
began to walk. She was twelve years old. Immediately they were
completely astounded. 43Jesus gave them strict instructions not to let
anyone know about this, and he told them to give her something to eat.

---

[36]In Aramaic.

6 1Jesus went from there to Nazareth, his hometown, with his disciples.
2On the Sabbath he started teaching in the synagogue, and the many
listeners were astonished. “Where did this man get these ideas from?”
they asked. “What is this wisdom he has been given, and this power to
do miracles? 3Is he not the carpenter, Mary’s son, the brother of James,
Joseph, Judas and Simon? Are not his sisters living here with us?” They
took offense at him. 4Jesus said to them, “A prophet is treated with
honor, but not in his hometown, among his own relatives, and within his
own family.” 5Consequently Jesus could not do any miracles there,
except to lay his hands on a few sick people and heal them. 6He was
amazed by their unbelief. He traveled around the villages, teaching as he
went.

7He called together the twelve disciples and sent them out two by
two. He gave them authority over evil spirits,[37] 8and instructed them to
take nothing with them except a walking staff — no bread, no bag, no
money. 9They were to wear sandals, but not take extra clothes. 10He said
to them, “When you are invited into a home, stay there until you leave
that town. 11Any place that does not welcome you or listen to you, shake
the dust off your feet as you leave as a testimony against them.” 12So they
traveled around preaching that people should repent.[38] 13They drove out
many demons, and anointed with oil many sick people and healed them.

14King Herod heard about Jesus, as his reputation had become well-
known. Some were saying, “John the Baptist has been raised from the
dead, and that is why these miraculous powers are at work in him.”
15Others said, “It is Elijah.” Still others said, “He is a prophet, like one of
the prophets of long ago.” 16But Herod kept saying, “John, the one I
beheaded, has been raised!”

17For Herod himself had had John arrested and imprisoned because of
Herodias. She was his brother Philip’s wife, whom Herod had married.
18John had been saying to Herod, “It is not lawful for you to marry your
brother’s wife.” 19Consequently Herodias resented John and wanted to
have him killed. But she could not arrange it 20because Herod respected

---

[37]A synonym for demons.

[38]They were of course preaching the same Gospel about the Kingdom which Jesus had preached. This is the true Gospel, including later, of course, as these events happened, the death and resurrection of Jesus (Mk. 1:14-15; Acts 10:34-43; 8:12; 19:8; 20:24-25; 28:23, 31; Lk. 4:43).

John as an upright and holy man. Herod protected John, and though he
was very confused at what John said, he still liked to listen to him.
21Herodias' opportunity came on Herod's birthday. He gave a banquet for
the nobles, military officers, and leaders of Galilee. 22Herodias' daughter
came in and danced, pleasing Herod and his dinner guests. He said to the
girl, 23"You can ask me for whatever you want, and I will give it to you!"
He promised with an oath, "I will give you up to half of my kingdom."
24So she went out and asked her mother, "What should I ask for?" Her
mother replied, "The head of John the Baptist." 25Immediately the girl
rushed back in and said to the king, "I want you to give me here and now
the head of John the Baptist on a platter." 26The king was very sorry, but
because of the oaths he had made in front of his guests, he did not want
to refuse her. 27So immediately the king sent an executioner with orders
to bring John's head. After beheading him in the prison, 28the executioner
brought John's head on a platter and gave it to the girl, and she gave it to
her mother. 29When John's disciples heard about this they came and took
his body and laid it in a tomb.

30The Apostles gathered together with Jesus and reported to him all
that they had done and taught. 31Jesus said to them, "Come with me to a
quiet place and rest for a while," because there were so many people
coming and going that they did not even have time to eat. 32So they went
away by boat to a quiet place to be by themselves.

33Many saw them leave and recognized them. So people from all the
surrounding towns ran ahead and got there before them. 34When Jesus
landed he saw a large crowd, and he felt compassion for them because
they were like sheep without a shepherd, so he began to teach them many
things. 35When it was already quite late, Jesus' disciples came to him.
"This place is far from anywhere," they said, "and it is already quite late.
36You had better tell the people to leave and buy themselves something to
eat in the surrounding countryside and villages." 37But Jesus responded,
"You give them something to eat." The disciples said, "We would need
over six months' pay to go and buy bread for them." 38Jesus asked, "So
how much bread do you have? Go and see." They went to find out, and
said to him, "Five loaves, and a couple of fish." 39Jesus directed everyone
to sit down on the green grass in groups. 40They sat down in groups of
hundreds and fifties. 41Then he took the five loaves and two fish. He
looked up to heaven and blessed the food and broke the bread. Then he

gave the bread to the disciples to distribute to the people, and he divided
the two fish up among them all. 42Everyone ate until they were satisfied.
43Then they collected up what was left of the bread and fish and filled
twelve baskets full. 44There were 5,000 men who ate.

45Immediately Jesus told his disciples to get back into the boat and to
go on ahead to Bethsaida on the other side of the lake, while he sent the
crowd away. 46After saying goodbye to them, he went to the mountain to
pray.

47Later that evening, the boat was out in the middle of the lake while
Jesus was alone on land. 48He could see them struggling to row, because
the wind was against them. About three a.m. Jesus came towards them,
walking on the sea. He would have passed them by, 49but when they saw
him walking on the sea, they thought it was a ghost and shouted out.
50They all saw him and were terrified. Immediately Jesus said to them,
"Courage! It is I. Do not be afraid!" 51He got into the boat with them and
the wind died down. They were completely astonished, 52because they
had not understood the meaning of the miracle of the loaves, because
their minds were closed.

53Having crossed the lake they arrived at Gennesaret and moored the
boat. 54As they got out of the boat, immediately people recognized Jesus,
55and they ran throughout the whole area to carry the sick on their mats to
where they heard Jesus was. 56Wherever he went, in the villages, in the
towns, or in the countryside, they were laying the sick in the
marketplaces and pleading with him that they might just touch the edge
of his coat. Everyone who touched it was healed.

7 1Some Pharisees and religious teachers gathered around Jesus when
they had come from Jerusalem. 2They saw that some of his disciples
were eating with impure, unwashed hands. 3The Pharisees and all Jews
do not eat until they have ceremonially washed their hands, following the
traditions of the elders. 4Also when they return from the market they do
not eat until they have washed themselves. They have many other rituals
they observe, like the washing of cups, pots, and pans. 5So the Pharisees
and religious teachers asked Jesus, "Why do your disciples not follow
the tradition of the elders, but eat their bread with impure hands?" 6Jesus
replied, "Isaiah was right when he prophesied about you hypocrites. As it
is written, 'These people honor me with what they say, but their hearts

are a long way from me. 7Their worship of me is in vain, because they
are teaching human rules as doctrines.' 8You have given up God's
commands and instead observe man-made traditions.

9"You are experts in setting aside God's clear command in order to
keep your own traditions! 10Moses said, 'Honor your father and mother.
Anyone who speaks evil of their father or mother is to be put to death.'
11But you say, 'If someone says to their father or mother, "Anything you
might have had from me is now Corban (that means a gift dedicated to
God),"' 12then you do not permit them to do anything more for their
mother or father. 13So you negate the word of God by your tradition
which you hand down, and you do many things like this."

14Jesus called the crowd to him again and said to them, "Everyone
listen to me and understand this: 15nothing which is on the outside and
goes into you can make you unclean. Instead it is what comes out that
makes you unclean. [16Whoever has ears to hear, listen!]"[39]

17When Jesus had left the crowd and gone into a house, his disciples
asked him about the parable. 18"Do you not understand either?" he asked
them. "Can you not see that whatever goes into a person from the outside
cannot make him unclean? 19For it does not go into his mind, but into his
stomach, and is then excreted." With this remark he pronounced every
kind of food clean.[40] 20He said, "It is what comes out of a person that

---

[39]Early manuscripts do not contain verse 16.

[40]Jesus abolished the Levitical food laws, and they realized this later. This is an editorial remark added by Mark, like the Markan comment in 3:30. Paul also, writing as a Jew and Christian, said that "nothing is unclean of itself… all things are clean" (Rom. 14:14, 20). Paul used the word *katharos*, "clean," which is the precise opposite of those foods listed in Lev. 11 as *akathartos*, "unclean," forbidden foods under the Torah of Moses. Paul spoke as a Jew and a Christian. Christians are now to be "within the Torah of Messiah" (Gal. 6:2; 1 Cor. 9:21). There is extensive instruction in Rom., Gal., Heb. and 2 Cor. 3 to teach that the Law is now spiritualized and not required of believers, in the letter of the Law of Moses (Rom. 7:6). See Gal. 3:19-29 for Paul's clear statement on the Law in the letter. Col. 2:16-17 emphatically and unequivocally calls the "trio" of Jewish calendar observances — holy day, new moon and sabbath — a single shadow replaced by the substance which is the sacrificial body of Messiah, who has come and is now exalted and present with us. The same shadow and body of Messiah contrast is found in Heb. 8:5 and 10:1. In 1 Cor. 9:20 Paul is "not under the Law" of Moses. He was free to accommodate himself with no sense of obligation, to win Jews for Christ. Attempts by Seventh-Day Adventists to remove the weekly Sabbath from Paul's list in Col. 2 are refuted by the fact that some 10 passages in the OT list the calendar as

makes him unclean. 21From inside, from people's minds, come evil
thoughts, sexual immorality, theft, murder, 22adultery, greed, wickedness,
deceit, indecency, envy, slander, pride and foolishness. 23All these evil
things come from inside and defile people."

24Then Jesus departed and went to the region of Tyre. He went into a
house and did not want anyone to know, but he could not avoid being
noticed. 25A woman whose young daughter had an evil spirit heard about
him, and she immediately came and fell at his feet. 26The woman was a
Gentile, of the Syrophoenician race, and she kept asking Jesus to cast out
the demon from her daughter. 27Jesus said to her, "First let the children
eat until they are full. It is not right to take the children's food and throw
it to the little dogs." 28She replied, "Yes, lord, but even the little dogs
under the table eat the crumbs from the children." 29He said to her,
"Because of your answer go on your way. The demon has gone out of
your daughter." 30She went home and found the child lying on the bed,
with the demon gone.

31Jesus left the region of Tyre and went through Sidon to the Sea of
Galilee in the region of Decapolis. 32There they brought him a deaf man
who had difficulty speaking. They begged Jesus to lay his hands on him.
33Jesus took him aside from the crowd, and put his fingers in his ears, and
after spitting, touched his tongue. 34He looked up to heaven with a sigh
and said to him, "Ephphatha," which means, "Be opened!" 35Immediately
the man's ears were opened, his speech returned, and he began speaking
clearly. 36Jesus gave them orders not to tell anyone, but the more he said
so, the more they kept spreading the news. 37They were absolutely
astonished and said, "He has done everything well. He even makes the
deaf hear and the mute speak."

8 1Around that time there was another large crowd with nothing to eat.
Jesus called the disciples together and said to them, 2"I feel
compassion for the people because they have already stayed with me for
three days and they have nothing to eat. 3If I send them home without
food, they will faint on the way, and some have come from far away."
4His disciples said, "Where could anyone find enough bread to feed them

---

annual, monthly and weekly observances. Paul spoke of annual, monthly, and weekly celebrations, the weekly Sabbath being of course Saturday. (See my *Law, Sabbath and New Covenant Christianity* at restorationfellowship.org for a fuller discussion.)

here in this isolated place?” 5He asked them, “How many loaves do you have?” They replied, “Seven.” 6He directed the crowd to sit down on the ground. Then, taking the seven loaves of bread and giving thanks, he broke the bread and gave the pieces to his disciples to serve to the crowd. 7They had a few small fish as well, so having blessed them, he ordered these to be served too. 8They ate until they were full, and then collected seven large baskets of leftovers. 9There were about 4,000 men there. After dismissing them, 10Jesus immediately got in the boat with his disciples and went to the Dalmanutha region.

11The Pharisees came and began to argue with him, wanting him to show them a miraculous sign from heaven, testing him. 12Sighing deeply in his spirit,[41] Jesus asked, “Why does this evil society seek a sign? I am telling you the truth: No sign will be given to this evil society.” 13So he left them behind, got into the boat, and went back across the lake.

14But the disciples had forgotten to bring bread with them. All they had in the boat was just one loaf. 15“Watch out!” he warned them. “Be careful of the yeast of the Pharisees and of Herod.” 16They began discussing with one another the fact that they had no bread. 17Jesus was aware of this and said, “Why are you discussing about not having bread? Do you still not know or understand? Do you have closed minds? 18You have eyes to see, have you not? And ears to hear? And do you not remember, 19when I shared five loaves among 5,000, how many large baskets full of leftovers did you pick up?” They replied, “Twelve.” 20“And the seven loaves for the 4,000 — how many baskets of leftovers did you take away?” They answered, “Seven.” 21He asked them, “Do you not understand yet?”

22They went to Bethsaida where some people brought a blind man to Jesus and begged him to touch him. 23Jesus took the blind man by the hand and took him outside the village. After spitting on the man’s eyes and laying his hands on them, Jesus asked him, “Do you see anything?” 24The man looked up. “I see people, but they look like trees walking around, ” he said. 25Jesus laid his hands on the man’s eyes again, and the man looked carefully around. He was healed and began to see everything

---

[41]That is, out of frustration at their culpable blindness and stubbornness (see Mt. 13:10-17; 2 Thess. 2:10; 2 Pet. 3:5; Acts 28:23-27).

clearly. 26 Jesus sent the man home and said to him, "Do not even go into
the village."

27 Jesus and his disciples left to go to the villages of Caesarea Philippi,
and on the way he asked his disciples, "Who do people say I am?" 28 They
answered, "Some say John the Baptist, some Elijah, and others one of
the prophets." 29 He then asked them, "But what about you? Who do you
say I am?" Peter answered, "You are the Messiah." 30 Jesus warned them
not to tell anyone about him.

31 Then Jesus began to teach them that the Son of Man would have to
suffer many things and be rejected by the elders, chief priests, and
religious teachers, and be killed, and three days later rise again.[42] 32 Jesus
told them this very clearly. Peter took him aside and started to reprimand
him. 33 Jesus turned around and, looking at his disciples, reprimanded
Peter. "Go away from me, you Satan," he said. "You are not setting your
mind on the things of God, but human things."

34 Jesus called over the crowd with his disciples and said to them, "If
anyone wants to come after me, he must deny himself, and take up his
cross and follow me. 35 Whoever wants to save his life will lose it, but
whoever loses his life for me and the Gospel[43] will save it. 36 What point
is there for anyone to get everything in the whole world, and lose his
life? 37 What would anyone give in exchange for his life? 38 Whoever is
ashamed of me and my words among this unfaithful and sinful society,[44]
the Son of Man will be ashamed of them when he comes in the glory of
his Father with the holy angels."

---

[42]Jesus mentioned his all-important death and resurrection here for the first time (cp. Mt. 16:21). He had been preaching the Gospel of the Kingdom for a long time prior to this. This will demonstrate that the Christian Gospel is more than belief in the death and the resurrection of Jesus. Its foundation is the coming Kingdom of God in which the believers will supervise the world with Jesus (Dan. 7:27; 1 Cor. 6:2; Rev. 2:26; 3:21; 5:10; 2 Tim. 2:12; Mt. 19:28). In Acts 20:24-25 Paul equates the Gospel of the grace of God with the proclamation of the Gospel of the Kingdom. There is no difference. There is only one saving Gospel in the NT preached equally by Jesus and Paul. It is the Gospel about the Kingdom and the name of Jesus Messiah (Acts 8:12).

[43]The Gospel of the Kingdom, once again the central core of the Christian faith. Without a clear definition of the Kingdom, there can be no true account of the faith.

[44]The present society is called "generation" by Jesus, meaning a society characterized by a common, in this case evil, quality. This evil system will persist until the return of Jesus to set up the Kingdom on a renewed earth. "Generation" has the same meaning in Matt. 24:34 and Luke 16:8.

9 1"I am telling you the truth," Jesus said to them, "there are some
standing here who will not die before they see the Kingdom of God
arriving with power."[45] 2Six days after saying this, Jesus took Peter,
James, and John with him and brought them up a high mountain by
themselves. His appearance was transformed before them. 3His clothes
shone brilliantly, brighter white than anyone on earth could wash them.
4Then Elijah and Moses appeared to them too, talking with Jesus. 5Peter
said to Jesus, "Rabbi, it is so good for us to be here! Let us make three
shelters — one each for you, Moses, and Elijah." 6He really did not know
what to say as they became so terrified. 7Then a cloud formed and spread
over them, and a voice came from the cloud: "This is My Son, the one I
love. Listen to him!" 8All of a sudden they looked around and saw
nobody with them except Jesus.

9As they were coming down the mountain Jesus gave them orders not
to tell anyone what they had seen[46] until after the Son of Man rose from
the dead. 10They kept this to themselves, but they did discuss with each
other what rising from the dead meant. 11"Why do the religious teachers
say that Elijah has to come first?" they asked him. 12"It is true that Elijah
comes first and restores all things," he explained. "So then why is it
written that the Son of Man has to suffer many things and be treated with
contempt? 13But I am telling you that Elijah has indeed come, and people
did to him as they wished, just as it is written about him."

14When they got back to the other disciples, they saw some religious
teachers arguing with them, surrounded by a large crowd. 15As soon as
the whole crowd saw Jesus they were amazed and ran to greet him.
16"What are you discussing?" Jesus asked them. 17One of the people in
the crowd said, "Teacher, I brought my son to you. He has an evil spirit
which makes him mute. 18Whenever it seizes him it throws him down,
and he foams at the mouth, grinds his teeth, and becomes stiff. I asked

---

[45]This prediction of the Kingdom was fulfilled in the *vision* (see Mt. 17:9, *orama*) provided at the transfiguration. Peter comments on and confirms this in 2 Pet. 1:16-18 where he says that the Parousia, the Second Coming which inaugurates the Kingdom, was seen in vision at the Transfiguration. Matthew calls this episode a vision (*orama*), not just "what you saw," as very inadequately translated in some versions.

[46]It was a *vision* (*orama*) of the future Kingdom as Matt. 17:9 says, and Peter in 2 Pet. 1:16-18 explains it also as a vision of the Parousia.

your disciples to cast it out, but they could not do it.” 19Jesus responded,
“You unbelieving society! How long will I be with you? How long will I
put up with you? Bring him here to me.” 20So they brought him to Jesus.
When the evil spirit saw[47] Jesus, it immediately sent the boy into a
convulsion and he fell on the ground, rolling around and foaming at the
mouth. 21“How long has this been happening to him?” Jesus asked the
boy’s father. “Since he was a little child,” the father replied.
22“Frequently it has thrown him into the fire, or tried to drown him in
water. But if you can do anything, please take pity on us and help us.”
23Jesus replied, “‘If you can’? All things are possible for the one who
believes!” 24Immediately the boy’s father cried out, “I do believe; help
my unbelief!” 25Jesus, seeing that the crowd was getting bigger,
reprimanded the evil spirit, “You spirit causing muteness and deafness, I
command you to come out of him and never enter him again.” 26After
screaming and throwing the boy into violent convulsions, the evil spirit
came out. The boy looked so dead that many of the people said, “He is
dead!” 27But Jesus took the boy by the hand and helped him up, and he
stood up. 28When Jesus came indoors, his disciples asked him in private,
“Why could we not cast the evil spirit out?” 29Jesus answered, “This kind
cannot come out except by prayer.”

30They left there and went through Galilee. Jesus did not want anyone
to know where he was 31because he was teaching his disciples: “The Son
of Man is to be betrayed to human authorities. They will kill him, but he
will rise three days later.” 32They did not understand what he was saying
and they were afraid to ask him about it.

33They arrived at Capernaum, and when they were indoors Jesus
asked them, “What were you discussing on the way?” 34But they kept
quiet because they had been discussing who was the most important.
35Jesus sat down and called the twelve disciples together. “If anyone
wants to be first, he has to be last of all, and the servant of all,” he said.

---

[47]Mark’s deliberate intention is to inform us that the demon is a non-human *personality*. The (grammatically neuter) demon is deliberately given personality by the use of a masculine participle, “seeing.” Demons are of course an indispensable part of the historical narrative. To explain them away is an assault on the integrity of Scripture, gets rid of a whole dimension of revealed truth, and hides the fact that our Christian struggle is first and foremost against evil spiritual powers, the “kosmocrats” of Eph. 6:12. “Demon” is a perfectly easy word with a clear meaning.

36He took a small child and set him in front of them. Taking the child in
his arms, he said to them, 37"Whoever welcomes a child like this in my
name welcomes me, and whoever welcomes me does not welcome me
but the One who sent me."

38John said to Jesus, "Teacher, we saw someone casting out demons
in your name, and we tried to stop him because he was not one of us."
39Jesus replied, "Do not stop him. No one who does miracles in my name
can quickly change and speak evil of me. 40Whoever is not against us is
for us. 41Whoever gives you a cup of water because you bear the name of
Messiah, I am telling you the truth: they will not lose their reward.

42"But if anyone causes one of these little ones who believe in me to
stumble, it would be better for them if they had a large millstone tied
around their neck and were thrown into the sea. 43If your hand leads you
to sin, cut it off. It is better to enter Life[48] as a cripple than to have both
hands and go into Gehenna fire, the fire which cannot be put out.[49] 45If
your foot leads you to sin, cut it off. It is better to enter Life lame than to
be thrown with two feet into Gehenna fire.[50] 47If your eye leads you to
sin, throw it out. It is better to enter the Kingdom of God with just one
eye than with both eyes to be thrown into Gehenna fire, 48where the
worm does not die and the fire is not put out.

49"Everybody will be 'salted' by fire. 50Salt is good, but if it is not
salty any more, how could you make it salty? Have salt in yourselves,
and be at peace with one another."

10 1Jesus departed and went to the regions of Judea and beyond the
Jordan. Again crowds flocked to him, and as was his custom he
was teaching them.

2Some Pharisees came to see him to try to test him, asking whether it
was lawful for a man to divorce his wife. 3"What did Moses command
you to do?" he asked in return. 4"Moses permitted a certificate of divorce

---

[48]The future Kingdom to be inaugurated when Jesus returns visibly to the earth (Lk. 21:31, etc).

[49]The penalty of the wicked is to be annihilated, burned up, not to suffer a conscious torture forever. Early manuscripts do not contain v. 44, 46 (identical to v. 48).

[50]Gehenna will be a place of total destruction by fire, certainly not a place of eternal, unceasing torture. Such a doctrine of unending suffering would make God a fiend of the worst type!

to be written and the woman sent away," they replied. 5But Jesus said to
them, "It was because of your hard-hearted attitude that Moses wrote this
command for you. 6But from the beginning, at creation, God made them
male and female.[51] 7That is why a man leaves his father and mother, 8and
the two become one flesh; so they are no longer two, but one flesh. 9No
one should separate what God has joined together."

10When they were indoors, the disciples asked him about this.
11"Whoever divorces his wife and marries another commits adultery
against her," he said to them, 12"or if a wife divorces her husband and
marries another she commits adultery."

13People were bringing children to Jesus so that he would touch and
bless them, but the disciples reprimanded them. 14When Jesus saw this he
was indignant and said to them, "Let the children come to me, and do not
stop them, because the Kingdom of God belongs to people like these
children. 15I am telling you the truth: whoever does not receive the
Kingdom of God like a child will certainly not enter it." 16He hugged the
children, and blessed them as he laid his hands on them.

17As Jesus was walking along, a man ran up and knelt before him.
"Good teacher," he asked, "what should I do to inherit the Life of the
Age to Come?"[52] 18Jesus responded, "Why do you call me good? No one
is absolutely good, except God alone.[53] 19You know the commandments:
do not murder, do not commit adultery, do not steal, do not lie, do not
defraud, honor your father and mother." 20The man replied, "Teacher, I
have kept all these from my youth." 21Looking at him, Jesus felt love for

---

[51]Certainly Jesus the Son was not the Creator! God rested on the seventh day (Heb. 4:4), and the Father, the one and only God, was unaccompanied at the creation (Isa. 44:24). Some 50 texts say that God was the Creator.

[52]That is, of course, a position of responsibility in the future Kingdom of God on earth, and immortality.

[53]With this clear statement Jesus of course warned against the false teaching that "Jesus is God." Jesus expressly denied being the One God here, and this merely echoes his definitive creedal statement in Mark 12:29, where agreeing with a Jew, Jesus defined the One God as a single Lord: "The Lord our God is one Lord" (as in Deut. 6:4). This verse is an essential indication of the distance Jesus, as a monotheist, put between himself and the only God. The proposition "Jesus *is* God" promotes of course two who are God and thus two Gods. The loss of Jesus' creed was a disaster which befell the Church, starting from the 2nd century. Jn. 17:3 is an unarguable text that only one Person can be the true God.

him and said, "You are just missing one thing. Go and sell everything
you own, give the money to the poor, and you will have treasure stored
in heaven. Then come and follow me." 22At these words the man's face
fell and he left very sad, because he was very wealthy.

23Jesus looked around and said to his disciples, "How hard it will be
for wealthy people to enter the Kingdom of God!" 24The disciples were
shocked at his words. But Jesus continued, "Children, how hard it is to
enter the Kingdom of God. 25It is easier for a camel to go through the eye
of a needle than for a rich person to enter the Kingdom of God." 26The
disciples were all the more astonished. "So who can be saved?" they said
to each other. 27Looking straight at them, Jesus replied, "With people it is
impossible, but not with God, because everything is possible with God."

28Peter started saying, "Look, we have left everything to follow you."
29Jesus responded, "I am telling you the truth: anyone who has left
behind their home, brothers, sisters, mother, father, children or land, for
the sake of me and the Gospel, 30will receive in this present age a
hundred times as many homes, brothers, sisters, mothers, children and
land — along with persecution. And in the Age to Come they will
receive the Life of that Age to Come. 31But many who are first will be
last, and the last will be first."

32As they were on their way up to Jerusalem, with Jesus walking
ahead, the disciples were apprehensive and those following were afraid.
Again he took the twelve disciples aside and began to tell them what was
about to happen to him. 33"Look, we are going up to Jerusalem, and the
Son of Man will be handed over to the chief priests and religious
teachers, and they will condemn him to death. They in turn will hand
him over to the Gentiles, 34and they will mock him, spit on him, flog him,
and kill him. But three days later he will rise again."

35James and John, Zebedee's sons, approached him. "Teacher," they
began, "we want you to do for us whatever we ask you." 36Jesus replied,
"What do you want me to do for you?" 37They said to him, "Grant that
one of us may sit on your right and one on your left in your glory." 38But
Jesus replied, "You have no idea what you are asking. Can you drink the
cup I drink? Can you be baptized with the baptism I experience?" 39They
assured him, "We can do it." Jesus said to them, "You will drink the cup
I drink, and you will be baptized with the baptism I experience. 40But to

sit on my right or on my left is not mine to give. These places are for
those for whom it has been prepared."
41When the other ten disciples heard this, they were upset with James
and John. 42Jesus called them together and said to them, "You know that
those who are recognized as rulers of nations oppress them, and their
leaders act like tyrants. 43But it is not to be like this among you. Whoever
wants to become important among you should be your servant, 44and
whoever wants to be first among you should be everyone's slave. 45For
even the Son of Man did not come to be served but to serve, and to give
his life as a ransom in place of many."[54]

46Then they arrived at Jericho. As Jesus and his disciples were
leaving the town, together with a large crowd, a blind beggar named
Bartimaeus, the son of Timaeus, was sitting by the road. 47When he heard
Jesus the Nazarene was there, he started shouting out, "Jesus, son of
David, have mercy on me!" 48Many told him to be quiet, but he shouted
even more, "Son of David, have mercy on me!" 49Jesus stopped and said,
"Call him over." So they called him over, saying to him, "Take heart and
stand up! He is calling you." 50Bartimaeus jumped up, threw aside his
coat, and came to Jesus. 51"What do you want me to do for you?" Jesus
asked him. "Rabbi," he said to Jesus, "I want to see again!" 52Jesus said
to him, "You can go. Your faith has healed you." Immediately he could
see, and he followed Jesus along the road.

11 1When they were near Jerusalem, at Bethphage and Bethany,
beside the Mount of Olives, Jesus sent two of his disciples 2with
these instructions: "Go into the village opposite, and immediately as you
enter you will find a colt tied up which no one has ever ridden. Untie it
and bring it here. 3If anyone asks you what you are doing, say, 'The lord
needs it and will return it soon.'" 4So they went off and found a colt tied
to a door, out on the street, and they untied it. 5Some people standing
there asked them, "What are you doing, untying that colt?" 6The
disciples replied just as Jesus had instructed them, and the people let
them take it. 7They brought the colt to Jesus and put their coats on it, and

---

[54]A foundational saying showing that the death of Jesus was in our place (*anti*), as a substitution, following the teaching of Isa. 53:6: "God laid on him the iniquity of us all." See also the "suffering servant" predictions of Jesus in Isa. 42, 49, 50, 52-53. Jesus did not die merely as a "good example." He died in our place.

Jesus sat on it. 8Many people spread their coats on the road, while others
spread leafy branches which they had cut from the fields. 9Those out in
front and those who followed were shouting, "Hosanna![55] Blessed is he
who comes in the name of the Lord! 10Blessed is the coming Kingdom of
our father David![56] Hosanna in the highest!"

11Jesus entered Jerusalem and went into the Temple. After looking
around at everything, since it was already evening, he went out to
Bethany with the twelve disciples. 12The next day, when they had left
Bethany, Jesus became hungry. 13From far away he saw a fig tree with
leaves, so he went to see if it had any fruit. But when he came to it, he
found only leaves, because it was not the season for figs. 14He said to the
tree, "May no one ever eat fruit from you again," and his disciples heard
what he said.

15They arrived in Jerusalem, and he went into the Temple and started
throwing out the people buying and selling in the Temple. He overturned
the moneychangers' tables and the dove sellers' chairs. 16He would not
let anyone carry merchandise through the Temple. 17And he was teaching
them, "Is it not written, 'My house will be called a house of prayer for all
nations'? But you turned it into a robbers' den!" 18The chief priests and
religious teachers heard what he said, and began looking for a way to kill
him because they were afraid of him, as the whole crowd was astonished
at his teaching.

19When evening came Jesus and his disciples used to leave the city.
20The following morning as they walked along, they saw the fig tree,
withered from the roots up. 21Peter, reminded of what had happened, said
to Jesus, "Rabbi, look, the fig tree that you cursed has withered." 22Jesus
replied, "Have faith in God and the faith taught by God through me.[57] 23I
am telling you the truth: if someone says to this mountain, 'Be taken up

---

[55]"Save us."

[56]The core of the Christian Gospel and the Christian faith.

[57]The Greek has "the faith of God," and this implies not only faith in God but the faith and Gospel as coming from God. Jesus came preaching God's Gospel, the Gospel of God, God's announcement of the Kingdom of God coming on earth. "God's Gospel" is found in Mk. 1:14-15; Rom. 1:1; 15:16; 2 Cor. 11:7; 1 Thess. 2:2, 8, 9; 1 Pet. 4:17, uniting the NT in the one and only saving Gospel of the Kingdom. This is the non-negotiable foundation of the Christian faith, including water baptism as practiced by Jesus (Jn. 3:22, 26; 4:1) and commanded by him until the end of the age (Mt. 28:19-20). Salvation is by obedience to Jesus (Heb. 5:9).

and thrown into the sea,' and does not doubt in his heart, but believes
that what he is asking will happen, then he will have it. 24So I am telling
you that whatever you are praying for, whatever you are asking, believe
that you have received it, and it will be yours. 25And whenever you are
praying, if you have something against anyone, forgive them, so that
your Father in heaven will also forgive you your sins." [26But if you do
not forgive, neither will your Father in heaven forgive your sins.][58]

27They arrived back in Jerusalem, and as he was walking in the
Temple, the chief priests, religious teachers, and the elders came to him.
28"By what authority are you doing all this?" they asked him. "Who gave
you this authority?" 29Jesus said to them, "I will ask you just one
question. You answer me, and I will tell you by what authority I do what
I do. 30Answer me: was the baptism of John from heaven or from
people?" 31They discussed it among themselves. "If we say it is from
heaven, he will reply, 'So why did you not believe him?' 32But if we say,
it is from people…" They were afraid of the people, because they were
all convinced that John was a real prophet. 33So they answered Jesus,
"We do not know." Jesus replied, "Then I am not telling you by what
authority I act."

12 1Then he began to speak to them using parables. "A man planted a
vineyard. He put a fence around it, dug a pit for a winepress, and
built a tower. Then he leased it to some farmers, and went away on a trip.
2At the time of the harvest, he sent a servant to the tenant farmers to pick
up some of the fruit from the vineyard. 3But they seized him, beat him
up, and sent him away empty-handed. 4So the man sent another servant.
They hit him on the head and abused him. 5He sent another, and this one
they killed. He sent many others — some they beat up, some they killed.
6He had one more to send, his beloved son. Finally he sent him, thinking
'They will respect my son.' 7But those farmers said to each other, 'Here
is the heir. If we kill him, we will get the inheritance!' 8So they took him
and killed him, and threw him out of the vineyard. 9Now what will the
owner of the vineyard do? He will come and kill those farmers, and give
the vineyard to others. 10Have you not read this Scripture: 'The stone
rejected by the builders has become the main cornerstone. 11This came

---

[58] Early manuscripts do not contain verse 26.

about from the Lord, and it is wonderful to see'?" 12The Jewish leaders
realized that the parable was directed at them, and so they tried to find a
way to arrest him, but they were afraid of the crowd. So they left him
and went away.

13Then they sent some Pharisees and Herodians to him, to try to catch
him out in conversation. 14They came and said to him, "Teacher, we
know you are a truthful person and you do not worry about what people
think of you. You show no partiality to anyone, but teach the way of God
in truth. So is it right to pay taxes to Caesar or not? 15Should we pay or
not?" Jesus, realizing their hypocrisy, asked them, "Why are you trying
to trap me? Bring me a denarius coin to look at." 16They brought one.
"Whose is this image and inscription?" Jesus asked them. "Caesar's,"
they answered. 17Jesus said to them, "Then give Caesar what belongs to
him, and give God what belongs to Him." They were astonished at what
he said.

18Then some Sadducees, who say there is no resurrection, came and
posed a question: 19"Teacher, Moses instructed us that if a man dies,
leaving a childless widow, then his brother should marry his widow and
have children on the dead man's behalf. 20Once there were seven
brothers. The first married, and then died without having children. 21The
second married his widow and then died, childless. The third did the
same. 22In fact all seven died without having any children. In the end the
woman died too. 23In the resurrection, whose wife will she be, because
she was the wife of all seven brothers?" 24Jesus said to them, "Does this
not prove you are mistaken, and do not understand the Scriptures nor the
power of God? 25For when the dead rise, they do not marry and are not
given in marriage, but are like the angels in heaven.[59] 26But about the fact
that the dead rise again, have you not read in Moses' writings, how God
spoke to him at the bush, 'I am the God of Abraham, and the God of
Isaac, and the God of Jacob'? 27He is not the God of the dead, but of the
living. You are badly mistaken!"

28One of the religious teachers came and heard them arguing, and
recognized that Jesus had given them a good answer. So he asked Jesus,

---

[59]Jesus here does not tell us about the capacities of evil, unholy angels. Thus Jesus' answer does not contradict the obvious fact that in Genesis 6:1-6 evil angels were involved in a disastrous sexual perversion. Peter speaks of the angels who sinned (2 Pet. 2:4; Jude 6).

"What commandment is the most important of all?" 29Jesus replied, "The
most important commandment is: 'Hear, O Israel! The Lord our God is
one Lord.[60] 30Love the Lord your God with all your heart, with all your
soul, with all your mind, and with all your strength.' 31The second is:
'Love your neighbor as yourself.' There is no more important
commandment than these." 32The religious teacher replied, "You are
right, teacher. It is true as you said that God is one Person,[61] and there is
no other besides Him,[62] 33and we are to love Him with all our heart, all
our mind, and all our strength, and to love our neighbor as ourselves.
That is far more important than all burnt offerings and sacrifices."
34Jesus, seeing that he had given an intelligent answer, said, "You are not
far from the Kingdom of God." After this no one was brave enough to
ask him any more questions.

35As Jesus continued teaching in the Temple, he asked, "How is it
that the religious teachers say that the Messiah is the son of David?
36David himself said, inspired by the holy spirit, 'The Lord said to my

---

[60]The greatest command is to hear and believe that God is one Person. This produces "the absolute simplicity of the entire inner life" (Lange). The Jewish scribe, who was not a Trinitarian (!), gives his wholehearted assent, repeating in other words exactly what Jesus had declared. Jesus confirms the scribe's correct understanding by commending him. The declaration of Jesus defining God roots Jesus in the Hebrew Bible and in the Jewish view of God. "Salvation," he said, is "of the Jews" (Jn. 4:22). The replacement of Jesus' central teaching by later "church fathers," turning God into a mysterious "Triune Being," represents a disastrous departure from the pristine faith of and in Jesus. It can be easily repaired as ordinary readers grasp the staggering yet simple implications of Mark 12:29 echoed in John 17:3, and 1300 NT references to God as the Father and not Jesus. Repentance and a return to the creed of Jesus is the greatest possible challenge to the uncritically accepted traditions of many churches, which nevertheless claim to be following the Bible! If Sola Scriptura (the Bible only) is to be more than a hollow boast, Christians need to be heeding the words of Jesus in Mark 12:28-34. By affirming and authorizing Deut. 6:4, "Jesus stood in complete and conscious agreement with Phariseeism" (Schlatter, *Das Wort Jesu*, p. 221).

[61]A plain statement that Jesus was a unitarian and not a Trinitarian!

[62]Neither Jesus nor the scribe could possibly have imagined God as a Trinity of three Persons. The concept of a triune God contradicts Jesus at the most fundamental level and disobeys him, substituting a definition of God which Jesus would never approve. 1300 occurrences of the word God to mean the Father in the NT simply confirm the easy concept that God is a single Person, the Father (cp. Mal. 2:10; Isa. 63:16; 64:8; 1 Cor. 8:4-6 where the one God of monotheism is the Father and Jesus is the one lord Messiah based on Ps. 110:1).

lord,[63] "Sit at My right hand until I put your enemies under your feet."'
37David himself calls him lord, so in what sense is he David's son?" The
large crowd enjoyed listening to what Jesus said.
38He continued his teaching by saying, "Beware of the religious
teachers who love to walk around in long robes, and to be given
respectful greetings in the marketplaces. 39They love to have seats of
honor in the synagogues and the best places at banquets. 40They cheat
widows out of their property, then try to make themselves look good
with long-winded prayers. They will receive heavy condemnation."
41Jesus sat down opposite the treasury collection box, watching
people putting in coins. Many rich people were putting in large numbers
of coins. 42Then a poor widow came and put in just two small coins,
amounting to only a penny. 43He called over his disciples and said to
them, "I am telling you the truth: this poor widow put in much more than
all the others. 44They all gave out of their abundance, but she gave from
her poverty all she owned, all she needed to live on."

13 1As Jesus was leaving the Temple, one of his disciples said to him,
"Teacher, look at these massive stones and magnificent
buildings!" 2Jesus responded, "You see all these great buildings? There
will not be left one stone on top of another. Everything will be
demolished."
3As he was sitting on the Mount of Olives opposite the Temple,
Peter, James, John, and Andrew asked him privately, 4"Tell us, when will

---

[63]The Hebrew for the second lord is *adoni*, and this must be translated "lord" and not "Lord." *Adoni* is the title given to non-Deity all 195 times it occurs in the Hebrew Bible. God is never addressed as *adoni*, my lord. The distinction between *Adonai* and *adoni* was well recognized when the text was read aloud, and this distinction is found in BC times long before the vowels were added to the consonantal text in the 7th century AD. The formal addition of the vowels merely recorded for posterity what had been traditionally read aloud for centuries. Jesus had just finished saying that God was one LORD (12:29). He now mentions a second lord, the Messiah, and that second lord logically cannot also be the Lord God, which would result in two Gods. The two Lords are always distinguished as in Lk. 2:11: "the Messiah lord" and 2:26: "the Lord God." When the post-biblical church turned the Son of God (Lk. 1:35) into God it demanded a confession of two (and later three) who are each God. It then sheltered under the alien idea that God is a single "essence" and not a single Person, as always in Scripture. Thus the meaning of God was changed and Jesus' creed was bypassed.

these things happen, and what will be the sign when all these things are
about to be fulfilled?"[64] 5Jesus began by saying to them, "Be careful that
no one deceives you. 6Many people will come in my name saying, 'I am
the Messiah,'[65] and they will mislead many. 7Do not be troubled when
you hear of wars and rumors of wars. These things must happen,[66] but
that is not yet the end.[67] 8Nation will fight against nation, and kingdom
against kingdom.[68] There will be earthquakes in various places, and
famines. These are the start of birth pains.[69]

---

[64]Many mistakes in Bible explanation derive from a failure to know and follow the OT background of the NT. Particularly is this true in the case of the Olivet Discourse, where Jesus expressly says that the Abomination of Desolation, the key figure in the events of the end of this age, is to be understood on the basis of what *Daniel* had written. In 13:4 we already have a clear reference to Dan. 12:6-7 in which Daniel had asked, "How long will it be to the end?" The angel had answered, "When the shattering of the power of the holy people comes to an end **all these things will be accomplished**." These are the exact words of 13:4 and we are invited to go back to Daniel for further information. Daniel had been asking about the final events of the final vision which ends in the resurrection. We know that the first resurrection will occur at the Second Coming of Jesus (1 Cor. 15:23, etc.). It is to Daniel that we must go to see how Jesus' Olivet Discourse is to be understood. Daniel understood after inquiry what "all these things" were. They were related to the "end-time," which is certainly not "the end of time"! The visions of Daniel, in ch. 2, 7, 8, 9, 11 and 12, end with the establishment of the Kingdom of God, when the power of evil and the deceptions of Satan will be cut off forever. Thus all the visions end at the same future point of time. They complement each other and the Olivet Discourse is the ultimate revealing commentary on them by Jesus. The chronological information which unites the prophecies is "a time, times and half a time" (Dan. 7:25; 12:7; see Rev. 11:2-3; 12:6, 14; 13:5). Daniel's great prayer in ch. 9 was a plea for the restoration of the city and sanctuary, and when that would be. To make either AD 33 or AD 70 the endpoint of the 490 years of Dan. 9:24-27 leaves Daniel's prayer unanswered and thus the whole biblical hope unresolved. The *Pulpit Commentary* says wisely that "our Lord correlates the destruction of Jerusalem with the end of the world" (*Daniel*, p. 335). Daniel 12:1-3, quoted by Jesus, provides the indispensable key to end-times teaching — Great Tribulation, resurrection, and immortality in the future Kingdom (Mt. 13:43).

[65]Or perhaps, "I represent Christ as a minister of his."

[66]This is an echo of Dan. 2:28ff and 2:45. These events must happen in the divine plan. "The end is yet to be at the appointed time" (Dan. 11:27).

[67]That is, "not yet the end of the age" which is the subject of their question and Jesus' answer (13:4; Mt. 24:3; Lk. 21:7; Dan. 9:27).

[68]Cp. 2 Chron. 15:6; Isa. 19:2.

[69]Leading to the rebirth of the world when the Kingdom will be established worldwide (Mt. 19:28; cp. Tit. 3:5).

9“Be on your guard! They will hand you over[70] to the courts, you will
be beaten in the synagogues, and you will have to stand before governors
and kings for my sake, as a testimony to them. 10The Gospel[71] must first
be preached to all the nations. 11When they come to arrest you, do not
worry about what you should say. Say what you are given to say at that
time, because it will not be you speaking, but the holy spirit. 12Brother
will betray brother to death, and a father his child. Children will rise up
against their parents and have them put to death. 13You will be hated by
everyone because of my name, but whoever endures until the end[72] will
be saved.

14“When you see the ‘Abomination of Desolation’ standing where
he[73] should not be (readers, understand!), then whoever is in Judea

---

[70]Cp. Dan. 7:25 where the saints are to be handed over to the last blasphemous king (ruler) for “a time, times and half a time.” This is evidently the same period as Dan. 9:27, the last half of the final seven-year period (heptad, a “seven” of years).

[71]Matthew defines it as “this Gospel about the Kingdom” (Mt. 24:14) and this is always what the Gospel means in the NT. There is only one saving Gospel and it is defined by Jesus as the Gospel of the Kingdom. See Acts 8:12 for the early, clear definition of what it means to become a Christian.

[72]For the endurance under persecution of the holy people, cp. Dan. 11:32 and 12:12. Dan. 11:35 says that this trial will go on until the end. The end in question in the whole discourse is the end of the age about which the initial question was asked. Dan. 12:1 is of course the future Great Tribulation at the end of which the faithful will be finally delivered. AD 70 was a disaster for Israel and certainly did not produce the Kingdom of God on earth. So-called preterism fails to understand the Gospel.

[73]The masculine participle (*esteekota*) shows that Mark and Jesus had in mind a *person* as the Abomination, or perhaps a statue of a person. A number of good modern translations make this point. Albrecht’s good translation in German states: “According to the original Greek, the Abomination is to be understood to be a male person” (my trans. from the German). Deut. 19:16-29 show how abominable acts attract the wrath of God, just as the homosexuality of Sodom brought destruction in the days of Lot. Lam. 4:6 speaks of “the iniquity of the daughter of my people being worse than the sin of Sodom, which was overthrown in a moment. The punishment of my dear people is greater than that of Sodom, which was overthrown in an instant, supernaturally.” A supernatural destruction will likewise eliminate the antichrist (2 Thess. 2:8; Isa. 11:4). Jesus describes the Abomination of Desolation as explicitly the Abomination described by Daniel in Dan. 9:27; 11:31; 12:11, and a parallel reference in Dan. 8:13. The time period indicated by Dan. 9:27 is clear. The sacrilege connected with the altar will continue “until the decreed end is poured out on the desolator.” The critically important words “final and decisive end” are found only here in Dan 9:27, in Isa. 10:23 and 28:22, in which God’s wrath falls on the whole earth, or land. Paul reads these same

should escape to the mountains. 15Whoever is on the roof should not go
back inside the house to get anything. 16Whoever is out in the fields
should not go home to get his coat. 17How hard it will be for those who
are pregnant or nursing babies at that time! 18You should pray that this
will not happen during the winter. 19For those will be days of tribulation[74]
as never before — not since the beginning of the creation which God
created until now, nor ever will be. 20If God does not cut short those
days, no one will survive, but for the sake of His elect, His chosen ones,
He has cut them short. 21If anyone says to you at that time, 'Look, here is
the Messiah,' or 'Look, there he is,' do not believe it. 22For false
Messiahs and false prophets will appear, and they will perform
miraculous signs and wonders to deceive God's elect, if possible. 23Stay
alert! I have told you everything before it happens.

---

words as a prophecy to be fulfilled at the return of Christ. Rom. 9:28: "a final and decisive end" (quoting the LXX) is a great key to the apostolic application of the phrase "final and decisive end" of Isa. 10:23, 28:22 and Dan. 9:27. The decisive and final end is to be when Jesus comes back, not earlier. All attempts to apply the end of the 70th week to AD 33 or AD 70 are thus incoherent. The final wicked person will be broken "without hand" (Dan. 8:25; cp. 11:45). He will "come to **his** end" (Dan. 9:26b). The same evil figure, the Man of Sin, will be supernaturally destroyed at the coming of Jesus, according to 2 Thess. 2:8, which cites the final destruction of the Assyrian of Isa. 11:4. This gives the clue to the national identity of the final wicker ruler, or at least to the general area in which he will be active, which is not Europe but the Middle East. Dan. 7:11 says that the final blasphemous beast will be destroyed by fire, the lake of fire of Rev. 19:20-21. The Assyrian is destroyed in the sulfurous lake of fire of Isa. 30:33. See also notes on Luke 21:21ff.

[74]The very days themselves will be characterized by unparalleled affliction and distress (see Zech. 13:8; 14:2; Jer. 30:7). "It will be the characteristic of those days that they are tribulation itself" (Lange). Matthew and Mark agree that the signs of the second coming will occur "immediately" after (Mt. 24:29) the tribulation of those days. This chronological precision rules out any concept of AD 70 being the stated time of "great tribulation." The great tribulation, days in which it will be impossibly difficult for pregnant and nursing women (v. 17), are the immediate precursors of the future arrival of Jesus to inaugurate the Kingdom of God worldwide. The 70th "week" of Dan. 9 is the time of the Abomination of Desolation, and Jesus by placing the Abomination just before the Second Coming obviously read that 70th "week" as future, just before the end of the age. A fulfillment of the 70th week in AD 33 or AD 70 is thus decisively excluded.

24“In those days, after that tribulation,[75] the sun will grow dark, and
the moon will not shine, 25the stars will fall from the sky, and the
heavenly powers will be shaken. 26Then everybody will see the Son of
Man coming in clouds with overwhelming power and glory. 27He will
send out the angels to gather together all his chosen ones from every
direction, from the most distant part of the earth to the furthest point of
heaven.

28“Learn a parable from the fig tree. When its branches become soft
and sprout leaves, you know that summer is near. 29In the same way,
when you see these things happening, you will know that it is near, right
at the door. 30I am telling you the truth: this present evil society[76] will not
pass away until all these things happen. 31Heaven and earth will pass
away, but my words will not pass away.

32“No one knows that day or hour, not even the angels in heaven, nor
the Son,[77] but the Father alone. 33Keep watching, stay awake — because
you do not know when the time will come. 34It is like a man going on a
trip, who before leaving his house gave his servants the authority to do

---

[75]The Great Tribulation connected with the appearing of the Abomination. There is only one Great Tribulation, and it was obviously not in AD 70, which was not followed by the Coming of Jesus.

[76]Much unnecessary speculation has been based on the false idea that “*genea*” here means a period of 40 or 70 years. In Acts 1:7 Jesus said that “the times and seasons” for the coming of the future Kingdom are not known. He could have said, “I told you it will be 40 or 70 years.” The word “*genea*” here means this evil society or world-system lasting until the Second Coming. This evil system will not come to an end before all the striking events outlined by Jesus have occurred. The same use of *genea* as “brood” or “group of people characterized by a similar quality” is found in Prov. 30:11-14, Lk. 16:8 and Mk. 8:38 where *genea* is equivalent to age.

[77]This statement of Jesus that the Son of God does not know the time of the Parousia rules out any dogma about Jesus being God Himself. Orthodox authorities were reduced to hopeless evasion on this verse. Athanasius says that Jesus did not know as a human being! Augustine said that Jesus did not know in such a way as to impart the information! Lange is frank enough to admit that “dogmatic theology has not reached the point of being able to do perfect justice to the economic and dynamic import of the Son’s not knowing,” which is a confusing way of conceding that once one says “Jesus is GOD,” nonsense is made of Jesus’ plain and easy statement that he, the Son of God, did not know! Jesus also increased in wisdom (Lk. 2:52), again showing that he was a human being and not “God the Son.” Jesus is Son of God explicitly based on Luke 1:35; Mt. 1:18, 20 (“begotten, fathered in her”). The idea of a “beginningless beginning” (eternal generation) is not a coherent concept.

what he instructed each of them, and commanded the doorkeeper to stay
alert. 35So be alert, because you do not know when the owner of the
house is coming back — during the evening, in the middle of the night,
at dawn, or in the morning. 36And you do not want him to come suddenly
and find you sleeping. 37What I am telling you, I am telling everyone:
Stay awake!"

14 1It was two days before Passover and the Feast of Unleavened
Bread. The chief priests and the religious teachers were trying to
find a crafty way to arrest Jesus and kill him. 2"Let us not do it during the
festival," they said to themselves, "so the people will not riot."
3When Jesus was in Bethany at Simon the leper's house, while he
was sitting eating, a woman came in with an alabaster jar of very
expensive pure nard perfume. She broke open the jar and poured the
perfume over Jesus' head. 4Some there were annoyed and said, "What
sense is there in wasting this perfume? 5It could have been sold for a
year's wages, which could have been given to the poor." And they were
scolding her. 6But Jesus said, "Leave her alone. Why are you bothering
her? She has done something good for me. 7You will always have the
poor with you, and you can help them whenever you want. But you will
not always have me. 8She did what she could — she anointed my body
beforehand for burial. 9I am telling you the truth: wherever the Gospel[78] is
preached anywhere in the world, what she has done will be
remembered."
10Then Judas Iscariot, one of the twelve disciples, went to the chief
priests to make arrangements to betray Jesus to them. 11When they heard
the plan they were delighted, and promised to pay him. So Judas began
looking for a good time to betray Jesus.
12On the first day of the Feast of Unleavened Bread, when the
Passover lamb was being sacrificed,[79] Jesus' disciples asked him, "Where

---

[78]About the Kingdom of God, Mt. 24:14.

[79]The time specified is exactly the day when the nation was to celebrate the Passover. There is no hint that Jesus was going to keep it on a different day! Jesus died on the day after the lambs were slain. The meal was eaten when the 15th Nisan began, after the sun had set, ending the 14th. Jesus was thus crucified on Friday the 15th Nisan. John does not disagree with this: He speaks of the Passover week and notes that the Friday on which Jesus died was the "Preparation Day in Passover Week" (Jn. 19:14, NIRV), not

do you want us to go and prepare for you to eat the Passover?"[80] 13He
sent two of his disciples, telling them, "Go into the city, and there you
will meet a man carrying a water pot. Follow him, 14and ask the owner of
the house he enters, 'The teacher asks, "Where is my guest room where I
may eat the Passover with my disciples?"' 15He himself will show you a
large upstairs room, all prepared, and you can get things ready for us
there." 16The disciples went into the city, and found things just as he had
told them. They prepared the Passover meal.

17In the evening Jesus came there with the twelve. 18While they were
sitting eating, Jesus said, "I am telling you the truth: one of you will
betray me — one who is eating with me now." 19They were saddened and
each one asked, "Surely it is not me, is it?" 20Jesus said, "It is one of the
twelve, one of you who is sharing this food with me. 21The Son of Man
will go just as it is written he would. But shame on the man by whom the
Son of Man is betrayed! It would be better for that man if he had never
been born."

22While they were eating, Jesus took some bread and after blessing it,
he broke it and gave it to them. "Take it. This is my body," he said.
23Then he took a cup, gave thanks, and gave it to them. They all drank

---

the preparation *for* the Passover meal which had taken place the evening before. It was the preparation day (Friday) of Passover week. Jesus was eating the final meal with his disciples when the nation was celebrating the Passover (see among many sources the appendix to A.T Robertson's *Harmony of the Gospels*). The soldiers did not want to enter the praetorium not because of a Passover meal (eating the lamb) on the evening of that day. Jesus was eating at the time of the Passover as the text says. They would be anyway clean by evening. They did not want to be unclean *in respect of the additional feasting to occur during the week of Passover*. John speaks of the Passover *week*, not just the first day. Standard commentary makes our point: "Generally *the Feast of Unleavened Bread* would refer to Nisan 15 (Friday), but the following reference to the sacrifice of the *Passover* lamb indicates that Nisan 14 (Thursday) was what Mark had in mind (Nisan = March 27 to April 25). The celebration of the Feast of Unleavened Bread lasted eight days, beginning with the Passover meal. The celebrations were so close together that at times the names of both were used interchangeably" (NET Bible Commentary).

[80]It was the Passover which he intended to eat with the disciples. The lord's supper was introduced at that meal. The lord's supper reminds us now of the covenant of Jesus to share rulership in the Kingdom with his disciples (Lk. 22:28-30).

from it. 24He said, "This is my blood of the covenant.[81] It is being poured
out[82] on behalf of many. 25I am telling you the truth: I will not drink the
fruit of the vine[83] until that day when I drink it new in the Kingdom of
God."[84] 26After singing a hymn, they left for the Mount of Olives.

27"You will all abandon me," Jesus said to them, "because it is
written, 'I will strike down the shepherd, and the sheep will be
scattered.' 28But after I have been raised, I will go ahead of you to
Galilee." 29But Peter said, "Even if everyone else abandons you, I will
not." 30Jesus said to him, "I am telling you the truth: this very night you
will deny me three times before a rooster crows twice." 31But Peter
insisted, "Even if I have to die with you, I will never deny you!" And
they all said the same thing.

32They came to a place called Gethsemane, and Jesus said to his
disciples, "Sit here while I pray." 33He took with him Peter, James, and
John, and began to be terribly disturbed and distressed. 34Jesus said, "I
am crushed with grief to the point of death. Remain here and keep
awake." 35He went a little further before falling to the ground. He was
praying that if it were possible he might be spared what was coming.
36"Abba, Father, everything is possible for You. Please take this cup of
suffering from me," he said. "But I will do Your will, not mine." 37Jesus
returned to find them sleeping. "Simon, are you asleep?" he asked Peter.
"Could you not stay awake for one hour? 38Stay awake and pray that you
will not give in to temptation. The spirit is willing, but the flesh is
weak." 39He left again and prayed using the same words. 40Then he
returned once more and found them asleep; they could not stay awake.

---

[81]All covenants are ratified with blood, and the New Covenant with the blood of Messiah. The death of the Son of God (Rom. 5:10) is proof positive that he cannot *be* God, since God cannot die. The famous line of the hymn "'Tis mystery all, the immortal dies," is witness to the incoherence inflicted on the church by philosophical traditions, which are post-biblical.

[82]Recalling the suffering servant in Isa. 53:12.

[83]The word means wine, not unfermented grape juice. Alcohol, in strict moderation of course, is part of biblical celebrations in both Testaments (see Deut. 14:26; Ps. 104:15).

[84]The Kingdom to come at the return of Jesus in glory. "Kingdom" in Mark refers to that future new government. Lk. 19:11-27 with Dan. 7:14, 18, 22, 27 are excellent passages for explaining this fundamental truth about the Gospel of the Kingdom. Lk. 21:31 is the great event of the one future, visible arrival of Jesus to rule the world from Jerusalem.

They did not know what to say to him. 41The third time he returned and
said to them, "Are you still asleep, still resting? Enough now, because
the time has come. Look around you — the Son of Man is about to be
betrayed into the hands of sinful people. 42Get up and let us go. Look, my
betrayer is approaching."

43Immediately, while he was still speaking, Judas, one of the twelve,
arrived with a crowd armed with swords and clubs, sent by the chief
priests, religious teachers, and elders. 44The betrayer had arranged a
signal with them: "He is the one whom I kiss. Seize him, and lead him
away under guard." 45So Judas came to Jesus immediately. "Rabbi," he
said, and kissed Jesus. 46They laid their hands on Jesus and arrested him.
47But someone standing nearby pulled out his sword and struck the high
priest's servant, cutting off his ear. 48"Have you come to arrest me as you
would some violent criminal, with swords and clubs?" Jesus asked them.
49"Every day I was with you, teaching in the Temple, and you did not
arrest me then. But this is happening to fulfill the Scriptures." 50Then all
his disciples abandoned Jesus and ran away.

51One young man was following Jesus, wearing only a linen cloth.
They seized him, 52but he ran off naked, leaving the cloth behind.

53They took Jesus away to the high priest's house, and all the chief
priests, elders, and religious teachers gathered there. 54Peter followed at a
distance, as far as the courtyard of the high priest's house. He was sitting
with the guards, warming himself by the fire. 55The chief priests and the
whole council were trying to find some evidence to put Jesus to death,
but they were not finding any. 56Many were giving false testimony
against him, but their testimonies did not agree. 57Some stood up to speak
falsely against Jesus: 58"We heard him say, 'I will destroy this Temple
which human hands built, and in three days I will build another without
hands.'" 59But even then their testimony did not agree. 60The high priest
stood up in the council and asked Jesus, "Are you not going to say
anything in reply to these charges made against you?" 61But Jesus
remained silent and gave no reply. So the high priest asked him, "Are
you the Messiah, the Son of the Blessed One?" 62Jesus replied, "I am,
and you will see the Son of Man sitting at the right hand[85] of Power, and

---

[85]The one predicted to be at the right hand is the second lord of the all-important Ps. 110:1. The second lord is *adoni* in the Hebrew, and *adoni* is invariably, all 195 times, the title of non-Deity. "Son of Man" means human being, thus confirming Jesus'

coming with the clouds of heaven." 63The high priest tore his clothes and
asked, "Why do we need any more witnesses? 64You heard the
blasphemy. What is your opinion?" They all condemned him as guilty
and deserving to die. 65Some started to spit at him, and they blindfolded
him, beat him with their fists and said, "Prophesy!" The officers took
him and beat him.

66Meanwhile Peter was down in the courtyard. One of the high
priest's servant girls came by, 67and seeing Peter warming himself,
looked straight at him. "You were with Jesus of Nazareth too!" she said.
68But Peter denied it. "I do not know what you are talking about. I do not
understand it," he said. Then he went out to the porch. 69The servant girl
saw him there, and repeated to those standing nearby, "He is one of
them!" 70Again Peter denied it. A little later they said to Peter again,
"You really are one of them because you are a Galilean too." 71Peter
started to curse and swear, "I do not know this man you are talking
about!" 72Immediately a rooster crowed a second time. Peter remembered
what Jesus had said to him: "Before a rooster crows twice, you will deny
me three times." And he broke down and wept.

15 1Early the next morning, the chief priests, elders, religious
teachers, and the whole council consulted together. They bound
Jesus and sent him away to be handed over to Pilate. 2Pilate asked him,
"Are you the king of the Jews?" Jesus replied, "It is as you say." 3The
chief priests were accusing him of many things. 4Pilate asked him, "Are
you not going to say anything? See how many charges they are bringing
against you!" 5But Jesus did not answer any more, which amazed Pilate.

6Because it was the Passover feast it was Pilate's custom to release
one prisoner to the people, whoever they asked him for. 7A man called
Barabbas had been imprisoned with a group of revolutionaries who had
committed murder during an uprising. 8The crowd went to Pilate and
asked him to release a prisoner as he usually did. 9"Do you want me to
release the king of the Jews to you?" he asked them, 10because he
realized that the chief priests had handed Jesus over to him because of

---

understanding of the second lord, not as Deity but a supremely exalted human being, the "man Messiah" of 1 Tim. 2:5; Lk. 2:11. Stephen as he died also saw the Son of Man, my lord, *adoni*, at the right hand of God (Acts 7:56). He was not wrong to address a prayer to him (see Jn. 14:14 where prayer to Jesus is authorized).

jealousy. 11But the chief priests incited the crowd to have him release
Barabbas to them instead. 12"So what do you want me to do with this
man you call the king of the Jews?" he asked them. 13"Crucify him!" they
shouted back. 14"Why?" Pilate asked them. "What crime has he
committed?" They shouted even louder, "Crucify him!" 15Pilate, wishing
to please the crowd, released Barabbas to them, and after having Jesus
flogged, handed him over to be crucified.

16The soldiers took him away to the palace, that is, the Praetorium,
where they called together the whole Roman cohort. 17They put a royal
purple robe on him, and wove together a crown of thorns, and crowned
him with it. 18Then they began to call out, "We salute you, king of the
Jews!" 19They kept beating him on the head with a rod, spat at him, and
mockingly knelt and bowed before him. 20When they had finished
mocking him, they took off the purple robe and put his own clothes on
him. Then they took him to be crucified. 21They forced a passer-by,
Simon of Cyrene, who was coming from the countryside, to carry his
cross. Simon was the father of Alexander and Rufus.

22Then they led Jesus to the place called Golgotha, which is translated
"Place of a Skull." 23They offered him wine mixed with myrrh, but he did
not take any. 24Then they crucified him. They divided up his clothes,
casting lots to decide what each man would get. 25It was 9 a.m. when
they put him on the cross. 26The charge against him read: "The King of
the Jews."

27They crucified two criminals with him, one on his right and one on
his left. [28And the Scripture was fulfilled which says: "He was numbered
with sinners."][86] 29People passing by ridiculed him, shaking their heads in
contempt: "Ha! You who are going to destroy the Temple and rebuild it
in three days, 30save yourself and come down from the cross!" 31In the
same way the chief priests and the religious teachers mocked him among
themselves: "He could save others, but he cannot save himself. 32Let this
Messiah, the king of Israel, now come down from the cross so that we
can see it and 'believe'!" The ones who were being crucified with him
also insulted him.

---

[86] Early manuscripts do not contain verse 28.

33At noon darkness spread over the whole land until three p.m. 34At
three p.m. Jesus cried out loudly, "Eloi, Eloi, lama sabachthani?"[87] which
translated means, "My God, my God, why have You abandoned me?"
35When some of those standing there heard this, they said, "Listen, he is
calling for Elijah." 36Someone ran and put a sponge soaked in sour wine
on a stick and held it up to Jesus to drink. He said, "Let us see if Elijah
will come to take him down." 37Then Jesus gave a loud cry, and breathed
his last. 38The Temple veil was torn in two from top to bottom. 39When
the centurion standing in front of him saw how he died, he said, "This
man really was the Son of God!"

40Among the women who were watching from a distance were Mary
Magdalene, Mary the mother of James the younger and of Joses, and
Salome. 41These were the women who had followed Jesus and taken care
of him when he was in Galilee, along with many other women who had
come with him to Jerusalem.

42When the evening of the Preparation Day came, the day before the
Sabbath,[88] 43Joseph of Arimathea, a leading member of the council, who
was himself waiting for the Kingdom of God,[89] gathered up courage to
go to Pilate and ask for Jesus' body. 44Pilate was surprised that Jesus was
dead so soon, so he called the centurion and asked him if Jesus had died
already. 45Once he found out from the centurion, he gave permission to
Joseph to take the body. 46Joseph bought a linen cloth, took Jesus down
from the cross, wrapped him in the sheet and placed him in a rock tomb.
Then he rolled a stone against the entrance. 47Mary Magdalene and Mary
the mother of Joses saw where he was laid.

16 1When the Sabbath was over, Mary Magdalene, Mary the mother
of James, and Salome bought spices[90] so that they could go and
anoint Jesus. 2Very early in the morning on the first day of the week, just

---

[87]In Aramaic.

[88]Greek *paraskeue*, the word for Friday as the day before the Sabbath. The preparation day for the weekly sabbath. Jesus rose on "the third day" since Friday, which is Sunday (Lk. 24:21 is decisive for this).

[89]He understood the Kingdom of God much more clearly than contemporary Bible readers and churchgoers. He knew that it meant a new world order and government with Messiah presiding in Jerusalem. It obviously had not already come! As a Christian disciple (Mt. 27:57) he was awaiting its arrival (cp. Heb. 10:13).

[90]Others had bought spices before the Sabbath began.

after sunrise, they went to the tomb. 3They were wondering, "Who will
roll away the stone for us from the entrance to the tomb?" 4But when
they arrived and looked, they saw that the very large stone had already
been rolled away. 5They went into the tomb and saw a young man sitting
to the right, wearing a white robe, and they were amazed. 6 "Do not be
amazed," he said to them. "You are looking for Jesus of Nazareth, who
was crucified. He has been raised; he is not here. 7Take a look at the
place where they laid him. Now go and tell his disciples and Peter, 'He is
going ahead of you to Galilee. You will see him there just as he told
you.'" 8They went out and ran from the tomb, because they were shaking
and terrified. They did not say anything to anyone because they were
afraid.[91]

9When he had risen early on the first day of the week, he appeared
first to Mary Magdalene, from whom he had cast out seven demons.
10She went and told those who had been with him, as they mourned and
wept. 11When they heard that he was alive and had been seen by her, they
did not believe it.

12Later he appeared in a different form[92] to two of them as they
walked on their way to the countryside. 13They went away and reported it
to the rest, but they did not believe them either.

14After that he appeared to the eleven disciples as they were eating.
He reprimanded them for their unbelief and hardness of heart, because
they had not believed those who had seen him after he had risen. 15He
said to them, "Go into all the world and preach the Gospel[93] to the whole

---

[91]The rest of Mark (16:9-20) is not found in some of the major early manuscripts.

[92]The Greek *morphe,* "form," means outward appearance and it is the word used of the historical and visible Jesus. It certainly does not refer to an invisible, so-called "preexistent," imagined Jesus in Phil. 2:6. The NIV translation there, "being in very nature God," is a seriously misleading departure from the meaning of the Greek text in the interest of promoting a pre-human and thus non-human Jesus.

[93]The saving Gospel should constantly and invariably be defined with reference to Jesus' own initial definition and preaching of the Christian Gospel in Mark 1:14-15. The Kingdom of God in Mark is without exception the Kingdom of God which has not yet come, and was expected by Joseph of Arimathea (15:43). Churches have continuously reduced this Messianic Kingdom to some sort of ethics "in the heart" or to a present "social gospel." The Messianic Kingdom of God expected and predicted by all the prophets, especially Daniel, needs to be reinstated at the heart of the saving Gospel; otherwise the Church will continue to reject Jesus, by rejecting his Gospel while claiming to "accept" him. The vague prospect of an afterlife as a disembodied

creation. 16Anyone who believes and is baptized[94] will be saved,[95] but
anyone who does not believe will be condemned. 17These signs will
accompany those who believe: In my authority they will cast out
demons, they will speak in new languages,[96] 18and they will pick up
snakes. If they drink any deadly poison it will not hurt them. They will
lay hands on the sick and they will recover."

19Then the lord Jesus, after he had spoken to them, was taken up into
heaven and took his seat at the right hand of God.[97] 20They went out and
preached the Gospel[98] everywhere, while the lord worked with them and
confirmed the Gospel-word by the accompanying signs.[99]

---

soul, at death, has replaced the Kingdom of God destined to come on earth, as understood and preached as Gospel by the earliest communities of Christians.

[94]In water, for the reception of the spirit. Water baptism is commanded as necessary obedience to Jesus throughout the NT (Mt. 28:19-20). "In one spirit we were all baptized into one body" (1 Cor. 12:13). This is the NT pattern throughout. There are never "two levels" of faith. Each believer must grow in grace in knowledge.

[95]Acts 8:12 is the model of the early church's theology of initiation into the body of Messiah. The essential information about the Gospel of the Kingdom and the identity of Jesus Messiah and the One God was required for initiation into the Church by water baptism.

[96]Fulfilled in a spectacular way in Acts 2 when the Apostles "began to speak in other languages," under the influence of the spirit. This was a demonstrable miracle to show where God was at work, and not intended to bridge the language gap, since Peter was able to communicate with them in his sermon in Greek, as the international language. Subsequent claims to the same "gift of languages" are not convincing and those who practice them in most cases never "pray to interpret" (1 Cor. 14:13). There must always be a verification of the miracle of real, intelligible language and communication, as in Acts 2. The phrase "speak in tongues" is misleading and does not reflect the Greek "speak in languages."

[97]As the *adoni*, my lord, not Lord, of Ps. 110:1. *Adoni* is in all of its 195 occurrences never the title of Deity. It defines the risen Messiah Jesus as the supremely exalted human being, certainly not a "second God" in a Trinity, which is a post-biblical development under the influence of Greek philosophy.

[98]Of the Kingdom and the things concerning Jesus (Acts 8:12).

[99]Miracles are of course possible any time God wills, but Heb. 2:3-4 notes that the accompanying signs were a special feature of the first generation of believers. See 2 Cor. 12:12 for miracles as the accrediting signs of Apostles. We do not today have Apostles at the level of the twelve. The miraculous must be carefully verified and not accepted gullibly, especially since the miraculous can be counterfeited (2 Thes. 2:9; Mt. 7:21-23).

Luke

1 1 Many have taken in hand to write up a narrative of the events which
have been fulfilled among us, 2 just as they were handed down to us
by those who from the beginning were eyewitnesses and servants of the
Gospel-Word.[1] 3 In view of this fact, since I have carefully investigated
everything from the beginning,[2] I also thought it would be good to write
out a clear account for you, most excellent Theophilus, 4 so that you may
know the absolute truth about the things you have been taught.

5 During the rule of Herod, king of Judea, there was a priest named
Zacharias, of the priestly division of Abijah.[3] He was married to
Elizabeth, who also came from the line of Aaron the priest. 6 They both
did what was right in God's eyes, following blamelessly all the Lord's
commandments and requirements. 7 They had no children since Elizabeth
could not become pregnant, and they were both growing old.

8 While Zacharias was fulfilling his priestly duties before God in his
division, 9 according to the priestly custom, he was chosen by lot to go
into the Lord's temple and burn incense. 10 A large crowd of people were

---

[1]The Gospel throughout the NT is always the Gospel about the Kingdom of God. It did not need to be repeated in its full title, just as we know that USA stands for United States of America and not the University of South Australia. The Gospel of the Kingdom of God is the saving Gospel as preached first by Jesus (Mk. 1:14-15; Heb. 2:3). Luke unites the pre-cross and post-cross preaching of the same Gospel by reminding us in Acts 1:3; 1:6; 8:12; 19:8; 20:24-25; 28:23, 30, 31 that until the end of the age (the Second Coming, Mt. 28:19-20) there is one saving Gospel, "the Gospel about the Kingdom and the things concerning the name of Jesus Christ." Acts 8:12 is an early summary creed, showing what was required for converts prior to baptism. The Gospel of the Kingdom appears in the shorthand, in-house phrase "word of God," "word of the Kingdom," and "word." The public is severely misled by not recognizing this rather easy fact. "Word of God" is not in Scripture just a synonym for the Bible. The Bible refers to itself as the Scriptures, holy writings. Jesus defined the limits of the Hebrew canon as the "Law, Prophets and Psalms/Writings" (Lk. 24:44).

[2]Luke was the model "Berean" who searched out everything conscientiously, talking to eye-witnesses. Even at common-sense level, we all know that eye-witnesses have an enormous advantage over those living centuries or millennia later! Scripture as we have it, Old and New Testaments, is the fixed basis for all discussion of Christianity as Jesus and his Apostles taught it.

[3]The 8th division of the 24 "courses" of priests (1 Chron. 24:10). 888 is the numerical value of Jesus in Greek (cp. 666 for Antichrist). 8 following 7 is a number of new beginnings.

outside praying at this time of offering incense. 11An angel of the Lord[4]
appeared to him, standing at the righthand side of the altar of incense.
12Zacharias was startled when he saw the angel, and he was afraid. 13But
the angel said to him, "Do not be afraid, Zacharias. Your prayer has been
heard, and your wife Elizabeth will bear you a son, and you are to name
him John. 14You will have joy and happiness, and many people will
celebrate his birth. 15He will be great in the eyes of the Lord. He will not
drink wine or any other alcoholic drink,[5] and he will be filled with holy
spirit[6] while still in his mother's womb.[7] 16He will bring many people of
Israel back to the Lord their God. 17He will go before Him[8] in the spirit

---

[4]I.e. the one Lord God of Israel, the GOD of biblical monotheism, the Father of our Lord Jesus Christ. The word *kurios* was used by the LXX and equally by the writers of NT Greek Scripture (the only Scripture we have for the New Covenant) to reproduce the Hebrew name of God YHVH. No NT writer makes any issue at all about preserving the Hebrew name (though they could have done this easily). It is therefore a corruption of and implied attack on Greek Scripture to insist on inserting it into the NT documents.

[5]This was a special regulation for Nazarites and certainly not for the people of Israel or the New Covenant community. Alcohol, used in proper moderation, was a God-given gift for celebration. Compare Jesus' turning 120 gallons of water into alcohol at the wedding in Cana. Some American fundamentalist churches turned that wine into grape juice, an equal "miracle"! *Oinos* in Greek does not mean grape juice. If it did, Paul would have said, "Do not get drunk on grape juice, but be filled with the spirit"! (Eph. 5:18).

[6]The divine, operational, creative presence and power of God — certainly not a "third Person," unknown to the NT. The imagined third Person is never worshiped and never prayed to and never sends greetings. The spirit of Jesus and of God in the NT is the operational presence and power of the Father and the exalted Son, very personal as coming from persons, as their outreach and influence, but never a "third Person" of a Trinity. The Comforter or *paraclete* of John's gospel is defined as the risen Jesus in 1 John 2:1. Jesus departed from the disciples and, not leaving them as orphans, was present with them, after he rose, as the holy spirit Comforter (cp. 2 Cor. 3:17-18).

[7]This is one of many scriptural testimonies to the fact that a fetus counts fully as a human person, before birth. The concept of taking the life of, thus murdering, the unborn is startlingly in opposition to the fact that the miracle of new life and personality takes place in the womb.

[8]The work of the lord Jesus Messiah is identified with the work of the Lord God. They work as one in purpose (Jn. 10:30). This does not of course mean that Jesus *is* the Father, as quite wrongly held by Oneness Pentecostals. Nor is Jesus a second God, as mistakenly later developed by "church fathers" and argued about for centuries! Jesus was a Jew and believed, as did his followers, in the One and Only God of Israel (Mk. 12:29; Jn. 17:3, etc). "God" means the Father some 1300 times in the NT.

and power of Elijah, to turn the hearts of parents to their children, and
the disobedient to the understanding of the upright, in order to make a
people ready for the Lord."
18"How will I know this is true?" Zacharias asked the angel. "I am an
old man, and my wife is elderly too." 19The angel answered, "I am
Gabriel. I stand in God's presence, and I was sent to bring you this good
news. 20Look — you will be mute, unable to speak, until what I have told
you happens, because you did not believe my words,[9] which will come
true at the proper time."
21The people outside were waiting for Zacharias, wondering why he
was taking so long in the temple. 22When he did come out he was not
able to speak to them, and they realized he had seen a vision in the
temple. He was making signs to them, and he was completely mute.
23When he had finished his period of priestly service, he went back
home.
24After this his wife Elizabeth became pregnant, and she stayed
hidden inside for five months. 25"The Lord has graciously done this for
me to take away my disgrace in people's eyes," she said.
26In the sixth month of Elizabeth's pregnancy God sent the angel
Gabriel to the town of Nazareth[10] in Galilee, 27to a young[11] virgin named
Mary. She was engaged to be married to a man named Joseph, of the
descendants of David. 28The angel came to her house and said,
"Greetings, you who are richly blessed! The Lord is with you." 29But
Mary was very confused at what he told her, wondering what this
greeting might mean. 30"Do not be afraid, Mary," the angel said,
"because you have found grace with God.[12] 31And listen: you will
become pregnant and give birth to a son, and you will name him Jesus.

---

[9]A crippling mood of "learned" unbelief continues to plague much of the theological enterprise. Scholars seem mesmerized by the notion that it is not possible ever to get back with certainty to the actual words of Jesus or the earliest witnesses. They fail to note that unless we have access to the real words of Jesus there is no Christian faith available, since Christianity in the NT is either based on the words of Jesus, and his Apostles and Bible writers, or is unknowable and lost. Not to believe what God has said brings its own penalty of non-comprehension (see 2 Thess. 2:10-14).

[10]This was hardly what we would call a town today. It was only recently found by archeologists and may have been about 4 acres in size!

[11]Most likely in her early teens.

[12]The One God of Israel and of the Bible.

32He will be very great, and he will be called the Son of the Most High.
The Lord God will give him the throne of his ancestor David, 33and he
will be king over the house of Jacob forever; his Kingdom will never
come to an end." 34Mary said to the angel, "How will this be possible
since I have never been with a man?" 35The angel answered, "Holy
spirit[13] will come upon you, and the power of the Most High will
overshadow you. For that reason precisely[14] the holy child to be
fathered[15] will be called the Son of God.[16] 36And Elizabeth, your relative,

---

[13]Holy spirit here is the operational presence and power of God to effect a biological miracle. The parallel phrase "power of the Most High" repeats and reinforces the meaning of "holy spirit." The disaster of later theological speculation is signaled by the amazing misunderstanding of Justin Martyr who believed that the power coming over Mary was a preexisting *Son* engineering his own conception! Thus the departure into a pagan, crypto-Gnostic Jesus was under way by 150 AD and earlier in the writings of Ignatius and others.

[14]"Precisely for this reason [and no other] he will be called the Son of God," meaning that this was who he was and is! The KJV is misleading with its "wherefore also," to promote by subtle insinuation the idea that there is *another* reason for being the Son of God! Luke is an embarrassment to later claims of "orthodoxy." Houdini-like, some attempt to escape the obvious here that the origin of the Son of God, Jesus, was in the womb of Mary. To posit a second "origin" either just before Genesis or in eternity is to give to the Son a double origin. Massive confusion then disturbs the Bible's beautiful and simple account of the origin of the Son of God. All humans originate in the womb of their mothers, and conception and begetting occur at the same time. "Orthodoxy" rejected these accounts of who Jesus is and invented a Son who because his origin was in eternity past could never by definition be genuinely human. 1 John 4:2, 2 John 7 were meant to warn against any Jesus who was not fully human. 1 John 4:3 reads, "Whoever does not believe in *that* Jesus…" i.e., the one defined as really human in 1 John 4:2. The threat to true faith arises from belief in a false Jesus, the invention of tradition and not the historical Jesus of Scripture.

[15]Begotten, which means brought into existence (*gennao*). Thus the "eternal begetting" of the Son is false to the Bible. As Trinitarian scholar McCleod notes, "It is uncertain what content if any may be given to the phrase 'eternal begetting.'" This is a "polite" admission of a nonsense phrase in the "orthodox" system, since one cannot have a "beginningless beginning." The only *biblical* begetting of the Son of God was in Mary (Mt. 1:20: "begotten in her," by miracle some 2000 years ago). This of course means that Luke and those he wrote about, and those to whom he described the true faith, were not believers in a triune God. The Son was the human being brought into existence by biological miracle in Mary.

[16]This is a fundamentally important defining of the term "Son of God," far removed from the post-biblical idea of a pre-human or "preexisting" Son, second member of a Trinity. Leading commentator Godet says: "We have here from the mouth of the angel

even she has become pregnant in her old age. The woman people said
could not conceive is now in her sixth month of pregnancy! 37For nothing
will be impossible with God." 38And Mary said, "I am the Lord's servant.
May your word to me come true." Then the angel left her.
39At that time Mary went in a hurry to a town of Judea in the hills,
40to Zacharias' house. She called out to Elizabeth as she entered the
home. 41When Elizabeth heard Mary's greeting, the baby leaped inside
her. Elizabeth was filled with holy spirit 42and cried out, "How blessed
you are among women, and how blessed is your baby! 43Why am I so
honored that the mother of my lord[17] would visit me? 44As soon as I
heard your greeting, my baby jumped for joy inside me. 45How blessed
you are for believing that what was spoken to you by the Lord will be
fulfilled."[18]

---

himself an authentic explanation of the term Son of God…After this explanation Mary could only understand the title [and so should we!] in the sense: a human being of whose existence God Himself is the immediate author. It does not convey the idea of preexistence [and thus makes impossible the later idea of 'God the Son']." The later "dogmatic" definition of the Son of God as "eternally begotten" suppressed the easy truth reported by Luke. That "eternal begetting" is foreign to the Bible is widely recognized by scholars. Once Jesus was given a pre-history, prior to his begetting in Mary, an appalling confusion about who Jesus is ensued. Van Buren deplored this ruination of the beautifully simple accounts of Matthew and Luke (and John when the later, post-biblical confusion is not read back into John 1): "If one were to make the claim of priority in a temporal sense for Jesus, one would be claiming that Jesus of Nazareth, born of Mary, had existed with God before the creation of the world. **That claim would be worse than unintelligible**; it would destroy all coherence in the essential Christian claim that Jesus was truly a human being, that the word *became* flesh. The humanity of Jesus could hardly be eternal in that sense and still be 'like us in all things, excepting sin' (Council of Chalcedon; Heb. 2:17). Jesus of Nazareth began his life, that is, began to exist at a definite time in history: the word became *flesh*" (*A Theology of the Jewish-Christian Reality*, p. 82).

[17]"My lord" is the title for the Messiah as foreseen in the divine oracle of Ps. 110:1. The Hebrew word *adoni*, my lord, is never in all 195 of its occurrences a title of Deity. It is always a reference to an exalted human being, occasionally an angel. "My lord" (Messiah) is the common description among the biblical community for God's uniquely begotten Son (Ps. 2:7; 2 Sam. 7:14). Jesus is "my lord," or "our lord," and these are the titles appropriate for the ultimate King of Israel, the Messiah, son of David. Jesus is lord, not Lord God some 200 times in the NT. He is the "lord Messiah" or "Messiah lord" (Lk. 2:11), as clearly distinguished from the Lord God (1 Tim. 2:5).

[18]This is the essence of NT faith — believing the words and promises of God. Zacharias had already been punished supernaturally for failing to believe the angel. This is a fair

46Mary said, "My soul praises the Lord, 47and my spirit is full of joy
in God my Savior, 48because He took notice of the low status of His
servant. From now on every generation will know I am blessed. 49The
Mighty One has done great things for me. Holy is His name, 50and His
mercy lasts for all generations to those who stand in awe of Him. 51With
the power of His strong arm He has done mighty works; He has scattered
those who were proud in their attitudes. 52He pulls down the powerful
from their thrones, and lifts up those who are humble. 53He fills the
hungry with all that is good, and sends the rich away empty-handed. 54He
has helped His servant Israel, in remembrance of His mercy, 55as He
spoke to our fathers, to Abraham and his descendants for the Age to
Come."[19] 56Mary stayed with Elizabeth for three months and then went
back home.

57The time came for Elizabeth to have her baby, and she gave birth to
a son. 58Her neighbors and relatives heard how the Lord had been so
mercifully kind to her, and they celebrated with her.

59On the eighth day it was time to circumcise the baby, and they were
going to name him Zacharias after his father. 60But his mother said, "No,
he is to be called John." 61They replied, "But none of your relatives has
that name." 62They gestured to Zacharias as to what he wanted to name
his son. 63He asked for something to write on and wrote, "His name is
John." They were all surprised. 64Immediately he could talk again, and he
spoke out loud, praising God. 65Everyone living nearby was in awe of
what had happened, and news spread throughout the hill country of
Judea. 66All who heard about it wondered and asked, "What will this
child grow up to be?" For the hand of the Lord was truly with him.

---

warning for us all. Angels are to be believed as divine messengers. Not to believe them is to imply that God has made a false promise! People often wind up in the same unbelief by twisting the words of Scripture to bring them into line with a much later doctrine originating in post-biblical councils.

[19]I take *eis ton aiona* to mean "in regard to the Age to Come," the Kingdom of God. God did not speak "forever," but more directly of the future Age to Come of the Kingdom of God to come on earth at the future Second Coming of Jesus to rule from Jerusalem, with the saints of all the ages (Dan. 7:14, 18, 22, 27, RSV). The Age to Come is contrasted everywhere in the NT with "the present evil age" which is under the domination of the very deceptive Satan, god of this system (2 Cor. 4:4; Gal. 1:4; Eph. 2:2; Rev. 12:9; 1 John 5:19). "Eternal life" means in fact "the life of the Age to Come" based on Dan. 12:2.

67Then his father Zacharias was filled with holy spirit and spoke this
prophecy: 68"Blessed be the Lord God of Israel, because He has taken
care of us and liberated His people. 69He has raised up a power of
salvation for us from the line of his servant David,[20] 70as He promised
through His holy prophets from the past: 71salvation from our enemies
and those who hate us. 72He shows mercy to our fathers and remembers
His sacred covenant — 73the oathbound promise He made to Abraham
our father. 74He rescues us from our enemies so that we can serve Him
without fear, 75by being holy and doing what is right before Him all our
days. 76And you, child, will be called the prophet of the Most High, for
you will go ahead of the Lord to prepare His ways, 77to give knowledge
of salvation to His people by the forgiveness of their sins. 78Because of
our God's tender heart of mercy, the sunrise from on high will visit us,
79to shine on those who sit in the dark and the shadow of death, to guide
our feet on the path of peace."

80The boy John grew and became strong in spirit, and he was in the
desert until the time came for his public appearance to Israel.

2 1In those days a decree went out from Caesar Augustus that a census
be taken of everyone in the empire.[21] 2This was a census prior to the
one under governor Quirinius of Syria.[22] 3All went to register for the
census, each to his native town. 4Since Joseph was of the house and
family of David, he traveled from Nazareth in Galilee to Bethlehem, the
city of David, in Judea, 5in order to register together with Mary, who was

---

[20]This inspired praise from Zacharias is delightfully free of the later fearful complications about the origin of Jesus, devised by post-biblical "church fathers" who turned the Messiah into a pre-human and thus essentially non-human person! Certainly Jesus was the unique expression of the One God, as His sinless Son, miraculously begotten. But he is never called "the Lord God," or "the Almighty," and never God the Son, nor the "God-man." The Father is called God, and often "**the** [one] God" about 1300 times in the NT. The definite article appearing often for the One God designates Him as *the* One God of Israel and of Abraham, Isaac and Jacob and of Jesus. Someone who has a GOD is not GOD! "The God" is the one true God of Israel and of Jesus, and that one God is to be carefully distinguished from all other "Gods."

[21]Literally, the whole world.

[22]Some render "The census happened before Quirinius was governor of Syria." See Nigel Turner, *Grammatical Insights into the New Testament*, pp. 23, 24.

engaged to him and was pregnant.[23] 6While they were there, the time
came for her to have her baby. 7She gave birth to her firstborn son, and
wrapped him up in strips of cloth and laid him in a feeding trough,
because there was no room for them in the guestroom.

8Nearby some shepherds were staying out in the fields, watching over
their flocks during the night. 9An angel of the Lord suddenly stood in
front of them, and the glory of the Lord shone all around them, and they
were terribly afraid. 10But the angel said to them, "Do not be afraid!
Listen, I am bringing you good news which will bring immense joy to
everyone. 11Today in the city of David has been born for you a Savior,
who is the Messiah lord.[24] 12Your sign of confirmation will be this: you
will find the child wrapped in strips of cloth and lying in a feeding
trough." 13Suddenly a large gathering of heavenly beings appeared with
the angel, praising God: 14"Glory to God in the highest, and on earth
peace to all people with whom He is pleased!"

15When the angels had gone away into heaven, the shepherds said to
each other, "Let us go straight to Bethlehem and see what has happened,

---

[23]This of course, as Luke has told us, was a supernatural pregnancy.

[24]Ps. 110:1: the second lord, *adoni*, my lord Messiah. This is the NT's favorite proof text for describing the relationship between the One God, the Father and the man Messiah Jesus (cp. 1 Tim. 2:5). The false capital on the second lord of Psalm 110:1 misleads many into thinking that the Hebrew word is *Adonai* (Lord God) when it is not! *Adoni* is the non-Deity title all 195 times. It is astonishing that even a brilliant commentator like Henry Alford could fail to distinguish between the Lord God and the lord Messiah ("I see no way of understanding this *kurios* [lord in 2:11] but as corresponding to the word Jehovah"). Ps. 110:1 should have prevented this appalling confusion. *Adoni* is "my lord" and Jesus is never called "the Lord GOD" or the Almighty. He is the supremely exalted human lord Messiah, descendant of David, second Adam, whose origin was in Mary by miracle. Luke 1:35 gives the explicit reason for Jesus being the Son of God, but later "orthodoxy" discarded these matchless accounts and substituted an alien God the Son, giving him a double origin, eternally and in recent times. This distorted the monotheism of Israel and of Jesus and the NT writers. Yahweh is the personal name of the Father and in no case can one say "my Yahweh"! Luke 1:43 confirms the correct understanding of who Jesus is. Elizabeth recognized Mary as "the mother of my lord" (from Ps. 110:1, the second lord, *adoni*), not the mother of my GOD! The lord Messiah is exactly the same as the King Messiah of Luke 23:2 (cp. Acts 2:34-36). "For the designation of Christ as lord, there is a special point of connection and explanation in Ps. 110:1. Cp. 1 Cor. 8:6, 'For us there is one God, the Father and one lord Jesus Messiah'" (Cremer, *Biblico-Theological Lexicon of the NT*, p. 383).

which the Lord has made known to us." 16They hurried off and found their way to Mary and Joseph, and the baby lying in the feeding trough. 17When they had seen this for themselves, they spread the news of the announcement given to them of this baby. 18Everyone who heard about it was astonished at what the shepherds told them, 19while Mary thought about these things and pondered them in her heart. 20The shepherds went back to the fields, honoring and praising God for everything they had heard and seen, just as it had been reported to them.

21After eight days the baby was circumcised and given the name Jesus, the name given by the angel before he was conceived.[25] 22When the time of ceremonial purification was completed according to the Law of Moses, his parents took him to Jerusalem to present him to the Lord 23(as it is written in the Law of the Lord: "Every mother's firstborn son is dedicated as holy to the Lord") 24and to offer a sacrifice according to the Law of the Lord: "a pair of turtledoves or two young pigeons."

25There was a man named Simeon living in Jerusalem. This man lived rightly and reverently, eagerly awaiting the restoration of Israel,[26] and holy spirit was with him. 26It had been revealed to him through the holy spirit that he would not die before he saw the Lord's Messiah.[27] 27In the spirit he came into the Temple, and when Jesus' parents brought the

---

[25]The name of Jesus is the only item which "preexisted" the actual existence of Jesus. As Son of God, Jesus was a special new creation by miracle in the womb of Mary. To add another, earlier existence to him is to confuse his identity. But "orthodoxy" gradually achieved just such a confusion.

[26]The Kingdom of God on earth in the future at the return of Jesus to the earth. This is the hallmark of sound NT faith. It is faith in the Gospel, as Jesus commanded it in Mark 1:14-15. Joseph of Arimathea was also waiting for the Kingdom after the death of Jesus (Mk. 15:43), and as a disciple he was not wrong! The disciples who had been thoroughly trained by Jesus and had themselves been preaching the Gospel of the Kingdom were also anxious in their famous last question in Acts 1:6 to know when the promised restoration and consolation of the nation of Israel would occur. Their question was the right one, although no times and seasons could be known as to how long it might be. Acts 3:21 points out that heaven must continue to retain the Messiah until the "time for the great restoration of all things predicted by the prophets" should eventually happen. This lies still in the future since Jesus has not yet returned to establish the Kingdom worldwide.

[27]"The anointed of the LORD." See for the background 1 Sam. 24:6, 10; 26:9, 16, 23; 2 Sam. 1:14, 16; 19:21. Jesus is the royal descendant of David and heir to the throne of David to be restored on earth when Jesus comes back (Acts 3:21; Mt. 19:28; Rev. 5:10).

little boy Jesus to be dedicated as the Law required, 28Simeon took Jesus
in his arms, thanked God, and said, 29"Lord, now You can let your
servant go in peace as You promised, 30because my eyes have seen Your
salvation 31that You have made available to everyone, 32a light of
revelation to the Gentiles, and the glory of Your people Israel."

33Jesus' father and mother were amazed at what was being said about
him. 34Simeon blessed them, and said to Jesus' mother Mary, "Listen,
this child is destined to be the downfall and rising of many in Israel, and
to be a sign which will be opposed. 35For you it will be like a sword
piercing right through your soul, so that the thoughts of many minds will
be revealed."

36And there was a prophetess named Anna there. She was the
daughter of Phanuel from the tribe of Asher, and she was very old. She
had been married for seven years, 37and then had been a widow to the age
of eighty-four. She was always in the Temple, serving night and day with
fasting and prayer. 38She came up at that moment and began thanking
God, talking about the child to everyone who was waiting for the
liberation of Jerusalem.[28]

39When they had completed everything required by the Law of God,
they went back to their hometown of Nazareth in Galilee. 40The little boy
continued to grow strong, becoming full of wisdom, with God's grace on
him.

41Every year Jesus' parents went to Jerusalem for the Passover
festival. 42When Jesus was twelve, they went to the festival as usual.
43When it was over and time to return home, the boy Jesus stayed behind
in Jerusalem, but his parents did not realize it. 44They thought he was
with everybody else traveling back. A day went by before they started
looking for him among their relatives and friends. 45When they did not
find him they returned to Jerusalem and looked for him there. 46Three
days later they found him in the Temple, sitting among the religious
teachers, listening to them and asking them questions. 47All the people
listening to him were amazed at his understanding and his answers. 48His

[28]This event lies yet in the future as is quite obvious from present conditions in the Middle East, where Jesus is not on the throne of David! It will occur in the future Messianic Kingdom on earth. Again, this is the hallmark of those who believe the saving Gospel about the Kingdom, God's great future for the earth, for which the Christian faith is now a preparation through trial and tribulation (Acts 14:22).

parents were astonished when they saw him, and his mother asked him,
"Son, why have you treated us like this? Look how worried we have
been, your father and I. We have been looking all over for you!" 49Jesus
replied, "Why were you looking for me? Did you not know I had to be
occupied in my Father's business?"[29] 50But they did not understand what
he was saying to them. 51Then he went back with them to Nazareth and
continued in obedience to them. His mother treasured up all these things
in her heart. 52Jesus kept advancing in wisdom and years, and in favor
with God and people.

3 1In the fifteenth year of the reign of Tiberias Caesar, when Pontius
Pilate was governor of Judea, Herod was tetrarch of Galilee, his
brother Philip was tetrarch of Iturea and Trachonitis, and Lysanius was
tetrarch of Abilene, 2when Annas and Caiaphas were high priests, the
word of God[30] came to John, son of Zacharias, in the desert.[31] 3And he
moved around the whole Jordan region, heralding a baptism of
repentance for the forgiveness of sins. 4This is as it is written in the book
of Isaiah the prophet: "A voice crying out in the desert, 'Prepare the way
of the Lord; make His paths straight. 5Every valley will be filled in, and
every mountain and hill will be leveled. The crooked ways will be
straightened, and the rough roads made smooth. 6All mankind will see
the salvation of God.'"

7John said to the crowds who came to him to be baptized, "You
brood of vipers, who warned you to flee from the coming judgment?
8Produce fruits consistent with repentance, and do not begin to say to

---

[29]Jesus defined with complete simplicity his primary task (and ours), that of preaching the Gospel about the Kingdom of God (4:43).

[30]The word of God is the NT shorthand for the Gospel about the Kingdom of God, preached by the NT community starting with Jesus (Heb. 2:3; Lk. 4:43). It is necessary to remind readers of the content of the NT Gospel because it has been popularly and very misleadingly reduced to facts about the death and resurrection of Jesus. Central as these are, they are not the whole of the saving Gospel. Jesus preached the Gospel of the Kingdom (Lk. 4:43; Mk. 1:14-15) long before saying a word about his death and resurrection (Mt. 16:21). Traditional Christianity is based on a very partial Gospel and this is signaled by the easily-spotted fact that "Gospel about the Kingdom" never appears in evangelistic tracts offering salvation. No one can "accept Jesus" without believing and practicing his words (Jn. 12:44ff; 3:36; 2 Jn. 7-9).

[31]Sparsely inhabited area.

yourselves, 'We are descendants of Abraham.' I am telling you that God could create children of Abraham from these stones. 9The axe is already being swung at the base of the trees, and every tree that does not produce good fruit will be chopped down and thrown into the fire."

10"So what should we do?" the crowds asked him. 11He answered, "If you have two coats, give one to the person who does not have any, and if you have food, do the same." 12Some tax collectors came to be baptized, and they also asked him, "Teacher, what should we do?" 13He replied, "Do not collect any more tax than you have been ordered to." 14Some soldiers asked, "What about us? What should we do?" He answered, "Do not demand money with violence, or accuse anyone falsely, and be satisfied with your wages."

15The people were in a state of eager anticipation, wondering if John himself was the Messiah. 16John responded, telling everybody, "As for me, I am baptizing you in water. But one is coming who is greater than I, and I am not worthy to untie his sandals. He will baptize you in holy spirit[32] and fire. 17With his winnowing tool in hand, he is ready to separate the wheat from the chaff on his threshing floor. He will gather the wheat into his barn, but will burn up the chaff with a fire which cannot be put out."[33]

18John gave many such warnings as he preached the Gospel[34] to the people. 19But because John reprimanded Herod the tetrarch for marrying Herodias, Herod's brother's wife, and for all the evil things Herod had done, 20Herod added to all this evil by imprisoning John.

21When all the people were baptized, Jesus was also baptized. As he prayed, heaven was opened, 22and the holy spirit came down upon him in

---

[32]Jesus imparted the spirit ("The words I have spoken to you are spirit and life," Jn. 6:63) long before Pentecost, when the Church received a special public blessing of spirit.

[33]That is, until it has consumed all that is thrown into it. The meaning is certainly not that there will be an endless perpetual torment for the wicked. This is not found in Scripture.

[34]John preached the same saving Gospel about the Kingdom of God/Heaven (no difference in meaning) as Jesus did (see Mt. 3:1; 4:17; 4:23; 9:35). Paul preached exactly the same Gospel of the Kingdom (see Acts 14:22; 19:8; 20:24-25; 28:23, 30, 31). There is only one saving Gospel in the NT.

the form of a dove. A voice came from heaven, "You are My Son,[35] the
one I love. I am delighted with you."

23 Jesus was about thirty years old when he began his ministry. He
was the son, as people thought, of Joseph, the son of Heli, 24 the son of
Matthat,[36] the son of Levi, the son of Melchi, the son of Jannai, the son of
Joseph, 25 the son of Mattathias, the son of Amos, the son of Nahum, the
son of Hesli, the son of Naggai, 26 the son of Maath, the son of Mattathias,
the son of Semein, the son of Josech, the son of Joda, 27 the son of Joanan,
the son of Rhesa, the son of Zerubbabel, the son of Shealtiel,[37] the son of
Neri, 28 the son of Melchi, the son of Addi, the son of Cosam, the son of
Elmadam, the son of Er, 29 the son of Joshua, the son of Eliezer, the son of
Jorim, the son of Matthat, the son of Levi, 30 the son of Simeon, the son of
Judah, the son of Joseph, the son of Jonam, the son of Eliakim, 31 the son
of Melea, the son of Menna, the son of Mattatha, the son of Nathan, the
son of David, 32 the son of Jesse, the son of Obed, the son of Boaz, the
son of Salmon, the son of Nahshon, 33 the son of Amminadab, the son of
Admin, the son of Ram, the son of Hezron, the son of Perez, the son of
Judah, 34 the son of Jacob, the son of Isaac, the son of Abraham, the son
of Terah, the son of Nahor, 35 the son of Serug, the son of Reu, the son of
Peleg, the son of Heber, the son of Shelah, 36 the son of Cainan, the son of
Arphaxad, the son of Shem, the son of Noah, the son of Lamech, 37 the
son of Methuselah, the son of Enoch, the son of Jared, the son of

---

[35]Jesus certainly did not become Son of God at his baptism! He was Son of God precisely because of the biological miracle worked in Mary by God (1:35). Isa. 9:6 had predicted that the Messiah would be the child begotten by God and the Son given to Israel. The two phrases "a child will be begotten" (i.e. by God, a divine passive) and "a Son will be given" reinforce each other and provide the biblical origin of the Son. Luke had worked out of that Messianic text in ch. 1 when he spoke of the Son as heir to the throne of his ancestor David and miraculously begotten in Mary. This miracle is expressly said to be the reason why Jesus is the Son (1:35). Matthew teaches exactly the same in Matt. 1:18 (*genesis*, origin) and 1:20: "what is begotten in her is from holy spirit," the creative activity of God. There is no mention in these books of the Son of God being a son "eternally begotten." Eternal begetting simply contradicts Ps. 2:7 and the whole of Scripture.

[36]Very possibly the grandfather of Joseph and Mary who were thus first cousins. Both were descended from David through Nathan.

[37]Selathiel, the uncle of Zerubbabel, appears too in the genealogy in Matthew and was transferred from the Nathan line when the Solomon line expired, when Jehoiakim was excluded from the royal lineage (see Jer. 22:24-30).

Mahalaleel, the son of Cainan, 38the son of Enosh, the son of Seth, the
son of Adam, the son of God.[38]

4 1Jesus, full of holy spirit,[39] returned from the Jordan and was led by
the spirit in the desert. 2For forty days he was tempted by the Devil.[40]
All that time he ate nothing, so at the end he became hungry. 3The Devil
said to him, "Since you are the Son of God, tell this stone to become
bread." Jesus answered him, 4"It is written, 'People are not to live by
eating bread only.'"

5Then the Devil took him up and showed him all the world's
kingdoms in a moment of time. 6The Devil said to Jesus, "I will give you
all this authority and the glory of these kingdoms, because it has been
handed over to me and I can give it to whoever I want. 7So if you bow

---

[38]The title "son of God" applies to Adam, too, as a uniquely created human being. "Son of God" is never in Scripture "God the Son." This title belongs to times after Scripture was completed. It became a pillar of the later creeds, which tragically obscured the much easier unitary monotheistic creed of Jesus (Mk. 12:29), endorsing his Jewish heritage from Deut. 6:4. God is the Father some 1300 times in the NT and no occurrence of the various words for "God" ever means a triune God.

[39]There is no definite article in the Greek. Holy spirit is the creative operational power and presence of the One God (and later of the risen Jesus). Holy spirit is thus defined in the Hebrew Bible which provides the indispensable background for understanding the NT. There is no "third Person" in the NT. And even in 325 AD the Church was uncertain about how to define the spirit. The mind of Christ is equated with the spirit of God in 1 Cor. 2:16, citing Isa. 40:13, LXX.

[40]The Devil or the Satan is positively not an internal tempter, i.e. human nature! He is always a person, and always external and not to be confused with sin in the human heart. He is the great deceiver of the world (Rev. 12:9), and one of his greatest achievements has been to deceive some Bible readers into believing that he does not exist. This is to wipe out the whole NT dimension of spiritual evil. Demons are supernatural non-human personalities who spoke to Jesus and he to them (Lk. 4:41, where the grammatical agreement shows even more clearly than in English that it was the demons who spoke to Jesus and were rebuked by him). The demons recognized, when the public generally did not, that Jesus was the promised Messiah. On no account should the demons be written out of the historical accounts. The word "demon" never means a human being, much less a mental disease. The demons can of course cause mental illness and evils of all kinds.

down and worship me, you can have all of it." 8Jesus replied, "It is
written, 'You shall worship the Lord your God[41] and serve only Him.'"
9Then the Devil led Jesus to Jerusalem, had him stand on the top of
the Temple, and said to him, "Since you are the Son of God, jump off
here. 10As it is written, 'He will command His angels to take care of you,
11to hold you up so you will not trip over a stone.'" 12Jesus replied, "It is
written, 'You should not test the Lord your God.'" 13When the Devil had
finished every temptation, he left Jesus until another opportunity arose.

14Jesus returned to Galilee in the power of the spirit. News about him
spread throughout the whole surrounding region. 15He was teaching in
their synagogues, and everyone was praising him.

16He arrived in Nazareth, where he had been brought up, and he went
into the synagogue on the Sabbath day as he always used to. He stood up
to read, 17and the scroll of the prophet Isaiah was handed to him. He
opened the scroll and found the place where it is written: 18"The Lord's
spirit is on me, because He anointed me to preach the Gospel to the poor.
He sent me to announce the release of those held captive and the
recovery of sight to the blind, to set free the downtrodden, 19and to
proclaim the year of the Lord's favor."[42]

20He rolled up the scroll, handed it back to the attendant, and sat
down. The eyes of everyone in the synagogue were fixed on him.
21"Today this Scripture is being fulfilled as you are hearing it read," he
said to them. 22Everybody was speaking well of him, and they were
amazed at the gracious words he spoke. "Is this not Joseph's son?" they
asked. 23Jesus responded, "I am sure you will quote me this proverb:
'Doctor, heal yourself!' and say, 'Do here in your own hometown what
we heard you did in Capernaum.' 24I am telling you the truth: no prophet
is welcome in his own hometown. 25I guarantee that there were many
widows in Israel during Elijah's time, when there was a drought for three
and a half years, causing a great famine throughout the country. 26Yet
Elijah was not sent to any of them, but to a widow in Zarephath in the
region of Sidon. 27And there were many lepers in Israel in the prophet
Elisha's time, but none of them was healed except Naaman the Syrian."

---

[41]Jesus of course was a unitarian believer in the One God of Israel and knew nothing of a post-biblical triune God.

[42]Jesus stopped his quotation of Isa. 61:2 and did not go on to mention the prophecy of the future day of God's vengeance and wrath.

28When they heard this everyone in the synagogue became furious.
29They got up and threw him out of the town, and dragged him to the top
of the hill their town was built on, in order to throw him off the cliff.
30But he passed through them and went on his way.

31Jesus then went to Capernaum, a city in Galilee. He was teaching
them on the Sabbath day, 32and they were amazed at his teaching because
his message carried such authority. 33There was a man in the synagogue
who was under the influence of the spirit of an evil demon.[43] He shouted
out, 34"Leave us alone! What do we have to do with each other, Jesus of
Nazareth? Have you come to destroy us? I know who you are — the holy
one of God!"[44] 35Jesus reprimanded him, "Be quiet and come out of
him!" Throwing him down in front of them, the demon came out of the
man without hurting him. 36Everyone was amazed and asked each other,
"What is this message? With power and authority he commands evil
spirits, and they leave." 37Word about Jesus spread everywhere in the
surrounding region.

38Jesus left the synagogue and went to Simon's house. Simon's
mother-in-law was suffering from a high fever, and they asked Jesus to
help her. 39Jesus stood over her and commanded the fever to leave her,
and it did. Immediately she got up and served them.

40While the sun was setting, people brought to Jesus everyone who
was sick from various diseases. One by one Jesus placed his hands on
them and healed them. 41Demons came out of many people, the demons
shouting,[45] "You are the Son of God!" But Jesus reprimanded the
demons and would not allow them to speak because the demons knew he
was the Messiah.[46]

---

[43]In the Greek world demons, spirits could be viewed as good or bad. But in Scripture they are strictly evil and opposed to God.

[44]According to Luke 1:35, a definitive verse for identifying Jesus, Jesus was holy, being the miraculously generated Son of God.

[45]The personality of the demons is quite clear and even clearer in the Greek here. It was the non-human demons who cried out and were able to recognize that Jesus was the Messiah. To say that these were just mentally deranged human persons is to make nonsense of the historical narrative.

[46]Once again the demons are perfectly clear in this historical narrative, and it is nothing less than an assault on the truth of the Bible to try to explain them away. The word "demon" in Greek means a supernatural, non-human personality, definitely not a

42When daylight came Jesus went out to a quiet place, but the crowds
searched him out and found him. They tried to stop him because they did
not want him to leave. 43But he said to them, "I must preach the Gospel
about the Kingdom of God to other towns also, because I was
commissioned for this purpose."[47] 44So he continued preaching the
Gospel in the synagogues of Judea.

5 1One day, as Jesus was standing beside the Sea of Galilee, a crowd of
people was pressing in on him to hear the Gospel-word of God.[48]
2Jesus noticed two boats lying by the lake. The fishermen had left them
and were washing their nets. 3Jesus got into one of the boats, which
belonged to Simon, and asked him to push off from shore a little way.
Jesus sat down in the boat and taught the crowd. 4When he had finished
speaking, he said to Simon, "Go out further into deeper water, and lower
your nets for a catch." 5Simon replied, "Master, we worked hard all night
and caught nothing. But if you say so, I will lower the nets." 6When they
had done this, the nets closed around a great number of fish, and their
nets began to break. 7They waved to their companions in the other boat
for them to come over and help. The others arrived, and all together they
filled both the boats with fish, so much so that the boats began to sink.
8When Simon Peter saw what happened, he dropped to his knees before
Jesus and exclaimed, "Please go away from me, lord, because I am a

---

human person, much less a mental disease. Cp. James 2:19: "The demons believe in the One God and tremble." This is self-evidently not true of mentally ill people.

[47]There is no clearer purpose statement in Scripture than this from the lips of Jesus. Preaching the Gospel of the Kingdom was his task and ought now to be the task of his body, the Church. But one can listen in vain to hear contemporary preachers and teachers define the Gospel as Jesus always did. Preaching the Gospel about the Kingdom of God is Jesus' and the whole Bible's programmatic statement of the content of the Christian faith. It is predominantly an announcement of God's great plan for the future of this planet. Without a true "eschatology" (understanding of the future) there can be no genuine Gospel. Jesus should be allowed to set the pace for and define the content of all Gospel preaching (Heb. 2:3). For further material on the Kingdom, please see our articles on the Kingdom at restorationfellowship.org and the 260 15-minute downloadable radio programs on the Kingdom. See also my *The Coming Kingdom of the Messiah: A Solution to the Riddle of the New Testament*.

[48]This verse and many others establish the fact that the Gospel of the Kingdom (4:43) is known as the "word" or "word of God." Matthew reminds us that it is the "word/Gospel of the Kingdom" (Mt. 13:19).

sinful man!" 9He and everyone with him were astounded by the catch
that they had landed together, 10as were James and John, the sons of
Zebedee, Simon's partners. "Do not be afraid," Jesus said to Simon.
"From now on you will be fishermen catching people!" 11When they had
pulled the boats up on shore, they left everything behind and followed
Jesus.

12While he was in one of the cities, a man with severe leprosy was
there. He bowed his face to the ground and begged Jesus, "lord, if you
are willing, you can heal me." 13Jesus reached out his hand and touched
the man. "I am willing," he said. "Be healed!" Immediately the leprosy
was gone. 14Jesus ordered him to tell no one, "But go and show yourself
to the priest and make the ceremonial offering which Moses
commanded, as a testimony to them." 15But the news about Jesus spread
even more, and large crowds came to hear him teach and to be healed of
their diseases. 16Jesus used to retreat into the desert and pray.

17One day when he was teaching, some Pharisees and religious
teachers were sitting there, who had come from every village of Galilee
and Judea and from Jerusalem. The Lord's healing power was with him,
18and some men brought a paralyzed man on a mat. They were trying to
bring him in and set him down in front of Jesus. 19But they could not find
any way through the crowd, so they went up on the roof and let the man
down on the mat through the roof tiles, right in front of Jesus in the
middle of the crowd. 20Jesus saw their faith, and said to the man, "Friend,
your sins are forgiven." 21The religious teachers and the Pharisees began
to argue. "Who is this speaking blasphemies?" they asked. "Who can
forgive sins except God alone?" 22Jesus knew what they were arguing
about, and said to them, "Why are you debating this in your minds?
23Which is easier — to say 'Your sins have been forgiven,' or to say 'Get
up and walk'? 24But so that you can be sure that the Son of Man does
have the authority on earth to forgive sins…" he said to the paralyzed
man, "I am telling you, get up, pick up your mat, and go home."
25Immediately the man stood up in front of them. He picked up the mat
he had been lying on and walked home, praising God. 26Everyone was
totally astonished. They praised God and, filled with awe, said, "We
have seen extraordinary things today."

27After this Jesus left, and he saw a tax collector named Levi sitting
in the tax booth. “Follow me,” Jesus said. 28And Levi left everything
behind, got up, and began to follow Jesus.

29Then Levi organized a large banquet for Jesus at his house, and a
big crowd of tax collectors and others were eating with them. 30The
Pharisees and their religious teachers complained to Jesus’ disciples.
“Why do you eat and drink with tax collectors and sinners?” they asked.
31“Healthy people do not need a doctor, but sick people do,” Jesus
answered. 32“I have not come to call to repentance those who live right,
but sinners.”

33They said to him, “John’s disciples often fast and pray, and the
Pharisees’ disciples do too, but your disciples are busy eating and
drinking.” 34Jesus said to them, “You cannot make the groomsmen fast
while the bridegroom is with them, can you? 35But the time is coming
when the bridegroom will be taken away from them. Then they will
fast.” 36Then he gave them a parable. “Nobody tears out a patch from
new clothes to mend old clothes. Otherwise he has torn the new clothes,
and the patch from the new does not match the old. 37And nobody puts
new wine into old wineskins, because if they did, the new wine would
burst the wineskins and spill out, and the wineskins would be ruined.
38New wine must be put into fresh wineskins. 39And nobody who is
drinking old wine wants new wine, because he says, ‘The old is good.’”

6 1One Sabbath day, as Jesus was walking through some grain fields,
his disciples picked some heads of grain and ate them, rubbing them
first in their hands to remove the husks. 2Some of the Pharisees asked,
“Why are you doing what is not lawful on the Sabbath?” 3Jesus replied,
“Have you never read what David did, when he and his men were
hungry? 4He went into the house of God, took and ate the consecrated
bread, and gave it to his men too. That is not lawful as the consecrated
bread is only for the priests.” 5Then he said to them, “The Son of Man is
lord of the Sabbath.”

6On another Sabbath he went into the synagogue and was teaching. A
man was there whose right hand was deformed and paralyzed. 7The
religious teachers and the Pharisees were watching Jesus closely to see if
he would heal on the Sabbath, so that they could have a reason to accuse
him. 8But Jesus knew what they were thinking, and he said to the man

with the deformed hand, "Stand up and come forward." The man stood
up and came forward. 9Then Jesus said to them, "Let me ask you: Is it
lawful to do good on the Sabbath, or to do harm? To save a life or to
destroy it?" 10After looking around at everyone he said to the man, "Hold
out your hand." The man did so, and his hand was healed. 11But the
religious teachers and the Pharisees became infuriated, and were
planning among themselves what action to take against Jesus.

12At this time Jesus went to a mountain to pray. He stayed there all
night, praying to God. 13In the morning he called together his disciples
and chose twelve of them as Apostles: 14Simon, who Jesus also called
Peter, Andrew his brother, James, John, Philip, Bartholomew, 15Matthew,
Thomas, James the son of Alphaeus, Simon who was called "the
revolutionary," 16Judas the son of James, and Judas Iscariot, who turned
traitor.

17Jesus came down the mountain with them and stood on some flat
ground. There a large crowd of his disciples and many other people from
all over Judea, Jerusalem, and the sea coast of Tyre and Sidon 18came to
listen to him and to be healed of their diseases. Those suffering from evil
spirits were also being healed. 19The whole crowd was trying to touch
him, because power was coming from him and healing everyone.

20Looking at his disciples, Jesus said, 21"Blessed are you who are
poor, because the Kingdom of God is yours. Blessed are you who are
hungry now, because you will be fully satisfied. Blessed are you who
weep now, because you will laugh. 22Blessed are you when people hate
you, reject you, insult you, and curse you as evil because of the Son of
Man. 23Be happy then and jump for joy, because great is your reward
stored up in heaven.[49] Remember that the ancestors of these people
mistreated the prophets in the same way. 24But alas for you who are rich,
because you are already living in comfort. 25Alas for you who are well-
fed now, because you will be hungry. Alas for you who laugh now,
because you will mourn and weep. 26Alas for you when everyone praises

---

[49]Rewards are in the NT currently stored up with God in heaven (Mt. 6:1) and will be given at the future coming of Jesus to the earth and enjoyed on the renewed earth of the future Kingdom. The NT does not teach that people go to heaven to be rewarded. They sleep the sleep of death (Ps. 13:3) until they are raised at the first resurrection which will occur at Jesus' Second Coming (1 Cor. 15:23, etc).

you. Remember that the ancestors of these people treated the false
prophets in the same way.

27"But I say to anyone who is listening: Love your enemies; do good
to those who hate you. 28Bless those who curse you; pray for those who
mistreat you. 29If someone hits you on one cheek, offer the other cheek,
and if someone takes your coat, do not keep your shirt from them. 30Give
to everyone who asks you, and if someone takes something from you, do
not demand it back. 31Do to others what you would want them to do to
you. 32If you love those who love you, what is so great about that? Even
sinners love those who love them. 33And if you are good to those who are
good to you, is that so great either? Sinners do that too. 34If you lend to
people you expect will repay you, how great is that? Sinners also lend to
sinners, expecting to get back what they lent. 35Instead love your
enemies, do good to them, and lend without expecting to receive
anything back. You will have a great reward, and you will be children of
the Most High, because He Himself is kind to ungrateful and evil people.
36Be merciful, just as your Father is merciful.

37"Do not judge, and you will not be judged; do not condemn, and
you will not be condemned; forgive, and you will be forgiven; 38give, and
it will be given to you generously. In fact when what you receive is
measured out, and pressed down so more can be added, it will spill out
over the top, falling into your lap! For whatever standard of measure you
use, it will be measured to you in return."

39Then he told them a parable to illustrate: "Can one blind person
lead another? Would they not both fall into a pit? 40A student does not
know more than his teacher, but when he has learned everything, then he
will be like his teacher. 41Why are you so concerned about the speck in
your brother's eye but do not notice the log in your own eye? 42How can
you say to your brother, 'Brother, let me take that speck out of your eye,'
when you cannot even see the log in your own eye? You hypocrite, first
take the log out of your own eye, and then you will be able to see clearly
to take the speck out of your brother's eye. 43For no good tree produces
bad fruit, and on the other hand no bad tree produces good fruit. 44Every
tree is recognized by the fruit it produces. No one picks figs from thorn
bushes, or harvests grapes from brambles. 45Whoever is good produces
good from what they have stored inside, and whoever is evil produces

evil from what they have stored inside. People speak what they are
thinking inside.
46“Why do call me ‘lord, lord,’ when you refuse to do what I say?
47Let me give you an illustration of someone who comes to me, listens to
my words, and does them. 48He is like a man who built a house. He dug
deep and laid the foundation on solid rock.[50] When the river burst its
banks and the flood rushed against that house, it did not damage it
because it was so solidly built. 49But someone who hears me teach but
does not do what I say is like a man who built his house without a
foundation. When the flood rushed against that house it immediately fell
down in total collapse.”

7 1After Jesus had finished speaking to the people, he went to
Capernaum. 2A Roman centurion was there who had a servant whom
he thought of highly, who was sick and about to die. 3When the centurion
heard about Jesus, he sent some Jewish elders to him, asking him to
come and save the life of his servant. 4When the elders came to Jesus,
they begged him, “He definitely deserves it, 5because he loves our people
and he even built us our synagogue.” 6Jesus went with them, and when
they were not far from the house, the centurion sent friends to Jesus to
tell him, “lord, you do not need to trouble yourself, because I am not
worthy that you would come under my roof. 7I did not even consider
myself worthy to go and see you. Just say the word, and my servant will
be healed. 8For I also am a man under authority, with soldiers under me.
I tell one to go and he goes, another to come and he comes, and I tell my
servant to do something and he does it.” 9When Jesus heard this he was
amazed at him. He turned to the crowd following him and said, “I tell
you, I have not found such great faith even in Israel.” 10The friends the
centurion had sent returned to the house and found the servant in
excellent health.
11Soon after that Jesus went to a town called Nain, and his disciples
and a large crowd went with him. 12As he approached the town gate he
met a funeral procession. The dead man was the only son of a widow. A
big crowd from the town was with her. 13When the lord saw her he was

---

[50]The NT Church is built on the solid rock of the teaching that Jesus is the Christ (Mt. 16:16), certainly not that he “is God,” which would violate the first commandment and the express creed of Jesus in Mark 12:29ff (cp. Jn. 17:3).

moved with compassion for her, and said, “Do not cry.” 14Jesus went up
to the coffin and touched it, and the pall-bearers stopped walking. He
said, “Young man, I tell you, arise!” 15The dead man sat up and began to
speak, and Jesus gave him back to his mother. 16A sense of awe gripped
everyone there, and they praised God, saying, “A powerful prophet has
arisen among us,” and “God has visited His people.” 17This news about
Jesus spread through the whole of Judea and the surrounding region.

18John’s disciples reported to him about all of this. 19John called on
two of his disciples to go to the lord and ask, “Are you the coming one,
or should we wait for someone else?” 20When they came to Jesus they
said, “John the Baptist sent us to ask you, ‘Are you the coming one, or
should we wait for someone else?’” 21Right at that time Jesus healed
many people of their sicknesses, diseases, and evil spirits, and gave sight
to many blind people. 22Jesus answered the men who had come to see
him, “Go and report to John what you saw and heard: The blind are
seeing, the lame are walking, the lepers are healed, the deaf are hearing,
the dead are raised back to life, and the poor have the Gospel preached to
them. 23Blessed is anyone who does not take offense at me.”

24When the messengers from John had left, Jesus started talking to
the crowds about John: “What did you go out to the desert to see? Some
dry stalk blown about by the wind? 25Well, what did you expect to see?
Someone dressed in fine clothes? Those who dress in rich clothes and
live in luxury are found in royal palaces! 26So what did you go out to see?
A prophet? Yes, I am telling you, and one who is more than a prophet.
27He is the one about whom it is written: ‘Look, I am sending My
messenger ahead of you to prepare your way before you.’ 28I am telling
you that no one born from women is greater than John, but even the least
significant person in the Kingdom of God[51] is greater than he is.” 29When
they heard this, everyone, even the tax collectors, acknowledged that
God’s way was right, because they had been baptized by John. 30But the
Pharisees and the experts in the Law rejected God’s purpose for them,[52]
having refused to be baptized by John.

---

[51]Referring to future status in the coming Kingdom, when the disciples will supervise the world with Jesus (1 Cor. 6:2; Rev. 2:26-27, etc).

[52]Showing that the Calvinistic idea of a double predestination is false. Jesus recognized that every human person must choose the Gospel or reject it. We are not robots but

31“What shall I compare the people of this evil society to? What are
they like?” Jesus asked. 32“They are like children sitting in the
marketplace, saying to each other, ‘We played the flute for you and you
did not dance; we sang sad songs and you did not weep.’ 33For John the
Baptist came eating no bread and drinking no wine, and you say, ‘He has
a demon!’ 34The Son of Man came eating and drinking with people, and
you say, ‘Look, a glutton and a drunkard, a friend of tax collectors and
sinners!’ 35Yet Wisdom is proved right by all her children.”

36One of the Pharisees invited Jesus to eat with him. Jesus went to the
Pharisee’s house and sat down to the meal. 37A woman in that town who
was a sinner learned that Jesus was eating in the Pharisee’s house, and
she brought an alabaster jar of perfume. 38She stood by Jesus weeping,
and with her tears she wet his feet, and with her hair she dried them. She
kissed his feet and poured the perfume on them. 39When the Pharisee
who had invited Jesus saw this he said to himself, “If this man was a
prophet he would know who this woman is who is touching him, and
what kind of person she is — a sinner!”

40Then Jesus answered his thoughts: “Simon, I have something to say
to you.” He responded, “Say it, Teacher.” 41“Once there were two people
in debt to a moneylender. One owed five hundred denarii and the other
fifty. 42Neither could pay him back, so he forgave both debts. Which one
will love him more?” 43Simon answered, “I assume the one he forgave
more.” Jesus said, “You have judged correctly.” 44Turning toward the
woman, he said to Simon, “You see this woman? I came into your house,
and you did not give me any water to wash my feet, but she washed my
feet with her tears, and wiped them dry with her hair. 45You did not give
me a kiss to greet me, but ever since I came in she has not stopped
kissing my feet. 46You did not put any oil on my head, but she poured
perfume over my feet. 47That is why I am telling you that her many sins
have been forgiven, so she loved much. But whoever is forgiven little
loves little.” 48Then Jesus said to the woman, “Your sins have been
forgiven.” 49Those who were sitting eating with him began saying among
themselves, “Who is this who even forgives sins?” 50And Jesus said to
the woman, “Your faith has saved you. Go in peace.”

---

charged with the responsibility of choice, in this case choosing life wisely, by heeding the teachings of Jesus Messiah.

8 1Soon after this Jesus traveled through the towns and villages, publicizing and preaching the Gospel about the Kingdom of God.[53] With him were the twelve disciples, 2and a number of women who had been healed from evil spirits and diseases: Mary called Magdalene from whom seven demons had gone out, 3Joanna, the wife of Chuza, Herod's administrator, Susanna, and many other women who helped by providing support from what they owned.

4A large crowd gathered from many towns to see Jesus. He spoke to them using a parable.[54] 5"A sower went out to sow his seed. As he sowed, some seed fell on the path where people walked on it, and birds ate it up. 6Other seed fell on rocky soil, and when it sprouted it dried up for lack of moisture. 7Other seed fell among thorns, and the thorns grew up with it and choked it out. 8Other seed fell on good soil, and grew up and produced a harvest a hundred times as much." When he told them this parable, Jesus would customarily shout out:[55] "Whoever has ears to hear, listen!"

9His disciples asked him what this parable meant. 10Jesus replied, "You have been given insight to know the mysteries[56] of the Kingdom of God, but the rest have parables, so that, 'Seeing, they do not really see; and hearing, they do not really understand.'

---

[53]Exactly as stated in the key text in 4:43, that preaching the saving Gospel of the Kingdom of God was the basis of all that Jesus came to teach and preach. It is thus equally the task of the Church until the end of the age, the return of Jesus (Mt. 28:19-20; 24:14; Acts 28:23, 31).

[54]A parable, a comparison basing a theological, spiritual truth on an observable truth of the natural creation.

[55]For emphasis on this the most fundamental of all teachings, showing that the parable of the sower lies at the heart of the saving Gospel of the Kingdom as preached by Jesus and Paul. The salvation process is just like a seed which must survive and grow and bear fruit. The doctrine of "once saved, always saved" is completely without foundation in the NT. Salvation is a process. We *were* saved, *are being* saved, and most importantly *will be* saved. Salvation is conditional on persistence to the end. "Some believe for a while," Jesus said (v. 13), but do not persist in their belief. Paul in Rom. 11:22 warns believers that if they do not remain within the kindness of God they will be cut off. "Salvation is now closer to us than when we first believed" (Rom. 13:11).

[56]These are not incomprehensible mystifications, but the revealed secrets of God's great immortality Kingdom program revealed in Jesus the Messiah.

11“This is what the parable means: The seed is the Gospel-word of
God.[57] 12The seeds on the path are like those who listen, but then the
Devil comes[58] and takes away the Gospel-word from their minds, so that
they do not believe it and so are not saved.[59] 13The seeds on the rocky soil
are those who listen and receive the Gospel-word with joy, but they do
not have any roots. They believe for a while,[60] but when difficult times
come they give up. 14The seeds that fell among thorns are those who
listen, but they are choked by life’s worries, wealth, and pleasure, and
they produce no fruit. 15But the seeds in the good soil are the ones who
listen to the Gospel-word with an honest and good heart. They hold onto
it and produce fruit with perseverance.

16“No one lights a lamp and covers it with a bucket or puts it under a
bed. Instead you put it on a stand, so that anyone who comes in may see
the light. 17For there is nothing hidden that will not be revealed; there is
nothing secret that will not become known and be made visible. 18So take
care how you listen. To whoever has, more will be given; whoever does
not have, even what he thinks he has will be taken away from him.”

19Then Jesus’ mother and brothers arrived, but they could not get
through the crowd to him. 20Jesus was told, “Your mother and your
brothers are standing outside, wanting to see you.” 21 Jesus replied, “My

---

[57]The Gospel of the Kingdom as defined first by Mk. 1:14-15 and Mt. 13:19 where understanding of the content of the saving Gospel begins. It is the foundation of true Christian faith.

[58]Reminding us of Satan’s constant policy of obstructing the progress of the Gospel of the Kingdom at every opportunity. Cp. Rev. 12:4 where the Devil’s object is to devour the true people of God, starting with Jesus. Those who hear the Gospel of the Kingdom of God as preached by Jesus are the ones “born again” by the reception of the word of the Kingdom (see 1 Pet. 1:22-25).

[59]This is one of the most fundamentally significant sayings of Jesus, showing that salvation is conditioned on an intelligent reception of the Gospel of the Kingdom, the word of the Kingdom (Mt. 13:19; Mk. 1:14-15; Lk. 4:43; Acts 8:12; 19:8; 28:23, 31, etc). Constant reference should be made by students of Jesus and his Gospel to 2 Thess. 2:10, where Paul in a spectacularly interesting passage about the Antichrist and the spirit of deception says that people are perishing “because a love of the truth they would not receive in order to be saved.” This is very much parallel to Lk. 8:12 where salvation and believing the Gospel of the Kingdom go together.

[60]Showing that the popular belief in “once saved always saved” is false to the teaching of Jesus. Paul warned believers that if we do not remain faithful we will be cut off (Rom. 11:21-22).

mother and my brothers are those who listen to the Gospel-word of God[61]
and do it."

22One day Jesus got into a boat with his disciples. "Let us cross over
to the other side of the lake," he said to them, and they set off. 23As they
were sailing along Jesus fell asleep, and a fierce gale came down on the
lake. The boat was swamped and they were in danger of sinking. 24They
went to Jesus and woke him up, saying, "Master, master, we are going to
drown!" Jesus got up and reprimanded the wind and the stormy waves;
they stopped and it became calm. 25"Where is your faith?" he asked
them. Afraid and amazed, they said to each other, "Who is this, who
commands even the winds and the water, and they obey him?"

26They sailed to the Gerasene region, across from Galilee. 27When
Jesus stepped out onto the shore, he was met by a demon-influenced man
from the town there. He had not worn clothes or lived in a house for a
long time. Instead he lived in the tombs. 28When he saw Jesus he
screamed, fell at his feet, and shouted, "What do we have to do with each
other, Jesus, Son of the Most High God? Do not torture me, I am
begging you!" 29For Jesus had already commanded the evil spirit to come
out of the man. Many times it had seized him, and even though he was
guarded and tied with chains and shackles, he would tear apart the chains
and be driven by the demon into the desert. 30"What is your name?" Jesus
asked him. "Legion," he replied, because many demons had entered him.
31The demons pleaded with Jesus not to order them into the abyss.

32A large herd of pigs was feeding on the hillside nearby, and the
demons begged him for permission to go into the pigs. He gave them
permission. 33The demons left the man and went into the pigs. The herd
stampeded down the steep bank into the lake and were drowned.

34The herdsmen who looked after the pigs ran away and reported
what happened in the town and the countryside. 35The people came to see
what had happened. When they came to Jesus and found the man from
whom the demons had gone out, sitting at Jesus' feet clothed and in his
right mind, they were alarmed. 36Those who had seen what happened told
them how the demon-influenced man had been healed. 37Then everyone
from the whole Gerasene region asked Jesus to leave because they were
gripped by terrible fear, so Jesus got into a boat and went back. 38The

---

[61]The saving Gospel of the Kingdom.

man from whom the demons had gone out begged Jesus to let him come
along, but Jesus sent him back. 39“Return home and describe what great
things God has done for you,” he said to him. So he went away,
announcing to the whole town what great things Jesus had done for him.

40When Jesus returned across the lake, a crowd of people welcomed
him, because they had all been waiting for him. 41A man named Jairus,
who was a synagogue leader, came and fell at Jesus’ feet. He begged him
to come to his house 42because his only daughter, about twelve years old,
was dying. As Jesus went, the crowds were pressing against him.

43A woman who had been sick with bleeding for twelve years was
there. No one had been able to heal her. 44She came up behind Jesus and
touched the edge of his clothes, and immediately her bleeding stopped.
45“Who touched me?” Jesus asked. Everybody denied it. “Master,” Peter
said, “people are crowding around you and pushing up against you.”
46But Jesus said, “Someone did touch me, because I know power went
out from me.” 47When the woman realized that she had not escaped
notice, she went forward trembling and fell down before him. She
explained in front of everybody why she had touched Jesus, and how she
had been immediately healed. 48Jesus said to her, “Daughter, your faith
has healed you. Go in peace.”

49While he was still speaking, someone came from the house of the
synagogue leader and said, “Your daughter has died. Do not bother the
teacher any more.” 50But Jesus heard this and said, “Do not be afraid.
Only believe, and she will be healed.” 51When Jesus came to the house he
did not let anyone else enter except Peter, John, James, and the girl’s
father and mother. 52Everyone was weeping and mourning for her, but
Jesus said, “Stop weeping, because she is not dead, but asleep.” 53They
laughed at him, because they knew she was dead. 54But Jesus held her
hand and said loudly, “My child, get up!” 55Her breath of life returned,
and she got up immediately. Jesus told them to give her something to eat.
56Her parents were astounded, but Jesus instructed them not to tell
anyone what had happened.

9 1Calling the twelve disciples together, Jesus gave them power and
authority over all the demons and to heal diseases. 2He sent them out
to proclaim the Gospel of the Kingdom of God and to heal the sick. 3“Do
not take anything with you for the journey,” he said to them, “no walking

stick, no bag, no bread, no money, nor a change of clothes. 4Whichever
house you go into, stay there until you leave that town. If people do not
accept you, shake the dust off your feet as you leave that town, as a
testimony against them." 6They left and traveled through the villages,
preaching the Gospel and healing everywhere.

7Herod the tetrarch heard about everything that was happening, and
he was thoroughly puzzled. Some said that John had risen from the dead;
8others said that Elijah had appeared; still others said that one of the
ancient prophets had risen from death. 9Herod said, "I myself had John
beheaded, so who is this man I am hearing about?" And he kept on
trying to see Jesus.

10When the Apostles returned they told Jesus all they had done. Then
he took them with him and went privately to a town called Bethsaida.
11But the crowds found out and followed him there. He welcomed them
and began speaking to them about the Kingdom of God,[62] and healing
those who needed it.

12As the day was coming to an end, the twelve came and said to him,
"Send the crowd away so they can go to the villages and countryside
around and find a place to stay and food to eat. We are in an isolated
place here." 13But Jesus replied, "You give them something to eat." They
said, "All we have are five loaves and two fish, unless we go and buy
food for all these people." 14There were about 5,000 men there. "Have
them sit down in groups of about fifty," he said to his disciples. 15So they
did, and all the people sat down. 16Jesus took the five loaves and the two
fish. He looked up to heaven, gave thanks, broke them in pieces, and
kept on giving them to the disciples to give to the people. 17They all ate
until they were full, and twelve baskets of leftovers were collected.

18One time when Jesus was praying privately with just his disciples
with him, he asked them, "Who do the crowds say that I am?" 19They
replied, "John the Baptist, or others say Elijah, and still others say one of
the ancient prophets risen from the dead." 20He asked them, "But what

---

[62]Exactly as Paul did always, see Acts 28:30-31. The Kingdom of God Gospel is the basis of the divine Plan to bestow immortality on human persons. It is astonishing that in our day the phrase "Gospel of the Kingdom," the basis of the whole mission of Jesus (Lk. 4:43), is never mentioned! A colossal suppression of the Kingdom Gospel has occurred. Paul was just as much as Jesus a tireless proclaimer of the Gospel of the Kingdom (Acts 19:8; 20:24-25; 28:23, 31).

about you — who do you say that I am?" Peter answered, "God's
Messiah." 21Jesus warned them, giving them strict instructions not to tell
this to anybody. 22"The Son of Man must suffer many things," he said.
"He will be rejected by the elders, chief priests, and religious teachers,
and be killed, and be raised up on the third day."[63]

23Jesus said to everyone, "If anyone wants to be my disciple, you
must deny yourself, pick up your cross daily, and follow me. 24For
whoever wants to save his life will lose it, and whoever loses his life for
my sake will save it. 25What use is it for anyone to gain the whole world
and then lose himself? 26Whoever is ashamed of me and my words, the
Son of Man will be ashamed of that person when he comes in his glory,
and the glory of the Father and of the holy angels. 27I am telling you the
truth: there are some standing here who will not die until they see the
Kingdom of God."[64]

28About eight days after saying this, Jesus took Peter, John, and
James and went up a mountain to pray. 29While he was praying, the
appearance of his face changed, and his clothing became a dazzling
white. 30Suddenly there were two men talking with him — Moses and
Elijah. 31They appeared in glorious splendor and were talking about
Jesus' death, which he was about to fulfill in Jerusalem. 32Peter and the
others were falling asleep, but they became fully awake and saw the
glory of Jesus[65] and the two men standing with him. 33Seeing that Moses
and Elijah were about to leave, Peter said to Jesus, "Master, it is so good
for us to be here. Let us make three shelters — one for you, one for
Moses, and one for Elijah." He did not really know what he was saying.
34As he was speaking a cloud came and spread out over them, and they
were afraid as they entered the cloud. 35A voice came from the cloud:
"This is My Son, My chosen one. Listen to him!"[66] 36When the voice

---

[63]Luke reckons inclusively, and the third day is Sunday, the third day after Friday (24:21; see 13:32-33).

[64]This prediction was fulfilled in the Transfiguration which happened 8 days later. 2 Pet. 1:16-18 confirms that the Parousia, the arrival of the future Kingdom was seen in vision. Mt. 17:9 calls the transfiguration a vision (*orama*).

[65]Glory is a description of the future Kingdom.

[66]A beautiful summary of the Christian faith as obedience to Jesus, the Son of God. Heb. 5:9 and John 3:36 and many other passages (2 John 7-9) summarize the faith in the same way. It is all about the obedience of faith (Rom. 1:5; 16:26), and the first command of Jesus is in Mk. 1:14-15 and the most important in Mk. 12:29.

finished speaking, only Jesus was there. They kept quiet about what
happened, and told no one at that time about what they had seen.
37The next day, when they came down from the mountain, a large
crowd met Jesus. 38A man in the crowd shouted out, “Teacher, I beg you
to help my son. He is my only child. 39A spirit takes hold of him and it
suddenly screams, making him convulse and foam at the mouth. It hardly
ever leaves him alone and is tormenting him severely. 40I begged your
disciples to drive it out, but they could not.” 41Jesus answered, “You
unbelieving and perverted society, how long will I stay with you and put
up with you? Bring your son here.” 42Even as the boy was coming, the
demon slammed him to the ground in convulsions. But Jesus
commanded the evil spirit and healed the boy, and gave him back to his
father. 43And they were all astounded at the greatness of God. While
everyone was marveling at everything Jesus was doing, he said to his
disciples, 44“Listen, and make sure these words sink in: the Son of Man is
going to be betrayed into human hands.” 45But they did not understand
this statement. Its meaning was hidden from them so they could not
grasp it, and they were afraid to ask him about it.
46Then they started arguing among themselves about which of them
would be the greatest. 47But Jesus, knowing the thoughts of their hearts,
picked up a child and placed him beside him. 48He said to them,
“Whoever welcomes this child in my name welcomes me, and whoever
welcomes me welcomes the One who sent me, because the least among
you is actually the greatest.”
49John said, “Master, we saw someone driving out demons in your
name, so we tried to stop him because he is not one of us.” 50But Jesus
said to him, “Do not stop him, because whoever is not against you is for
you.”
51As the time approached for his ascension, Jesus was determined to
go to Jerusalem. 52He sent messengers on ahead. They arrived at a
Samaritan village to get things ready for him, 53but the people there
would not welcome him because he was determined to go to Jerusalem.
54When his disciples James and John realized this, they asked, “lord, do
you want us to command fire to come down from heaven and burn them
up?” 55But Jesus turned and reprimanded them [and said, “You do not
know what spirit you are of, because the Son of Man did not come to

destroy people's lives, but to save them."][67] 56And they went on to
another village.

57As they were walking, someone said to Jesus, "I will follow you
wherever you go!" 58Jesus said to him, "Foxes have dens, and wild birds
have nests, but the Son of Man has nowhere even to lay his head." 59He
said to another man, "Follow me." But the man replied, "lord, first let me
go and bury my father." 60Jesus replied, "Let the dead bury their own
dead. But you are to go and announce the Gospel of the Kingdom of
God."[68] 61Another person said, "lord, I will follow you! But first let me
go and say goodbye to my family." 62But Jesus said to him, "Nobody
who has started plowing and then looks back is fit for the Kingdom of
God."

10 1After this the lord appointed seventy others, and sent them ahead
in pairs to every town and place that he intended to visit. 2"The
harvest is abundant, but the workers are few," he said to them. "So pray
to the Lord of the harvest to send out workers into His harvest fields.
3Now go — I am sending you like sheep among wolves. 4Do not take a
money belt or bag or extra shoes, and do not stop to talk with people on
the way. 5When you enter a house, first say, 'Peace to this house.' 6If a
person of peace is living there, your peace will rest on them; if not, it
will come back to you. 7Stay in the same house, eating and drinking
whatever they give you, as workers deserve their pay. Do not go from
house to house. 8Whatever town you enter, if the people there welcome
you, eat what is set before you. 9Heal the sick people there and say to
them, 'The Kingdom of God has come near to you.'[69] 10But whatever
town you enter, if the people do not welcome you, go into their streets
and tell them, 11'We are wiping off against you even the dust of your
town that sticks to our feet. Yet be sure of this: The Kingdom of God has
come near.' 12I tell you, it will be better in the Day of Judgment for
Sodom than for that town.

13"Shame on you, Chorazin! Shame on you, Bethsaida! If the
miracles that happened in you had been performed in Tyre and Sidon,
they would have repented a long time ago, sitting in sackcloth and ashes.

---

[67]Early manuscripts do not contain the text in brackets.

[68]The one saving Gospel preached throughout the NT.

[69]That is, in the persons of its ambassadors.

14That is why it will be better for Tyre and Sidon in the judgment than for
you. 15And you, Capernaum, you will not be exalted to heaven. No, you
will be brought down to Hades. 16Whoever listens to you listens to me,
and whoever rejects you rejects me, and whoever rejects me rejects the
One who commissioned me."[70]

17The seventy returned with joy, saying, "lord, even the demons are
submitting to us in your name!" 18So Jesus replied, "I was watching
Satan falling from heaven like lightning.[71] 19Look, I have given you
authority to tread on snakes and scorpions, and over all the power of the
enemy, and nothing will harm you. 20But do not rejoice that the spirits
submit to you; instead rejoice that your names are written down in
heaven."[72]

21At that very time Jesus was filled with joy in the holy spirit, and
said, "I praise you, Father, Lord of heaven and earth, because You have
hidden these things from the wise and clever people and revealed them to
children! Yes, Father, You are pleased to do things this way.
22Everything has been handed over to me by my Father. No one
understands who the Son is except the Father, and who the Father is
except the Son,[73] and anyone to whom the Son chooses to reveal Him."

23Jesus turned to the disciples and said privately, "How blessed are
the eyes which see what you see! 24I tell you that many prophets and
kings wanted to see the things you are seeing, but they did not see them,
and to hear the things you are hearing, but they did not hear them."[74]

25An expert in the Law stood up to test Jesus. "Teacher," he asked,
"what should I do to inherit the Life of the Age to Come?" 26Jesus asked
him, "What is written in the Law? How do you interpret it?" 27The man

---

[70]In this way Thomas eventually understood that seeing and hearing Jesus is equivalent to seeing and hearing God, since Jesus was God's unique emissary (Jn. 20:28; cp. 14:7).

[71]The remark of Jesus here refers to the fall of Satan's kingdom when demons are driven out. Satan "fell" as the disciples were able to expel demonic powers. Or perhaps Satan rushed to the defense of his kingdom.

[72]In the citizen list of the future Kingdom, in which the saints will rule with Jesus on a renewed earth (Dan. 7:18, 22, 27; cp. Isa. 4:3; Rev. 5:10).

[73]This statement has nothing whatsoever to do with a "Trinitarian" relationship of Father and Son!

[74]Reminiscent of the parable of the sower in ch. 8, where seeing and understanding the Gospel of the Kingdom is the measure of true understanding and a right relation to Jesus and the faith taught by Jesus.

answered, "You should love the Lord your God with your whole heart,
your whole self, your whole strength, and your whole mind; and love
your neighbor as yourself." 28Jesus said to him, "You have answered
correctly. Do this and you will live." 29But the man, wanting to prove
himself right, asked Jesus, "And who is my neighbor?"

30Jesus said in reply, "There was a man who was going from
Jerusalem to Jericho. He was attacked by robbers who stripped him and
beat him. They left him half dead. 31A priest happened to be going down
that road. When he saw the man, he passed by on the other side of the
road. 32In the same way a Levite, when he got to the place and saw the
man, also passed by on the other side. 33But then a Samaritan came
along. When he saw the man he felt compassion for him. 34He went over
to him and bandaged his wounds, treating them with oil and wine. Then
he put the man on his own donkey and took him to an inn where he took
care of him. 35The next day he gave two denarii to the innkeeper and said
to him, 'Take care of him, and whatever you spend more than this, when
I return I will pay you back.' 36So which one of these three people do you
think proved to be a neighbor to the man attacked by robbers?" 37The
man replied, "The one who showed kindness to him." Jesus said to him,
"Then go and do the same."

38As they were traveling along, Jesus went into a village, and a
woman named Martha welcomed him into her home. 39She had a sister
named Mary, who sat at the lord's feet to listen to his Gospel-word.
40Martha was preoccupied with getting the meal ready, and she came up
to Jesus and said, "lord, do you not care that my sister has left me alone
to do all the work? Tell her to come and help me." 41But the lord
answered, "Martha, Martha, you are anxious and bothered about many
things. 42But only one thing is really needed here. Mary has chosen what
is best, and it will not be taken away from her."

11 1When Jesus was praying in a certain place, after he finished, one
of his disciples said to him, "lord, teach us to pray, just as John
taught his disciples." 2So Jesus said to them, "When you pray, say,
'Father, holy is Your name.[75] May Your Kingdom come.[76] 3Give us the

---

[75]Your whole immortality program. "Name" stands for everything that God is — His nature, character and agenda, everything He does.

bread we need every day. 4Forgive us our sins, as we forgive everyone
who sins against us. And keep us from temptation.'"
5Then he said to them, "If you have a friend and you go to him in the
middle of the night and say, 'My friend, lend me three loaves of bread
6because a friend of mine on a journey has come to visit me, and I do not
have anything to give him.' 7Your friend might answer from inside the
house, 'Do not bother me. I have already locked the door, and my
children and I have gone to bed. I cannot get up to give you anything
now.' 8I tell you, even though he will not get up and give you anything
because he is your friend, yet because of your persistence your friend
will get up and give you everything you need.
9"So I say to you, keep asking, and you will receive; keep seeking,
and you will find; keep knocking, and the door will be opened to you.
10For everyone who keeps asking, receives; and everyone who keeps
seeking, finds; and everyone who keeps knocking has the door opened to
them. 11Which of you fathers, if your son asks for a fish, gives him a
snake instead of a fish? 12Or if he asks for an egg, do you give him a
scorpion? 13So if you, being evil, know how to give good gifts to your
children, how much more will your heavenly Father give holy spirit[77] to
those who ask Him?"
14Jesus was driving out a demon that caused muteness. When the
demon had gone out, the man who was mute spoke, and the crowds were
astonished. 15But some of them said, "He is casting out demons by the
power of Beelzebul, the ruler of the demons." 16Others wanted to test
Jesus by demanding from him a miraculous sign from heaven. 17But he
knew their thoughts and said to them, "Any kingdom which is divided
against itself is destroyed, and a house divided against itself falls. 18If
Satan was divided against himself, how would his kingdom stand? You

---

[76]The request is for the kingdoms of this present evil system (Gal. 1:4) to be replaced by the coming Messianic Kingdom to be introduced at the future, post-Great Tribulation arrival of Jesus in power and glory. There is no double second coming, thus no pre-tribulation rapture.

[77]Holy spirit in the Bible is not a "third Person." The holy spirit is the very personal operational presence and power of God (or in the NT) of Jesus — their outreach to us, expressed in different ways. 2 Cor. 3:17 states that "the lord is the spirit" (i.e. Jesus in action and influence). In 1 John 2:1 the "Comforter" of John's gospel is defined as Jesus, at the right hand of the Father. Jesus left the earth to go (not go back!) to his Father but he came to be with the disciples in spirit, by his holy spirit.

say that I am casting out demons by the power of Beelzebul. 19If I am
casting out demons by the power of Beelzebul, by whose power do your
people cast them out? They will be the judges of what you have said.
20But if I cast out the demons by the finger of God, then the Kingdom of
God has come upon you.[78] 21When a strong, fully armed man guards his
own house, everything he has is safe. 22But if a stronger man attacks him
and overpowers him, then the stronger takes from him all the weapons he
relied on, and shares out all his possessions. 23Whoever is not with me is
against me, and whoever does not gather with me, scatters.

24"When an evil spirit goes out of someone, it goes through waterless
places looking for rest, and when it finds none it says, 'I will go back to
my house I left.' 25When it returns, it finds its old home all clean and
tidy. 26So it goes and finds seven other spirits more evil than itself, and
they go in and live there, and the final state of that person is worse than
the first."

27While Jesus was saying this a woman in the crowd shouted out,
"Blessed is the womb that carried you and the breasts that nursed you."
28But he said, "Better to say, blessed are those who listen to the word of
God[79] and obey it."

29As the crowds were growing larger, he began saying, "This is an
evil society.[80] It is looking for a miraculous sign, but no sign will be

---

[78]The presence of the Kingdom in this case is not to be confused with the massive number of verses which describe the Kingdom as the great event of the future, its worldwide establishment at the future Second Coming (Parousia) of Jesus. When a demon is expelled the authority of Jesus replaces that of the demon. All the OT prophets predict the future empire of the Messiah with its capital in Jerusalem. Jer. 23:3-8 is a marvelous summary of the future Kingdom and the heart of the Gospel. The public revealing of the Kingdom worldwide awaits the Second Coming when all nations will become the Kingdom of our God and His Messiah (Rev. 11:15-18; cp. Lk. 21:31).

[79]One of many examples where "the word of God" means the saving Gospel of the Kingdom as Jesus and Paul preached it (Lk. 4:43; Mk. 1:14-15; Acts 8:12; 19:8; 28:23, 31, etc).

[80]The Greek word *genea* means society. It is not necessarily limited to a period of 40 or 70 years. Thus when Jesus predicted that "this *genea* will not pass" until the events of the second coming take place (21:32), he meant the present evil society which will continue until Jesus comes back. Jesus never set a date for his future coming. This is proven by Acts 1:6 where he told the disciples that time periods in relation to the Parousia (second coming) have not been revealed, but are known only to the Father.

given to it except the sign of Jonah. 30Just as Jonah was a sign to the
Ninevites, so will the Son of Man be a sign to this society. 31The Queen
of the South will rise up with the people of this society at the judgment
and will condemn them, because she came from the ends of the earth to
hear the wisdom of Solomon, and there is someone greater than Solomon
here! 32The people of Nineveh will be raised in the judgment with this
society, and will condemn it, because they repented at Jonah's preaching,
and there is someone greater than Jonah here!

33"No one lights a lamp and puts it away in the cellar or under a
bucket. No, you put it on a lampstand so that everyone coming into the
house may see the light. 34The lamp of your body is your eye. When your
eye[81] is clear, your whole body is full of light. But when your eye is bad,
your whole body is in darkness. 35Make sure that the light in you is not
really darkness. 36If your whole body is full of light and no part of it is in
darkness,[82] it will be completely lit up, just as a lamp shining brightly
gives you light."

37When Jesus had finished speaking a Pharisee asked him to have
lunch with him. So Jesus went and sat down to a meal. 38The Pharisee
was surprised did not ceremonially wash before the meal. 39So the lord
said to him, "You Pharisees clean the outside of the cup and the plate,
but inside you are full of theft and evil. 40You foolish people, do you not
think that He who made the outside made the inside also? 41But give
from the heart inside to those in need, and everything will be clean to
you.

42"Shame on you Pharisees! You pay tithes on all kinds of herbs and
plants, but ignore justice and the love of God. That is what you should
have done, while not leaving these other things undone. 43Shame on you
Pharisees! You love the chief seats in the synagogues, and being greeted
with respect in the marketplaces. 44Shame on you! You are like
unmarked graves that people walk over without knowing."

---

[81]The eye stands for the faculty of spiritual enlightenment and understanding. "Jesus came to give us an understanding so that we may come to know God" (1 John 5:20). "By his knowledge, my upright servant will make many upright" (Isa. 53:11; cp. Dan. 12:3).

[82]Some students of the Bible arrive at a large measure of truth, but remain blind in some important areas of truth.

45One of the experts in the Law responded, "Teacher, when you say
this you are insulting us also." 46He said, "Shame on you experts in the
Law as well! You load people down with burdens too hard to carry, but
you do not help carry those burdens even with your little finger. 47Shame
on you! You build memorial tombs for the prophets, but it was your own
ancestors who killed them! 48So you prove that you approve of what your
ancestors did — they killed the prophets and you build their tombs!
49That is why the wisdom of God said,[83] 'I will send them prophets and
Apostles. Some of them they will kill and persecute.' 50This is so that the
blood of all the prophets shed since the beginning of the world will be
charged against this wicked society,[84] 51from the blood of Abel to the
blood of Zechariah,[85] who was killed between the altar and the house of
God. Yes, I tell you, it will be charged against this evil society.[86] 52Shame
on you, experts in the Law! You have taken away the key of
knowledge;[87] so you did not go in yourselves, and you kept others from
going in."

53When he left there the religious teachers and the Pharisees began to
be very hostile, questioning him closely on many subjects, 54lying in wait
to trap him in something he might say.

12 1Meanwhile so many thousands of people had gathered that they
were trampling on each other. Jesus began saying to his disciples
first of all, "Watch out for the yeast of the Pharisees, which is hypocrisy.
2There is nothing concealed that will not be revealed; nothing hidden that

---

[83]"The wisdom of God said" illustrates the fact that wisdom and word can be personified, spoken of as if a person but really just the one God in action. So in John 1:1, we find the word/wisdom of God with God and fully expressive of Him. When Jesus the Son was begotten that wisdom was embodied in a fully human being.

[84]Generation, meaning evil society or in this case "evil brood" of religious leaders.

[85]That is, all those killed for the truth, from Genesis (Abel) to 2 Chronicles where a prophet Zechariah (not the Bible prophet Zechariah) was murdered. Jesus' Bible had the same books as we have in the OT, but in a different order. See Jesus' reference to this in Luke 24:44: Law, Prophets and Psalms (Writings), what Jews refer to under the acronym TaNaKh, Torah, Nevi'im, Ketuvim.

[86]This evil society as it is right up to the Second Coming of Jesus — not just his contemporaries. The word *genea* carries the sense of a group of people characterized by a common quality, in this case evil (see Mk. 8:38).

[87]The parallel in Matthew (23:13) shows that the Kingdom of God and understanding it as the heart of the Gospel is the necessary key.

will not be known. 3Whatever you have said in the dark will be heard in
the light, and whatever you whispered in private will be shouted from the
rooftops.

4"I say to you, my friends, do not be afraid of those who can kill the
body, because after that there is nothing more they can do. 5Let me warn
you who you should fear: Fear the One who after killing, has the
authority to throw into Gehenna-fire.[88] Yes, I tell you, fear Him! 6Are not
five sparrows sold for two pennies? Yet not one sparrow is forgotten in
God's sight. 7Even the hairs on your head have been counted. So do not
be afraid; you are worth more than many sparrows!

8"I say to you, everyone who confesses me before people, the Son of
Man will confess them before the angels of God, 9but whoever denies me
before people will be denied before the angels of God. 10Everyone who
speaks against the Son of Man will be forgiven, but anyone who
blasphemes against the holy spirit[89] will not be forgiven. 11When they
bring you before synagogues and leaders and authorities, do not worry
about what to say in your defense, 12because the holy spirit will instruct
you at that time what you should say."

13Someone in the crowd said to him, "Teacher, tell my brother to
divide the family inheritance with me." 14But Jesus replied, "Man, who
made me a judge or arbitrator over you?" 15Then Jesus said to the people,
"Be careful to avoid all greedy thoughts and actions, because a person's
life is not made up of how many possessions they have, even if they are
rich." 16He told them a parable.[90] "There was a rich man whose land was
very productive," he began. 17"The man thought to himself, 'What shall I
do, because I have nowhere to store my crops.' 18He decided, 'This is
what I will do: I will tear down my barns and build bigger ones, and
there I will store all my grain and my possessions. 19Then I will say to
myself, "Self, you have enough for many years, so take it easy, eat, drink
and have fun!"' 20But God said to him, 'Foolish man! This very night
your life will be demanded of you, and then who will get everything you

---

[88]That is, by destroying by annihilation in fire. There is no doctrine of eternal torture for the wicked in Scripture.

[89]Those who in the face of demonstrable and unarguable evidence of the spirit of God at work, refuse to acknowledge God's activity.

[90]A comparison.

have stored up?' 21That is what it is like for people who collect wealth for
themselves but are not rich toward God."

22He said to his disciples, "That is why I am telling you, do not worry
about life — about what to eat, or what clothes to put on your body.
23Life is more than food, and the body more than clothes. 24Consider the
crows: they do not sow or reap, have no storeroom or barn, but God
feeds them. You are much more valuable than birds! 25And can any of
you live even a little longer by worrying about it? 26If you cannot do
anything about these things, why worry about the rest? 27Consider the
lilies and how they grow: they do not work hard or spin yarn. But I am
telling you, not even Solomon in all his glory was as beautifully dressed
as they are. 28And if God clothes wildflowers growing in a field so
beautifully, which are here today but tomorrow are thrown in a furnace,
how much more will He clothe you, you who have little faith? 29So do
not be preoccupied about what you are going to eat or drink, and do not
be anxious. 30These are the things that everybody in the world seeks, and
your Father knows you need them. 31But seek His Kingdom,[91] and these
things will be provided for you. 32Do not be afraid, little flock, because
your Father is delighted to give you the Kingdom.[92]

33"Sell what you have and give to the poor. Make yourselves money
bags which do not wear out, an unfailing treasure stored up in heaven,[93]
where no thief comes near and no moth destroys. 34For where your
treasure is, there your heart will be also.

---

[91]The Kingdom of God is the heart of the true, saving Gospel and is therefore to be believed. In much popular preaching the Kingdom and the Gospel about it has been replaced by a vacuous and vague disembodied existence in "heaven." Such an idea is destructive of belief in the true Gospel as Jesus preached it. Luke 8:12 and many verses make an intelligent grasp of the word/Gospel of the Kingdom (Mt. 13:19) the basic condition for salvation.

[92]To be given the Kingdom means to inherit it when Jesus returns and to be granted a position of management responsibility in the Kingdom of God on a renewed earth (1 Cor. 6:2; 2 Tim. 2:12; Mt. 19:28; Rev. 5:10; 2:26; 3:21; Dan. 7:14, 18, 22, 27).

[93]Future reward, the inheritance of the Kingdom on earth when Jesus returns, is now prepared and promised by God. In the same way Jesus asked for his reward, at the completion of his work, the reward which had been stored up with God from long ago (Jn. 17:5; cp. 17:22, 24 where the same glory had been given in prospect to disciples not yet born).

35“Be ready for action, and keep your lamps burning. 36Be like
servants waiting for their master to return from the wedding feast, ready
to open the door quickly for him when he comes and knocks. 37Blessed
are those servants whom the master will find on the alert when he comes.
I am telling you the truth: he will get himself ready, have them sit down
for a meal, and come and serve them. 38Even if he comes in the middle of
the night, or just before dawn, they will be blessed if he finds them
watching.

39“Remember this: if the head of the house knew what time a thief
was coming, he would not allow his house to be broken into. 40In the
same way you should be ready, because the Son of Man will come at a
time you do not expect.”

41Peter asked, “lord, are you directing this parable to us, or to
everyone else as well?” 42The lord said, “So who is the trustworthy and
wise supervisor, the one his master puts in charge of his servants, to
share out their food allowance at the right time? 43Blessed is that servant
when his master comes and finds him doing as he should. 44I am telling
you the truth: the master will put him in charge of everything he has.[94]
45But if that servant says to himself, ‘My master will take his time in
returning,’ and begins to beat the other servants, both men and women,
and to feast and get drunk, 46then that servant’s master will return
unexpectedly one day, and will cut him in pieces, and assign him a place
with the unbelievers. 47A servant who knew what his master wanted, and
yet did not prepare or carry out his instructions, will be severely beaten;
48but the servant who did not know, but did things deserving punishment,
will be beaten only lightly. From everyone who has been given much,
much will be required, and from anyone who is entrusted with much,
more will be expected.

49“I came to bring fire to the earth, and I wish it was already burning!
50But I have a baptism to go through, and how I am suffering until it is
accomplished! 51Do you think that I came to bring peace on earth? No, I
am telling you that I bring division. 52From now on a household of five
will be divided, three against two and two against three. 53They will be
divided, father against son and son against father; mother against

---

[94]Cp. 19:17: “Be governor of ten cities.”

daughter and daughter against mother; mother-in-law against daughter-
in-law and daughter-in-law against mother-in-law."
54To the crowds, Jesus said, "When you see a cloud coming up in the
west you immediately say, 'A shower is coming,' and so it does. 55And
when a south wind blows, you say, 'It will be a hot day,' and it is. 56You
hypocrites, how is it that you know how to analyze the earth and sky, but
you do not analyze this present time?
57"Why do you not judge for yourselves and decide what is right? 58It
is as if you are going with your opponent to a magistrate. While on the
way you should be working to settle the matter so that you will not be
dragged before the judge, and the judge hand you over to the officer, and
the officer throw you into prison. 59I tell you, you will not get out of there
until you have paid the very last penny."

13 1At that same time some people told Jesus about the Galileans who
had been killed by Pilate even while they were offering sacrifices.
2Jesus said to them, "Do you think that those Galileans were the worst
sinners of all Galileans because they suffered like this? 3I tell you, no!
But unless you repent, you will all perish as well. 4Or what about those
eighteen people who were killed when the tower in Siloam fell on them?
Do you think they were more guilty than all the other people who live in
Jerusalem? 5I tell you, no! But unless you repent, you will all perish as
well."
6Then he told them this parable: "There was a man who had a fig tree
planted in his vineyard. He came looking for fruit on it, but did not find
any. 7So he said to the gardener, 'Look, for three years running I have
been checking for fruit on this fig tree, but I found none. Chop it down.
Why should it just take up space?' 8The gardener replied, 'Leave it alone,
sir, for just one more year, and I will dig the soil around it and put in
some fertilizer. 9If it gives fruit next year, that is good. If not, then you
can have it chopped down.'"
10Jesus was teaching in one of the synagogues on the Sabbath. 11A
woman was there who for eighteen years had suffered with a sickness
caused by a spirit. She was bent over and unable to straighten up at all.
12When Jesus saw her, he called her over and said to her, "You are set
free from your sickness." 13He laid his hands on her, and immediately she
was able to stand up straight, and she began giving glory to God. 14But

the synagogue leader was angry that Jesus had healed on the Sabbath,
and said to the crowd, "There are six days when work should be done, so
come during those days and be healed, not on the Sabbath day." 15But the
lord answered him, "You hypocrites, does not each of you on the
Sabbath untie your ox or donkey from the stall and take it to give it a
drink? 16So should not this woman, this daughter of Abraham who has
been tied up by Satan for eighteen years, have been untied from the chain
that bound her on the Sabbath day?" 17When he said this, all his
opponents were shamed, and the whole crowd was delighted by the
wonderful things he was doing.

18So Jesus said, "What is the Kingdom of God like? What should I
compare it to? 19It is like a mustard seed which a man planted in his
garden. It grew and became a tree, and the birds nested in its branches."[95]

20Again he said, "What should I compare the Kingdom of God to? 21It
is like yeast which a woman put in three measures of flour, until the
whole dough rose."

22Jesus traveled through towns and villages, teaching as he made his
way to Jerusalem. 23Someone asked him, "lord, are only a few going to
be saved?" He said, 24"Struggle[96] to enter through the narrow doorway,
because I am telling you that many will try to go in and will not be able.
25Once the head of the house gets up and shuts the door, you will be
standing on the outside knocking on the door, saying, 'lord, open the
door for us!' He will reply, 'I do not know where you are from.' 26Then
you will say, 'We ate and drank with you, and you taught in our streets.'
27He will say, 'I am telling you, I do not know where you come from. Get
away from me, all you evil people!' 28There will be weeping and
grinding of teeth when you see Abraham, Isaac, Jacob and all the
prophets in the Kingdom of God but yourselves being thrown out.
29People will come from east and west, north and south, and will sit down
at the banquet table in the Kingdom of God. 30Indeed the last will be first,
and the first will be last."

31Right at that time some Pharisees came up to Jesus and said, "Get
away from here, because Herod is trying to kill you." 32He said to them,

---

[95]Referring to the future Kingdom of God prophesied in Dan. 2:44. For the same Kingdom see Dan. 7:14, 18, 22, 27; cp. Lk. 21:31.

[96]This saying exposes the popular misconception that salvation, being by grace and faith alone, requires no effort or work on our part! The very opposite is true.

"Go and tell that fox,[97] 'Look, I am driving out demons and healing
people today and tomorrow, and on the third day[98] I will reach my goal.
33Even so I must continue my journey today, tomorrow, and the day after,
because a prophet cannot die outside Jerusalem!' 34Oh Jerusalem,
Jerusalem, who kills prophets and stones those sent to her! How often I
wanted to gather your children together, just as a hen gathers her chicks
under her wings, and you would not![99] 35Look, your house is being
abandoned. I tell you that you will not see me again until the day comes
when you say, 'Blessed is he who comes in the name of the Lord!'"[100]

14 1One Sabbath Jesus went to the house of one of the leaders of the
Pharisees to have a meal, and they were watching him closely.
2Right in front of him was a man suffering from limbs swollen with fluid.
3So Jesus asked the experts in the Law and the Pharisees, "Is it lawful to
heal on the Sabbath or not?" 4But they kept quiet. Jesus touched the man,
healed him, and sent him on his way. 5Then Jesus said to them, "If your
son or your ox fell into a well on a Sabbath day, would you not
immediately go and pull him out?" 6And they were not able to answer.

7Then he told a parable to the guests who had been invited to the
meal, as he had noticed that they were choosing the seats of honor:
8"When you are invited by someone to a wedding reception, do not sit in
the place of honor, in case someone more important than you may have

---

[97]The use of animal terms for persons is parallel to the use of "serpent" for the person Satan, the Devil.

[98]This is an important statement showing how Jesus reckons inclusively: "today, tomorrow and the third day." That sequence fits perfectly the Friday crucifixion followed by the resurrection on the third day, Sunday (24:21). Sunday is the third day since Friday. The followers of Jesus kept the Sabbath on Saturday and the resurrection was on Sunday. "Sabbath was approaching…And on the sabbath they rested" (23:54-56).

[99]This statement shows that Jesus was not a Calvinist. Jesus thought of his enemies as having freedom of choice to reject what God wanted them to do.

[100]A remnant of the people of Israel will eventually accept the Messiah when he returns. This will be after a remnant has been refined in the future Great Tribulation. Paul spoke in Romans 9-11 of a future, collective conversion of now blinded national, natural Israel. Israel is destined for a time of great distress as defined by Zechariah 13 and 14. Note particularly Zech. 12:3, LXX and Lk. 21:24; Rev. 11:1-2. Eventually a remnant will be refined and allowed to enter the Kingdom. There is no salvation for anyone apart from the acceptance of Jesus and obedience to him (Jn. 3:36).

been invited. 9Your host may come and say to you, 'Give this person
your place,' and then you will be embarrassed to have to move to the last
seat. 10Instead, when you are invited somewhere, go and sit in the last
seat, so that when your host comes in, he may say to you, 'My friend,
please move up to a better seat.' Then you will be honored in front of all
the guests. 11For those who exalt themselves will be humbled, and those
who humble themselves will be exalted."

12He went on to say to the one who had invited him, "When you give
a lunch or dinner party, do not invite your friends, brothers, relatives or
rich neighbors, because they may invite you in return, and you would be
paid back. 13Instead, when you give a banquet, invite the poor, disabled,
lame, and blind, 14and you will be blessed, because they have no way of
repaying you. But you will be repaid at the resurrection of the
righteous."[101]

15When one of those eating at the table with him heard what he said,
he said to Jesus, "How blessed are those who will feast in the Kingdom
of God!" 16Jesus said to him, "There was a man who was giving a great
banquet, and he invited many people. 17At the time of the dinner he sent
his servant to say to everyone who had been invited, 'Come, because the
banquet is ready.' 18But they all began to make excuses. The first one
said, 'I have bought a field and I have to go and see it. Please excuse
me.' 19Another said, 'I have bought five pairs of oxen and I am going to
try them out. Please excuse me.' Another said, 20'I just got married and
so I cannot come.' 21So the servant returned and told his master what
they said. Then the head of the house became angry and said to his
servant, 'Go out at once into the streets and alleys of the town, and bring
in here the poor, disabled, blind and lame.' 22Then the servant said,
'Master, I did what you commanded me, and there is still room.' 23So the
master said to the servant, 'Go out on the roads and paths, and urge

---

[101]This is a critically important statement showing that the first resurrection, of all the faithful of all the ages, will occur at the future coming of Jesus (1 Cor. 15:23). Only at that time will rewards be given. This of course contradicts the popular notion that rewards are received immediately at death. The biblical point of view is that the dead are currently "sleeping," unconscious, unaware of the passage of time. They will be woken from the sleep of death (Ps. 13:3) at the resurrection of the upright and rewarded with positions in the Messianic Kingdom of the future Age (the first stage of the future Kingdom of God on earth is the millennium, Rev. 20:1-6).

people to come, so that my house may be full. 24I tell you, not one of
those people who were invited will taste my banquet.'"
25Large crowds were going along with Jesus, and he turned and said
to them, 26"If anyone comes to me and does not hate[102] his own father and
mother, wife and children, and brothers and sisters — and even his own
life — he cannot be my disciple. 27Whoever does not carry his own cross
and follow me cannot be my disciple. 28If you wanted to build a tower,
would you not first sit down and calculate how much it would cost, to
see if you have enough to finish it? 29Otherwise, after you laid a
foundation and then were not able to finish it, everyone watching would
laugh at you and say, 30'This person started building but could not
finish.' 31What king who is going to battle with another king, does not
first sit down and work out if he and his 10,000 men are strong enough
against the one coming against him with 20,000? 32If not, he will send
representatives while the other king is still a long way off, and ask for
peace terms. 33In the same way, you cannot be my disciple unless you
give up all that you have.
34"So salt is good, but if it becomes tasteless, how do you make it
taste again? 35It is no good for the soil or the manure pile; you just throw
it out. Whoever has ears to hear, listen!"

15 1All the tax collectors and sinners were gathering around Jesus to
listen to him. 2The Pharisees and religious teachers complained,
"This man welcomes sinners and eats with them."
3So Jesus told them this parable: 4"If a man has a hundred sheep and
loses one, would he not leave the ninety-nine in the open pasture and go
looking for the lost one until he finds it? 5When he finds it, he puts it on
his shoulders with joy. 6When he gets home he calls together his friends
and neighbors and says to them, 'Celebrate with me, because I have
found my lost sheep!' 7I tell you that in the same way there will be more
joy in heaven over one sinner who repents than over ninety-nine upright
people who do not need to repent.
8"Or if a woman has ten silver coins and loses one, would she not
light a lamp, sweep the house, and look carefully until she finds it?

[102]The sense is that one must value discipleship to Jesus and his teachings above loyalty to family and friends.

9When she finds it, she calls together her friends and neighbors and says,
'Celebrate with me, because I found the coin that I lost.' 10I am telling
you that there is joy just like this among God's angels over one sinner
who repents."

11Jesus said, "There was a man who had two sons. 12The younger one
said to his father, 'Father, please give me my inheritance early.' So the
man divided what he had between them. 13A few days later the younger
son gathered all he had and left for a distant country. There he wasted all
his wealth by living a wild life. 14When he had spent all he had, a severe
famine took place in that country, and he started to be in need. 15So he
went and got a job from one of the landowners there, who sent him into
his fields to feed pigs. 16He was so hungry that he would have eaten the
seed pods which the pigs were eating, but no one gave him anything.
17When he came to his senses he said to himself, 'How many of my
father's workers have more than enough to eat, and I am here dying of
hunger? 18I am going to get up and go to my father and say to him,
"Father, I have sinned against heaven and against you. 19I am no longer
worthy to be called your son. Please hire me as one of your workers."'
20So he got up and went to his father. When he was still a long way away,
his father saw him and his heart went out to his son. He ran and hugged
him and kissed him. 21The son said to him, 'Father, I have sinned against
heaven and against you. I am no longer worthy to be called your son.'
22But the father said to his servants, 'Quickly bring out the best robe and
put it on him. Put a ring on his finger and shoes on his feet. 23Bring the
calf we have been fattening up and kill it. Let us feast and celebrate,
24because this son of mine was dead and has come to life again; he was
lost and has been found.' So they started celebrating.

25"Now the older son was out in the fields, and as he headed towards
the house, he heard music and dancing. 26He called one of the servants
and asked what was happening. 27'Your brother has come home, and
your father has killed the fattened calf, because he has come back safe
and well,' the servant said to him. 28But the brother became angry and
refused to go in, so his father came out and encouraged him to join them.
29He answered his father, 'Look, I have served you all these years and
never disobeyed any of your commands, but you never gave me even a
young goat to have a party with my friends. 30But this son of yours comes
back, who has spent your money on prostitutes, and you kill the fattened

calf for him!' 31His father said to him, 'Son, you are always here with me, and everything I have is yours. 32But we had to celebrate and be happy now, because this brother of yours was dead and has come back to life; he was lost and has been found.'"

16 1Jesus also said to his disciples, "Once there was a rich man, whose manager was accused of wasting the rich man's money. 2So the rich man called the manager in and said, 'What is this I hear about you? Give me your management report, because you will not be managing any more.' 3The manager said to himself, 'What am I going to do, now that my master is taking away the management job from me? I do not have strength to go digging, and I am ashamed to beg. 4I know what I will do, so that when I am dismissed as manager, people will welcome me into their homes.' 5He asked each person who owed his master to come and see him. He asked the first one, 'How much do you owe my master?' 6He replied, 'A hundred units of oil.' The manager said to him, 'Take your bill, quickly sit down and write fifty.' 7Then he said to another, 'And how much do you owe?' The man answered, 'A hundred measures of wheat.' He said to him, 'Take your bill and write eighty.' 8His master commended the defrauding manager because he acted cleverly, because people of this age[103] act more cleverly in dealing with their own kind than do the children of light. 9I am telling you, make friends for yourselves using the wealth of this corrupt world, so that when it is used up they will welcome you into the homes of the coming age![104]

10"Whoever can be trusted with small things can also be trusted with big things, and whoever is dishonest in small things will also be dishonest in big things. 11So if you are not trustworthy when it comes to worldly wealth, who will trust you with true riches? 12And if you are not trustworthy with what belongs to someone else, who will give you anything of your own? 13No one can be a servant of two masters. Either he will hate one and love the other, or he will be devoted to one and look down on the other. You cannot serve both God and money."

---

[103]The present evil world system which will persist until it is replaced by the new Age of the coming Kingdom of God on earth (see Mt. 19:28; Acts 3:21).

[104]A home belonging to the Age to Come. Jesus is speaking with irony here, since money will never achieve a place in the coming Kingdom of the Age to Come.

14Now the Pharisees, who loved money, had been listening to all this,
and they began mocking Jesus. 15He said to them, "You justify
yourselves in front of people, but God knows your hearts. What is highly
respected by people is detestable in the sight of God.

16"The Law and the prophets were until John; from then on the
Gospel about the Kingdom of God is being preached, and everyone is
urgently invited to enter it. 17But it is easier for heaven and earth to pass
away than for the smallest detail of the Law to fail.[105]

18"Anyone who divorces his wife and marries another commits
adultery, and he who marries a woman who is divorced commits
adultery.[106]

19"There once was a rich man who wore expensive purple and fine
linen clothes, and lived a life of luxury. 20A poor man named Lazarus lay
at his gate, covered in sores, 21longing to be fed from the scraps which
fell from the rich man's table. And besides, the dogs came and licked his
sores. 22The poor man died, and he was carried away by the angels to
Abraham's bosom.[107] The rich man died too and he was buried.
23Tormented in Hades, he looked up and saw Abraham a long way away
with Lazarus at his side. 24'Father Abraham,' he cried out, 'have mercy
on me and send Lazarus so that he could dip the tip of his finger in water
and cool my tongue, because I am in agony in this flame.' 25But Abraham
said, 'Child, remember that during your life you received your good
things, just as Lazarus received bad things. But now he is being
comforted here, while you are in agony. 26And besides all that, between

---

[105]The law in the New Covenant is in the spirit and not the letter (see Rom. 7:6; Col. 2:16-17; Eph. 2:14-15).

[106]An exception, for infidelity, which allows for divorce and thus remarriage, is given in Matt. 19:9.

[107]The phrase "Abraham's bosom" would suggest to readers of the NT the coming banquet at which Abraham and Isaac and Jacob and the prophets will celebrate in the coming Kingdom when Jesus returns. However the story about Lazarus and the rich man pictures a conscious embodied existence with rewards and punishments before the future judgment. The wicked are within earshot of the saved. According to Josephus the Pharisees of the 1st century believed in the immortality of the soul (an unbiblical belief) and hence in a conscious intermediate state for the righteous and the wicked between death and future resurrection. The Jewish Talmud refers to Abraham's bosom and it is clear that in some Jewish circles Abraham was thought to be alive and well, immediately after death.

us and you there is a huge chasm set, so that those who want to go from
here to you cannot do so, and no one can cross over from there to us.'
27The rich man said, 'Father, I am begging you, then please send him to
my father's house. 28I have five brothers and he could warn them, so that
they will not also come to this place of torment.' 29But Abraham replied,
'They have Moses and the prophets. Let them listen to them.' 30But he
said, 'No, father Abraham, but if someone goes to them from the dead,
they will repent!' 31But Abraham said to him, 'If they will not listen to
Moses and the prophets, they will not be persuaded even if someone
rises from the dead.'"[108]

17 1Jesus said to his disciples, "Stumbling blocks are sure to come,
but alas for those through whom they come! 2It would be better for
such people for a millstone to be hung around their neck and be thrown
into the sea, rather than to cause one of these little ones to stumble. 3Be
on your guard! If your brother sins, reprimand him; and if he repents,[109]
forgive him. 4Even if he sins against you seven times a day, and seven
times comes back to you and says 'I repent,' then forgive him."

---

[108]On no account should this one story by used, as it often is, to contradict the whole of the rest of Scripture which teaches that the dead are unconscious till the future resurrection (Ecc. 9:5, 10; Jn. 11:11, 14). In this story, one well known to Jews, the characters are not disembodied "souls" or "spirits." Thus taken literally it gives no support at all to the traditional idea that the dead are currently disembodied, without bodies, in heaven or underground in hell! Rewards are given at the future resurrection of the upright, Jesus had said earlier in 14:14. It would be highly confusing to pit Luke 16 against Luke 14, and ch. 20, and against the rest of the Bible. The biblical view of death is established by such clear texts as Ps. 88:11-12: death is "the land of forgetfulness"; Ecc. 9:5, 10 "the dead know nothing at all…there is no activity or planning or knowledge or wisdom in Sheol/Hades." Man in death "ceases to be" (Job 7:21). Ps. 115:17: "The dead do not praise the Lord, nor do any who go down into silence." Jesus in this story uses a measure of irony, using the Pharisees' story against themselves. In the same context a few verses earlier, Jesus had used sarcasm: "Use the wealth of this world to make friends for yourselves so that when it is gone, you will be welcomed into an eternal home!" (16:9).

[109]There are conditions for repentance and forgiveness. Even those who murdered Jesus have to repent, as we all have to. It is a myth to say that love is unconditional. If so God would automatically forgive everyone without any need for repentance. This would destroy the NT Gospel (Mk. 1:14-15).

5The Apostles said to the lord, "Help us to have more faith!" 6The
lord said, "Even if your faith was as small as a mustard seed, you could
say to this mulberry tree, 'Be uprooted and be planted in the sea,' and it
would obey you.

7"If you have a servant plowing or looking after sheep, would you
say to him when he comes in from the field, 'Please come immediately
and sit down for a meal'? 8No, you tell him, 'Prepare a meal for me and
get yourself ready to serve me while I eat and drink, and then after that
you can eat and drink.' 9And you do not thank the servant because he did
what he was commanded, do you? 10So you too, when you have done
everything you are commanded, say, 'We are servants who do not
deserve special praise. We have just done what we ought to have
done.'"[110]

11As he was on the way to Jerusalem, he passed between Samaria and
Galilee. 12As he entered a village, ten men with leprosy met him. 13They
stood at a distance and called out, "Jesus, master, please have mercy on
us!" 14When he saw them, Jesus said to them, "Go and show yourselves
to the priests." As they went to do so they were healed. 15One of them,
when he saw that he had been healed, turned back, praising God loudly.
16He fell down at Jesus' feet and thanked him. And he was a Samaritan.
17"Were there not ten men healed?" Jesus asked. "So where are the other
nine? 18Did no one come back to give glory to God except this
foreigner?" 19Then he said to him, "Get up and go on your way. Your
faith has healed you."

20The Pharisees came and asked Jesus when the Kingdom of God
would come. He answered, "The Kingdom of God does not come with
your careful observing. 21Nor will people say, 'Look, here it is' or 'There
it is,' because the Kingdom of God will be all over, in the midst of
you."[111]

---

[110]This leaves no room for boasting! After all what talent do you have that God did not give you? It is our duty and a requirement for entering the Kingdom, being saved, that we develop our talents in the service of Jesus and his Gospel about the Kingdom.

[111]This verse has been badly abused to teach a Kingdom only in the heart. Some suggest that Jesus is referring to himself as the king of the Kingdom among (not "within") them. It is much more likely that he is saying that the arrival of the Kingdom in v. 24 will be visible and universally seen, not hidden. Some will mislead by saying "the Kingdom is here or there." He explains this to the disciples in the verses which follow describing the future day of the Son of Man, the Messiah, at his future arrival. A secret

22Then Jesus said to the disciples, “The time is coming when you will
long to see one of the days of the Son of Man, but you will not see it.
23People will say to you, ‘Look, there he is’ or ‘Look, here he is,’ but do
not go running off or follow them. 24For just as the lightning flashes from
one side of the sky to the other, so will be the Son of Man in his day.[112]
25But first he must suffer many things and be rejected by this evil
society.[113] 26Just as it was in the days of Noah, so it will be in the days of
the Son of Man. 27People were eating, drinking, marrying and being
given in marriage, until the day Noah went into the ark. Then the flood
came and destroyed them all. 28It was just the same in the days of Lot.
People were eating and drinking, buying and selling, planting and
building. 29But on the day when Lot left Sodom, it rained fire and
brimstone from heaven and destroyed them all. 30It will be just the same
on the day when the Son of Man will be revealed. 31On that day, the one
who is on the roof of the house must not go down to get his belongings;
and the one out in the fields must not go back to the house. 32Remember
Lot’s wife! 33Whoever tries to keep his life will lose it, but whoever loses
his life will save it. 34I tell you, on that night there will be two in one bed;
one will be taken[114] and the other will be left. 35Two women will be
grinding grain together; one will be taken and the other will be left.”
[36Two men will be in the field; one will be taken and the other will be
left.][115] 37They asked him, “Where, lord?” He said to them, “Vultures
gather where the carcass is.”[116]

---

so-called *pre*-tribulation rapture/resurrection is nowhere taught in the Bible and offers a completely false hope.

[112]That is, when he comes to establish his Kingdom on earth. For the timing of the Kingdom of God see our “The Kingdom of God: Present or Future?” at restorationfellowship.org

[113]Generation, i.e., “evil society.” This is true of all present societies of the present evil age (Gal. 1:4). They will become the Kingdom of God only at the future Second Coming of Jesus at the last trumpet (Rev. 11:15-18).

[114]That is, taken to meet the descending lord Jesus in the air and escort him to the earth where he will inaugurate his worldwide Kingdom (Dan. 2:44; 7:14, 18, 22, 27; Rev. 5:9-10, etc).

[115]Early manuscripts do not contain verse 36.

[116]Possibly a reference to the bird feast which will occur at the destruction of the Antichrist (2 Thess. 2:8; Isa. 11:4).

18 1Jesus told them a parable to teach them to pray always and not
give up. 2He said, "There was once a judge in a certain town who
did not fear God or respect people. 3A widow in the same town kept on
going to him, saying, 'Give me justice against my opponent.' 4For some
time the judge refused, but after a while he said to himself, 'Even though
I do not fear God or respect people, 5because this widow keeps bothering
me I will ensure she receives justice, so that she does not wear me out by
her repeated visits.'" 6The lord[117] said, "Listen to what the unjust judge
said. 7Do you not think that God will bring about justice for His chosen
ones, who cry out to Him day and night? Do you think He will keep
them waiting? 8I tell you, He will bring about justice for them quickly.
But when the Son of Man comes, will he find the faith on the earth?"[118]
9He also told this parable to some people who trusted in their own
self-righteousness, and looked down on everyone else: 10"Two men went
to the Temple to pray. One was a Pharisee, the other a tax collector.
11The Pharisee stood up and prayed to himself, 'God, I thank you that I
am not like everybody else — swindlers, crooks, adulterers, or like this
tax collector here. 12I fast twice a week, and I pay tithes on everything I
receive.' 13But the tax collector stood at a distance and did not want to
even raise his eyes towards heaven. Instead he beat himself on the chest
and prayed, 'God, please be merciful to me because I am a sinful man.'
14I tell you, it was this man who went home right in God's eyes rather
than the other, because everyone who exalts himself will be humbled,
but he who humbles himself will be exalted."
15People were bringing even their babies to Jesus so that he would lay
hands on them and bless them. But when the disciples saw this, they
scolded the people. 16But Jesus called them to come to him. "Allow the
little children to come to me," he said. "Do not stop them, because the
Kingdom of God belongs to people like them. 17I am telling you the

---

[117]The lower case "lord" is deliberate as referring to Jesus, the non-Deity *adoni* of Ps. 110:1. In some cases in the NT it is not clear whether the Lord God or the lord Messiah Jesus is meant. This is not a problem since they work in perfect harmony.

[118]Jesus was doubtful whether the true faith in the One God and in him as Messiah would survive until his return. This saying hardly suggests a universal acceptance of the true faith prior to the coming of Jesus.

truth: whoever does not receive the Kingdom of God like a child will not enter it."[119]

18One of the leaders asked Jesus, "Good teacher, what should I do to inherit the Life of the Age to Come?" 19Jesus replied, "Why do you call me good? No one is good except God alone.[120] 20You know the commandments: do not commit adultery, do not murder, do not steal, do not lie, honor your father and mother." 21The man responded, "I have kept all these from the time I was young." 22When Jesus heard this reply, he said to the man, "You still fall short in one thing. Sell everything you own and distribute it to the poor, and you will have treasure stored up in heaven. Then come and follow me." 23But when the man heard this he became very sad, because he was extremely rich. 24Seeing his reaction, Jesus said, "How hard it is for those who are wealthy to enter the Kingdom of God![121] 25It is easier for a camel to go through the eye of a needle than for a rich person to enter the Kingdom of God." 26The people listening said, "Then who can be saved?" 27But Jesus said, "Things that are humanly impossible are possible with God."

28Peter said, "Look, we abandoned everything to follow you!" 29Jesus said to them, "I am telling you the truth: there is nobody who has left home, wife, brothers, parents, or children for the sake of the Kingdom of God 30who will not receive many times more in this age, and in the Age to Come the life of that future age."

31Jesus took the twelve aside and said to them, "Listen, we are going up to Jerusalem, and everything written through the prophets about the

---

[119]This verse is fundamentally important as defining salvation. An intelligent grasp of the Gospel of the Kingdom of God is essential for salvation. Jesus was the original preacher of the Kingdom Gospel (Heb. 2:3) and his first command to us is that we are to repent and believe the Gospel about the Kingdom of God (Mk. 1:14-15; see Acts 10:34-43). The coming Kingdom is not something to be argued with, but accepted in childlike faith. See Mk. 4:11-12 and Lk. 8:12, where an intelligent grasp of the Kingdom is needed for repentance and salvation.

[120]This is a typical unitary monotheistic statement of Jesus, whose creed was the unitarian creed of Israel (Mk. 12:29). Jesus was sinless, but only the One God, the Father is absolutely good. To claim that Jesus was here claiming to *be* God would involve belief in two GODS, violating the first commandment. The Bible requires believing that Jesus is the unique Son of God and Luke 1:35 defines how and why he is the Son of God.

[121]Equivalent to "the life of the age to come" in v. 18.

Son of Man will be fulfilled: 32He will be handed over to the Gentiles,
and will be mocked, abused, and spit on. 33After they have beaten him
they will kill him, and on the third day he will rise again." 34But the
disciples did not comprehend any of this. It was hidden from them, and
they did not understand what was said.

35As Jesus was approaching Jericho a blind man was sitting by the
road begging. 36Hearing a crowd going by, he asked what was happening.
37They told him that Jesus of Nazareth was passing by. 38He called out,
"Jesus, son of David,[122] please have mercy on me!" 39Those at the front of
the crowd sternly told him to be quiet, but he shouted even louder, "Son
of David, please have mercy on me!" 40Jesus stopped and commanded
the man to be brought to him. When he came near, Jesus asked him,
41"What do you want me to do for you?" He said, "lord, I want to see
again." 42Jesus said to him, "See again; your faith has healed you."
43Immediately the man regained his sight and began following Jesus,
praising God. And all the people who saw it gave praise to God.

19 1Jesus entered Jericho and was walking through the town. 2A man
named Zaccheus was there, a chief tax collector who was rich. 3He
was trying to see who Jesus was,[123] but he could not because of the crowd
and the fact that he was short. 4So he ran on ahead and climbed up into a
sycamore tree to see Jesus, because he was going to come that way.
5When Jesus got there, he looked up and said, "Zaccheus, hurry and
come down, because today I must stay at your house." 6He came down
quickly and with joy took Jesus home with him. 7When the people saw
this they complained, "He has gone to be the guest of a sinner."
8Zaccheus stopped and said to the lord, "Look, lord, I will give half of all
I own to the poor, and to anybody I have cheated of anything, I will
repay them four times as much." 9Jesus said to him, "Salvation has come

[122]Throughout the NT the recognition of Jesus as the human Messiah, son of David, commends those who have this faith in the true Jesus.

[123]This is the key question for us all. Jesus is the promised Messiah, Son of God (Lk. 1:35; Mt. 1:18: *genesis*, origin; 1:20). Certainly not God the Son, which is a post-biblical concept only possible when the unitarian creed of Jesus (Mk. 12:29; Jn. 17:3) was left behind, shaking the foundations of the Bible. The results in splintered denominations are obvious. Unity among believers will be possible only when we all agree to the first command of Jesus that "the LORD our God is one LORD" (Mk. 12:29).

to this house today, because he too is a son of Abraham. 10The Son of
Man came to seek and save what was lost."

11While they were listening, Jesus went on to tell a parable, because
he was near Jerusalem and the people were thinking that the Kingdom of
God was going to appear immediately.[124] 12So he said, "There was a
nobleman who went to a distant country to receive a kingdom for
himself, and to return. 13He called ten of his servants and gave them each
10 minas. 'Invest this money in business until I come back,' he said to
them. 14But the people of his country hated him, and sent a group after
him. 'We do not want this man to be king over us,' they said.[125] 15When
the king returned, after receiving the kingdom,[126] he ordered that his
servants be brought to him. He wanted to know what they had gained by
investing the money he had given them. 16The first servant came and
said, 'Master, your mina has made ten more minas.' 17The king said to
him, 'Well done, good servant! Because you were faithful in a small
way, I am now putting you in charge of ten towns.' 18The second servant
came and said, 'Master, your mina has made five more minas.' 19The
king said, 'And I am putting you in charge of five towns.' 20Another
servant came and said, 'Master, here is your mina which I kept wrapped
in a cloth. 21I was afraid of you, because you are a harsh man. You take
out what you did not put in, and you harvest what you did not sow.'
22The king replied, 'I will judge you by your own words, you worthless
servant. You say you know I am a harsh man, who "takes out what I did
not put in, and harvests what I did not sow." 23If that is the case, then

---

[124]The assumption that the Kingdom of God would be inaugurated when the Messiah was near the capital of the Kingdom, Jerusalem, was of course absolutely right and biblical. The crowd was well educated in the Messianism of the Hebrew Bible. The Kingdom will appear at the future Second Coming of Jesus. Jesus is coming back to the earth and will then inherit the throne of David. Many Bible readers have been taught mistakenly that Jesus does not really come back to the earth! This would be a sort of "drive-by." In fact, the saints will go out to meet the returning lord in the air (1 Thess. 4:13ff) and escort him to his residence on the earth. Jesus has a one-way ticket when he returns from his present session at the right hand of the One God in heaven (Ps. 110:1).

[125]This is the chronic attitude of all those who despise Jesus and his claims to Messiahship as Son of God miraculously begotten in Mary (Lk. 1:35; Mt. 1:20: "begotten in her").

[126]Placing the Kingdom of God, as typically in the NT, at the return of Jesus. The Gospel is also about that great future event (see Dan. 7:18, 22, 27).

why did you not at least put my money in the bank, so that when I came back I could have collected it with interest?' 24The king said to his attendants, 'Take the mina away from him and give it to the one who has ten.' 25They replied, 'But master, he already has ten minas.' 26The king said, 'I tell you that to everyone who has, more will be given, but from whoever does not have, even what they have will be taken away. 27But as for my enemies who did not want me to be king over them, bring them here and slaughter[127] them in front of me.'"

28After he had said these things, Jesus went towards Jerusalem, walking on ahead. 29As he got close to Bethphage and Bethany, near the hill called the Mount of Olives, he sent two disciples, 30saying, "Go into the village up ahead, and as you enter you will find a colt tied there which no one has ever ridden. Untie it and bring it here. 31If anyone asks you, 'Why are you untying it?' just say, 'The lord needs it.'" 32So the two disciples went and found everything just as Jesus had told them. 33As they were untying the colt, its owners asked, "Why are you untying the colt?" 34They answered, "The lord needs it." 35They led the colt to Jesus and threw their coats over it, and Jesus sat on top. 36As he went along, they were spreading their coats on the road. 37As he reached the place where the road descends the Mount of Olives, the whole crowd of disciples began to shout joyful praises to God for all the miracles they had seen. 38"Blessed is the king who comes in the name of the Lord. Peace in heaven and glory in the highest!" they shouted. 39Some of the Pharisees from the crowd said to Jesus, "Teacher, reprimand your disciples." 40But Jesus answered, "I tell you, if they become silent then the stones will shout aloud!"

41As he got closer to Jerusalem, Jesus saw the city and wept over it. 42"If you had realized today, even you, the things which would lead to peace!" he said. "But now they are hidden from your sight. 43For the time

---

[127]Showing that the time for judgment and punishment will come at the future return of Jesus to establish the Kingdom on earth. The book of Revelation, inspired by Jesus (1:1) gives much fuller detail about the future arrival of Jesus in glory. Revelation unpacks the final "week" of Daniel's famous prophecy of 70 "weeks," the last half of the last 7 years being critically important (Rev. 11:1-2, etc). That final period of trouble is introduced often in the OT, especially the LXX of Zech. 12:3, cited by Jesus in Luke 21:24 and Rev. 11:2. A savage attack on the city and sanctuary in Jerusalem will precede the coming of Jesus (cp. Mt. 24:21; Mk. 13:14, where the Abomination is a person "standing where *he* ought not to"). See Zech. 13:8-9; 14:2.

is coming when your enemies will besiege you, surround you and shut
you in on every side. 44They will level you to the ground with your
children within your walls, and they will not leave in you one stone on
another, because you did not recognize the time of your visitation."

45Jesus went into the Temple and started throwing out the people
selling there. 46"It is written," he said to them, "'My house will be a
house of prayer,' but you have turned it into a robbers' den."

47He was teaching every day in the Temple. But the chief priests, the
religious teachers and the leading men among the people kept on trying
to find a way to get rid of him. 48However they could not find a way to
do this, because all the people were hanging on to every word he said.

20 1One day when Jesus was teaching the people in the Temple and
preaching the Gospel, the chief priests and religious teachers with
the elders confronted him 2and asked, "Tell us — by what authority do
you do these things? Who gave you this authority?" 3Jesus answered, "I
will also ask you a question. Tell me — 4was the baptism of John from
heaven or from people?" 5They discussed this among themselves: "If we
say 'From heaven,' he will ask, 'So why did you not believe John?' 6And
if we say 'From people,' then all the people will stone us to death
because they are convinced that John was a prophet."[128] 7So they replied,
"We do not know where it came from." 8Jesus said to them, "Neither will
I tell you by what authority I do these things."

9Then he told the people this parable: "A man planted a vineyard,
rented it out to tenant farmers, and went on a journey for a long time.
10At harvest time he sent a servant to the farmers to get some of the fruit
from the vineyard. But the farmers beat the servant and sent him away
with nothing. 11So the owner sent another servant, but they beat him too
and treated him badly, and sent him away with nothing. 12Then he sent a
third servant, but they wounded him and threw him out. 13The owner of

---

[128]Bible readers today find themselves similarly on the horns of a dilemma when asked, "Is the creed of Jesus in Mark 12:29 a unitarian or Trinitarian creed?" If they say "unitarian," then the question arises as to why they do not believe and affirm this central teaching of Jesus. If they say, it was a Trinitarian creed, then it may be asked, how is it that a Jewish expert could have believed in the Trinity? The question about the creed of Jesus will reveal the awful fact that Christians are not too concerned with the teaching of Jesus even when he defined the true God as the Father alone.

the vineyard wondered, ‘What should I do? I will send my beloved son.
Maybe they will respect him.’ 14But when the farmers saw the son, they
talked among themselves and decided, ‘This is the owner’s heir. Let us
kill him so we can take his inheritance.’ 15They threw him out of the
vineyard and killed him. So what will the owner of the vineyard do to
them? 16He will come and destroy those farmers and give the vineyard to
others.” When they heard this they said, “That should never be!” 17But
Jesus looked at them and said, “Why then is it written, ‘The stone the
builders rejected became the chief cornerstone’? 18Everyone who falls on
that stone will be broken to pieces, but whoever it falls on will be ground
to dust.’”[129]

19At that very time the religious teachers and the chief priests tried to
arrest Jesus. They realized that Jesus had directed this parable against
them, but they feared the people. 20So they watched Jesus and sent spies
who pretended to be sincere, to try to catch him in something he said, so
that they could hand him over to the rule and the authority of the
governor. 21They asked him, “Teacher, we know that you speak and
teach correctly, and are not influenced by what others think, but teach the
way of God in truth. 22Is it lawful for us to pay taxes to Caesar, or not?”
23But he saw through their trick question and said to them, 24“Show me a
denarius coin. Whose image and inscription is on it?” They replied,
“Caesar’s.” 25He said to them, “Then pay to Caesar what belongs to
Caesar, and to God what belongs to God.” 26They were not able to catch
him out in front of the people. They were amazed at his response and
became silent.

27Then some Sadducees came to him. They say that there is no
resurrection. They asked him this question: 28“Teacher, Moses wrote for
us that if a married man dies childless, then his brother should marry his
widow and raise up children for his brother. 29Now there once were seven
brothers. The first married and died without having children. 30The
second brother 31and then the third married the widow. Likewise all
seven married her without having children. 32Finally the woman died too.
33So in the resurrection whose wife will she be, because she was married
to all seven brothers?”

---

[129]Conversion involves the breaking of our human wills in order to obey God and Jesus. This is a good thing, compared with being ground to dust if we refuse obedience.

34Jesus said to them, “People in this age marry and are given in
marriage, 35but those who are considered worthy to attain to that future
age[130] and the resurrection from the dead do not marry or are given in
marriage. 36They cannot die any more, because they are like the angels,
and they are sons of God by resurrection. 37As to whether the dead will
be raised, even Moses proved this at the burning bush when he called the
Lord ‘the God of Abraham, the God of Isaac, and the God of Jacob.’ 38He
is not the God of the dead but of the living, for all live[131] to Him.” 39Some
of the religious teachers said, “Teacher, you gave a good answer.” 40And
no one was brave enough to ask him any more questions.

41He then asked them, “How is it that people say that the Messiah is
the son of David? 42For David himself says in the book of Psalms, ‘The
Lord said to my lord,[132] “Sit at My right hand 43until I make your enemies
a footstool for your feet.”’[133] 44So David calls him ‘lord,’ and how is he
his son?”

---

[130]The Coming Age of the Kingdom of God at the future return of Jesus in visible power and glory.

[131]That is, they will come to life from death by the future resurrection. At present they are dead (Ecc. 9:5, 10; Jn. 11:11, 14).

[132]*adoni*, my lord, not Lord. All 195 times this title (*adoni*) is a non-Deity title, applied to human superiors and occasionally to angels. This gives rise to the NT’s constant use of “our lord” for Jesus and also the frequently used title Son of Man for Jesus. Jesus constantly called himself Son of Man, and the NT creed giving the simple relationship between Jesus and God is 1 Tim. 2:5: “There is one God and one mediator between God and humans, the human being Messiah Jesus.” This creedal statement preserves the unique position of God the Father as the One God of the Bible, of Israel, of Abraham, Isaac and Jacob, of David and of Jesus and of course of the whole NT. The idea of a triune God is unknown to Scripture. It took a learned Church historian, Rev. Charles Bigg, DD, Regius Professor of church history at Oxford, to point out the obvious fact that when Paul calls Jesus “lord” (1 Cor. 8:6), “we are not to suppose that the Apostles identified Christ with Jehovah; there were passages which made this impossible: Ps. 110:1; Mal. 3:1…It was God who gave Jesus the ‘name which is above all names’ (Phil. 2:9) and who *made* Jesus lord (Acts 2:36 [quoting Ps. 110:1])…It would be rash to conclude that Peter meant to identify Jehovah with Christ. No such identification can be clearly made out in the NT” (*International Critical Commentary* on 1 Peter, pp. 191, 127). Ps. 110:1 has been suppressed, since it clashes with the later “coequal” “orthodoxy” of church councils.

[133]This verse, coupled with Ps. 8 which describes the destiny of man, under whose feet God subjects everything, forms the backbone of all that is taught in the NT about the

45While all the people were listening, he said to his disciples, 46"Watch out for the religious teachers, who like to walk around in long robes, and love respectful greetings in the market places, chief seats in the synagogues and places of honor at banquets. 47They cheat widows out of their property and then pretend to be pious by praying long prayers. They will receive more severe condemnation."

21 1Looking up, Jesus saw rich people putting their gifts into the Temple treasury collection box. 2He also saw a poor widow put in two small copper coins, 3and he said, "I am telling you the truth: this poor widow put in more than everyone else, 4because they gave from their excess, but she gave from her poverty everything she had to live on."

5Some people there were speaking about the Temple — how wonderful the stonework was, and how beautiful the donated gift offerings. Jesus said, 6"As for these things you are looking at, the days will come when not one stone will be left on top of another; everything will be torn down."

7They asked him, "Teacher, when will these things happen, and what will be the sign when these things are about to take place?"[134] 8Jesus said, "Watch out that you are not deceived, because many people will come in my name, saying, 'I am the Messiah!' and 'The time is close!' Do not go after them. 9When you hear of wars and disturbances, do not be terrified, because such things have to come first, but the end will not follow immediately."

10He continued, "Nation will fight against nation, and kingdom against kingdom. 11There will be massive earthquakes, famines and

---

identity of Jesus as the Son of Man (human being), certainly not GOD Himself, but the unique, sinless, virginally begotten Son of God (Lk. 1:35).

[134]The common assumption of Jesus and the disciples, based on Daniel's prophecy, is that trouble in the Temple and the immediately following Second Coming are connected. Jesus did nothing in his reply to undermine or correct this correct understanding of prophecy. A temple in which an Abomination of Desolation will stand where "he ought not to" (Mk. 13:14) is to be expected, based on Daniel, Jesus and Paul who spoke of the Man of Sin sitting in the Temple. When Paul means by "temple" the individual believer or the church body, he does not introduce them as "the temple," but "a temple." When in 2 Thess. 2:4 he speaks of "**the** temple" he is understood most naturally as speaking of a building.

epidemics in various places, terrifying things happening and great signs in the sky.

12“But before all this, they will seize you and persecute you, delivering you to the synagogues and prisons, bringing you before kings and governors for my name’s sake. 13This will lead to an opportunity for your testimony. 14So make up your minds not to prepare in advance to defend yourselves, 15because I will give you words to speak and wisdom which none of your enemies will be able to oppose or contradict. 16You will be betrayed even by parents, brothers, relatives, and friends, and they will kill some of you.[135] 17You will be hated by everyone because of my name. 18Yet not a single hair of your head will perish. 19By your endurance you will gain your lives.

20“When you see Jerusalem surrounded by armies, then know that her desolation is near.[136] 21Then those in Judea should flee[137] to the mountains, and those in the city should leave, and those in the country should not go into the city, 22because these are days of punishment, so that everything written will be fulfilled. 23Alas for those who are pregnant or nursing babies at that time, because there will be great distress[138] in the land and anger against this people. 24They will be cut down by the sword and taken away as prisoners into all the nations.

---

[135]Scripture states that some who are weak will need to be refined in the Great Tribulation in the future. Others will be permitted to escape and thus not go through the Great Tribulation. But such escape will certainly not be by a prior rapture/resurrection 7 or 3 1/2 years before the public arrival of Jesus.

[136]This is Luke’s equivalent of “when you see the Abomination of Desolation standing where **he** ought not to” (Mk. 13:14). The days of vengeance which this event introduces are the days of the Great Tribulation of Matt. 24:21. 2 Thess. 2:8 speaks of the destruction of the final evil Man of Sin, the antichrist (cp. 1 John 2:18). Luke 17:26-31 connects the flood and the destruction of Sodom with end-time events. Zech. 12:3 in the LXX (not Hebrew) is key to the thinking of Jesus since he alludes to it in Luke 21:24 and Rev. 11:2, referring to the last half of Daniel’s final “week” (Dan. 9:24-27).

[137]The flight here recalls the flight of Lot from Sodom and the flight of Dan. 12:1. The time of extreme trouble may be avoided by escape but certainly not by a so-called PRE-Tribulation rapture, of which the NT knows nothing. Jesus gathers his people “after the tribulation” (Mt. 24:29ff).

[138]The equivalent exactly of the Great Tribulation of Matt 24:21 and Mark 13:19. The Dead Sea Scrolls also refer to the time of final tribulation, which is worse than any preceding time. Cp. Isa. 33:2: “Be our salvation, rescue in time of trouble.”

Jerusalem will be trampled underfoot by the Gentiles[139] until the
appointed times of the Gentiles[140] have been fulfilled.
25“There will be signs in the sun, moon, and stars, and on the earth
the nations will be in turmoil, bewildered by the roaring of the sea and its
waves. 26People will be fainting because of fear, terrified about what is
coming upon the world, for the powers of heaven will be shaken. 27Then
they will see the Son of Man coming on a cloud with power and brilliant
glory. 28When these things start to happen, stand up and lift up your
heads, because your redemption is about to come.”[141]
29Then he told them a parable: “Look at the fig tree and all the trees.
30When you see them growing new leaves, you know that summer is
near. 31In the same way, when you see these things happening, know that
the Kingdom of God is near.[142] 32I am telling you the truth: this evil
society[143] will not pass away until all these things happen. 33Heaven and
earth will pass away, but my words will not pass away.
34“Watch out! Make sure you do not get preoccupied with partying or
drinking or the worries of life, or that day will catch you suddenly like a
trap. 35For that day will come on everyone who lives on the face of the
whole earth. 36But keep on the alert at all times, praying that you may
have strength to escape all these things that are going to happen, and to
stand before the Son of Man.”

---

[139]Under foreign control.

[140]The times when a final oppression of Israel by the Gentiles will occur. This verse is highly significant. It is a quotation from the LXX of Zech. 12:3 which says that “all the nations will gather against Jerusalem and will mock the city and trample it under foot.” Jesus understands this to describe the final punishment of Israel, and in Rev. 11:2-3 he links it to the Abomination of Desolation of Dan. 9:26-27 where the prince who is to come will desecrate the city for the final 3 ½ years of the final period of 7 years. Thus Luke 21:24, Dan. 9:26-27 and Rev. 11:2-3 must be kept closely together as they interpret each other.

[141]Salvation is very often an event of the future in the NT. Christians are now being saved and will be finally saved at the return of Jesus to the earth. “He who endures to the end will be saved” (Mt. 24:13).

[142]This is one of many plain statements of Jesus showing that the Kingdom of God means primarily the new world order on a renewed earth when Jesus returns and appoints the saints to administer the world with him (Mt. 19:28; 1 Cor. 6:2; 2 Tim. 2:12; Rev. 2:26; 5:10; 3:21; Dan. 7:14, 18, 22, 27, etc).

[143]Paul refers to this as the present evil age (Gal. 1:4). Society is governed by Satan who is deceiving the whole world (Rev. 12:9).

37 During the day Jesus was teaching in the Temple, and every
evening he would go out and spend the night on the hill known as the
Mount of Olives. 38 All the people would get up early to come and listen
to him in the Temple.

22 1 The Feast of Unleavened Bread,[144] called the Passover,[145] was
approaching. 2 The chief priests and the religious teachers were
trying to find a way to kill Jesus, for they were afraid of the people.
3 Then Satan entered into Judas who was called Iscariot, one of the
twelve. 4 He went and discussed with the chief priests and officers how he
might betray Jesus to them. 5 They were delighted and offered to pay him.
6 He agreed, and started looking for a good opportunity to betray Jesus to
them when the crowd was not there.
7 The first day of Unleavened Bread arrived, when the Passover lamb
had to be sacrificed.[146] 8 Jesus sent Peter and John, saying to them, "Go

---

[144] "Luke identifies Passover (with its Passover lamb) and Unleavened Bread (with its week starting with Passover in which Jewish people were required to keep totally separate from leaven and leavened bread)" (*Word Biblical Commentary*, Luke 18:35-24:53, p. 1027).

[145] Passover is the name of the entire festival of 8 days, not only the name of the day of the paschal lamb which opens the festival towards the end of the 14 Nisan. Readers of Luke would not be familiar with the Jewish calendar and so needed this explanation.

[146] That is, as laid down by the Law. On the eve, i.e. towards the end, of the 14th Nisan the Passover lamb was killed and then eaten on the same evening (after sunset) which was the 15th Nisan. It is perfectly clear from Mathew, Mark and Luke that Jesus and the disciples were planning their meal for the same time that the nation was celebrating the Passover supper. John can be harmonized with this fact; see notes on John. Lange's protest against false views is appropriate: "It is really an enigma how one could ever have found in this chronological datum of Luke and in the words of Matt. 26:18 a ground for the entirely unprovable conjecture that our Savior ate the Passover a day earlier than other Israelites. Upon every impartial person the beginning of this section makes far more the impression that Luke speaks here of the definite day on which, according to the appointment of the Law, the Passover lamb had to be slaughtered. Only on this day was the disciples' question perfectly natural…Be it only granted to us to express our conviction — the result of special and repeated investigation — that as well according to the Synoptics as according to John, our Lord, on the 14th Nisan, at the same time with the other Jews, and at the time appointed by the Law, ate the Passover, and on the 15th suffered the death on the cross…The last Passover celebration of the Old Covenant coalesces with the institution of the Holy Communion…In the same way

and prepare the Passover meal for us so we can eat it together." 9They asked him, "Where do you want us to prepare it?" 10He said to them, "When you go into the city a man carrying a pitcher of water will meet you. Follow him and go into the house he enters, 11and say to the owner of the house, 'The teacher asks you, "Where is the room where I may eat the Passover with my disciples?"' 12He will show you a large furnished upstairs room. Prepare the meal there." 13They went and found everything just as he had told them, and they prepared the Passover.[147]

14When the time came, he sat down with the Apostles. 15He said to them, "I have been longing to eat this Passover meal with you before I suffer. 16For I tell you, I will not eat it again until it is fulfilled in the Kingdom of God."[148] 17He took a cup, and after giving thanks he said, "Take this and share it among yourselves. 18I tell you that I will not drink of the fruit of the vine[149] from now on until the Kingdom of God comes."[150] 19He took some bread, and after giving thanks, he broke it and gave it to them. "This is my body given for you; remember me by doing this," he said to them. 20In the same way he took the cup after supper and said, "This cup is the New Covenant ratified by my blood which is being poured out for you. 21But notice that the hand of the one betraying me is with mine on the table. 22For the Son of Man will go as it has been determined, but alas for that man by whom he is betrayed!" 23They began

---

Jesus did away with circumcision [in the flesh] when it was accomplished on himself on the eighth day (Lk. 2:21)" (Lange, *Commentary on Luke*, p. 332).

[147]It is perfectly obvious that the Passover meal was the one to be kept by the nation according to the law (Ex. 12). There is not a shred of evidence that Jesus was keeping it a day earlier than the nation.

[148]That is, at the Second Coming, the Parousia.

[149]*Oinos* in Greek is a fermented drink, not grape juice. Alcohol was used by Jews as prescribed by God in the OT and Jesus turned 120 gallons of water into wine (John 2). The "temperance movement" was wrongly named since they enforced *prohibition*, not temperance. Drunkenness is of course a completely different issue since the Bible condemns this always. To insist on the prohibition of all alcohol is to be more righteous than Jesus, and many churchgoers would "piously" condemn Jesus at the wedding in Cana. "Fruit of the vine" is Septuagint idiom (Deut. 22:9; Isa. 32:12, LXX) and is found in Jewish literature as a blessing over wine.

[150]These are critically important verses for showing that the Kingdom of God, the heart of the Christian Gospel, is firstly and predominantly a new world order of the future, dependent on the return of Jesus.

to discuss among themselves which one of them it might be who was going to do this.

24They also began to dispute about which of them would be
considered the greatest. 25Jesus said to them, "Gentile kings lord it over
their subjects, and those with authority are even called 'benefactors.'
26But you are not to be like that. Whoever is greatest among you should
become like the lowest, and the leader should be like a servant. 27For who
is greater — the one at the table, or the one serving? Is it not the one at
the table? But I am among you as the one serving.

28"You are the ones who stayed with me through my trials. 29Just as
my Father covenanted[151] a Kingdom to me, I covenant a Kingdom to you,
30that you may eat and drink at my table in my Kingdom, where you will
sit on thrones governing the twelve tribes of Israel.[152]

---

[151]The Greek is "covenant," not just give. The disciples are given the right to rule in the Kingdom. This shows that the gift of the Kingdom and rulership in it is the heart of the New Covenant. Jesus describes to the disciples what that covenanted Kingdom will mean for their future activity. The promise of the future Kingdom is made to all believers (Lk. 12:32; 1 Tim. 2:12; James 2:5; 1 Cor. 6:2; Dan. 7:18, 22, 27: "serve and obey them"; Rev. 1:6; 2:26; 3:21; 5:10; 20:6). The Kingdom is given to the saints (Lk. 12:32). "The time comes when the saints possess the Kingdom" (Dan. 7:22). The Kingdom of God in OT times was "in the hands of the sons of David" (1 Chron. 28:5; 2 Chron. 13:8). Thus the Church, destined to inherit the Kingdom with Jesus, are the royal family in training to administer the new world coming on earth when Jesus returns. Some Bible readers have a vacuous and vague idea of the Kingdom, which has little content. This needs to be corrected if we truly believe the Gospel of the Kingdom and all that this means. This text in Luke 22:29 proves, too, that there are surviving mortals in the Kingdom, to be supervised by the immortalized saints. Immortals will not rule over immortals! (Cp. Zech. 14:16-21; Isa. 24:6; 65:17ff). The whole question of the definition of the Christian hope is at stake here, and hope is the *foundation* of love and faith (Col. 1:4). Without a clear understanding of the content of Christian hope, love and faith are diminished and depleted.

[152]See Acts 1:6-8 and Matt. 19:28. The Christian reward is to administer the coming new world of the Kingdom of God on earth, based principally on the amazing promises of Dan. 7:14, 18, 22, 27; Ps. 37:9, 11, 18, 22, 34. This Messianic hope, coming from Messiah's words, is far removed from the non-substantial "hope" of strumming harps in heaven (where Jesus will not be!) as a disembodied soul at death! Christians are to prove themselves now, fully exercising their talents in the service of Messiah and his Kingdom Gospel. Their skills will be fully harnessed when Jesus appoints them to positions of administrative authority in the Kingdom to come (1 Cor. 6:2; 2 Tim. 2:12; Rev. 2:26; 3:21; 5:10; 20:1-6; Lk. 19:17, 19). The wicked will be judged and destroyed (Lk. 19:27). Some will repent and be allowed into the Kingdom as mortals (Isa.

31“Simon, Simon, Satan has demanded to sift you all like wheat, 32but
I have prayed for you that your own faith might not fail. When you have
turned back, strengthen your brothers.” 33But Peter replied, “lord, I am
ready to go with you, to prison and to death!” 34Jesus said, “I am telling
you, Peter, the rooster will not crow today until you have denied three
times that you know me.”

35He asked them, “When I sent you out without a money belt, bag, or
sandals, did you need anything?” They answered, “No, nothing.” 36He
said to them, “But now, let everyone who has a money belt take it, and a
bag as well. And if you do not have a sword, sell your coat and buy one.
37For I am telling you, this Scripture must be fulfilled in me: ‘He was
considered among the criminals.’ Indeed what is written about me is now
being fulfilled.” 38They said, “Look, lord, here are two swords.”[153] He
replied, “That is enough.”

39He left and went as usual to the Mount of Olives, and the disciples
followed. 40When he got there he said to them, “Pray that you may not
enter into temptation.” 41He left them and went about a stone’s throw
away, where he knelt down and prayed, 42“Father, if You are willing,
please take this cup of suffering from me; yet not my will, but Yours be
done.” 43Then an angel appeared from heaven to strengthen him. 44In
agony, he prayed even harder, and his sweat became like drops of blood
falling onto the ground. 45When he rose from prayer he went over to the
disciples and found them asleep, worn out from sorrow. 46“Why are you
sleeping?” he asked them. “Get up and pray so that you do not give in to
temptation.”

47While he was still speaking, a crowd arrived, led by Judas, one of
the twelve. Judas went up to Jesus to kiss him. 48But Jesus said to him,
“Judas, are you going to betray the Son of Man with a kiss?” 49When
those with Jesus saw what was going to happen they said, “lord, shall we

---

65:17ff). Some will have to be severely disciplined by Jesus as the then King of the Kingdom (Zech. 14:16-21). The pagan doctrine of the immortal soul has disastrously interfered with the biblical hope of resurrection of the whole person, when Jesus comes back (1 Cor. 15:23). See my *What Happens When We Die?*

[153]The provision of swords is here said to be for the purpose of fulfilling the prophecy that the Messiah would be seen as a common freedom fighter. Even the defensive sword of Peter was condemned by Jesus: “Put your sword back in its sheath, for all who take the sword will perish with the sword” (Mt. 26:52).

use our swords?" 50And one of them struck the high priest's servant and
cut off his right ear. 51At this Jesus said, "Stop! No more of this." He
touched the man's ear and healed him. 52Then Jesus said to the chief
priests, officers of the Temple, and elders who had come against him,
"Did you need to come out with swords and clubs as if you were coming
after a criminal? 53When I was with you every day in the Temple, you did
not arrest me. But this time and the power of darkness are yours."

54They seized him and led him away, and brought him to the high
priest's house. Peter followed at a distance. 55They lit a fire in the middle
of the courtyard and sat around it. Peter sat there with them. 56A servant
girl noticed him as he sat there in the firelight, and stared at him. 57"This
man was with him," she said. But Peter denied it. "Woman, I do not
know him," he replied. 58A little while later someone else looked at him
and said, "You are one of them too!" But Peter said, "No, I am not!"
59About an hour later, another person insisted, "I am certain that this man
also was with him. He is clearly a Galilean." 60But Peter replied, "Man, I
do not know what you are talking about!" And immediately, while he
was still speaking, a rooster crowed. The lord turned and looked at Peter,
61and Peter remembered the lord's word, how he had said to him, "Before
a rooster crows today, you will deny me three times." 62And he went out
and wept bitterly.

63The men holding Jesus prisoner were mocking him and beating
him. 64They put a blindfold on him and said to him, "Prophesy — who
just hit you?" 65They blasphemed with many other insults against him.

66When day came[154] the elders' council assembled, including chief
priests and religious teachers, and led him away to their council
chamber. They said, 67"If you are the Messiah, tell us." But Jesus said to
them, "If I tell you, you will not believe, 68and if I ask a question, you
will not answer. 69But from now on the Son of Man will be seated at the
right hand of the power of God."[155] 70They all said, "So are you the Son

---

[154]This was Friday morning, 15th Nisan.

[155]Fulfilling the key OT verse from the NT, alluded to in the NT more than any other verse from the OT, Ps. 110:1 where YHVH gives a prophetic utterance about *adoni*, my lord (Messiah).

of God then?"[156] He replied, "Yes, I am." 71They said, "Why do we need
any more evidence from others? We have heard it for ourselves from his
own mouth."

23 1Then the whole council got up and took him to Pilate. 2They
began to accuse him. "We discovered this man misleading our
nation, forbidding them to pay taxes to Caesar, and claiming to be
Messiah, a king,"[157] they said. 3So Pilate asked him, "Are you the King of
the Jews?" He answered, "As you say." 4Pilate said to the chief priests
and the crowds, "I do not find this man guilty of anything." 5But they
kept on insisting and said, "He stirs up the people with his teaching all
over Judea, starting from Galilee all the way here." 6When he heard this,
Pilate asked if Jesus was a Galilean. 7When he realized that Jesus came
under Herod's jurisdiction, he sent him to Herod who was also in
Jerusalem at that time.

8Herod was very happy when he saw Jesus, because he had been
wanting to see him for a long time. He had heard a lot about him and
hoped to see him perform a miracle. 9So he questioned him for a long
time, but Jesus did not reply at all. 10The chief priests and religious
teachers stood there, accusing him vigorously. 11Herod and his soldiers
humiliated and mocked Jesus, dressed him in a royal robe, and then sent
him back to Pilate. 12That day Herod and Pilate became friends with each
other; before that they had been enemies.

13Pilate summoned the chief priests, the rulers, and the people, 14and
said to them, "You brought this man before me, accusing him of inciting

---

[156]"Son of God" in the New Testament context is nothing at all to do with the Church's later mutation of this very Messianic title into "God the Son," second member of a triune God who is unknown to Scripture.
The worst that they could charge him with was that he claimed to be the Messiah, Son of God and the one destined to sit at the right hand of the One God in heaven, the overarching prophecy of Ps. 110:1 which controls the entire definition of Jesus in relation to God. The second "lord" in Ps. 110:1 is *adoni*, my lord, which in all of its 195 occurrences never means Deity. The word is properly rendered "my lord" (*kurios mou*) in the LXX and thus also in NT Scripture.

[157]This is exactly "the lord Messiah" who had been born in Bethlehem (Lk. 2:11). God cannot be born! No one accused Jesus of claiming to *be* YHVH. The worst they could say was that he claimed to be the Messiah, Son of God and of David, who would be seated in heaven with the Father.

the people to rebellion. I have examined him in your presence, and I do
not find him guilty of the charges you bring against him. 15Herod did not
find him guilty either, because he sent him back to us. Indeed he has
done nothing worthy of the death penalty. 16So I will have him flogged
and let him go." 17[Now he was meant to release one prisoner to them at
the feast.][158]

18But the whole crowd shouted all together, "Away with this man,
and release Barabbas for us." 19He was a man who had been thrown into
prison for a rebellion in the city, and for murder. 20Pilate, wanting to
release Jesus, spoke to them again, 21but they went on shouting, "Crucify
him! Crucify him!" 22For the third time Pilate asked them, "Why? What
has he done wrong? I do not find him worthy of the death sentence, so I
will have him flogged and release him." 23But they kept insisting, loudly
demanding that he be crucified, and their shouts won out. 24Pilate
pronounced sentence as they demanded. 25He released the man they were
asking for, who had been imprisoned for rebellion and murder, while he
handed Jesus over to them, to do what they wanted with him.

26As they led him away, they seized a man, Simon from Cyrene, who
was coming in from the countryside, and placed the cross on him to carry
it behind Jesus. 27A large crowd of people followed him, and women
mourning and lamenting him. 28But Jesus turned to them and said,
"Daughters of Jerusalem, stop weeping for me, but weep for yourselves
and your children, 29because the time is coming when people will say,
'Blessed are those who are childless, and those who never had babies,
and those who never nursed them.' 30Then they will be saying to the
mountains, 'Fall on us!' and to the hills, 'Cover us up!' 31For if they are
doing these things when the tree is alive, what will happen when it is
withered?"

32Two others, who were criminals, were also being led out to be put
to death with Jesus. 33When they came to the place called the Skull they
crucified him there with the criminals, one on the right and the other on
the left. 34Jesus said, "Father, forgive them, because they do not know
what they are doing." They threw dice to divide up his clothes among
them. 35The people stood there watching, while the leaders ridiculed him:
"He saved other people, so let him save himself if he really is the

---

[158]Early manuscripts do not contain v. 17.

Messiah of God, His chosen one." 36The soldiers also mocked him,
coming up to him and offering him sour wine. 37"If you are the King of
the Jews, then save yourself!" they jeered. 38Above Jesus was a sign
which read, "This is the King of the Jews."

39One of the criminals hanging there insulted Jesus: "Are you not the
Messiah? Then save yourself and us!" 40But the other criminal
reprimanded him: "Do you not even fear God when you are condemned
to die? And in our case the sentence is correct because we are getting
what we deserve for what we did, but this man has done nothing wrong."
42And he said, "Jesus, remember me when you come bringing in your
Kingdom." 43Jesus said to him, "Truly I tell you today, you will indeed
be with me in paradise."[159]

44It was then about noon, and it became dark over the whole land
until three o'clock. 45The sun stopped shining, and the Temple veil was
torn in two. 46Jesus cried out, "Father, into Your hands I commit my
spirit,"[160] and then he breathed his last. 47When the centurion saw what
happened he praised God and said, "There is no doubt that this man was
innocent." 48And all the crowds who had gathered to watch, when they
saw what happened went back beating their chests with grief. 49All who
knew him, and the women who had accompanied him from Galilee,
watched from a distance.

50There was a man named Joseph, a council member, a good and
honest man. 51He had not agreed to the plan and actions of the council.
He was from the Jewish town of Arimathea, and he was waiting for the

---

[159]The future paradise is mentioned in Rev. 2:7. The promised future restoration of paradise on earth was guaranteed by Isa. 51:3, where "garden" is paradise in the Greek LXX. Jesus was not in that Kingdom the day he died (he was asleep in the tomb). On the following Sunday he had still not yet ascended to the Father. And in Acts 2:31-32 Peter said that God had not abandoned the person Jesus to the realm of the dead, but had brought him back to life and out of "gravedom," the world of the dead by resurrection which occurred on the third day (Sunday).

[160]This request has nothing to do with a conscious survival of Jesus at death. He is simply putting himself into God's hands as he dies, knowing that God will resurrect him on the third day (Sunday). David used the same language when not dying, simply commending himself to God's care (Ps. 31:5). Stephen, the whole person, fell asleep in the sleep of death (Ps. 13:3) and had similarly entrusted himself to GOD (Acts 7:59-60).

Kingdom of God.[161] 52He went to Pilate and asked for Jesus' body. 53He took it down and wrapped it in a linen cloth. He laid Jesus in a tomb cut into the rock, which had not been used before. 54It was preparation day, and the Sabbath day was about to begin.[162] 55The women who had come with Jesus from Galilee followed and saw the tomb and how his body was laid. 56Then they went home and prepared burial spices and perfumes. On the Sabbath[163] they rested according to the commandment.[164]

24 1At dawn on the first day of the week, the women went to the tomb, carrying the spices they had prepared. 2They discovered that the stone had been rolled away from the tomb entrance, 3so they went in, but they did not find the body of the lord Jesus. 4As they were bewildered about this, suddenly two men in dazzling white clothes appeared. 5The women were terrified and bowed down with their faces to the ground. They said to the women, "Why are you looking for the living

---

[161]Showing clear evidence that the Kingdom, the heart of the Christian Gospel, was something which had not yet arrived, even after the death of Jesus. The expectation and hope of original Christianity is for the future arrival of the world government and Kingdom of Messiah which he will introduce at his return to the earth. This good news for a suffering and distracted world is the core of the Christian Gospel. Belief in that Kingdom was the subject of Jesus' first, foremost and fundamental command (Mk. 1:14-15).

[162]The afternoon of Friday which was preparation day. Sabbath began at sunset.

[163]The article on "the sabbath" here points back naturally to the sabbath mentioned in v. 54. Luke would be an extremely poor and confusing historian and writer if he intended two different "sabbaths"! Some have claimed, very confusingly, that there was a sabbath on Thursday and another on Saturday. No reader of Luke could possibly have imagined this. The NT speaks only of Saturday as Sabbath (even in Jn. 19:31, where the reference is to the weekly Sabbath falling in Passover week and being of special importance for that reason). Friday is *prosabbaton* or *paraskeue* (preparation). Jesus was crucified on Friday and raised on "the third day," Sunday. Luke 24:21 is decisive and definitive on this point, since Sunday is the third day since Friday. Matt. 12:40 is a Hebraic idiom where three days and nights stand for part of that total.

[164]As the New Covenant was later offered to Gentiles of all nations, the requirements of the calendar law in the letter were changed to obedience in the spirit. Thus in Col. 2:16-17 the Jewish calendar is a single "trio" of observances constituting a mere shadow of what was to come. What came, as the context in Col. 2 shows, was Christ and his exaltation to the right hand of the Father. Paul worked hard against those who advocated a regression to the letter of the law given to Moses.

among the dead? 6He is not here, but he has been raised. Remember that
he told you, while he was still in Galilee, 7that the Son of Man must be
betrayed into the hands of evil men, be crucified, and on the third day[165]
rise again." 8And they remembered Jesus' words. 9They returned from
the tomb and reported everything to the eleven and all the others. 10It was
Mary Magdalene, Joanna, Mary the mother of James, and the other
women with them who told the Apostles what had happened. 11But it
seemed like nonsense to them, and the Apostles would not believe them.
12But Peter got up and ran to the tomb. He bent down and looked in and
saw only the linen wrappings. So he went home, wondering what had
happened.

13That same day two of the disciples were going to a village named
Emmaus, about seven miles from Jerusalem. 14They were discussing with
each other everything that had happened. 15As they were talking and
discussing, Jesus himself came up and began walking together with
them. 16But their eyes were prevented from recognizing him. 17He asked
them, "What are you talking about as you walk along?" They stopped in
their tracks, their faces sad. 18One of them, named Cleopas, answered,
"Are you just a visitor to Jerusalem? You must be the only person not to
know what has happened there lately." 19Jesus asked them, "What has
happened?" They said to him, "It is about Jesus of Nazareth, who was a
prophet mighty in actions and words before God and all the people. 20The
chief priests and our leaders handed him over to be sentenced to death,
and crucified him. 21But we were hoping he was the one who was going
to rescue Israel.[166] And, what is more, today is the third day since these
things happened.[167] 22In addition, some of the women in our group

---

[165]Sunday being the third day since Friday as predicted by Jesus and confirmed by Luke's inclusive reckoning (cp. 13:32-33: "today, tomorrow and the third day").

[166]This of course was the right, Messianic, biblical expectation, confirmed in Acts 1:6-7 by Jesus as the time when the Apostles and the faithful would be rewarded as servant-governors in the coming Kingdom (Mt. 19:28), administering the 12 tribes regathered in the land. This of course was the major hope and vision of all OT prophecy. Future hope for Christians had and has nothing at all to do with departing to heaven. The land of Israel and the world restored is the constant and unchanging hope of the Bible.

[167]The disciples here expect the third day after the crucifixion, Sunday, to be resurrection day — and of course it was! Luke makes much of the third day as resurrection day. In v. 7 the angels designate the third day as resurrection day, and Jesus makes the same point in v. 46.

amazed us. 23They went to the tomb at dawn and did not find his body
there. They came back saying they had seen a vision of angels who said
that he was alive. 24Some of those who were with us went to the tomb,
and found it just as the women said, but they did not see him." 25Jesus
said to them, "How foolish you are, and how slow to believe all that the
prophets have said! 26Was it not necessary for the Messiah to suffer these
things[168] and to enter into his glory?" 27Then beginning with Moses and
all the prophets, he explained to them everything in Scripture about
himself.

28As they approached the village where they were going, he acted as
if he were going farther. 29But they urged him, "Please stay with us,
because it is nearly evening and the day is almost over." So he went in to
stay with them. 30When he sat down to eat with them, he took the bread
and blessed it, broke it, and gave it to them. 31At that point their eyes
were opened and they recognized him. Then he vanished. 32They said to
each other, "Were not our hearts burning within us[169] as he was speaking
to us on the road, as he opened up the Scriptures to us?" 33They got up
that very hour and went back to Jerusalem. There they found the eleven
and the others gathered together. 34They were saying, "The lord has
really risen and has appeared to Simon." 35Then the two disciples related
what had happened on the road, and how they recognized him when he
broke the bread.

36While they were telling these things, Jesus himself stood among
them and said, "Peace to you." 37Startled and afraid, they thought they
were seeing a spirit. 38"Why are you afraid, and why do you doubt?" he
asked them. 39"Look at my hands and my feet; you can see it is I myself.
Touch me and look, because a spirit does not have flesh and bones as
you can see I have." 40When he had said this, he showed them his hands
and his feet. 41Since they still could not believe because of their joy and
amazement, he asked them, "Do you have anything here to eat?" 42They

---

[168]The Greek implies this divine necessity, just as in Luke 4:43 Jesus was compelled by his divine commission to preach the saving Gospel about the Kingdom of God. This is the one Christian Gospel (Acts 8:12; 19:8; 20:24-25; 28:23, 30, 31).

[169]The fire of the holy spirit transmitted by the words of Jesus (cp. Jer. 23:28-36).

gave him a piece of cooked fish,[170] 43which he took and ate in front of
them.

44He said to them, "These were my words while I was still with you
— that everything which is written about me in the Law of Moses, the
Prophets, and the Psalms[171] must be fulfilled." 45Then he opened their
minds so that they could understand the Scriptures.[172] 46He said to them,
"It is written that the Messiah would suffer and rise from the dead on the
third day, 47and that repentance for the forgiveness of sins[173] would be
proclaimed in his name[174] to all nations, beginning in Jerusalem. 48You
are witnesses of these things. 49I am about to send you the promise of my
Father, but wait in the city until you are empowered from on high."

50He led them as far as Bethany, and he lifted up his hands and
blessed them. 51While he was blessing them, he left them and was taken
up to heaven. 52They bowed in worship to him, and then returned to
Jerusalem with great joy. 53There they were praising God all the time in
the Temple.

---

[170]Jesus was not a vegetarian. Seventh Day Adventists have been, in this respect, taught to be more "righteous" than Jesus! This ought to prod them into investigation of other treasured traditions. Jesus was also not a teetotaler as seen from the wedding in Cana.

[171]The threefold division of the Hebrew Bible — the Law (*Torah*), prophets (*Neviim*) and Psalms, often called the Writings (*Ketuvim*). Jesus' Bible and the Bible of the synagogue had the same books as our OT but in a different order. So today the Jewish Bibles are arranged as Law, Prophets and Writings (TaNaKh, the acronym for *Torah, Neviim, Ketuvim*). Jesus obviously worked out of an authoritative Scripture of the Hebrew canon, and by analogy it is obvious that there must be an authoritative canon of Greek New Testament Scripture. The constant demand of the Apostles that we not abandon "the faith once delivered to the saints" (Jude 3) logically implies that we can have access to the original faith of the earliest Christians. Scripture ensures that we do. Paul urges Christians "all to say the same thing and be perfectly united in one mind and judgment" (1 Cor. 1:10). The chaos of so many denominations points to the loss of basic, essential truths, primarily the Gospel of the Kingdom (Mk. 1:14-15; Acts 20:25), which is more than the death and resurrection of Jesus. These are part of the Gospel only (1 Cor. 15:3).

[172]The same process was used by Paul in opening the eyes of Lydia, bringing her to conversion in Acts 16:13-15.

[173]Repentance for the forgiveness of sins should never be separated from baptism in water (immersion) as necessary Christian obedience (Acts 2:38; Heb. 5:9).

[174]On his authority and in response to his Gospel of the Kingdom.

John

1 1In the beginning was the word,[1] and the word[2] was with[3] God, and
the word was fully expressive of God Himself. 2This was with God in

---

[1]Footnote 1 for John 1:1 is at the end of the gospel, beginning on p. 304.

[2]The NET Bible Commentary remarks on the meaning of "word" in Ps. 33:6-11: "The LORD's 'word' refers to the decrees whereby He governs His dominion." Only when *logos* in John 1:1 is made into a second Person, the Son, do all the problems arise. Jesus defined God in Mark 12:29: "The Lord our God is one Lord," not two or three! It would be a fatal contradiction to introduce a second "God, Person" in John 1. In John 17:3 Jesus was a strict monotheist declaring the Father to be "the only one [*monos*] who is true God [*theos*]." This is unitary not Trinitarian monotheism. Note Schonfield, *Authentic New Testament*: "In the beginning was the expressed concept." If we read "In the beginning was the SON" we make two who are GOD, and this breaks the fundamental and easy, express monotheism of Jesus (Mk. 12:29; 1 Cor. 8:4-6) and the whole of the Bible. Sadly John 1:1 has been used to contradict Jesus in John 17:3 and the detailed birth narratives of Matthew and Luke, and the more than 1300 NT references to GOD as the Father. There are thousands of references to God in Scripture as a single Person, defined by singular personal pronouns. The God of the Bible is a single divine "someone," "self." The moment someone *else*, the Son, is said to *be* God, two Gods are posited; the universe is "tinkered with" and idolatry is introduced (cp. 1 John 5:20-21 for fair warning).

[3]The same Greek word *pros* (with) occurs in the phrase "the things concerning God," *ta pros ton theon.* Thus "the word" reflects the heart of God's thinking, His concern. The Aramaic word *memra* (word) was used by Jews as expressing likewise the activity and wisdom of God. John naturally reflects his Jewish background, as does the whole NT. BBE has "This Word was from the first in relation with God." Note *Thayer's Lexicon:* "things respecting, pertaining to God" (Rom. 15:17; Heb. 2:17, 5:1). Philo speaks of three kinds of life, one of which is "*pros theon,*" related to God, characteristic of God (*Quis rer. div. haer.* 9, *International Critical Commentary, John*, Vol. 1, p. cxli). Similarly the Gospel remains "with [*pros* as in Jn. 1:1] the disciples," Gal. 2:5, that is, in their minds. Philo speaks of things "*pros theon*" as things *pertaining to* God, belonging to Him. John does not speak here of person to person, for which he uses the prepositions *para* or *meta*. "Elsewhere John uses *para* to express the idea of proximity of one person to another (Jn. 1:39; 4:40; 8:38; 14:17, 23, 25; 19:25; cp. 14:23…never *pros*" (see *Dictionary of New Testament Theology*, Vol. 3, p. 1205.) Dan. 2:22 tells us that "light dwells with God," or "light is with Him" (LXX). No one imagined light to be a second divine Person, making two GODs! Jesus, the Son of God, is not a second GOD, destroying the first commandment and the Shema! (Deut. 6:4; Mk. 12:29). The Bible knows of no "God the Son." Ps. 36:9 similarly says that "the fountain of life is **with** You. In Your light we see light." Cp. Jer. 2:13. As Dr. Colin Brown of Fuller Seminary wisely said: "To read John 1:1 as if it said 'In the beginning was *the Son*' is patently wrong" (*Ex Auditu*, 7, 1991, p. 89).

the beginning. 3Everything came into existence through it, and without it
nothing of what came into being existed.[4] 4In it there was life and that life
was the light of men. 5And the light shines in the darkness and the
darkness does not overwhelm it.[5]

6There came on the scene of history a man sent from God.[6] His name
was John. 7This man came as a witness[7] so that he might bear witness to
the Light and that everyone might believe through him. 8He was not the
Light himself, but he witnessed concerning the Light.

9This was the genuine Light, which enlightens every person, coming
into the world.[8] 10He was in the world and the world came into existence
through him, and the world did not recognize him,[9] the Light. 11He came
to his own land and his own people did not accept him. 12As many,
however, as did accept him, to these he gave the right to become children
of God[10] — namely the ones believing in his Gospel revelation. 13These

---

[4]There is an obvious parallel to John 1:1-3 at Qumran, the Dead Sea Scrolls, I QS 11.11: "By his knowledge everything has been brought into being. And everything that is, He established by His purpose and apart from Him nothing is done." If we look for parallels in the Hebrew OT, we find "the word of the Lord was with him" (2 Kings 3:12), or "with whom is a dream" (Jer. 23:28). In no case does word mean a person in the OT. The word or dream can be "with" a person, meaning that a person has the word in his mind, or that he experiences a dream. Cp. "with" connected to plan in Job 10:13; 12:13; 23:14; 27:11.

[5]The light here is neuter, "it," not yet a person. In v. 10 the historical Jesus is in the world and the light is then given a masculine gender (*auton*), "him." "The true light which comes into the world" (v. 9) is fully expressed in the man Messiah. The impersonal light became a person only when Jesus was born.

[6]"Sent from God" has nothing to do with so-called "preexistence"! John the Baptist was sent from God, i.e. commissioned, as was Jesus. Literally, "sent from beside God." Nicodemus did not think of preexistence when he confessed that Jesus had "come from (*apo*) God" (Jn. 3:2). Cp. 1 John 4:1, where the true Jesus is fully human.

[7]Preacher of the Gospel of the Kingdom (Mt. 3:2).

[8]To "come into the world" is to be born. Jesus came into the world in a unique way, having God as his Father.

[9]Now that Jesus is on the scene the light which was "it" in v. 5 has been given personality and is described appropriately in the Greek as "him" (*auton*).

[10]Believers who are born again become "genetically" related to GOD as sons and daughters. They are not just "adopted," but true members of God's family by rebirth in contact with the word/Gospel of the Kingdom.

were born not from blood, nor from the desire of the flesh, nor from the
desire of a male, but from God.[11]
14 And the word became a human being[12] and tabernacled among us,
and we saw his glory, the glory such as a uniquely begotten[13] Son enjoys
from his Father,[14] full of grace and truth. 15 John gave his witness

---

[11]The earliest quotations of this verse in the church fathers, earlier than any of our Greek manuscripts of the NT, give a reading which applies this statement to Jesus, not to believers. It would then be a clear statement of the virginal begetting of Jesus. The Jerusalem Bible and French Jerusalem Bible put that reading into the text and other scholars have supported it strongly. It seems very labored to say that the spiritual rebirth of Christians is "not from the flesh or the desire of the male." A much more natural and easy understanding is that v. 13 is a reference to the supernatural beginning/begetting of Jesus in Mary's womb. Thus John, in complete harmony with Matthew and Luke, recorded the virginal begetting of the Son (cp. 1 John 5:18: the Son was begotten in time, caused to come into existence; Ps. 2:7; cp. the first Adam in Gen. 2:7). The earliest reading "who [Jesus] was begotten…" is found in the Verona codex, which is Old Latin, the *Epistula Apostolorum*, and by four early church fathers — Tertullian, Justin Martyr, Irenaeus and Origen. The idea of "eternal generation" of the Son makes nonsense of all this! John would thus be deliberately in agreement with Matthew and Luke and the rest of the NT on the supernatural origin of the Son as the beginning of the New Creation. Trinitarianism makes all this impossibly confused, and in the course of the post-biblical councils suppressed the easy accounts of the origin of the Son in Matthew and Luke. The *Albrecht New Testament* in German notes "I am following in v. 13 ["Jesus who was begotten"] Irenaeus and Tertullian, and elsewhere dominant also from the 2nd to the 4th century in the west and leaving traces in the east. John emphatically recognizes the miraculous begetting of the Son, agreeing with Matthew and Luke" (8th edition, 1957).

[12]In the gospel of John "word" means the Gospel message and words/teaching of Jesus, given to him by the Father. Jesus does not say "I am the word/Word." This might encourage a confusion of "word" with a preexisting Son, which inevitably leads to polytheism. John 17:3 is a perfectly plain unitary monotheistic statement backed by 1300 NT references to God as the Father (cp. Mal. 2:10). John 1:14 is the announcement that personification (word) has become a person for the first time, the incarnation of grace and truth (v. 17). Similarly Jews thought of Moses as the incarnation of the law (Philo, *Life of Moses* I, 162). The Son comes into existence, as in Luke 1:35. The NT is thus perfectly harmonious in presenting the Son as the miraculously generated second Adam.

[13]This is exactly the teaching of Luke 1:35. Jesus is uniquely the Son of God, because of the miracle which procreated him, as the second Adam. Adam was also son of God (Lk. 3:38).

[14]Cp. Moffat who captures the sense. This image is based on the description of Israel as Son of God. Cp. Ps. Sol. 18:4; 13:8: "Your chastisement is upon us as on a firstborn

concerning him and cried out with these words, “This was the one of
whom I said, ‘The one coming after me has now moved ahead of me,
because he always was my superior.’”[15] 16For from his fullness all of us
have received grace and more grace.[16] 17For the Law was given through
Moses, but grace and truth came through Jesus Messiah. 18No one has
seen God at any time. A uniquely begotten Son,[17] one who is in the
bosom[18] of the Father — he has explained God.[19]

19And this is the witness of John, when the Jews sent a commission of
priests and Levites to him from Jerusalem to ask him, “Who are you?”

---

only son.” II Esdras 6:58: “We Your people whom You have called Your firstborn, Your only-begotten, Your beloved.” So also Ex. 4:22; Ps. 89:27; Jer. 31:9; Sirach 30:4: “When the father dies it is as if he were still alive, for he has left a copy of himself behind.” This profound truth is lost if Jesus is really an “eternally begotten,” essentially non-human, pre-human person.

[15]*Protos mou* means here “my superior,” but many translations force a meaning on it which would contradict the rest of Scripture, i.e., “he was before me,” or “existed before me.” If we translate in harmony with the creed of Jesus in Mark 12:29 and John 17:3 we must understand: “A follower of mine has taken precedence of me for he (always) was my superior.” “Some take ‘first’ to mean not ‘first in time’ but ‘first in importance’” (Leon Morris, *New International Critical Commentary on John,* p. 109). He suggests “he [Jesus] was my Chief.” Schonfield, *Authentic New Testament*: “After me will come a man who ranks before me; for he is my superior.”

[16]There was grace in the Old Covenant, but in Christ and the New Covenant there is a more intensive grace expressed in Jesus who is the second Adam, the head of a new type of human being. The whole point of Scripture is lost if Jesus is really God! He is in fact the ultimate Human Being, Son of Man, second Adam.

[17]Some manuscripts say “a god.” It is much disputed as to whether John wrote that word. If he did the text does not say that the Son was “God the Son” from eternity. A person who is begotten is brought into existence and this is not true of the One God. The Father in John 17:3 is in the plain words of Jesus “the only one who is true God.” This is an explicitly unitarian proposition, quite unarguable. Dr. Hort says that if “an only begotten god” is right, “it would point to the highest form of derived being.” This is certainly not GOD in the Trinitarian sense.

[18]Jesus was in the most intimate relationship with GOD. The present participle (“being”) indicates that this is nothing to do with a so-called past preexistence.

[19]“No one has seen God, but we all saw Jesus who is God” would be incoherent! The word GOD means the Father some 170 times in the writings of John and 1300 times in the NT. This points to the massive evidence for unitary monotheism by which the Father is “the only one who is true GOD” (Jn. 17:3). This verse is a sort of “crime scene,” since Augustine, to justify the later Trinity, had to forge the text by moving the phrases to say “You, Father *and Jesus Christ* whom you sent, the only true God” (see his *Homilies on John*).

20And he confessed and did not deny, "I am not the Messiah." 21And they
asked him, "Who are you? Are you Elijah?" And he said, "I am not."
"Are you the expected prophet?" He answered, "No." 22And they said to
him, "Who are you? Tell us so that we can give an answer to those who
sent us. What do you say about yourself?" 23He said, "I am the voice of
one crying out in the wilderness, 'Make straight the way of the Lord,' as
Isaiah the prophet spoke."

24The ones sent were from the Pharisees. 25And they asked him a
further question, "Why do you baptize if you are not the Messiah, or
Elijah or the prophet who was to come?"[20] 26John answered them, "I am
baptizing in water. Among you there stands one whom you do not
recognize — 27the one coming after me, the thongs of whose sandals I
am not worthy to untie." 28These things happened in Bethany beyond the
Jordan where John was baptizing.

29The next day John saw Jesus coming towards him and he said,
"This is the lamb of God, the one who removes the sin of the world.[21]
30This is the one of whom I said, 'After me there comes a man who has
now moved ahead of me, because he was always my superior.'[22] 31And I
did not recognize him, but so that he might be recognized by Israel, for
that reason I came baptizing with water." 32And John witnessed with
these words: "I saw the spirit descending as a dove out of heaven and
remaining on him, 33and I did not recognize him. But the one who sent
me to baptize in water spoke to me and said, 'The one on whom you see
the spirit descending and remaining on him, he is the one who is
baptizing with holy spirit.'[23] 34And I saw this, and I have witnessed to the
fact that this is the Son of God."[24]

---

[20]As predicted by the critically important text, defining the expected Messiah, in Deut. 18:15-18, cited by Peter in Acts 3:22 and Stephen in Acts 7:37. No one could imagine a Messiah who is GOD from this text.

[21]Jesus died for every human being (1 Tim. 2:4, etc), contrary to the fearful doctrine that Jesus died only for some, predestined apart from any choice they might make.

[22]The *New International Critical Commentary on John* by Dr. Leon Morris suggests "He was my Chief."

[23]Since the words of Jesus "are spirit and life," the whole of his ministry was a baptizing in spirit. At the ascension the spirit came in a new way from the resurrected, exalted Messiah (Jn. 7:39).

[24]Literally "the Son of **the** God," i.e. the Son of the one God whom we know. Certainly not an imagined "God the Son" which would break the first principle of all true religion

35The next day John stood with two of his disciples, 36and seeing
Jesus walking by, he said, "This is the lamb of God." 37And John's two
disciples heard him speaking and followed Jesus. 38Jesus, turning round
and seeing them following him, said, "What are you looking for?" They
said, "Rabbi (which translated means teacher), where are you staying?"
39And he said to them, "Come and see." And so they went and saw where
he was staying and remained with him that whole day. It was about four
in the afternoon. 40This was Andrew, the brother of Simon Peter, one of
the two who had heard from John and followed Jesus. 41He first found his
brother Simon and said to him, "We have found the Messiah" (which
translated[25] means the Christ). 42He brought him to Jesus, and Jesus
looked at him and said, "You are Simon the son of John. You will be
called Cephas," which translated[26] means Peter.

43The next day Jesus wanted to go to Galilee, and he found Philip and
said to him, "Follow me." 44Now Philip was from Bethsaida, the town of
Andrew and Peter. 45Philip then found Nathanael and said to him, "The
one about whom Moses wrote in the Law[27] and whom the prophets

---

and the creed of Israel and of Jesus, that God is a single Divine Person (Mk. 12:29: "The Lord our God is one Lord"). John wrote his whole Gospel for the purpose of convincing us that "Jesus is the Messiah, the Son of God" (Jn. 20:31). No one imagined that the Messiah would threaten the monotheism of Hebrew Scripture! Everyone understood Messiah to be a unique human being. Thus Dr. Matthews: "It must be admitted by everyone who has the rudiments of an historical sense that the doctrine of the Trinity **formed no part of the original message**. St. Paul did not know it, and would have been unable to understand the meaning of the terms used in the theological formula on which the Church ultimately agreed" (*God in Christian Experience*, p. 180).

[25]The Hebrew *Mashiach*, anointed one, applies to kings and also the patriarchs in Ps. 105:15. The Greek equivalent is *christos*, Christ. No reader of the NT would imagine that the Christ, as God's anointed one, was also fully GOD. They knew that GOD was one Person and that God cannot be born or die.

[26]It is perfectly right, following the example of New Covenant Scripture, to translate names from one language to another. A vast amount of wasted energy has been spent by some disputing over the translation of proper names!

[27]Moses in Deut. 18:15-18 had predicted the future Messiah as a human person, an Israelite like Moses, and God had warned that anyone who did not respond obediently to that Messiah would be cut off from the people. Peter quoted this key text in Acts 3:22 and Stephen in Acts 7:37. The Israelites had requested that *God* not speak directly to them any more. To claim that the agent was, after all, also God would make no sense. God responded to their request with the promise that He would use an ultimate Israelite human person as His agent and commissioner.

predicted, we have found, Jesus, the son of Joseph from Nazareth."
46Nathanael said to him, "Can anything good come from Nazareth?"
Philip said, "Come and see." 47Jesus saw Nathanael coming towards him
and remarked, "Look, a genuine Israelite in whom there is no guile."
48Nathanael said to him, "How is it that you know me?" Jesus answered
him, "Before Philip called you, I saw you under the fig tree."[28]
49Nathanael answered him, "Rabbi, you are the Son of God; you are the
King of Israel."[29] 50Jesus answered him with these words: "Because I told
you that I saw you under the fig tree, you are a believer? You will see
greater things than this." 51And he said to him, "I tell you on the higest
authority: you will see heaven opened and the angels of God ascending
and descending on the Son of Man."[30]

2 1Now on the third day[31] there was a wedding in Cana of Galilee, and
the mother of Jesus was there. 2Jesus also was invited to the wedding
with his disciples. 3When they ran out of wine, Jesus' mother said to him,
"They have no more wine." 4Jesus said to her, "Lady, of what concern is
this to you and me? My hour[32] has not yet come." 5His mother said to the
servants, "Whatever he tells you to do, do." 6There were six water jars
standing there for the Jewish rites of purification, each holding about 20
or 30 gallons. 7Jesus said to them, "Fill the water pots with water." And
they filled them to the brim, 8and he said to them, "Now pour some out
and bring it to the head steward of the wedding," and they did this.
9When the head steward tasted the water which had become wine,[33] and

---

[28]Possibly the location for school, when Nathaniel was younger.

[29]This gives us the essentially Messianic meaning of Son of God, a highly politically-charged term, since the Messiah as Son of God will rule the world at his return to the earth. Ps. 2 is key in this respect. Matt. 16:16 as *the* key to Christian confession is repeated in 1 John 5:1, 5.

[30]Jesus is thus the unique bridge between heaven and earth, between God and man. Jesus enjoyed intimate contact with God, his Father and spoke for the Father as His unique agent.

[31]A tradition noted that in Genesis the third day had been pronounced "good" and thus a suitable day for weddings (Gen. 1:12)!

[32]Of his death.

[33]Various attempts to avoid the obvious fact that this was alcohol should be abandoned! Everyone knows that *oinos* is wine and certainly not grape juice! It was the falsely named "temperance" (actually prohibition) movement which caused the considerable confusion over this easy matter. See also Deut. 14:26.

he did not know how this had happened (but the servants who had
poured out the water knew), the steward called the bridegroom and said,
10“Everybody serves the good wine at the beginning, and when everyone
has drunk sufficiently, poorer wine. But you have kept the best wine
until now.”

11Jesus performed this, the first of his symbolic miracles, at Cana in
Galilee, and he displayed his glory[34] and his disciples believed in him.
12After this he, his mother, his brothers and his disciples went down to
Capernaum and they stayed there for a few days.

13And the Jewish Festival of Passover[35] was approaching, and Jesus
went up to Jerusalem 14and he found in the temple those selling cattle,
sheep and doves. 15He made a little whip and drove them, both the sheep
and the cattle, out of the temple and overturned the tables, 16and said to
those selling the doves, “Take these things out of here. Do not make my
Father’s house into a market place.” 17And the disciples remembered
what Scripture had said: “A passion for Your House consumes me.” 18So
the Jews answered Jesus with these words: “What sign are you going to
show us, to prove your authority for doing these things?” 19Jesus replied,
“Destroy this temple and in three days I will raise it up.” 20The Jews
answered, “This temple has been under construction for 46 years, and
you say that you are going to raise it up in three days?” 21But he was
speaking of the temple of his body. 22When Jesus was later raised from
the dead, his disciples remembered that he had said these words, and
they believed the Scripture and the word which Jesus had spoken.[36]

23Now when he was in Jerusalem at the Passover festival many
believed in his name[37] when they saw the signs which he was doing.
24But Jesus did not commit himself to them because he understood the

---

[34]As the image of God and ideal man. Man is supposed to reflect the image and glory of God (1 Cor. 11:7). Image and glory are the visible qualities of the man Jesus (Jn. 1:14). No hint of a pre-non-human life.

[35]John speaks of the entire festival of Passover lasting a week, not just the single day on which the lamb was slain.

[36]Believing the word, Gospel, and words of Jesus is the basis of Christianity. It ought not to be necessary to mention such an elementary fact, but many churchgoers think of Jesus as only one who died and rose and not as rabbi/teacher. As one commentator noted, the public thinks of Jesus as “nice but not smart.” This is a huge misunderstanding, especially in view of John 12:44ff.

[37]His claims and his Gospel teaching, everything he stands for, his whole agenda.

nature of all people. 25And he did not need anyone to testify about mankind, because he knew what was in mankind.

3 1There was a man of the Pharisees named Nicodemus, a Jewish ruler. 2He came to see Jesus by night[38] and said to him, "Rabbi, we recognize that you are a teacher commissioned by God.[39] No one can possibly do these miraculous signs which you are performing unless God is with him." 3Jesus replied to him, "I tell you on the authority of God, unless a person is born again,[40] he is unable to see the Kingdom of God."

4Nicodemus replied, "How is it possible for a person to be born when he is old? Surely he cannot enter his mother's womb a second time and be born?" 5Jesus answered, "On the authority of God I tell you that unless a person is born from water and spirit, he will be unable to enter the Kingdom of God. 6What has been born of flesh is fleshly and what has been born of spirit is spiritual. 7Do not be amazed that I told you that

---

[38]It would have been dangerous to be seen in public with the "heretic" Jesus. The same fear may exist today, but we have to be unashamed of the teachings of Jesus. Jesus will be ashamed of those who are ashamed of his words (Mk. 8:38).

[39]This certainly does not mean that Nicodemus thought that Jesus preexisted his birth. The same language about being sent from beside God is used of John the Baptist (Jn. 1:6).

[40]Or born from above, that is, with God as the author of this regeneration dependent on our belief in the truth and repentance. Rebirth is thus the non-negotiable basis for becoming a Christian. In the synoptic gospels, Matthew, Mark and Luke, spiritual rebirth is described as the new life springing from the seed of the Gospel (Lk. 8:11). Thus with Nicodemus Jesus uses the biological metaphor and with the public who heard the parable of the sower, the agricultural metaphor. These are beautifully combined in 1 Pet. 1:22-25 where being born again is based on the seed which is the Gospel. Thus the NT contains a single united theology for becoming a believer. It starts with belief in Jesus' Gospel of the Kingdom (Mk. 1:14-15). The Gospel is given the "shorthand" form "word," or "word of God." This Gospel of the Kingdom contains the essential seed of immortality and conveys to us the creative life of God, the *logos*, the word preached as Gospel by all NT evangelists and writers. We become children of God by the infusion of His seed in us (1 John 3:9). The spiritual parallel with the natural reproduction by "seed" (*sperma* and *sporos*) is obvious. One might think of a human head as an ovum and the Gospel of the Kingdom must penetrate it through the ear, conveying understanding. The parable of the sower is indispensable for understanding all the parables (Mk. 4:13). The parable of the sower teaches us about the essential "new root of personality in rebirth" (Hastings Dictionary of the Bible, Vol. 4, p. 216), created by the regenerating seed.

you must be born again. 8The wind blows where it wishes and you hear
its sound, but you do not know where it comes from and where it goes.
So it is with anyone who has been born from the spirit."[41]
9Nicodemus responded, "How can these things happen?" 10Jesus
replied, "Are you a teacher in Israel, and you do not understand these
things? 11On God's authority I assure you, we speak the things which we
know about and witness to the things we have seen, but you do not
accept our Gospel-witness. 12If I have told you about earthly things and
you do not believe them, how will you believe heavenly things[42] if I tell
you about them? 13And no one has ascended to heaven[43] except the one
who has his origin in God, the one who is the Son of Man.[44] 14And just as
Moses lifted up the snake in the wilderness, in the same way the Son of
Man must be lifted up, 15so that all who believe in him may gain the life
of the Age to Come.[45]
16"God loved the world in this way: that He gave His uniquely
begotten Son,[46] so that every person who believes in him should not

---

[41]Rebirth must happen now, and it depends on the invisible activity of the creative spirit/word/Gospel of God. Nowhere does the NT say that rebirth can happen only in the future resurrection. James (1:18), using a different metaphor says that God has "brought us forth" (the image is of a mother bearing a child). Peter says that Christians have been born again and as newborn babes must then seek the genuine milk of the Gospel (1 Pet. 1:23-2:2).

[42]The great spiritual truths of the Gospel, originating from God in heaven. Nothing to do with an imagined "going to heaven" at death about which the Bible has nothing to say. The saints will rule and govern on earth (Rev. 5:10; Dan. 7:14, 18, 22, 27; 2:44).

[43]i.e. gained access to the secrets of God. Jesus is the bridge between heaven and earth.

[44]The human being seen in advance in a vision in Daniel 7.

[45]The life of the future Kingdom, much too vaguely translated as "eternal life." The phrase originates in Dan. 12:2 where it describes "the life of the [future] age," following the resurrection to immortality. That life must be tasted now in advance by believing the Gospel as Jesus preached it, and thereby receiving a downpayment or foretaste of the Kingdom in the spirit.

[46]All sons are begotten in the Bible and so "son" implies a begetting, coming into existence. This is described in detail, following the declaration about the begetting of the Son in Ps. 2:7, in Matthew's and Luke's birth narratives. See Matthew 1:18, 20 ("begotten in her") and Luke 1:35 ("being begotten") which provide the definition of Son of God. The begetting of the Son was long before predicted in Isa. 9:6 where the Son/child "will be begotten" (brought into existence by God, begotten by God). 1 John 5:18 records the same event in time: the fathering of the unique Son of God, Jesus (cp. 2 Sam. 7:14; 1 Chron. 17:13-15).

perish but have the life of the Age to Come. 17For God did not send His
Son into the world[47] for the purpose of condemning the world, but so that
the world might be rescued through him. 18The person who believes in
him is not condemned. But the one who does not believe has been
condemned already, because he has not believed in the revelation and
whole agenda[48] of God's uniquely begotten[49] Son. 19This is the reason for
condemnation: the light has come into the world and human beings loved
darkness rather than light, because their activities were wicked. 20Every
person who does wicked things hates the light and will not come to the
light, so that his works will not be exposed. 21But the one who performs
truth comes to the light, so that his works may be demonstrated as
performed under God's direction."

22After these things Jesus and his disciples came into Judea and he
stayed there with them and was baptizing[50] people. 23And John the
Baptist was baptizing in Aenon near Salim, because there were many
springs there, and people were coming to get baptized. 24John the Baptist
had not yet been thrown into prison.

25There arose a dispute amongst the disciples of John with a Jew
about purification. 26So they came to John and asked him, "Rabbi, the
one who was with you on the other side of the Jordan, the one you bore
witness to,[51] he is baptizing and a lot of people are joining him." 27John
replied, "A person can receive nothing unless it is granted him from
heaven. 28You yourselves will confirm the fact that I said, 'I am not the
Messiah, but I have been sent ahead of him.' 29The one who has the bride
is the bridegroom. But the friend of the bridegroom who stands and

---

[47]To be sent into the world means to be commissioned with the task of preaching to it. The disciples were sent out in the same way as Jesus (20:21). All prophets were "sent."

[48]Lit., the name, which entails the whole character and activity of God.

[49]Jesus the Son of God was uniquely begotten, fathered, brought into existence by biological miracle in the womb of Mary. Luke 1:35 provides this basic truth precisely in the authoritative words of the angel Gabriel and Matt. 1:18, 20 speak of the origin (*genesis*), not just birth, of the one who is "begotten in her" (Mt. 1:20, *to gennethen*). The Son is the one begotten in 1 John 5:18.

[50]It is important to note that Jesus baptized in water with his disciples, see 4:1. Jesus himself was baptized in water, as required obedience to God. Salvation is given to those who obey Jesus (Heb. 5:9).

[51]That is, "the one you said is the Messiah."

listens to him has great joy hearing the bridegroom's voice. I am
therefore full of joy. 30He must increase, while I must decrease.
31"The one who comes from above[52] is superior to all. The one who
comes from the earth is of the earth and speaks from the earth. The one
coming from heaven[53] is above all. 32He bears witness to what he has
seen and heard. But no one accepts his witness.[54] 33The person who does
accept his Gospel-witness sets his seal on the fact that God is truthful.
34For the one whom God sent as His agent speaks the words of God, for
he does not give out the spirit by measure. 35The Father loves the Son and
has given him power over everything. 36The person who believes in the
Son has the Life of the Age to Come. The one who refuses to obey the
Son[55] will not see that life. Rather, the righteous fury of God hangs over
him."[56]

4 1Now when Jesus learned that the Pharisees had heard that Jesus was
making and baptizing more disciples than John 2 — although Jesus
himself was not actually performing the baptisms, but his disciples were,
as his agents[57] — 3he left Judea and went back to Galilee. 4But he had to
go through Samaria. 5So he came to a town in Samaria called Sychar,
near the plot of ground Jacob had given to his son Joseph. 6Jacob's well

---

[52]Whose origin is from God by supernatural miracle in Mary (Lk. 1:35). The one who is divinely authorized.

[53]This is idiomatic for someone who is God's gift since "all good gifts come down from heaven" (James 1:17; 3:15). This is nothing to do with a pre-human person, who by definition could not be the promised lineal descendant of David, the necessary qualification for Messiahship.

[54]Gospel of the Kingdom.

[55]Refusal to obey the Son is the opposite of believing in the Son. This gives us the most fundamental of all biblical truths about salvation. Salvation is given only to those who obey the Son (Heb 5:9; 1 Tim. 6:3; 2 Jn. 7-9; Jn. 12:44ff, etc). Paul uses the summary phrase "obedience of faith" (framing the whole book of Romans: Rom. 1:5; 16:26).

[56]That is, threatening him with destruction unless he responds by repenting and believing the Gospel of the Kingdom as preached by Jesus and every NT writer (Mk. 1:14-15; Acts 8:12, etc).

[57]Paul followed this practice in 1 Cor. 1:14-16. The importance of water baptism in the NT cannot be overemphasized. Unbaptized people were not considered part of the NT community. A form of "ultra-dispensationalism" has tended to confuse this easy matter for some people.

was there, and Jesus, tired from the journey, sat down by the well. It was
about noon.
7A Samaritan woman came to draw water and Jesus said to her,
"Give me a drink." 8His disciples had gone into the town to buy food.
9The Samaritan woman said to him, "How can you, a Jew, ask me, a
Samaritan woman, for a drink?" (For Jews have no dealings with
Samaritans.) 10Jesus answered her, "If you knew the gift of God and who
it is who requests a drink from you, you would have asked him and he
would have given you living water." 11The woman said to him, "Sir,[58]
you do not even have a bucket and the well is deep; where then can you
get this living water? 12Are you a greater man than our father Jacob, who
gave us this well and drank from it himself with his sons and his cattle?"
13Jesus replied, "Everyone who drinks this water will be thirsty again.
14But whoever drinks the water I will give will never thirst: the water I
will give him will become in him a spring of water welling up to the Life
of the Age to Come."
15The woman said to him, "Sir, give me this water so that I will not
get thirsty and have to keep coming here to draw water." 16Jesus said to
her, "Go and get your husband." 17The woman answered, "I have no
husband." 18Jesus said, "The fact is, you have had five husbands, and the
man you are now living with is not your husband. What you have just
said is true." 19The woman said to him, "Sir, I see that you are a prophet.
20Our ancestors worshiped on this mountain, but you say that the place
where people must worship is in Jerusalem." 21Jesus said, "Believe me,
woman, the hour is coming when you will worship the Father neither on
this mountain nor in Jerusalem. 22You people worship what you do not
understand; we worship what we understand, because salvation comes
from the Jews.[59] 23Yet a time is coming, and has now come, when the true

---

[58]Note that she addresses him as "lord" but no one imagines that calling Jesus "lord" implied he was Deity! So in Ps. 110:1, which controls the thinking of the entire NT, the second lord (*adoni*) is not God. Jesus is the supremely exalted human Messiah, the second Adam (1 Cor. 15:45-49; 1 Tim. 2:5). That God is a single and only Lord is repeated constantly in the NT. Jesus is the Messiah, and that is the key to understanding the Christian faith. Denial of Jesus as Messiah is the greatest of all falsehoods (1 John 2:22)

[59]This is one of the great confirmations of the non-Trinitarian faith of Jesus and the Bible. The idea that God is one Essence in three Persons is utterly foreign to Scripture.

worshippers will worship the Father in spirit and truth, for the Father is
looking for such people to worship Him. 24God communicates through
spirit,[60] and those who worship Him must worship Him on the basis of
spirit and truth." 25The woman said, "I know that the Messiah (called
Christ) is coming. When *he* comes, he will tell us everything." 26Jesus
replied "I am he, that Messiah,[61] the one speaking to you."

27At this point his disciples returned and were amazed to find him
speaking to a woman, but none of them asked, "What do you want from
her, or what are you talking to her about?" 28The woman left her water jar
and went into the town and said to the people, 29"Come and meet a man
who told me everything I ever did! Could this be the Messiah?" 30They
left the town and were on their way to see Jesus.

31Meanwhile the disciples were urging him, "Rabbi, eat something."
32But he said, "I have food to eat that you do not know about." 33So the
disciples said to one another, "Could someone have brought him
something to eat?" 34Jesus said, "My food is to do the will of the One
who commissioned me and to complete His work. 35Do you not say,
'Four months and then the harvest'? Well, I tell you, look around, look at
the fields; they are ripe, ready for harvest! 36Already the reaper is being
paid his wage; already he is bringing in fruit for the Life of the Age to
Come, so that sower[62] and reaper can rejoice together. 37You know the
saying, 'One sows and another reaps.' 38I sent you to reap a harvest you
have not labored for. Others have labored for it; and you have shared the
rewards of their labor."

The God of the Hebrew Bible and thus of Jews, and the God of Jesus, is the one and only true God (Jn. 17:3; Mk. 12:29, etc).

[60]Literally "God is spirit," meaning that he communicates via spirit. The meaning is not "God is *a* spirit." God is love, and God is light are parallel statements. Salvation is based on "a love of the truth in order to be saved" (2 Thess. 2:10).

[61]The phrase "I am he" in John is John's vivid way of making his main point that all he writes is directed to proving that Jesus is the Messiah (20:31). The meaning of "I am he" (as here, for the first time in 4:26), "I am the one" is "I am the Christ, the Messiah." It is nothing to do with the OT "I am the one who is," "I am the self-existing one" of Ex. 3:14 (LXX) or "I am who I am" (Heb.), spoken by God. Jesus here in John did not repeat the Greek of Ex. 3:14: "I am the self-existing one." His claim is to be Messiah (cp. 1 John 5:1-2; 2:22).

[62]All fruit in the NT is born from the word of the Kingdom Gospel (Mt. 13:19; Lk. 8:11-12; 1 Pet. 1:23-25).

39And many of the Samaritans of that town believed in him because
of the words of the woman who testified, “He told me everything I ever
did.” 40When the Samaritans came to him, they invited him to stay with
them; and he stayed there two days. 41Many more believed because of his
word[63] 42and they said to the woman, “We no longer believe because of
your word; for we have heard for ourselves, and we are convinced that
this is truly the Savior of the world.”

43When the two days were over Jesus left for Galilee. 44For Jesus
himself testified that a prophet has no honor in his own country. 45So
when he came to Galilee, the Galileans welcomed him, after seeing all
the things that he did in Jerusalem at the feast; for they themselves also
went to the feast.

46Once more Jesus visited Cana in Galilee, where he had turned the
water into wine. And there was a certain royal official whose son lay sick
at Capernaum. 47When he heard that Jesus had arrived in Galilee from
Judea, he went to him and asked him to come down and heal his son,
who was close to death. 48Jesus said to him, “Unless you people see signs
and wonders, you will not believe.” 49The royal official said, “Sir, come
down before my child dies.” 50Jesus said to him, “You may go; your son
will live.” The man believed what Jesus said to him[64] and departed.
51While he was on his way home, his servants met him and told him that
his boy was alive. 52He asked them at what time he began to recover.
They said to him, “The fever left him yesterday, about one in the
afternoon.” 53Then the father realized that this was the exact moment at
which Jesus had said to him, “Your son is going to live.” So he and all
his household believed. 54This was the second symbolic miracle which
Jesus performed, on his return from Judea to Galilee.

---

[63]The Gospel of the Kingdom from the lips of Jesus. “Word” is the standard shorthand for the word/Gospel of the Kingdom (Mt. 13:19; Lk. 8:11-12), the saving Gospel (see Acts 8:12; 19:8; 20:24-25; 28:23, 31). The essential non-negotiable basis of true Christian faith is believing and obeying Jesus (Jn. 3:36; Heb. 5:9).

[64]The great key to Christian success: believing and obeying what Jesus says. This is more than just “accepting Jesus” as the one who died for us all. The death and resurrection of Jesus are central to the Gospel, but never to the exclusion of obedience to the words of Jesus (12:44ff).

5 1After this there was a Jewish[65] festival and Jesus went up to
Jerusalem. 2Now in Jerusalem at the sheep-gate there is a pool called
in Aramaic Bethsaida with five colonnades. 3A mass of sick people lie
there, blind, crippled and paralyzed, waiting for the moving of the
waters. 4For an angel of the Lord used to go down at certain seasons into
the pool and stir up the water. Whoever first stepped in when the water
was stirred was cured from whatever disease he was afflicted with.
5There was one man there who had been sick for 38 years. 6Jesus saw
him lying there, and knowing he had been an invalid for a long time,
asked him, "Do you want to be healed?" 7The sick man answered, "Sir, I
have no one to take me down into the pool when the water is stirred up.
As I try to go down, someone else goes down in front of me." 8Jesus said
to him, "Pick up your bed and walk," 9and immediately the man was
healed and picked up his bed and began to walk. Now that day was the
Sabbath.

10So the Jews said to the man who had been healed, "It is Sabbath,
and it is not permissible for you to carry your bed." 11But he answered
them, "The one who healed me said, 'Take up your bed and walk.'"
12They said to him, "Who is this man who told you to get up and walk?"
13The man who had been healed did not know who it was, because Jesus
had left since there was a crowd at that place. 14After this Jesus found
him in the temple and he said to him, "Look, you are healed now. Do not
sin any more. If you do, a worse thing might happen to you." 15The man
went away and announced to the Jews that Jesus was the one who had
made him well. 16So then the Jews persecuted Jesus, because he had done
these things on the Sabbath. 17Jesus replied to them, "My Father is
working up to now and I am working too." 18For this reason the Jews
were seeking all the more to kill him, because not only had he broken the

---

[65]Not Christian, but Jewish festival. John did not identify the feasts of the OT calendar with the practice of Christians. See Col. 2:16-17 for the NT teaching that the Old Testament calendar is a single shadow — annual festivals, monthly new moons and weekly Sabbaths. That shadow is negatively contrasted with the Messiah who has come. The Messiah is the reality of which the calendar was a shadow. Paul urged that the tri-fold calendar not be imposed on Christians under the New Covenant.

Sabbath, but he was calling God his own Father and putting himself on a
par with God.[66]
19So Jesus answered them, "I am telling you the truth: the Son is
unable to do anything on his own authority. He can do only what he sees
the Father doing. Whatever his Father does, the Son does likewise.
20Because the Father loves the Son He has shown him what He is doing,
and He will show him greater things, so that you may marvel. 21For just
as the Father raises the dead and makes them alive, so also the Son
makes alive whom he wishes. 22The Father judges no one but has put all
judgment into the hands of the Son,[67] 23so that everyone may honor the
Son as they honor the Father. The one who does not honor the Son does
not honor the Father, who commissioned him as His agent.
24"I tell you on the highest authority that the one who hears[68] my
Gospel-word and thus believes the One who commissioned me has the
Life of the Age to Come,[69] and will not come into judgment, but he has
been transferred from death to life. 25I am telling you the truth: the hour
is coming, and now already is, when the dead will hear the voice of the
Son of God and those who hear will come back to life. 26Just as the
Father has life in Himself, so also He has granted the Son to have life in
himself, 27and He has given him authority to carry out judgment, because
he is the Son of Man.[70] 28Do not be amazed at this, because the hour is
coming when all who are in their graves will hear the voice of the Son of
Man. 29They will come out of their graves, the ones who have done what

---

[66]Jesus as the unique, sinless, virginally begotten human being had a functional equality with God, always expressing and carrying out the will of his Father. This certainly does not make Jesus a coeternal part of a triune God. The irony is that Trinitarians do put the Son in a position of complete equality with God, exactly what the hostile Jews accused him of, and which he firmly rejected (cp. 10:33).

[67]For a wonderful statement confirming this, see Acts 17:31.

[68]Implying obedience, of course, cp. Heb. 5:9 and John 3:36, etc.

[69]The life of the Kingdom of God, tasted now in the spirit, and fully experienced when the future Messianic Kingdom arrives at the return of Jesus.

[70]Who eventually judges, governs and administers the whole world at his return (see Dan. 7:14, 18, 22, 27; Isa. 32:1; 16:5).

is good to a resurrection of life[71] and those who have done what is evil to
a resurrection of judgment.[72]

30"I can do nothing on my own authority. As I hear I judge, and my
judgment is fair, because I do not seek my own will but the will of the
One who commissioned me as His agent. 31If I witness about myself, my
witness is not true. 32There is another who witnesses about me, and I
know that the witness He gives about me is true.

33"You sent messengers to John and he witnessed to the truth. 34I do
not accept witness from people, but these things I am telling you so that
you can be saved. 35He was a bright shining light and you were willing to
rejoice in his light for a time.

36"But I have a much greater witness than John, because the works
which the Father has given me to do, these works witness to the fact that
the Father has commissioned me. 37And my Father who commissioned
me has witnessed about me. You have never heard His voice or seen His
form at any time. 38And you do not have His Gospel-word[73] living in
your heart, because the one whom the Father commissioned — him you
do not believe.[74]

39"You search the Scriptures because you think that you have the Life
of the Age to Come in them. These are the very Scriptures which bear
witness to me. 40But you are not willing to come to me to have that life.
41I do not receive praise from people, 42but I know that you do not have
God's love in you. 43I have come in the name of my Father, as His agent,
and you do not receive me. Yet if another comes in his own name, you
will receive him. 44How can you possibly believe when you accept praise
from one another, and you fail to seek the praise which comes from the
only One who is God?[75] 45Do not imagine that I will accuse you before

---

[71] Indestructible life, immortality in the future Kingdom on earth.

[72] The second resurrection of Rev. 20:11ff where all the rest of the dead (20:5), i.e. those not worthy of the first resurrection, will come back to life. Many have lived and died without even hearing of Jesus.

[73] The "word" is the indispensable Gospel of the Kingdom preached by Jesus (Mk. 1:14-15; Lk. 8:12, etc).

[74] Obedience, of course, is implied (Heb. 5:9).

[75] This is significantly and dramatically true of the people who, failing to believe Moses' definition of the One God in Deut. 6:4, that He is a single Lord, fail to believe Jesus' affirmation of that unitary monotheistic creed, when Jesus declared it to be the most

the Father. There is one who will accuse you and that is Moses, in whom
you claim to have placed your hope. 46If indeed you believed Moses you
would believe me, because he wrote about me. 47But if you will not
believe his writings, how can you possibly believe my words?"[76]

6 1After this Jesus crossed to the other side of the Lake of Galilee (or
Tiberias) 2and a large crowd was following him because they had
seen the miraculous signs which he was performing for sick people.
3Jesus then went up a hillside and sat there with his disciples. 4The
Jewish[77] annual festival of Passover was approaching. 5Jesus looked out
on the large crowd which was coming to him, and he said to Philip,
"Where are we going to buy food for these people to eat?" 6He said this
as a test for Philip because he knew what he was intending to do. 7So
Philip answered, "200 denarii worth of bread would be not enough, even
for each of them to have a small portion." 8One of his disciples, Andrew,
brother of Simon Peter, said, 9"There is a young lad here who has five
loaves of bread and two fish, but this is hardly sufficient for such a
crowd." 10Jesus said, "Tell the people to sit down." There was a lot of
grass at that place, and so about 5,000 men were seated. 11Jesus then took
the loaves and having given thanks distributed them to the people who
were seated. He did the same with the fish, as much as they wanted.
12When the people had eaten their fill, he said to the disciples, "Collect
the remaining pieces of bread so that nothing is wasted." 13So they
gathered what was left of the five barley loaves, filling twelve baskets.
14When the people saw the miraculous sign that Jesus had performed they
were saying, "This must truly be the prophet who was to come into the

---

important of all commands (Mk. 12:29; Jn. 17:3). The One God is the Father some 1300 times in the NT and thousands of times in the Bible.

[76]Note the constantly repeated theme: that faith in Jesus is genuine only if it recognizes obedience to Jesus (Jn. 3:36, etc; cp. Heb. 5:9), which involves of course an intelligent grasp of Jesus' words.

[77]Not Christian. The Jewish festival lasted for 8 days, including the opening marked by the slaying of the Passover lamb. The first high day followed on the 15th Nisan and ended with another celebration on 21st Nisan. Jesus ate his final meal when the nation was celebrating the Passover meal. He died the following day (still the 15th Nisan).

world."[78] 15So Jesus, knowing that they were about to come and seize him
and make him king,[79] withdrew again to the mountain alone by himself.

16And when it was late the disciples departed in a boat 17and crossed
the lake to Capernaum, and it was already getting dark and Jesus had not
yet come to them. 18The sea was becoming rough because a strong wind
was blowing. 19When they had rowed about 3 or 4 miles they saw Jesus
walking on the sea and approaching them, and they were frightened. 20He
said to them, "It is me,[80] do not be scared." 21They wanted to take him
into the boat, and immediately the boat arrived at the shore where they
were headed.

22The next day the crowd standing on the other side of the lake saw
only one[81] small boat there. They noticed that Jesus had not gone in the
boat with his disciples, but that the disciples had left on their own.
23Other small boats came from Tiberias near the place where they had
eaten the bread after the lord had given thanks. 24When they saw that
Jesus was not there nor the disciples with him, they got into small boats

---

[78]Deut. 18:15-18, quoted twice in Acts as defining the expected Messiah, who certainly was not expected to be GOD, but God's unique agent and representative, the second Adam and Son of God. To come into the world means to be born.

[79]The crowd acted on the basis of all OT expectation, which is certainly not rescinded in the NT! What they did not understand was that the Messiah was destined to suffer and die first, then be exalted to heaven and only then at his Second Coming (*Parousia*) take up his position as King of a new society on earth. The Messianic drama which pervades the whole Bible is largely lost on churchgoers today.

[80]The Greek idiom is "I am [he]." Certainly he is not claiming to be GOD, here or in any other occurrence of this self-identification. The meaning of "I am [he]" in John 8:58 and other places has been carefully established by John when he introduces this phrase and clearly gives it the meaning "I am he, the Messiah" (Jn. 4:25-26). John wrote the whole book to convince us that "Jesus is the Messiah, the Son of God" (20:31), certainly with no intention of proving that Jesus was God, which would have contradicted the unitary monotheistic creed of Jesus in John 17:3; 5:44. If Jesus were God, and we all know that the Father is God, that would amount to two who are God, which is two Gods and violates the first commandment so strongly emphasized by Jesus in Mark 12:29. The creed of Jesus should always provide the indispensable heart of all theology and teaching claiming to be biblically Christian.

[81]The phrase "only one" is perfectly clear and produces no discussion whatsoever. The same language defines God as "the only one who is true God" (Jn. 17:3) and "there is no one else besides him" (Mk. 12:32). There was only one boat there, and no other besides it. Thousands of singular personal pronouns define God as one single divine Person, and only one Person.

and went to Capernaum looking for Jesus. 25Finding him across the lake,
they said to him, “Rabbi, when did you get here?”
26Jesus answered, “I tell you on the highest authority, you are looking
for me not because you saw the miracles but because you were given
food and were satisfied. 27Do not work for perishable food, but for the
food which remains for the Age to Come,[82] which the Son of Man[83] will
give you because the Father, who is God,[84] has authorized him to provide
this.” 28So they said to him, “What shall we do to work the works of
God?” 29Jesus answered, “This is the work of God: that you believe in
the one whom God has commissioned as His representative.” 30So they
said to him, “What sign are you going to give us so that we may
understand and believe you? What will you do? 31Our ancestors ate the
manna in the wilderness as it is written in Scripture: “He gave them
bread from heaven to eat.” 32So Jesus said to them, “I tell you on the
highest authority: it was not Moses who gave you that bread from heaven
but my Father who gives you the genuine bread from heaven, 33for God’s
bread is the bread coming from heaven and it gives Life[85] to the world.”
34So they said to him, “lord, keep on giving us this bread.”
35Jesus said to them, “I am that bread of life. Everyone who comes to
me will not be hungry and the one believing in me will never again be
thirsty. 36But I said to you that you have seen me and still do not believe.
37Everyone whom my Father gives to me comes to me, and the person
who comes to me I will never turn away, 38because I have come down

---

[82]The food which will gain you immortality and which guarantees a place in the future Kingdom.

[83]The human being, Jesus’ favorite self-designation. It is based on the Messianic human figure in Daniel 7.

[84]This is one of 1300 references in the NT to the Father, who is the One God of biblical monotheism. The evidence for unitary, not Trinitarian monotheism is massive in both Testaments. Later developments under pagan influence and leading to a triune God at the Council of Nicea are far removed from the Bible. Jesus was a confessed unitary monotheist, as is proven by Mark 12:29.

[85]Christians receive the germ of immortality now by believing the truth of the teachings of Jesus and of the New Covenant Scripture introduced by Jesus, and they gain immortality, Life forever and Life indestructible, only at the future resurrection when Jesus returns to the earth (1 Cor. 15:23).

from heaven[86] not to do my own will but the will of the One
commissioning me. 39This is the will of the One who commissioned me:
that everyone given to me by God should not be lost, but I will resurrect
him on the final day of this age. 40This is the will of my Father, that
everyone who sees the Son and believes in him should gain the Life of
the Age to Come,[87] and I will resurrect him on the final day of this age."

41This caused the Jews to grumble at him because he said, "I am the
bread which comes down from heaven." 42They were saying, "Surely this
is Jesus the son of Joseph whom we know, whose father and mother we
know? How then can he say that he came down from heaven?" 43Jesus
answered them, "Do not grumble among yourselves. 44No one is able to
come to me unless the Father who commissioned me draws him, and I
will resurrect him on the final day of this age. 45It stands written in
Scripture in the prophets: 'They will all be taught by God.' Everyone
who has heard and learned from the Father comes to me, 46not that
anyone has seen the Father. Only the one who is from the Father has
truly seen[88] the Father. 47I tell you on the highest authority, the one who
believes has the Life of the Age to Come. 48I am the bread of life. 49Your
ancestors ate the manna in the wilderness and died. 50This is the bread
which comes down from heaven so that you may eat it and not die. 51I am
the life-giving bread which came from heaven. If someone eats this
bread he will live in the Age to Come,[89] and the bread which I will give
is my flesh,[90] and it is for the life of the world."

52So the Jews were arguing among themselves, "How can this person
give us his flesh to eat?" 53Jesus replied, "I tell you on the highest

---

[86]To "come down from heaven" is Hebrew idiom for being God's gift to us. James says that "every good gift comes down from heaven" and noted that true wisdom "comes down from heaven" (1:17; 3:15).

[87]Immortality in the future Kingdom on earth, at Jesus' return to rule and govern the world.

[88]John uses the verb "see" in a figurative sense to mean "see with the mind," "understand and know."

[89]Not "go to heaven" as a disembodied soul at death, which contradicts the biblical hope and Gospel.

[90]It is highly important to note that it is the *human being* Jesus, as flesh, who came down from heaven. The descending bread is the human Jesus, not a preexistent God or angel figure.

authority: unless you eat the flesh of the Son of Man[91] and drink his
blood you have no life in yourselves. 54The one 'chewing on' my flesh
and 'drinking my blood' has the Life of the Age to Come, and I will
resurrect him on the last day of this present age. 55For my flesh is the
genuine food and my blood is genuine drink. 56The one 'chewing on my
flesh' and 'drinking my blood' remains in me and I in him. 57Just as the
living Father commissioned me, so I live because of the Father, and the
one 'chewing on me'[92] will live because of me. 58This is the bread[93]
which came down from heaven — not like your ancestors who ate and
died. The one chewing this bread will live in the Coming Age."[94] 59This
was Jesus' message as he taught in the synagogue in Capernaum.

60Many of his disciples who heard this said, "This is a difficult
teaching. Who can grasp it?" 61Jesus, conscious of the fact that they were
grumbling over his teaching, said to them, "Are you offended by this
too? 62What if you should see the Son of Man ascending to where he was
before?[95] 63It is the spirit which gives life; the flesh gains you nothing.
The words which I have spoken to you *are* spirit and are life. 64But there
are some among you who refuse to believe." Jesus knew from the
beginning which ones would not believe and who would betray him, 65so
he was saying, "That is why I said to you, no one can come to me unless
it is granted to him by the Father."

66Because of these words many of his disciples left him and no longer
continued to associate with him. 67So Jesus said to the twelve, "Are you
wanting to leave also?" 68Simon Peter replied, "Master,[96] who would we

---

[91]*The* human being, based on Daniel 7. This was Jesus' favorite title for himself.

[92]Absorbing, ingesting my teachings, "chewing" on them, feeding on the Kingdom teachings of Jesus as the essential food which alone can lead us to immortality.

[93]The flesh of Jesus, his human person "came down from heaven." This is not a reference to preexistence, since no one thinks the *human* Jesus preexisted. To "come down from heaven" means to be God's gift to the world (cp. James 1:17; 3:15).

[94]The future Kingdom on earth.

[95]Note carefully that the subject of his ascent is the *human being*. The reference is to the Son of Man in Daniel 7, who had previously been seen in *a vision* of the future, with God in heaven. Jesus went to heaven at his ascension.

[96]The Greek is *kurios*, lord, and means of course, "lord, rabbi, teacher." Jesus is the lord *Messiah* who was born (Lk. 2:11), and the lord, son of David (Mt. 15:22; 20:30) — certainly not the Lord *God*, who is the Father. There is only one Lord God, the Father, and so Jesus cannot be Lord God, which makes two!

join? You have the words of the Life of the Age to Come,[97] and 69we
believe and have come to know that you are God's Holy One." 70Jesus
replied, "Have I not chosen you twelve, yet one of you is a devil?"[98] 71He
was referring to Judas Iscariot. He was one of the twelve and was about
to betray Jesus.

7 1After this, Jesus went from place to place in Galilee. He did not want
to stay in Judea, because the Jews were looking for an opportunity to
put him to death. 2Now the Jewish festival of Tabernacles[99] was near. 3So
his brothers said to him, "Leave here and go to Judea so that your
students may observe the miraculous works you are doing. 4For no one
does things secretly if he wants to be in the public eye. If you are doing
these things, let the world see what you are doing." 5For even his own
brothers did not believe in him. 6Jesus then said to them, "My decisive
moment is still to come, but any time is right for you. 7It is not possible
for you to be hated by the world; but I am hated by it, because I am
witnessing to the fact that its activities are evil. 8You go on up to the
festival: I am not going up to the festival now because the right time for
me has not fully come." 9With these words, he stayed behind in Galilee.

10But after his brothers had gone up to the festival, he went up, not
publicly, but in secret. 11At the festival the Jews were looking for him
and asking, "Where is he?" 12And there was much complaining about
him among the people. Some said, "He is a good man," but others said,
"No, he is deceiving the people." 13But no one said anything about him
openly, for fear of the Jews.

14Now in the middle of the festival Jesus went up to the Temple and
began teaching. 15Then the Jews were astonished and said, "Where did
this man get all this knowledge[100] from? He has never been to school
formally." 16Jesus gave them this answer: "It is not my own teaching, but

---

[97]That is, the teachings of Jesus, when believed and obeyed, give us access to immortality in the future Kingdom of God on earth.

[98]Not "the Devil" who is the supernatural external tempter in Scripture, but "a devil" manifesting the same evil qualities as Satan, the Devil.

[99]Not a "Christian festival."

[100]An astonishingly neglected if not suppressed text is Isa. 53:11: "By his knowledge my righteous servant will make many right."

it comes from the One who commissioned me. 17If anyone is willing[101] to
do God's will he will fully recognize this teaching and where it comes
from — from God or from my own initiative. 18The man whose teachings
come from himself is looking for glory for himself, but he who is
looking for the glory of Him who sent him — that man is genuine, and
there is nothing false about him.

19"Did not Moses give you the Law? Even so, none of you keeps the
Law. Why are you wanting to put me to death?" 20The people answered,
"You have a demonic spirit! Who wants to put you to death?" 21Jesus
answered, "I have performed one miraculous work and you are all
shocked by it. 22Moses gave you circumcision — not that it comes
actually from Moses, but from the patriarchs — and on that account you
circumcise a male child on the Sabbath. 23If a child is circumcised on the
Sabbath so that the Law of Moses is not broken, why are you angry with
me because I made a whole man healthy on the Sabbath? 24Stop basing
your decisions on appearance, and make honest judgments."

25Then some of the people of Jerusalem said, "Is not this the man
whom the authorities are trying to kill? 26And here he is talking openly
and they say nothing to him! Is it possible that the rulers know in fact
that this really is the Messiah? 27However, it is clear to us where this man
comes from, but when the Messiah comes no one will know where he
comes from." Then, while teaching in the Temple, 28Jesus shouted out:
"You know about me. You know where I came from; and I have not
come on my own authority; but there is One who has commissioned me;
He is true, but you have no knowledge of Him. 29I know Him because I
came from Him[102] and He commissioned me." 30Then they wanted to
seize him, but no one arrested him because his hour was still to come.
31And many of the people believed in him, and they said, "When the
Messiah comes will he do more signs than this man has done?"

---

[101]This shows that salvation is dependent not only on God's gracious offer but on a human being's willingness to work with God in response (Phil. 2:12-13). Jesus noted that the Pharisees "resisted God's will for themselves" (Lk. 7:30), and Jesus lamented the fact that his enemies refused to listen to him, although he earnestly desired that they would (Mt. 23:37). These are clear indications of a synergism, a working together of God and man. See also Rev. 22:17, where a man must desire to follow Jesus, that is, must choose to do so. "God wants everyone to be saved" (1 Tim. 2:4), but not everyone will be saved, because they chose not to be saved.

[102]His origin was in the virginal begetting (Lk. 1:35; Mt. 1:18, 20).

32 This discussion among the people came to the ears of the Pharisees,
and the chief priests and the Pharisees sent temple police to seize him.
33 Then Jesus said, “I will be with you a little longer, and then I am going
to Him who commissioned me. 34 You will be looking for me, and you
will not find me: and where I am going you may not come.” 35 So the
Jews said among themselves, “Where is he going where we will not be
able to see him? Will he go to the Jews living among the Greeks and
become the teacher of the Greeks? 36 What does he mean by this: ‘You
will be looking for me and will not see me, and where I am going you
may not come?’”

37 On the great, last day of the feast of Tabernacles, Jesus stood up and
shouted out, “If any of you is thirsty let him come to me and let him
drink. 38 He who believes and obeys me, out of his inner person,[103] as
Scripture has said, will come rivers of living water.” 39 He meant by this
the spirit which would be given to those who believed and obeyed him.
For the spirit was not yet present[104] because Jesus had not yet been
glorified.

40 Hearing these words some of the people said, “This certainly must
be *the* prophet.”[105] 41 Others were saying, “This is the Messiah.” But
others said, “That is not right; will the Messiah come from Galilee?
42 Does not Scripture tell us that the Messiah is a descendant of David and
from Bethlehem, the little town where David lived?” 43 So there was a
division among the people because of him. 44 And some of them wanted
to seize him, but no one laid hands on him.

45 Then the temple police went back to the chief priests and Pharisees,
who said to them, “Why did you not bring him with you?” 46 The police
officers replied, “No one ever spoke like this man.” 47 So the Pharisees
said to them, “Are you being deceived just like the others? 48 Have any of
the rulers believed in him, or any one of the Pharisees? 49 But these
people who are ignorant of the Law are cursed.” 50 Nicodemus, the one
who had come to Jesus earlier — and he was one of the ruling Pharisees
— said to them, 51 “Is a man to be judged by our law before it is heard
what he has to say, and before we know what he has done?” 52 This was

---

[103]Literally, “out of his belly.” This means the innermost part of the person, and so the spirit will pour from the true believer.

[104]From the risen Messiah, now at the right hand of God (Ps. 110:1).

[105]Predicted by Deut. 18:15-18, and quoted of Jesus in Acts 3:22 and 7:37.

their answer: "Are you also one of those people from Galilee? Do some
research, and you will see that no prophet comes out of Galilee." 53And
they all went to their homes.[106]

8 1Jesus went out to the Mount of Olives. 2At dawn he made his way to
the temple complex again and all the people were coming to hear him
teach. He sat down and began teaching them. 3Then the religious teachers
and Pharisees brought a woman caught in adultery and made her stand in
front of them. 4They said to him, "Teacher, this woman was caught in the
very act of committing adultery. 5According to the law, Moses
commanded us to stone women like this. So what do you propose?"
6They asked this in order to trap Jesus, so that they might have evidence
to accuse him. Jesus stooped down and began writing on the ground with
his finger. 7When they persisted with their question, he stood up and said
to them, "Whoever is without sin among you should be the first to throw
a rock at her." 8Then Jesus stooped down again and continued to write on
the ground. 9When they saw this they left one by one starting with the
older men. Only Jesus was left, with the woman standing with him.
10When Jesus stood up he said to her, "Woman, where are your accusers?
Has no one condemned you?" 11She answered him, "No one, lord." Jesus
said, "I do not condemn you either. So leave, but do not sin anymore."

12Then Jesus spoke to them again: "I am the light[107] of the world.
Anyone who follows me and my teaching will never walk in the
darkness but will have the light of life." 13So the Pharisees said to him,
"You are testifying about yourself, so your testimony is invalid." Jesus
answered, 14"Even if I testify about myself, my testimony is indeed valid,
because I know where I came from and where I am going, but you do not
know where I come from or where I am going. 15You are using external,
unspiritual standards to judge. I am judging no one. 16But if I do judge,
my judgment is true because I am not alone, but I and the Father who
commissioned me are united in our judgment. 17Even in your law it is

---

[106]The earliest manuscripts do not include John 7:53-8:11.
[107]Cp. the prologue where the "word," which is expressive of God, contains light. Jesus is what that light became.

written that the witness of two men[108] is valid. 18I am the one who
testifies about myself, and the Father who commissioned me testifies
about me also." 19So then they were asking him, "Where is your father?"
Jesus answered, "You recognize neither me nor my Father. If you knew
me you would also recognize my Father."[109] 20He spoke these words by
the treasury, while teaching in the temple complex. But no one arrested
him, because his decisive hour had not yet come.

21Then he said to them again, "I am going away; you will search for
me and you will die in your sins. Where I am going, you cannot come."
22So the Jews said again, "Is he going to kill himself, since he says,
'Where I am going you cannot come'?" 23Jesus replied, "You are from
below; I am from above. You are of this world; I am not of this world.
24That is why I told you that you will die in your sins. For if you do not
believe that I am he, the Messiah,[110] you will die in your sins." 25They
asked him, "Who are you?" Jesus replied, "Precisely what I have been
telling you from the very beginning. 26I have a lot more things to say to
you which judge you, but the One who commissioned me is true, and
what I have heard from him — that is what I am announcing to the
world." 27They did not know that he was speaking to them about the
Father. 28So Jesus said this, "When you lift up the Son of Man, then you
will know that I am he, the Messiah, and that I do nothing on my own,
but just as the Father taught me, so I speak. 29The one who commissioned
me is with me. He has not left me alone, because I continuously do what
pleases Him." 30As he was saying these things, many came to believe in
him.

31So Jesus said to the Jews who had believed him, "If you continue in
my Gospel-word, then you really are my disciples. 32And you will know

---

[108]Jesus and God are two individuals, as much so as any two individuals. If both Father and Son are equally God, that makes two who are God and thus two Gods, which is not monotheism.

[109]Thus Thomas in 20:28 eventually came to understand that in seeing the Son you also see the Father: "my lord and my God," an address to two persons, the Father recognized in the Son ("the lord of me and the God of me," a double article and possessive pronoun suggesting two subjects).

[110]The meaning of the Greek *ego eimi*, "I am [he]" is established by its first occurrence in a series. This is found in John 4:26, where the meaning is obviously "I am the Messiah." John wrote his whole book to demonstrate this fact that Jesus is the Messiah (20:31).

the truth[111] and that truth will set you free." 33They answered, "We are
descendants of Abraham, and we have never been enslaved to anyone.
How then can you say, 'You will become free'?"

34Jesus responded, "I assure you of this: everyone who commits sin is
a slave of sin. 35A slave does not remain a member of the household
forever, but a son does remain forever. 36Therefore if the son sets you
free, you really will be free. 37I recognize that you are descendants of
Abraham, but you are trying to kill me because my Gospel-word makes
no progress in you.[112] 38I speak what I have learned and understood[113] in
the presence of my Father, and you do what you have heard from *your*
father."

39They said, "Our father is Abraham!" Jesus replied to them, "If you
were Abraham's children, you would be doing what Abraham did, 40but
in fact you are trying to kill me, a man who has told you the truth, the
truth which I heard from God. Abraham certainly did not do this! 41You
are doing exactly what your father does." They said, "We were not born
of sexual immorality.[114] We have one Father – God."[115] 42Jesus said to
them, "If God really was your Father, you would love me, because I
originated from God[116] and I have come here. I did not come on my own,

---

[111]"The truth" is elsewhere a designation of the saving Gospel, otherwise described as "the word," or "the word of God." It must never be forgotten that the saving word/Gospel of Jesus is his Gospel about the Kingdom of God. Belief in that Gospel and in Jesus as Messiah is the basis of the whole Christian faith announced by Jesus in Mark 1:14-15. In Mark's account the Kingdom means invariably the Kingdom which will arrive in the future at Jesus' Second Coming. Without a clear view of the future (eschatology) there can be no grasp of the saving Gospel of the Kingdom as preached by Jesus.

[112]The true believer is one in whom the Gospel of the Kingdom word of Jesus takes hold. The death and resurrection of Jesus are of course equally indispensable.

[113]There is no reference to a pre-human life here. Jesus learned from his Father during the course of his life. Similarly his enemies learned from the Devil, their father.

[114]With the vicious insinuation that Jesus *was* born illegitimately.

[115]Their claim was to be monotheists in the sense taught by the Hebrew Bible: "Do we not all have one Father? Has not one God created us?" (Mal. 2:10). Jesus of course was a Jewish monotheist in the same sense, but the church in post-biblical times changed the meaning of "God" to denote a triune God, which Jesus would not have recognized.

[116]The origin (*genesis*) of Jesus is clearly laid out in Matt. 1:18, 20 and expressly also in Luke 1:35. John had these gospels before him and certainly agreed with his colleague writers of NT Scripture.

but He commissioned me. 43Why are you incapable of understanding
what I am saying to you? It is because you cannot listen to and grasp my
Gospel-word. 44You are the products of your father the Devil, and your
desire is to carry out your father's wishes. He was a murderer from the
beginning and has not remained in the truth, because there is no truth in
him. When he tells a lie, he speaks from his own nature, because he is a
liar and the father of liars. 45Yet because I tell you the truth you refuse to
believe me. 46Who among you can convict me of sin? If I tell you the
truth, why are you not believing me? 47The person who is of God listens
to and grasps God's words. This is why you do not listen to those words,
because you are not of God."

48The Jews responded to him, "We are certainly right to say that you
are a Samaritan and have a demon." 49Jesus answered, "I do not have a
demon. On the contrary I am honoring my Father and you are
dishonoring me. 50I am not seeking my own glory. There is One who
seeks glory and judges. 51I tell you, if anyone keeps my Gospel-word he
will ultimately not see death." 52Then the Jews said, "Now we know for
certain that you have a demon. Abraham died and so did the prophets.
But you say, 'If anyone keeps my Gospel-word he will never experience
death'! 53Are you greater than our father Abraham who died? Even the
prophets died. Who do you think you are?" 54Jesus answered, "If I glorify
myself my glory amounts to nothing. My Father — of whom you say He
is our God — He is the one who glorifies me. 55You have never come to
know Him, but I know Him. If I were to say I do not know Him, I would
be a liar just like you. But I do in fact know Him, and I keep His Gospel-
word. 56Your father Abraham was overjoyed at the prospect that he
would see my day. He saw it and rejoiced looking forward to the future."
57The Jews replied, "You are not even fifty years old yet, and yet you
have *seen* Abraham?" 58Jesus said to them, "Let me assure you on the
highest authority, before Abraham ever existed, I am the Messiah."[117]

---

[117]That is, the Messiah planned in God's great design for humanity. The "I am [he]" of John 4:26 retains the meaning John assigned to it at its first occurrence — "I am the Messiah." It is also possible to translate the Greek, "Before Abraham comes to be [in the resurrection] I am already alive." Thus Jesus proved his superiority to Abraham by alone being resurrected on the third day. Abraham will rise from death at the future resurrection when Jesus returns (1 Cor. 15:23).

59Hearing those words, they picked up rocks to throw at him. But Jesus
was hidden and left the temple complex.

9 1As Jesus was passing by he noticed a man blind from birth. 2His
disciples questioned him: "Rabbi, who was it who sinned, this man or
his parents, to cause him to be born blind?" 3Jesus answered, "Neither
this man or his parents sinned. This blindness came about so that God's
works might be displayed in him. 4We are required to do the works of the
One who commissioned me while it is still day. Night is coming when no
one can work. 5As long as I am in the world, I am the light of the world."
6After making these remarks he spat on the ground, made some mud
from the saliva and spread the mud on the blind man's eyes. 7Then he
said to him, "Go and wash in the pool of Siloam" (which translated
means "commissioned"). So he left, washed and came back seeing. 8His
neighbors and those who had earlier seen him as a beggar said, "Is this
the man who used to be sitting begging?" 9Some said, "Yes, he is the
one." Others were saying, "No, but he does look like him." He kept
saying, "I am he!"[118] 10So they asked him, "Then how do you now see?"
11He answered, "The man called Jesus made some mud, spread it on my
eyes and told me to go to Siloam and wash. So I went and washed, and
now I can see." 12They asked him, "Where is he?" He said, "I do not
know."

13They brought the man who had been blind to the Pharisees. 14The
day that Jesus had made mud and opened the blind man's eyes was the
Sabbath. 15So again the Pharisees were asking him how he received his
sight. He explained to them, "He put mud on my eyes. I washed and now
I can see." 16Therefore some of the Pharisees said, "This man cannot be
from God: he is not keeping the Sabbath!" But others were saying, "How
can a sinful man perform signs like this?" And so there was a division
among them. 17Again they asked the blind man, "What do you say about
him since he was able to give you your sight?" He said, "He is a
prophet."

---

[118] *Ego eimi* ("I am he"), said by the blind man, is the same as Jesus' language: "I am he." Jesus means in every case "I am the **Messiah**" as the first and explanatory occurrence in John 4:26 demonstrates. Jesus did not say, "I am the self-existing one" (*Ego eimi ho ohn*). These are the words of the One God in Ex. 3:14.

18The Jews were not willing to believe this about him — that he had
been blind and had received his sight — until they summoned the parents
of the man who had gained his sight. 19They asked them, “Is this your
son, the one you claim was born blind? How is he able to see now?”
20His parents answered, “We know this is our son and we know he was
born blind, 21but we do not understand how he is now able to see, and we
do not know who gave him his sight. Why not ask him yourselves? He is
an adult. He can speak for himself.” 22They said these things because
they were scared of the Jews, since the Jews had already agreed that if
anyone confessed Jesus as Messiah he would be banned from attending
the synagogue. 23That is why his parents said, “He is an adult; ask him.”

24So they summoned the formerly blind man a second time and said
to him, “Give glory to God by telling the truth. We know that this man is
a sinner!” 25He answered, “Whether or not he is a sinner, I have no idea.
One thing I do know is that I was blind and now I can see!” 26Then they
asked him, “What did he do to you? How did he give you sight?” 27He
said, “I already told you, and you did not listen. Why do you want me to
tell you again? Are you perhaps wanting to become his disciples?”
28They ridiculed him. “You must be that man’s disciple, but we are the
disciples of Moses. 29We know that God has spoken to Moses. But this
man, we have no idea where he is from.” 30The man replied, “This is an
amazing thing. You do not know where he is from, yet he was able to
give me my sight! 31We know that God does not listen to sinners, but if
anyone is God-fearing and does God’s will, God does listen to him.
32Throughout history no one has ever heard of someone giving sight to a
person born blind. 33If this man were not from God, he would not be able
to do anything.” 34They replied, “You were a sinner from birth, and you
are trying to teach *us*?” Then they threw him out.

35When Jesus heard that they had expelled the man, he found him and
asked, “Do you believe in the Son of Man?” 36He asked, “Who is he,
sir,[119] so that I can believe in him?” 37Jesus replied, “You have seen the
Son of Man; in fact he is the one speaking to you now.” 38He said, “I do
believe, sir,” and he bowed before him in deep respect.[120] 39Jesus said, “I
was born into the world for judgment, in order that those who do not see

---

[119] Literally “lord,” showing the title lord does not have to imply Deity! Jesus is the lord Messiah (Lk. 2:11; Ps. 110:1), not the Lord GOD.

[120] “Worshiped” him, clearly not as GOD but as “the Son of Man,” as he just said.

may see, and those who see may become blind.” 40Some of the Pharisees
were with him and heard this. They asked him, “We are not blind too,
are we?” 41Jesus said to them, “If you were blind, you would not be
guilty of sin. But because you say that you can see, your sin remains.”

10 1I tell you on the highest authority: “Anyone who does not enter
the sheep pen by the door but climbs in by some other way is a
thief and robber. 2The one who enters by the door is the shepherd of the
sheep. 3The doorkeeper opens the door for him, and the sheep hear his
voice. He calls his own sheep by name and leads them out. 4When he has
brought all his own sheep outside, he goes ahead of them; the sheep
follow him because they recognize his voice. 5They will never follow a
stranger. They will run away from him, because they do not recognize
the voice of strangers.” 6Jesus gave them this illustration, but they did not
understand the point of what he was telling them.

7So Jesus said again, “I tell you on the highest authority: I am the
door of the sheep. 8All who came before me are thieves and robbers,[121]
but the sheep did not listen to them. 9I am the door. If anyone enters
through me, he will be saved and will come in and go out and find
pasture. 10A thief comes only to steal and kill and destroy. But I have
come so that they may have life and have it in thc greatest abundance.

11“I am the good shepherd. The good shepherd lays down his life for
the sheep. 12The hired man, because he is not the shepherd and does not
own the sheep, abandons them and runs away when he sees a wolf
coming. The wolf then snatches them and scatters them. 13This happens
because he is a hired man and does not care about the sheep. 14I am the
Good Shepherd.[122] I know my own sheep well, and they know me, 15as
the Father knows me, and I know the Father. I lay down my life for the
sake of the sheep. 16But I have other sheep who are not of this fold; I
must bring them along also, and they will listen to my voice. Then there
will be one flock and one shepherd. 17This is why my Father loves me,
because I am giving up my life so that I may take it up again. 18No one
takes my life from me, but I lay it down on my own. I have the right to

---

[121] I.e. false claimants to Messiahship.

[122] That is, the Good Pastor.

give it up, and I have the right to resume it again. I have received this
authority from my Father."

19Once again a division took place among the Jews because of these
words of Jesus. 20Many of them were saying, "He obviously has a
demon. He is crazy! Why do you even listen to him?" 21Others were
saying, "These are certainly not the words of a demon-influenced person.
Can a demon open the eyes of blind people?"

22Then the Festival of Dedication[123] took place in Jerusalem, 23and it
was wintertime. Jesus was walking in the temple complex in Solomon's
colonnade. 24Then the Jews surrounded him and asked, "How long are
you going to keep us in suspense? If you really are the Messiah, tell us
plainly." 25Jesus replied to them, "I did tell you, and you do not believe
me. The works which I do on the authority of my Father testify about
me. 26But you do not believe, because you are not my sheep. 27My sheep
hear my voice, I know them, and they follow me and 28I give them the
Life of the Age to come, and they will never, ever perish! No one will be
able to snatch them out of my hand.[124] 29My Father, who has given them
to me, is greater than all. No one can possibly snatch them out of the
Father's hand. 30The Father and I are working in complete unity."[125]

31Again the Jews picked up rocks to stone him. 32Jesus replied, "I
have demonstrated to you many good works from the Father. Which of
these good works are you trying to stone me for?" 33The Jews answered,
"We are not stoning you for a good work, but for blasphemy, because
you — who are only a man — are making yourself out to be God."[126]

---

[123]Hanukkah.

[124]This is "one side of the coin." Other passages teach that we must resolve to remain in the teaching of Jesus until the end. Our free will is not suspended by Jesus' statement here.

[125]"I and the Father are one" (neuter in Greek), one thing, not one Person. The sense is that they are in perfect agreement, hand in glove. The relationship of unity is predicated of true believers in 17:11, 22 and so the statement in 10:30 has nothing whatsoever to do with a unity in the Trinity. Jesus endorsed the unitary monotheism of his Jewish heritage (Mk. 12:29; Jn. 17:3, etc.). This text is not remotely connected to the idea of "one philosophical essence." 1 Cor. 3:8 shows that those who "plant" and those who "water" for the Gospel are "one."

[126]Or "a god." If Jesus were GOD, as "God the Son," this would have been the ideal moment to state this. But instead he very logically describes himself as the unique agent of the One God. It is the supreme irony that Trinitarians finally agreed that Jesus was in fact God, exactly what the hostile Jews accused him of, and they made this the heart of

34 Jesus said to them, "Is it not stated in your own Law, 'I said, you are
gods'? 35 If God called those[127] to whom the word of God came 'gods' —
and the Scripture cannot be broken — 36 are you telling me I am
blaspheming because I, the one whom the Father set apart[128] and
commissioned to go into the world, said 'I am the Son of God'?[129] 37 If I
am not doing my Father's works, do not believe me. 38 But if I am doing
them and you do not believe me, at least believe the works. This way you
will come to know and understand that the Father is in me and I am in
the Father."[130] 39 Then they were trying once again to arrest him, but he
was able to elude their grasp.

40 So Jesus departed again across the Jordan to the place where John
had been baptizing earlier, and he remained there. 41 Many came to him
and said, "John did not do any miraculous signs, but everything John
said about this man has turned out to be true." 42 And many believed in
Jesus there.

11 1 Now there was a sick man, Lazarus, from Bethany, the village
where Mary and her sister Martha lived. 2 Mary was the woman
who later anointed the lord with fragrant oil and wiped his feet with her
hair. It was her brother Lazarus who was sick. 3 So the sisters sent a
message to Jesus: "lord, the one you love is sick." 4 When Jesus heard
this, he said, "This sickness is not going to end in death, but it is for the

---

their rejection of him. Jesus, however, as a strict monotheist (Mk. 12:29; Jn. 17:3) explained that as the Son of God he was the supreme and final *agent* of the One God, not the One God Himself, which would of course make two who are God, thus two Gods. The same accusation was made against Jesus by hostile Jews in 5:18.

[127]I.e. leaders or judges in Israel.

[128]I.e. that is by a virginal begetting. The word here is "sanctified" and it was the miracle in Mary which constituted Jesus holy and uniquely the Son of God (Lk. 1:35; Mt. 1:20: "what is begotten in her is from holy spirit," the divine creative activity of the One God, the Father). The loss of the biblical definition of Jesus as Son of God in Luke 1:35 is the disaster which allowed post-biblical definitions of him as "God the Son" to develop. Monotheism was fatally tampered with. Recovery will begin when Bible teachers root themselves again in Luke 1:35 and Matt. 1:18, 20.

[129]A decisive and clear definition of who Jesus is, by Jesus himself! And he knew who he was! A Son of God, in the most ideal and unique sense, always obeying his Father, not "God the Son." John calls Jesus "Son of God" and distinguishes him from Christians by referring to the latter as "children of God."

[130]This is the sense in which Father and Son are one (10:30).

glory of God, so that the Son of God may be glorified through it." 5Jesus
loved Martha, her sister, and Lazarus. 6So when he heard that Lazarus
was sick he stayed two more days where he was. 7After this he said to the
disciples, "Let us go to Judea again." 8The disciples said, "Rabbi, the
Jews have just recently been trying to stone you, and you are proposing
to go there again?" 9Jesus answered, "Are there not twelve hours in a
day? If anyone walks during the day, he does not stumble, because he
sees the light of this world. 10If anyone walks during the night, he does
stumble, because there is no light in him." 11He said this, and then he said
to them, "Our friend Lazarus has fallen asleep and is sleeping,[131] but I am
going to wake him up." 12Then the disciples said to him, "lord, if he has
fallen asleep he is going to get well." 13Jesus, however, had spoken about
his death, but they thought he was talking about natural sleep. 14So Jesus
then told them plainly, "Lazarus is dead. 15I am glad for you that I was
not there, so that you may believe. But let us go to him." 16Then Thomas
("the twin") said to his fellow disciples, "Why should we not go too, so
that we may die with him?"

17When Jesus arrived he found that Lazarus had already been in the
tomb for four days. 18Bethany was close to Jerusalem, about two miles
away. 19Many of the Jews had come to Martha and Mary to console them
about their brother. 20As soon as Martha heard that Jesus was coming she
went out to meet him. But Mary stayed in the house. 21Martha then said
to Jesus, "lord, if you had been here my brother would not have died.
22Yet even now I know very well that whatever you ask from God, God
is going to give it to you." 23Jesus reassured her, "Your brother will rise
again." 24Martha said to him, "I know that he is going to rise again in the
resurrection on the last day."[132] 25Jesus said to her, "I am the resurrection
and the life. The one who believes in me, even though he has died, will
live again in the resurrection. 26Everyone who lives and believes in me
will never die — ever.[133] Do you believe this?" 27She replied, "Yes, lord,
I believe absolutely that you are the Messiah, the Son of God, who was
destined to be born into the world."[134]

---

[131]"And is sleeping" is implied by the Greek verb tense. "The sleep of death" (Ps. 13:3).
[132]1 Cor. 15:23 refers to this first resurrection at the return of Jesus.
[133]That is, never die again after being resurrected.
[134]Luke 1:35 and Matt. 1:18, 20 should be constantly consulted to learn of the true origin of the Son of God.

28After saying this she went back and called her sister Mary, and spoke to her in private, “The teacher is here and is calling for you.” 29As soon as Mary heard this, she got up immediately and went to him.

30Jesus had not yet come into the village, but was still at the place where Martha had met him. 31The Jews who were with her in the house consoling her saw Mary get up quickly and go out. So they followed her, thinking that she was going to the tomb to weep there. 32When Mary arrived where Jesus was and saw him, she fell at his feet and said to him, “lord, if you had been here, my brother would not have died!” 33When Jesus saw her crying and the Jews who had come with her crying, he was indignant[135] and his spirit was deeply moved. 34He asked, “Where have you put him?” They said, “lord, come and see.” 35Jesus wept. 36So the Jews were saying, “Look how much he loved him!” 37But some of them said, “Why could he who opened the blind man’s eyes not also have prevented this man from dying?”

38Then Jesus, indignant again, arrived at the tomb. It was a cave, and the stone was lying against it. 39Jesus said, “Remove the stone.” Martha, the dead man’s sister, said, “lord, he is already stinking. It has been four days.” 40Jesus said to her, “Did I not tell you that if you believed you would see the glory of God?” 41So they removed the stone. Then Jesus raised his eyes and said, “Father, I thank you that you heard me. 42I know that you always hear me, but because of the crowd standing here I said this, so that they may believe that You commissioned me.” 43After that he shouted with a loud voice, “Lazarus, come out!” 44And the man who had died[136] came out bound hand and foot with linen strips and with his face wrapped in a cloth. Jesus said to them, “Free him and let him go.”

45Therefore many of the Jews who came to Mary and saw what Jesus was doing believed in him. 46But some of them went to the Pharisees and told them what Jesus had done.

---

[135] Perhaps indignant at the manifestation of Satan’s kingdom of evil.

[136] And was still dead! That is, the dead man came out alive. Note the grammatical parallel with Rev. 20:4: “Those who had been beheaded…came to life [in resurrection].” This is a real coming back to life after being dead, nothing whatsoever to do with being converted to spiritual life! Amillennialism fails entirely on this point, and also because all references to the saints ruling with Jesus are in the future tense in the NT. Paul warned in 1 Cor. 4:8 that it was dangerous to imagine that the saints are *now* ruling! In Rev. 2:8 the resurrection of Jesus is described with the same word: “came to life.”

47So then the chief priests and the Pharisees convened the Sanhedrin
and said, "What are we going to do in view of all the miraculous signs
this man is performing? 48If we let him go on like this everybody is going
to believe in him! But that will mean that the Romans will come and
remove our holy place and our nation." 49One of them, Caiaphas, who
was High Priest that year, said to them, "You know nothing at all! 50You
do not understand that it is to your advantage that one man should die for
the people[137] rather than that the whole nation should perish." 51He did
not say this on his own initiative, but as High Priest that year he
prophesied that Jesus was going to die for the nation, 52and not for the
nation only, but also to unite the scattered children of God. 53So from that
day onwards they plotted to kill Jesus. 54Jesus was no longer able to walk
around in public among the Jews, but departed from there to the
countryside close to the sparsely inhabited areas, to a town called
Ephraim. And he remained there with his disciples.

55The Jewish Passover festival was near, and many people went up to
Jerusalem from the countryside to purify themselves before the Passover
season. 56They were looking for Jesus and asking one another as they
convened in the Temple complex, "Do you think he is going to come up
to the festival?" 57The chief priests and Pharisees had given strict orders
that anyone who knew where Jesus was must report it so they could
arrest him.

12 1Six days before the Passover season[138] began, Jesus came to
Bethany where Lazarus was, the one he had resurrected from
death. 2So they gave a dinner party for him there, and Martha was
serving them. Lazarus was one of those reclining at the table with him.
3Then Mary took a pound of costly perfumed oil and she anointed Jesus'
feet and wiped them with her hair. And the house was filled with the
fragrance of the oil. 4Then one of the disciples, Judas Iscariot (who was
about to betray Jesus) said, 5"This fragrant oil should have been sold for
300 denarii and given to the poor." 6He said this not because he cared
about the poor but because he was a thief. He was in charge of the
money bag and used to steal part of what was put in it. 7Jesus answered,

---

[137] A substitionary death (cp. Mk. 10:45; Isa. 53:4-6, 8, 12).

[138] When John says "Passover" he refers to the entire festival lasting a week.

"Leave her alone. She has kept this for my burial day. 8You will always
have the poor with you, but you will not always have me with you."

9Then a large crowd of the Jews learned that Jesus was there. They
came not only to see Jesus, but also to see Lazarus, the one he had
resurrected from death. 10Therefore the chief priests decided also to kill
Lazarus, 11because he was the main reason many of the Jews were
deserting them in order to give their loyalty to Jesus.

12The next day a large crowd which had come to the festival heard
that Jesus was coming to Jerusalem, 13and gathered some palm branches
and went out to meet him. They kept shouting: "Hosanna![139] Blessed is
the one who comes in the name of the Lord God — the King of Israel."
14Jesus found a young donkey and mounted it, just as it is written, 15"Do
not be afraid any more, daughter Zion. Look, your King is coming
mounted on the donkey's colt." 16The disciples did not at first understand
these things. However when Jesus was later glorified, then they
remembered that these words had been written about him, and that they
had done these things to him. 17Meanwhile the crowd, who had been with
him when he called Lazarus out of the tomb and resurrected him from
death, continued to give their testimony. 18This is also why the crowd
came to meet him, because they had heard that he had performed this
miraculous sign. 19Then the Pharisees said to one another, "You see? You
have achieved nothing. The whole world is following him!"

20Now there were some Greeks among the people who went up to
worship at the festival. 21So they came to Philip, who was from Bethsaida
in Galilee, and they requested of him, "Sir, we want to see Jesus."
22Philip went and told Andrew. Then Andrew and Philip went and told
Jesus. 23Jesus replied to them, "The time has come now for the Son to be
glorified. 24I tell you on the highest authority: Unless a grain of wheat
falls into the ground and dies, it remains by itself. But if it dies it
produces a large crop. 25The person who loves his own life will lose it,
and the person who hates his life in this evil world-system will keep it
for the Life of the Age to Come. 26If anyone serves me he must follow
me. Where I am, there my servant will be also. If anyone serves me, the
Father will honor him.

---

[139] "Save us, now!"

27“Now I am experiencing deep distress. What should I say: 28Father, rescue me from this hour of crisis? But for this purpose I came to this hour. Father, glorify your name.”[140] Then a voice was heard from heaven: “I have glorified it and I am going to glorify it again!” 29The crowd standing there heard the voice and said it sounded like thunder. Others said, “An angel must have spoken to him.” 30Jesus replied, “This voice did not come for my benefit but for you. Now the judgment of this evil world-system has come. 31Now the ruler of this world-system is going to be thrown out. 32As for me, when I am lifted up from the earth, I will draw all people[141] to myself.” 33He said this in order to signify what kind of death he was about to die. 34So then the crowd replied to him, “We have heard from the Law that the Messiah is going to remain forever. So what do you mean when you say, ‘The Son of Man has to be lifted up’? Who is this Son of Man?” 35Jesus replied, “The Light will be with you only a little longer. Walk while you still have the Light, so that darkness does not overcome you. The person who walks in darkness does not know where he is going. 36While you still have the Light, believe in the Light so that you may become children of light.”[142] When he had said this, Jesus went away and hid himself from them.

37Even though Jesus had performed so many symbolic miracles in their presence, they still refused to believe in him. 38And this was a fulfillment of the word of Isaiah the prophet who said: “Lord, who has believed our Gospel message? And who has the arm of the Lord been revealed to?”[143] 39And this is why they were unable to believe, because Isaiah also said, 40“God has blinded their eyes and hardened their hearts, so that they would not see with their eyes nor understand with their hearts, and be converted, and I would heal them.”[144] 41Isaiah said these

---

[140]Your whole plan and agenda, the great salvation drama worked out through Jesus.

[141]This would imply those myriads of human beings who had never heard of him. He died for the whole world and this implies a wider hope for some in the second resurrection (Rev. 20:5: Rom 2:14-16). Zech. 7:12 gives us the same truth. David is the model of good spirituality (2 Sam. 23:1-2).

[142]That is, enlightened people, people whose minds grasp truth.

[143]The sense of this fascinating text from Isa. 6:9-10 (cp. Isa. 53:1) is quoted 5 times in the NT and is a standing protest against the way human beings set their hearts “like flint” against believing the words of Scripture.

[144]This in no way diminishes human responsibility for failure to believe and obey. Isaiah said, “They have closed *their* eyes” (Isa. 6:10, LXX; Mt. 13:15; Acts 28:27). If

things because he saw Messiah's glory[145] and spoke about him.
42Nevertheless many of them did believe in him even among the rulers in
the Sanhedrin, but because of the Pharisees they were afraid to confess
him openly, so that they would not be banned from the synagogue.
43They loved praise from people more than praise from God.

44Then Jesus called out,[146] "The person who believes in me does not
believe in me,[147] but in the One who commissioned me. 45And the one
who sees and understands me sees and understands Him who
commissioned me. 46I was born into the world[148] as a light, so that
everyone who believes in me would not remain in darkness. 47If someone
hears my words and does not obey[149] them, I do not judge him. For I did
not come to judge the world, but to save the world.[150] 48The person who

---

we refuse truth we are liable to a greater judgment, that of becoming more and more blinded and hardened (2 Thess. 2:10ff).

[145]The vision of the glory of his Kingdom which Isaiah spoke of often, especially in Isa. 4:5; 24:16, 23; 40:5; 44:23; 62:2; 66:18-19. This is not a reference to Isaiah seeing the Lord God (*Adonai*) in ch. 6. Jesus is never called the Lord of Hosts. This is a title used only of the Father, the one God. John cites two references to Isaiah. Jesus nowhere claimed to be the Lord God and is never called "the Lord God," nor the Almighty. Rev. 1:8 is no exception (though some red-letter Bibles wrongly lead readers to think that Jesus is called the Almighty there), since the Almighty is the Father there as distinct from the Messiah.

[146]Jesus raised his voice for special emphasis. It is of the highest significance that he repeats the basis of the Christian faith as obedience to his words/Gospel/teaching. Cp. Luke 8:8 where again he raises his voice to impress on the audience the supreme importance of his words. Immortality was at stake, success or failure in the Christian endeavor.

[147]That is, "does not believe ultimately in me, but in the Father who commissioned me as the *final* word to the world" (Heb. 1:1-2).

[148]"I have come as a light into the world." "To come into the world" is to be born. Nicodemus knew that Jesus was a man come from God (3:2), i.e. born to be God's servant and messenger.

[149]The phrase "obedience of faith" beautifully combines belief and obedience. Paul uses this phrase to frame his whole treatise in Romans (1:5; 16:26). Salvation is "given to those who obey Jesus" (Heb. 5:9). Failure to believe and obey the words of Jesus is the fatal trap to be avoided at all costs (2 John 7-9; 1 Tim. 6:3). Jesus expressed the concept of obedience and faith beautifully and succinctly in John 3:36. Refusal to obey is unbelief.

[150]This does not exclude the fact that in the future Jesus has been appointed judge of all men (Acts 17:30-31). Obedience to Jesus and his Gospel teaching, all his words, is the basis of salvation.

rejects me and refuses to accept my teachings has this as his judge: the
Gospel-word[151] I have spoken will judge him on the last day of this
age.[152] 49For I have not spoken on my own initiative, but the Father
Himself who commissioned me has given me a command as to what I
should say and what I should speak. 50And I know that His command
means Life in the Coming Age.[153] So the things I speak I speak just as the
Father instructed me."

13 1Now before the Passover festival[154] Jesus knew that his hour had
arrived to depart from this world[155] and to go to the Father. Having

---

[151]The basis of Christianity as Jesus defined it in Mark 1:14-15, making intelligent belief in the Kingdom of God the basis of true faith. In Luke 4:43 Jesus defined his whole mission as the preaching of the Gospel about the Kingdom (cp. Acts 1:3, 6; 8:12; 19:8; 20:24-25; 28:23, 30, 31). The Gospel of the Kingdom is the scaffolding upon which the whole NT is built. It is strikingly absent from contemporary presentations of what is popularly but misleadingly called "the gospel." Tracts offering salvation invariably do *not* mention the Kingdom of God at all. Jesus made belief in God as "the one who alone is true God" (Jn. 17:3) the standard for a successful entrance into salvation and immortality: "This is the Life of the Age to come: that they believe in You, Father, the only one who is true God, and in Jesus Messiah whom you commissioned."

[152]Acts 17:30-31 is a definitive statement about God's appointment of the man Messiah as judge of the whole of humanity. The resurrection of Jesus is the guarantee that this is going to happen.

[153]"Life in the Coming Age" is synonymous with the Kingdom of God. John's account of Jesus is not less emphatic about the Kingdom of God than Matthew, Mark and Luke. He uses different vocabulary to express the same truth about the Gospel. Jesus' statement that God's commandment *is* the Life of the Age to Come is parallel in its supreme significance to his statement that "This *is* the Life of the Age to Come: to come to know that the Father is the only one who is true God [unitary monotheism], and Jesus Christ whom [God] sent" (Jn. 17:3; cp. Mk. 12:29).

[154]When John uses the word Passover he refers to the entire feast of 7 days. John does not disagree with Matthew, Mark and Luke about which day Jesus was crucified. As Dr. Torrey of Yale observed, "The author of the Fourth Gospel was perfectly familiar with the clear and repeated assertion of the Synoptics that the Last Supper was the paschal meal, and that the crucifixion took place on the 15th Nisan. He knew that the gospels of Mark and Matthew (at least) were before the public; doubtless also that they were familiar to many of those for whom John was writing" (*The Date of the Crucifixion According to the Fourth Gospel*, p. 241).

[155]A human being comes into the world at birth and departs at death, in the case of Jesus to rest in the grave from Friday to Sunday. All others rest in the sleep of death

loved his own people who were in the world, he loved them to the end.
2 Now by supper-time[156] the Devil had already put it into the mind of
Judas, Simon Iscariot's son, to betray him. 3 Jesus knew that the Father
had given everything into his hands, that he had come from God[157] and
that he was going[158] to God. 4 So he got up from supper, laid aside his
robe, picked up the towel, and tied it around himself.

5 Next he poured some water into a basin and began washing his
disciples' feet, drying them with the towel tied around him. 6 He came to
Simon Peter, who asked him, "lord, are you going to wash my feet?"
7 Jesus answered him, "What I am doing now you do not understand, but
afterwards you will understand." 8 Peter said, "You will never wash my
feet — never." Jesus replied, "If I do not wash your feet you have no part
with me." 9 Simon Peter said to him, "lord, then not only my feet, but also
my hands and my head." 10 Jesus replied, "One who has had a bath does
not need to wash anything except his feet, but he is completely clean.
You disciples are clean, but not all of you." 11 For Jesus knew who was
going to betray him. That is why he said, "You are not *all* clean."

12 When Jesus had washed their feet and put on his robe again, he
reclined and said to them, "Do you know what I have done for you?
13 You call me teacher and lord. You are right to do this, because that is
what I am. 14 So if I, your lord and teacher, have washed your feet you
also ought to wash one another's feet. 15 I have given you an example that
you should do just as I have done to you. 16 On the highest authority I tell
you, a servant is not greater than his master, and the messenger is not
greater than the one who commissions him. 17 If you understand these
things you are blessed indeed if you do them. 18 I am not speaking about
all of you; I know the ones I have chosen. But the Scripture has to be
fulfilled: 'The one who eats food with me has turned against me.' 19 I am
telling you this now before it happens, so that when it does happen you

---

(Ps. 13:3) until the resurrection of the sleeping dead, at the return of Jesus to the earth at his Second Coming.

156 This was the occasion of the Passover meal described in the other gospels.

157 By the miraculous begetting in Mary (Lk. 1:35; Mt. 1:18, 20; 1 John 5:18). Cp. Isa. 9:6: "A son has been begotten [past tense of prophecy] for us," i.e., by God (divine passive).

158 Not "going *back*." See also 16:28; 20:17.

will believe that I am he, the Messiah.[159] 20I tell you on the highest authority: the person who receives someone I commission receives me, and the person who receives me receives the One who commissioned me."[160]

21When Jesus had said this he was inwardly troubled[161] and gave this testimony, "On the highest authority I tell you, one of you is going to betray me." 22The disciples began looking at one another, uncertain about which one he had in mind. 23One of his disciples, the one Jesus loved, was reclining at table close beside Jesus. 24Simon Peter motioned to him to find out who it was Jesus was talking about. 25So he leaned back against Jesus and asked him, "lord, who is it?" 26Jesus replied, "It is the one I give the piece of bread to after I have dipped it." 27After dipping the bread, he gave it to Judas, Simon Iscariot's son. After Judas ate the piece of bread, Satan entered him. Therefore Jesus said to him, "What you are intending to do, do quickly." 28None of those reclining at the table understood why he said this to him. Since Judas was the one who kept the money bag, 29some thought that Jesus was instructing him, "Buy what we need for the festival," or that he should give something to the poor. 30After receiving the piece of bread Judas went out immediately. And it was night.[162]

31When Judas had gone out, Jesus said, "Now the Son of Man is glorified, and God is glorified in him. 32If God is glorified in him, God will also glorify him in Himself, and He will glorify him at once.[163] 33My children, I am with you for a little while longer. You will be looking for

---

[159]Believing that Jesus is the Messiah (certainly not GOD the Son, making two GODs) is the great core teaching of the NT, the foundation of the Church (Mt. 16:16-18; 1 John 5:1, 5; 2:22) and the whole point of John's writing his gospel (20:31).

[160]The principle of agency. Jesus is the agent of his Father, the one God. They act in perfect harmony and purpose. This is the ideal for all human beings — to obey the Father by obeying the Son, to learn the Father's "business," and to represent the Father and reflect Him as the image of God.

[161]Troubled in his spirit.

[162]Thursday night by our reckoning. Jesus was crucified the next day, Friday.

[163]These are past tenses with a future sense. The glorification of Jesus happened in his death and following resurrection. This is true of the glory promised to Jesus in 17:5. That same glory had been given (past tense) to disciples not yet born when Jesus spoke these words (17:22). We see at work the principle that God can speak "of things which are not as though they were" (Rom. 4:17).

me, and just as I told the Jews, 'Where I am going you cannot come,' I
am now telling you the same. 34I am giving you a new commandment:
love one another. Just as I have loved you, you must also love one
another. 35This is how everyone will know that you are my disciples, if
you have love for one another."[164]

36Simon Peter said to him, "lord, where are you going?" Jesus
replied, "Where I am going you cannot follow me now, but you will
follow me later."[165] 37Peter asked, "lord, why may I not follow you now?
I will gladly lay down my life for you!" 38Jesus replied, "Will you lay
down your life for me? I tell you on the highest authority: the rooster will
not crow until you deny me three times."

14 1"Your heart must not be in turmoil. Keep on believing in God,
and keep on believing also in me.[166] 2In my Father's household
there are many dwelling places and positions. If not, I would have told
you. So I am now going away to prepare a place for you.[167] 3If I go away
and prepare a place for you, I will come back[168] and receive you to
myself, so that where I will be[169] you may be with me.[170] 4And you know
the way where I am going." 5Thomas said, "lord, we do not know where
you are going. How can we know the way?" 6Jesus said to him, "I am the
way, the truth and the life. No one can come to the Father except through

---

164This should raise the soul-searching question as to why it is right for Christians to fight international wars in which inevitably they take the lives of fellow believers in other countries. Do the laws of Jesus cease to be relevant in war time?

165A reference to Peter's later martyrdom.

166The obvious contrast is between God and someone who is not God! It would be quite unwarranted to imagine that Jesus thinks that he *is* God.

167In the future Kingdom of God on earth, just as James and John asked about places prepared for believers in the coming Kingdom (Mk. 10:40).

168At his future Second Coming, the Parousia, to rule on earth with the saints (Rev. 5:10). He was in the meanwhile going to prepare their positions in that future Kingdom which is the heart of the Christian Gospel (Mk. 1:14-15; Lk. 4:43).

169The Greek has "where I am," and the sense of the idiom is "where I will be." The same usage of a present for a future is found in John 7:34, 36: "Where I am you cannot come" = "where I will be..."

170Jesus will be back on earth and so anyone wanting to be with him will not be in heaven, because Jesus will not be there! He is coming back to the earth.

me. 7If you have come to know me you will also know my Father. From
now on you do know Him and have seen[171] Him."
8Philip said, "lord, show us the Father and that will be enough for
us." 9Jesus said to him, "Have I been with you all this time without your
knowing me, Philip? The person who has seen me has seen the Father.[172]
How then can you say, 'Show us the Father'? 10Do you not believe that I
am in the Father and the Father is in me? The words I speak to you I do
not speak on my own initiative. The Father who lives in me is doing His
works through me. 11Believe me, that I am in the Father and the Father is
in me.[173] Otherwise believe because of the works themselves. 12I tell you
on the highest authority: the person who believes in me will also do the
works that I do. And he will do even greater works than these,[174] because
I am going to the Father. 13Whatever it is you ask in my name I will do it,
so that the Father may be glorified in the Son. 14If you ask me anything in
my name, I will do it.[175]

---

[171]Not literally "see" because no one has literally seen the Father. The Father is "seen" in a different sense, in Jesus. A Christian who continually sins, is not genuinely converted, has not "seen Him or known Him" (1 John 3:6). This is a spiritual "seeing" with the mind.

[172]Thus in John 20:28, Thomas who was present at the conversation here in ch. 14, finally sees God in Jesus and realizes this when he addresses Jesus as "my lord" and "my God," seeing the One God in Jesus. This is the sequel to and resolution of the problem which Philip and Thomas had in not realizing how God the Father is seen in the Son.

[173]It is in this sense that "I and the Father are one" (10:30). The same unity is the ideal for all believers who are to be of one mind and purpose with the Father and Son (17:11, 22).

[174]It is a false assumption to think that by "greater works" Jesus means more spectacular miracles. The teaching of Jesus' Gospel on a more extensive scale, after he went to the Father, is probably the point.

[175]This text is proof that prayer requests to Jesus are appropriate. Prayer is of course addressed to the Father through Jesus, but it is not a fixed rule without exception. Paul thanked Jesus for putting him in ministry (1 Tim. 1:12). Doxologies are offered to the risen Messiah, who is worshiped alongside the One God (Rev. 5:13). And the Corinthians are described by Paul as "those who call on the name of the Lord Jesus Christ" (1 Cor. 1:2). Many appealed to Jesus to grant them requests, notably the Canaaanite woman and the two blind men who appealed to Jesus with the words "lord, son of David, have mercy on us" (Mt. 15:22; 20:30).

15“If you love me you will keep my commands.[176] 16And I will ask the
Father, and He will give you another Counselor to be with you forever.
17This is the spirit of the truth. The world is incapable of receiving it,
because it does not see it or know it, but you do know it, because it
remains with you and will be in you.

18“I will not leave you as orphans; I am coming to you.[177] 19In a little
while the world will not see me any longer, but you will see[178] me.
Because I am going to be alive, you will be alive.[179] 20That day you will
know that I am in my Father, and you are in me, just as I am in you.
21The person who has my commands and carries them out is the one who
loves me[180] and the one who loves me will be loved by my Father. I will
also love him and reveal myself to him.” 22Judas (not Judas Iscariot) said
to him, “lord, how is it that you are going to reveal yourself to us and not
to the world?” 23Jesus replied, “If anyone loves me, he will preserve and
obey my Gospel-word.[181] My Father will love him, and we will come to
him and make our residence with him. 24The one who does not love me
will not keep my words. The Gospel-word which you hear is not mine
but it is the Father’s who commissioned me.

---

[176]His commands include everything Jesus taught. His first and fundamental command is that we are to “repent and believe the Gospel of the Kingdom” message (Mk. 1:14-15). Jesus also commanded belief in the One Lord God of his Hebrew heritage, and makes this “the most important” of all commands (Mk. 12:29). It should be a matter of urgent public concern that later “church fathers” replaced Jesus’ definition of God with an alien concept of a triune God, not known to Jesus or the Apostles.

[177]i.e. Jesus will “return” in spirit presence. “The lord is the spirit” (2 Cor. 3:17).

[178]There will be no literal seeing of Jesus until his Second Coming, but he is understood and known through the spirit which he promised would remain with believers.

[179]The life of the risen Jesus would be present with them as the Counselor, not a third “Person” but the exalted Jesus coming to be with them in spirit (cp. 2 Cor. 3:17-18; 1Jn. 2:1).

[180]This is exactly the “obedience of faith” taught by the whole NT (Rom. 1:5: 16:26; Jn. 3:36; Heb. 5:9). An example of required obedience is water baptism, commanded by Jesus till the end of the age. This is an integral and essential element of the Great Commission (Mt. 28:19-20). Obedience is required in those “difficult” areas of behavior such as loving enemies, which cannot include killing them!

[181]“word” is the shorthand NT expression for the Gospel of the Kingdom, the “word of the Kingdom” in Matt. 13:19. This is the essential seed of immortality (Lk. 8:11), and the agent of Christian rebirth.

25“I have spoken these things to you while I am still with you. 26But
the Counselor, the holy spirit, which the Father will send as representing
and reproducing my presence, will teach you all things and remind you
of everything I have told you. 27Peace I leave with you. My peace I give
to you. I do not give it to you as the world gives. Stop letting your minds
be troubled or cowardly. 28You have heard me say, ‘I am going away and
I am coming back to you.’[182] If you loved me, you would rejoice that I
am going to the Father, because the Father is greater than I am. 29I tell
you now before this happens, so that when it does happen you may
believe. 30I will not be talking with you much longer, because the ruler of
the world[183] is coming. He has no power over me. 31On the contrary, so
that the world may know that I love the Father, I am doing just as the
Father commanded me. Let us get up and leave this place.”

15 1“I am the genuine vine,[184] and my Father is the vineyard keeper.
2Every branch in me which does not produce fruit[185] my Father
removes, and He prunes every branch that produces fruit so that it will
produce more fruit. 3You are already clean[186] because of the Gospel-word
I have spoken to you.[187] 4Remain in me, and I in you. Just as a branch is
unable to produce fruit by itself unless it remains on the vine, so neither

---

[182]The reference is to the “return” of Jesus as the paraclete, Counselor, as constant support for believers. The Messiah is identified with the “Counselor” in 1 John 2:1. And in 2 Cor. 3:17-18 “the lord is the spirit.”

[183]The Devil, the external supernatural being who opposes God’s plan in Messiah.

[184]The vine in the Hebrew Bible is the symbol of Israel, and so Jesus represents the ideal Israel, what Israel should have been. The true international body of believers is now the “Israel of God” (Gal. 6:16) and “the true circumcision” (Phil. 3:3), as distinct from now blinded “Israel of the flesh” (1 Cor. 10:18). Paul, of course, and much OT prophecy expects a future national conversion of a remnant of now blinded Israel, consequent upon the Second Coming. Israel will yet declare, “Blessed is the one coming in the name of the Lord God” (Lk. 13:35), i.e. the Messiah at his return. This has certainly not happened yet. The present return of Israel as a nation in unbelief does not correspond to the biblical prophecy of the conversion of Israel.

[185]Christian fruit is borne only from the seed Gospel message of the Kingdom as taught by Jesus clearly in the parable of the sower. That seed Gospel Message is the essential foundation of the faith. If the seed is not present, true fruit cannot be borne.

[186]Cp. “Blessed are the pure [clean, cleansed] in heart” (Mt. 5:8).

[187]The Kingdom of God Gospel is the basis for all effective and genuine faith in God and His Messiah.

can you produce fruit unless you remain in union with me. 5I am the
vine; you are the branches. The person who remains in me and I in him,
produces much fruit, because you can do nothing without me. 6If anyone
does not remain in me, he is thrown aside like a branch, and he withers.
Then they gather them, throw them into the fire and they are burned. 7If
you remain in me and my words remain in you,[188] you can ask whatever
you want and it will be done for you. 8My Father is glorified by this: that
you produce much fruit and thus prove to be my disciples. 9Just as the
Father has loved me I have also loved you. So remain in my love. 10If
you keep my commands[189] you will remain in my love just as I have kept
my Father's commands and remain in His love. 11I have spoken these
things to you so that my joy may be in you and your joy may be
complete.

12"This is my command: love one another as I have loved you. 13No
one has greater love than this, that someone would be willing to lay
down his life for his friends. 14You are my friends if you do what I
command you. 15I am not calling you servants any longer because a
servant does not know what his master is doing. I have called you
friends, because I have made known to you everything I have heard from
my Father. 16You did not choose me, but I chose you. And I appointed
you to go out and produce fruit so that your fruit should remain, such
that whatever you ask the Father based on my authority, as representing
me, He will give it to you. 17This is what I command you: love one
another.

18"If the world hates you, understand that it hated me before it hated
you. 19If you belonged to this world-system the world would love you as
its own. However, because you do not belong to this world-system, but I
have chosen you out of the world, the world hates you. 20Remember the
statement I made to you: a servant is not greater than his master. If they

---

[188]The claim to be "in Christ" is vain, unless **the words** of Christ are deeply rooted in the heart. Christians must sound like Jesus in their teaching and behave like Jesus.

[189]The constant repetition of the need for obedience is striking. Obedience begins with an obedient believing response to Jesus' opening command to "repent and believe the Gospel about the Kingdom" (Mk. 1:14-15). Equally essential is an intelligent, obedient response to Jesus' command: "Listen, Israel, the Lord our God is one Lord" (Mk. 12:29). It is that God, the God of Jesus and of Israel, whom we are commanded to serve.

persecuted me they will certainly also persecute you. If they have kept
and obeyed my Gospel-word, they will also keep yours. 21But they will
do all these things to you on account of my name and agenda, and
everything I stand for,[190] because they do not know the One who
commissioned me. 22If I had not come and spoken to them they would
not be guilty of sin.[191] As it is they now have no excuse for this sin. 23The
one who hates me also hates my Father. 24If I had not performed the
works among them which no one else has done, they would not be guilty
of sin.[192] Now they have seen and yet hated both me and my Father. 25But
this happened so that the statement written in their law might be fulfilled:
'They hated me for no reason.'

26"When the Counselor comes, the one I will send you from the
Father, the spirit of the truth[193] which proceeds from the Father, this
Counselor will testify about me. 27You also are going to bear witness
because you have been with me from the beginning."

16 1"I have told you these things in advance to keep you from
stumbling and losing faith. 2They will reject you from the
synagogues. In fact, the time is coming when anyone who kills you will
think he is rendering a service to God.[194] 3They will do these things
because they have not come to know and understand the Father or me,

---

[190]Giving the sense of "name" which is unclear to most readers. "Name" is everything a person stands for and represents.

[191]This shows the brilliant insight that judgment and culpability are according to what can be known. As truth comes to us we are responsible for embracing it, and we are in danger if we refuse it.

[192]Guilt is on a sliding scale, depending on the degree of knowledge a person has been exposed to.

[193]There is no "third Person" of a Trinity in the NT. The spirit is very personal as being the operational presence and power of the risen Jesus, as well as the outreach of the Father. The holy spirit is never worshiped in the Bible and never sends greetings at the opening of Paul's letters. The spirit is never prayed to. Ask your friends: Is the "spirit of Elijah" a different person from Elijah? No. The spirit of Elijah is the mood, disposition, personality of Elijah (Lk. 1:17). The same is true of "the spirit of Jesus" (Acts 16:7). The Counselor/Comforter is identified with Jesus (1 Jn. 2:1).

[194]This statement proves that false religion is a terrific power, causing a deception so profound that its adherents are unable to see the difference between truth and error. Jesus had warned that multitudes would find out one day that their supposed adherence to Christianity was false and misguided (Mt. 7:21-23).

4but I told you these things so that when the time comes you may
remember that I told you. I did not tell you these things from the
beginning, because I was still with you.

5"Now I am going away[195] to Him who commissioned me, and none
of you asks me, where are you going? 6Yet because I have spoken these
things to you, your hearts are filled with sorrow. 7Nevertheless I am
telling you the truth. It is for your benefit that I am going away, because
if I do not go away the Counselor[196] will not come to you. If I go, I will
send him to you. 8When he comes he will convict the world about sin,
doing right, and judgment: 9about sin, because sin is the failure to believe
in and obey me; 10about being and doing right, because I am going to the
Father and you will no longer see me; 11and about judgment, because the
ruler of this world-system has been judged.[197]

12"I still have many things to tell you, but you are not able to bear
them now. 13When that spirit of the truth[198] comes, it will guide you into
all the truth.[199] The spirit will not speak on its own initiative, but it will
speak whatever it hears, and it will also declare to you what is going to
happen in the future. 14It will glorify me because it will receive from me
and show it to you. 15Everything which the Father has is mine. That is
why I told you that the spirit will take from what is mine and declare it to
you.

16"In a little while you will see me no longer, and yet in a little while
you will see me." 17So some of the disciples said to one another, "What
does he mean by this, 'A little while and you will not see me again and a
little while and you will see me,' and 'because I am going to the Father'?

---

[195]Not "going back" or "returning," but "going," a very great difference.

[196]Jesus is identified as the Counselor, the Paraclete, in 1 John 2:1. In the Gospel of John the paraclete is the replacement of Jesus who was leaving. He returned to them as his own spirit presence, the spirit of Jesus. There is no *third* Person in the NT. The "Holy Spirit" of later theology is absent from the NT, where the spirit is never worshiped or prayed to, and never sends greetings.

[197]Satan will be bound and imprisoned, so that he can no longer deceive the world, at the beginning of the future millennium (Rev. 20:2-3).

[198]The spirit of the truth is the personal presence and operation of Jesus, who is now absent literally but present with us if we obey him (Acts 5:32). Jesus is identified with the Counselor in 1 John 2:1. In this verse the spirit of truth is designated as "that person" (*ekeinos*, masculine).

[199]Further truth was indeed revealed through Paul and the other writers of the NT.

18What is the meaning of this saying ‘a little while’? We do not
understand what he is talking about.” 19Jesus knew that they were
wanting to question him, so he said to them, “Are you asking one
another about what I meant by ‘a little while and you will not see me,
and again a little while and you will see me’? 20I tell you on the highest
authority: you will weep and wail, but the world will rejoice. You will
become sorrowful, but your sorrow will turn to joy. 21Whenever a woman
is in labor she has pain because her time for delivery has come. But
when she has given birth to a child, she no longer remembers the
suffering, on account of the joy that a person has been born into the
world.[200] 22Therefore you also have sorrow now, but I will see you again.
Your hearts will rejoice, and no one will be able to rob you of your joy.

23“In that day you will not need to ask me anything. I tell you on the
highest authority: Anything you ask the Father in my name He will give
you. 24Until now you have asked nothing in my name. Ask and you will
receive so that your joy may be complete.

25“I have spoken these things to you in obscure, metaphorical speech.
But the time is coming when I will no longer speak to you in figurative
language, but I will tell you plainly about the Father. 26In that day you
will ask in my name. I am not telling you that I will make requests to the
Father on your behalf, 27for the Father Himself loves you, because you
have loved me, and you believed I came from God.[201] 28I came from the
Father and have come into the world.[202] Again, I am leaving the world
and going[203] to the Father.”

29His disciples said, “Now you are speaking plainly and not using
figurative language. 30Now we know that you know everything and do
not need anyone to question you. By this we believe that you came from

---

[200]To come into the world or to be born into the world is what every human being experiences. The same language is used of Jesus’ origin and so there is no reference to a pre-life in heaven, which would contradict the birth narratives of Matthew and Luke and the rest of Scripture.

[201]Jesus’ origin from God is spelled out explicitly in Matt. 1:18 (origin, *genesis*) and 1:20 (“begotten in her”) and with complete clarity also in Luke 1:35, where the “Son of God” is beautifully defined.

[202]His origin and birth is in the Father who miraculously brought him into existence (Lk. 1:35; Mt. 1:18, 20).

[203]Going to the Father, certainly not going *back* or returning to the Father. The NIV and other translations are misleading on this point as also in 13:3 and 20:17.

God." 31Jesus replied to them, "Do you now finally believe? 32Look, the
hour is coming and has already come when each of you will be scattered
to his own home, and you will leave me on my own. Yet I am not alone,
because the Father is with me. 33I have told you these things so that in me
you would have peace. You will have suffering in this world, but be full
of courage. I have conquered the world."

17 1Jesus spoke these words and then looked up to heaven and said,
"Father, the hour has arrived. Glorify Your Son so that the Son
may glorify You, 2just as You gave him authority over all mankind, so
that he may grant the Life of the Age to Come to all You have given
him. 3This is the core and essence of the Life of the Age to Come,[204] that
they may know You, the only one who is true God,[205] and the one You

---

[204]That is, this is how a human being may attain to immortality. Jesus' unitarian definition of God is the most fundamental of all saving truths. Jesus' words are a summary, concentrated on a single idea, expressed in the Greek as "This **is** the life of the Age to Come…"

[205]Because John 1:1 has been misleadingly translated to give the impression that the Son of God existed eternally (the capital on Word is not warranted by the Greek text), it is essential to point out that scholars recognize that the Bible does not teach the "eternal generation" of the Son. Many also recognize that John "is as undeviating a witness as any NT writer to unitary monotheism" (Rom. 3:30; James 2:19; Jn. 5:44; 17:3" (Dr. J.A.T. Robinson, *Twelve More New Testament Studies*, p. 175). All the Bible writers were obviously unitarians. The later move away from Jesus to an alien definition of God as Triune is one of the most remarkable shifts away from and loss of essential information, in the history of (mis)communication. Jesus expressed his unitarian confession of faith here by asserting that the "Father is the only one who is true God." This text merely repeats the 1300 NT references to GOD as the equivalent of the Father. Jesus declares himself to be not GOD, which would make two Gods, but God's unique human agent. The simplicity of the confession in John 17:3 may be illustrated like this: "You (singular), Father (singular), are (singular) the (singular) only (singular and exclusive) true (singular) God (singular)." Standard commentary finds itself obliged to write: "How often may these last solemn words of Jesus have stirred the soul of John. To this corresponds the self-consciousness, as childlike as it is simple and clear in its elevation, the victorious rest and peace of this prayer, which is the noblest and purest pearl of devotion in the whole New Testament. For plain and simple as it sounds, so deep rich and wide it is that none can fathom it" (Luther). "Spener never ventured to preach on it because he felt that its true understanding exceeded the ordinary measure of faith; but he caused it to be read to him three times on the evening before his death" (Meyer, 1884, p. 475). Meyer comments, "Only one, *the Father*, can be termed absolutely 'the only true God,' 'the one who is above and over all" (Rom. 9:5), not at

---

the same time Christ (who is not even in 1 John 5:20 the true God)." Meyer says that the Son is in unity with the Father, works as His commissioner (10:30) and is His representative (14:9, 10). Meyer loses himself in a befuddling confusion over the "genetic subsistence" of the Son, but he has already admitted to the unitarian statement of Jesus. The famous commentary by Barrett notes that in Wisdom literature (Prov. 11:9) "through knowledge the righteous will be saved," and that the world will eventually be "filled with the knowledge of the glory of the Lord" (Hab. 2:14), and that "my people are destroyed for lack of knowledge" (Hos. 4:6; Isa. 5:13). "Clearly then the notion of knowledge as the ground of salvation is very widespread...knowledge and believing are not set over against each other but are correlated. The God whom to know is to have eternal life is the only being who may properly be so described; He, and it must follow, He alone is truly God" (*Commentary on John*, pp. 419-20). This is straightforward unitary, non-Trinitarian monotheism. Professor Loofs described the process of the early corruption of biblical Christianity: "The Apologists ['church fathers' like Justin Martyr, mid-2nd century] laid the foundation for the **perversion/corruption** (*Verkehrung*) of Christianity into a revealed [philosophical] teaching. Specifically, their Christology affected the later development disastrously. By taking for granted the transfer of the concept of Son of God onto the preexisting Christ, they were the cause of the Christological problem of the fourth century. They caused a shift in the point of departure of Christological thinking — *away from the historical Christ* and onto the issue of preexistence. They thus shifted attention away from the historical life of Jesus, putting it into the shadow and promoting instead the Incarnation [i.e., of a preexistent Son]. They tied Christology to cosmology and could not tie it to soteriology. The Logos teaching is not a 'higher' Christology than the customary one. It lags in fact far behind the genuine appreciation of Christ. According to their teaching it is no longer God who reveals Himself in Christ, but the Logos, the inferior God, a God who as God is subordinated to the Highest God (inferiorism or subordinationism). In addition, the suppression of economic-trinitarian ideas by metaphysical-pluralistic concepts of the divine triad (*trias*) can be traced to the Apologists" (Friedrich Loofs, *Leitfaden zum Studium des Dogmengeschichte* [*Manual for the Study of the History of Dogma*], 1890, part 1 ch. 2, section 18: "Christianity as a Revealed Philosophy. The Greek Apologists," Niemeyer Verlag, 1951, p. 97, translation mine). Those who are dedicated to restoring the identity of the biblical Jesus, Son of God, may take heart from the incisive words of a leading systematic theologian of our times. He restores the biblical meaning of the crucial title "Son of God," rescuing it from the millennia-long obscurity it has suffered from Platonically-minded church fathers and theologians. Professor Colin Brown, general editor of the *New International Dictionary of New Testament Theology*, writes, "The crux of the matter lies in how we understand the term Son of God...The title Son of God is not in itself an expression of personal Deity or the expression of metaphysical distinctions within the Godhead. Indeed, to be a 'Son of God' one has to be a being who is *not* God! It is a designation for a creature indicating a special relationship with God. In particular, it denotes God's representative, God's vice-regent. It is a designation of kingship, identifying the king as God's Son...In my

have commissioned, Jesus Messiah.[206] 4I have glorified You on the earth
by completing the work You gave me to do. 5Now, Father, glorify me at
Your side[207] with the glory I had as a promise[208] with You before the
world existed.

6"I revealed Your character, plan and agenda to the men You gave
me from the world. They were Yours, and You gave them to me, and
they have kept Your Gospel-word. 7Now they have come to know that
everything You have given me is from You, 8because the words which
You gave me I have given to them. And they received those words and

---

view the term 'Son of God' ultimately converges on the term 'image of God' which is to be understood as God's representative, the one in whom God's spirit dwells, and who is given stewardship and authority to act on God's behalf…It seems to me to be a fundamental mistake to treat statements in the Fourth Gospel about the Son and his relationship with the Father as expressions of inner-Trinitarian relationships. But this kind of systematic misreading of the Fourth Gospel seems to underlie much of social Trinitarian thinking…It is a common but patent misreading of the opening of John's Gospel to read it as if it said, 'In the beginning was the *Son,* and the *Son* was with God, and the *Son* was God.' What has happened here is the substitution of *Son* for Word (Gk. *logos*) and thereby the Son is made a member of the Godhead which existed from the beginning" ("Trinity and Incarnation: Towards a Contemporary Orthodoxy," *Ex Auditu*, 7, 1991, pp. 87-89).

[206]Augustine, finding this creedal statement incompatible with the Trinitarian creed of the post-biblical Church, actually dared to alter the order of the sentence and fraudulently twist the words of Jesus. In his *Homilies on John* he said that John 17:3 ought to read: "This is eternal life, that they know you [Father] and Jesus Christ whom you sent as the only true God." Reader, take careful note. The "church father" Gregory of Nyssa (335-394) conceded that the Trinity, of which he was an architect, "does not harmonize with the Jewish dogma" (he was referring to the strict monotheistic creed of Jesus and Israel in Deut. 6:4; Mk. 12:29). He thought that the Trinity destroyed "each heresy," i.e. the unitary monotheism of Jesus and Israel and the pagan polytheism of the non-Jewish world, "and yet accepting what is useful from both [the Shema and paganism]. He argued that the Trinity was a truth which passes in the mean between the two positions [Jewish and pagan]." Gregory unashamedly condemned Jesus' unitarian view of God as a "Jewish dogma" needing to be replaced.

[207]Jesus is not returning to a position relinquished but one he had not previously occupied, i.e. in the presence of the Father, at his side (Ps. 110:1).

[208]"to have with God" (*para theo*) is a common Hebrew idiom for having something as promised and stored up for the future as a reward (see Mt. 6:1-2). Cp. Isa.49:4: "the justice due to me is with the LORD, and my reward with my God" and 2 Cor. 5:1: "we **have**" a spiritual body, i.e. prepared for the future when we receive it.

have become convinced that I came forth[209] from you. They have
believed that You commissioned me. 9My request is for them. My
request is not for the world but for those whom You have given me,
because they belong to You. 10All my things belong to You and Yours
belong to me, and I have been glorified in them. 11I am to be no longer in
the world, but they are in the world, and I am coming to You. Holy
Father, protect them by Your authority and power, which You have
given me, so that they may be one in mind and purpose as we are.
12While I was with them, I was keeping them in your name, the name[210]
You have given me. I guarded them and not one of them has been lost,
except the one destined for destruction, so that the Scripture may be
fulfilled.

13"Now I am coming to You, and I am speaking these things in the
world so that they may share completely in my joy. 14I have given them
your Gospel-word. The world hated them because they do not belong to
this world-system just as I do not belong to this world-system. 15I am not
praying that You should take them out of the world, but I am asking You
to protect them from the Evil One. 16They do not belong to this world-
system, just as I do not belong to that world. 17Make them holy through
the truth. Your Gospel-word is the truth.[211] 18As You commissioned me to
go into the world, I also have commissioned them to go into the world.
19I make myself holy on behalf of them, so that they may be made holy in
harmony with the truth.

20"I am not praying only for these but also for the ones who are going
to believe in me in the future through their Gospel message. 21I am
praying that they all may be one in mind and purpose as You, Father, are
in me and I am in You. May they also be one in mind and purpose[212] in
us, so that the world may believe that You commissioned me.

---

[209]A word connoting birth. Jesus' origin in the womb of Mary was by miracle (Lk. 1:35 is decisive as defining the term Son of God for Jesus).

[210]Name stands for the whole Gospel agenda of Jesus, which he preached on behalf of God, his Father.

[211]Reminding us of Paul's impassioned statement about the love of the truth in order to gain salvation. He noted that people are "on their way to ruin and loss because they refused to accept a love of the truth in order to be saved" (2 Thess. 2:10).

[212]The same request for unity in the one Church was made by Paul in 1 Cor. 1:10.

22“I have given them[213] the same glory which you have given me.[214] I want them all to be one, just as we are one in mind and purpose; 23I in them, and You in me, so that they may be brought to maturity in one mind, that the world may come to know that You sent me and that You loved them just as You loved me. 24Father, it is my desire that those You have given me[215] be with me where I will be.[216] Then they will see my glory, the future glory[217] which You have promised to give me,[218] because You loved me before the world’s foundation.

25“Righteous Father, the world has not recognized or understood You. However I have known You, and these have known that You commissioned me. 26I made known to them Your authority and power,[219] and will continue to make it known to them, so that the love You had for me may be in them, and I may be in union with them.”

18 1After Jesus had offered this prayer he went out with his disciples across the Kidron Valley where there was a garden, into which he and his disciples entered. 2Judas, who betrayed him, also knew of this place, because Jesus often met there with his disciples. 3So Judas took a detachment of soldiers and some Temple police from the chief priests and the Pharisees, and they came there with lanterns, torches and weapons. 4Then Jesus, knowing exactly what was about to happen to

---

[213]I.e. “I promise to give them.” This is glory in prospect and promise as in 17:5.

[214]“Promised to give me.” Again this is glory as promised for the future.

[215]I.e. “promised to give me,” all disciples past and future to Jesus’ time on earth.

[216]Literally “where I am,” meaning where I will be in the future when the disciples will have been glorified. Note the past tense of glorified in Rom. 8:30. The future is certain and can be expressed as having already happened (“as good as done”). Jesus is coming back to the earth!

[217]The future glory which is the future Messianic Kingdom on earth.

[218]As guaranteed by promise in God’s plan and thus “possessed” even before the creation as in 17:5. “The lamb was slain before the foundation of the world” (Rev. 13:8), that is, in God’s plan.

[219]Literally “Your name,” a concept foreign to our western minds. “Name” stands for the whole agenda of God, His revealed character and intention, in fact the saving Gospel of the Kingdom which offers immortality to presently mortal man, through the one “man Messiah Jesus” (1 Tim. 2:5), who is the unique Son and agent of that One God, the Father. Jesus’ whole commission to preach the Gospel of the Kingdom was defined in Luke 4:43. That commission is now the task of the Church, the body of Christ.

him, went out and said to them, "Who is it you are looking for?" 5They
answered, "Jesus the Nazarene." Jesus said, "That is me."[220] Judas who
betrayed him was also standing with them 6when he said to them, "It is
me." They stepped backward and fell to the ground.[221] 7Then he asked
them again, "Who are you looking for?" They said, "Jesus the
Nazarene." 8Jesus replied, "I told you, that is me. So if you are looking
for me, let these men go." 9This was to fulfill the words Jesus had
spoken: "I have not lost one of those You have given me." 10Then Simon
Peter, who had a sword, drew it and struck the high priest's slave, cutting
off his right ear (the slave's name was Malchus). 11Jesus' response to
Peter was, "Put away your sword! Am I not to drink the cup which my
Father has given me?"

12Then the detachment of soldiers, the commander, and the Jewish
temple police arrested Jesus and tied him up. 13First they led him to
Annas. He was the father-in-law of Caiaphas who was High Priest that
year. 14Caiaphas was the one who had advised the Jews that it was to
their advantage that one man should die for the people.

15Meanwhile Simon Peter was following Jesus, along with another
disciple. That disciple was an acquaintance of the high priest; so he went
with Jesus into the High Priest's courtyard. 16But Peter remained standing
outside at the gate. So that other disciple, the one known to the High
Priest, went out and spoke to the girl who was the doorkeeper, and
brought Peter in. 17Then the slave girl, the doorkeeper, said to Peter, "Are
you not also one of this man's disciples?" He replied, "I am not." 18Now
the slaves and the temple police had made a charcoal fire because it was
cold. They were standing there warming themselves, and Peter was
standing with them warming himself.

19The High Priest questioned Jesus about his disciples and about his
teaching. 20Jesus answered him, "I have been speaking openly to the

---

[220]Literally "It is I," *ego eimi*. The appearance of this identifying marker should alert readers that the phrase "*ego eimi*" on the lips of Jesus does not mean "I am God." The blind man also identified himself with the phrase *ego eimi* — it's me. Jesus' constant self-designation is "I am the Messiah," and the first occurrence of the phrase *ego eimi* in John 4:26 establishes its important meaning in John. The Samaritan lady had referred to the Samaritan expectation of a coming Messiah. Jesus then says, "I, the one speaking to you, am he" — obviously affirming that he is that expected Messiah.

[221]Reminding us of the Messianic Psalm 45 where the enemies of the King Messiah fall backwards in his presence.

world. I have always taught in the synagogue and in the temple complex
where Jews congregate, and I have not spoken anything in secret. 21 Why
are you questioning me? Why not question those who heard what I said
to them? They certainly know what I said." 22 When he said this one of
the temple police standing by slapped Jesus in the face and said, "Is this
the way you answer the High Priest?" 23 Jesus replied, "If I have spoken
wrongly, give evidence about the wrong. But if I have spoken rightly,
why are you hitting me?" 24 Then Annas sent him bound to Caiaphas the
high priest.

25 Now Simon Peter was still standing and warming himself. They
said to him, "You are not one of his disciples too, are you?" He denied it
and said, "I am not." 26 One of the high priest's slaves, a relative of the
man whose ear Peter had cut off, said, "I believe I saw you with him in
the garden, didn't I?" 27 Peter then denied it again. And immediately the
rooster crowed.

28 Then they took Jesus from Caiaphas to the governor's residence,
and it was early morning.[222] They did not enter the headquarters
themselves, because then they would be defiled and unable to eat the
Passover.[223] 29 Then Pilate came out to them and said, "What charge are
you bringing against this man?" 30 They answered him, "If this man was
not an evildoer we would not have handed him over to you." 31 Pilate said
to them, "Take him yourselves and judge him in accordance with your
law." The Jews said, "It is not legal for us to put anyone to death."
32 They said this so that Jesus' words might be fulfilled when he
announced what sort of death he was going to die.

33 Then Pilate went back into his residence, summoned Jesus and said
to him, "Are you the King of the Jews?" 34 Jesus answered, "Are you
asking this on your own initiative, or have others told you about me?"
35 Pilate replied, "I am not a Jew, am I? It was your own nation and the
chief priests who handed you over to me. What have you done?" 36 Jesus
said, "My Kingdom does not belong to or originate from this world-

---

[222]On Friday, the 15th Nisan.

[223]That is, take part in the Passover *week* celebrations. The Passover meal when the lamb was eaten had taken place already. Jesus had eaten the Passover with the disciples the evening before.

system.[224] If my Kingdom did belong to this world-system, my servants
would be fighting, so that I would not be handed over to the Jews. As it
is, my Kingdom does not take its origin from this system." 37So Pilate
asked, "You are a king then?" Jesus replied, "You rightly say that I am a
king. I was born for that very purpose, and I have come into the world to
testify to that truth.[225] Everyone who belongs to that truth listens to my
voice."

38Pilate asked, "Truth? What is that?" After he had said this, he went
out to the Jews again and said to them, "I find no grounds for charging
him. 39You have a custom that I release one prisoner to you at the
Passover season. So do you want me to release the King of the Jews to
you?" 40They shouted back, "Not this man, but Barabbas." Now
Barabbas was a revolutionary.[226]

19 1Then Pilate took Jesus and had him flogged. 2The soldiers twisted
together a crown of thorns, put it on Jesus' head, and threw a
purple robe around him. 3Then they repeatedly insulted him: "Hail, King
of the Jews!" and they were slapping him in the face. 4Pilate went outside
again and spoke to them. "Look, I am bringing him outside to you, to let
you know that I find no grounds for charging him." 5Then Jesus came out
wearing the crown of thorns and the purple robe. Pilate said to them,
"Here is the man!" 6When the chief priests and the temple police saw
him, they shouted, "Crucify him! Crucify him!" Pilate responded, "Take
him and crucify him yourselves. I find no grounds for charging him."
7The Jews replied to him, "We have a law, and according to that law he
must be put to death, because he claimed to be the Son of God."

8When Pilate heard this statement, he was more afraid than ever. 9He
went back into his residence and asked Jesus, "Where are you from?"
But Jesus did not give him an answer. 10So Pilate said to him, "You are
apparently not willing to talk to me? Do you understand that I have

---

[224]This one saying has given some an excuse to eliminate the whole Messianic hope of the future Kingdom of God on a renewed earth when Jesus comes back! Jesus' point is about the origin of the Kingdom. Its location will be on earth from the time of the Parousia.

[225]Jesus stated in Luke 4:43 that his entire mission was to announce the Gospel about the Kingdom of God, which includes of course his own kingship in that Kingdom.

[226]Probably what we would call a freedom fighter, and a threat to the Romans.

authority to release you and authority to have you crucified?” 11Jesus
answered him, “You would have no authority over me at all, if it had not
been granted you from above. This is why the one who handed me over
to you has the greater sin.” 12From that moment on Pilate made every
effort to release Jesus. But the Jews shouted, “If you release this man,
you are no friend of Caesar’s. Any self-appointed king opposes Caesar!”

13When Pilate heard these words, he brought Jesus outside. He sat
down on the judge’s bench at a place called the Stone Pavement (in
Hebrew, Gabbatha). 14It was the preparation day[227] of Passover week, and
it was about six in the morning. Then Pilate told the Jews, “Here is your
King!” 15But they yelled, “Take him away! Remove him! Crucify him!”
Pilate said to them, “Should I really crucify your King?” The chief
priests answered, “We have no king except Caesar!”

16So then, because of this, he handed Jesus over to them to be
crucified. 17So they took Jesus away. Carrying his own cross, he went out
to what is known as Skull Place, which in Hebrew is called Golgotha.
18There they crucified him and two others with him, one on either side,
with Jesus in the middle. 19Pilate also had a sign made and put on the
cross. The inscription read: “Jesus the Nazarene, King of the Jews.”
20Many of the Jews read this sign, because the place where Jesus was
crucified was near the city, and it was written in Hebrew, Latin, and
Greek. 21So the Jewish chief priests said to Pilate, “Do not write, the
King of the Jews, but that he *said*, I am the King of the Jews.” 22Pilate
replied, “What I have written, I have written.”

23When the soldiers crucified Jesus, they took his clothes and divided
them into four parts, one part for each soldier. They also took his tunic,
which was seamless, woven in one piece from the top. 24They then said
to one another, “Let us not tear it, but toss for it, to see who gets it.”
They did this to fulfill the Scripture which says: “They divided my
clothes among themselves and cast lots for my clothing.” 25And this is
what the soldiers did. Standing close to the cross of Jesus were his

---

[227]Friday, preparation day, of Passover week (see NIB, NIRV, GWN) not the preparation for the Passover *meal*, which had taken place the evening before, when Jesus ate the meal at the same time as the nation, introducing the Lord’s Supper (see Matthew, Mark and Luke for the clear evidence that Jesus ate the meal at the time the nation was keeping the Passover. John does not in any way contradict this).

mother, his mother's sister, Mary, the wife of Clopas, and Mary
Magdalene.
26When Jesus saw his mother and the disciple he loved standing
there, he said to his mother, "Woman, this is your son." 27Then he said to
the disciple, "This is your mother." And from that moment the disciple
took her to live in his home.
28After this, when Jesus knew that everything was now accomplished
in accordance with the fulfillment of Scripture, he said, "I am thirsty!"
29A jar full of sour wine was sitting there; so they put a sponge full of
sour wine on a hyssop plant and held it up to his mouth. 30When Jesus
had taken the sour wine, he said, "It is finished!" Bowing his head, he
expired.
31Since it was the preparation day of Passover week,[228] the Jews did
not want the bodies to remain on the cross on the Sabbath, for that
Sabbath day[229] was a special Sabbath.[230] They requested that Pilate have
the men's legs broken and that their bodies be taken away. 32So the
soldiers came and broke the legs of the first man and of the other one
who had been crucified with Jesus. 33When they came to Jesus they did
not break his legs since they saw that he was already dead. 34But one of
the soldiers pierced his side with a spear, and at once blood and water
came out. 35He who saw this happen has witnessed to that fact. His
purpose is that you also may believe. His testimony is true, and he knows
he is telling the truth. 36These events happened so that the Scripture
would be fulfilled: "Not one of his bones will be broken." 37And another
Scripture says: "They will look at the one they have pierced."
38After this, Joseph of Arimathea, who was one of Jesus' disciples —
but secretly, because of his fear of the Jews — asked Pilate that he might
remove Jesus' body. Pilate gave him permission, so he came and took his
body away. 39Nicodemus, who previously had visited Jesus at night, also
came, bringing a mixture of myrrh and aloes, weighing about 75 pounds.
40Then they took Jesus' body and wrapped it in linen cloths with the
aromatic spices, following the burial custom of the Jews. 41There was a

---

[228]All four gospels agree that Jesus died on Friday. *Paraskeue* and *prosabbaton* are words for Friday. Other days were in NT times called first day, second day, third day, etc.

[229]Saturday (sabbath).

[230]As the Saturday (sabbath) of Passover week.

garden in the place where he was crucified. A new tomb was in that
garden; no one had yet been placed in it. 42They laid Jesus there because
of the Jewish preparation day[231] and since the tomb was nearby.

20 1On the first day of the week Mary Magdalene came to the tomb
early while it was still dark. She noticed that the stone had been
removed from the tomb. 2So she ran to Simon Peter and the other
disciple, the one Jesus loved, and said to them, "They have taken the lord
out of the tomb, and we do not know where they have put him!" 3So then
Peter and the other disciple went out, heading for the tomb. 4The two
were running together, but the other disciple outran Peter and got to the
tomb first. 5Stooping down he saw the linen cloths lying there, but he did
not go in. 6Then, following him, Simon Peter arrived. He entered the
tomb and saw the linen cloths. 7The wrapping which had been on Jesus'
head was not lying with the linen cloths but folded up in a separate place
by itself. 8The other disciple, who had reached the tomb first, saw and
believed. 9For they still did not understand the Scripture which said that
he must rise from the dead. 10Then the disciples went home again.

11But Mary stood outside facing the tomb, weeping. Still sobbing, she
stooped down to look into the tomb. 12She saw two angels in white sitting
there, one at the head and one at the feet, where the body of Jesus had
been lying. 13The angels said to her, "Woman, why are you weeping?"
She replied to them, "Because they have taken away my lord,[232] and I do
not know where they have put him." 14With these words she turned
around and saw Jesus standing there, though she did not know it was
Jesus. 15Jesus said to her, "Woman, why are you weeping? Who are you
looking for?" Imagining that he was the gardener, she replied, "Sir,[233] if
you have removed him, tell me where you have put him, and I will take
him away." 16Jesus said to her, "Mary!" Turning round, she said to him

---

[231]Friday of Passover week. The Jewish preparation day for the weekly sabbath.

[232]Messiah, my lord, *adoni* of Ps. 110:1. This is the all-important verse from the Psalms for identifying Jesus not as Deity, but as "my lord," the Messiah. *Adoni*, my lord, not Lord, never refers to God. Jesus and Peter used this verse as a master-key (Mk. 12:35-37; Acts 2:34-36). So should we! When Jesus was born he was identified as the "lord Messiah" (Lk. 2:11). The reason for his being uniquely God's Son is given definitively in Luke 1:35. It was because God was his Father by miracle.

[233]*kurie*, lord, a title flexible enough to be applied to God and a gardener!

in Hebrew “Rabboni,” which means “teacher.” 17Jesus said to her, “Stop clinging to me; I have not yet ascended to the Father.[234] But go to my brothers and tell them that I am ascending[235] to my Father and your Father — to my God[236] and your God.” 18Mary Magdalene went and announced to the disciples, “I have seen the lord!” And she told them what he had said to her.

19In the evening of that first day of the week, the disciples were gathered together with the doors locked because of their fear of the Jews. Then Jesus came and stood among them and said to them, “Peace be with you!” 20With these words, Jesus showed them his hands and his side. The disciples were filled with joy when they saw the lord. 21Jesus said to them again, “Peace be with you! As the Father has commissioned me, I am also now commissioning you.” 22With these words he breathed on them and said, “Receive holy spirit. 23If you forgive the sins of any, they are forgiven; if you retain the sins of any they are retained.”

24But one of the twelve, Thomas (called the twin), was not with them when Jesus came. 25So the other disciples kept telling him, “We have seen the lord.” But Thomas said to them, “If I do not see the nail marks in his hands, put my finger into the nail marks, and put my hands into his side, I will never believe!”

26After eight days his disciples were in the house again, and Thomas was with them. Even though the doors were locked, Jesus came and stood among them and said, “Peace to you!” 27Then he said to Thomas,

---

[234]Showing that Jesus had not yet been to the Father. He had been dead, unconscious, while in the tomb. Resurrection is the only biblical way out of death.

[235]Note the very misleading translation of NIV and others which make Jesus speak of “returning” to the Father rather than going to the Father, as the Greek states. The same misleading rendering is found in John 16:28 and 13:3.

[236]This statement of Jesus proves that he cannot be GOD! God cannot have a God. One eternal Person cannot be the God of another eternal Person! The God of Jesus is the one God of Israel, the Father and that same one God is also the God of Jesus and of Christians. The creed of Christendom represents an amazing departure from the creed of Jesus and the Bible. Jesus gave us the one and only true creed in Mark 12:29. “The Lord our God is one Lord.” One Lord is not two or three Lords! The Father is “the only one who is true God” as Jesus stated in John 17:3 (cp. 5:44). The phrase “my lord” cannot be “my Yahweh,” since Yahweh (YHVH) can never take a possessive pronoun. Jesus is never once called “the Lord God” and never called “the Almighty.” The word “God” never means a triune God in Scripture. No Bible writer ever meant a triune God when he wrote “God.” These are staggeringly interesting facts.

"Put your fingers here and inspect my hands. Extend your hand and put it
into my side. Stop being an unbeliever, and believe." 28Thomas
responded, "My lord and my God!"[237] 29Jesus said, "Because you have
seen me,[238] you have believed. Blessed indeed are those who have not
seen, but yet believe without seeing!"[239]

30Jesus performed many other miracles in the presence of his
disciples, but these are not recorded in this book. 31The ones recorded
here are to persuade and convince you to believe that the Messiah is
Jesus, the Son of God,[240] and by believing this you may gain Life in
Jesus' name.[241]

---

[237]Finally seeing what he had earlier in ch. 14 missed, that in seeing Jesus you see God the Father in action and word. This of course does not mean that Jesus *is* the Father! No son is his own father! Thomas certainly did not think that the creed of Israel and Jesus (Mk. 12:29) was suddenly destroyed! John 17:3 defines the Father as "the only one who is true GOD." John wrote his whole book to prove that Jesus is the Messiah (20:31).

[238]And thus, Jesus implies, you have seen God in seeing me. This is what Thomas had earlier in ch. 14 not believed, i.e., that Jesus is the perfect image of his Father who is the only true God (17:3).

[239]That is, as we might say, "Congratulations, bravo to those who are believers without having seen Jesus alive literally."

[240]1 John 5:1, 5; 2:22; 4:1-4; 2 John 7. The confession is not here or anywhere else "that you may believe that Jesus is GOD," which would violate the first commandment and contradict the rest of the NT, especially John 17:3 and Mark 12:29. Celebrated experts on Christology admit that the Trinitarian concept of God has a serious flaw. Dr. J. A Dorner (Prof. of Theology at the University of Gottingen) wrote, "It must of course be allowed that the doctrine of the Trinity, as laid down even by the Nicene Fathers, leaves much to be desired...How shall we determine the nature of the distinction between the God who became man and the God [how many Gods?] who did not become man, without destroying the unity of God, on the one hand, or interfering with Christology on the other? Neither the Council of Nicea, nor the Church Fathers of the fourth century satisfactorily answered this question" (*History of the Development of the Doctrine of the Person of Christ*, T & T Clark, 1989, Division 1, Vol. 2, p. 330). Note these statements also: "It must be admitted by everyone who has the rudiments of an historical sense that the doctrine of the Trinity *formed no part of the original message*. St. Paul did not know it, and would have been unable to understand the meaning of the terms used in the theological formula on which the Church ultimately agreed" (Dean Matthews, DD, D. Litt., *God in Christian Experience*, p. 180). "The evolution of the Trinity: No responsible NT scholar would claim that the doctrine of the Trinity was taught by Jesus or preached by the earliest Christians or consciously held by any writer of the NT. It was in fact slowly worked out in the course of the first few centuries in an attempt to give an intelligible doctrine of God" (Dr. A.T. Hanson, Professor of

21 1After this, Jesus revealed himself again to his disciples at the sea of Tiberias. This is how it happened: 2Simon Peter, Thomas, whose name means twin, Nathanael from Cana of Galilee, Zebedee's sons, and two others of his disciples were together. 3Simon Peter said to them, "I am going fishing." They responded, "We are coming with you." They went out and got into the boat, but that night they caught nothing.

4When daybreak came, Jesus was standing on the shore. However, the disciples did not know that it was Jesus. 5Jesus called out to them, "Lads, you have not got any fish, have you?" They answered, "No." 6He said to them, "Then cast the net to the right side of the boat, and you will get some." So they did this, and they were unable to haul in the net because of the large number of fish. 7Therefore that disciple, the one Jesus loved, said to Peter, "It is the lord!" When Simon Peter heard that it was the lord, he tied his outer garment around him (he was practically naked) and plunged into the sea. 8But since they were not far from land (about a hundred yards away) the other disciples came with the boat, dragging the net full of fish.

9When they got out on land, they saw a charcoal fire there with fish cooking on it and bread. 10Jesus said to them, "Bring some of the fish you have just caught." 11So Simon Peter went aboard and hauled the net ashore, full of large fish — 153 of them. Even though there were so many fish, the net was not torn.

12Jesus said to them, "Come and have breakfast." None of the disciples dared to ask him, "Who are you?" because they knew it was the lord. 13Jesus came, took the bread, and gave it to them. He did the same with the fish. 14This was now the third time Jesus had appeared to the disciples after he was resurrected from the dead.

Theology, University of Hull, *The Image of the Invisible God*, SCM Press, 1982). "It might tend to moderation and in the end agreement, if we were industrious on all occasions to represent our own doctrine [the Trinity] as wholly *unintelligible*" (Dr. Hey, *Lectures in Divinity*, 2, 235).

[241]"Name" in this Hebrew environment means everything a person stands for, i.e. his whole agenda, the Kingdom Gospel preaching of Jesus the Messiah — God's logos plan offering human beings immortality through Christ and obedience to him and his teachings.

15When they had finished breakfast, Jesus asked Simon Peter, "Simon, son of John, do you love me more than these others do?" He said to him, "Yes, lord, you know that I love you." He said to him, "Feed my lambs." 16A second time Jesus asked him, "Simon, son of John, do you love me?" He replied, "Yes, lord, you know that I love you." Jesus said, "Pastor my sheep." 17He asked him a third time, "Simon, son of John, do you love me?" Peter was upset that he asked him the third time, "Do you love me?" He said, "lord, you know everything! You know that I love[242] you." "Pastor my sheep," Jesus said.

18"I assure you on the highest authority:[243] when you were young, you used to fasten your own belt and go wherever you wanted. But when you grow old, you will stretch out your hands, and someone else will tie you up and carry you where you will not want to go." 19Jesus said this to signify by what kind of death Peter would glorify God. After saying this, he said to him, "Follow me!"

20So Peter turned round and saw the disciple Jesus loved following them. The disciple was the one who had leaned back against Jesus at the supper and asked, "lord, who is the one who is going to betray you?" 21When Peter saw him, he asked Jesus, "lord, what about this man?" 22Jesus answered, "If I want him to remain alive until I come back, what does that matter to you? Just make sure you follow me." 23So this report spread among the brothers, that this disciple was not going to die. But Jesus had not said that he would not die. He had said only, "If I want him to remain alive until I come back, what does that matter to you?"

24This is the disciple who witnesses to these events and who wrote them down. We know that his testimony is genuine.[244] 25And there are also many other things Jesus did, which, if they were all recorded one by one, I doubt that the world itself would have enough space to contain the books which would have to be written.

---

[242]There appears to be no recognizable difference in the two Greek words translated "love" here. John sometimes uses synonymous terms, without any distinction.

[243]"Amen, amen, I tell you."

[244]Authentic, as opposed to what is fictitious, counterfeit, imagined or pretended.

Note on John 1:1

The "word" or design of course was the plan to have Jesus, in the fullness of time, born to Mary. Elsewhere in the NT "word" is the Christian Gospel of the Kingdom, the word, which as Gospel, alone can cause the rebirth of those who are to achieve salvation (see 1 Pet. 1:23-25; cp. Mt. 13:19; Lk. 8:11-12). Jesus as preacher of that saving word, Gospel of the Kingdom (Lk. 4:43), embodied and announced the saving message. John provided his own commentary on these opening words of his Gospel, in 1 John 1:1-2. He explains there that "**what** [not 'he who'] was from the beginning" was "the word, promise of eternal life," and that "life was with [*pros* as in Jn. 1:1] the Father." In 1:1c the word was *God* (emphatic), i.e. God Himself, not someone else! The word is thus understood by John 1:1 in the Gospel not as the Son, who was not yet born, not yet in existence, but the promise of the Life of the Age to Come, the essence of the Christian Gospel of the Kingdom — the promise of immortality for man if he obeys God and Jesus (Heb. 5:9; Jn. 3:36; Rom. 1:5; 16:26, etc.). This Life in the Age to Come was said to be *pros ton patera,* "with the Father" (1 John 1:2, the same preposition as in *pros ton theon,* "with God," Jn. 1:1 and Rom. 8:31: "concerning," "about these things"). It (not He) was manifested in Jesus the Son when Jesus began to exist, miraculously begotten in Mary (Lk. 1:35; Mt. 1:18, 20). 1 John 5:18 (not KJV) carefully describes the Son as the "the one who was **brought into existence**, begotten." (The NT says nothing at all about an "eternal generation" of the Son.) John himself in 1 John 5:18 speaks of a beginning in time for the Son, exactly as does Matt. 1:20, where the Son was "the one begotten, brought into existence, in her [Mary]." There was no Son of God prior to the beginning of the life, the procreation of the Son by miracle in Mary. Luke 1:35 declares explicitly that "Son of God" is the title for Jesus "*precisely because of" (dio kai)* his origin in Mary by biological miracle. God's word is in its Jewish background God's mighty command, reminding us of the first creation in Genesis, where God spoke things into existence. Here, like Matthew (1:1; 1:18, 20), John is describing the new Creation, which is the procreation of the unique Son of God, Jesus (from Jn. 1:14). There is no "God the Son" in Scripture. Dr. Caird at Oxford makes our point about "word" succinctly: "How is John 1:1 to be translated? The solution is that *logos* for John primarily means 'purpose.' 'In the beginning was the purpose, the purpose in the mind of God, the purpose which was God's own being.' It is surely a conceivable thought that God is wholly identified with His purpose of love and that this purpose took human form in Jesus of Nazareth" (Dr. G.B. Caird, *New Testament Theology*, p. 332). "The Apostles did **not identify Jesus with Yahweh**. There were passages which made this impossible, for example Ps. 110:1; Mal. 3:1, 'the lord' (NAB)" (Charles Bigg, DD, Regius Prof. of Ecclesiastical History, University of Oxford, in *International Critical Commentary on 1 Peter*, 1910, pp. 99, 127). He writes also: "It would be rash to conclude that St. Peter identified Jehovah with Christ" (citing Prof. Hort, *Dissertations*).

"The wisdom of God said" in Luke 11:49 illustrates the fact that wisdom and word can be personified, spoken of as if a person but really just the One God in action. So in John 1:1 we find the "word/wisdom of God with God" and fully expressive of Him.

When Jesus the Son was begotten that wisdom was embodied in a fully human being. It is a mistake to read "word" or "wisdom" as another person than the Father. Personification of the word does not imply *personalizing* the word before the conception of the person of the Son, in Mary. F.F. Bruce, in correspondence with me (1981), raised exactly the same question with this remark: "On the preexistence question, one can at least accept the preexistence of the eternal Word or Wisdom of God, **which** (who?) became incarnate in Jesus." Bruce went on to say that on balance he thought John was in favor of the Son's preexistence but that he was very uncertain about Paul's believing in a preexisting Son. For 50 translations which did not assume that *logos* was a second Person, see *Focus on the Kingdom* of July, 2004, at restorationfellowship.org. These translations give us the pronoun "it," not "he" for word. Note the important words of the leading Christologist Dr. James Dunn on Paul in 1 Cor. 8:6 and John 1: "Christ is being identified here **not with a pre-existent being** but with the creative power and action of God...There is **no indication** that **Jesus thought or spoke of himself** as having **pre-existed with God prior to his birth**" (*Christology in the Making*, p. 182, 254).

Dr. James Dunn, *Unity and Diversity in the NT*: "Jesus thought of himself as Wisdom's messenger, a self-understanding reflected particularly in Matt. 11:25-27; Luke 7:31-35; 11:49-51. Now here we must recall that within Judaism Wisdom was only a way of speaking about God's action in creation, revelation and redemption without actually speaking about God. Wisdom, like the name of God, the spirit of God and *logos* (word), etc., denotes the immanent activity of God, without detracting from God's wholly other transcendence. For pre-Christian Judaism Wisdom was neither an inferior heavenly being (one of the heavenly council) nor a divine hypostasis (as in the later Trinitarian conception of God). Such a development would have been (and in the event was) unacceptable to Judaism's [and Jesus'] strict monotheism [Mk. 12:29; Jn. 17:3]. Wisdom is no more than a personification of God's immanence, no more to be regarded as a distinct person within the Godhead than the rabbinic concept or talk of pre-existing Torah." Paul never uses the name Jesus for the preexistent one. "Jesus was the man that preexistent Wisdom became...Even in John here as with Paul, Jesus is to be thought of as the man which preexistent Logos became, that is the man who brings God to expression more than any other man...There is no good evidence that Jesus thought of himself as a preexistent being...The importance of Ps. 110:1 lies in the double use of *kurios*. The one is clearly YHVH, but who is the other? Clearly *not* YHVH, but an exalted being whom the writer calls lord (1 Cor. 8:5-6, Eph 4:5, 6). Here Christianity shows itself as a developed form of Judaism, with its monotheistic confession as one of the most important parts of its Jewish inheritance. For in Judaism the most fundamental confession is 'God is one.' There is only one God (Deut. 6:4). Hence also Rom. 3:30; Gal. 3:20; 1 Tim 2:5; cf. James 2:19. Within Palestine and the Jewish nation such an affirmation would have been unnecessary — Jew and Christian shared a belief in God's oneness. But in the Gentile mission this Jewish presupposition within Christianity would have emerged to prominence, in face of the wider belief in 'gods many.' The point for us to note is that Paul can hail Jesus as **lord not in order to identify him with God, but rather if anything to distinguish him from God** (cp. particularly 1 Cor. 15:24-28)...For Paul even the title 'lord' becomes a way of

distinguishing Jesus from God rather than identifying him with God (Rom. 15:6; 1 Cor. 8:6; 15:24-28; 2 Cor. 1:3; 11:31; Eph. 1:3, 17; Phil. 2:11; Col. 1:3). Paul was and remained a monotheist" (p. 221, 223, 225, 53, 226).

Thus also Karl-Heinz Ohlig on the later development of the Trinity: "No matter how one interprets the individual steps, it is certain the doctrine of the Trinity, as it in the end became 'dogma,' both in the East and even more so in the West, possesses no Biblical foundation whatsoever and also has no 'continuous succession' [i.e. a link back to the NT]" (*One or Three? From the Father of Jesus to the Trinity*, p. 130). *TDNT*: "John attributes divine generation to Jesus (1 John 5:18; John 1:13)" (Vol. 1, p. 671). This state-of-the-art document recognizes that John 1:13 refers to the virgin birth, thus harmonizing John beautifully and easily with Matthew and Luke.

Dr. Dunn gives us a fair warning: "To speak of *Christ* as himself preexistent, coming down from heaven, and so forth, has to be seen as metaphorical; **otherwise it leads inevitably to some kind of polytheism**...Even to speak of the incarnation of the Son of God can be **misleading**, unless the Son Christology of John is seen as it was probably intended, as an expression of the same Wisdom/Word Christology; otherwise, **there is the danger of a too literal translation of Father-Son language once again into a form of polytheism** — that very abandoning of the oneness of God of which Jews and Muslims accuse Christians. The incarnation doctrine which comes to expression in the New Testament is properly understood only if it is understood as the incarnation of God's self-revelation [*logos*, word, not Word. Cp. "Behold, they say to me, 'Where is the word of the LORD? Let it come!'" (Jer. 17:15, ESV)]. The issue which **caused the breach** with Jewish thought and with Judaism is the charge against the Johannine Jesus that 'you being a man, make yourself God' (Jn. 10:33)" (Dunn, *The Christ and the Spirit*, 1998, p 47). Jesus is in 1 Cor. 1:30 the wisdom which came from God. Jesus is the human being who expresses the wisdom/word of God, as well as "righteousness, sanctification and redemption." Jesus is not a "God the Son" who came from God. Jesus is what wisdom/word became. If Matthew and Luke had been believed, none of the arguments over the Trinity would have arisen. The key is not to make John contradict Matthew and Luke (and Peter and Paul, of course) — and never to contradict Mark 12:29, John 17:3 and Luke 1:35.

Acts

1 1The first account I wrote, Theophilus, was about all that Jesus began
to do and to teach 2until the day that he was taken up into heaven,
after he had given commands through holy spirit[1] to the Apostles he had
chosen. 3To them also he showed himself to be alive, after he suffered,
by many convincing proofs. Over a period of forty days he was seen by
them, and he spoke to them about the Kingdom of God.[2] 4While he was
meeting with them he commanded, "Do not depart from Jerusalem, but
wait for what the Father promised, which you heard about from me. 5For
John baptized in water, but you will be baptized in holy spirit in a few
days."

6And so when they had come together they were asking him, "lord, is
this the time when you are going to restore the Kingdom to Israel?"[3] 7He

---

[1]In the NT the holy spirit is the operational presence and power of God or Jesus Messiah, expressed in different ways and activities. In 1 John 2:1 the paraclete is identified as Jesus the mediator. Jesus said that he would be going away and in the same breath promised that he would come to them, in his invisible spirit-presence (Jn. 14:16-18). Hence it can be said "the lord [Jesus] is the spirit" (2 Cor. 3:17). There is no third Person. The Spirit is never worshipped or prayed to, and never sends greetings.

[2]**The first Kingdom text in Acts**. The Kingdom of God is the core of his teaching and the label given to his saving Gospel. His whole purpose, as ours today also must be, was to announce the Gospel of the Kingdom. Acts 8:12 provides a brilliant summary of the faith needed to be believed before water baptism into the church. See also Acts 19:8; 20:24-25; 28:23, 31. For Kingdom see always Dan. 2:44; 7:18, 22, 27; Lk. 4:43; 19:11ff; Rev. 15:15-18. The Gospel begins with the preaching of John the Baptist, who introduced Jesus (Lk. 16:16; Jn. 1:17). Heb. 2:3 shows how the New Covenant had its beginning with the teaching of Jesus.

[3]**The second Kingdom text in Acts**. The Gospel about the Kingdom includes not only the promise of world peace and international disarmament but also the important promise of a restored remnant of Israel (along with Egypt and Assyria, then converted, Isa. 19:23-25) being in that future Kingdom. The international church will be immortalized and supervise this new world with Jesus (1 Cor. 6:2; Rev. 5:10). The restoration of the Kingdom is a simple, political hope and is so recognized in the OT when in 2 Chron. 11:1 the Kingdom was to be restored. The meaning is clear, and so also here where Jesus is the great expected King of Israel (Mt. 19:28). The restoration is political and very spiritual since Jesus will be ruling in Jerusalem. The fundamental error in much Bible reading is to think that spiritual things belong only to the invisible. But Christians are going to have a "spiritual body" (1 Cor. 15:44). Jesus had a spiritual body, too, but he was still visible and palpable and he ate food! (Lk. 24). At present much scholarship and commentary simply contradicts Jesus' definition of the Kingdom

replied, "It is not for you to know times or periods which the Father has
set by His own authority. 8But you will receive power when holy spirit
has come upon you. You will then be my witnesses in Jerusalem, in all
Judea and Samaria, and to the farthest regions of the earth."

9When he had said these things, as they were watching, he was lifted
up and a cloud caused him to disappear from their sight. 10While they
were looking intently into the sky as he went up, suddenly two men in
white clothes stood next to them. 11They said, "Men of Galilee, why are
you standing gazing into the sky? This same Jesus who was taken up
from you into heaven will come back in just the same way as you saw
him going into heaven."[4]

12Then they returned to Jerusalem from the mountain known as
Olives which is near Jerusalem, a distance of a Sabbath day's journey.
13When they had come into the city, they went up to the upstairs room
where they were staying: Peter, John, James, Andrew, Philip, Thomas,
Bartholomew, Matthew, James the son of Alphaeus, Simon the Zealot,
and Judas the son of James. 14All these were devoting themselves to
prayer continually with one mind, along with the women, and Mary the
mother of Jesus, and his brothers.

15It was in those days that Peter stood up in the midst of the disciples
(there were about 120 believers gathered) and said, 16"Brothers, it was
necessary that this scripture be fulfilled which the holy spirit prophesied
through David, about Judas, who guided those who arrested Jesus. 17For

---

as the restoration of the Davidic throne in Jerusalem (Acts 3:21; Lk. 22:28-30, etc.). Dr. Geoffrey Lampe is at his most misleading when he asserts that Jesus taught in Acts 1:6 a "reinterpretation of the Kingdom." "The disciples learned," Lampe maintains quite wrongly, "that the Gospel was not to include the restoration of the Davidic kingdom in Israel, but that the Messiah's reign was to be established through the witness which they themselves would bear to him from Jerusalem to the ends of the earth" (*God as Spirit*, 1976, p. 9). The plain fact is that the disciples' question, after extensive instruction from Jesus on the Kingdom, was the right one, and indeed looked forward to a future political empire in Israel. That fact was not doubted by Jesus. The *time* when it would come was not to be known. Unbelieving commentary is a tragic repetition of Calvin's regrettable comment on Acts 1:6: "there are as many errors in the disciples' question as words"! See my article "Acts 1:6 and the Eclipse of the Biblical Kingdom," *Evangelical Quarterly* 66:3 (1994) at focusonthekingdom.org

[4]Certainly and positively not a **pre-tribulation** rapture/resurrection! There will be one single visible return of Jesus and it will happen after the Great Tribulation and the heavenly signs. Matt. 24:29 settles all argument.

he was one of us and had a part in this ministry." 18(Now this man Judas
bought a field with the money which he took for his wickedness, and
falling headlong, his body burst open and all his intestines gushed out.
19This fact became known to everyone living in Jerusalem, so that in their
language that field was called 'Hakeldama,' that is, 'Field of blood.')
20"For it is written in the book of Psalms, 'Let his house become empty;
may no one live in it' and 'Let someone else take his office.'

21"So then, of the men who have accompanied us all the time that the
lord Jesus was with us[5] — 22beginning from his baptism by John to the
day when he was taken up from us — of these men one must become a
witness with us of his resurrection." 23So they put forward two: Joseph
called Barsabbas, who was also called Justus, and Matthias. 24They
prayed, "You, Lord,[6] who know the hearts of everyone, show us which
one of these two You have chosen 25to take part in this ministry and hold
the office of Apostle from which Judas fell away to go to his own place."
26They drew lots for them, and the lot fell on Matthias, and he was added
to the eleven Apostles.

2 1When the day of Pentecost had come and was being fulfilled,[7] they
were all together in one place. 2Suddenly there came from the sky a
sound like the rushing of a strong wind, and it filled the whole house
where they were sitting. 3There appeared flames of fire distributed to
them, one sitting on each of them. 4They were all filled with holy spirit
and began to speak foreign languages,[8] as the spirit gave them the ability
to speak.

---

[5]The necessary qualification for an Apostle at the level of the 12 is that he must have personally seen Jesus. Paul qualified for the office of Apostle in the same way.

[6]The prayer may be directed to the Lord God or the lord Messiah. Most prayer in the NT goes to the Father through the Son, but prayer to the Son is approved by John 14:14 and 1 Cor. 1:2. Paul thanks Jesus (1 Tim. 1:12).

[7]The Greek suggests that it not only came but was being fulfilled, the calendar day being superseded by its spiritual fulfillment (see Col. 2:16-17; Heb. 8:5; 10:1). "Adam *is* a type of the one to come" (Rom. 5:14) and the tri-fold calendar — holy days, new moons and weekly Sabbaths — are a shadow of the Messiah who has come.

[8]The narrative is quite clear that it was not a miracle of hearing on the part of the audience, but a miraculous ability on the part of the Apostles (and others, up to 120) to speak in real foreign languages (v. 6, 8, 11). They were the languages of various nationalities attending the Feast. "Every man heard them speaking in his own language"

5Now there were devout Jews living in Jerusalem from every nation
on earth. 6When this sound was heard a crowd gathered, bewildered
because each one heard them speaking his own native language.
7Amazed and confused, they exclaimed, “Look, are not all those who are
speaking Galileans? 8How are we hearing them speak our own native
languages? 9Parthians, Medes and Elamites; people from Mesopotamia,
Judea and Cappadocia, Pontus and the province of Asia, 10Phrygia and
Pamphylia; Egypt and the area of Libya around Cyrene; visitors from
Rome, both Jews and proselytes, 11Cretans and Arabs — we hear them
speaking in our own languages about the mighty works of God.” 12They
continued to be astonished and perplexed, and said to one another,
“What does this mean?” 13But others mocked and said, “They are drunk
with sweet wine!”

14But Peter, standing up with the eleven, raised his voice and spoke to
them: “People of Judea and all of you living in Jerusalem, let this be
known to you and pay attention to my words. 15These men are not drunk,
as you suppose, as it is only nine in the morning! 16But this is what was
spoken through the prophet Joel: 17‘It will be in the last days,’ says God,
‘that I will pour out from My spirit on all people. Your sons and
daughters[9] will prophesy. Your young men will see visions, and your old

---

(v. 6). It is misleading to translate *glossa* as other than “language.” On no account should the miracle be moved from the Apostles to their international audience. “There is no evidence whatever of [the languages in Acts or at Corinth] being mere gibberish as distinct from *language.* All that Paul said to the Corinthians is fully applicable to any language spoken when there were none present who understood it” (*Pulpit Commentary*, *Acts*, p. 50). The miracle points to a time when all persons including angels will be united in Christ. This reversed the Tower of Babel. Paul covers the extent of the language gift when he refers to “human or angelic languages” (1 Cor. 13:1). He was no friend of unintelligibility and tried to expose a hidden false “tongue” by telling the speaker to pray in order to interpret for the benefit of the church (1 Cor. 14:13). Today’s claims to foreign language supernaturally spoken need to be verified. Such claims to be speaking in “tongues” (really foreign language unlearned) require inspection and verification (“prove all things”). Otherwise there is the great danger of self-deception and false claims, an exercise in dishonesty. The situation is aggravated when the claim to “tongues” is made *the* sign of having the holy spirit, leading the one who has the “tongues” to consider all who do not have the “tongues” to be without holy spirit, and thus not Christian, since every true believer must have the spirit (Rom. 8:9).

[9]Showing that the spirit and its gifts were not limited to the men! So also in 1 Cor. 12 and 14. Both men and women exercised their gifts in church.

men will dream dreams. 18On My servants, both male and female, I will pour out from My spirit in those days, and they will prophesy. 19I will show wonders in the sky above and signs on the earth beneath — blood, fire, and billows of smoke. 20The sun will be darkened and the moon will appear like blood before that great and glorious Day of the Lord will come. 21And it will be that everyone who calls on the name of the Lord will be saved.'

22"People of Israel, listen to my words: Jesus from Nazareth, a man[10] fully accredited to you by God by the miracles, wonders and signs that God did through him among you, as you well know — 23this man was delivered up by the predetermined counsel and foreknowledge of God, and using godless men, you nailed him to a cross and killed him. 24But God raised him up, freeing him from the agony of death, because it was impossible for him to be held in death's grip. 25For David refers to Jesus' experience: 'I saw the Lord always before me, because He is on my right hand so that I will not be shaken. 26So my heart was glad and my tongue rejoiced, and my body will rest in hope 27because You will not leave my soul in the grave, nor will You allow Your holy one to see decay. 28You made known the ways of life to me. You will make me full of gladness with Your presence.'

29"Brothers, I confidently tell you that the patriarch David both died and was buried, and his tomb is with us to this very day. 30Being a prophet, David knew that God had sworn an oath to him that He would seat one of his descendants on his throne. 31Foreseeing this he spoke about the resurrection of the Messiah: that he was not abandoned to the grave[11] nor did his body experience decay. 32This Jesus, God resurrected, and we are all witnesses of that fact. 33So now that he has been exalted to the right hand of God,[12] and has received from the Father the promised

---

[10]Peter knew nothing about a "GOD-man," which is the product of post-biblical theology confusing the central doctrine of Jesus and of Scripture that "the Lord our God is one Lord" (Mk. 12:29) and that the Father is "the only one who is true God" (Jn. 17:3; 5:44).

[11]I. e. "gravedom," the world of all the dead, both good and evil, *Sheol* in Hebrew and *Hades* in Greek.

[12]Fulfilling Ps. 110:1 where the Messiah is *adoni*, my lord (not LORD!) and thus not Deity but a supremely exalted man. This is the easy early creed of the Christians (1 Tim. 2:5). *Adoni*, my lord, is never a title of Deity, all 195 times. When occurring in

holy spirit, he has poured out this which you now see and hear. 34For it
was not David who went up to heaven,[13] but David himself said, ‘The
Lord said to my lord,[14] “Sit at My right hand 35until I make your enemies
a footstool for your feet.”’ 36Let the whole house of Israel therefore know
with absolute certainty that God has made him both lord and Messiah,
this Jesus whom you crucified.”[15]

37Hearing this, they were very troubled and asked Peter and the rest
of the Apostles, “Brothers, what are we to do?” 38Peter said to them,
“Repent and be baptized,[16] each one of you, in the name of Jesus
Messiah[17] for the forgiveness of your sins, and you will receive the gift
of holy spirit. 39For this promise is for you and for your children, and for

---

contrast to GOD, it is regularly rendered *kurios mou,* my lord. There is no uncertainty or evidence of corruption in the Greek text here.

[13]David was obviously not then alive in heaven! This demonstrates the pervasive teaching of the Bible that the dead are non-conscious until the future resurrection (Dan. 12:2). The dead know nothing at all and there is no activity in Sheol/Hades, the place of all the dead (Ecc. 9:5, 10; Jn. 11:11, 14).

[14]The key term is *adoni*, my lord, which in all 195 occurrences is never the title of Deity. This shows how confusing the later philosophical, non-biblical attempt was to say that Jesus was co-equal God and member of a triune God not once recognized in the Bible. The word “God” in the NT refers to the Father of Jesus over 1300 times and none of the various words for God in Scripture (*Adonai*, YHVH, *Elohim*, *Theos*) ever means a triune God. Jesus as founder of the Christian faith (Heb. 2:3) was not a Trinitarian, because he and a fellow Jew were in complete agreement on the unitarian creed of the Hebrew Bible (see Mk. 12:28ff). The capital letter on the second lord of Ps. 110:1 is most misleading, forcing the reader to believe that the second lord is *Adonai*, the Lord GOD — a second GOD! *Adoni* is never a title of Deity. *Adonai* always is.

[15]The Bible’s Jesus is just that, “the lord Messiah” who was born in Bethlehem (Lk. 2:11) and is also the LORD’s, Yehovah’s Messiah (Lk. 2:26). See Ps. 2 where Yehovah has put His Messiah on the hill at Jerusalem, that is He will do this when Jesus returns.

[16]The command was to be baptized in water of course, and this is a standing order for all believers according to Scripture. It is commanded equally by Jesus in the Great Commission and is an issue of obedience. Disobedience would be a gravely dangerous mistake (Heb. 5:9; Jn. 14:15; 3:36).

[17]That is, based on the teaching of Messiah and his authority. The name of a person in Scripture means all that that person stands for and represents — certainly not how to pronounce the name in Hebrew! Yahweh, YHVH, is the personal name of the One God. The *meaning* of His name is given us in Greek in Rev. 1:4, 8; 11:17; 16:5, but not the name in Hebrew, which is found nowhere in the NT Greek scripture. An attempt was made by some Jews who translated the LXX to reproduce the divine name in Hebrew, but this is never attempted in NT Scripture.

all who are far off — as many as the Lord our God will invite to
Himself."[18] 40With many other words Peter continued to testify, and he
warned them, "Save yourselves from this crooked society!"[19] 41So those
who received his word were baptized,[20] and there were added that day
about 3,000 persons. 42They devoted themselves to the Apostles'
teaching and to fellowship in the breaking of bread and in prayer.

43Awe came on everyone, and many miracles and signs were
performed by the Apostles. 44All who had believed were together and had
all things in common. 45They sold their property and belongings and
shared with all, as anyone had a need. 46Day after day they met regularly
and with one mind in the Temple courts, and breaking bread from house
to house, they were eating their meals together with joy and humble
hearts, 47praising God and finding favor with all the people. The Lord
was adding to their number daily those who were being saved.

3 1Peter and John were going up to the Temple at the hour of prayer,
three in the afternoon. 2A man crippled from birth was being carried.
They used to set him down every day at the Temple gate which is called
"Beautiful," so that he could beg from people going into the Temple.
3When he saw Peter and John about to go into the Temple, he begged for
a gift. 4But Peter fastened his eyes on him, as did John, and said, "Look
at us!" 5He stared at them expectantly, hoping to receive something from
them. 6Peter said, "Money I do not have, but what I do have I give you.
In the name of Jesus Messiah of Nazareth, walk!" 7Peter took him by the
right hand and raised him up. Immediately his feet and ankles became

---

[18]Acts 17:30 states that "God now commands all men everywhere to repent." He also "wants all men to be saved" (1Tim. 2:4). Calvinism is opposed to this universal invitation of God to salvation in Jesus. Matt. 13:15 states the problem of blindness cannot be blamed on God: "*They* have closed their eyes." In Acts 13:46 Paul told his opponents who refused the Gospel that *they* were "counting *themselves* unworthy of salvation in the age to come."

[19]The Greek word *genea* means evil society right up to the time of the Second Coming. See Mark 8:38 where Jesus compared the present evil *genea* with the future age of the Kingdom to begin at the Second Coming. Note the use of *genea* to mean "brood" or type of person in Prov. 30:11-14: and Luke 16:8.

[20]In water of course, as a public demonstration of their becoming part of the body of Messiah. Baptism in water is an essential part of the salvation process (Acts 8:12), as "the response of a clear conscience" (1 Pet. 3:21).

strong, 8and he leapt to his feet and began walking. He entered the temple
with them, walking, leaping and praising God. 9All the people saw him
walking and praising God. 10They recognized him as the one who used to
sit begging for gifts at the Beautiful Gate of the Temple, and they were
filled with wonder and astonishment at what had happened to him.

11He held on to Peter and John. All the people, in utter amazement,
ran together to them to the porch called Solomon's Porch. 12When Peter
saw this he addressed the people: "People of Israel, why are you
amazed? Why are you staring at us as though by our own power or
godliness we had made this man walk? 13The God of Abraham, Isaac,
and Jacob, the God of our fathers,[21] has glorified His servant[22] Jesus,
whom you delivered up and denied in the presence of Pilate, when he
had determined to release him. 14But you denied the holy and righteous
one, and asked that a murderer be released to you instead. 15You killed
the leader of life, whom God raised from the dead, and we are witnesses
of that fact. 16Based on faith in Jesus' name,[23] that name has strengthened
this man,[24] whom you see and know. The faith which comes through
Jesus[25] has given this man perfect health in the presence of all of you.

17"Now, brothers and sisters, I know that you did this in ignorance, as
did your rulers also. 18But the things which God foretold through all the
prophets, that His Messiah would suffer, He has in this way fulfilled.
19Repent therefore and turn back, so that your sins may be blotted out and
so that there may come times of refreshing from the presence of the
Lord, 20and that He will send Jesus, the Messiah appointed for you.

---

[21]This of course is the One God of Israel, a single Divine Person, the Father. It is certainly not the triune God of much later Greek-philosophically influenced theology.

[22]The famous servant of Isaiah, of course, who was to be the ideal Israelite, loving and obeying God.

[23]"Name" in Scripture stands for all a person is, his identity, character, agenda, teaching and authority. There is nothing in the sound of the name itself, but it is what stands behind the name, the whole person, who counts.

[24]The risen lord Jesus Messiah is of course intensively active in the Church, then as now, where the truth is being discovered. God is to be worshipped in spirit and truth (Jn. 4:24), and obscurity over the definition of God and the Son of God impedes clear thinking about and worship of the Father.

[25]The faith in the work and teachings of Jesus, the faith modeled by Jesus as well as faith in him.

21Heaven must retain him until the time for the restoration of all things,[26]
which God announced long ago through His holy prophets. 22Moses said,
'The Lord God will put on the scene of history a prophet like me from
among your brothers.[27] You are to listen to and obey him, everything he
says to you. 23Everyone who will not listen to and obey that prophet will
be utterly destroyed from among the people.' 24And all the prophets who
have spoken have announced these days, from Samuel and those who
followed after. 25You are the children of the prophets, and of the
covenant which God made with your fathers, promising to Abraham, 'All
the families of the earth will be blessed through your offspring.' 26God
produced His servant[28] and sent him to you first to bless you, by turning
every one of you away from your wickedness."

4 1As they were speaking to the people, the priests, the captain of the
temple guard, and the Sadducees came up to them. 2They were
disturbed because they were teaching the people and proclaiming the
resurrection from the dead through Jesus. 3They arrested them and put
them in jail until the next day, since it was already evening. 4But many of
those who had heard the Gospel-word believed it, and the number of
men came to about 5,000.

5The next day, their rulers, elders, and religious teachers gathered
together in Jerusalem. 6Annas the high priest was there, as well as
Caiaphas, John, Alexander, and other relatives of the high priest. 7They
made Peter and John stand in the middle of them, and inquired, "By what

---

[26]With this single statement about the *apokatastasis* (restoration) of everything which the prophets announced (see for example Isa. 1:26), Peter expects us to understand the whole promise of peace on earth (Isa. 2; 65:17ff; Rev. 20:1-6), a restored nation of Israel (Isa. 19) and the Kingdom of God worldwide on earth, with Jesus on the throne of David restored, in short the whole basis of the Christian Gospel of the Kingdom. It entails of course the raising of the faithful dead and their participation in the Kingdom as then immortalized rulers with Jesus (Dan. 7:18, 22, 27; 1 Cor. 6:2, etc.).

[27]The reference is to the marvelous promise of Messiah in Deut. 18-15-18 whom no one reading would imagine to be a second GOD! The Messiah must originate from the family of Israel and be like Moses. His origin is described in Luke 1:35 and Matt 1:18, 20; 1 John 5:18 ("begotten," "brought into existence"). There is no "God the Son," an eternally begotten Son, anywhere in the Bible.

[28]By miracle in Mary (Lk. 1:35) which explicitly constituted him uniquely the Son of God, the second Adam, pioneer of the way to immortality for all who choose (1 Tim. 2:4-5).

power or in what name have you done this?" 8Then Peter, filled with
holy spirit, said to them, "Rulers and elders of the people, 9if we are
being tried today for a good thing done to a crippled man — how this
man has been healed — 10let it be known to you all, and all the people of
Israel, that it was by the name and authority of Jesus Messiah of
Nazareth, whom you crucified and whom God resurrected from the dead,
that this man stands here before you in good health. 11He is 'the stone
which was rejected by you, the builders, but has become the
cornerstone.' 12There is salvation in no one else, as there is no other name
in the whole world given among people by which we must be saved."[29]

13When they saw the courage of Peter and John, and found out that
they were unlearned, ordinary men, they were astonished. They
recognized that they had been with Jesus. 14Seeing the man who had been
healed standing with them, there was nothing they could say. 15But when
they had commanded them to leave the council they conferred among
themselves: 16"What should we do with these men? A notable miracle
has been done through them, as can be plainly seen by everyone living in
Jerusalem, and we cannot deny it. 17But so that this spreads no further
among the people, let us warn them not to speak to anyone in this name
from now on." 18They called them in and commanded them not to speak
or teach at all in the name of Jesus.[30] 19But Peter and John answered
them, "Whether it is right in the sight of God to obey you rather than
God, you can judge for yourselves. 20We cannot possibly stop speaking
about what we have seen and heard." 21When they had further threatened
them, they let them go, since they could find no way to punish them
because of the people, as everyone was praising God for what had
happened. 22For the man who had been healed by this miraculous sign
was more than forty years old.

23When Peter and John had been released, they came to the other
believers and reported all that the chief priests and elders had said to
them. 24When they heard it, with one mind they raised their voices to
God: "Lord of all, You are the One who made the heaven and earth and
sea, and all that is in them. 25You said by holy spirit through our father,
Your servant David, 'Why do the nations rage, and the people plot futile

---

[29]Definitively ruling out all modern ideas about "many different paths to God."

[30]I.e. everything Jesus stood for, his whole teaching and character.

opposition? 26The kings of the earth take a stand, and the rulers gather
together against the Lord and against His Messiah.' 27Truly in this city
both Herod and Pontius Pilate, along with the Gentiles and the people of
Israel, did gather together to oppose Your holy servant Jesus, whom You
anointed. 28They did whatever Your authority and Your plan
predetermined to happen. 29Now, Lord, notice their threats and give to
Your servants the ability to speak Your Gospel-word with all boldness,
30while You stretch out your hand to heal, and cause signs and wonders
to happen through the name of Your holy servant Jesus." 31When they
had prayed, the place where they were gathered was shaken. They were
all filled with holy spirit, and they spoke the Gospel-word[31] of God with
boldness.

32The group of those who believed were of one mind and heart. Not
one of them claimed that any of his belongings was his own, but they
shared all their property in common. 33With great power the Apostles
were giving their testimony to the resurrection of the lord Jesus, and
great grace was on them all. 34No one among them lacked anything,
because all who owned lands or houses sold them and brought the money
from the sales, 35and laid it at the Apostles' feet to be distributed
according to anyone's need.

36Joseph, who the Apostles also called Barnabas, which translated
means "son of encouragement," was a Levite and a native of Cyprus.
37He sold some land that he owned, brought the money and laid it at the
Apostles' feet.

5 1A man named Ananias, with his wife Sapphira, sold a piece of land.
2He kept back part of the money for himself, and his wife was fully
aware of it. He brought part of the money and laid it at the Apostles'
feet. 3But Peter said, "Ananias, why has Satan filled your heart to lie to
the holy spirit and to keep back part of the price of the land? 4Before you
sold it, was it not your own? And after it was sold, was the money not
still under your control? Why have you conceived this plan in your
heart? You have not lied to people but to God!" 5As he heard these
words, Ananias collapsed and died. Great fear seized all who heard about

---

[31]The Gospel of the Kingdom, as Jesus had first announced it in Mark 1:14-15 (cp. Lk. 4:43; 9:11).

it. 6The young men got up, covered him up, and carried him out to bury
him.

7About three hours later his wife came in, not knowing what had
happened. 8Peter asked her, “Did the two of you sell the land for such
and such a price?” She answered, “Yes, that was the price.” 9Then Peter
asked her, “Why have you both agreed to test the Lord’s spirit? Look,
the feet of those who have buried your husband are at the door, and they
will carry you out too!” 10She collapsed immediately at his feet and died.
The young men came in and found her dead, and they carried her out and
buried her next to her husband. 11Great fear seized the whole church, as
well as everyone who heard about it.

12Through the hands of the Apostles many signs and wonders were
performed among the people. With one mind they were meeting together
in Solomon’s porch. 13None of the rest dared to join them, yet the people
thought highly of them. 14And more believers were being added to the
lord, multitudes of both men and women. 15They even carried out the
sick into the streets and laid them on beds and mats, so that as Peter
came by at least his shadow might fall on any of them. 16A crowd also
came together from the towns around Jerusalem, bringing sick people
and those tormented by unclean spirits, and every one of them was
healed.

17But the high priest took a stand and all those with him (the sect of
the Sadducees) as they were filled with jealousy. 18They arrested the
Apostles and put them into the public jail. 19But during the night an angel
of the Lord opened the prison doors and brought them out and said,
20“Go and stand and speak to the people in the Temple the whole
message of this Life.”

21When they heard this, they entered the Temple about daybreak and
were teaching. But the high priest and his associates called together the
Sanhedrin, the whole council of the Israelites, and sent to the jail to have
the Apostles brought in. 22But the officers did not find them in the prison,
and they returned and reported, 23“We found the prison securely locked
and the guards standing at the doors. But when we opened them, we
found no one inside.” 24Now when the captain of the temple guards and
the chief priests heard this, they were deeply perplexed about what was
going on. 25Then someone came and told them, “The men you put in
prison are standing in the Temple, teaching the people!” 26Then the

captain went with the officers and brought them without violence,
because they were afraid of being stoned by the people.
27When they had brought them in, they stood them before the
Sanhedrin. 28The high priest demanded, "We strictly commanded you not
to continue teaching on the basis of this name, but you have filled
Jerusalem with your teaching, and you intend to bring the guilt of this
man's death on us." 29But Peter and the Apostles answered, "We must
obey God rather than people. 30The God of our ancestors resurrected
Jesus, whom you killed by hanging him on a cross. 31He is the one whom
God exalted to His right hand as leader and savior,[32] to give repentance
to Israel and forgiveness of sins. 32We are his witnesses of these things,
and so is the holy spirit, which God has given to those who obey[33] Him."
33Hearing this, they became infuriated and were determined to kill
them. 34But a Pharisee named Gamaliel stood up in the council, a teacher
of the Law respected by all the people, and he commanded the men to be
put outside for a little while. 35Gamaliel then spoke to the council: "Men
of Israel, be careful about what you do with these men. 36For some time
ago Theudas rose up, making himself out to be somebody, and about
four hundred men joined up with him. But he was killed and all those
who were persuaded by him dispersed and came to nothing. 37After him
Judas of Galilee rose up in the days of the census, and led away some
people to revolt. He also was killed, and all who were persuaded by him
were scattered. 38So I tell you in this case, stay away from these men and
leave them alone. If this plan or work originates with people it will not
succeed. 39But if it is from God, you will not be able to overthrow it, and
you might even be found fighting against God."
40They were persuaded by him. Summoning the Apostles, they beat
them and ordered them not to speak in the name and authority of Jesus,

[32]Reference to the key OT verse in Ps. 110:1 defining the status of Jesus as the Messiah, the *adoni*, my lord of that verse. *Adoni*, my lord, not my Lord, in all of its 195 occurrences is never a title of Deity. Ps 110:1 provides the perfect paradigm instructing us in the relationship of the human Messiah (Son of Man) to the one God.

[33]A key concept: the spirit is given to the obedient. This is exactly John 3:36 and Heb. 5:9. There is no true faith without obedience, hence the all-important phrase "obedience of faith" which frames Romans (1:5; 16:26; cp. 1 Tim. 6:3). The reception of the spirit comes to all at conversion and baptism, as is clearly stated in 1 Cor. 12:13. The "charismatic" idea that the spirit is a second level of conversion received later creates a fatal two-class system in the Church and is entirely foreign to the NT.

and let them go. 41So they left the council, rejoicing that they had been
counted worthy to suffer shame for the name.[34] 42And every day in the
Temple and from house to house, they never stopped teaching and
evangelizing that the Messiah is Jesus.

6 1At that time, when the number of disciples was multiplying, a
complaint arose among the Greek-speaking believers against the
Hebrews, because their widows were being neglected in the daily
distribution of food. 2So the twelve Apostles summoned all the disciples
and said, "It is not appropriate for us to neglect the Gospel-word of God[35]
in order to serve tables. 3So select from among you, brothers, seven men
with good reputations, full of the spirit and wisdom, whom we may
appoint over this work. 4But we will devote ourselves to prayer and the
ministry of the Gospel-word." 5These words pleased the whole group.
They chose Stephen, a man full of faith and holy spirit, Philip,
Prochorus, Nicanor, Timon, Parmenas, and Nicolaus, a proselyte from
Antioch. 6They brought them before the Apostles, who prayed and laid
their hands on them.

7The Gospel-word of God kept spreading and the number of disciples
greatly increased in Jerusalem. Many of the priests became obedient to
the faith. 8Stephen, full of grace and power, performed great wonders and
miraculous signs among the people. 9But some from what was known as
the synagogue of the freedmen, including Cyrenians, Alexandrians, and
people from Cilicia and the province of Asia, started to dispute with
Stephen. 10They were unable to resist the wisdom and the spirit by which
he spoke. 11Then they secretly induced some men to say, "We have heard
him speak blasphemous words against Moses and against God." 12They
stirred up the people, the elders and the religious teachers, and they came
and seized Stephen and brought him before the council, the Sanhedrin.
13They set up false witnesses who said, "This man never stops speaking
against this holy place and the Law. 14For we have heard him say that this
Jesus of Nazareth will destroy this place, and will change the customs
which Moses delivered to us." 15All those sitting in the council fixed their
eyes on Stephen, and saw his face as if it were the face of an angel.

---

[34]"Name" in scripture refers to the whole cause and agenda of a person, in this case the Christian faith taught by Jesus.

[35]About the Kingdom, as defined in Mark 1:14-15 as a summary of the Christian faith.

7 1The high priest asked, "Are these things true?" 2Stephen said,
"Brothers and fathers, listen to me! The God of glory appeared to our
father Abraham when he lived in Mesopotamia, before he lived in Haran,
3and said to him, 'Leave your country and your relatives, and come into
the land which I am going to show you.'[36] 4Then he left the land of the
Chaldeans and lived in Haran. From there, after his father died, God
moved him to this land where you are now living. 5But He gave him no
inheritance in it, not even a square foot of land. Yet, even when he had
no children, He promised that He would give it to him as his possession,
and to his descendants. 6God told him that his descendants would live as
aliens in a foreign land, and that they would be enslaved and mistreated
for four hundred years. 7God said, 'I Myself will punish the nation that
held them in bondage, and after that they will come out and serve Me in
this place.'[37] 8Then He gave Abraham the covenant of circumcision. So
Abraham became the father of Isaac, and circumcised him on the eighth
day, and Isaac became the father of Jacob, and Jacob became the father
of the twelve patriarchs.

9"The patriarchs were jealous of Joseph and sold him into Egypt. But
God was with him, 10and delivered him out of all his trials. He gave him
favor and wisdom in the sight of Pharaoh, king of Egypt, who made him
governor[38] over Egypt and all his household.

---

[36]This is the model of the Christian faith. We give up the things closest to us for the only cause which ultimately counts: inheriting the land/Kingdom when Jesus returns (Mt. 5:5; Ps. 37: 9, 11, 18, 29). Abraham will gain his inheritance in that future resurrection with all the saints of all the ages.

[37]This pattern of events will happen again when the nation of Israel will be severely punished by Gentile nations, during the future period of the Great Tribulation (Mt. 24:21; Rev. 7:14). See for the details Zech. 13 and 14. From that time of unprecedented suffering a remnant of Israel will return to the land, and Jesus will govern them together with the then converted nations of Egypt and Assyria (Isa. 19:22-25). Zech 12:3, LXX describes the severe trouble to be experienced in Israel, and that suffering will be relieved by the return of Jesus. Jesus alludes to Zech. 12:3, LXX in Luke 21:24 and again in Rev. 11:2. A temple will be desecrated and Jerusalem severely punished by invasion.

[38]Governorship is promised to believers in the Kingdom to come. Judges and Kings in the OT are likewise a foreshadowing of the future rulership of the saints with Jesus in the Kingdom (1 Cor. 6:2; Dan. 7:14, 18, 22, 27; Rev. 3:21; 2:26; 5:10). We are to learn not to make the mistakes of the kings who failed, and emulate those who did well.

11"Then a famine came over all Egypt and Canaan, bringing great
hardship, and our fathers could not find food. 12So when Jacob heard that
there was grain in Egypt, he sent our fathers there the first time. 13On
their second visit, Joseph let his brothers know who he was, and Pharaoh
found out about Joseph's family. 14Joseph sent and invited Jacob his
father and all his relatives to come — seventy-five persons in all. 15So
Jacob went down to Egypt, and he and our fathers died there. 16They
were brought back to Shechem and laid in the tomb which Abraham had
bought for a certain amount of money from the sons of Hamor in
Shechem.

17"As the time for the fulfillment of the promise[39] which God had
pledged to Abraham came close, the people grew and multiplied in
Egypt. 18There arose another king over Egypt who knew nothing about
Joseph. 19This king took advantage of our nation and mistreated our
fathers, forcing them to put their newborn babies outdoors so they would
not survive. 20At that time Moses was born. He was beautiful to God, and
he was raised for three months in his father's house. 21When he was set
outdoors, Pharaoh's daughter took him in and brought him up as her own
son. 22So Moses was instructed in all the learning of the Egyptians, and
he was powerful in words and actions. 23But when he was about forty
years old, it occurred to him to visit his brothers, the Israelites. 24When
he saw one of them being mistreated, Moses defended him and avenged
the mistreated person by striking down the Egyptian. 25He thought his
people would understand that God was giving them deliverance through
him, but they did not understand. 26The next day, Moses found two
Israelites fighting. He tried to make peace between them by saying,
'Men, you are brothers! Why are you hurting one another?' 27But the one
who was mistreating his neighbor pushed Moses away and said, 'Who
made you a ruler and judge over us? 28Do you intend to kill me as you
killed the Egyptian yesterday?' 29When he heard this Moses fled and
became a resident alien in the land of Midian, where he became the
father of two sons.

---

[39]This of course was not the ultimate fulfillment of the promise that Abraham would inherit the land/Kingdom forever. This will happen at the resurrection when Jesus returns (Acts 3:21, etc).

30“Forty years later, an angel[40] appeared to him in the desert of Mount
Sinai, in the flame of a burning bush. 31When Moses saw it, he was
astonished at the sight. He went closer to look, and the voice of the Lord
came to him: 32‘I am the God of your fathers, the God of Abraham, Isaac
and Jacob.’ Moses trembled and did not dare to look. 33But the Lord said
to him, ‘Take off your sandals, because the place where you are standing
is holy ground. 34I have indeed seen the oppression of My people in
Egypt, and I have heard their groaning. I have come down to rescue
them. Now come, and I will send you to Egypt.’

35“This Moses whom they refused by saying, ‘Who made you a ruler
and judge?’ is the one whom God sent as both a ruler and a deliverer,
through the angel who appeared to him in the bush. 36This Moses led
them out, performing wonders and miraculous signs[41] in Egypt, at the
Red Sea, and in the desert for forty years. 37Moses is the one who said to
the Israelites, ‘God will put on the scene of history a prophet like me
from among your brothers.’ 38Moses is the one who was in the assembly
in the desert with the angel who spoke to him on Mount Sinai. He was
with our fathers, and he received living oracles to give to you. 39Our
fathers refused to obey him, but they pushed him away and in their hearts
turned back to Egypt. 40They said to Aaron, ‘Make gods for us, who will
go before us. As for this Moses who led us out of Egypt, we do not know
what has happened to him.’ 41At that time they made a calf, and brought
a sacrifice to the idol, and celebrated what they had made with their own
hands. 42But God turned away from them and gave them over to worship
the host of heaven. As it is written in the book of the prophets: ‘It was
not to Me that you offered animals and sacrifices for those forty years in
the wilderness, was it, O house of Israel? 43You carried the tabernacle of
Moloch and the star of the god Rephan, the figures which you made to
worship. But I will send you away beyond Babylon.’

---

[40]This was evidently an angel and not an imagined pre-human Jesus. If Jesus had been alive in the OT he would not qualify as Messiah, who must be a descendant of, not older than David! Heb. 1:5, 13 explicitly and lucidly opposes the idea that the Messiah was ever an angel! The Jehovah’s Witnesses’ idea that Jesus was Michael the archangel is utterly impossible on this argument from Hebrews (and much else). Dan. 10:13 designates Michael as “*one* of the chief angel-princes,” and Jesus is absolutely not one in a class exactly like him.

[41]Jesus as the “new Moses” was also accredited by the amazing signs and wonders he performed. Jesus is also judge and savior of the world (17:30-31).

44"Our fathers had the tabernacle of testimony in the wilderness, just
as the One who spoke to Moses commanded him to make it according to
the pattern he had seen. 45Our fathers, in their turn, brought it in with
Joshua when they captured the land from the nations which God drove
out before them, until the time of David. 46David found favor in God's
sight and requested that he might build a house for the God of Jacob.
47But it was Solomon who built a house for Him. 48However the Most
High does not live in buildings made by human hands. As the prophet
said, 49'Heaven is My throne, and the earth is My footstool. What kind of
house will you build for Me?' says the Lord, 'or what place is there
where I can rest? 50Did not My hand make all these things?'

51"You stubborn people, who are uncircumcised in hearts and
hearing! You continuously resist the holy spirit, just as your fathers did!
52Which of the prophets did your fathers not persecute? They killed those
who foretold the coming of the righteous one, and now you have
betrayed and murdered him. 53You received the Law as ordained through
angels, but you did not obey it."

54When they heard this, they became infuriated and gnashed their
teeth at him in rage. 55But Stephen was full of holy spirit, and he looked
intently up to heaven and saw the glory of God, and Jesus standing at the
right hand of God.[42] 56He said, "Look, I see the heavens opened, and the
Son of Man standing at the right hand of God!" 57But they shouted and
covered their ears. All together they rushed at him, 58drove him out of the
city, and began stoning him. The witnesses placed their coats at the feet
of a young man named Saul. 59They continued to stone Stephen as he
called out, "lord Jesus, receive my spirit."[43] 60Then he fell to his knees

---

[42]Another key reference to the most important Ps. 110:1, the umbrella text over the whole NT, defining the position and status of Jesus as Messiah seated beside the One God of Israel and of Jesus. The *adoni,* my lord, of Ps. 110:1 is defined as a human being, Son of Man. This proves that the Hebrew text is precisely right and the "my lord" of the NT correctly renders the original Hebrew.

[43]This is nothing to do with an "immortal spirit" living on after Stephen died. Stephen merely committed himself to the care of Jesus. David also committed his spirit to God, when he was not dying (Ps. 31:5)! So committing the spirit is not remotely to do with passing on or "passing away" conscious to another world at death. Stephen expected to be raised from the sleep of death in the future resurrection of Jesus at his Second Coming to bring in his Kingdom on the earth.

and cried out, "lord, do not hold this sin against them!" When he had
said this, he fell asleep in death.[44]

8 1Saul fully agreed with killing Stephen. And a severe persecution
broke out that very day against the church in Jerusalem. Except for
the Apostles, they were all scattered throughout the regions of Judea and
Samaria. 2Devout men buried Stephen and lamented him loudly. 3But
Saul began to destroy the church, entering house after house and
dragging both men and women off to prison.

4Those who had been scattered went around proclaiming the Gospel-
word.[45] 5Philip went to the principal city in Samaria and proclaimed the
Messiah[46] to them. 6The crowds listened with one mind to what Philip
said, when they heard and saw the miraculous signs he was performing.
7For evil spirits, shrieking loudly, were coming out of many, and many
others who were paralyzed and lame were healed. 8So there was great joy
in that city.

9But there was a man named Simon who used to practice sorcery in
that city and amazed the people of Samaria, claiming to be some great
one. 10They all paid attention to him, from the least to the greatest, and
said, "This man is that Great Power of God." 11They listened to him
because for a long time he had amazed them with his sorceries. 12But
when they believed Philip as he was heralding the Gospel about the
Kingdom of God and the name of Jesus the Messiah, they were being

---

[44]Death is spoken of throughout the Bible as unconscious sleep. Ecc. 9:5, 10: "The dead know nothing at all…and there is no activity in Sheol ["gravedom," the world of all of the dead] where you are going." Jesus spoke of the dead Lazarus as sleeping and he intended to wake him up from death (Jn. 11:11, 14). This simple view of death was in post-biblical times replaced by the pagan notion of an immortal soul which could not die and thus must continue to remain conscious either in heaven or a torturing hell. Stephen committed himself to God as he died, and he (Stephen, not just his body!) fell asleep in the sleep of death (Ps. 13:3). Resurrection of the whole person is the only way back from death to life (Dan. 12:2, Lk. 14:14; 1 Cor. 15:23).

[45]The "word" is the Gospel of the Kingdom as defined by v. 12 and Mark 1:14-15; 2:2; Luke 8:12 with Matt. 13:19. There is only one saving Gospel for everyone, the Gospel of the Kingdom as originally preached by Jesus (Mk. 1:14-15; Heb. 2:3).

[46]"Proclaiming the Messiah" is brilliantly defined in context by v. 12, "preaching the Gospel of the Kingdom." Verse 4 describes the same activity as "preaching the word as Gospel." Thus the content of the saving Gospel is precisely defined by Luke.

baptized, both men and women.[47] 13Even Simon himself believed and
was baptized.[48] He continued on with Philip, constantly amazed at the
signs and great miracles he saw.

14When the Apostles in Jerusalem heard that Samaria had received
the Gospel-word of God, they sent Peter and John to them, 15They went
and prayed for them so that they might receive holy spirit. 16For as yet it
had not fallen on any of them; they had simply been baptized into the
name of the lord Jesus. 17Then Peter and John laid their hands on the
Samaritans, and they were receiving holy spirit. 18When Simon saw that
the spirit was given through the laying on of the Apostles' hands, he
offered them money 19and said, "Give me this authority too, so that
everyone I lay my hands on may receive holy spirit." 20But Peter said to
him, "May you and your money be destroyed, because you thought that
you could get God's gift with money! 21You have nothing to do with this
matter, because your heart is not right before God. 22Therefore repent of
this wickedness of yours, and pray to the Lord that the thought of your
heart may perhaps be forgiven. 23For I can see that you have fallen into
the bitterness of envy and the bondage of sin." 24But Simon answered,
"You pray to the Lord for me, so that none of the things which you have
said will happen to me."

25When Peter and John had solemnly testified and spoken the Gospel-
word of the Lord, they returned to Jerusalem, preaching the Gospel to
many villages of the Samaritans on the way. 26An angel of the Lord
spoke to Philip: "Get up and go south on the road which goes down from
Jerusalem to Gaza." (This is a desert road.) 27So he got up and went. And
there was a eunuch from Ethiopia, a court official under Queen Candace

---

[47]**The third Kingdom text in Acts**. This is a brilliant early creedal statement showing what was expected of believers coming to the faith. An intelligent grasp of Jesus' own Gospel of the Kingdom (Mk. 1:14-15) was needed before they were ready to be baptized in water to become officially members of the body of Messiah. Few verses in the NT summarize so lucidly how salvation was embarked on. The idea that the Gospel as preached by Jesus was different from that preached by the Apostles is exposed as nonsense by this and many other verses. The idea that NT salvation is a kind of "free ticket out of hell" is false. We have to cooperate with Jesus by obeying him. The parable of the sower lays out Jesus' own theology of evangelism.

[48]This is baptism in water of course, as commanded by Jesus in the Great Commission until the end of the age, the return of Jesus (Mt. 28:19-20). It is a matter of non-negotiable obedience to the Messiah.

of Ethiopia, who was in charge of her whole treasury. He had come up to
Jerusalem to worship. 28He was returning home, sitting in his chariot and
reading the prophet Isaiah. 29The spirit said to Philip, "Go and join that
chariot." 30So Philip ran up and heard him reading Isaiah the prophet. He
asked, "Do you understand what you are reading?" 31The man replied,
"How can I unless someone explains it to me?" And he asked Philip to
come up and sit with him. 32Now the passage of Scripture he was reading
was this: "He was led as a sheep to the slaughter. As a lamb with its
shearer is silent, so he did not open his mouth. 33In humiliation justice
was denied him. Who will tell about his descendants? For his life was
removed from the earth."

34The eunuch asked Philip, "Please tell me, who is the prophet talking
about? About himself, or someone else?" 35So Philip opened his mouth
and beginning with this Scripture, he preached the Gospel of Jesus[49] to
him. 36As they went along the road, they came to some water, and the
eunuch said, "Look, here is water! What is preventing me from being
baptized?"[50] 38He commanded the chariot to stop, and they both went
down into the water, both Philip and the eunuch, and Philip baptized
him.[51] 39When they came up out of the water the lord's spirit snatched
Philip away. The eunuch did not see him any more, but went on his way
full of joy. 40But Philip found himself at Azotus, and as he passed
through the region he kept preaching the Gospel to all the towns until he
came to Caesarea.

---

[49]In the NT this always means both the Gospel of the Kingdom as Jesus preached it and the facts about the death and resurrection of Jesus. Notice that Philip "opened his mouth," which is an idiom for speaking in a somewhat formal way, by a teacher or one in authority (see Matt. 5:2; 13:35; Acts 10:34; 18:14; Eph. 6:19; Rev. 13:6).

[50]Most manuscripts do not contain verse 37.

[51]Water baptism is of course one of the easiest and most fundamental practices of NT Christianity. It is simply a matter of obedience to Jesus, who was himself baptized and who baptized others using his agents. Water baptism is mandated in the Great Commission until the end of the age (Mt. 28:19-20). Today many decide to get rebaptized when they come to understand that God is one Person, that Jesus is the Son of God as defined by Luke 1:35 and that the Gospel involves a firm, clear belief in the Kingdom of God as well as the substitutionary death of Jesus for our sins (Mk. 10:45) and his resurrection on the Sunday following his Friday crucifixion.

9 1Saul, still breathing out threats of murder against the disciples of the
lord, went to the high priest 2and requested letters from him to the
synagogues in Damascus, so that if he found any who belonged to the
Way, either men or women, he would bring them in chains to Jerusalem.
3As Saul came near Damascus, suddenly a light from the sky flashed
around him. 4He fell to the ground and heard a voice saying to him,
"Saul, Saul, why are you persecuting me?" 5Saul asked, "Who are you,
lord?" He answered, "I am Jesus, whom you are persecuting. 6Get up and
enter the city, and then you will be told what you have to do." 7The men
traveling with Saul stood speechless, hearing the voice but seeing no
one. 8Saul got up from the ground, and though his eyes were open he
could not see anything. The men with him led him by the hand and
brought him into Damascus. 9He was without sight for three days, and
had no food or drink.

10There was a disciple in Damascus named Ananias, and the lord said
to him in a vision, "Ananias!" He responded, "Yes, lord, here I am."
11The lord said to him, "Get up and go to Straight Street and inquire at
the house of Judas for a man named Saul from Tarsus. He is praying,
12and in a vision he has seen a man named Ananias coming in and laying
his hands on him so that he might regain his sight." 13But Ananias
replied, "lord, I have heard from many people about this man, about how
much harm he did to your saints in Jerusalem. 14And here in this city he
has authority from the chief priests to put in chains all who call on your
name." 15But the lord said to him, "Go, because he is my chosen
instrument to carry my name before Gentiles and kings and Israelites.
16For I will show him how much he must suffer for my name's sake."
17So Ananias departed and entered the house. He laid his hands on Saul
and said, "Brother Saul, the lord Jesus, who appeared to you on the road
as you were coming here, has sent me so that you may regain your sight
and be filled with holy spirit." 18Immediately something like scales fell
from his eyes, and he regained his sight, and got up and was baptized.
19He ate some food and was strengthened. For several days Saul stayed
with the disciples in Damascus.

20Immediately in the synagogues he began to herald Jesus, saying,
"He is the Son of God."[52] 21All who heard him were amazed and said, "Is
this not the one who in Jerusalem destroyed those calling on this name?
And did he not come here intending to bring them in chains before the
chief priests?" 22But Saul was being filled with power, confounding the
Jews living in Damascus by proving that Jesus is the Messiah.

23After several days the Jews made a plan to kill him, 24but their plot
became known to Saul. They were also watching the city gates day and
night in order to kill him, 25but his disciples took him at night and let him
down through a hole in the wall, lowering him in a large basket.

26When Saul came to Jerusalem, he tried to associate with the
disciples, but they were all afraid of him because they did not believe
that he was a disciple. 27But Barnabas took him and brought him to the
Apostles. He explained to them how Saul had seen the lord on the road,
that Jesus had spoken to him, and how in Damascus he had spoken
boldly in the name of Jesus. 28And Saul stayed with them, associating
with them freely in Jerusalem, 29speaking out boldly in the name of the
lord. He talked and disputed with the Greek-speaking Jews, but they
were trying to kill him. 30When the brothers heard about this they brought
him down to Caesarea and sent him off to Tarsus. 31The churches
throughout Judea, Galilee, and Samaria enjoyed peace and were being
built up. As they continued in the fear of the lord and in the comfort of
the holy spirit, their numbers increased.

32As Peter was traveling around he came to the saints living in Lydda.
33There he found a man named Aeneas who had been bed-ridden for
eight years because he was paralyzed. 34Peter said to him, "Aeneas, Jesus
the Messiah heals you! Get up and make your bed!" Immediately he got
up. 35Everyone living in Lydda and Sharon saw him, and they turned to
the lord.

36In Joppa there was a disciple named Tabitha (Dorcas in Greek).
This woman's life was continually full of kind works and charity. 37At
that time she became sick and died. When they had washed her body
they laid her in an upstairs room. 38As Lydda was near Joppa, the
disciples in Joppa, hearing that Peter was in Lydda, sent two men to him

[52]Son of God is beautifully defined by Luke 1:35 as the miraculously fathered Son of God. The Son of God is of course the Messiah of Israel (Ps. 2:7-9; Mt. 16:16-18).

imploring him to come to them without delay. 39So Peter got up and went
with them. When he arrived they brought him into the upstairs room. All
the widows were standing by him weeping, and showing him all the
clothes which Dorcas used to make while she was still with them. 40But
Peter sent them all out and knelt down and prayed. Turning to the body,
he said, "Tabitha,[53] get up." She opened her eyes, and when she saw
Peter she sat up. 41He gave her his hand and raised her to her feet. Calling
the saints and widows, he presented her to them alive.[54] 42This became
known all over Joppa, and many believed in the lord. 43Peter stayed in
Joppa for many days with a tanner named Simon.

10 1There was a man in Caesarea named Cornelius, a centurion of
what was called the Italian cohort. 2He was a devout man who
feared God along with all his household, who gave gifts generously to
the needy, and who was constantly in prayer to God. 3At about 3 p.m. he
clearly saw in a vision an angel of God come in and say, "Cornelius!"
4Alarmed, Cornelius fixed his eyes on him and responded, "What is it,
lord?" He said to him, "Your prayers and your gifts to the needy have
gone up and been remembered in God's presence. 5Now send men to
Joppa, and send for a man named Simon, who is also called Peter. 6He is
staying with a tanner named Simon whose house is by the sea." 7When
the angel who had spoken to him had departed, Cornelius summoned two
of his servants and a devout soldier, one of his personal attendants. 8After
explaining everything to them he sent them to Joppa.

9The next day, as they were on their journey and nearing the city,
Peter went up on the housetop at about noon to pray. 10He became hungry
and wanted to eat, but while they were preparing food he went into a
trance. 11He saw heaven opened and descending to him something like a
large sheet let down by four corners to the earth. 12In it were all kinds of
four-footed animals, crawling creatures and birds. 13A voice came to him:
"Get up, Peter, kill and eat!" 14But Peter said, "No, lord! I have never
eaten anything unholy or unclean." 15A voice came to him again: "What

---

[53]Reminiscent of Jesus' words as he raised the little girl back to life: "Talitha koum."

[54]Reminiscent of the appearance of the risen Jesus in Acts 1:3.

God has cleansed, do not consider unclean!"[55] 16This happened three
times, and immediately the sheet was taken up into heaven.
17While Peter was at a loss to know what the vision might mean, right
then the men who had been sent by Cornelius arrived at the gate, after
asking for directions to Simon's house. 18They asked whether Simon,
also called Peter, was staying there. 19While Peter was still pondering the
vision, the spirit said to him, "Look, three men are asking for you. 20Get
up, go down and go with them without hesitation, because I have sent
them." 21So Peter went down to the men and said, "I am the one you are
looking for. Why have you come?" 22They replied, "Cornelius, a
centurion, an upright man who fears God and is well spoken of by all the
Jewish nation, was directed by a holy angel to invite you to his house
and to listen to what you have to say." 23So Peter invited them in as
guests and showed them hospitality. The next day Peter got up and went
with them, and some of the brothers from Joppa accompanied him.
24The next day they entered Caesarea. Cornelius was waiting for
them, having called together his relatives and close friends. 25When Peter
entered the house, Cornelius met him, fell at his feet and bowed down to
him. 26But Peter lifted him to his feet and said, "Stand up! I am also a
man." 27As Peter talked with him, he went in and found many others
gathered there. 28He said to them, "You yourselves know that it is
unlawful for a Jew to associate with or visit a Gentile. But God has
shown me that I should not call anyone unholy or unclean. 29That is why
I came without any objection when I was sent for. So I ask, Why did you
send for me?"
30Cornelius explained, "Four days ago to the hour, I was praying in
my house at three o'clock in the afternoon. Suddenly a man stood in
front of me in shining clothes. 31He said, 'Cornelius, your prayer has
been heard, and your gifts to the needy have been remembered before
God. 32So send someone to Joppa and invite Simon, who is also called
Peter. He is staying in the house of a tanner named Simon by the sea.'
33So I immediately sent for you, and it was kind of you to come. And so

---

[55]Jesus in Mark 7:19 was later understood to have "cleansed all foods," thus putting an end to the law of clean and unclean in Lev. 11. The social divisions caused by these temporary laws were inappropriate in the New Covenant and Paul taught the same freedom in Rom. 14:14, 20, where "all things are clean." He uses the word *katharos*, which is the exact opposite of the unclean *akathartos* foods listed in Lev. 11.

now we are all here present in the sight of God, to listen to everything
that you have been commanded by the lord to say."
34Opening his mouth, Peter began to speak: "I now truly understand
that God does not show favoritism, 35but He welcomes from every nation
the person who fears Him and does what is right. 36You know the
Gospel-word which He sent to the Israelites, proclaiming the Gospel of
peace through Jesus Messiah — he is lord of all.[56] 37And you know what
happened throughout Judea, beginning in Galilee, after the baptism
which John proclaimed — 38Jesus from Nazareth, whom God anointed
with holy spirit and with power, went around doing good and healing all
who were oppressed by the Devil, because God was with him. 39We are
witnesses of everything he did, both in Judea and in Jerusalem. They
killed him by hanging him on a cross. 40But God resurrected him on the
third day, and allowed him to be revealed, 41not to all the people, but to
eyewitnesses who were chosen ahead of time by God — to us who ate
and drank with him after he rose from the dead.[57] 42And he commanded
us to herald to the people, and to testify solemnly that this is the one
appointed by God as the judge of the living and the dead.[58] 43All the
prophets testify about him, that through his name everyone who believes
in him receives forgiveness of sins."
44While Peter was still speaking these words, the holy spirit fell on all
those who were listening to the Gospel-word.[59] 45The Jewish believers
who had come with Peter were amazed, because the gift of the holy spirit
was poured out on the Gentiles. 46For they heard them speaking foreign
languages[60] and praising God. 47Then Peter said, "Surely no one can
refuse the water for these people to be baptized, since they have received

[56]"The lord Messiah" of Luke 2:11. For "Gospel of peace" see Eph. 6:15.

[57]One of the most beautiful and convincing evidences of the resurrection, promised also for Christians when Jesus returns (1 Cor. 15:23). Christianity is based not on emotion or guesses but on the first-hand witnesses of the resurrection. It is the height of arrogance to suppose that 2,000 years later, one knows better than Luke, Paul and Peter, what actually happened!

[58]Acts 17:31 repeats this divine plan of God with equal simplicity and clarity. Note the reference to the risen Jesus as a man, in contrast to the One God.

[59]About the Kingdom of God and the things concerning Jesus, as in Acts 8:12.

[60]A supernatural gift of speaking a language they did not know, as in Acts 2. There is no reason to imagine that Luke without warning changes the meaning of "speaking in languages"! These were real languages, as also in 1 Cor. 12-14.

the holy spirit just as we did?" 48And he commanded that they be
baptized in the name of Jesus Messiah. Then they asked him to stay for a
few days.

11 1The Apostles and the brothers and sisters throughout Judea heard
that the Gentiles[61] had also received the Gospel-word of God. 2So
when Peter came up to Jerusalem, the Jewish believers challenged him:
3"You visited uncircumcised men and ate with them." 4But Peter told
them the whole story: 5"I was in the city of Joppa praying, and in a trance
I saw a vision. Something that looked like a large sheet was being let
down from heaven by its four corners, and it came down to me. 6I kept
looking intently at it and I saw four-footed animals, wild animals,
crawling creatures, and birds. 7I also heard a voice saying to me, 'Get up,
Peter; kill and eat.' 8But I said, 'No, lord! Nothing unholy or unclean has
ever entered my mouth!' 9But a voice from heaven spoke again, 'What
God has cleansed, do not consider unclean!' 10This happened three times,
and then everything was drawn up again into heaven. 11At that very
moment, three men arrived at the house where I was staying. They had
been sent from Caesarea to me. 12The spirit told me to go with them
without hesitation. These six brothers also accompanied me, and we
entered the man's house. 13He told us how he had seen an angel standing
in his house and saying, 'Send someone to Joppa and bring Simon, also
called Peter, 14who will speak words to you by which you will be saved,
you and all your household.' 15Then as I began to speak, the holy spirit
fell on them, just as on us at the beginning. 16And I remembered the
lord's word, how he used to say, 'John baptized in water, but you will be
baptized in holy spirit.'[62] 17If then God gave them the same gift as to us
after believing in the lord Jesus Messiah, who was I to stand in God's
way?" 18When the Jewish believers heard this, they fell silent, and then
glorified God, saying, "Then God has given even to the Gentiles
repentance leading to Life."

19The ones who had been scattered by the persecution following the
death of Stephen traveled as far as Phoenicia, Cyprus, and Antioch,

---

[61]That is, Gentiles, non-Jews.

[62]Note that being baptized in spirit in no way removes the obligation to undergo water baptism. To negate baptism in water would be a dangerous and direct refusal of a clear command of Jesus till the end of the age (Mt. 28:19-20).

speaking the Gospel-word to Jews only. 20But some of them, men from
Cyprus and Cyrene, came to Antioch and spoke to the Greeks also,
proclaiming the lord Jesus' Gospel. 21The hand of the lord was with
them, and a great number believed and turned to the lord. 22The report
about them came to the attention of the church in Jerusalem, and they
sent Barnabas to Antioch. 23When he arrived and saw the grace of God,
he was overjoyed. He encouraged them all to remain true and faithful to
the lord with determination. 24He was a good man, full of holy spirit and
faith. Many people were brought to the lord. 25Then Barnabas went to
Tarsus to look for Saul, 26and when he had found him he brought him to
Antioch. For a whole year they met with the church there and taught
large numbers of people. It was in Antioch that the disciples were first
called "Christians."[63]

27At that time some prophets came from Jerusalem to Antioch. 28One
of them named Agabus stood up and prophesied by the spirit that there
was about to be a terrible famine all over the inhabited world. And this
famine happened in the reign of Claudius. 29In proportion to each
disciple's ability, they decided to donate to the relief of the brothers and
sisters living in Judea. 30So they did this, sending it to the elders by the
hands of Barnabas and Saul.

12 1About that time King Herod had some members of the church
arrested to harm them. 2He had James, the brother of John,
beheaded. 3When he saw that this pleased the Jews, he arrested Peter
also. It was during the days of Unleavened Bread. 4He had Peter seized
and put in prison with four squads of four soldiers each to guard him. He
intended to bring him out for a trial before the people after the Passover.
5While Peter was kept in prison, the church was earnestly praying to God
for him.

6The very night before Herod was about to bring him out for trial,
Peter was sleeping between two soldiers, bound with two chains. Guards
at the door were keeping watch over the prison. 7Suddenly an angel of
the Lord appeared and a light shone in the cell. The angel struck Peter on
the side to wake him up and said, "Stand up quickly!" And his chains fell
off his hands. 8The angel said to him, "Put on your belt and your

---

[63]That is, Messianists, Messiah people.

sandals." He did so. The angel then said, "Put on your cloak and follow
me." 9Peter went out following him. He did not know that what the angel
was doing was real, but thought he was seeing a vision. 10When they
were past the first and second guard posts, they came to the iron gate
which leads out to the city. It opened automatically. They went out and
down one street, and immediately the angel left him. 11When Peter had
come to his senses, he said, "Now I truly understand that the lord has
sent his angel and delivered me from Herod's hand, and from everything
that the Jewish people were expecting." 12Realizing that, he went to the
house of Mary, the mother of John who was also called Mark, where
many had gathered and were praying. 13When Peter knocked at the gate,
a servant girl named Rhoda came. 14When she recognized Peter's voice,
she did not open the gate for sheer joy, but ran in and reported that Peter
was standing at the gate. 15They said to her, "You must be crazy!" But
she insisted that it was Peter. They said, "It must be his angel."[64] 16But
Peter continued knocking. When they opened the gate and saw him they
were astonished. 17He gestured to them with his hand to be silent, and
described to them how the lord had brought him out of the prison. "Pass
on this news to James and the brothers," he said. Then he left and went
to another place.

18As soon as it was day, there was great agitation among the soldiers
over what could have become of Peter. 19When Herod had a search made
for him and did not find him, he questioned the guards and commanded
that they be put to death. Then Herod went from Judea to Caesarea and
stayed there.

20Now Herod was enraged with the people of Tyre and Sidon. They
came in a united body to him, and having won over Blastus, the king's
personal aide, they asked for a reconciliation because their region
depended on the king's region for food. 21On an appointed day, Herod,
dressed in his royal clothing, sat on his judgment seat and began giving a
speech to them. 22But the crowd kept shouting, "The voice of a god and
not of a man!" 23And immediately an angel of the Lord struck Herod
down because he did not give God the glory, and he was eaten by worms
and died.

---

[64]The Jewish idea was that each person had a personal guardian angel.

24But the Gospel-word of God continued to grow and multiply.[65]
25Barnabas and Saul returned from Jerusalem when they had completed
their service, taking along with them John, who was also called Mark.

13 1In the church at Antioch there were prophets and teachers:
Barnabas, Simeon who was called Niger, Lucius from Cyrene,
Manaen, who had been brought up with Herod the tetrarch, and Saul. 2As
they were serving the Lord and fasting, the holy spirit said, "Set apart
Barnabas and Saul for the work to which I have called them." 3Then,
when they had fasted, prayed, and laid their hands on them, they sent
them out.

4So, sent by the holy spirit, Barnabas and Saul went to Seleucia and
from there they sailed to Cyprus. 5When they reached Salamis, they
proclaimed the Gospel-word of God in the Jewish synagogues. John was
with them as their assistant. 6When they had traveled through the whole
island as far as Paphos, they met a magician, a Jewish false prophet
whose name was Bar-Jesus. 7He was with the proconsul, Sergius Paulus,
who was a man of intelligence. Sergius Paulus summoned Barnabas and
Saul, desiring to hear the Gospel-word of God. 8But Elymas the magician
(that is the translation of his name) resisted them, trying to turn the
proconsul away from the faith. 9But Saul, who was also called Paul,
filled with holy spirit, fixed his eyes on him and said, 10"You son of the
Devil, full of all deceit and fraud, you enemy of all righteousness! Will
you not stop making crooked the straight ways of the Lord? 11Now look,
the hand of the Lord is on you, and you will be blind, unable to see the
sun for a time!" Immediately a mist and darkness fell on him, and he
went around trying to find people to lead him by the hand. 12When the
proconsul saw what had happened, he became a believer, astonished at
the teaching of the lord.

13Then Paul and those with him set sail from Paphos and went to
Perga in Pamphylia, but John left them and returned to Jerusalem. 14Then
they left Perga and arrived at Antioch in Pisidia. They went into the

---

[65]Repeating the illuminating pattern of Acts 8:12 which shows the constant stress on the Gospel of the Kingdom of God as preached originally by Jesus (Mk. 1:14-15; Lk. 4:43; Heb. 2:3) and then by Paul (Acts 19:8; 20:24-25; 28:23, 31). By believing the Gospel of the Kingdom we respond in obedience to Jesus' primary, summary command in Mark 1:14-15.

synagogue on the Sabbath day and sat down. 15After the reading from the
Law and the Prophets, the synagogue officials said to them: "Brothers, if
you have any word of exhortation to the people, speak to us." 16So Paul
stood up, and gesturing with his hand said, "Men of Israel, and you
Gentiles who fear God,[66] listen to me. 17The God of this people Israel
chose our fathers, and made the people increase when they were living as
resident aliens in Egypt, and with uplifted arm He brought them out of
Egypt. 18For about forty years He put up with them in the desert. 19When
He had destroyed seven nations in the land of Canaan, God gave His
people their land as an inheritance. All this was about 450 years. 20After
this He gave them judges[67] until Samuel the prophet. 21Then they asked
for a king, and God gave them Saul, son of Kish of the tribe of
Benjamin, for forty years. 22After He had removed Saul, He raised up
David, putting him on the scene to be their king. About David He
testified, 'I have found David the son of Jesse, to be a man after My own
heart, who will carry out ally My will.' 23From David's descendants,
fulfilling His promise, God has brought a Savior to Israel, Jesus. 24Before
his coming on the scene, John had first preached a baptism of repentance
to the people of Israel. 25As John was completing his work, he kept
saying, 'Who do you think I am? I am not he. But look, there is one
coming after me whose sandals I am not worthy to untie.'

26"Brothers, descendants of Abraham, and all those Gentiles among
you who fear God: to us the Gospel-word of this salvation has been sent.
27For those living in Jerusalem and their rulers, because they did not
recognize Jesus or the words of the prophets read every Sabbath, fulfilled
those words by condemning him. 28They found no reason to put him to
death, but they still asked Pilate to have him killed. 29When they had
fulfilled everything written about him, they took him down from the
cross and laid him in a tomb. 30But God raised him from the dead, 31and
he appeared over many days to those who had come with him from

---

[66]"God" in the NT is the One God of Israel and of Jesus. "God" defines the Father more than 1300 times. The definite article, "the God," specifies God as the one true God of Abraham, Isaac and Jacob.

[67]The judges were leaders and governors and are a foreshadowing of the activity to be assigned to the saints in the coming Kingdom (1 Cor. 6:2, etc). The OT is largely a book about governors and kings (Judges, 1 and 2 Samuel, 1 and 2 Kings, 1 and 2 Chronicles).

Galilee to Jerusalem, the ones who are now his witnesses to the people.
32And we bring you the Gospel of the promise made to the fathers,[68]
33which God has fulfilled to us, their children, by putting Jesus on the
scene of history. As it is written in the second Psalm, 'You are My Son;
today I have fathered you.'[69] 34And as for the fact that God resurrected
him from the dead, never to die again, He has spoken: 'I will give all of
you the holy and sure promises decreed to David.' 35And in another
psalm: 'You will not allow Your holy one to experience decay.' 36For
David, after he had served the purpose of God in his own generation, fell
asleep in death, and was laid with his fathers, and did experience decay.
37But the one whom God resurrected did not experience decay.
38Therefore, brothers, let it be known to you that through him forgiveness
of sins is proclaimed to you. 39And through him everyone who believes is
made right from all things from which you could not be made right by
the Law of Moses. 40So be careful that what is spoken about in the
prophets does not happen to you: 41'Look, you who scorn, be amazed and
die! For the work I am doing in your days you would never believe, even
if someone tells you.'"

42As Paul and Barnabas were going out of the synagogue, the people
kept begging that this topic might be preached to them the next Sabbath.
43After the meeting in the synagogue, many of the Jews and the God-
fearing Gentile proselytes followed Paul and Barnabas, who spoke to
them and urged them to continue in the grace of God.

---

[68]The Gospel of the land promise to Abraham becomes the Gospel of the Kingdom in the New Covenant. Jesus promises the land forever, in the age to come, when he returns to rule on earth. This is the substance of the Christian Gospel along of course with the facts about the death and resurrection of Jesus.

[69]This text describes the coming into existence, the begetting, fathering, in the case of Jesus by miracle (Lk. 1:35: Mt. 1:18, 20; cp. 1 Jn. 5:18 and probably Jn. 1:13: see the Jerusalem Bible translation, "who was," the Son of God, i.e. Jesus at his virginal begetting, not "who were"). Acts 13:34 describes, by contrast to v. 33, the further fact of his resurrection *from the dead.* The KJV obscures this easy fact by adding the word "again" in v. 33, leading readers to think of the resurrection in that verse. But the resurrection of Jesus is proven from the quotation in v. 34. His coming into existence in Mary is predicted by Ps. 2:7 which prophesied the begetting of the Son. This is the fulfillment of the promise in Isa. 9:6 where the child/Son will be begotten. The so-called "eternal generation" of the Son is entirely alien to the Bible.

44The following Sabbath almost the entire city gathered to hear the
Gospel-word of the Lord.[70] 45But when the Jews saw the crowds, they
were filled with jealousy and contradicted what Paul was saying by
slandering him.[71] 46Paul and Barnabas spoke out boldly: "It was
necessary that God's Gospel-word be spoken to you first. But now that
you are rejecting it and judging yourselves unworthy of the Life of the
Age to Come[72] — we are turning to the Gentiles. 47For that is what the
Lord commanded us: 'I have appointed you as a light to the Gentiles, so
that you may bring salvation to the farthest regions of the earth.'"[73]

48When the Gentiles heard this they rejoiced and gave glory to the
Gospel-word of the Lord. All who were appointed to the Life of the Age
to Come believed. 49And the Gospel-word of the Lord was spreading
throughout the region. 50But the Jews stirred up the devout and prominent
women and the leading men of the city to persecute Paul and Barnabas,
and they drove them out of that region. 51So they shook off the dust of
their feet against them and went on to Iconium. 52And the disciples were
continually filled with joy and with holy spirit.

14 1Similarly, in Iconium Paul and Barnabas spoke in the Jewish
synagogue in such a way that large numbers of both Jews and
Greeks believed.[74] 2But the Jews who refused to believe stirred up the
Gentiles and embittered their minds against the brothers. 3So Paul and
Barnabas stayed there a long time, speaking boldly for the Lord, who
testified to the Gospel-word of His grace by granting miraculous signs
and wonders to be done through them. 4But the people of the city were
split, with some siding with the Jews and some with the Apostles. 5When
some of the Gentiles and the Jews, with their rulers, made an attempt to

---

[70]As always, the Gospel of the Kingdom, the Christian Gospel.

[71]Blaspheming.

[72]Paul's statement here excludes a Calvinism which seems to eliminate human choice and free will in the acceptance of salvation. See 1 Tim. 2:4-5 to learn that "God wishes everyone to be saved and come to the knowledge of the truth, namely that there is one God, and one mediator between God and man, Messiah Jesus, himself man."

[73]A quotation from the suffering servant prophecies of Isaiah (49:6), showing that believers are part of the corporate figure which applies firstly of course to Jesus.

[74]Of course this means believing and obeying Jesus' Gospel of the Kingdom, accepting his substitutionary, sacrificial death for the sins of the world and all the teachings of Jesus summed up as the "obedience of faith" (Rom 1:5; 16:26; Heb. 5:9; Jn. 3:36, etc).

mistreat and stone them, 6Paul and Barnabas became aware of it and fled
to the cities of Lystra and Derbe in Lycaonia and the surrounding region,
7where they continued to proclaim the Gospel.[75]
8At Lystra there was a man who had no use of his feet. He had been
lame from birth and had never walked. 9He sat there listening to Paul
speak, and Paul fixed his eyes on him and saw that he had faith to be
healed. 10Paul said loudly, "Stand up on your feet!" The man leaped up
and began to walk. 11When the crowds saw what Paul had done, they
shouted in the language of Lycaonia, "The gods have taken on human
form and come down[76] to us!" 12They began calling Barnabas Zeus, and
Paul Hermes, because he was the main speaker. 13The priest of the
temple of Zeus, which was just outside the city, brought oxen and flower
wreaths to the city gates; he and the crowds wanted to offer sacrifices to
them. 14But when the Apostles Barnabas and Paul heard this, they tore
their clothes and rushed into the crowd, shouting, 15"Men, why are you
doing these things? We are human beings like you. We preach the
Gospel to you, so that you turn from these futile things to the living God
who made the sky, the earth, and the sea, and everything in them. 16In
generations gone by He allowed all the nations to follow their own ways,
17yet He never left Himself without witness, by doing what is good,
giving you rain from the sky and harvest seasons, satisfying you with
food and your hearts with gladness." 18Even by saying this they barely
managed to persuade the crowds not to offer a sacrifice to them.
19But some Jews came from Antioch and Iconium and won over the
crowds, who then stoned Paul and dragged him outside the town,
thinking that he was dead. 20But as the disciples stood around him, he got
up and entered the city. The next day he went with Barnabas to Derbe.
21After they had preached the Gospel[77] to that city and made many
disciples, they returned to Lystra, Iconium, and Antioch. 22They
strengthened the disciples and encouraged them to continue in the faith.
They said, "It is through many trials that we must enter the Kingdom of

[75]Of the Kingdom and the things concerning Jesus (Acts 8:12; Mk. 1:14-15).

[76]"Gods" coming down to the earth has some affinity with the "orthodox" doctrine of the Trinity and Incarnation. The Biblical view, however, is that God begat his Son, the Messiah in the womb of Mary (Lk. 1:35; Mt. 1:18, 20) and then commissioned him to reveal the true faith to us and also to die and be resurrected.

[77]Of the Kingdom and the things concerning Jesus Messiah (8:12).

God."[78] 23When they had appointed elders for them in every church, they
prayed and fasted and entrusted them to the lord in whom they had
believed.
24They passed through Pisidia and came to Pamphylia. 25When they
had spoken the Gospel-Word[79] in Perga, they went to Attalia. 26Then they
sailed back to Antioch, where they had been committed to the grace of
God for the work which they had now completed. 27When they arrived
and gathered the church together, they reported all the things that God
had done with them, and that He had opened a door of faith to the
Gentiles. 28They stayed there with the disciples for a long time.

15 1Some men came from Judea to Antioch and began teaching the
brothers, "Unless you are circumcised following the custom of
Moses,[80] you cannot be saved." 2Paul and Barnabas had a strong
disagreement and debate with them, so the brothers appointed Paul and
Barnabas and some others to go up to Jerusalem to talk with the Apostles
and elders about this issue. 3They were sent on their way by the church,
and they passed through Phoenicia and Samaria, reporting on the
conversion of the Gentiles. They brought great joy to all the brothers and
sisters. 4When they came to Jerusalem they were received by the church,
the Apostles, and the elders. They gave an account of everything that
God had done with them. 5But some from the sect of the Pharisees, who
had become believers, stood up and said, "It is essential to circumcise the
Gentile converts and command them to keep the Law of Moses."

---

[78]**The fourth Kingdom text in Acts.** Another golden text proving that the coming Kingdom of God on a renewed earth, with Jesus present here as ruler, is the great hope of Christianity, so very different from vague promises of "heaven when you die," about which Scripture says nothing.

[79]The word of God is of course the shorthand for "the word of the Kingdom" (Mt. 13:19), the Gospel as preached first by Jesus (Heb. 2:3) and always by the Apostles. Acts 8:12 is a constant reminder for us not to mis-define the Gospel.

[80]Exactly the same pro-Moses tendency persists in our time by the so-called Jewish roots movement, which in various ways undermines Paul's clear definition of New Covenant faith. Under the New Covenant there is no obligation for believers to keep the kosher laws of Lev. 11 and certainly no obligation to sabbath, holy day and new moon observance (Col. 2:16-17; Mt. 12:5-6). The whole book of Galatians warns about mixing Moses and Jesus, as does 2 Cor. and much of Hebrews. Christians should insist on the spiritual freedom from the letter of the law. Paul teaches this vigorously in Gal. 4 and 5, comparing the 10 commandments in the letter to Hagar and bondage.

6The Apostles and elders gathered together to consider this matter.
7After much discussion, Peter stood up and said to them, “Brothers, you
know that in the early days God made a choice among you, that through
me the Gentiles would hear the word of the Gospel[81] and believe. 8God,
who knows everyone’s thoughts, gave His approval to them by giving
them the holy spirit just as He did to us. 9He made no distinction between
us and them, by purifying their hearts by faith. 10So now why are you
testing God by putting a yoke on the neck of the disciples that neither our
forefathers nor we have been able to bear? 11But we believe that we are
being saved through the grace of the lord Jesus, just as they are.”
12Everyone kept silent as they listened to Barnabas and Paul reporting the
miraculous signs and wonders that God had done among the Gentiles
through them.

13After they had finished speaking, James replied, “Brothers, listen to
me. 14Simeon has reported how God first intervened to choose from
among the Gentiles a people for His name. 15This agrees with the words
of the prophets, as it is written: 16‘After these things I will return; I will
rebuild the royal house of David which has fallen; I will rebuild its ruins
and restore it, 17so that the rest of mankind may seek the Lord, all the
Gentiles who I have called to be Mine, 18says the Lord who makes these
things known from long ago.’ 19Therefore my judgment is this: that we
do not trouble those from among the Gentiles who are turning to God,
20but that we write to them that they abstain from things polluted by
idols, from sexual immorality, from what is strangled and from blood.
21For Moses from generations past has had in every city those who
proclaim him, since he is read out loud in the synagogues every
Sabbath.”

22Then it seemed good to the Apostles and the elders, with the whole
church, to choose men from among them and send them to Antioch with
Paul and Barnabas: Judas called Barsabbas and Silas, leaders among the
brothers. 23They sent this letter with them: “From the Apostles and
elders, your brothers, to the Gentile brothers and sisters in Antioch,
Syria, and Cilicia, greetings! 24We have heard that some of our number,
who had no instructions from us, have troubled you with their words,

---

[81]The one Gospel is always the Gospel of the Kingdom taught by Jesus (Mk. 1:14-15; Acts 8:12, etc).

unsettling you. 25It seemed good to us, having come to a unanimous
decision, to select men and send them to you with our beloved Barnabas
and Paul, 26who who have risked their lives for the name of our lord
Jesus Messiah. 27So we are sending Judas and Silas, who themselves will
also tell you the same things. 28For it seemed good to the holy spirit and
to us to lay no greater burden on you than these essential things: 29that
you abstain from meat sacrificed to idols, from blood, from things
strangled, and from sexual immorality. If you keep yourselves free from
these things, it will go well with you. Farewell."

30So when they had been sent off, they went to Antioch. Having
gathered the group of believers together, they delivered the letter. 31When
they had read it out loud, the group rejoiced over its encouragement.
32Judas and Silas, who were prophets themselves, encouraged and
strengthened the brothers with a long talk. 33After they had spent some
time there, they were sent back in peace by the believers to those who
had sent them.[82] 35But Paul and Barnabas stayed on in Antioch, teaching
and proclaiming the Gospel-word of the Lord, along with many others.

36After some days Paul said to Barnabas, "Let us return now and visit
our brothers and sisters in every town in which we proclaimed the
Gospel-word of the Lord, to see how they are." 37Barnabas wanted to
take John, who was called Mark, with them also. 38But Paul did not think
that it was a good idea to take with them someone who had left them in
Pamphylia, and had not continued with them in the work. 39The
disagreement became so sharp that they separated from each other.
Barnabas took Mark with him and sailed to Cyprus. 40But Paul chose
Silas, and as they left the brothers and sisters committed them to the
grace of the Lord. 41Paul went through Syria and Cilicia, strengthening
the churches.

16 1Paul came to Derbe and then to Lystra, where he met a disciple
named Timothy. He was the son of a Jewish woman who was a
believer, but his father was a Greek. 2The brothers at Lystra and Iconium
spoke highly of him. 3Paul wanted Timothy to travel with him, so he
took him and circumcised him because of the Jews[83] in the area, as they

---

[82]Early manuscripts do not contain verse 34.

[83]The phrase "because of the Jews" is most significant. It was for the purpose of not causing unnecessary trouble. On a later occasion when misled believers tried to insist

all knew that his father was Greek. 4As they went on their way through
the towns, they delivered the decisions from the Apostles and elders in
Jerusalem for the Gentile believers to follow. 5So the churches were
being strengthened in the faith and increasing in number daily.

6They went through the region of Phrygia and Galatia, after they
were prevented by the holy spirit from speaking the Gospel-word in the
province of Asia. 7After they went to Mysia they tried to go into
Bithynia, but the spirit of Jesus[84] did not permit them. 8So they passed by
Mysia and went to Troas. 9There Paul had a vision one night of a man
from Macedonia standing and begging him, "Come over to Macedonia
and help us!" 10When Paul had seen this vision, we[85] immediately made
every effort to go to Macedonia, concluding that God had summoned us
to proclaim the Gospel to them.

11Setting sail from Troas, we made a straight course to Samothrace,
and the next day to Neapolis, 12and from there to Philippi, a Roman
colony and a leading city in that district of Macedonia. We stayed some
days in this city. 13On the Sabbath day we went out of the city gates to
the riverside where we assumed that there would be a place of prayer.
We sat down and spoke to the women who had gathered there.

14A woman named Lydia, a seller of purple cloth from the town of
Thyatira, one who worshiped God, listened to us. The Lord opened her
mind to respond to what Paul was saying. 15After she and her household
had been baptized,[86] she urged us, "If you consider me to be a believer in
the lord, come and stay at my house." So she persuaded us.

---

on circumcision, Paul resisted them strongly and wrote an entire book on Christian freedom from the letter of the Law — Galatians. Gal. 5:1ff warns against the danger of any insistence on physical circumcision for religious purposes.

[84]The spirit of Jesus is of course the same as the holy spirit (cp. 2 Cor. 3:17) and this is the operational presence of Jesus at work in the Church. Holy spirit is equally, in other passages, the spirit of the Father, since Father and Son work in complete harmony.

[85]The "we" indicates that Luke was accompanying Paul. This proves Luke to be a most faithful and accurate witness to NT Christianity. Luke wrote slightly more of the NT than any other writer and uniquely recorded the Christian faith in his two books, Luke and Acts. Luke documented events both before and after the cross. He gave a definitive designation of Jesus as the Son of God miraculously brought into existence by God (Lk. 1:35). This text if believed would quickly unite the conflicting denominations.

[86]Baptism in water being part of essential obedience to Jesus who commanded it in the Great Commission to the end of the age (Mt. 28:19-20). Salvation is granted to those who obey Jesus (Heb. 5:9).

16As we were going to the place of prayer, we were met by a slave girl who had a spirit that enabled her to foretell the future. She brought her masters much money by fortune-telling. 17Following Paul and us, she kept crying out, "These men are servants of the Most High God, and are proclaiming to you the way of salvation!" 18She continued this for many days. Paul became very annoyed and turned and said to the spirit,[87] "I command you in the name of Jesus Messiah to come out of her!" The spirit came out that very moment.

19But when her masters saw that their source of profit was gone, they seized Paul and Silas and dragged them into the marketplace before the authorities. 20When they had brought them to the magistrates, they said, "These Jewish men are disturbing our city, 21advocating customs which it is not lawful for us Romans to accept or observe."

22The crowd joined in the attack against them. The magistrates had them stripped and beaten with rods. 23After they had beaten them severely, they threw them into prison, ordering the jailer to guard them securely. 24The jailer followed his orders. He threw them into the innermost part of the prison and secured their feet with chains.

25About midnight Paul and Silas were praying and singing hymns to God, and the other prisoners were listening to them. 26Suddenly there was a great earthquake, and the foundations of the prison were shaken. Immediately all the doors were opened and everyone's chains fell off. 27The jailer awoke, and when he saw the prison doors open he drew his sword and was about to kill himself, thinking that the prisoners had escaped. 28But Paul shouted, "Do not harm yourself — we are all here!" 29The jailer called for lights, rushed in, and fell down trembling with fear before Paul and Silas. 30He brought them out and said, "Sirs, what do I have to do to be saved?"

31They responded, "Believe in the lord Jesus,[88] and you will be saved, you and your household." 32Then they spoke the Gospel-word of the

---

[87] Showing, just as in the gospels (Lk. 4:41; Mk. 9:20, where the demon saw the child coming), that demons are supernatural evil personalities. On no account should Scripture be violated by any attempt to extract them from the historical narrative, in the interest of some modern, rationalizing tendency.

[88] Believing in the lord means believing and obeying his teachings and Gospel of the Kingdom, not just the facts about his death and resurrection which of course are also essential. Paul preached the death and the resurrection of Jesus as "among things of first

lord[89] to him and to all who were in his house. 33He took them that same
hour of the night and washed their wounds, and was immediately
baptized, he and his household. 34He brought them to his house and
served them food. The jailer and his household were full of joy because
they had come to believe in God.[90]

35When day came the magistrates sent their officers, saying, "Let
those men go." 36The jailer reported these words to Paul, saying, "The
magistrates have sent word to let you go. So then come out and go in
peace." 37But Paul said to them, "They have beaten us publicly without a
trial, and we are Roman citizens. They threw us into prison! And now
they intend to send us away secretly? No, certainly not! Let them come
themselves and bring us out!" 38The officers reported these words to the
magistrates, who were afraid when they heard that Paul and Silas were
Roman citizens, 39and they came and apologized to them. When they had
brought them out they kept begging them to depart from the city. 40So
when they had gone out of the prison they went to Lydia's house. When
they saw the brothers and sisters, they encouraged them and then
departed.

17 1When Paul and Silas had passed through Amphipolis and
Apollonia, they came to Thessalonica, where there was a Jewish
synagogue. 2As he usually did, Paul went to the Jews in the synagogue
and for three Sabbath days spoke to them from the Scriptures. 3He
explained and showed evidence that the Messiah had to suffer and rise
from the dead. He said, "This Jesus I am proclaiming to you is the
Messiah." 4Some of them were convinced and joined Paul and Silas,
along with a large number of God-fearing Gentiles and quite a few of the
leading women. 5But the other Jews became jealous and took some
wicked men loitering in the marketplace to form a mob, and set the city
in an uproar. They attacked the house of Jason and tried to bring Paul
and Silas out to the assembly. 6When they did not find them, they

---

importance" (1 Cor. 15:3), not as the whole Gospel. See also Acts 19:8; 20:24-25; 28:23, 31.

89The Gospel of the Kingdom as Jesus had always preached it.

90Not of course a vague theism, but wholehearted belief in and commitment to the Gospel of the Kingdom and everything pertaining to the lord Jesus Messiah (Acts. 8:12; Mt. 13:19; Heb. 2:3).

dragged Jason and some of the brothers before the city authorities, shouting, "These men who have stirred up rebellion all over the world have come here also. 7Jason has welcomed them, and they are all acting contrary to the decrees of Caesar, saying that there is another king, Jesus." 8So they stirred up the crowd and the city authorities. 9When the city authorities had received bail money from Jason and the others, they released them.

10The brothers immediately sent Paul and Silas by night to Berea. When they arrived they went to the Jewish synagogue. 11These people were more noble-minded than those in Thessalonica, so that they received the Gospel-word with great eagerness and examined the Scriptures every day to see whether these things were so. 12As a result many of them became believers, along with quite a few respected Greek women and men. 13But when the Jews in Thessalonica heard that the Gospel-word of God was also being proclaimed by Paul in Berea, they went there to agitate and stir up the crowds. 14Immediately the brothers sent Paul off to the coast, while Silas and Timothy remained in Berea. 15Those escorting Paul took him all the way to Athens, and then Paul told them to tell Silas and Timothy to come to him as soon as possible.

16While Paul was waiting for them in Athens, his spirit was troubled as he saw the city full of idols. 17So he spoke in the synagogue to the Jews and the God-fearing Gentiles, and in the marketplace every day with the people who happened to be there.[91] 18Some Epicurean and Stoic philosophers also were conversing with him. Some of them said, "What is this ignorant show-off trying to say?[92]" Others said, "He seems to be advocating foreign gods," because Paul was preaching Jesus and the resurrection. 19So they brought him to the Areopagus and said, "May we

---

[91]The modern equivalent of this public forum for debating and explaining the Christian faith is the internet — websites, forums, blogs, Facebook, etc. A large proportion of the world can now be reached by the miracle of technology. This makes the command in Matt. 24:14 about the Gospel of the Kingdom being announced worldwide a real possibility. As technology for translating improves, the various language barriers will be overcome. A good command of English remains a most valuable asset for all Gospel of the Kingdom preachers, and of course a thorough immersion in Scripture.

[92]Literally in the Greek, "one who picks up scraps of information." The word is *spermologos*, "seed-word person." Ironically, and I am sure Luke did not miss the humor here, Paul and Jesus were both preachers of the seed-word Gospel of the Kingdom (Lk. 8:11, Mt. 13:19; cp. 1 Pet. 1:22-25).

know what this new teaching of yours is? 20For you are bringing some astonishing things to our ears, and we want to know what they mean." 21All the Athenians and foreigners living there used to spend all their time either telling or hearing some new thing.

22So Paul stood up in the middle of the Areopagus and said, "People of Athens, I see that you are very religious in all ways. 23For as I was walking around and looking at the objects of your worship, I even found an altar with this inscription: 'To an Unknown God.' So then what you unknowingly worship I am announcing to you: 24The God who made the world and everything in it, the Lord of heaven and earth, does not live in temples made with hands. 25And He is not served by human hands as if He needed anything, since He Himself gives to everyone life and breath and all things. 26He made from one man every nation of mankind to live on the whole earth, having set their appointed times and the boundaries of their lands. 27God wanted people to seek Him, if perhaps they might reach out for Him and find Him — though He is not far from each one of us. 28For in Him we live, move, and exist. As some of your own poets have said, 'We are all his children.'[93] 29So since we are the children of God, we should not think that the Deity is like gold or silver or stone, an image designed by the skill and creativity of humans. 30So then God has overlooked the times of ignorance, but now He commands all people everywhere to repent,[94] 31because He has set a day when He will judge the world with justice through a man He has appointed, and He gave proof of this to everyone by resurrecting him from the dead."

32When they heard about the resurrection from the dead, some ridiculed him, but others said, "We want to hear more from you about this." 33So Paul left the Areopagus. 34But some people joined him and became believers, including Dionysius, who was a member of the council of the Areopagus, as well as a woman named Damaris, and others.

---

[93]It is a remarkable thing to consider that every human being is related, and we all have Adam and Eve as our parents. Imagine what the family tree of the whole human race would look like!

[94]The Calvinist idea of a limited atonement or limited call to salvation is plainly refuted by Paul's words here.

18 1After this Paul departed from Athens and went to Corinth, 2where
he met a Jew named Aquila, from Pontus. He had recently come
from Italy with his wife Priscilla, because Claudius had commanded all
the Jews to leave Rome. Paul went to see them, 3and because they
practiced the same trade, he stayed with them and worked. By trade they
were tentmakers. 4Paul spoke in the synagogue every Sabbath, trying to
persuade both Jews and Gentiles.

5When Silas and Timothy came from Macedonia, Paul devoted his
time completely to the Gospel-word, testifying to the Jews that Jesus was
the Messiah. 6When they opposed and slandered him, he shook out his
clothes in protest and said to them, "Your blood be on your own heads! I
am innocent of it. From now on I will go to the Gentiles." 7Then he
departed from the synagogue and went to the house of Titius Justus, a
God-fearing Gentile whose house was next to the synagogue. 8Crispus,
the leader of the synagogue, believed the lord with all his household.
Many of the Corinthian people heard, believed, and were baptized.[95] 9The
lord said to Paul in a vision at night, "Do not be afraid, but keep on
speaking and do not be silent, 10because I am with you, and no one will
attack and harm you, as I have many people in this city." 11So Paul lived
there for eighteen months, teaching the Gospel-word of God among
them.

12But when Gallio was the proconsul of Achaia, the Jews
unanimously made an attack on Paul and brought him before the
judgment seat. 13They said, "This man is persuading people to worship
God in a manner contrary to the Law." 14But when Paul was about to
open his mouth to respond, Gallio said to the Jews, "If it were a matter of
evil or a serious crime, I would have a reason to accept a legal complaint
from you Jews. 15But since it is a dispute about words and names and
your own Law, see to it yourselves. I refuse to be a judge of these
matters!" 16And he had them thrown out of the court. 17So they all seized
Sosthenes, the leader of the synagogue, and beat him in front of the
judgment seat, but Gallio ignored all of this.

---

[95]Baptism in water being an essential element of obedience to the Gospel. Jesus was baptized and he also baptized others (Jn. 3:26; 4:1). Peter and Paul always instructed converts to be baptized. The standard procedure followed and should still follow the example in Acts 8:12.

18Paul stayed for many days longer in Corinth and then said goodbye
to the brothers. He sailed for Syria, together with Priscilla and Aquila.
He had his head shaved in Cenchrea because he had made a vow. 19They
came to Ephesus, and Paul left them there. Then he himself entered the
synagogue and addressed the Jews. 20When they asked him to stay longer
he declined, 21but as he left them he said, "I will return to you if God
wills." Then he set sail from Ephesus.
22When he had landed at Caesarea he went and greeted the church,
and then went to Antioch. 23After spending some time there, he departed
and went through the region of Galatia and Phrygia, strengthening all the
disciples.
24A Jew named Apollos, from Alexandria, came to Ephesus. He was
an eloquent speaker and powerful in using the Scriptures. 25He had been
taught the way of the Lord, and he spoke zealously and taught accurately
the things about Jesus, although he knew only the baptism of John. 26He
began to speak boldly in the synagogue, but when Priscilla and Aquila
heard him, they took him aside and explained the way of God to him
more accurately. 27When Apollos wanted to go to Achaia, the brothers
encouraged him and wrote to the disciples to welcome him. When he
arrived he greatly helped those who had believed through grace, 28as he
powerfully refuted the Jews in public debate, showing from the
Scriptures that the Messiah was Jesus.

19 1While Apollos was in Corinth, Paul traveled through the inland
country and came to Ephesus, where he found some disciples. 2He
asked them, "Did you receive holy spirit when you believed?"[96] They
answered, "No, we have not even heard that there is holy spirit given."
3So Paul asked, "Into what then were you baptized?" They answered,
"Into John's baptism." Paul then said, 4"John baptized with a baptism of
repentance, telling people that they should believe in the one who was to
come after him — that is, in Jesus." 5When they heard this, they were
baptized into the name of the lord Jesus. 6And when Paul laid his hands

---

[96]Not "since you believed," but "when you (first) believed." There is no "second level" of Christian faith in the NT. The holy spirit is given to those who obey Jesus by hearing and obeying the Gospel (Acts 5:32; Heb. 5:9; cp. Gal. 3:2-3; the Gospel contains the spirit which must be received by the convert).

on them, the holy spirit came on them and they began to speak foreign
languages and prophesy. 7There were about twelve men in all.

8Paul entered the synagogue and spoke boldly for a period of three
months, addressing and persuading them about the Kingdom of God.[97]
9But when some stubbornly refused to believe, insulting the Way before
the people, he left them and took the disciples with him. Then he spoke
to them daily in the lecture hall of Tyrannus. 10This continued for two
years, so that all those living in the province of Asia heard the Gospel-
word of the Lord, both Jews and Gentiles.

11God worked extraordinary miracles through Paul, 12so that even
handkerchiefs or aprons were carried from his body to the sick, and their
diseases left them and the evil spirits went out of them. 13But some Jews
who were traveling around casting out demons tried to use the name of
the lord Jesus over those who had evil spirits, saying, "I solemnly
command you by Jesus whom Paul preaches." 14There were seven sons
of Sceva, a Jewish chief priest, who were doing this. 15The evil spirit
answered them, "I recognize Jesus, and I know about Paul, but who are
you?" 16And the man, in whom the evil spirit was, leapt on them,
overpowered all of them and beat them, and they fled out of that house
naked and wounded. 17This became known to everyone who lived in
Ephesus, both Jews and Gentiles. Fear fell on them all, and the name of
the lord Jesus was being honored. 18Many of those who had believed
came and confessed, openly admitting their former practices. 19And many
of those who had practiced magic brought their books and burned them
up in the sight of all. They calculated their value and found it to be
50,000 silver coins. 20So the Gospel-word of the Lord was growing
powerfully and increasing.

21After all this, Paul decided that when he had passed through
Macedonia and Achaia, he would go to Jerusalem. He said, "After I have
been there, I must also go to Rome." 22So after sending into Macedonia
two of those who helped him, Timothy and Erastus, he himself stayed for
a while in the province of Asia.

23About that time there arose a great disturbance concerning the Way.
24For a man named Demetrius, a silversmith who made silver shrines of
the goddess Artemis, was bringing in a great deal of business to himself

---

[97]**The fifth Kingdom text in Acts.**

and the other craftsmen. 25Demetrius gathered them together, along with
the workmen in similar trades, and said, "Men, you know that our wealth
depends on this business. 26And you see and hear that not only in
Ephesus, but almost throughout the whole province of Asia, this Paul has
persuaded and led away many people, by saying that the gods made with
hands are not gods at all. 27Not only is there a danger that our trade might
lose its good reputation, but also the temple of the great goddess Artemis
will be counted as nothing and her majesty lost, she whom all the
province of Asia and the world worship."

28When they heard this they were furious and began to shout, "Great
is Artemis of the Ephesians!" 29The city was filled with confusion, and
people rushed together into the amphitheater, seizing Paul's traveling
companions Gaius and Aristarchus who were from Macedonia. 30But
when Paul wanted to go in among the people, the disciples would not
allow him. 31Even some of the provincial officials, who were Paul's
friends, sent word to him and begged him not to risk entering the
amphitheater. 32Some people were shouting one thing and some another.
The crowd was in complete confusion. Most of them did not know why
they were there. 33Some of them thought Alexander was the reason,
because the Jews had pushed him to the front. Alexander gestured with
his hand and was intending to make a defense to the crowd. 34But when
they realized that he was a Jew, they all shouted in unison for about two
hours, "Great is Artemis of the Ephesians!" 35When the city clerk had
quieted the crowd down, he said, "People of Ephesus, is there anyone
who does not know that the city of the Ephesians is the guardian of the
temple of the great Artemis and of her image that fell from heaven?
36Since these are undeniable facts, you ought to be calm and do nothing
rash. 37For you have brought these men here, who are neither robbers of
temples nor blasphemers of our goddess. 38So then if Demetrius and the
craftsmen with him have a complaint against anyone, the courts are open
and there are proconsuls. Let them bring charges there. 39But if you
require anything beyond this, it will be settled in a lawful assembly.
40Indeed we are in danger of being accused of a riot because of today's
events, and there is no cause for it. We will not be able to give a single
reason for this commotion." 41After speaking these words, he dismissed
the crowd.

20 1After the uproar had stopped, Paul sent for the disciples, and after
encouraging them he said goodbye and departed for Macedonia.
2He passed through that region and spoke many encouraging words to
the believers there, and then went on to Greece. 3When he had spent
three months there, a plot was made against him by the Jews as he was
intending to set sail for Syria, so he decided to return through Macedonia
instead. 4He was accompanied by Sopater from Berea, the son of
Pyrrhus; Aristarchus and Secundus from Thessalonica; Gaius from
Derbe; Timothy; and Tychicus and Trophimus from the province of
Asia. 5These had gone on ahead and were waiting for us at Troas. 6After
the days of Unleavened Bread we sailed from Philippi, and met them
five days later in Troas, where we stayed seven days.

7On the first day of the week[98] when we gathered together to break
bread, Paul began to speak to the people, intending to depart the next
day, and continued his speech until midnight. 8There were many lamps in
the upstairs room where we were meeting. 9A young man named
Eutychus was sitting in the window and began to sink into a deep sleep.
As Paul kept on talking he was overcome by sleep and fell down from
the third floor and was picked up dead. 10But Paul went down and fell
upon him, and embracing him said, "Do not be troubled. He is still
alive." 11Paul went back upstairs, broke bread and ate, and talked with
them a long while, even until daybreak, and then he departed. 12They
took the young man home alive, and were greatly comforted.

13After going on ahead to the ship we set sail for Assos, intending to
take Paul aboard there. He had arranged this, intending to go there by
land. 14When he met us at Assos we took him aboard and went to
Mitylene. 15Sailing from there we came the next day offshore from
Chios, and the next day we approached Samos, and the following day we
arrived at Miletus. 16Paul had determined to sail past Ephesus and not
spend time in the province of Asia, because he was in a hurry to reach
Jerusalem, if possible, by the day of Pentecost.[99]

98Resurrection day after a Friday crucifixion. A suitable beginning of the new covenant, the 8th day, Sunday. In 1 Cor. 16:2, it appears that collections were made in the church treasury at meetings every Sunday, according to the personal choice of those giving (not Levitical tithing). The reason was, as Paul said, that there should be no collections when he later arrived.

99A festival would guarantee a large audience needing to hear the Gospel.

17From Miletus he sent word to Ephesus and summoned the elders of the church. 18When they came he said to them, "You yourselves know, from the first day I set foot in the province of Asia, the way I lived the whole time I was with you, 19serving the Lord with all humility, with many tears, and with the troubles brought on me by the plots of the Jews. 20I did not hold back from declaring to you anything that was profitable, teaching you publicly and from house to house. 21I testified to both Jews and Gentiles about repentance towards God and faith in our lord[100] Jesus Messiah. 22Now I am going, compelled by the spirit, to Jerusalem, not knowing what will happen to me there. 23All I know is that in every town the holy spirit testifies to me that prison and troubles await me. 24But I consider my life worth nothing to me, so that I may finish my task and the ministry which I received from the lord Jesus: to testify to the Gospel of the grace of God. 25Now I know that you all, among whom I went around heralding the Gospel of the Kingdom,[101] will see me no more. 26So then I testify to you today, I am innocent of the blood of all of you, 27because I have not held back from declaring to you the whole plan of God.[102]

28"Be alert for yourselves and for all the flock, in which the holy spirit has made you overseers, to shepherd the church of God which He acquired with the blood of His own Son. 29I know that after my departure savage wolves will come in among you, not sparing the flock. 30Even from among your own number men will arise who will pervert the truth in order to draw away the disciples after them. 31So be on guard! Do not forget that for a period of three years I never ceased to warn every one of

---

[100]It is important to remember that the constant phrase "our lord Jesus" tell us that Jesus is not here receiving the title YHVH, the sacred name. It is impossible in Hebrew to say "my YHVH" or "our YHVH." The title "lord" for Jesus is based upon the famous Ps. 110:1 where he is "my lord" (not Lord), a title (*adoni*) which is never used for Deity.

[101]**The sixth Kingdom text in Acts.** This is a fundamentally important verse for establishing the easy fact that the Gospel of the grace of God is not in any way different from the Gospel of the Kingdom, as preached by Jesus and Paul. "Preaching the Gospel of the grace of God" (v. 24) is synonymous with "announcing the Gospel of the Kingdom" (v. 25; cp. 19:8; 28:23, 30, 31).

[102]These are warning words for believers and especially teachers at all times. On no account is part of the counsel of God to be omitted or played down for reasons of popularity or pressure from others whose understanding is flawed or weak. "He who loves relatives more than me is not worthy of me," Jesus had said (Mt. 10:37).

you, night and day, with tears. 32And now I entrust you to God and to the
Gospel-word of His grace,[103] which is able to build you up and give you
the inheritance among all those who are holy. 33I have desired no one's
silver, gold or clothing. 34You yourselves know that these hands of mine
provided for my own needs, as well as the needs of those who were with
me. 35In everything I did, I showed you that laboring in this way we
ought to help the weak, and remember the words of the lord Jesus when
he himself said, 'It is more blessed to give than to receive.'"

36When he had said these things, he knelt down and prayed with them
all. 37They all wept freely and hugged Paul and kissed him. 38They were
especially sad because of what he had said about seeing him no more.
Then they accompanied him to the ship.

21 1When we had torn ourselves away from them, we set sail on a
straight course to Cos, and the next day to Rhodes and from there
to Patara. 2After finding a ship crossing over to Phoenicia, we went
aboard and set sail. 3When we had come within sight of Cyprus, leaving
it on our port side, we sailed to Syria and landed at Tyre, because the
ship was to unload her cargo there. 4Finding the disciples, we stayed
there for a week. They kept urging Paul through the spirit not to set foot
in Jerusalem. 5When our days there were over, we departed and
continued on our journey. All the believers, with wives and children,
accompanied us until we were out of the city. Kneeling down on the
beach, we prayed. After saying goodbye to each other, 6we boarded the
ship and they returned home.

7Continuing the voyage from Tyre, we arrived at Ptolemais. We
greeted the brothers and sisters and spent a day with them. 8The next day
we departed and went to Caesarea. We stayed at the house of Philip the
evangelist, who was one of the seven. 9Philip had four virgin daughters
who were prophetesses.[104] 10While we stayed there for many days, a
prophet named Agabus came from Judea. 11Coming to us and taking
Paul's belt, he bound his own hands and feet and said, "This is what the
holy spirit says: In this way the Jews in Jerusalem will bind the man who
owns this belt, and will deliver him over to the Gentiles." 12When we

---

[103]Synonymous with the Gospel of the Kingdom in v. 24-25.

[104]Not necessarily prophetesses in the predictive sense, but ladies who were thoroughly involved in the ministry of edifying and encouraging (1 Cor. 11:4-5; 14:3ff).

heard this, we and the believers there begged Paul not to go up to
Jerusalem. 13Then Paul answered, "What are you doing, weeping and
breaking my heart? For I am ready not only to be bound, but also to die
in Jerusalem for the name of the lord Jesus." 14Since we could not
persuade him, we said no more except, "The Lord's will be done."
15After these days we made preparations and started on our way to
Jerusalem. 16Some of the disciples from Caesarea also went with us,
bringing us to the house of Mnason from Cyprus, a disciple from the
early days, with whom we were going to stay.
17When we had come to Jerusalem, the brothers and sisters there gave
us a warm welcome. 18The following day Paul went with us to see James,
and all the elders were present. 19After he had greeted them, Paul
recounted in detail everything that God had done among the Gentiles
through his ministry. 20When they heard it they glorified God. Then they
said to Paul, "You see, brother, how many thousands of Jews have
become believers, and they are all zealous for the Law. 21They have been
informed about you, that you teach all the Jews living among the
Gentiles to forsake Moses, telling them not to circumcise their children
and not to follow the customs. 22What should be done then? Doubtless,
they will hear that you have come. 23So then do what we tell you: We
have four men who have taken a vow. 24Take them and purify yourself
with them, and pay their expenses to have their heads shaved. Then all
will know that there is no truth in what they have heard about you, but
that you yourself live in conformity with the Law. 25But about the
Gentiles who have believed, we have written our decision that they
should avoid meat sacrificed to idols, blood, the meat of strangled
animals, and sexual immorality." 26So Paul took the men, and the next
day purified himself with them and went into the Temple[105] and gave

---

[105]This episode suggests that Paul's understanding was more radical than James', but Paul was willing to be diplomatic on this occasion. In Galatians and Colossians the imposition of the Law of Moses in the letter on any believer was opposed by Paul, and in Rom. 14:14, 20 Paul spoke as a Jew and a Christian in a way that could not possibly mean that he was teaching the food laws of Lev. 11. Paul in Galatians speaks of circumcision in the flesh as unnecessary for Jew or Gentile (Gal. 5:2, 3, 11). He said vehemently that if anyone insisted on obeying the law of circumcision in the flesh, one would have to keep the whole Law.

notice of the completion of the days of purification, when the sacrifice
would be offered for each of them.

27When the seven days were almost completed, the Jews from the
province of Asia, seeing Paul in the Temple, stirred up the whole crowd
and laid hands on him, 28shouting, "People of Israel, help! This is the
man who is teaching everyone everywhere against our people, the Law,
and this place. And he has even brought Greeks into the inner Temple
courts and has defiled this holy place!" 29For they had seen Trophimus
the Ephesian with Paul in the city and assumed that Paul had brought
him into the inner Temple courts. 30Then the whole city was stirred up
and the people came running together. They seized Paul and dragged him
out of the Temple. Immediately the doors were shut. 31As they were
trying to kill him, a report was sent to the commander of the Roman
cohort that all Jerusalem was in an uproar. 32Instantly the commander
took soldiers and centurions and ran down to the people. When the
crowd saw the commander and the soldiers, they stopped beating Paul.
33Then the commander came up, arrested Paul, ordered him to be bound
with two chains, and asked who he was and what he had done. 34But
some of the crowd were shouting one thing and some another. When the
commander was unable to get the facts because of all the noise, he
ordered Paul to be brought into the barracks. 35When Paul came to the
stairs, he actually had to be carried by the soldiers because of the
violence of the mob, 36as a crowd was following them, shouting, "Away
with him!"

37As Paul was about to be brought into the barracks, he asked the
commander, "May I speak to you?" The commander said, "Do you speak
Greek? 38Then you are not the Egyptian who stirred up a rebellion and
led 4,000 of the 'Assassins' into the desert some time ago?" 39Paul
replied, "I am a Jew, from Tarsus in Cilicia, a citizen of a significant
city. I request permission to speak to the people." 40When the commander
had given him permission, Paul stood on the stairs and gestured with his
hand to the people. A great silence fell over them, and he addressed them
in Aramaic:

22 1"Brothers and fathers, listen to the defense which I now present to
you." 2When they heard that he was speaking to them in Aramaic,
they became even quieter. 3He continued, "I am a Jew born in Tarsus of

Cilicia, but brought up in this city. I was educated with strictness by
Gamaliel according to the Law of our forefathers, and was zealous for
God, just as you all are today. 4I persecuted this Way to the death,
chaining up and putting in prison both men and women. 5The high priest
and the whole Sanhedrin can testify to this. I received from them letters
to the brothers in Damascus, and was traveling there to arrest and bring
the prisoners in chains to Jerusalem to be punished.

6"As I was on my journey, near Damascus at about noon, suddenly a
bright light from the sky flashed all around me. 7I fell to the ground and
heard a voice say to me, 'Saul, Saul, why are you persecuting me?' 8I
answered, 'Who are you, lord?' He said to me, 'I am Jesus of Nazareth,
whom you are persecuting.' 9Those who were with me saw the light, but
they did not understand the voice speaking to me. 10I asked, 'What shall I
do, lord?' The lord said to me, 'Get up and go to Damascus. There you
will be told about everything which has been assigned for you to do.'
11Since I was unable to see because of the intensity of that light, I was led
by the hand of those who were with me, and so I came to Damascus.

12"A man named Ananias, who was devout according to the Law, and
spoken highly of by all the Jews living in Damascus, came to me. 13He
stood beside me and said, 'Brother Saul, regain your sight!' At that very
moment I looked up at him and was able to see. 14He said, 'The God of
our forefathers has selected you to know His will, to see the Righteous
One, and to hear from him. 15You will be his witness to all people of
what you have seen and heard. Now why wait? 16Get up, be baptized, and
have your sins washed away, calling on his name.'

17"When I had returned to Jerusalem, while I was praying in the
Temple, I went into a trance, 18and saw Jesus saying to me, 'Hurry! Get
out of Jerusalem quickly, because they will not accept your testimony
about me.' 19I responded, 'lord, they themselves know that I used to
imprison and beat in the synagogues those who believe in you. 20And
when Stephen your witness was murdered, I myself was standing by
approving, and guarding the coats of those who were killing him.' 21Then
he said to me, 'Go, because I am going to send you far from here to the
Gentiles.'"

22The people listened to him until he said that, but then they shouted,
"Rid the earth of this man — he should not be allowed to live!" 23As they
shouted they threw off their coats and flung dust into the air. 24The

commander ordered Paul to be brought into the barracks and interrogated
under the lash, so that he could find out why the crowd was shouting
against Paul. 25When they had stretched him out to be lashed, Paul
asked the centurion standing there on duty, "Is it lawful for you to lash
a Roman citizen who has not had a trial?" 26When the centurion
heard this, he went and reported to the commander, "What are you about
to do? This man is a Roman citizen." 27The commander came and asked
Paul, "Are you a Roman citizen?" Paul replied, "Yes." 28The commander
said, "I obtained my citizenship with a great deal of money." Paul
replied, "But I was actually born a Roman citizen." 29Immediately those
who were about to interrogate Paul by lashing stepped back from him.
The commander was afraid when he discovered that Paul was a Roman
citizen, because he had put him in chains.

30The next day, desiring to know the truth about why Paul was being
accused by the Jews, the commander released him and ordered the chief
priests and all the Sanhedrin to come together. He brought Paul and
made him stand before them.

23 1Paul looked directly at the Sanhedrin and said, "Brothers, I have
lived with a clear conscience before God to this day." 2Hearing
that, the high priest Ananias commanded those standing by Paul to strike
him on the mouth. 3Paul said to him, "God will strike you, you
whitewashed wall! Are you sitting here to judge me according to the
Law, and contrary to the Law you command me to be struck?" 4Those
standing by said, "Are you maligning God's high priest?" 5Paul
responded, "I did not realize, brothers, that he was the high priest. As it
is written, 'You are not to speak evil of a ruler of your people.'"

6Paul realized that some of the Sanhedrin were Sadducees and the
others Pharisees, and he shouted out, "Brothers, I am a Pharisee, a son of
Pharisees. I am on trial for the hope of the resurrection of the dead!"
7When he said this, an argument began between the Pharisees and
Sadducees, and the assembly was divided. 8For the Sadducees say that
there is no resurrection, nor angels, nor spirits, but the Pharisees believe
in all of these. 9The noise level rose and some of the Pharisee religious
teachers stood up and argued strongly, "We find no wrong in this man!
What if a spirit or an angel has spoken to him?" 10When the argument
became fierce, the commander, fearing that they would tear Paul to

pieces, commanded the soldiers to go and seize him away from them by
force, and bring him to the barracks.

11The following night the lord stood by Paul and said, "Do not be
afraid. As you have testified to my cause in Jerusalcm, so you must also
testify in Rome."

12When day came some of the Jews banded together and bound
themselves under an oath, swearing that they would not eat or drink until
they had killed Paul. 13More than forty people were part of this plot.
14They went to the chief priests and the elders and said, "We have put
ourselves under a solemn oath to eat or drink nothing until we have
killed Paul. 15Therefore you and the Sanhedrin inform the commander
that he should bring Paul down to you, as if you were going to examine
his case more carefully. We are ready to kill him before he gets here."

16But Paul's nephew heard about their plot and went to the barracks
and told Paul. 17Paul summoned one of the centurions and said, "Take
this young man to the commander, because he has something to tell
him." 18So the centurion took Paul's nephew and led him to the
commander and said, "The prisoner Paul summoned me and asked me to
bring this young man to you, as he has something to tell you." 19The
commander took the young man by the hand, drew him aside and asked
him privately, "What is it that you want to tell me?" 20He replied, "The
Jews have conspired to ask you to bring Paul to the council tomorrow, as
though they were going to examine his case more carefully. 21But do not
be persuaded to do this, because more than forty of them will be lying in
wait for him. They have bound themselves under an oath not to eat or
drink until they have killed him. They are ready now, just waiting for
you to agree to their request." 22The commander let the young man leave,
ordering him, "Do not tell anyone that you have reported this to me."

23Then he called in two centurions and said, "Get 200 soldiers ready
to go to Caesarea, along with 70 soldiers on horseback and 200 more
armed with spears. Have them ready to leave at nine o'clock tonight.
24Provide horses for Paul to ride to take him safely to Governor Felix."
25He wrote a letter that said: 26"From Claudius Lysias to His Excellency
Governor Felix, greetings! 27This man was seized by the Jews and was
about to be killed by them, when I came with soldiers and rescued him,
after learning that he was a Roman citizen. 28Wanting to know what their
accusations were, I took him to their council. 29I found that he was being

accused on matters concerning their law, but I found no charge worthy of
death or imprisonment. 30When I was informed that there was a plot
against this man, I sent him to you immediately, directing his accusers to
bring their charges against him before you."

31So the soldiers carried out their orders and took Paul by night to
Antipatris. 32The next day they left the horsemen to go on with him, and
they returned to the barracks. 33When the horsemen came to Caesarea
they delivered the letter to the governor and also presented Paul to him.
34When the governor had read the letter, he asked what province Paul
was from. On learning that he was from Cilicia, he said, 35"I will give
you a hearing when your accusers arrive." Then he commanded that Paul
be held under guard in Herod's palace.

24 1After five days the high priest Ananias came with some of the
elders and an attorney named Tertullus, to present their case
against Paul before the governor. 2When Paul was called, Tertullus began
his formal accusation, saying to the governor, "We are enjoying much
peace because of you, and reforms are being made in this nation because
of your foresight. 3Most Excellent Felix, we always and everywhere
acknowledge this with deepest gratitude. 4But not wanting to delay you, I
ask you in your kindness to give us a brief hearing. 5We have found this
man to be a troublemaker, an instigator of insurrections of all the Jews
all over the world. He is a ringleader of the Nazarene sect. 6He even tried
to profane the Temple, so we arrested him.[106] 8When you examine him
yourself you will find out about all these things of which we are accusing
him." 9The Jews joined in the charges, insisting that they were true.

10When the governor had gestured to him to speak, Paul replied,
"Because I know that you have been a judge of this nation for many
years, I cheerfully make my defense. 11You can verify the fact that not
more than twelve days ago I went up to Jerusalem to worship. 12My
accusers did not find me disputing with anyone or stirring up a crowd
either in the Temple courts or in the synagogues or anywhere in the city.
13And they cannot prove to you what they are accusing me of doing.
14But I confess this to you: According to the Way which they call a sect, I
serve the God of our forefathers, believing everything written in the Law

---

[106]Early manuscripts do not contain verse 7.

and the prophets. 15I have the same hope in God as they have — that
there will be a resurrection of both the just and the unjust. 16That is why I
do my best to always have a clear conscience before God and before
people. 17After some years, I came to bring gifts for the poor of my
nation and to give offerings. 18While I was doing this they found me in
the Temple, ritually purified, without any crowd or disturbance. 19But
some Jews from the province of Asia ought to be here before you, to
make an accusation if they have anything against me. 20Otherwise let
these men here say what crime I committed when I stood before the
council, 21other than this one statement that I shouted when I stood before
them: 'It is for the resurrection of the dead that I am on trial before you
today.'"

22Then Felix, who had a more accurate understanding of the Way,
adjourned the hearing and said, "When Lysias the commander comes I
will decide your case." 23He ordered the centurion to keep Paul in
custody but to let him have some freedom, and not to forbid any of
Paul's friends from serving and visiting him.

24After some days Felix came with his wife Drusilla, who was
Jewish. He sent for Paul and listened to him talk about faith in Messiah
Jesus. 25While Paul was discussing uprightness, self-control and the
coming judgment, Felix became alarmed and said, "Go now, and when it
is convenient for me I will send for you." 26He was also hoping that Paul
would give him money, so Felix sent for Paul as often as possible and
talked with him. 27After two years Felix was succeeded by Porcius
Festus. Because he wanted to do the Jews a favor, Felix left Paul in
prison.

25 1Three days after Festus had come to the province he left Caesarea
for Jerusalem. 2So the chief priests and Jewish leaders brought
formal charges against Paul to him there. 3They begged Festus as a favor
to have Paul brought to Jerusalem, because they were plotting to ambush
and kill him on the way. 4Festus replied that Paul was being kept in
custody in Caesarea and that he himself would be going there soon. 5He
said to them, "Let your leaders go with me. and if this man has
committed any crime, they may bring their accusations against him."

6When he had stayed there among them for eight or ten days, Festus
went to Caesarea. The next day he sat on the judgment seat and

commanded Paul to be brought in. 7When Paul came in, the Jews who had come from Jerusalem stood around him, bringing many serious accusations against him which they could not prove. 8Paul said in his defense, “I have done nothing against the Law of the Jews, against the Temple, or against Caesar.” 9But Festus, wanting to do the Jews a favor, asked Paul, “Are you willing to go to Jerusalem and be put on trial before me there on these charges?” 10Paul responded, “I am standing before Caesar’s judgment seat, where I ought to be tried. I have done no wrong to the Jews, as you know very well. 11If I have done wrong and committed a crime worthy of death, I am not trying to escape the death penalty. But if none of their charges against me is true, then no one can give me over to them. I appeal to Caesar!” 12Festus, after conferring with his council of advisors, responded, “You have appealed to Caesar, so to Caesar you will go!”

13After several days, King Agrippa and his sister Bernice arrived in Caesarea on an official visit to Festus. 14They stayed there several days, and Festus presented Paul’s case to the king for consideration. “There is a man left here as a prisoner by Felix,” he began. 15“When I was in Jerusalem, the Jewish chief priests and elders made accusations against him, asking for a guilty verdict. 16I replied to them that it is not the custom of the Romans to hand anyone over before he has met his accusers face to face and has had an opportunity to make his defense against the charges. 17So when his accusers came here with me, I did not delay, but the next day I sat on the judgment seat and commanded the man to be brought before me. 18When his accusers stood up they did not charge him with the wrongdoing that I expected. 19Instead they had several points of disagreement with him about their own religion, and about a dead man named Jesus who Paul said was alive. 20I was at a loss to know how to investigate these matters, and so I asked him if he was willing to go to Jerusalem to stand trial there. 21But Paul appealed that his case be tried before the emperor, so I commanded him to be kept in custody until I could send him to Caesar.” 22Agrippa said to Festus, “I would like to hear this man myself.” Felix replied, “Tomorrow you will hear him.”

23So the next day Agrippa and Bernice arrived with great pageantry at the auditorium, along with the military commanders and leading men of the city. Then Festus ordered Paul to be brought in. 24Festus said, “King

Agrippa, and all of you who are present with us, you see this man about
whom all the Jewish people petitioned me, both in Jerusalem and here in
Caesarea. They shouted that he should not be allowed to live any longer.
25But I found that he had done nothing that deserved death, and since he
appealed to His Majesty the Emperor, I determined to send him there.
26But I have nothing certain to write about him to my lord the emperor.
Therefore I have brought him before you all, and especially before you,
King Agrippa, so that after this hearing I may have something definite to
write. 27For it seems to me unreasonable to send a prisoner without
specifying the charges against him."

26 1Agrippa said to Paul, "You may speak for yourself." Then Paul
extended his hand and made his defense: 2"Regarding all these
accusations by the Jews, I consider myself fortunate, King Agrippa, that
I can make my defense before you today, 3because you are very
knowledgeable about all the Jewish customs and controversial
arguments. Therefore I request you to hear me patiently.

4"All the Jews know my way of life from my youth onwards —
beginning among my own people and then in Jerusalem. 5They have
known me in the past, and if they are willing to testify they will confirm
that I lived as a Pharisee, the strictest sect of our religion. 6Now I stand
here on trial for my hope in the promise made by God to our forefathers,
7the promise which our twelve tribes hope to reach as they earnestly
worship God night and day. It is for this hope[107] that I am being accused
by the Jews, Your Majesty! 8Why do any of you here think it is
unbelievable that God resurrects the dead?

9"I myself used to be convinced that I ought to do as much as
possible against the name and cause of Jesus from Nazareth. 10And I did
this in Jerusalem. I not only locked up many of the saints in prisons, after
I received authority from the chief priests, but also when they were being
sentenced to death I voted against them. 11I punished them often in the
synagogues and tried to make them blaspheme. Because I was extremely
enraged against them, I traveled to persecute them even in foreign cities.

---

[107]The hope of the Christian Gospel of the Kingdom that Jesus will return to the earth (Mt. 5:5; Rev. 5:10) to rule and govern with the faithful in a renewed society (Dan. 2:44; 7:14, 18, 22, 27; Mt. 19:28; Acts 3:21).

12“And so I was traveling to Damascus with the authority and
commission from the chief priests. 13About noon, Your Majesty, along
the road I saw a light from the sky, brighter than the sun, shining all
around me and those traveling with me. 14When we had all fallen to the
ground, I heard a voice speaking to me in Aramaic, ‘Saul, Saul, why are
you persecuting me? You are hurting yourself by stubbornly resisting.’
15So I asked, ‘Who are you, lord?’ The lord said, ‘I am Jesus, whom you
are persecuting. 16But get up on your feet. I have appeared to you for this
purpose: to appoint you as a servant and a witness, both of the things
which you have seen and of the things which I will reveal to you. 17I will
rescue you from your own people and from the Gentiles, to whom I am
sending you. 18You are to open their eyes so that they may turn from
darkness to light and from the domain of Satan to God, so that they may
receive forgiveness of sins and an inheritance among those who are
made holy by faith in me.’

19“Therefore, King Agrippa, I was not disobedient to this heavenly
vision, 20but I declared first to the people in Damascus, then in Jerusalem
and throughout Judea, and also to the Gentiles, that they should repent
and turn to God, doing works consistent with repentance. 21For this
reason the Jews seized me in the Temple courts and tried to kill me. 22But
God has helped me to this day, so I am standing here to testify to people
of every status, stating nothing except what the prophets and Moses said
was going to happen: 23that the Messiah would suffer, and as the first to
be resurrected from the dead he would proclaim light both to our people
and to the Gentiles.”

24As Paul was saying these things in his defense, Festus interrupted
loudly, “Paul, you have lost your mind! Your great learning is making
you insane!” 25But Paul replied, “I have not lost my mind, most excellent
Festus, but I am declaring true and reasonable words. 26For the king
knows about these things, and I am speaking openly to him. I am
convinced that none of these events has escaped his notice, because none
of it has been done in a corner. 27King Agrippa, do you believe the
prophets? I know that you do.” 28Agrippa said to Paul, “In a short time
you will persuade me to become a Christian!” 29Paul replied, “Whether it
takes a short or a long time, I pray to God that not only you, but also
everyone hearing me today, might become like me — except for these
chains!”

30The king stood up, along with the governor and Bernice, and the
others sitting with them. 31As they were leaving they said to each other,
"This man is doing nothing worthy of death or imprisonment." 32Agrippa
said to Festus, "This man could have been set free if he had not appealed
to Caesar."

27 1When it was determined that we would sail to Italy, they
transferred Paul and some other prisoners to a centurion named
Julius of the Augustan cohort. 2Boarding a ship from Adramyttium
which was going to sail to ports along the coast of the province of Asia,
we set sail. Aristarchus, a Macedonian from Thessalonica, was with us.
3The next day we stopped at Sidon. Julius treated Paul kindly and gave
him permission to go to his friends and receive their hospitality. 4Setting
out from there we sailed under the shelter of the island of Cyprus
because the wind was against us. 5When we had sailed across the sea off
Cilicia and Pamphylia, we came to Myra in Lycia. 6There the centurion
found an Alexandrian ship sailing for Italy, and he put us on board.
7After sailing slowly for many days we arrived with difficulty off
Cnidus. Because the wind did not allow us to go on, we sailed under the
shelter of the island of Crete, off Salmone. 8With difficulty we sailed
along the coast of Crete and reached a place called Fair Havens, near the
town of Lasea.

9A long time had gone by, and the voyage was now unsafe because
the fast[108] was already over. Paul warned them, 10"Men, I can see that this
voyage will end in disaster and heavy loss — not only of the cargo and
the ship, but also of our lives." 11But the centurion was more persuaded
by the captain and the owner of the ship than by what Paul said. 12As the
harbor was not fit to winter in, the majority decided to set sail from there
and see if they could reach Phoenix and spend the winter there. This was
a harbor of Crete which faced southwest and northwest.

13When a light wind began to blow from the south, thinking their plan
would work, they weighed anchor and sailed along the coast of Crete,
staying close to the shore. 14But before long a hurricane-strength wind
called a "northeaster" swept down from the island. 15The ship was caught
in it, and since she could not face the wind we gave way and allowed

---

[108]The Jewish day of atonement in the fall. Dangerous winter winds would be coming.

ourselves to be driven along. 16As we passed under the shelter of a small
island called Clauda, we were able with great difficulty to get the ship's
rowboat under control. 17After hoisting it on board, the sailors used
undergirding cables to brace the ship. Fearing that they would run
aground on the sands of Syrtis, they lowered the sea anchor and allowed
the ship to be carried along. 18The next day, because we were being so
violently beaten by the storm, they started throwing the cargo overboard.
19And on the third day, the sailors threw the ship's tackle overboard.
20For a number of days we did not see the sun nor the stars and the storm
continued to rage, until finally all hope of being saved disappeared.

21Since many of them had no desire to eat, Paul stood up among them
and said, "Men, you should have listened to me and not sailed from
Crete. Then you would have escaped this damage and loss. 22But now I
advise you to maintain your courage, because there will be no loss of
life, but only of the ship. 23For last night an angel of the God to whom I
belong and whom I worship stood by me 24and said, 'Have no fear, Paul.
You must stand before Caesar, and God has graciously given you the
lives of all those sailing with you.' 25So keep up your courage, men,
because I believe God. It will be exactly as I have been told. 26But we
must run aground on some island."

27On the fourteenth night, while we were being driven across the
Adriatic Sea, about midnight the sailors suspected that land was close by.
28When they took soundings they measured a depth of twenty fathoms,
and a little farther on they again took soundings and it was fifteen.
29Afraid that we might run aground on rocks, they let down four anchors
from the stern and wished for daylight to come. 30Then the sailors were
trying to escape secretly from the ship, and had lowered the ship's
rowboat into the sea, pretending that they were going to let down
anchors from the bow. 31But Paul said to the centurion and the soldiers,
"If these men do not remain in the ship, you yourselves cannot be
saved." 32So the soldiers cut the boat's ropes and let it drift away.

33Just before daybreak Paul urged all of them to eat something,
saying, "Today is the fourteenth day that you have been constantly on
watch and going without any food, 34so I urge you to eat something to
regain your strength. For not one of you will lose a hair of his head!"
35Then he took bread and gave thanks to God in the presence of all, and
he broke it and began to eat. 36They were all encouraged and ate also.

37There were 276 persons on the ship. 38When they had eaten enough,
they lightened the ship by throwing the grain into the sea.

39When day came they could not recognize the land, but they spotted
a bay with a sandy beach, where they decided to run the ship aground if
possible. 40So they released the anchors and left them in the sea. At the
same time they loosened the ropes holding the rudders, and hoisting the
foresail to the wind, they headed for the beach. 41But they struck a
crosscurrent and ran the ship aground. The bow stuck and could not be
moved, while the stern began to break in pieces from the beating of the
waves. 42So the soldiers planned to kill the prisoners to stop them from
swimming away and escaping. 43But the centurion wanted to save Paul
and prevented their plan. He ordered all who could swim to jump
overboard first and get to land, 44and the rest to follow, some on boards
and others on broken pieces of the ship. And in this way all were brought
safely to land.

28 1When we had been brought to safety, we learned that we were on
the island of Malta. 2The local people showed us unusual kindness.
Because of the rain and the cold, they built a fire and welcomed us all.
3When Paul gathered a bundle of sticks and put them on the fire, a
poisonous snake came out because of the heat and fastened itself on his
hand. 4When the local people saw the snake hanging from his hand, they
said to one another, "This man is undoubtedly a murderer, and though he
has escaped from the sea, the goddess Justice has not allowed him to
live!" 5But Paul shook the snake off into the fire and was not harmed.
6They were expecting that he was about to swell up or suddenly fall
down dead. But after they waited for a long time and saw nothing
unusual happen to him, they changed their minds and said he was a
god.[109]

7Nearby were fields belonging to Publius, the leading Roman official
of the island. He welcomed us and showed us hospitality for three days.
8Publius' father was sick in bed with fever and dysentery. Paul went to

---

[109]This is humorous, showing the pitiful superstition of ignorant people. Luke, recording the life of Paul so brilliantly, seems to tower above this ignorance. Paul was able to take charge of a whole ship and based on what God told him, comfort and encourage them all. Such is the power of truth and biblical wisdom.

see him, and after praying, he laid his hands on him and healed him.[110]
9After that, the rest of the sick people on the island came and were
healed. 10They honored us greatly, and as we were preparing to set sail
they provided us with everything we needed.

11After three months we set sail on a ship from Alexandria which had
wintered at the island, and which had the twin gods as its figurehead.
12We landed at Syracuse and stayed there three days. 13From there we
cast off and arrived at Rhegium. The next day a south wind began to
blow, and the following day we arrived at Puteoli. 14There we found
some brothers, and they invited us to stay a week with them. And in this
way we came to Rome. 15When the brothers from Rome heard of our
arrival, they came to meet us[111] as far as the Forum of Appius and Three
Taverns. When Paul saw them, he thanked God and was encouraged.

16When we entered Rome, Paul was allowed to live by himself, with
the soldier who was guarding him. 17Three days later Paul invited the
local Jewish leaders to come to see him. When they had assembled he
said to them, "Brothers, though I had done nothing against our people or
the customs of our forefathers, I was turned over to the Romans in
Jerusalem as a prisoner. 18The Romans held a hearing and wanted to set
me free because there was no basis for a death sentence against me. 19But
when the Jews objected to my release, I was forced to appeal to Caesar,
yet not because I had any accusation to bring against my own people.
20So then I asked to see you and speak to you, because it is for the hope
of Israel[112] that I am tied with this chain." 21They responded, "We
received no letters from Judea about you, nor did any of the brothers
there come here to report or say anything negative about you. 22But we
would like to hear what your beliefs are, because we know that this sect
is spoken against everywhere."

---

[110]This reminds us of the immediate healing by Jesus of Peter's mother-in-law's high fever in Matt. 8:14-15.

[111]They went out to meet the distinguished visitor and accompanied him to his destination. This is exactly the same procedure as in 1 Thess. 4:16-18, where Christians will be caught up (after the Great Tribulation, not before it) to meet Jesus and escort him to the earth. A further parallel is found in Matt. 25:1, 6.

[112]The Christian Gospel of the Kingdom of God to be established on earth at the Second Coming of Jesus, for which Christians must now prepare with all urgency and zeal.

23They set a day to meet with him, and then they came in even greater numbers to the place where he was staying. From morning till night Paul explained to them, solemnly testifying about the Kingdom of God[113] and trying to convince them about Jesus from both the Law of Moses and the prophets. 24Some of them were persuaded by what Paul said, but others refused to believe.[114] 25They were unable to agree among themselves and they began to leave, after Paul had spoken one final word: "The holy spirit rightly spoke through Isaiah the prophet to your forefathers: 26'Go to this people and say, "You will keep on hearing but never understand, and you will keep on looking but never see. 27For the minds of these people have become hardened, and they are barely able to hear with their ears, and they have shut their eyes tight.[115] Otherwise they might see with their eyes and hear with their ears, and understand with their minds, and turn, and I would heal them."'[116] 28So then let it be known to you that this

---

[113]**The seventh Kingdom text in Acts**. The grand climax and conclusion of Luke's marvelous account is to inform us that Paul was following exactly the same Gospel of the Kingdom preaching as Jesus. This is the task of all believers, until the end of the age (Mt. 28:19-20).

[114]Compare John 3:36, where refusal to obey Jesus and believe in him or acceptance of him by obeying him is the central question in Christian faith and salvation. Being persuaded is the same as believing and believing and obeying are inseparable. One cannot have faith or belief without obedience. Isa. 53:11 reminds us that the Messiah, God's servant makes people righteous not only by his saving death and resurrection but also by his knowledge. The same importance is attached to knowledge in Dan. 12:3, 10. "People perish for lack of knowledge" (Hos. 4:6; Isa. 5:13: "My people go into exile for lack of knowledge").

[115]This is certainly not Calvinism! The responsibility for believing the Gospel of the Kingdom rests with your human choice. We are not robots but are faced with a choice. If we close our eyes, we are responsible for the dreadful consequences of disobedience to the Gospel (Mk. 1:14-15).

[116]This is precisely the same saving Gospel as preached by Jesus and expanded in the parable of the sower. Repentance and forgiveness of sin are conditioned upon an intelligent reception of the Gospel of the Kingdom of God (Mt. 13:19; Mk. 4:11-12), abbreviated in shorthand form as "the word" often in Acts and in the parable of the sower in Matt. 13, Mark 4 and Luke 8. Luke 8:12 and Acts 8:12, easily memorized, are marvelous summary statements of the Gospel and our necessary response to that Gospel of the Kingdom, for salvation.

salvation of God[117] has been sent to the Gentiles, and they will listen to it!"[118]

30Paul stayed two full years there at his own expense, and he welcomed everyone who came to him, 31proclaiming the Gospel of the Kingdom of God and teaching about the lord Jesus Messiah with complete openness and without restriction.[119]

---

[117]God's Gospel about the Kingdom (Mk. 1:14-15; Lk. 4:43; Mt. 4:23).

[118]Early manuscripts do not contain v. 29: "When he had spoken these words, the Jews departed, in a great dispute among themselves."

[119]**The eighth Kingdom text in Acts.** Thus Paul ends where Jesus began, welcoming the people and preaching God's Gospel about the Kingdom of God. Jesus did exactly this in Luke 9:11: He "welcomed the people and spoke to them about the Kingdom of God" (cp. Heb. 2:3). For our 260 15-minute radio programs on the Kingdom of God, please go to restorationfellowship.org. There are also many articles there on the Kingdom and the Gospel.

Romans

1 1From Paul, a servant of Messiah Jesus, called to be an Apostle, set
apart for God's Gospel.[1] 2He promised this Gospel in advance
through His prophets in the Holy Scriptures,[2] 3about His Son, who came
into existence as a physical descendant of David,[3] 4and was marked out
to be the Son of God with power by his resurrection from the dead,[4]
according to the spirit of holiness, Jesus Messiah our lord.[5] 5Through him

---

[1]"God's Gospel" appears 8 times in the NT: Mk. 1:14; Rom. 1:1; 15:16 (framing the book of Romans); 2 Cor. 11:7; 1 Thess. 2:2, 8, 9; 1 Pet. 4:17. We know from Mark 1:14-15 that God's Gospel is the Gospel of the Kingdom of God as first proclaimed by Jesus. Preaching the Gospel of the Kingdom was the purpose and point of Jesus' entire work for God (Lk. 4:43 summarizes the faith of Jesus and must characterize ours also). Obedience to the words of Jesus is the fundamental point of the Christian faith (Jn. 12:44ff; 3:36; 2 Jn. 7-9; 1 Tim. 6:3; Heb. 2:3; Acts 10:36-37). Christianity did not begin at the cross or at Pentecost, but with the preaching of John the Baptist who introduced Jesus (Lk. 16:16; Jn. 1:17). Jesus was the mediator of the New Covenant, not the Law of Moses (Heb. 8:6; 9:15; 12:24; 1 Tim. 2:5).

[2]The Hebrew prophets speak constantly of restoration, salvation, peace and consolation in Jerusalem and thus of the coming Kingdom of God on earth. This is the Christian Gospel of the Kingdom as preached by Jesus and all the NT writers. Isa. 52:7 and context is a fine example of the content of the Gospel of the Kingdom, the revealed reign of God through Messiah.

[3]Paul used an unusual word to describe the origin of the Son of God and Son of David. He said that Jesus "came into existence" (*genomenon*) from the seed of David. He meant of course from the miracle God worked in Mary, who was of the seed of David. By this process Jesus was from his birth at the same time Son of God and son of Mary. He became Son of God *with power* at his resurrection. Acts 13:33 speaks of his being begotten, brought into existence, being raised up as was David in 13:22 (and the Messiah in 3:22; 7:37). 13:33 points to the moment when God fathered him in Mary. His resurrection by contrast is proven by a different OT text in Acts 13:34. The KJV is misleading in v. 33.

[4]He certainly did not first become the Son of God at his resurrection, a popular fallacy. He is named Son of God from his conception (begotten, Mt. 1:20) and he calls himself Son of God in the Gospels, frequently referring to God as his Father. Note that in this summary statement, which is decisive for Paul's understanding of Jesus, the Son of God begins, comes into existence, as the descendant of David (exactly as Mt. 1 and Lk. 1 say). He is further declared to be Son of God *with power* at the resurrection. Many readers overlook the fact that it is in Paul's definition here **the Son of God** (v. 3) whose origin is from the line of David. God became the Father of that Son by miracle in Mary. Paul knows of no eternal Son, no eternal generation.

[5]"our lord" is based on the key OT oracle defining the Messiah in relation to the Lord God. The Messiah is the *adoni*, our lord, the king of Israel. *Adoni* in all 195 occurrences

we have received grace and Apostleship, to bring about the obedience of
faith[6] among all the Gentiles for his name.[7] 6And you are included among
those invited to belong to Jesus the Messiah. 7To all of you in Rome
beloved by God and invited to be saints: Grace and peace to you from
God who is our Father and from the lord Jesus Messiah.

8First of all I thank my God through Jesus Messiah for all of you,
because your faith is being proclaimed throughout the entire world. 9God
is my witness, whom I serve in my spirit in the Gospel of His Son,[8] how
I constantly remember you, 10always requesting in my prayers that by the
will of God I may be finally enabled to visit you. 11For I long to see you
so that I may give you a spiritual blessing to strengthen you — 12that is,
we may be encouraged mutually by the other's faith, both yours and
mine. 13I want you to know, brothers and sisters, that I often have
planned to visit you, but I was prevented so far. I wanted to harvest some
spiritual fruit[9] among you also, just as among other Gentiles. 14I am
obligated to the Greeks and all the other nations, to the educated and the
uneducated. 15And that is why I am eager to proclaim the Gospel to you
also who live in Rome.

---

is never the Lord God. Luke carefully distinguishes the lord Messiah (Lk. 2:11) from the LORD's (Yahweh's) Messiah (Lk. 2:26). Elizabeth visited the "mother of my lord" in Luke 1:43 and Mary Magdalene did not know where they had put "my lord" (Jn. 20:13). Jesus is the Messiah, the Son of God (Lk. 1:35) not the Lord God, which would make the unthinkable — two who are GOD, two Gods!

[6]A critically important and useful phrase showing that faith without obedience to Jesus is not real faith. It "frames" the book of Romans and appears at the very end in 16:26. It is the constant theme of the NT.

[7]"Name" signifies all that Jesus stands for, his whole agenda and Gospel of the Kingdom preaching and teaching.

[8]The Gospel of God's Son is the Gospel of the Kingdom as preached by both Jesus and Paul (Mk. 1:14-15; Lk. 4:43; Heb. 2:3; Acts 19:8; 20:24-25; 28:23, 30, 31; Mt. 24:14). It contains the information, too, about the saving death and resurrection of Jesus. It is necessary, to avoid misunderstanding, to paraphrase the Gospel of the Son as both the Gospel he preached and the Gospel about him. See Heb. 2:3 where Jesus is the original preacher of the saving Gospel.

[9]Reminding us of the parable of the sower, where fruit is born based on the seed which is the "word of the Kingdom" (Mt. 13:19). Paul preached the same Gospel of the Kingdom as Jesus had.

16For I am not ashamed of the Gospel, because it contains the power
of God[10] leading to salvation for everyone who believes it, for Jews first
and also for Gentiles. 17In the Gospel God's way of being right is
revealed, by faith from start to finish. As it is written, "The upright will
live by faith."[11]

18For the righteous anger of God is revealed from heaven against
every form of godlessness and wickedness of people who suppress the
truth with their wickedness, 19because what can be known about God is
evident to them, since God has shown it to them. 20For since the creation
of the world, His invisible attributes of everlasting power and divine
nature are clearly seen, because they can be perceived in the things He
has made, and so people have no excuse. 21For even though they knew
God, they did not glorify Him as the God He is or thank Him, but their
arguments turned into stupidity, and their empty minds were filled with
darkness. 22They claimed to be wise but became fools, 23and exchanged
the glory of the immortal God for images looking like mortal human
beings, birds, animals, and reptiles.

24In response, God gave them over in the lusts of their hearts to
impurity, to dishonor their bodies among themselves. 25They exchanged
the truth of God for the lie, and worshiped and served creatures rather
than the One who created them, who is blessed for all ages! Amen.

26That is why God gave them over to vile passions. Their women
exchanged the natural sexual function for what is against nature. 27In the
same way the men, leaving the natural function with women, burned
with lust for each other. Men committed shameful acts with other men,
and as a result they received in themselves the just penalty of their error.

---

[10]The Gospel is what energizes (see 1 Thess. 2:13). It is the creative activity of God, God's energizing word. It functions with the energy of a life-imparting seed (Lk. 8:11). Much contemporary preaching simply ignores Jesus as the preacher of the Gospel, reducing the faith to a "gospel of sin management," gutting it and depriving it of its central content, the Kingdom. A revival will occur when we return to the Gospel preaching of Jesus about the Kingdom which is the foundation of the faith (Mk. 1:14-15). Obedience to Jesus begins with our intelligent response to Jesus in Mark 1:14-15. Equally important is our intelligent compliance with the creed of Jesus defining God as a single Lord GOD (Mk. 12:29). Jesus knew nothing of a triune God.

[11]Belief in God's revealed immortality plan found in the Gospel of the Kingdom preached first by Jesus (Heb. 2:3) and then by all the NT writers.

28Because they refused to have God in their knowledge, God gave
them over to a reprobate mind, to do things that should not be done.
29They are filled with every form of unrighteousness, wickedness, greed,
and evil. They are full of envy, murder, strife, deceit, and hatred. They
are gossips, 30slanderers, haters of God, insolent, arrogant and boastful.
They are inventors of new forms of evil. They dishonor their parents.
31They are without understanding.[12] They are promise-breakers, unloving,
and unmerciful. 32Though they know well God's sentence — that those
who practice these things deserve to die — they not only do them, but
fully approve[13] others who practice them.

2 1So then everyone who passes judgment, whoever you are, has no
defense. For by judging another you condemn yourself, because you
practice the same things. 2We know that the judgment of God is based on
truth against those who practice such things. 3Do you imagine, whoever
you are, when you judge those who do such things and yet do them
yourself, that you will escape the judgment of God? 4Or do you show
contempt for the riches of His kindness, tolerance, and patience, failing
to understand that the kindness of God is meant to lead you to
repentance? 5But because of your stubbornness and unrepentant heart,
you are storing up for yourselves anger for the day of anger, the day of
the revelation of God's just judgment.[14] 6He will repay everyone
according to their works: 7Those who by perseverance in doing what is
good seek glory, honor, and immortality, will receive the Life of the Age
to Come.[15] 8But those who are self-seeking and do not obey the truth, but

---

[12]Knowledge is an indispensable key to salvation. Isa. 53:11 states that the Messiah will "make people right through his knowledge." Isa. 5:13 and Hos. 4:6 lament the fact that people are destroyed for lack of knowledge.

[13]Applauding others who indulge in these various forms of evil conduct means guilt by association.

[14]Acts 17:31 is a definitive text, telling us that God has planned to judge the world using His agent and Son Jesus, and God has proven that He intends to do this by raising His Son from the dead.

[15]This is the biblical definition of the Christian destiny. The Bible has not a word to say about "going to heaven when you die." "'Heaven' is never in fact used in the Bible for the destination of the dying" (Dr. J.A.T. Robinson, *In the End God*, p. 104).

obey unrighteousness, will receive anger and fury.[16] 9There will be
affliction and suffering for everyone who does what is evil, the Jew first
and also the Gentile, 10but glory, honor and peace for everyone who does
what is good, the Jew first and also the Gentile. 11For with God there is
no favoritism.

12For all who have sinned[17] outside the Law will also perish without
the Law, while those who have sinned under the Law will be judged by
it. 13For it is not the hearers of the Law who are right before God, but the
doers of the Law will be declared right.[18] 14For when Gentiles[19] who do
not have the Law do by nature[20] the things of the Law, these who do not

---

[16]This foundational truth of the Gospel was expressed often by Jesus, notably in John 3:36; 12:44ff.

[17]I.e. without any of the redeeming features of those Gentiles who do at least some of the things of the law by nature. They have a sense of God and His demands by recognizing God in creation. They do "what is fitting," and not what is "against nature."

[18]In the light of the rest of Paul's teaching, he does not mean that Christianity is just a repeat of the Law of Moses. In Galatians he says that no one is made right by the law. Paul in fact distinguishes the Law of Moses from the Law of Messiah (1 Cor. 9:21; Gal. 6:2), summed up as love. The law in the spirit is the basis of Christianity and this excludes observance of the calendar of Israel (Col. 2:16-17), food laws (Rom. 14:14, 20; Mk. 7:19) and physical circumcision. Paul warns against being physically circumcised, lest one then be obligated to keep the whole law! (Gal. 5:3). In Genesis 17 by comparison every Jew and Gentile wanting to be in covenant with God had to be circumcised. This illustrates the sharp difference between the covenants. Paul teaches that mixing the law in the letter, of Moses, with the law in the spirit of Messiah is fatal. "If I still preached circumcision, why am I being persecuted?" (Gal. 5:11).

[19]That is, Gentiles, not "the Gentiles" as a whole but some Gentiles, what Jews knew as pious Gentiles.

[20]By nature, guided by conscience. These are positively not Christians of whom it would never be said that they are operating "by nature." These are people who had no contact with Israel, but lived up to such light as they had. This is a highly significant part of Paul's Gospel, and bears on the second resurrection, which is not just a mass destruction of the wicked! (see Rev. 20:12-15). Paul speaks of the wicked as acting "against nature" when they practice homosexuality. There are some Gentiles however who do have a high ethical standard, without being exposed to the true faith. "God wants all to be saved and come to the knowledge of the truth" (1 Tim. 2:4) and He did not mean just people who happened to live after the coming of Jesus! This implies logically that there must be a way for the "righteous Gentile" to be saved. To burn people up for not knowing and obeying Jesus when they clearly had no opportunity of knowing Jesus would present God as a cruel monster, rather like the appalling popular doctrine of "eternal torture" for the wicked. Those whose names are written in the book

have the Law are a law to themselves. 15They show the demands of the
Law written in their hearts, as their consciences bear witness and their
thoughts either accuse or excuse them, 16on the day when God will judge
the secrets of mankind through Messiah Jesus, according to my Gospel.[21]
17If you bear the name "Jew," rest on the Law, boast in God, 18know
His will, and approve the things that are important, being instructed from
the Law — 19and if you are confident that you yourself are a guide to the
blind, a light to those in darkness, 20an instructor of the foolish, a teacher
of "children," because you have in the Law the embodiment of
knowledge and truth — 21you who teach others, do you not teach
yourself? You who proclaim that people must not steal, do you steal?
22You who say that people must not commit adultery, do you commit
adultery? You who detest idols, do you rob temples? 23You who boast
about the Law, do you dishonor God by disobeying the Law? 24As it is
written, "The name of God is blasphemed among the Gentiles because of
you."
25For circumcision has value if you practice the Law.[22] But if you
break the Law, your circumcision has become uncircumcision. 26So then
if the uncircumcised keep the requirements of the Law, will they not be

---

of life at the second resurrection are certainly not confined to those who become converted during the millennium. Of these it would never be said that they were doing good things just "by nature." In fact they will have had the Torah of Messiah operating in them during the millennial reign.

[21]Acts 17:30-31 is the classic statement of God's intention to judge the world through the man Messiah Jesus. The proof that this is going to happen is the historical fact that God brought Jesus back to life after his crucifixion, and Peter and others "ate with him after he rose from death" (Acts 10:41). Failure to believe this witness is the culpable failure of faith in reliable testimony. Paul said that if we fail to believe in the resurrection we are implying that God and the Apostles were false witnesses, liars (1 Cor. 15:15). Zacharias was struck dumb for 9 months when he failed to believe what the angel said (Lk. 1:20).

[22]Paul's definition of Law must be understood from all he writes on that subject. He is against the Torah in the letter and tried to move people forward to a spiritual understanding of Torah — Torah in the spirit and not the letter. Circumcision and other Jewish ways of life, sabbath, holy days and food laws, are replaced by "the law of Messiah" appropriate to the New Covenant. Paul struggled to get Jews especially to see that the New Covenant is not just a repeat of the Old. Rom. 7:6 announces the new principle of spirit as distinct from the letter.

regarded as circumcised?[23] 27And those who are physically
uncircumcised but keep the Law will judge you who, though having the
letter of the Law and circumcision, break the Law. 28For a person is not a
Jew who is one on the outside, and true circumcision is not external and
physical, 29but a person is a Jew who is one on the inside, and true
circumcision is of the heart — in the spirit, not in the letter.[24] This
person's praise comes not from people but from God.

3 1So then what advantage does the Jew have? Or what profit is there in
circumcision? 2Much, in many ways! First of all, the Jews were
entrusted with God's oracles.[25] 3But what if some of them did not
believe? Will their lack of faith negate the faithfulness of God?
4Absolutely not! Let God be proved true even if every human being is
proved a liar. As it is written, "so that You will be found right in Your
words, and triumph when You are criticized."

5But if our unrighteousness shows the righteousness of God, what
can we say? Is the God who inflicts His anger on us unjust? (I am
speaking from a human perspective.) 6Absolutely not! For how then
could God judge the world? 7For if through my lie God's truth increases
to His glory, why am I still being condemnded as a sinner? 8Why not, as
we are slanderously reported to say, "Let us do evil so that good may
result"? Those who say this deserve to be condemned.[26]

9So then, are we Jews better than others? No, in no way! We already
charged that both Jews and Gentiles are all under sin. 10As it is written,
"There is no one who is righteous, not one. 11There is no one who

---

[23]One of the great Pauline themes of the New Covenant is to show that the law of Messiah is in the spirit and not the letter. Gen. 17 mandates obligatory physical circumcision equally for both Jews and Gentiles. Paul reverses that by making circumcision a matter of the heart, not in the letter and the flesh. Paul spoke as the Apostolic emissary of Jesus.

[24]The distinction between the spirit of the Law and the letter of the Law is the essential key to understanding how Paul can appear to be both pro-Law and anti-Law. The same distinction appears in 7:6. Sabbath and the whole calendar in the letter are a mere shadow of the Messiah who has come (Col. 2:16-17). In the same context in Col. 2:11 circumcision in the letter has been replaced by circumcision in the spirit, of the heart.

[25]Scripture as defined by Jesus in Luke 24:44. In the NT Peter treats Paul's writings as Scripture (2 Pet. 3:16). Luke 10:7 is also called Scripture in 1 Tim. 5:18.

[26]That is, they have a plainly silly argument!

understands; there is no one who seeks God. 12They have all gone astray;
they have together become useless. There is no one who does good, not a
single one. 13Their throats are like open tombs; with their tongues they
deceive; the poison of snakes is in their lips. 14Their mouths are full of
cursing and bitterness; 15their feet are swift to shed blood. 16Destruction
and misery are in their ways, 17and the way of peace they have never
known. 18There is no fear of God before their eyes."

19Now we know that whatever the Law says, it speaks to those who
are under the Law, so that every mouth may be shut, and the whole
world may be held accountable to God. 20For by the works of the Law no
one will be made right in His sight, because through the Law comes the
knowledge of sin.

21But now, apart from the Law, God's way of being right has been
revealed, attested by the Law and the Prophets. 22That is, God's way of
being right is through the faith of Jesus Messiah[27] for everyone who
believes, and there is no distinction. 23For all have sinned and fall short of
the glory of God. 24We are all made right freely by His grace[28] through
the redemption that is in Messiah Jesus.[29] 25God displayed him publicly
as the atoning sacrifice by his blood,[30] effective through faith. This was
to demonstrate His righteousness, because in His forbearance God
passed over prior sins. 26And He demonstrates His righteousness at this

---

[27]"The faith of Jesus" means everything believed and taught by Jesus. See the same phrase in v. 26; Gal. 2:16, 20: 3:22; Eph. 3:12; Phil. 3:9; Rev. 14:12 (cp. 4:16: "the faith of Abraham"). Jesus is the model Christian and we are to believe what he believed. Start with Mark 1:14-15 for the entry point into Christ-like faith. Also, for the right definition of God, start with Mark 12:28-34.

[28]It is important always to remember that the Gospel of the grace of God is synonymous with the Gospel of the Kingdom. Acts 20:24-25 could if intelligently believed correct a whole systematically mistaken evangelicalism.

[29]Isa. 53:11 should be kept in mind at all times, since it bases our "being made right with God" on the Messiah's **knowledge** and not on his death and resurrection alone. "By his knowledge my righteous servant will make people right [righteous]." So also in Dan. 12:3. People are destroyed and even exiled for lack of knowledge (Hos. 4:6; Isa. 5:13).

[30]The blood of Messiah is the key factor in the official ratification of the New Covenant, which is based on the words of Jesus. All covenants are sealed with blood. The terms of the New Covenant are the Law of Messiah (1 Cor. 9:20; Gal. 6:2).

present time, that He is right, and He makes right those who have the
faith of Jesus.[31]

27Where then is boasting? There is no place for it. By what kind of
law? Of works? No, but by the law of faith. 28For we maintain that
people are made right by faith[32] and not by works of the Law. 29Or is God
the God of Jews only?[33] Is He not the God of Gentiles also?[34] Yes, of
Gentiles also, 30because God is only one Person,[35] and He will make the
circumcised right by faith and the uncircumcised right through the same
faith. 31Are we then negating the Law by faith? Absolutely not! No, we
are upholding the Law.

4 1What then shall we say that Abraham,[36] our physical ancestor, has
discovered? 2If Abraham was made right by his works, he has
something to boast about, but not before God. 3What does Scripture say?
"Abraham believed God,[37] and it was credited to him as making him

---

[31]NT faith in Messiah entails not just believing in him but believing what he believed and taught (Heb. 5:9; 2 Jn. 7-9; 1 Tim. 6:3; Jn. 3:36). It is "the faith of Jesus" as well as "faith in Jesus" (see 3:22; cp. 4:16: "the faith of Abraham").

[32]The basic principle of "obedient faith" frames the book of Romans (1:5; 16:26) and is repeated throughout the NT. Note especially Heb. 5:9 which makes salvation depend directly on obeying Jesus. Jesus stated this in clear terms everywhere in the gospels and succinctly in John 3:36 and 12:44ff.

[33]As defined by Jesus in agreement with a Jew in Mark 12:29: "The Lord our God is one Lord" — certainly not two or three lords!

[34]The tragedy of Christianity is that its definition of God is different from Jesus' own definition of God given as the most important of all truths in Mark 12:29 and John 17:3, etc.

[35]God is one, *eis* in Greek. In the masculine gender this is the equivalent in English of "one person." Dr. James Dunn's remark is highly revealing: "'God is one' is certainly intended as an evocation of the basic creed of Jewish monotheism: 'The Lord our God is one Lord' (Deut. 6:4); Paul takes it up again in 1 Cor. 8:6; cp. Mark 12:29 = Deut. 6:4; James 2:19: 'God is one'" (*Word Biblical Commentary, Romans 1-8*, p. 189). Dunn apparently sees no difficulty with the fact that this admitted Jewish monotheism is not that of the Church. How is it that the Church has abandoned the Jewish, unitary, non-Trinitarian monotheism of Israel and of Jesus?

[36]Abraham is the model of this new scheme of obedient faith in Messiah. Abraham is thus rightly the "father of the faithful" and true faith is called in 4:16 "the faith of Abraham."

right.” 4Now to a person who works, his wage is not credited as a
gracious gift, but as his due. 5But to a person who does not work, but
believes in the One who makes the ungodly right, his faith is credited as
making him right. 6David also speaks of the blessing on the person
whom God credits as right apart from works: 7“Blessed are those whose
iniquities are forgiven, whose sins are covered. 8Blessed is the one whom
the Lord will by no means charge with sin.”

9So is this blessing for the circumcised, or for the uncircumcised
also? We have just said that faith was credited to Abraham as making
him right.[38] 10When was it credited? When Abraham was circumcised or
uncircumcised? Not while he was circumcised, but while he was still
uncircumcised! 11He received the sign of circumcision as a seal of being
made right by the faith which he had while he was still uncircumcised.
The purpose was that he would be the father of all the uncircumcised[39]
who believe, and thus being right is credited to them. 12He is also the
father of the circumcised, who are not just circumcised but who also
follow in the steps of the faith our father Abraham had while he was still
uncircumcised.

13For the promise to Abraham and to his descendants that he would
inherit the world[40] was not through the Law, but through being made
right by believing.[41] 14If the heirs[42] are those who follow the Law, then

---

[37]Cp. beginning our Christian life by obeying Jesus’ command to us to “believe the Gospel” about the Kingdom (Mk. 1:14-15). That is where the faith begins — with the words of Jesus (Heb. 2:3).

[38]Abraham responded in obedient faith to God’s invitation that he leave the things nearest and dearest to him —country and family — and go in faith to a land he had not seen. This is exactly the challenge of Jesus to us all, when he summons us to believe the Gospel of the Kingdom of God, and give up all in pursuit of the goal of the Kingdom, inheriting the land/earth (Mt. 5:5; Rev. 5:10).

[39]That is, they are not circumcised in the flesh.

[40]Certainly there is no promise here, or elsewhere, about going as a disembodied soul to heaven, or indeed ever about “heaven” as the reward. The promise is the inheritance of the world, exactly as Jesus promised the meek that they “will inherit the earth” (Mt. 5:5). This will happen when Jesus returns to rule on the earth (Rev. 5:10).

[41]Abraham’s initial obedient faith is recorded in Gen. 12:1-4. This is a model of Christian faith in the Gospel of the Kingdom as preached first by Jesus (Mk. 1:14-15).

[42]Heirs of the world (v. 13), the promise of the Kingdom or the earth, as promised by Jesus (Mt. 5:5; Rev. 5:10). Cp. Ps. 2:8; Isa. 9:7; 1 Cor. 3:21-22.

belief is made void and the promise is negated. 15For the Law brings about God's anger, but where there is no law, there is no violation of it.

16That is why inheriting the promise is based on belief,[43] so that it may rest on grace, and that way the promise will be guaranteed to all the descendants, not only to those who are of the Law, but also to those who are of the faith of Abraham, who is the spiritual father of us all.[44] 17As it is written, "I have made you the father of many nations." This was in the presence of the God he believed, who gives life to the dead and calls things that are not as though they already are.[45] 18Abraham hoped against hope and believed, and as a result he became the father of many nations, as had been promised: "So countless your descendants will be!" 19His faith never became weak even though he considered his own body which was already worn out (he was about a hundred years old), and the deadness of Sarah's womb. 20Nevertheless, looking to the promise of God, he did not waver through unbelief, but grew strong in belief, giving glory to God. 21He was fully convinced that what God had promised He was able to do. 22So that belief was credited to him as making him right. 23The statement "it was credited to him" was not written for Abraham's sake alone, 24but also for our sake, to whom it will be credited, we who believe the One who raised Jesus our lord from the dead. 25Jesus was delivered over for our sins, and was resurrected to make us right.

---

[43]Starting with Jesus' first summary command that we are to "repent and believe God's Gospel about the Kingdom" (Mk. 1:14-15).

[44]Again this shows that Christianity cannot be understood apart from a grasp of the faith and obedience of Abraham.

[45]This text gives the important principle of the "past tense of prophecy," by which God speaks of some events as past although they are predictions of the future. Thus "Unto us a child was born; unto us a Son was given" (Isa. 9:6). The sense is of course that the child/Son will be given *by God.* Heb. 2:8 says that "all things **have been put** under the control of man…yet we do not yet see all things under man." Jesus in John 17:5 spoke of receiving at the end of his ministry the glory which he "had" with God before the foundation of the world. In the same context that same glory "had already been given" to disciples not yet born! (17:22, 24). Paul can say that "we have" a glorified body (2 Cor. 5:1) but he means that it is promised to us by God for the future. Jesus spoke of us "having" (present tense) no reward with God if we pray in the wrong manner (Mt. 6:1). Rewards are promised to us, as they were to Jesus. They are said to be "with God," stored up with Him to be bestowed in the future. Thus Jesus asked as his reward the glory which he "had with God," i.e. promised by God, existing in promise and prospect (Jn. 17:5).

5 1So then, having been made right by belief,[46] we now have peace with
God through our lord Jesus Messiah. 2It is through Jesus that we have
our access by belief into this grace in which we now stand, and we
rejoice in the hope of the glory of God.[47] 3Not only this, but we are also
rejoicing in our sufferings, knowing that suffering produces
perseverance. 4Perseverance in turn produces proven character, and
proven character, hope. 5And hope will not disappoint us, because the
love of God has been poured out into our hearts through the holy spirit
which was given to us.[48]

6For while we were still powerless, at the right time Messiah died[49]
for the ungodly. 7Hardly anyone would die for even an upright person,
though perhaps for a good person someone might possibly dare to die.
8But God demonstrates His own love for us in this way: while we were
still sinners, Messiah died for us. 9Much more then, being now made
right by his blood,[50] we will be saved through him from God's anger.
10For if while we were His enemies we were reconciled to God through
the death of His Son; much more now, having been reconciled, we will
be saved by the life of His Son. 11Not only this, but we also rejoice in
God through our lord Jesus Messiah, through whom we have now
received this reconciliation.

12So then, just as sin entered the world through one man, and death
through sin, death came to all people because all sinned. 13For before the

---

[46]That is by obedient faith, obeying and believing Jesus. Hence Paul's key phrase in 1:5 and 16:26: "the obedience of faith." Heb. 5:9 should be consulted continuously, since it links obedience to salvation.

[47]The Kingdom of God, to appear at the 7th trumpet when Jesus returns (Rev. 11:15-18; 5:9-10; Mt. 5:5).

[48]1 Cor. 12:13 is the key verse showing that the spirit is received at baptism into the body of Christ. It is never a "second level" which only certain believers attain to (the notion that speaking in languages is the chief sign of having received the spirit is false). The situation in Acts 8:14-16 is not the NT pattern. In that passage only Apostles from Jerusalem could bring the spirit to them. This is impossible today.

[49]The idea of "GOD dying" should appear impossible and alien to readers of the NT! Jesus as Son of God died (v. 10), and Jesus the Son must have been mortal. God cannot die: He is immortal (1 Tim. 6:16).

[50]The death of Jesus not only provides an atonement for our sins, it also inaugurates the New Covenant, ratified in Messiah's blood, and this covenant offers us rulership in the Kingdom to come (Lk. 22:28-30).

Law sin was in the world, but sin is not charged when there is no law.
14But death reigned from Adam until Moses, even over those whose sins
were not like Adam's disobedience. Adam is[51] a shadow of the one who
was to come.

15But the gracious gift is not like the sin. For if through the sin of the
one man many died, much more did the grace of God and the gift by the
grace of the one man, Jesus Messiah, multiply to many! 16And the gift is
different from the effect of Adam's sin. For judgment after one sin led to
condemnation, but the free gift after many sins led to us being made
right. 17For if as a result of one man's sin, death reigned through that one
man, so how much more will those who receive the abundance of grace
and the gift of being made right reign in Life[52] through the one man,
Jesus Messiah!

18In conclusion then, just as through one sin all were condemned, in
the same way through one right act all may be made right leading to
Life. 19Just as through one man's disobedience many were made sinners,
in the same way through one man's[53] obedience many will be made right.
20The Law entered in to increase sin, but where sin increased grace
multiplied much more. 21So just as sin reigned, meaning death for us,
grace will reign, making us right with God, leading to the Life of the Age
to Come through Jesus Messiah our lord.[54]

---

[51]Literally "Adam *is* a type of the one to come." The sense in English is that Adam was a direct parallel of the one to come. In the same way in Col. 2:17 the Jewish calendar *is* a shadow of what was to come (and has now come). The sense as in Romans is that the calendar *was* only a shadow of the Messiah who has now come. The calendar shadow is now superseded. Adam and Jesus are equally human beings, which is untrue if Jesus had an origin outside the human race. Jesus is "the second man" (1 Cor. 15:47) and "the last Adam" (15:45). Paul is keen to tell us that Jesus did not precede Adam, but the other way round (1 Cor. 15:45-47).

[52]This is a central doctrine of the Gospel that we will reign as kings with Messiah in the Kingdom to be established on earth when Jesus comes back (Dan. 2:44; 7:14, 18, 22, 27; Mt. 19:28; Lk. 19:17; 1 Cor. 6:2; 2 Tim. 2:12; Rev. 2:26; 3:21, 5:10; 20:1-6). Cp. Wisdom of Solomon 3:8; 5:15-16.

[53]The parallel between Adam and Jesus, both human beings, is inescapable. The post-biblical equating of Jesus with a preexisting Deity spoiled the simplicity of the divine program, obscuring monotheism and the human Messiah, the second Adam.

[54]Reflecting, as must be continuously stressed, the "my lord" (*adoni*, 195 times never a title of Deity) of Ps. 110:1. It is the umbrella text over the whole NT and defines Jesus as the human king Messiah (Lk. 2:11). Cp. 1 Tim. 2:5 which confirms this in an easy

6 1What are we to say then? Should we continue in sin so that grace may increase? 2Absolutely not! How could we who died to sin still live in it? 3Do you not understand that all of us who were baptized[55] into Messiah Jesus were baptized into his death? 4So then we were buried with him through baptism into death, so that just as Messiah was resurrected from the dead through the glory of the Father, we also can live a new life. 5For if we have become one with him in a death like his, then certainly we will be in a resurrection like his. 6We know that our old self was crucified with him, so that the body of sin might be abolished, and we would no longer be in slavery to sin. 7For one who has died has been freed from sin.

8If we died with Messiah, we believe that we will also live with him. 9We know that Messiah, having been resurrected from the dead, will never die again. Death no longer has any power over him. 10For the death he died, he died to sin once and for all, but the life he lives, he lives to God. 11So too consider yourselves dead to sin, but alive to God in Messiah Jesus.

12So do not let sin reign in your mortal body, so that you obey its lusts, 13and do not present any parts of yourself to sin as tools for evil. Instead present yourselves to God as alive from the dead, and the parts of yourself as tools for what is right. 14For sin is not to have mastery over you, because you are not under law but under grace.

15So then, does that mean we are to sin because we are not under law but under grace? Absolutely not! 16Do you not understand that when you present yourselves as servants and obey someone, you are the servants of the one you obey? If you are servants of sin, it leads to death; if you are servants of obedience, it leads to being right. 17But thanks be to God that although you used to be servants of sin, you then became obedient from the heart to that pattern of teaching in which you were instructed. 18Having been set free from sin, you became servants of what is right. 19I am using a human illustration because of the weakness of your human nature. For just as you presented yourselves as servants to impurity and

---

creedal statement, and John 17:3 where the Messiah is distinct from the Father who is "the only one who is true God" (cp. Mk. 12:29).

[55]Water baptism is the NT public demonstration of our intended commitment to faith in Messiah Jesus, and the Gospel he preached (Heb. 2:3; Lk. 4:43; 9:11).

wickedness, leading to more wickedness, so now present yourselves as
servants to what is right, leading to being holy.

20For when you were servants of sin, you were free in relation to what
is right. 21What fruit did you have at that time from the things of which
you are now ashamed? For the result of those things is death. 22But now,
since you have been set free from sin and have become servants of God,
you have your fruit in becoming holy, and the final result is the Life of
the Age to Come.[56] 23For the final result of sin is death, but the gift of
God is the Life of the Age to Come in Messiah Jesus our lord.

7 1Do you not understand, brothers and sisters (for I am speaking to
people who know the Law), that the Law has authority over people
only for as long as they live? 2For instance, a married woman is bound
by the Law to her husband as long as he lives, but if her husband dies,
she is freed from that marriage law. 3So then, if while her husband is
alive she is joined to another man, she would rightly be called an
adulteress. But if her husband dies she is free from that law, and if she
marries another man, she would not be guilty of adultery.

4So, my brothers and sisters, you also died to the Law through the
body of Messiah, so that you could be joined to another, to the one who
was resurrected from the dead, in order that we would produce fruit for
God.[57] 5For when we were under the power of human nature, the sinful
passions aroused by the Law worked in every part of us to produce fruit
to death. 6But now we have been freed from the Law, because we have

---

[56]In the future Kingdom of God on earth when Jesus comes — certainly not in an imagined post-death experience in "heaven." The life of that future age (wrongly translated "eternal life" but corrected to "the life of the age to come" in N.T. Wright's *Kingdom New Testament*) is experienced *now* in advance through the spirit given to Christians, as a foretaste and downpayment of the future Kingdom.

[57]That productive life would include making disciples and thus bearing spiritual fruit in terms of new spiritual family. The whole concept of rebirth is parallel to seeds in nature. The seed is the package of energy which produces new life. The Gospel is the seed of God (Lk. 8:11) which must bear fruit. One can imagine the human head as an ovum, which must be penetrated by the living seed (*sperma*, *sporos*) of the Gospel of the Kingdom (cp. 1 Pet. 1:22-25; 1 John 3:5). The Gospel is the creative, energetic word of God at work in believers (1 Thess. 2:13).

died to what held us in bondage, so that we serve in the newness of the
spirit and not the oldness of the letter.[58]

7So what shall we say then? Is the Law sin? Absolutely not! Certainly
I would not have known sin except through the Law. For I would not
have known about coveting unless the Law had said, “Do not covet.”
8But sin, finding its opportunity through this commandment, produced in
me all kinds of coveting. For apart from the Law, sin is dead. 9I was alive
apart from the Law once, but when the commandment came, sin became
alive and I died. 10And so I found that the commandment which was
meant to lead to life led to death. 11For sin, seizing an opportunity
through the commandment, deceived me, and through it killed me. 12So
then, the Law is holy, and the commandment holy, right, and good.
13Then did what is good become death to me? Absolutely not! But sin, so
that it might be shown as sin, was producing death in me through what is
good, so that through the commandment sin would be revealed as
extremely sinful.

14For we know that the Law is spiritual, but I am unspiritual, sold as a
slave to sin. 15For I do not understand what I do. I do not do what I want,
but I do what I hate. 16When I do what I do not want, I acknowledge that
the Law is good. 17But now it is no longer I who do it, but sin which lives
in me. 18For I know that nothing good lives in me, that is, in my human
nature. For I have the will but not the power to do what is good. 19The
good I want to do, I do not do, but the evil I do not want to do, I do! 20But
if I am doing what I do not want to, then it is no longer I who do it, but
sin living in me.

21I find then the principle that when I want to do what is good, evil is
with me. 22For I delight in God’s Law in my inner self, 23but I see a
different law at work in the parts of my body, warring against the law of
my mind, and bringing me into captivity under the law of sin which is
within me. 24What a wretched person I am! Who will rescue me from this
body of death? I thank God through Jesus Messiah our lord! 25So then,
with my mind I myself am serving God’s Law, but with my human
nature I am serving a law of sin.

---

[58]This is the key to the distinction between Torah (Law) in the letter and Law in the spirit. The New Covenant spiritualizes the letter of the Law, hence the major changes it introduces, in regard to the calendar, circumcision and food laws.

8 1So then there is now[59] no condemnation for those who are in Messiah
Jesus, 2because the law of the spirit of life in Messiah Jesus has set
you free from the law of sin and death. 3What the Law could not do
because it was weak due to human nature, God did. By commissioning[60]
His own Son in the likeness of sinful human nature,[61] and for sin, He
condemned sin in human nature 4so that the requirement of the Law[62]
may be fulfilled in us, who live not following human nature but
following the spirit. 5For those who live according to human nature have
their mindset shaped by human nature, but those who live according to
the spirit have their mindset shaped by the spirit. 6The mindset of human
nature results in death, but the mindset of the spirit results in life and
peace. 7For the mindset of human nature is hostile to God because it does
not and cannot submit to the law of God. 8Those who are under human
nature cannot please God.

9But you are not controlled by human nature, but by the spirit, if
indeed that spirit of God lives in you. But if anyone does not have the
spirit of Messiah, that person does not belong to him.[63] 10But if Messiah
is in you, the body is dead because of sin, but the spirit is life because of
being and doing right. 11And if the spirit of the One who resurrected
Jesus from the dead lives in you, the One who resurrected Messiah Jesus
from the dead will also raise your mortal bodies through His spirit living
in you.

12So then, brothers and sisters, we are not under obligation to human
nature, to live by its standard. 13For if you live by such a standard, you

---

[59]Paul certainly did not consider the sad situation in ch. 7 to be the continuous experience of the converted Christian. The triumph must be demonstrated in our present lives, since we "have been set free from the law of sin and death" (8:2).

[60]"Sending someone is established in Judeo-Christian thought as a way of expressing the messenger's or prophet's authorization, without any reference to his place of origin (e.g. Ps. 105:26; Jer. 1:7; Mic. 6:4; Lk. 4:26; 20:13)" (James Dunn, *Word Biblical Commentary, Romans*, p. 420).

[61]Jesus himself had to learn obedience through the things which he suffered (Heb. 5:8). God obviously could not learn obedience! Jesus was like us in every way, except that he was sinless.

[62]The law in the spirit and not the letter (7:6).

[63]That is, they are not Christian in the biblical sense. This means that Jehovah's Witnesses exclude themselves from a biblical definition of a Christian, unless they claim (rarely) to be part of the special group which they name the 144,000.

are going to die. But if by the spirit you are putting to death the actions
of your lower nature, you will live.[64] 14For all who are being led by the
spirit of God are the children of God. 15For you did not receive a spirit of
slavery, leading you back to fear, but you received a spirit of sonship, by
which we cry, "Abba, dear Father!" 16The spirit itself testifies with our
spirit that we are children of God. 17And since we are children, then we
are heirs — heirs of God and fellow heirs with the Messiah — if we
suffer with him so that we may share in the glory with him.[65]

18For I am convinced that the sufferings of this present time are not
even worth comparing with the coming glory which is going to be
revealed in us.[66] 19For the creation is eagerly waiting for the public
revealing of the children of God. 20For the creation was subjected to
futility, not of its own accord but because of the One who subjected it, in
hope 21that the creation itself will also be set free from the bondage of
decay and share the freedom of the glory of God's children. 22For we
know that the whole creation is groaning and suffering birth pains
together until now. 23Not only creation, but we ourselves also, who have
the first fruits, namely the spirit, groan within ourselves as we wait for
God to give us sonship,[67] the redemption of our whole selves. 24For we
were saved in hope.[68] Yet hope which is seen is not hope at all, because

---

[64]Both now and eventually by resurrection or surviving till Jesus comes back, you will live forever by gaining indestructible life.

[65]2 Tim. 2:12: "If we suffer with him we will also reign as kings with him" (cp. Dan 7:14, 18, 22, 27; Mt. 19:28). Achieving salvation in the Kingdom means gaining the honor of administering the world with Jesus in the first ever successful world government. To this the whole Bible looks forward with breathless excitement and anticipation.

[66]Not just revealed "to us," but revealed "in us," since we are going to be glorified in the future Kingdom of glory on earth. "Then the righteous will shine forth like the sun in the Kingdom of their Father" (Mt. 13:43, citing Dan. 12:3).

[67]Christians are of course born again now, and are thus spiritual sons now, when they accept the Gospel of the Kingdom (as in Acts 8:12), but sonship is completed finally at the future coming of Jesus, when immortality is conferred on the faithful. A foretaste of that future life can be enjoyed now in the spirit as a downpayment or first installment (2 Cor. 1:22; 5:5).

[68]Salvation is in three tenses of the verb — past, continuing in the present (we are being saved) and completed in the future. The doctrine of "once saved always saved" is entirely foreign to the NT.

who hopes for what they already see? 25But if we hope for what we do
not see, we eagerly wait for it and persevere.

26In the same way, the spirit helps us in our weakness. For we do not
know how we should pray, but the spirit itself intercedes for us with
groans that cannot be uttered.[69] 27And He who searches our hearts knows
the mind of the spirit, because the spirit intercedes for the saints
according to the will of God.

28We know God works for good[70] in all things for those who love
God, who are called according to His purpose. 29For those God
foreknew,[71] He also predestined to be conformed to the image of His
Son, so that the Son would be the firstborn among many brothers and
sisters. 30And those whom He predestined, He also called; and those He
called, He also made right; and those He made right, He also glorified.[72]

31So then what should we say about[73] these things? If God[74] is for us,
who can be against us? 32Since God did not spare His own Son, but gave
him up for all of us,[75] how will He not also, along with him, freely give

---

[69]This is certainly not a reference to "speaking in tongues," since "languages" are words and utterances and not groans.

[70]This statement is certainly not a promise that bad things cannot happen to Christians. But the assurance given here is that God and Jesus continue to work in whatever circumstances believers experience.

[71]This is not the Calvinism of double-predestination. Jesus noted that the Pharisees "resisted the will of God" (Lk. 7:30), and Paul charged those who refused his preaching with "counting themselves unworthy of the Life of the Age to Come" (Acts 13:46). Christian choice and persistence to the end is needed for final salvation.

[72]Note that future glory is expressed in the past tense, just as in John 17:5, where the glory Jesus "had with" God is the promised glory of the future. That same glory had already been given to believers who had not yet been born when Jesus promised it to them in John 17:22, 24. Matt. 6:1 speaks of a reward already stored up with God. We have it, and yet it will be given to us in reality in the future.

[73]"About" here is *pros* in the Greek, that is, "concerning." Cp. the word which is concerning or about (*pros*) God in John 1:1.

[74]As very often in the NT "God" in Scripture is "*the* God," the One God of the Bible, of Israel and of Jesus and certainly not the triune God who appears nowhere in the Bible as God. The only God recognized by Jesus is the "one God" of the creed of Israel, affirmed by Jesus in Mark 12:29, agreeing with a unitarian Jew.

[75]Since God cannot die (1 Tim. 6:16), it is quite obvious that Jesus, the Son of God, cannot *be* God, making two who are God.

us everything? 33Who will bring any charge against God's chosen ones?[76]
It is God who makes us right,[77] 34so who will condemn us? It is Messiah
Jesus who died — even more, who was resurrected — who is now at the
right hand of God,[78] interceding for us. 35Who will separate us from the
love of Messiah? Will oppression, distress, persecution, famine,
nakedness, danger or violence? 36Just as it is written, "For your sake we
are being killed all day long; we are considered as sheep to be
slaughtered." 37No, in all these things we are completely victorious
through Him who loved us. 38For I am convinced that neither death nor
life, nor angels, nor demons, nor the present, nor the future, nor powers,
39nor height, nor depth, nor any other created thing will be able to
separate us from the love of God in Messiah Jesus our lord.

9 1I am telling you the truth in Messiah. I am not lying! My conscience
is testifying with me in holy spirit 2that I have great sadness and
unceasing distress in my heart. 3For I could even wish that I myself were
cursed, cut off from Messiah for my people's sake, my physical relatives,
4the Israelites. To them belong the sonship, the glory, the covenants, the
giving of the Law,[79] the temple service, and the promises. 5To them
belong the fathers, and from them is the Messiah by physical descent.[80]
May God who is over all be blessed for all ages. Amen.[81]

6But it is not as though the Gospel-word of God has failed. For not all
who are descended from Israel are the true Israel, 7nor are they
Abraham's children just because they are his descendants. Instead,
"Through Isaac your descendants will be counted." 8That is, it is not the
children of physical descent who are the children of God, but the

[76]Note that the elect as in Matt. 22:14 and 24:31 are not presently unconverted Jews, but the international church, the saints. The elect, the saints, the true people of God will be gathered to meet Jesus after (post) the time of the Great Tribulation in the future.

[77]This making us right is a process, ongoing and reaching finality when we gain immortality at the resurrection and return of Jesus to this earth.

[78]The *adoni*, my lord, not Lord of Psalm 110:1. *Adoni* is the non-Deity title, all 195 times. It is never a reference to God who is Adonai, the supreme Lord.

[79]The Torah.

[80]See 1:3-4 where God's Son is son of Mary, of David and of God as Luke 1:35, Matt. 1:18, 20 define him. Luke 1:35 is an all-sufficient definition of the title Son of God for Jesus. "God the Son" is alien to Scripture and appears not once.

[81]This is a doxology to God as shown by the parallels in 1:25; 11:36; 2 Cor. 11:31.

children of the promise are counted as true descendants.[82] 9For these are
the words of the promise: "About this time next year I will return and
Sarah will have a son." 10Not only that, but Rebekah conceived twins by
one man, by our forefather Isaac. 11Even before the twins were born,
before either had done anything good or bad — so that the purpose of
God in election might stand, not by works but by Him who calls[83] —
12Rebekah was told, "The older brother will serve the younger one." 13As
it is written, "Jacob I loved, but Esau I hated."

14What shall we say then? Is there injustice with God? Absolutely
not! 15As He said to Moses, "I will have mercy on whom I have mercy,
and I will have compassion on whom I have compassion." 16So then, it
does not depend on human will or efforts, but on God who has mercy.
17For Scripture says to Pharaoh: "For this very purpose I caused you to be
put on the human scene, so that I would show through you My power,
and so that My name would be proclaimed throughout all the earth." 18So
then, God has mercy on those whom He wants to have mercy, and He
hardens those He wants to.[84]

19You will say to me, "Then why does God find fault? For who can
resist His will?"[85] 20But who are you, a human being, to talk back to God
in this way? Will the thing formed ask the one who formed it, "Why did
you make me like this?" 21Does not the potter have the right to make
from the same lump of clay one vessel for special use and another for
ordinary use?[86] 22But what if God, although willing to show His anger

---

[82]Paul made the same point in Gal. 6:16, calling the international believers the "Israel of God" (cp. Phil. 3:3).

[83]But it does of course entail our cooperating obedience to God by believing and obeying the Gospel. The Pharisees "resisted God's will for themselves" (Lk. 7:30), showing that man has a free will to choose or refuse good.

[84]It is seldom observed that Pharaoh himself also hardened his own heart (Ex. 7:14; 8:32; 9:34; cp. 9:27 where Pharaoh accepts responsibility).

[85]This statement is not a contradiction of Jesus who said that "the Pharisees resisted the will of God for themselves" (Lk. 7:30).

[86]This one verse in Romans should never be taken to mean that God deliberately hardens people's hearts and then punishes them for it! This would be to eliminate any concept of free will and choice. God commands us to "choose" and it would be deceptive if we are unable to choose. The hardening of the heart is a rejection of divine grace. There are always two sides to a coin, when it comes to God's dealings with us. God initiates the Gospel call and we must decide to respond. The Hebrew mind can work with a "two sides of one coin" principle. For example John 12:44: "He who

and make His power known, has endured with much patience vessels of
wrath ready for destruction? 23He is willing to do this to make known the
riches of His glory on vessels of mercy which He prepared ahead of time
for glory — 24us whom He called, not from the Jews only, but also from
the Gentiles. 25As He says in Hosea, "I will call them 'My people' who
were not My people, and 'My beloved' who were not beloved. 26It will be
that in the very place where it was said to them, 'You are not My
people,' there they will be called 'children of the living God.'"

27Isaiah calls out concerning Israel: "Although the number of the
children of Israel is like the sand of the sea, it is only a remnant that will
be saved. 28For the Lord will quickly and decisively finish His work of
judgment on the earth."[87] 29As Isaiah predicted, "Unless the Lord of
Hosts had left us descendants,[88] we would have become like Sodom, and
would have been like Gomorrah."

30What shall we say then? That the Gentiles, who did not pursue the
way of being right, attained to it — being right based on belief. 31But
Israel pursued being right based on the Law and did not attain to it.

---

believes in me does not believe in me..." Belief is ultimately in God but always through Jesus. So with free will: one side of the coin is that God draws us with the Gospel. The other is that we must respond (Mt. 23:37). This passage in Romans provides no support for Calvin's double predestination. Human beings are responsible for choosing to cooperate with God. "Work out your own salvation because God is at work in you" (Phil. 2:12-13). By isolating "one side of the coin" and ignoring the other, many readers fall into misunderstanding. God "desires **all** men to be saved" (1 Tim. 2:4). Some, however, will be lost. God is at work, but we must work with Him and Jesus. By isolating one side of the coin and ignoring the other, it is possible to become blind to texts like Lk. 7:30: "The Pharisees resisted and frustrated God's purposes for themselves" (cp. Mt. 23:37; Lk. 13:34). In Acts 13:46, some were "making themselves unworthy of the life of the age to come." It was *their* choice to refuse salvation and not God's. Paul teaches that a person wanting to be a holy vessel for God must purify himself! (2 Tim. 2:21). Pharaoh hardened his own heart (Ex. 8:15, 32; 9:34), and God responded to His stubbornness. Responsibility is on a "sliding scale," as Jesus told the Pharisees in John 15:22, 24.

[87]Note here the deliberate quotation of Isa. 10:23 and 28:22 and especially Dan. 9:27, showing that Paul understands the final 70th "week" of 7 years to end with the Second Coming, not earlier in AD 33 or 70. "His end" in Dan. 26b will not fit with Titus!

[88]Literally "seed," a remnant, the international church in the New Covenant (Gal. 6:16; Phil. 3:3) as the ones who have accepted the seed Gospel message of the Kingdom. This of course involves people of every nation, including Jews who have accepted that Jesus is the Messiah, and believe the Gospel teaching of Jesus (Mk. 1:14-15).

32Why? Because they did not pursue it by belief, but, as if it were
possible, by works. They stumbled over the stumbling stone, 33just as is
written: "Look, I am placing in Zion a stumbling stone, a rock of offense.
But the person who believes in him will not be put to shame."

10 1Brothers and sisters, my heart's desire and my prayer to God for
the Israelites is that they may be saved. 2For I testify to this fact
about them: they have a zeal for God, but it is not based on knowledge.[89]
3For they are ignorant of God's way of being right, and seeking to
establish their own way, they have failed to subject themselves to God's
way of being right. 4For Messiah is the fulfillment and end of the Law, to
make right everyone who believes.

5For Moses writes about the way of being right based on the Law:
"The one who does these things will live by them." 6But the way of being
right based on belief says this: "Do not say in your heart, 'Who will
ascend to heaven?' (that is, to bring Messiah down), 7or 'Who will
descend to the abyss?' (that is, to bring Messiah up from the dead)." 8But
what does it say? "The word[90] is near you, in your mouth and in your
heart" — that is, the Gospel-word of faith that we are proclaiming.[91] 9For
if you confess with your mouth that Jesus is lord[92] and believe in your
heart that God raised him from the dead, you will be saved. 10For with
the heart one believes, resulting in being right, and with the mouth one
confesses, resulting in salvation. 11As Scripture says, "Whoever believes
in him will not be put to shame." 12For there is no distinction between
Jew and Gentile, as the same Lord is Lord of all, and is rich to all who

---

[89]Cp. "My people are destroyed for lack of knowledge" (Hos. 4:6; see Isa. 5:13). This gives added strength to the important teaching of Isa. 53:11 that the Messiah "causes many to be righteous by his knowledge" (cp. 1 John 5:20; Dan. 12:3). See also Proverbs with its heavy emphasis on knowledge, 40 times.

[90]Of the Gospel of the Kingdom as Jesus and Paul preached it (Mk. 1:14-15; Lk. 4:43; Heb. 2:3; Acts 19:8; 20:24-25; 28:23, 30, 31).

[91]As reported in Acts 19:8; 20:24-25; 28:23, 30, 31 — the Gospel of the Kingdom as in Mark 1:14-15 and Acts 8:12.

[92]And believe his Gospel of the Kingdom. One cannot believe in Jesus and not believe his words and Gospel. Mark 1:14-15 is Jesus' first command and the basis for our belief in him. See John 12:44ff for Jesus' maximum emphasis on the fatal danger of not believing Jesus' words.

call on Him. 13For "everyone who calls on the name of the Lord[93] will be saved."

14How then will people call on him unless they have believed him? And how will they believe him unless they have heard him preaching the Gospel?[94] And how will they hear it unless someone preaches it to them? 15And how are they to preach it unless they are sent? As it is written, "How beautiful are those who preach the Gospel!" 16But they did not all obey the Gospel. As Isaiah says, "Lord, who has believed our message?" 17So then belief is based on hearing — hearing the Gospel Message preached by the Messiah.[95]

18But I ask, has Israel not heard? Yes, they have. "Their voice went out throughout all the earth, their words to the ends of the world." 19I ask, did Israel not understand? First Moses says, "I will provoke you to jealousy with what is really not a nation; I will make you angry by a nation without understanding." 20And Isaiah says boldly, "I was found by those who did not seek Me; I revealed Myself to those who did not inquire about Me." 21But about Israel God says, "All day long I have stretched out My hands to a disobedient and stubborn people."[96]

11 1I ask this then: God has not rejected His people, has He?[97] Absolutely not! For I too am an Israelite, a descendant of

---

[93]Joel 2:32 quoted here refers to the Lord God. It is applied to Jesus, the lord Messiah, in the NT, since Jesus works as the perfect agent of the one God, and as Son perfectly represents his Father.

[94]Note that one must hear the Gospel *preached by Jesus* for salvation. It is not a matter of hearing *about* Jesus (NIV is misleading here) but one must hear *him*, i.e. preaching the Gospel. Paul is thinking about an important Kingdom verse here, since he quotes from Isa. 52:7 concerning the future Kingdom on earth, the core of the Gospel along with the death and resurrection of Jesus (Acts 8:12).

[95]This is the basis of Christian salvation as commanded by Jesus in Mk 1:14-15; cp. Heb. 2:3.

[96]There is no Calvinism here. Paul lays the blame squarely upon Israel's culpable, stubborn refusal to obey God. Jesus was met with the same refusal on the part of many Jews, especially the religious establishment. See Mt. 23:37 for Jesus' despair at their stubbornness. 2 Thess. 2:10 demonstrates human responsibility for not believing the truth in order to be saved.

[97]The topic is obviously not the church but now blinded Israel. Paul calls the international church the "Israel of God" (Gal. 6:16) as distinct from the "Israel of the

Abraham, from the tribe of Benjamin. 2God has not rejected His people whom He foreknew. Do you not know what the Scripture says about Elijah, how he complains to God about Israel? 3"Lord, they have killed Your prophets and have broken down Your altars. I alone am left, and they are seeking to kill me!" 4But how did God respond to him? "I have reserved for Myself 7,000 people who have not bowed the knee to Baal." 5In the same way then, at this present time also, there is a remnant chosen by grace. 6And if by grace, then it is no longer by works, or grace would no longer be grace.

7What shall we say then? What Israel was seeking they did not obtain. The chosen ones obtained it, but the rest were hardened. 8As it is written, "God gave them a spirit of sleepiness, eyes that would not see and ears that would not hear, up to this very day." 9And David says, "Let their feasts become a snare and a trap, a stumbling block and a just punishment for them. 10Let their eyes be darkened to not see, and always keep their backs bent over."

11I ask then, did they stumble in order to completely fall? Absolutely not. But by their sin, salvation has come to the Gentiles, to make Israel jealous. 12Now if their sin means riches for the world and their loss means riches for the Gentiles, how much more will their inclusion mean? 13Now I am speaking to you who are Gentiles. Since I am an Apostle to the Gentiles, I will make the most of my ministry 14so that somehow I might provoke my own people to jealousy, and save some of them. 15For if their rejection means the reconciling of the world, what would their acceptance mean but life from the dead![98] 16If the piece of dough offered as firstfruits is holy, so is the whole batch; if the root is holy, so are the branches.

---

flesh" (1 Cor. 10:18). The church is also the true spiritual circumcision, i.e. the true Jews (Phil. 3:3).

[98]A future spiritual revival of Israel is mentioned in Ezek. 37 and this is one of many prophecies of a recovery of a remnant of now blinded natural, national Israel. In the meantime, the international church has become the true Israel of God (Gal. 6:16) and true circumcision of the spirit (Phil. 3:3). Paul refers to unconverted national, natural Israel as the "Israel of the flesh" (1 Cor. 10:18) or "Israelites" (Rom. 9:4; 2 Cor. 11:22). The contrast with the international believers is obvious in Gal. 6:16, the Israel of God, the true people of God. Paul still sees in the future a national, collective conversion of now blinded Israel. This will happen under the pressure and refining effects of the future Great Tribulation (see Zech. 13:8-9; 14:2).

17But if some of the branches were broken off, and you Gentiles, a
wild olive, were grafted in among them, and now share the rich root of
the olive tree, 18then do not boast over the other branches. But if you
boast, remember that it is not you who support the root, but the root that
supports you.[99] 19You will say, "Branches were broken off so that I could
be grafted in." 20That is correct: they were broken off because of their
unbelief, and you are standing because of your faith. Do not be arrogant,
but fear, 21because if God did not spare the natural branches, neither
would He spare you.[100] 22Reflect then on the kindness and severity of
God: severity towards those who fell, but God's kindness towards you —
if you continue in His kindness. Otherwise you too will be cut off.[101]
23And if Jews do not continue in their unbelief they will be grafted in,
because God is able to graft them in again. 24For if you were cut from
what is by nature a wild olive tree, and were grafted against nature into a
cultivated olive tree, how much more will these who are the natural
branches be grafted into their own olive tree?

25For I do not want you to be ignorant, brothers and sisters, of this
previously hidden truth, so that you will not be arrogant: A partial
hardening has happened to Israel, until[102] the full number of the Gentiles
has come in. 26This is how all Israel[103] will then be saved. As it is written,
"There will come from Zion the deliverer, and he will banish all evil
from Jacob. 27This will be My covenant with them, when I take away
their sins."

---

[99]Not to be confused with contemporary "Messianic roots" systems which muddle Moses and Jesus.

[100]Showing that Paul disagreed entirely with modern theories about "once saved, always saved," and Paul was no Calvinist. Salvation depends on our willing cooperation with God (Phil. 2:12-13).

[101]This and many other verses deliver a death knell to the popular but erroneous teaching about "once saved always saved." Salvation is conditional on successful persistence to the end. This too is the warning given by Jesus in the parable of the sower, where "some believe for a while" (Lk. 8:13). These verses make any doctrine of double predestination impossible, thankfully!

[102]"Until" of course is an adverb of time and implies "and then…"

[103]Referring not to every Jew just because he is a Jew, but a collective national conversion of a remnant of Jews. This will happen at the future Second Coming of Jesus, after the future Great Tribulation which will have the effect of refining those who go through it. A collective remnant of Jews will finally say to the Messiah, "Blessed is the one coming in the name of the LORD" (Mt. 23:39).

28They are presently enemies of the Gospel for your sake, but they are
still potentially the chosen people, beloved for the fathers' sake. 29For
God does not take back His gifts and calling. 30Just as you in time past
were disobedient to God, but now have obtained mercy as a result of
their disobedience; 31in the same way they are currently disobedient, so
that by the mercy shown to you they may also obtain mercy. 32For God
delivered all to disobedience, so that He may show mercy to all.

33Oh, the depth of the riches of the wisdom and the knowledge of
God! How unsearchable are His judgments, and how undiscoverable His
ways! 34Who has known the mind of the Lord? Or who has been His
advisor? 35Who has first given to God so that God would pay it back?
36For everything is from Him, through Him, and to Him. To Him be the
glory for the ages! Amen.

12 1So I urge you, brothers and sisters, by the mercies of God, to
present your whole selves[104] as a sacrifice which is living, holy
and pleasing to God. This is your service for the Gospel-word.[105] 2Do not
be conformed to this present age, but be transformed by the renewing of
your mind, so that you may discern the will of God — what is good,
well-pleasing and perfect.

3For through the grace given to me I say to every one of you not to
think of yourself more highly than you ought to think, but to think
sensibly, as God has given to each of you a measure of faith. 4For just as
there are many parts in one body, and all the parts do not have the same
function, 5so we, who are many, are one body in Messiah, and we all
belong to one another. 6We each have different gifts according to the
grace given to us: If it is prophecy, then use that gift according to the
proportion of your faith. 7If it is service, then serve; if it is teaching, then
teach; 8if it is exhortation, then exhort; if it is giving, then do it

---

[104]"Bodies" in the Greek here stands for the whole person, the self. In Heb. 10:5-10 Jesus carried out the will of God by offering himself as a sacrificial person. Christians "have been sanctified through the offering of the body [the person] of Jesus Messiah once for all" (Heb. 10:10). In the same way the calendar of Israel — annual holy days, new moons and weekly Sabbath — which was only a shadow, was replaced by the person of Jesus (Col. 2:16-17).

[105]"The word" in the NT is shorthand for the Gospel of the Kingdom, Jesus' own Gospel (Heb. 2:3; Lk. 8:11-12; Mt. 13:19).

generously; if it is leadership, then lead diligently; if it is showing mercy, then do it cheerfully.

9Let love be without hypocrisy. Hate what is evil; cling to what is good. 10Be devoted to one another in love, honoring each other above yourselves. 11Do not lack diligence; be enthusiastic in spirit; serve the Lord. 12Rejoice in hope; persevere in trials; persist in prayer. 13Contribute to the needs of the saints; practice hospitality.

14Bless those who persecute you; bless them, and do not curse them. 15Rejoice with those who rejoice; weep with those who weep. 16Live in peace with each other. Do not be haughty, but associate with people of low status. Do not be wise in your own eyes. 17Do not repay evil for evil to anyone. Consider what is right in the sight of all people. 18If possible, as much as it is up to you, be at peace with everyone. 19Do not avenge yourselves,[106] beloved, but leave room for the wrath of God,[107] because it is written, "Vengeance belongs to Me; I will repay," says the Lord. 20Instead, "if your enemy is hungry, feed him; if he is thirsty, give him a drink. In doing this you will be piling coals of fire on his head." 21Do not be overcome by evil, but overcome evil with good.

13 1Let every person be in subjection to the government authorities. For there is no authority except from God, and the authorities which exist have been ordained by God. 2So then those who resist authority oppose what God has ordained, and they will be judged accordingly. 3For rulers are not a threat to good behavior, but to evil. Do you want to have no fear of authority? Do what is good, and you will have its approval, 4because government is a servant of God for your good. But if you do what is wrong, live in fear, because government does not have the power of the sword for nothing. It is God's servant, an avenger that brings wrath on the one who does wrong. 5So then you need

---

[106]Paul sees the state as a tool of vengeance in 13:4, but he never imagined that believers assume that role. NT believers are not part of the present political world-system. They are resident aliens, and should not be fighting in the wars of this world-system. Satan's kingdoms become the Kingdom of God only at the future seventh trumpet which signals the arrival of Messiah to rule with the saints (Rev. 11:15-18). Jesus did not attempt to interfere with politics at his first coming.

[107]God will see that justice is ultimately done and Ps. 149 shows that the saints will in the future be involved in executing that justice. But they should not do this now (cp. Lk. 19:27; Rev. 2:26-27; Dan. 7:27).

to be in subjection, not only because of their wrath, but also for your own conscience' sake. 6And this is why you must also pay taxes, for the authorities are servants of God, doing the work of governing. 7Give to everyone what is owed: taxes to whom taxes are due; revenue to whom revenue is due; respect to whom respect is due; honor to whom honor is due.

8Owe nothing to anyone, except to love one another, because the one who loves his neighbor has fulfilled the Law. 9For the commandments, "Do not commit adultery, do not murder, do not steal, do not covet," and whatever other commandments there are, are all summed up in this: "Love your neighbor as yourself." 10Love does no wrong to a neighbor; so love fulfills the Law.

11Do this, knowing the time, that it is already time for you to awake from sleep. For salvation is now nearer to us than when we began to be believers.[108] 12The night is nearly gone, and the day is near. So let us throw off the works of darkness and put on the armor of light. 13Let us behave suitably as in the daylight, not in wild parties and drunkenness, not in sexual immorality and sensuality, not in rivalry and jealousy. 14Instead put on the lord Jesus Messiah, and do not cater to the lower nature and its lusts.

14 1Accept the one who is weak in the faith, but not to dispute over opinions. 2One person believes in eating everything, while the weak person eats only vegetables.[109] 3The one who eats everything must not look down on the one who does not, and the one who does not eat everything must not judge the one who eats everything, because God has accepted him. 4Who are you to judge someone else's servant? He stands or falls before his own master. And he will stand, because the Lord is able to make him stand.

---

[108]In popular evangelicalism salvation is constantly spoken of as something only in the past: "when I got saved." In the NT the balance of the salvation statements is in favor of a yet future, final salvation. The NT says too that we "are being saved" (1 Cor. 1:18; 2 Cor. 2:15).

[109]Paul allowed time for people to reexamine their thinking. In the case of both eating meat and drinking wine, the proof lay close at hand that Jesus was not a vegetarian, nor did he abstain from the moderate use of alcohol (cp. Deut. 14:26).

5One person considers one day as more holy than other days, while
another person considers every day alike. Each person must be fully
convinced in his own mind.[110] 6The one who observes the day observes it
for the lord. The one who eats everything eats for the lord, because he
gives thanks to God. The one who does not eat everything does it for the
lord, and gives thanks to God. 7For none of us lives for himself, and none
dies for himself. 8If we live, we live for the lord, or if we die, we die for
the lord. So then, whether we live or die, we are the lord's. 9For this
reason Messiah died and came to life — so that he may be the lord of
both the dead and the living.

10But why does one who eats only vegetables judge his brother or
sister? And why does one who eats everything look down on his brother
or sister? For we will all stand before the judgment seat of God.[111] 11For it
is written, "As I live, says the Lord, to Me every knee will bow, and
every tongue will praise God." 12So each one of us will give account of
ourselves to God.

13So then let us not pass judgment on one another any more, but
rather determine this: never put an obstacle or a stumbling block in a
brother or sister's way. 14I know and am persuaded in the lord Jesus that
nothing is unclean in itself.[112] But if someone considers something to be
unclean, to him it is unclean. 15For if because of what you eat your
brother or sister is upset, you are no longer behaving in love. Do not
destroy with your food anyone for whom Messiah died. 16And do not let
what you regard as good be spoken of as evil, 17because God's

---

[110]Paul urges the weak to become strong, but they must be dealt with gently as they progress in understanding. Paul sets the right model by showing that distinctions in food (Lev. 11) are of no consequence to the strong and mature (Rom. 14:14, 20).

[111]Compare "the judgment seat of the Messiah" (2 Cor. 5:10). Not that the Messiah *is* God, but as Jesus said, "The Father judges no one but has put all judgment into the hands of the Son" (John 5:22). See also Acts 17:31.

[112]This is proof positive that Paul is not enforcing in any sense the food laws of Lev. 11. He is speaking as a Jew and a Christian. Jesus had, as they later fully realized (Mark's comment) "cleansed all foods" (Mk. 7:19). Paul's statement here obviously dispenses with the food laws observed under the Law of Moses. Paul here sets the standard of Christian maturity, into which we must all grow in unity. Paul rightly changed his tone entirely and strongly rejected any who taught that Sabbath keeping and Jewish calendar or physical circumcision are mandated in the New Covenant (Col. 2:16-17; Gal. 4 and 5; Eph. 2:14-15).

Kingdom[113] is not primarily about eating and drinking, but about living right, having peace and joy in holy spirit. 18Anyone who serves the Messiah in this way is pleasing to God and approved by people. 19So let us pursue what leads to peace and building one another up. 20Do not tear down God's work for the sake of food. All things are clean, but it is wrong to eat anything that causes another to stumble. 21It is good not to eat meat, drink wine, or do anything which causes your brother or sister to stumble. 22The faith you have, keep as your own conviction before God. Blessed is the one who has no reason to condemn himself for what he approves. 23But the one who doubts is condemned if he eats,[114] because the eating is not from faith, and whatever is not from faith is sin.

15 1We who are strong ought to bear with the frailties of the weak and not just please ourselves. 2Each of us should please his neighbor for his good, to build him up. 3For the Messiah did not please himself, but as it is written, "The insults of those who insult You fall on me." 4For everything that was written in the past was written for our learning, so that through perseverance and the encouragement of the Scriptures we might have hope. 5Now may the God of perseverance and encouragement grant you to be of the same mind with one another, following Messiah Jesus, 6so that with one mind you may with one voice glorify the God and Father of our lord Jesus Messiah.

7So accept one another, just as the Messiah also accepted us, to the glory of God. 8For I tell you that Messiah has become a servant to the Jews for the truth of God, to confirm the promises made to the fathers, 9and so that the Gentiles glorify God for His mercy. As it is written, "So then I will praise You among the Gentiles, and sing to Your name." 10Again it says, "Rejoice, you Gentiles, with His people!" 11And "Praise the Lord, all you Gentiles! Let all peoples praise Him." 12And again

---

[113]Meaning here the whole Christian faith which is preparation now for entry into the Kingdom to be established when Jesus comes back. The Christian life now, therefore, requires Kingdom principles.

[114]Those who are weak in the faith (v. 1). They are urged to follow Paul and become strong.

Isaiah says, "There will come the shoot of Jesse,[115] the one who arises to rule over the Gentiles.[116] In him the Gentiles will hope." 13May the God of hope fill you with all joy and peace in believing, so that you may overflow with hope in the power of holy spirit.

14I myself am persuaded about you, my brothers and sisters, that you are full of goodness, filled with all knowledge, and able to instruct one another. 15But I have written boldly to you on some points to remind you. This is because of the grace that was given to me by God 16to be a minister of Messiah Jesus to the Gentiles. I serve as a priest of God's Gospel,[117] so that my offering up of the Gentiles may become acceptable, being made holy by the holy spirit. 17So then my boasting is in Messiah Jesus in things pertaining to God. 18For I will not dare to speak of anything except what Messiah worked through me leading to the obedience of the Gentiles, in word and work, 19in the power of signs and wonders, in the power of God's spirit. So from Jerusalem as far as Illyricum, I have fully proclaimed the Gospel of the Messiah.[118] 20And it was my goal to proclaim the Gospel in places where Messiah was not already named, so that I would not be building on another's foundation, 21but as it is written, "Those who had no news of him will see, and those who have not heard will understand."

22That is why I was prevented on many occasions from coming to you. 23But now, with nothing more to keep me in these regions, and since I have for many years wanted to come to you, 24when I travel to Spain I will visit you. For I hope to see you on my journey and to be helped on my way there by you, after first enjoying your company for a while. 25But now I am going to Jerusalem to serve the saints, 26because it has been the good pleasure of Macedonia and Achaia to make a contribution for the poor among the saints in Jerusalem. 27Yes, they were delighted to

---

[115]The promised Messiah (Isa. 7, 9, 11). Isa. 9:6 predicted the begetting of the Son by God: "To us a child was begotten [by God]; to us a Son was given." These are past tenses of prophecy, certain to occur and promised by God.

[116]The promise of the Kingdom of God to be inaugurated worldwide when Jesus returns (Mk. 1:14-15). The Kingdom is the central theme of the Gospel, along, of course, with the sacrificial death and resurrection of Jesus.

[117]God's Gospel, or the Gospel of God, appears 8 times in the NT: Mk. 1:14; Rom. 1:1; 15:16 (framing the book of Romans); 2 Cor. 11:7; 1 Thess. 2:2, 8, 9; 1 Pet. 4:17.

[118]The Gospel of the Kingdom as preached by Jesus (Mk. 1:1, 14, 15) and the Gospel about him. Paul of course preached that same Gospel (Acts 19:8; 20:24-25; 28:23, 31).

do this, and they are in debt to those Jerusalem saints. For if the Gentiles
have shared in their spiritual things, they owe it to them to serve them in
material things. 28So when I have accomplished this and have delivered
this contribution to them, I will see you on my way to Spain. 29I know
that when I come to you, I will come in the fullness of the blessing of the
Messiah.

30I urge you, brothers and sisters, through our lord Jesus Messiah and
through the love of the spirit, to join me earnestly in prayer to God for
me. 31Pray that I may be delivered from those who are disobedient in
Judea, and that my ministry in Jerusalem will prove acceptable to the
saints, 32so that by the will of God I will come to you in joy and in your
company find rest and refreshing. 33May the God of peace be with you
all. Amen.

16 1I recommend to you Phoebe our sister, who is a servant[119] of the
church at Cenchrea. 2I want you to welcome her in the lord in a
way worthy of the saints, and assist her in whatever she needs from you,
because she has been a helper of many, and of myself.

3Greet Prisca and Aquila, my fellow workers in Messiah Jesus, 4who
risked their lives for me. I am thankful for them, as are all the churches
of the Gentiles. 5And greet the church in their house. Greet Epaenetus,
my dear friend, who is the first convert to Messiah from the province of
Asia. 6Greet Mary, who worked hard for you. 7Greet Andronicus and
Junia,[120] my relatives and fellow prisoners. They are noteworthy in the
eyes of the apostles, and were in Messiah before me. 8Greet Ampliatus,
my dear friend in the lord. 9Greet Urbanus, our fellow worker in
Messiah, and Stachys, my dear friend. 10Greet Apelles, approved in
Messiah. Greet those in the household of Aristobulus. 11Greet Herodion,
my countryman, and those of the household of Narcissus who are in the
lord. 12Greet Tryphaena and Tryphosa, workers in the lord, and my dear
friend Persis, who labored hard in the lord. 13Greet Rufus, chosen in the
lord, and his mother who has been a mother to me as well. 14Greet

---

[119]She was most probably a financial supporter and thus a patroness of the church there. Paul did not ordain women as elders/pastors (1 Tim. 3:1). But women spoke, educated, and encouraged in the church setting (1 Cor. 11:4-5).

[120]Junia is apparently the name of a woman and since women "prayed and prophesied" in the church (1 Cor. 14:5), Junia may have been traveling and teaching.

Asyncritus, Phlegon, Hermes, Patrobas, Hermas, and the believers who are with them. 15Greet Philologus and Julia, Nereus and his sister, Olympas, and all the saints with them. 16Greet one another with a holy kiss. All the churches of Messiah greet you.

17Now I urge you, brothers and sisters, watch out for those who are causing divisions and obstacles contrary to the teachings which you learned. Turn away from these people, 18because they are not serving our lord Messiah[121] but their own desires, and by their smooth and flattering speech they deceive the minds of unsuspecting people. 19Your obedience has become known to all, so I am rejoicing over you, but I want you to be wise in what is good and innocent in what is evil. 20The God of peace will quickly crush Satan[122] under your feet. The grace of our lord[123] Jesus be with you.

21Timothy, my fellow worker, sends greetings, as do Lucius, Jason, and Sosipater, my countrymen. 22I, Tertius, who am writing this letter, greet you in the Lord. 23Gaius, my host and host of the whole church,

---

[121]Our lord Messiah is of course Paul's abbreviated form of "our lord Jesus Messiah." The phrase is exactly that of Luke in 2:11, where "the lord Messiah" was born in Bethlehem. No one in NT times imagined that God was born! The lord Messiah is the second lord of Ps. 110:1, and the lord (*adoni* in Heb.) is certainly not a second GOD. He is "the man Messiah Jesus" of Paul's constant creed (1 Tim. 2:5), the human Messiah whom Paul discusses in Phil. 2:5ff where he is not talking about a pre-human (i.e. non-human) person, but the historical lord Messiah who took the status of a servant, as a model for us. Cp. Isa. 53:12: "poured out himself," as did Paul in Phil. 2:17.

[122]The Satan is a fallen angel who "fell into condemnation" (1 Tim. 3:6). God permits this morally responsible angel who by choice became evil. The Christadelphian idea that the "serpent" was not morally responsible, just a snake, implies a terrible indictment of God, making God the author of the lie! Founder of Christadelphianism, John Thomas, said that "the serpent lied *but did not intend to lie*." This very cleverly traces the lie to God, making God the author of the lie. However, the serpent, the Satan, was deliberately punished by God for his transgression. God did not punish the innocent.

[123]"Our lord" is the Messianic title for Jesus based on Ps. 110:1, "my lord," *adoni*. It is a plain fact that no one in the Hebrew Bible wrote "my YHVH, or "our YHVH." Calling Jesus lord means that he is the Messiah, the *adoni* of Ps. 110:1, and *adoni* in all of its 195 occurrences is never a reference to Deity. Thus the critical difference between God and *not* God can be inspected 645 times — *Adonai* 450 and *adoni* 195 times.

greets you. Erastus, the city treasurer, greets you, as does our brother
Quartus.[124]

25Now to the One who is able to establish you according to my
Gospel[125] and the preaching of Jesus Messiah, according to the revealing
of the secret which has been hidden from past ages, 26but now is
manifested, and through the Scriptures of the prophets, following the
command of the God of the ages, has been made known to all the
nations, to bring about the obedience of faith[126] — 27to the only wise
God,[127] through Jesus Messiah, be the glory to the ages! Amen.

---

[124]Early manuscripts do not contain v. 24: "The grace of our lord Jesus Messiah be with you all. Amen."

[125]There was no special Gospel revealed only to Paul. The same Gospel was revealed to all the Apostles (Eph. 3:5), and of course was initially preached by Jesus (Heb. 2:3: Mk. 1:1, 14, 15).

[126]This is the key phrase with which Paul opens the book in 1:5 and so it frames the book of Romans. Faith without obedience is not faith, agreeing with James of course that salvation, being made right with God, is not by faith alone (James 2:24). Obedience is to be defined according to the New Covenant and not in the letter of the Torah. Those Jewish identity markers like circumcision in the flesh, sabbath and other calendar observances (cp. Col. 2:16-17, which is definitive) and food laws are of no consequence for Paul. Obedience properly defined is the basis of NT salvation, as Heb. 5:9 says echoing the words of Jesus in John 3:36. See also 1 Tim. 6:3, 2 John 7-9. All the complex and unnecessary arguments about faith and works are resolved once "obedience of faith" is taken as the key.

[127]This is a typical Jewish and NT Christian statement of unitary, non-Trinitarian monotheism. Cp. James 2:19: "God is one Person" (cp. Gal. 3:20, "God is only one Person," Amplified Version). Jesus fully endorsed the creed of his Hebrew heritage in Mark 12:29, agreeing with a scribe (cp. Jn. 17:3). Trinitarianism is a post-biblical creation of Greek philosophically minded Gentiles, and should never be read back into Scripture. The word God (often "the God") refers to the Father over 1300 times. No verse with "GOD" anywhere in the Bible (about 11,000 times: YHWH, *Adonai, Elohim, Theos*) means a triune God. Evangelicals have become confused by tradition which they imagine to be in the Bible. While claiming *sola scriptura,* they inadvertently read their tradition back into the Scripture and make it describe a triune God when it does not. Jesus was not a Trinitarian (Mk. 12:29; Jn. 17:3), so why are his followers? The essence of deception is failure to follow the teachings of Jesus (1 Tim. 6:3; Heb. 5:9).

1 Corinthians

1 1From Paul, called to be an Apostle of Messiah Jesus through the will
of God, and Sosthenes, our brother, 2to the church of God in Corinth,
those who are made holy in Messiah Jesus, invited to be saints,[1] with all
those everywhere who call on the name of our lord Jesus Messiah,[2] their
lord and ours: 3Grace and peace to you from God who is our Father[3] and
from the lord Jesus Messiah.[4]

4I am always giving thanks to my God for you because of the grace
of God given to you in Messiah Jesus. 5I am thankful that in him you
have been enriched in gifts, in all speech and all knowledge. 6In this way
the testimony of Messiah was confirmed among you, 7so that you are not
lacking in any spiritual gift as you expectantly wait for the revelation[5] of
our lord Jesus Messiah. 8He also will keep you strong to the end, so that
you will be blameless on the Day of our lord Jesus Messiah. 9God is
faithful, who invited you into fellowship with His Son, Jesus Messiah
our lord.[6]

10Brothers and sisters, I urge you by the authority of our lord Jesus
Messiah to all agree and have no divisions among you, but to develop a
united mind and purpose. 11For it has been reported to me, my brothers
and sisters, by some of Chloe's household that there are rivalries among
you. 12What I mean is this: You are each making different claims: "I am
with Paul," or "I am with Apollos," or "I am with Peter," or "I am with
Messiah." 13Is Messiah divided? Was Paul crucified for you? Or were
you really baptized into the name of Paul? 14I am thankful to God that I

---

[1]That is, "holy ones." The root meaning has to do with being holy.

[2]Strongly suggesting prayer to Jesus. Although prayer is generally to the Father through Jesus, appealing to Jesus or requesting things from him is not excluded in the NT. John 14:14 (not KJV) invites us to make requests of Jesus, who promises to answer.

[3]This is one of 1300 unitarian references to God as the Father.

[4]"The lord Jesus Messiah" is based on the *adoni*, "my lord" (not Lord) of Ps. 110:1 — a key verse throughout the NT. The simplicity of the creed is given us by Paul in 1 Tim. 2:5. The One God is the Father, and Jesus is the human being elevated to sit next to God.

[5]The revelation of Jesus at his future coming to establish the Kingdom on earth. Elsewhere the Parousia, arrival of Jesus.

[6]The "my lord," *adoni,* of Ps. 110:1. *Adoni* is never a title of Deity. It occurs 195 times in the Hebrew Bible.

did not baptize any of you except Crispus and Gaius,[7] 15so that nobody
can claim that you were baptized into my name. 16I do remember that I
also baptized the household of Stephanas — I do not remember whether
I baptized anyone else. 17For Messiah did not commission me to do
baptisms,[8] but to preach the Gospel, and not with words of elegant
human wisdom; otherwise the cross of the Messiah would be deprived of
its power.

18For the message of the cross is stupidity to those who are being lost,
but to us who are being saved[9] it is the power of God. 19As it is written, "I
will destroy the wisdom of the wise, and I will set aside the learning of
the learned."[10] 20Where is the wise person, the scholar, and the debater of
this age? Has not God made stupid the wisdom of this world? 21For since
in God's wisdom the world did not know God through its wisdom, God
was pleased to save those who believe the "stupidity" of the preaching.
22For Jews demand miraculous signs and Greeks search for wisdom, 23but
we preach about a Messiah[11] killed on a cross, which is a stumbling
block to Jews and stupidity to Gentiles. 24Yet to those who are called,
both Jews and Gentiles, Messiah is the power of God and the wisdom of
God. 25For the "foolishness" of God is wiser than human wisdom, and
the "weakness" of God is stronger than human strength.

26Brothers and sisters, reflect on your circumstances when you were
called. Not many of you were wise from a human point of view; not
many were powerful; not many were of noble birth. 27Instead God has

---

[7]This verse should never be twisted to imply that Paul minimized the crucial importance of Christian baptism. Just as Jesus had, he used his agents to carry out the baptizing in water (Jn. 4:1-2).

[8]Readers should be keenly aware that Paul was in no way disparaging Christian obedience expressed in water baptism, which is expressly commanded by Jesus in Matt. 28:19, the Great Commission and practiced always in apostolic Christianity, and by Jesus himself (Jn. 4:1).

[9]Salvation, which is based on obedience to Jesus (Heb. 5:9; Jn. 12:44ff), is a process and not a once and for all event. That is, we "were saved, are being saved, and will be saved." The majority of references in the NT are to our future salvation. "Salvation," Paul said, "is now closer to us than when we first believed" (Rom. 13:11).

[10]Referencing Isa. 29:14.

[11]Paul evidently does not suddenly, in complete contradiction to Jesus and to himself elsewhere, reduce the Gospel to just news about the Messiah's death! The term "Messiah" implies all that Jesus taught, starting with Jesus' first command to repent and believe the Gospel about the Kingdom (Mark 1:14-15).

chosen what the world considers stupid to shame the wise; He has chosen what the world considers weak to shame the powerful. 28God chose what the world considers unimportant and looks down on, what the world regards as nothing, to reduce to nothing what it regards as something, 29so that no human being can ever boast in the presence of God. 30It is because of Him that you are in union with Messiah Jesus, who became wisdom to us from God, and uprightness, holiness and redemption, 31so that, as it is written, "Let the one who boasts, boast in the Lord."

2 1When I came to you, brothers and sisters, I did not come with excellence in speech or human wisdom, as I proclaimed the testimony of God to you. 2For I was determined to be concerned about nothing among you except Jesus Messiah, and him crucified.[12] 3I was with you in weakness, in fear and much trembling. 4My speech and my Gospel proclamation were not with persuasive words of human wisdom, but with a demonstration of spirit and power. 5In this way your faith would not be based on human wisdom but on the power of God.

6We do speak wisdom, however, among those of us who are full-grown believers, yet it is a wisdom not of this age or of the rulers of this age, who are coming to nothing. 7But we speak God's wisdom in a now-revealed mystery,[13] the wisdom which had been hidden, which God predetermined before the ages[14] for our glory. 8None of the rulers of this age has understood this wisdom. If they had, they would not have crucified the lord of glory.[15] 9But as it is written, "Things that no eye has

---

[12]This of course does not mean that he omitted the resurrection of Jesus or the Kingdom of God from the content of his Gospel.

[13]The unfolding immortality program which God planned for human beings, the mystery of the Kingdom of God preached first by Jesus (Heb. 2:3; cp. Acts 8:12; 19:8; 20:24-25; 28:23, 31).

[14]Cp. "In the beginning was the word or wisdom" (Jn. 1:1), God's creative immortality plan for the world. Cp. William Tyndale's translation and others which preceded the KJV of 1611. These translated *logos* as "word," not "Word."

[15]It is the epitome of insanity to kill the only one who has the solutions to all man's problems and who announced the secret of gaining immortality! Jesus at his return to the earth will reorganize the world on godly principles (Isa. 2:1-4), assisted by the saints who are now the royal family, the aristocracy of the future world system, in

seen, and no ear has heard, things which have not occurred to human
minds; all these God has prepared for those who love Him."[16] 10To us
God revealed these things through the spirit, because the spirit searches
all things, even the deep things of God.

11Among human beings, who knows the things of a person except the
spirit of that person, which is in him? In the same way no one knows the
things of God except the spirit of God. 12We did not receive the spirit of
the world, but the spirit which comes from God, so that we may know
the things that are graciously given to us by God. 13And we speak these
things not in words taught by human wisdom, but in words taught by
spirit, explaining spiritual truths with spiritual words.

14Now an unconverted person does not receive the things of the spirit
of God, because they are stupidity to him, and he cannot understand
them, because they are spiritually discerned. 15The person who is
spiritual evaluates all things,[17] but he himself is not subject to evaluation
by anyone. 16For "Who has known the mind of the Lord, so as to teach
Him?" But we have the mind of Messiah.[18]

---

training. They will rule and reign with Jesus on the earth (Rev. 5:9-10; Dan. 7:18, 22, 27, etc).

[16]The things of the future including rewards for the faithful are prepared by God and "with Him," meaning that they are presently stored up with GOD. Jesus asked to be rewarded with the glory which was stored up in God's promise, and which Jesus thus "had" before the foundation of the world (Jn. 17:5). Matt. 6:1 speaks likewise of a reward which believers "have" stored up with God in His plan.

[17]1 Thess. 5:21.

[18]The Hebrew of Isa. 40:13 cited here has "spirit" and the LXX which Paul cites has "mind." This shows that mind and spirit (and often "heart") are more or less synonymous. The spirit is never a third Person in the NT. The spirit never sends greetings and is never worshiped. If Christians have the mind of Messiah they ought to sound like him and act like him, reflecting his words and thoughts and teachings based on the Gospel of the Kingdom. Any theology which tries to remove the words and mind of Jesus from believers is dangerously deceptive. A typical example is the attempt to remove the eschatological teachings of Jesus in Matt. 24 from believers! Jesus was not just talking to Jews! They were disciples and through the apostles Jesus speaks to us. There is no PRE-Tribulation rapture in Matt. 24, nor in any passage of the NT. A major error is to separate Jesus from his words (Jn. 12:44ff), as illustrated by C.S. Lewis' amazing claim that the Gospel is not in the gospels (Introduction to J.B. Phillips, *Letters to Young Churches*, p. 9).

3 1Brothers and sisters, I could not speak to you as spiritual people but
as fleshly people, as babies in Messiah. 2I fed you with milk and not
solid food, because you were not yet ready for it. Indeed, you are not
ready even now, 3because you are still fleshly. Since there is jealousy and
division among you, are you not influenced by the flesh and acting like
unconverted people? 4For when one of you says, "I am with Paul," and
another says, "I am with Apollos," are you not being fleshly and merely
human?

5Who after all is Apollos? And who is Paul? Only servants through
whom you became believers, as the Lord gave opportunity in ministry to
each of us. 6I planted, Apollos watered, but God caused the growth. 7So
neither the person who plants is anything, nor the one who waters, but
God who causes the growth. 8The one who plants and the one who
waters are one,[19] but each will receive his own reward for his own work.
9We are co-workers who belong to God. You are God's field, His
building.

10Through the grace of God given to me, like a skillful master builder
I laid a foundation, and someone else is building on it. But let each
person be careful how he builds. 11For no one can lay any other
foundation than the one which has been laid, which is Jesus Messiah. 12If
anyone builds on that foundation with gold, silver, precious stones, or
wood, hay, or straw, 13each builder's work will be seen clearly. For the
Day will make it plain, because it will be revealed by fire, and the fire
will test what sort of work each builder has done. 14If a builder's work
still stands, he will receive a reward. 15If a builder's work is burned up,
he will suffer loss, but he himself will be saved as if through fire.[20]

16Do you not understand that you all are a temple of God[21] and that
the spirit of God lives in you? 17If anyone destroys God's temple, God
will destroy him, because God's temple is holy, and that is what you are.

---

[19]They are one in mind and purpose, the same expression used of God and Jesus in John 10:30: "I and the Father are one."

[20]The topic here is the building of churches, not the salvation of an individual. A believer who shows no fruit and has done nothing with his talent is excluded from salvation. In Matt. 25:14-30 the unproductive Christian is rejected from the Kingdom, not saved.

[21]Paul introduces the church as "a temple," not "the temple." When, however he describes the end-time appearance of the antichrist he says that he will sit in "*the*

18Let no one deceive himself. If someone among you thinks he is wise in this age, let him become "stupid" so that he can become wise! 19For the wisdom of this world-system is stupidity to God. As it is written, "He catches the wise in their own trickery," 20and "The Lord knows the reasonings of the wise; they are pointless."[22] 21So let no one boast about people. For everything belongs to you — 22whether Paul, Apollos, or Peter, the world, life, death, things present, or things to come — everything belongs to you, 23and you belong to Messiah, and Messiah belongs to God.

4 1You are to think of us in this way: as Messiah's servants and stewards of God's revealed mysteries.[23] 2And it is required of stewards that they be found faithful. 3So for me it is unimportant that I am judged by you or by any human court. Indeed I do not even judge myself. 4For I am not aware of anything against myself, but this does not make me right. It is the lord[24] who judges me. 5So do not keep passing judgment before the time — until the lord comes. He will bring to light things hidden in darkness, and reveal the intentions of hearts. Then each person will receive praise from God.[25]

6Brothers and sisters, I have used Apollos and myself as illustrations for your benefit, so that you will learn not to go beyond what is written, so that none of you will be arrogant and follow one person over another. 7For who made you better than others? What do you have that you were not given?[26] If you did receive it, why do you brag as if you had not received it?

---

temple" (2 Thess. 2:4). There the reference is not a metaphor, but based on the teaching of Dan. 11:31; 12:11; 9:24-27; 8:13-14.

[22]Reminding us of Isa. 29:13-21 where tradition mounted against the Bible leads to futile arguments (vv. 13, 21).

[23]The unfolding immortality plan revealed in Messiah and obedience to him (Heb. 5:9; Jn. 6:63). For "mystery" see also Dan. 2:28, 29, 47.

[24]Either God or Jesus, who work in perfect harmony. In this context of the second coming, Paul probably refers to the lord Messiah.

[25]Reminding us of Jesus' words: "Well done, good and faithful servant" (Mt. 25:21, 23).

[26]Every believer should ask, "What talent do I have that God did not give me?" The critical issue is the development, for the sake of the Christian cause, of the talents which God has given to each one.

8You are already filled. You have already become rich. You have
begun to reign as kings without us! I wish indeed that you were really
reigning as kings, so we would also be reigning as kings with you![27] 9For
I think that God has put us Apostles on display last of all, as men
sentenced to death. We have become a public spectacle to the world,
both to angels and to human beings. 10We are fools for Messiah, but you
are wise in Messiah. We are weak, but you are strong. You receive
honor, but we receive dishonor. 11Right up to this present hour we are
hungry and thirsty, poorly clothed, harshly treated, and homeless. 12We
are toiling, working hard with our own hands. When people curse us, we
bless them. When we are persecuted, we endure it. 13When we are
slandered, we respond with kindness. Even now we are regarded as the
scum of the earth, the trash of the world.

14I am not writing these things to you to shame you, but to warn you
as my beloved children. 15Even if you had 10,000 tutors in Messiah, you
do not have many fathers, because in Messiah Jesus I became your father
through the Gospel.[28] 16So then I appeal to you to be imitators of me.
17That is why I have sent Timothy to you, my beloved and faithful child
in the lord. He will remind you of my ways in Messiah, just as I teach
everywhere in every church. 18Some of you have become arrogant, as if I
were not coming to you. 19But I will come to you shortly, if the lord is
willing. I will find out, not only about the words of these arrogant
people, but also about their power. 20For the Kingdom of God is not a
matter of words, but of power. 21What do you want? Should I come to
you with a rod to discipline you, or with love and a spirit of gentleness?

5 1It is actually reported that there is sexual immorality among you,
worse than even among unbelievers. One of you has his father's wife!

---

[27]Rev. 2:26; 3:21; 5:10; 20:1-6; 1 Cor. 6:2; Dan. 7:14, 18, 22, 27. This text is strong proof against an "amillennial" or "postmillennial" view, the illusion that the faithful are ruling the world *now*, before Jesus returns. Paul's whole point is that the future Kingdom, of which the first stage is the millennium (Rev. 20:1-6) cannot begin before the future return of Jesus to the earth at his Parousia.

[28]The Gospel of the Kingdom being the seed which causes rebirth (Lk. 8:11; Mt. 13:19; 1 Pet. 1:23-25). Paul is the agent of their rebirth, becoming their spiritual father, as he was also of Timothy.

2You have become arrogant, when you should have mourned and
removed the one who did this from among you.
3Even though I am absent in body but present in spirit, I have
already, as if I were present, judged him who has done this. 4When you
are gathered together in the name of our lord Jesus, with me there in
spirit, and with the power of our lord Jesus, 5you are to deliver this man
to Satan[29] for the destruction of his flesh, so that his spirit may be saved
on the day of the Lord.
6Your boasting is not good. Do you not understand that a little yeast
works its way through the whole batch of dough? 7Get rid of this old
yeast so that you can become a new batch, because you are in fact
unleavened. For Messiah, our Passover lamb, has been sacrificed. 8So let
us be celebrating the festival continuously,[30] not with the old yeast, the
yeast of sin and wickedness, but with the unleavened bread of
genuineness and truth.
9In my previous letter I wrote to you not to associate with sexually
immoral people. 10I certainly did not mean the immoral people of this
world, or the covetous and thieves or idolaters, because in that case you
would have to leave the world completely! 11What I meant was not to
associate with any so-called brother or sister who is sexually immoral,
covetous, an idolater, a slanderer, a drunkard, or a thief. Do not even eat
with such a person. 12For what business of mine is it to judge those
outside the church? Should you not be judging those who are in the
church? 13But God will judge those who are outside the church. "Expel
that wicked man from among you."

6 1How dare any of you who has a dispute with another go to court
before the unrighteous and not before the saints! 2Do you not

[29]The point would be that the ravages of Satan's attack on the man might lead him to repentance.

[30]The present continuous sense of the verb here shows that Paul is not urging them to observe the OT calendar. The feasts are spiritualized, along with the Sabbath, in the NT (Col. 2:16-17). John refers to the feasts as feasts "of the Jews." He refers to the Friday prior to the Sabbath as "the preparation day of the Jews" (Jn. 19:42).

understand that the saints are going to govern and manage the world?[31] If
you are going to manage the world, are you not able to judge less
important matters? 3Do you not understand that we will be judging[32]
angels? Then why not matters related to this present life! 4So if you have
such disputes, do you take them to people who have no standing in the
church? 5I say this to shame you. Is there no one among you wise enough
to decide between fellow believers? 6Instead does a believer sue a
believer, and before unbelievers?

7Actually it is already a defeat for you that you have lawsuits with
each other. Why not rather be wronged? Why not rather allow yourself
to be defrauded? 8No, but you yourselves do wrong and defraud, even to
your fellow believers.

9Do you not understand that the unrighteous will not inherit the
Kingdom of God? Do not be deceived. Neither the sexually immoral, nor
idolaters, nor adulterers, nor male prostitutes, nor homosexuals, 10nor
thieves, nor greedy, nor drunkards, nor slanderers, nor swindlers will
inherit the Kingdom of God.[33] 11Some of you were such people,[34] but you
were washed; you were made holy; you were made right in the name of
the lord Jesus Messiah and in the spirit of our God.

12"All things are lawful for me" — but not everything is helpful. "All
things are lawful for me" — but I will not be controlled by anything.
13"Food is for the stomach, and the stomach is for food, but God will do
away with both of them." The body is not meant for sexual immorality

---

[31]This is the destiny of the true believers and it is taught throughout the NT and OT, most obviously in Dan. 2:44; 7:14, 18, 22, 27: "all nations will be subject to the saints." So also Matt. 19:28; Luke 22:28-30; Rev. 2:26; 3:21; 5:10; 20:1-6; 2 Tim. 2:12. For Paul this was an elementary truth of the faith which they should have fully understood — hence his surprise at their ignorance. In popular thinking today all this has been replaced by a very non-specific reward for disembodied souls in heaven. The Kingdom of the LORD should be referred always to 2 Chron. 13:8. It is to be a political Kingdom and empire.

[32]Or perhaps managing, governing.

[33]The popular language about "going to heaven" is found nowhere in the Bible. The Christian destiny is always to enter and inherit the future Kingdom of God when Jesus returns, and rule with him in it. The pagan notion of the disembodied immortal soul has been responsible for suppressing the real Christian view of the future. The clarity of the genuine Christian hope is eliminated. Love and faith, as a consequence, are diminished (Col. 1:4-5).

[34]Showing that former homosexuals, too, can recover from that and any other sin.

but for the lord, and the lord for the body. 14God not only has resurrected the lord, but also will resurrect us by His power. 15Do you not understand that your bodies are members of Messiah? Should I take the members of the Messiah and make them members of a prostitute? Absolutely not! 16Or do you not understand that a person who joins himself to a prostitute becomes "one body" with her?[35] For He says, "The two will become one flesh." 17But the one who joins himself to the lord becomes one spirit with him. 18Avoid all sexual immorality. All other sins which people commit are outside the body, but the sexually immoral person sins against his own body. 19Or do you not understand that your body is a temple[36] of the holy spirit which is in you, which you have from God? You are not your own, 20because you have been bought with a price. So glorify God with your body.

7 1Now concerning the matters you wrote about: "It is good for a man not to have sexual relations with a woman." 2However, because of sexual immorality, each man should have sexual relations with his own wife, and each woman with her own husband. 3The husband should meet his wife's sexual needs, and the wife her husband's. 4A wife does not have authority over her own body, but her husband does; and in the same way a husband does not have authority over his own body, but his wife does. 5Do not deprive each other, unless it is by consent for a time, so that you may devote yourselves to prayer. Then come together again so that Satan does not tempt you because of your lack of self-control. 6This I am saying by way of concession, not command. 7I wish that everyone was unmarried like me,[37] but each person has his or her own gift from God; one has this gift, one has another.

8But this I say to the unmarried and to the widowed: it is good for them if they remain as I am. 9But if they do not have self-control, let them get married, because it is better to marry than burn with passion.

---

[35]A severe warning also against any involvement with pornography.

[36]When Paul introduces the idea of the believer as a temple, he refers to "**a** temple." When referring to a literal temple building he calls it "**the** temple of God" in which the Man of Sin, the Antichrist will sit (2 Thess. 2:1-12; Dan. 9:26-27).

[37]Paul certainly never advocated celibacy for all! His statement is hyperbole for the sake of effect as in 14:5: "I wish you all spoke in tongues (languages)." But he had already made it clear that not everyone has that gift (12:30).

10But to the married I command — not I, but the lord[38] — that the
wife is not to leave her husband. 11But if she does leave, she should not
marry someone else, but rather be reconciled to her husband; and the
husband should not divorce his wife.

12But to the rest of you I — not the lord — say: if a believing man has
an unbelieving wife and she is content to continue living with him, he is
not to divorce her. 13And if a woman has an unbelieving husband, and he
is content to continue living with her, she should not divorce him. 14For
the unbelieving husband is made holy because of his wife, and the
unbelieving wife is made holy because of her husband. Otherwise your
children would be unholy, but as it is they are holy. 15Yet if the
unbeliever leaves, allow it to happen. The brother or sister is not bound[39]
in such cases, but God has called you to live in peace. 16Wife, how do
you know whether you will save your husband? And husband, how do
you know whether you will save your wife?

17As the lord has assigned to each one, and as God has called each, let
them live. This is what I command in all the churches. 18Was anyone
called already circumcised? He is not to try to reverse it. Was anyone
called while uncircumcised? He is not to get circumcised. 19Circumcision
means nothing and uncircumcision means nothing,[40] but what matters is
keeping the commandments of God.[41] 20Let everyone remain in the
condition in which they were called.

---

[38]Paul quotes an explicit ruling of the lord Jesus, reflecting Jesus' own words in Mark 10:2-12 and parallels. There is no possibility of divorce for believers. (Jesus had made a single exception, that of unrepented, continuing adultery, Mt. 19:9.) If for some unfortunate reason one of the marriage partners separates, he or she is to remain single, that is, unmarried to anyone else, with a view to becoming reconciled to his or her husband or wife. It is clear that separation definitely does not imply a divorce. It is entirely impossible that Paul had in mind some Roman law which allowed divorce by separation! His whole point here (i.e. that of Jesus who speaks in him) is that a separated believer is *not* to marry someone else. He or she is to remain unmarried, or be reconciled (see any standard commentary on this point).

[39]Implying the dissolution of such a marriage and thus a right to remarry.

[40]This shows a striking and significant difference between the Old and New Covenants. In Gen. 17 every male — Israelite and Gentile — had to be circumcised physically, to be fully part of God's people. This is radically changed under the New Covenant.

[41]A resounding statement of the basic NT teaching about the "obedience of faith" (Jn. 3:36; 12:44ff; Heb. 5:9, etc).

21Were you called when you were a slave? Do not let that trouble
you, but if you get an opportunity to become free, take it. 22For the
person who is called in the lord while a slave is the lord's free man. In
the same way the person who is called while free is Messiah's slave.
23You were bought with a price; do not become slaves of anyone.
24Brothers and sisters, in whatever condition you were when you were
called, remain in that condition with God.

25Now concerning virgins, I have no command from the lord, but I do
give my opinion as one who by the mercy of the lord is trustworthy. 26I
think that because of the distressing time we are currently living in, it is
good to remain just as you are. 27Are you married? Do not seek to be
freed. Are you unmarried? Do not seek to be married. 28But if you marry,
you have not sinned. And if a virgin marries, she has not sinned. But you
will have difficulty in this life, and I want to spare you this. 29I say this,
brothers and sisters: the time is short, and from now on those who are
married should be as though they were unmarried, 30and those who weep
as though they did not weep, and those who rejoice as if they did not
rejoice, and those who buy as though they did not own possessions, 31and
those who use the world as though they did not use it to the full, because
the form of this present world[42] is passing away.

32I want you to be free from worries. He who is unmarried is
concerned with the things of the lord, and how he may please the lord.
33But a man who is married is concerned with the things of the world,
and how he may please his wife. 34As a result his devotion is divided. A
widow or a virgin is concerned with the things of the lord, in order to be
holy both in body and spirit. But a married woman is concerned with the
things of the world, and how she may please her husband. 35This I say for
your own benefit, not to limit you, but to promote what is appropriate,
ensuring devotion to the lord without distraction.

36If a man thinks he is behaving inappropriately in regard to his virgin
daughter, if she is past her youth and if it seems necessary, he is not
sinning by letting her marry.[43] 37But the one who stands firm in his

---

[42]Rev. 12:9 states that Satan is now deceiving the whole world-system.

[43]Alternatively this may be about a "betrothed" whom a man wants to marry. In that case the sense is: "If anyone thinks that he is not behaving properly toward his betrothed, if his passions are strong, and it has to be, let him do as he wishes: let them marry — it is no sin" (ESV).

purpose, having no urgency but power over his own will, and is
determined in his own mind to keep his daughter unmarried, he does
well. 38So the man who gives his daughter in marriage does well, and the
one who does not give her in marriage does better.

39A wife is bound to her husband as long as he is living. But if her
husband falls asleep in death, she is free to marry whomever she wishes,
but only if he is in the lord.[44] 40But in my opinion she would be happier if
she stays as she is, and I think that I too have the spirit of God.

8 1Now concerning food sacrificed to idols, we know that we all have
knowledge. This knowledge puffs up, but love builds up. 2If anyone
thinks he knows something, he does not yet know it as he should. 3But if
anyone loves God, that person is known by Him.

4So then concerning the eating of food sacrificed to idols, we know
that an idol in the world is nothing, and that there is no God except for
the one God.[45] 5Even though there are some called "gods," either in
heaven or on earth — as in fact there are many "gods" and many "lords"
— 6yet for us there is only one God, who is the Father,[46] from[47] whom are
all things, and we are for Him; and one lord[48] Messiah Jesus,[49] through[50]
whom are all things, and we are through him.

---

[44]That is, marriage should be strictly to those of the same biblical, Christian faith.

[45]Defined as the Father 1300 times in the NT and expressly so in the creedal statement of Jesus in John 17:3 and Mark 12:29. This is exactly the proposition given us by the Jew who agreed with Jesus on the greatest of all commandments (Mk. 12:29). That one and only God is defined here in v. 6 as the Father.

[46]The word "God," very often in the NT "*the* God" (of Israel), occurs some 1300 times and means the Father and not the Son. Mal. 2:10 sums up the biblical definition of God: "Do we not all have one Father? Has not one God created us?" The later concept of God as Trinity is completely unknown in the Bible. Jesus defined God as did all Jews, based on Israel's central creedal statement in Deut. 6:4 (see Mk. 12:29; Jn. 17:3). "The Lord our God is one Lord," not two or three lords.

[47]The Father, who is God, is here as everywhere else said to be the source and origin of the creation. Col. 1:16 is no exception, since the creation there was "because of Christ" (a *causal* use of the Greek word *en*, "in," Moulton, *A Grammar of NT*, Vol. 3, p. 253).

[48]The lord Messiah is never ever to be confused with the Lord God! The two lords are carefully distinguished in the oracle in Ps. 110:1. YHVH is of course the one God, and the second lord of Ps. 110:l (falsely capitalized in many versions) is the human being, *adoni*, "my lord," the Messiah. *Adoni* is never a title of Deity, but always of non-Deity. Jesus is called "**our** lord Messiah" scores of times, and everyone knows that "**our**

YHVH" is a language impossibility appearing nowhere. Luke 2:11 defines the lord Messiah who was born, and of course no one in the Bible imagined that God could be born (or die!). Dr. James Dunn makes our point well: "Paul speaks of God not simply as the God of Christ but as 'the God of our *Lord* Jesus Christ.' Even as Lord, Jesus acknowledges his Father as his God. Here it becomes plain that *kyrios* (lord) is not so much a way of identifying Jesus with God, but if anything more a way of *distinguishing* Jesus from God" (*The Theology of Paul the Apostle*, p. 254). Cp. 1 Cor. 3:23, "You are Christ's and Christ is God's," and 11:3, "the head of Christ is God." Ps. 110:1 had made all that very clear, but little or no attention has been paid to the two lords in that verse, the second of whom is non-Deity. It ought to be easy to see that "God speaking to God" shatters monotheism.

[49]It is one of the most disastrous misunderstandings of the NT to claim with some exegetes today that Paul has "split the shema" (the creed of Deut. 6:4) between God and the Son, calling Jesus YHVH and the Father GOD! This is an assault on biblical monotheism (and common sense!), which is always unitary monotheism and not Trinitarian. The master key to good understanding is that there are two "lords" based on Ps. 110:1, the second of whom is not YHVH! The title "lord" for Jesus is derived from Ps. 110:1, where the second lord (my lord, *adoni*) provides the indispensable information by which Jesus is entitled to be the "lord Messiah" (Lk. 2:11; Col 3:24: "you are serving the lord Messiah"). In Acts 2:34-36 Peter makes Ps. 110:1 the key to defining the exalted position of Jesus now at the right hand of the One God: Jesus is "*made* lord and Messiah." One obviously cannot be *made* YHVH! Ps. 110:1 is by far the most often quoted or alluded to verse from the OT in the NT. Its significance cannot be overemphasized. Here Paul is in perfect agreement with the unitary monotheism of Jesus which he emphasized in Mark 12:29 and John 17:3. Both Jesus and Paul have the Shema as the pillar and foundation of their theology. This simple truth was blurred and lost from the second century on.

Moreover Jesus (Mk. 14:62) and Stephen (Acts 7:56) knew well that the one at the right hand of God was the Son of Man, the Human Being. This was certainly not "God at the right hand of God," destroying monotheism! When proper attention is paid to the all-important Ps. 110:1 we can expect a return to biblical monotheism, the creed of Jesus. The simplicity of the NT creed is found in Paul's summary statement that the truth needed for salvation is that "there is one God, and one mediator between God and man, Messiah Jesus, himself man" (1 Tim. 2:4-5). The whole point of the Bible is lost if Jesus is not a real human being. It is through "a man" that God has planned to judge the world (Acts 17:31), and that man is now an immortalized man! This too is the destiny of believers — to gain immortality at the resurrection. Placing the man Messiah (*adoni* of Ps. 110:1, a human person) next to God does not in any way alter the Shema, the creed of Jesus and of all Scripture. Paul spoke of "turning to the one God and waiting for His Son from heaven" (1 Thess. 1:9-10). God is still the Father alone. The idea of "redefining" the creed of the Bible in *one* verse in Paul is one of the most preposterous attempts of some to justify the post-biblical development of the Trinity.

7But this knowledge is not possessed by all. Some have been so used
to idols, that they still think of the food they are eating as being
sacrificed to an idol, and their conscience, being weak, is violated. 8But
food will not make us pleasing to God! If we do not eat this food, we are
not worse off, and if we do eat this food, we are not better off. 9But be
careful: on no account should this liberty of yours become a stumbling
block to the weak. 10For if a weak believer sees you who have knowledge
eating food in an idol temple, will he not be encouraged to eat food
sacrificed to idols and so violate his conscience? 11And through your
knowledge one who is weak is destroyed, a brother or sister for whom
Messiah died. 12In this way you sin against other believers by causing
them to violate their weaker consciences, and you sin against the
Messiah. 13So if eating food sacrificed to idols causes my fellow believer
to stumble, I will never eat such meat again, so that I will not cause any
believer to stumble.

9 1Am I not free? Am I not an Apostle? Have I not seen Jesus our
lord?[51] Are you not my work in the lord? 2If to others I am not an
Apostle, at least I am to you, because you are the evidence of my office
as Apostle in the lord.

3My defense to those who are investigating me is this: 4Do we not
have a right to our food and drink? 5Do we not have a right to take along
a believing wife, just like the rest of the Apostles, the brothers of the
lord, and Peter? 6Or do only Barnabas and I have to work another job?
7What soldier ever serves at his own expense? Who plants a vineyard and
does not eat its fruit? Who takes care of a flock and does not drink its
milk?

---

[50]The things which are "through" Messiah are the things of the new creation. Jesus is also the human expression of God's "wisdom," the perfect embodiment of God's eternal wisdom and plan. The "word," God's self-expression, not Word, became flesh when the Messiah, Son of God, came into existence (Jn. 1:14; Lk. 1:35; Mt. 1:20; 1 Jn. 5:18).

[51]An essential qualification for being an Apostle, along with the accrediting miraculous signs of an Apostle (2 Cor. 12:12). Jesus does not now appear literally since Paul was the last to see him in that sense (1 Cor. 15:8). The Apostles did not ordain their successors and so the Apostolic office does not exist now. The claims of some to be Apostles are not sustainable.

8Am I saying these things based only on human authority, or does the Law not say the same thing? 9For it is written in the Law of Moses, "You are not to put a muzzle on an ox while it is treading out the grain." Is God here concerned about oxen? 10Or does He say this for our sake? Yes, this was written for us, because the one who plows ought to plow in hope, and the one who threshes ought to thresh in hope of sharing the harvest. 11If we sowed spiritual seed in you, are we not entitled to harvest some material support from you? 12If others have this right to receive support from you, should we not all the more? Yet we did not use this right, but we endure everything so that we will not hinder the Gospel of the Messiah. 13Do you not understand that those who perform sacred service eat food from the temple, and those who serve at the altar receive a portion of the sacrifice on the altar? 14In the same way the Lord directed that those who proclaim the Gospel should earn their living by the Gospel.

15But I have not used any of these rights, and I do not write so that these things should be done in my case. I would rather die than allow anyone to make my boasting empty! 16For if I proclaim the Gospel I have nothing to boast about, because it is something I am compelled to do.[52] Alas for me if I do not proclaim the Gospel! 17If I do this willingly, I receive a reward. But if unwillingly, it is still my responsibility. 18What then is my reward? That when I proclaim the Gospel I may present the Gospel without charge, so as not to make full use of my rights in the Gospel.

19Though I am free and a slave to no one, I have made myself a slave to everyone, so that I may win more people. 20To the Jews I became like a Jew, so that I may win Jews. To those who are under the Law I became like someone under the Law — even though I myself am not under the Law — so that I may win those under the Law. 21To those outside the Law I became like one outside the Law, not myself being outside the Law of God, but within the Law of Messiah,[53] so that I may win those

---

[52]Just as in Luke 4:43 Jesus expressed his divine compulsion to carry out his divinely given task of announcing and preaching the Gospel about the Kingdom everywhere. Paul preached exactly the same Gospel of the Kingdom (Acts 19:8; 20:24-25; 28:23, 31).

[53]The Torah of Messiah as distinct from the Torah of Moses. Paul is free from the Torah of Moses because he is under the Torah of Messiah. Even some rabbis

who are outside the Law. 22To the weak I became weak, so that I may
win the weak. I have become all things to all people, so that I may by all
means save some. 23I do all this for the Gospel, so that I may participate
in its blessings.

24Do you not understand that in a race everyone runs, but only one
receives the prize? Then run so that you will win. 25Everyone who
competes in the games must exercise self-control in everything. They do
it to receive a crown which will not last, but we a lasting one. 26So then I
do not run like someone running without a goal. I do not fight like a
boxer hitting the air. 27But I discipline my body and bring it into
submission, so that after I have preached to others, I myself will not be
disqualified.[54]

10 1For I do not want you to be ignorant, brothers and sisters. Our
ancestors were all under the cloud, and they all passed through the
sea. 2Symbolically, they were "baptized into Moses" in the cloud and in
the sea. 3They all ate the same spiritual food 4and drank the same
spiritual drink, because they drank from a spiritual, "typical" rock that
followed them. That rock was a foreshadowing of the Messiah.[55] 5But
with most of them God was not pleased, and they were struck down in
the wilderness.

6Now these things happened as examples and "types"[56] for us, so that
we would not lust for evil things, as they lusted. 7So do not be idolaters,
as some of them were, as it is written: "The people sat down to eat and
drink, and stood up to play." 8Let us not act immorally, as some of them
did, and in a single day 23,000 died. 9Let us not test the Lord, as some of
them did, and they were killed by snakes. 10And do not grumble, as some

---

recognized that there would be a Torah superior to that of Moses, to be introduced by Messiah. The Jewish comment on Ecc. 11:8 reads: "The Torah which a man learns in this world is nothing compared to the Torah of Messiah" (Strack-Billerbeck, *Kommentar zum Neuen Testament*, Vol. 3, p. 577).

[54] The fact that Paul entertained this idea as a possibility is another clear proof against the popular doctrine of "once saved always saved" (cp. Rom. 11:22).

[55] Paul did not believe in a literal Messiah living in OT times! His language is clear here: the rock and other events and items in the history of Israel were foreshadowings of the NT and of Messiah. There was no literal "walking rock." Baptism is not literally in a cloud — or in the Red Sea!

[56] A foreshadowing, looking forward to the future reality in Messiah (cp. Col. 2:16-17).

of them did, and they were killed by the destroying angel. 11These things
happened to them as "types" and examples, and were written down as
instruction for us, on whom the ends of the ages have come. 12So then if
you think you stand, be careful that you do not fall. 13No temptation has
come to you except what is common to humans. God is faithful, and will
not allow you to be tempted beyond what you are able to bear, but with
the temptation will provide a way of escape so that you will be able to
endure it.

14So then, my beloved, run from idolatry. 15I am speaking as to
discerning people, so decide for yourselves: 16The cup of blessing which
we bless,[57] is it not a sharing in the blood of Messiah? The bread which
we break, is it not a sharing in the body of Messiah? 17Because there is
one bread, we who are many are one body, since we all share the one
bread. 18Think about the Israel of the flesh:[58] do not those who eat the
sacrifices participate in the altar? 19What am I saying then? That meat
sacrificed to idols is anything, or that an idol is anything? 20No, but I am
saying that the things which the pagans sacrifice, they are sacrificing to
demons[59] and not to God. I do not want you to participate with demons!
21You cannot drink the cup of the lord and the cup of demons; you cannot
eat from the lord's table and the table of demons. 22Are we trying to
provoke the lord to jealousy? Are we stronger than he is?

23"Everything is lawful" — but not everything is beneficial!
"Everything is lawful" — but not everything builds others up! 24No one
should seek his own good, but the good of others. 25Whatever is sold in

---

[57]This memorial celebration of the lord's death and reminder of his future Kingdom was not kept just once a year but at church gatherings. "As often as you do it" (11:26) points to an indefinite time, certainly not just annually.

[58]Meaning natural, national, now unconverted Israel. This shows of course that Paul recognized a "spiritual Israel" of the Church whom he called "the Israel of God" in Gal. 6:16 and the "true circumcision" (Jew) in Phil. 3:3. The international body of believers has been grafted into the true olive tree.

[59]The demons of course, the power behind the idols, are very real, and the synoptic record as part of the historical narratives documents the activity of supernatural, evil personalities with intelligence, the demons. The demons cried out and the demons recognized Jesus to be the Messiah (see Lk. 4:41). Jesus rebuked the demons. On no account should the records be violated by confusing the demons with the demoniacs! Demon never means in the Bible a human person and certainly not a mental disease! James notes that "the demons believe in the One God and tremble" (James 2:19). Nonsense is made of this categorical statement if demons do not exist!

the meat market you can eat without asking any questions for the sake of
conscience, 26because "the earth belongs to the Lord, and everything on it
is His." 27If an unbeliever invites you to a meal, and you decide to go, eat
whatever is set before you without asking any questions for the sake of
conscience. 28But if someone says to you, "This food was offered to an
idol," do not eat it for the sake of the one who told you, and for the sake
of conscience. 29I mean his conscience, not your own. For why is my
personal freedom being judged by another's conscience? 30If I eat with
thankfulness, why am I to be blamed for something I give thanks for?

31So whether you eat or drink or whatever you do, do it for the glory
of God. 32Give no offense, either to Jews or to Gentiles or to the church
of God, 33just as I am trying to please everyone in all things. I do not seek
my own good, but the good of the many, so that they may be saved.

11 1Follow my example, just as I follow the example of Messiah. 2I
praise you because you remember me in all things, and hold to the
traditions just as I handed them on to you. 3But I want you to know that
the Messiah is the head of every man, the man is the head of a woman,
and God is the head of the Messiah. 4A man praying or prophesying[60]
with his head covered dishonors his head. 5But a woman praying or
prophesying with her head uncovered dishonors her head, because it is
the equivalent of having her head shaved. 6For if a woman's head is not
covered, then let her hair be cut off. But if it is shameful for a woman to
have her hair cut off or shaved, then she should have her head covered.
7A man should not have his head covered, because he is the image and
glory of God, but the woman is the glory of the man. 8For man is not
from woman, but woman from man; 9and man was not created for the
woman, but woman for the man. 10So the woman ought to have a sign of
authority on her head, because of the angels.[61] 11Nevertheless the woman
is not independent of the man, nor the man independent of the woman, in
the lord. 12For as woman came from the man, so man comes through
woman, but everything comes from God. 13Decide for yourselves: is it
appropriate for a woman to pray to God with her head uncovered? 14Does
not even common sense teach you that if a man has long hair it is a

---

[60]Prophesying has the general sense of encouraging and edifying (see 14:3).
[61]The exact point in relation to the angels is disputed by commentary.

dishonor to him? 15But if a woman has long hair it is a glory to her,
because her hair is given to her as a covering. 16If anyone wants to argue
about this, we have no other practice, nor do the churches of God.

17In giving you the instructions which follow I do not praise you,
because when you come together it is not for the better but for the worse.
18First of all, when you come together as a church, I hear that there are
divisions among you, and I partly believe it. 19For there must be divisions
among you so that those who are approved may become known. 20So
then, when you meet together it is not really the lord's supper that you
are eating, 21because when it is time to eat each one takes his own supper
first, leaving one hungry and another drunk. 22What? Do you not have
houses to eat and drink in? Or do you show contempt for God's church
and shame those who have nothing? What should I tell you? Should I
praise you? In this I certainly do not praise you.

23For I received from the lord what I handed on to you: the lord Jesus,
on the night[62] he was betrayed, took bread. 24When he had given thanks,
he broke it and said, "This bread represents my body, which is for you.
Do this in memory of me." 25In the same way he took the cup after
supper, with these words: "This cup represents the New Covenant
ratified by my blood. Do this, as often as[63] you drink it, in memory of
me." 26For as often as you eat this bread and drink from this cup, you are
proclaiming the lord's death until he comes.

27So then, whoever eats the bread or drinks from the lord's cup in an
unworthy way will be guilty of the body and blood of the lord. 28Let each
person first examine themselves, and then eat the bread and drink from
the cup. 29For the person who eats and drinks without regard for the body
eats and drinks judgment on himself. 30This is the reason why many of
you are weak and sick, and some have fallen asleep in death. 31But if we

---

[62]The Thursday evening before his Friday crucifixion, followed by his resurrection on the third day, Sunday (Lk. 24:21; cp. 9:22; 13:32; 18:33). That Friday in the year of the crucifixion was the 15th day of Nisan, and the Passover meal had been eaten by Jesus and the nation when the 15th began at sunset.

[63]Indicating an indefinite frequency, certainly not just once a year since this is a new Christian celebration. The Jehovah's Witness practice of excluding ordinary members (other than the so-called 144,000) from the communion is in fact a way (not intentional) of excommunicating them! It is fanciful to base a whole "two-class" system in the church on the passages in Rev. 7, 14. Jesus and Paul would have argued against this vehemently.

examined ourselves rightly, we would not be judged. 32But when we are judged, we are disciplined by the lord, so that we will not be condemned along with the world.

33So, my brothers and sisters, when you come together to eat the lord's supper, wait for one another. 34If anyone is hungry, let him eat at home, so that your coming together will not bring judgment. About the other matters, I will instruct you when I come.[64]

12 1Now concerning spiritual gifts, brothers and sisters, I do not want you to be ignorant. 2You know that when you were pagans, you were being led away to those mute idols, however you may have been led. 3So I want you to understand that no one speaking by God's spirit says, "Jesus is accursed." And no one can say, "Jesus is lord"[65] but by holy spirit.

4Now there are different spiritual gifts,[66] but the same spirit. 5And there are different services, but the same lord. 6And there are different activities, but the same God, who works all things in everyone. 7To each person is given the evidence of the spirit for the benefit of all. 8One person is given through the spirit a word of wisdom. Another person[67] is given a word of knowledge in harmony with the same spirit. 9To another is given faith by the same spirit, and to another gifts of healings by the one spirit. 10To another is given the ability to perform miracles; to another prophecy; to another discernment of spirits; to another the ability to speak different languages,[68] and to another the translation of those

---

[64]The lord's supper was obviously not once a year, but at church meetings. Paul had to pay urgent attention to correcting the abuse of the lord's supper by letter, and he was going to visit them within a year.

[65]The confession is not "Jesus is God" which would make two Gods. Jesus is everywhere in the NT "the lord Messiah" (Lk. 2:11) based on the *adoni* (my lord) of Ps. 110:1. *Adoni,* "my lord," is in all 195 occurrences never a title of Deity.

[66]There are different gifts (*charismata*), services and activities.

[67]Paul emphasizes the fact that not every member has the same gift! It is a disastrous misreading to say that every church member ought to be able to operate all the varieties of gifts, which are given, obviously, on a principle of distribution.

[68]These were intelligible languages but needing to be translated. At Pentecost, foreigners heard the Apostles speaking their native languages supernaturally. This was a demonstrable miracle of speaking, not a miracle of hearing! The Apostles "began to speak in other languages" (Acts 2:4). The faith was now going universally, and the tower of Babel (Babylon) was being reversed. "Tongues" ought always to be rendered

languages. 11But the one and the same spirit produces all of these, distributing to each person as he[69] desires.

12As the human body is one but has many parts, and although there are many parts of the body, they are still one body, so also is the Messiah. 13For in one spirit we were all baptized into one body,[70] whether Jews or Gentiles, slaves or free; we all were made to drink of one spirit.

14For the body is not one part, but many. 15If a foot were to say, "Because I am not a hand, I am not part of the body," that does not make it any less a part of the body. 16If an ear were to say, "Because I am not an eye, I am not part of the body," that does not make it any less a part of the body. 17If the whole body were an eye, where would the hearing be? If the whole body were an ear, where would the sense of smell be? 18But God has set each part in the body just as He desired. 19If they were all one part, where would the body be? 20So there are many parts, but one body. 21The eye cannot say to the hand, "I do not need you," or the head say to the foot, "I do not need you." 22On the contrary, some of those parts of the body that seem weaker are truly necessary. 23And those parts of the body we consider to be less honorable, to those we give more honor, and our less presentable parts become much more presentable, 24while our presentable parts have no such need. God has perfectly arranged the body, giving greater honor to its apparently inferior parts. 25This is so that there would be no division in the body, but the parts should have the same care for one another. 26When one part suffers, all the other parts of the body suffer with it, and when a part is honored, then all the other parts of the body rejoice with it.

27Now you are the body of Messiah, and each one of you is a part of it. 28God has appointed in the church: first Apostles,[71] second prophets,

---

"languages," and claims to "tongues" must be verified to see that actual languages are being spoken. Otherwise there is a very real danger of self-deception.

69There is no third Person. The spirit of God or Jesus is at work among believers.

70This is not a "second level" of conversion but the common initiation of every true believer into the Church. There is no noun phrase "baptism of the holy spirit" in the NT, but being immersed in spirit is the common experience of all NT believers. It is the essential mark of becoming a believer. Water baptism was the required public sign of joining the body of Messiah.

71Apostles, at the level of the twelve, ceased when the Apostles died. Jesus did not reappear after he appeared last to Paul. Apostles must have seen Jesus literally and also have the accrediting signs of an Apostle (2 Cor. 12:12).

third teachers; then miracles, then gifts of healings, of helping,
leadership, and different languages. 29Are all Apostles? No. Are all
prophets? No. Are all teachers? No. Do all perform miracles? No. 30Do
all have gifts of healing? No. Do all speak in different languages?[72] No.
Do all translate languages? No. 31But you should earnestly desire the
higher gifts. And now I will show you the most excellent way.

13 1If I were to speak in the languages of humans and of angels, but
do not have love, I have become just a noisy gong or a clanging
cymbal. 2If I have the gift of prophecy, and understand all mysteries and
all knowledge, and if I had complete faith so that I could move
mountains, but do not have love, then I amount to nothing. 3If I give
away all my possessions, and if I even give up my body, but do not have
love, then I gain nothing.

4Love is patient and kind, and is not envious. Love does not brag and
is not arrogant. 5Love does not behave inappropriately, or seek its own
way. Love is not easily angered and keeps no record of wrongs. 6Love
does not rejoice in evil, but rejoices in the truth.[73] 7Love bears all things,
believes all things, hopes all things, and endures all things.

8Love will never end. But the gift of prophecy will be done away
with. The gift of languages will cease. The gift of knowledge will be set
aside. 9For we know in part and we prophesy in part, 10but when what is
complete comes, then what is incomplete will be done away with.
11When I was a child, I spoke as a child, thought as a child, and reasoned
as a child. Now that I am an adult I have put away those childish ways.
12For now we see as if looking at a reflection in a mirror, but then[74] we
will see face to face. Now I know in part, but then I will know fully, just

---

[72]It should be perfectly obvious then that the idea of a universal "prayer language" is in direct contradiction to Scripture. Believers are to have different gifts. The idea that one gift could be exercised by all believers is in direct contradiction of this passage. When Paul speaks of "all speaking in languages," he means of course those who have that particular gift.

[73]"A love of the truth in order to be saved" is one of Paul's most significant teachings (2 Thess. 2:10).

[74]At the future resurrection to occur when Jesus comes back, certainly not before. There is no conscious "intermediate" state in Scripture. The dead are asleep in the "sleep of death" (Ps. 13:3). They will awake to the Life of the Age to Come when Jesus returns (Dan. 12:2; 1 Cor. 15:23; Rev. 11:15-18; 20:1-6).

as I was fully known. 13So now faith, hope, and love remain — these three. And the greatest of these is love.

14 1Keep on pursuing love[75] and earnestly desire the spiritual gifts, especially the ability to prophesy.[76] 2For one who speaks in another language speaks not to people but to God, because nobody understands him; in the spirit he is speaking secret truths.[77] 3But one who prophesies speaks to people for their edification, encouragement and consolation. 4One who speaks in another language builds himself up, but one who prophesies builds up the church. 5I would like it if you all spoke in languages,[78] but I prefer that you would prophesy.[79] One who prophesies is more important than one who speaks in languages, unless he translates, so that the church may be built up.

6Brothers and sisters, if I come to you speaking in other languages, what benefit would I be to you unless I speak to you either with revelation, or knowledge,[80] or prophesying, or teaching? 7Even with non-living things which make sounds, like a flute or a harp, if there is no distinction in the notes, how would you know what is being played? 8If the trumpet gives an unclear sound, who would prepare for battle? 9So you too, unless you speak a language that everyone understands, how will it be known what you are saying? For you would just be speaking into the air. 10There are many different languages in this world, and none of them is without meaning. 11If I do not understand a language, I will be

---

[75]Including the important characteristic of love, that it celebrates the truth (13:6), the polar opposite of error (cp. 2 Thess. 2:10).

[76]Seek to prophesy, which in the NT is not confined to prediction but is defined as v. 3 explains as the ability "to speak to people for edification, encouragement and consolation."

[77]Paul never endorses the idea that the gift of language remain permanently untranslated or private. He urges all who have that gift to "pray that they may interpret" (v. 13). The object is that all may hear what the spirit is saying. Paul also defines "languages" as a sign to unbelievers. This is a public miracle and certainly not confined to the prayer closet. "Languages" are spoken publicly in Acts.

[78]That is, those who have that particular gift. He has already explained that this gift is not given to all (12:30).

[79]In the sense defined by verse 3.

[80]The importance of knowledge is stressed by the under-quoted verse Isa. 53:11 which teaches us that the Messiah "makes people right through his knowledge" (cp. Dan. 12:3).

a foreigner to those who speak it, and they will be foreigners to me. 12So
also you, since you are zealous for spiritual gifts, seek to excel in those
that build up the church.

13So then, let the one who speaks in another language pray that he
could translate it.[81] 14If I pray in another language, my spirit prays, but
my understanding bears no fruit for other people.[82] 15What is my
conclusion then? I will pray with my spirit, and I will pray with my
understanding also. I will sing praises with my spirit, and I will sing
praises with my understanding also. 16Otherwise if you give thanks in the
spirit, how can ungifted people say "Amen" after your prayer of thanks,
since they do not know what you said? 17You may have thanked God
well, but the other people have not been helped! 18I thank God that I
speak in languages more than all of you.[83] 19But in the church I would
rather speak five words with my understanding, so that I can instruct
others, than ten thousand words in another language.

20Brothers and sisters, do not think like children. Be as innocent as
babies in regard to evil, but in your thinking become mature. 21As it is
written in the Law, "By people speaking foreign languages, by the
mouths of foreigners, I will speak to this people, but even then they will
not listen to Me, says the Lord." 22Speaking in foreign languages, then, is
a miraculous sign, not for believers, but for unbelievers.[84] But
prophesying is not for unbelievers, but for believers. 23If the whole
church is gathered and everyone speaks in other languages, and
unbelievers or uninformed people come in, will they not say that you are
crazy? 24But if everyone prophesies, and an unbeliever or uninformed
person comes in, he will be convicted by all and called to account by all.

---

[81]Paul is no friend of unintelligibility. He does not recognize a "language" which never comes to public notice by translation. The language-gifted person is expected to be able to translate or have access to a person with the companion gift of translation. The latter procedure seems to be the norm. The point is that "languages" are not proven to be the genuine thing if they forever remain untranslated. How does anyone know, in that case, if the "gift" is genuine or not? It might just be a form of self-deception.

[82]That is, benefits no one else.

[83]It is mistakenly assumed that Paul means speaking languages in private prayer!

[84]This marvelous definition of "tongues" (languages) should be rigorously applied to what goes under the name of "tongues" today. The vast majority of so-called tongues speakers have never known what they say and have translated their language to no one.

25The secrets of his heart are revealed, and so he will fall on his face and
worship God, declaring that God is truly among you.

26What is my conclusion then, brothers and sisters? When you come
together, each one of you has a song, a teaching, a revelation, another
language, or translation of it. Let all these things be done to build each
other up. 27If someone speaks in another language, let it be two, or at the
most three, and one at a time,[85] and someone must translate. 28But if there
is no translator, those who speak in languages should keep silent in the
church and speak to themselves and to God.

29Let two or three prophets speak, and let the others evaluate what
was said. 30If a revelation is made to another who is sitting down, then
the person speaking should finish. 31For you can all prophesy, one at a
time, so that all may learn and all may be encouraged. 32The spirits of
prophets are subject to the prophets themselves, 33because God is not a
God of confusion but of peace, as in all the churches of the saints.

34Let the women be quiet in the churches, because it is not permitted
for them to be talking except in submission, as the Law also says. 35If
they want to inquire about something, let them ask their own husbands at
home, because it is improper for a woman to be speaking in church.[86]
36Did the Gospel-word of God[87] begin with you Corinthians? Or are you
the only people it has reached?

37Anyone who thinks he is a prophet or spiritual, let him recognize
that the things I am writing to you are the Lord's command. 38But if
anyone does not recognize this, he is not recognized.

---

[85]A "chorus" of "tongues" is thus forbidden.

[86]The remarkable fact is that just 3 chapters earlier in 11:5 Paul wants women to pray and prophesy. This indicates his statement here cannot be read as a blanket ban on women speaking in church. It seems possible from the context that women in the church at Corinth were questioning and arguing. This would be part of the disorder he mentions, and this may be the issue Paul is addressing here. Others have suggested that 14:34-35 is the practice of some in the church at Corinth, and Paul is quoting them before refuting their argument. On no account should the instructions in 11:5 be overlooked! The gifts, many of which involve public speaking, were given to men and women alike. Paul, however, did not ordain women to be church leaders (1 Tim. 3:1-2).

[87]The Gospel of the Kingdom, the saving Gospel (cp. Acts 8:12 for an early creed and guide to salvation).

39So then, brothers and sisters, earnestly desire to prophesy, and do
not prohibit speaking in languages. 40But let everything be done in a
proper and orderly way.

15 1Now I declare to you, brothers and sisters, the Gospel I preached
to you, which you received, on which you stand firm. 2It is by this
Gospel that you are being saved[88] — if you hold firmly to the Gospel-
word which I preached to you. Otherwise you have believed for nothing.
3For among matters of first importance,[89] I delivered to you what I
also received: that Messiah died for our sins according to the Scriptures;
4that he was buried and that he was raised on the third day,[90] according to
the Scriptures; 5and that he appeared to Peter, then to the twelve. 6After
that he appeared to over 500 brothers and sisters at once, most of whom
are still alive now, though some have fallen asleep in death.[91] 7Then he
appeared to James, and then to all the Apostles. 8And last of all, as

---

[88]Salvation in the NT is in three tenses of the verb. We were saved, and since we must continue, we are being saved, and most importantly we will be saved at Messiah's return. The proof of this point is in Paul's defining statement that "salvation is now closer to us than when we first believed" (Rom. 13:11). Salvation is a race to the finish, and no one gets a gold medal when the starting gun goes off!

[89]Paul mentions central, non-negotiable aspects of the Gospel, but he says expressly that these are "are *among* items of first importance" (Thayer's Lexicon: "among the first things delivered to you by me"), not that they are the whole of the Gospel. The Kingdom of God is the basis and beginning of the Gospel, from Jesus who first preached it (Mk. 1:14-15; Heb. 2:3; Acts 10:34-37) onwards. Paul always preached the Gospel of the Kingdom (Acts 19:8; 20:24-25; 28:23, 30, 31). Thus the death and resurrection of Jesus are among the key elements of the Gospel, but not the whole Gospel, since Jesus preached the Kingdom as Gospel long before even mentioning his death which he first did in Matt. 16:21. 1 Cor. 15:1-3 has been misused constantly to deprive Jesus of his role as preacher of the Gospel and also disastrously to pit Paul against Jesus! The one fatal thing is to suppress or eliminate the words/teaching/Gospel preached by Jesus (1 Tim. 6:3; 2 John 7-9). The NT constantly warns against this fatal pitfall. A most strikingly misleading statement is that of C.S. Lewis: "The Gospel is not in the gospels" (Introduction to *Letters to Young Churches*, by J.B. Phillips). This is the diametric opposite of the truth.

[90]Sunday is the third day since Friday and Luke 24:21 puts this fact beyond doubt. See Luke 13:32-33 for Jesus' own inclusive reckoning: "today, tomorrow, and the third day" (cp. Hos. 6:2).

[91]For the sleep of death see Ps. 13:3; Ecc. 9:5, 10; Jn. 11:11, 14 and my *The Amazing Aims and Claims of Jesus*, appendices 4 and 5.

though to a child born at the wrong time, he appeared to me also. 9For I
am the least of the Apostles, who is not worthy to be called an Apostle
because I persecuted the church of God. 10But by the grace of God I am
what I am. His grace which was given to me was not for nothing, but I
have worked more than all of them — though not I, but the grace of God
with me. 11So whether it is I or they, so we proclaim and so you believed.

12Now if it is preached that the Messiah has been raised from the
dead, how are some among you saying that there is no resurrection of the
dead?[92] 13If there is no resurrection of the dead, then Messiah has not
been raised from the dead either. 14And if Messiah has not been raised,
then our preaching is pointless, and your faith is pointless too. 15Indeed
we would be false witnesses of God because we would have testified
against God that He raised Messiah, whom He did not raise if the dead
are not raised! 16For if the dead are not raised, then Messiah has not been
raised either, 17and if Messiah has not been raised, then your faith is
useless, and you are still in your sins. 18Then also those who have fallen
asleep in death in Messiah have perished.[93] 19For if we have hoped in
Messiah in this life only, we should be pitied more than anyone!

20But now Messiah has been raised from the dead, the first fruits of
those who have fallen asleep in death. 21For since death came through a
human being, the resurrection of the dead also comes through a human
being.[94] 22For just as in Adam all die, so in the Messiah all will be made
alive.[95] 23But each in his own order: Messiah the first fruits, then those
who belong to Messiah at his coming.[96] 24Later comes the end, when he

---

[92]Showing a tragic instability among some believers. The need for Paul's apostolic call to return to sanity is obvious.

[93]Proving that Paul did not believe in a post-mortem survival, but that gaining immortality depended entirely on the future resurrection of believers (v. 23; Lk. 14:14, etc).

[94]Showing that Jesus is the second Adam, the head of God's new creation, but not an eternal God the Son. Adam was the son of God (Lk. 3:38) and Jesus is the Son of God, as defined by Luke 1:35. Jesus is the head of the new race of human beings. He came into existence from a woman (Gal. 4:4; Rom. 1:3).

[95]This of course implies that before coming back to life, being made alive, they are dead and unconscious — not alive as disembodied spirits. The latter idea is entirely foreign to Scripture.

[96]That is, at his Second Coming, his *Parousia*. This is a single event, not divided into two events separated by 7 years. The 70th "week" is certainly future based on Dan. 9:24-27 but there is no PRE-Tribulation rapture/resurrection. Jesus made no mention of

will hand over the Kingdom[97] to God who is the Father, after abolishing
all rule, authority, and power. 25For Messiah is destined to reign[98] until he
has put all his enemies under his feet. 26The last enemy to be abolished is
death. 27For "He has put[99] all things in subjection under his feet." Of
course when it says "all things" are put in subjection, it is evident that
this does not include the One who subjected all things to him. 28And
when all things are subjected to him, then the Son himself will be
subjected to the One who subjected all things to him, so that God may be
all in all.

29Otherwise what do some of you mean by being baptized for the
dead? If the dead are not raised at all, why then are people baptized for
them? 30And why do we live in danger every moment? 31Brothers and
sisters, I affirm by the pride in you which I have in Messiah Jesus our
lord, I face death daily. 32If I fought with wild animals at Ephesus for
human purposes, what did it benefit me? If the dead are not raised, "Let
us eat and drink, because tomorrow we die"! 33Do not be deceived: "Bad
company corrupts good morals." 34Become sober and right-minded, and
stop sinning. For some have no knowledge of God — I say this to your
shame.

---

any PRE-Tribulation rapture/resurrection in Matt. 24, Mark 13, Luke 21, nor did Paul in Thessalonians. The future resurrection of all the faithful will occur at the last trumpet, the seventh trumpet of Rev. 11:15-18. Paul promised relief for Christians "at the revelation of Jesus from heaven in flaming fire taking vengeance on his enemies" (2 Thess. 1:7-8). No one writing thus could possibly have imagined a "secret rapture/resurrection" seven years earlier! And Jesus speaking to us Christians through the Apostles warned his followers to flee to the mountains when the onset of the future Great Tribulation was about to happen. The key sign for this is "when you see the Abomination of Desolation standing where HE ought not to…" (Mk. 13:14). The participle *estekota* is masculine to signify a person as the Abomination. In Daniel this antichrist is the King of the North and in Isaiah the Assyrian who will be destroyed by the brightness of Jesus' coming (see 2 Thess. 2:8, citing Isa. 11:4).

[97]The Kingdom here is its first stage, the millennium as revealed in Rev. 20:1-6. Jesus will reign for that 1000 years and then present the Kingdom to God (v. 28). Rev. 5:10 summarizes the Kingdom program.

[98]That is, Messiah will rule in the future millennial Kingdom, prior to the second resurrection (Rev. 20:1-6).

[99]A past tense of prophecy from Ps. 8:6. We do not yet see everything subject to Jesus (Heb. 2:8). Cp. Isa. 9:6: "To us a child has been born; a son has been given," expressed in the past tense but a prophecy of the future.

35But someone will say, "How are the dead raised? What kind of
body will they have?" 36You foolish person! What you sow does not
sprout into life unless it dies. 37And when you sow, you do not sow the
plant it will grow into, just the bare seed, whether wheat or something
else. 38But God gives it a body as He has planned, and each kind of seed
grows into a different plant. 39All bodies are not the same, but humans
have one kind of body, animals another, birds another, and fish another.
40There are also heavenly bodies and earthly bodies, and the brightness of
the heavenly bodies differs from that of the earthly bodies. 41The sun has
one kind of brightness, the moon another, and the stars another. And one
star differs from another star in brightness.

42So it is with the resurrection of the dead. The body is sown mortal;
it is resurrected immortal. 43It is sown in dishonor; it is raised in honor
and glory. It is sown in weakness; it is raised in power. 44It is sown a
natural body; it is raised a spiritual body. If there is a natural body, there
is also a spiritual body. 45So as it is written, "The first man, Adam,
became a living person"; the last Adam became a life-imparting spirit.
46Yet the spiritual did not come first, but the natural. Then the spiritual
came after that.[100] 47The first man is of the earth, made of dust. The
second man is of heaven.[101] 48As is the one made from dust, so also are
those made from dust, and as is the man of heaven, so also are those who
are of heaven. 49As we have borne the image of the man of dust, we will
also bear the image of the man of heaven.

50Now I say this to you, brothers and sisters: Flesh and blood[102]
cannot inherit the Kingdom of God;[103] the perishable does not inherit the

---

[100]Showing of course that the first Adam came first and the spiritual man next, in that order. The idea of a preexistent or pre-human Jesus would be in direct contradiction to Paul here.

[101]The now immortal Jesus will arrive from heaven at his return. "From his resurrection onwards Messiah became to human faith the 'man of heaven'" (G.G. Findlay, *Expositor's Greek New Testament*).

[102]"Flesh and blood": as we are presently constituted.

[103]The inheritance of the Kingdom of God is always something for Christians which lies in the future. We can obtain a taste of it now by receiving the spirit of the Kingdom as a downpayment and guarantee. But the inheritance of the Kingdom on earth refers to the time when believers will possess the Kingdom and rule and reign with Messiah in it (see Dan. 7:18, 22, 27, RSV). "Fear not, little flock, because your Father is delighted to give you the Kingdom," Jesus said (Lk. 12:32).

imperishable. 51Listen, I am revealing a mystery to you: We will not all
fall asleep in death,[104] but we will all be changed, 52in a moment, in the
blink of an eye, at the last trumpet.[105] For the trumpet will sound, and the
dead will be resurrected unable ever to die again, and we will be
changed.[106] 53For this perishable body must put on the imperishable, and
this mortal body must put on immortality. 54When this perishable will
have put on the imperishable, and this mortal will have put on
immortality, then will happen the saying that is written: "Death has been
swallowed up by victory. 55Death, where is your victory? Death, where is
your sting?" 56The sting of death is sin, and the power of sin is the Law.
57But thanks be to God, who gives us the victory through our lord Jesus
Messiah. 58So my beloved brothers and sisters, be firm, immovable,
always abounding in the lord's work, knowing that your labor in the lord
is not for nothing.

16 1Now concerning the collection for the saints, as I commanded the
churches in Galatia, you do also: 2On the first day of every week
let each one of you set aside and place in the church treasury some
money, as you have been blessed. I do not want there to be any
collections when I come.[107] 3When I arrive I will send with letters of

---

[104]The current popular phrases "pass away," "pass on," or "pass" are highly deceptive. They mislead people into thinking that death is not really the cessation of life, but merely passing in a different form to a different condition. This is the Devil's original falsehood: "you will surely not die" (Gen. 3:4). Resurrection in the Bible means a return from the state of death (which is not life!) to life which will be endless., i.e. immortality and indestructibility. This is the Christian hope, on which faith and love depend (Col. 1:4-5).

[105]The seventh and final trumpet of Rev. 11:15-18. This is the resurrection of the faithful of all the ages (Dan 12:2).

[106]That is, from mortal to immortal, the staggering objective of God's whole Gospel of the Kingdom immortality plan (Jn. 1:1; Mk. 1:14-15).

[107]The fact that Paul did not want collections to be made when he arrived tells us that the money was collected weekly, every first day of the week, in church. "It may be added that since Paul urges this course (collection for the poor) 'so that no collections be made when I come' and as the whole work is described in v. 1 as a collection (*logia*) it is most natural to infer that there was not only a setting apart of gifts, but also a paying into a local fund week by week. This strengthens the view that v. 2 incidentally gives evidence of early movements towards the setting up of the Lord's day as an institution, especially when taken along with Acts 20:7. For when could the

introduction whomever you approve to carry your gift to Jerusalem. 4If it
is appropriate for me to go too, they will go with me.

5Since I am intending to go through Macedonia, I will come to you
after that. 6I may stay with you for a while, maybe through the winter, so
that you can send me on my way to wherever I go. 7For I do not want to
see you now just in passing, but I hope to stay with you for some time, if
the lord permits. 8I will stay in Ephesus until Pentecost, 9because a
productive door has opened wide for me, but there are many enemies.

10Now if Timothy comes, see to it that you make him feel welcome
among you, because he is doing the work of the lord as I am. 11So do not
let anyone look down on him. Send him on his journey in peace so he
may come to me, because I expect him to come with the brothers.

12Concerning our brother Apollos, I strongly urged him to come to
you with the other brothers, but he did not want to do so now. He will
come when he has an opportunity.

13Be alert. Stand firm in the faith. Be courageous. Be strong. 14Let all
that you do be done in love.

15You know the household of Stephanas were among the first
converts in Achaia, and they have dedicated themselves to serve the
saints. I urge you, brothers and sisters, 16to be in subjection to them, and
to everyone who helps the work with such dedication. 17I rejoice in the
coming of Stephanas, Fortunatus, and Achaicus, because they have made
up for your absence. 18They have refreshed my spirit and yours, so
recognize such people.

---

contributions of the people be better collected in readiness for the Apostle than at their meetings on the special day of worship?" (*Dictionary of Apostolic Church*, Vol. 1, p. 707). "Some have interpreted the words *par eauto* (by himself) to mean at home. But then why mention doing it on Sunday [actually *every* Sunday], when they could just as well do it regularly at home at other times? The meaning must rather be that the Christians were to bring their offerings to church on Sunday, since that was the day they assembled for worship (Acts 20:7; Justin Martyr mentions this practice in his Apology 1, 67. 6)" (*New International Dictionary of New Testament Theology*, Vol. 2, p. 329). "'Every first day of the week.' This is the first piece of evidence to show that the Christians habitually observed that day (a custom from the start, Jn. 20:19, 26; Acts 20:7). Paul expressly deprecates the collecting of the money when he arrives (which would be necessary if they all had it laid by *at home*). It is better perhaps to think of it as being stored in the church treasury. Paul indicates no definite amount, no exact proportion of one's income" (Leon Morris, *Tyndale Commentary*, p. 238).

19The churches in the province of Asia send their greetings. Aquila
and Prisca send their hearty greetings in the lord, together with the
church that meets in their house. 20All the brothers and sisters send
greetings. Greet one another with a holy kiss.

21This greeting comes from me, Paul, in my own handwriting. 22If
anyone does not love the lord, let him be cursed. Maranatha — may our
lord[108] come!

23The grace of the lord Jesus be with you. 24My love be with all of
you in Messiah Jesus. Amen.

---

[108]The title "our lord" is proof positive that Jesus is not YHVH! The name YHVH is the personal name of the One God, and "my YHVH" and "our YHVH" are impossible phrases found nowhere. Jesus however is the "my lord, our lord" (*adoni*) of Ps. 110:1. This is the Messianic title *par excellence*, and Ps. 110:1 is an umbrella text pervading the whole NT. The second lord of Ps. 110:1 is *adoni* in the Hebrew, and in all 195 occurrences of this word it never refers to Deity. It is a shattering violation of Scripture to speak of two who are YHVH! It assaults the first commandment and the centrally important "*shema*" ("Hear, O Israel") of Deut. 6:4, repeated as the foundation of all true religion by Jesus in Mark 12:29.

2 Corinthians

1 1From Paul, an Apostle of Messiah Jesus by the will of God, and Timothy our brother, to the church of God in Corinth, and all the saints living in the whole of Achaia: 2Grace and peace to you from God who is our Father and from the lord Jesus Messiah.[1]

3Blessed be the God and Father of our lord Jesus Messiah, the Father of compassion and God of all comfort. 4He comforts us in all our trials, so that we may be able to comfort those experiencing any trial with the comfort with which we ourselves are comforted by God. 5For as we share abundantly in the sufferings of the Messiah, in the same way we share abundantly in comfort through the Messiah. 6If we are troubled, it is for your comfort and salvation. If we are comforted, it is for your comfort, which you experience when you patiently endure the same sufferings which we are also undergoing. 7Our hope for you is well-founded, since we know that as you share in our sufferings you will also share in our comfort.

8For we do not want you to be uninformed, brothers and sisters, about the trouble we had in the province of Asia. We were extremely weighed down beyond our strength, so much that we despaired even of life. 9We felt as if a sentence of death was on us; this was to make us rely not on ourselves but on God, the One who resurrects the dead. 10He rescued us from such a great risk of death, and He will rescue us. On Him we have set our hope that He will yet again rescue us, 11as you join in helping us by praying. Then many people will give thanks on our behalf for the gracious favor given to us through many people's prayers.

12For our confidence is this: the testimony of our conscience, that in simplicity and sincerity from God, not in worldly wisdom but in the grace of God, we have behaved in the world, and especially toward you.

---

[1]Jesus is defined in Scripture as the "lord Messiah" (Lk. 2:11; Rom. 16:18; Col. 3:24) certainly not the Lord God. This is because only one Person is the Lord God. The creed of Israel and of Jesus is clear: "The Lord our God is one Lord" (Mk. 12:29, quoting the Shema of Deut. 6:4). Jesus is the *adoni*, "my lord" of Ps. 110:1 which is the master key text from the OT in the NT. *Adoni* in all of its 195 occurrences is never the title of Deity. No one in NT times imagined Jesus to be a second Yahweh. The Messianic title "my lord" (*adoni*) becomes the "our lord Jesus Messiah" of the NT. In 1 Cor. 8:4-6 Jesus is not God, but the lord Jesus Messiah. The idea that Paul has split the Shema between God and Jesus is entirely unwarranted.

13For we write to you only what you can read and understand.[2] And I
hope you will understand completely, 14as you have partially understood
us, so that we will be your reason for pride, as you will be ours, on the
Day of our lord Jesus.

15In this confidence I was determined at first to come to you so that
you might have the blessing of two visits, 16as I wanted to visit you on
my way to Macedonia, and then return from Macedonia to you, and be
helped by you on our way to Judea. 17Since I originally intended to do
this but changed my plan, was I being indecisive? Or do you think I
make plans like a worldly person, saying yes and no at the same time?
18But as God is faithful, our Gospel-word to you has not been yes and no.
19For the Son of God, Messiah Jesus, the one who was preached among
you by us — me, Silvanus, and Timothy — was not yes and no, but it is
always yes in him! 20For every one of God's promises has its "yes" in
him. That is why it is through him that we say "Amen" to the glory of
God. 21God is the One who establishes us with you in Messiah and
anointed us.[3] 22He is also the One who sealed us and gave us the spirit in
our hearts as a down-payment.

23God is my witness: the reason I did not come to Corinth again was
to spare you. 24It is not that we are trying to control your faith, but we are
fellow workers with you for your joy, as you stand firm in the faith.

2 1So I determined in my own mind that I would not come to you again
in sorrow. 2For if I cause you sorrow, then who will make me happy?
It will not be those I have made sad. 3I wrote this very thing to you, so

---

[2]This principle applies in general to the NT and the whole Bible. Trinitarianism is a fearfully and alarmingly complicated attempt to impose on the Hebrew unitarian Scriptures the later, post-biblical idea of the triune God. There is no way to make three into one. God is never one "essence" or one "What" in Scripture, but always one divine Person or Self, the Father of the lord Jesus Messiah, the God of Jesus. The appalling complications and complexities, on the admission even of those who attempt to explain it, are the strongest evidence of a large-scale failure to maintain the Bible as the sole source of faith. The claim that "Jesus is GOD" violates, complicates and confuses the greatest of all commandments, that only one single divine Self is the true God. There is no other except He, and this is stated on almost every page of Scripture, while there is not a single reference to "God" in the Bible meaning a triune GOD.

[3]Christians as "Messianists" have received the Messiah's anointing spirit and are charged with representing the Messiah, reflecting his life and teachings.

that when I came I would not have sorrow from those who should make
me happy. I am confident in you all that my joy would be shared by all
of you. 4For out of much affliction and anguish of heart I wrote to you
with many tears, not to make you sad, but so you would know how much
love I have for you.

5But if anyone has caused sorrow, he has caused sorrow not only to
me, but in some degree to all of you — not to put it too severely. 6This
punishment from the majority has been sufficient for this person, 7so now
you should forgive him and comfort him. Otherwise he may be
overwhelmed by excessive sorrow and give up. 8So I urge you all to
reaffirm your love toward him. 9That is also why I wrote, so that I might
test whether you are obedient in everything. 10Anyone you forgive, I
forgive. Indeed what I have forgiven, if I have forgiven anything, was for
your sakes in the presence of the Messiah. 11In this way Satan will not be
able to take advantage of us, as we are not ignorant of his schemes.

12Now when I came to Troas to proclaim the Gospel of the Messiah,[4]
a door of opportunity was opened for me in the lord. 13But I experienced
no peace of mind because I did not find Titus my brother there. So I said
goodbye to them and went to Macedonia.

14But thanks be to God, who always leads us in triumph in the
Messiah, and reveals through us the sweet aroma of his knowledge in
every place! 15For we are a sweet aroma of Messiah to God among those
who are being saved[5] as well as those who are perishing. 16To those who
are dying it is a stench of death which leads to death, while to the others
it is a sweet aroma of life which leads to life. And who is competent for
this work of ministry? 17For we are not like so many who peddle the
Gospel-word of God[6] for profit, but we speak in the Messiah before God
from pure motives, as persons sent from God.

---

[4]The Gospel about the Kingdom as first preached by Jesus and constantly preached by the Apostles (Heb. 2:3; Mk. 1:14-15; Lk. 4:43; 9:11; Acts 28:23, 31).

[5]"Being saved" shows, unlike popular evangelistic language today, that salvation is a process. Very often we hear the language, "I got saved" — but almost never, with Scripture, I am "being saved and hope to be saved in the future."

[6]The Gospel of the Kingdom of God, as originally preached by Jesus in Mark 1:14-15. It is abbreviated very often in the NT as "word" or "word of God." Readers should always think of the Gospel of the Kingdom when they read "word" or "word of God." "The word" is not just a synonym for the Bible as a whole, which is known as the Scriptures (2 Tim. 3:15-16). Mk. 4:11-12 makes an intelligent understanding of the

3 1Are we beginning to commend ourselves again? Or do we need, as
do some, letters of recommendation to you or from you? 2You are our
letter of recommendation, written on our hearts, to be known and read by
all. 3You reveal that you are a letter of the Messiah, delivered by us,
written not with ink but with the spirit of the living God; not on stone
tablets but on tablets of human hearts.

4This confidence we have through the Messiah before God. 5It is not
that we are competent in ourselves to consider anything as coming from
ourselves, but our competence is from God. 6He made us competent to be
servants of a new covenant, not of the letter, but of the spirit, because the
letter kills, but the spirit gives life.[7]

7The ministry of death, written in letters carved on stone tablets,
came with glory, so that the children of Israel could not look steadily at
the face of Moses because of its glory, even though that glory was
fading. 8Since that was so, will not the ministry of the spirit have even
more glory? 9For if the ministry of condemnation had glory, the ministry
of making people right has much more glory. 10For certainly what once
had glory[8] now has no glory at all. because of the glory which surpasses
it. 11For if the one which was fading away had glory, the one which
continucs has much more glory.

12So then, since we have that hope, we speak very boldly. 13We are
not like Moses, who used to put a veil over his face so that the children
of Israel would not look intently at the end of the glory which was fading
away. 14But their minds were closed, and even today when they hear the
reading of the Old Covenant, the same veil remains. Only in Messiah is
it taken away. 15Yet to this day, when Moses is read, a veil lies over their
minds. 16But when a person turns to the lord,[9] the veil is removed. 17Now

---

Kingdom Gospel (Mt. 13:19, "the word") a prerequisite and condition for repentance and forgiveness.

[7]The change from the Old Covenant Torah in the letter to the spiritual New Covenant in Messiah was such a huge revolution in thinking that it took whole books to detail it. Romans, Galatians and Hebrews are largely concerned with this subject which to this day still causes difficulty due to Bible readers' frail understanding and preoccupation with unnecessary or misleading tradition. Gal. 3:19-29 provide an exact explanation.

[8]In the time of Moses and under the Law of Moses.

[9]"Accepting the lord" is pointless and deceptive apart from accepting his Gospel teaching. "Why do you call me 'lord, lord,' and do not do the things I say?" (Lk. 6:46).

the lord is the spirit,[10] and where the spirit of the lord is, there is freedom.
18And all of us, with our faces unveiled, reflecting like mirrors the glory
of the lord, are being transformed into the same image, from glory to
more glory. This comes from the lord, the spirit.

4 1So since we have this ministry by God's mercy, we do not lose heart.
2But we have renounced the hidden ways of shame. We do not
behave craftily nor distort the Gospel-word of God,[11] but by clearly
proclaiming the truth, we commend ourselves to every person's
conscience in the sight of God. 3And if our Gospel is veiled, it is veiled
only to those who are perishing. 4In their case the god of this age[12] has
blinded the minds of the unbelieving, so that they would not see the light
of the Gospel of the glory of Messiah, who is the image of God. 5For we
are not proclaiming ourselves, but Messiah Jesus as lord,[13] and ourselves
as your servants for Jesus' sake. 6For God who said, "Light will shine out
of the darkness" is the One who has shone in our minds to give us the
light of the knowledge of the glory of God in the face of the Messiah.

7But we are like clay jars holding this treasure,[14] so that the supreme
greatness of the power is shown to be from God and not from ourselves.
8We are afflicted from every side, but not crushed. We are perplexed, but
not in despair. 9We are persecuted, but not forsaken. We are hurt, but not
destroyed. 10In our bodies we always carry the threat of dying violently
as Jesus did, so that the life of Jesus may also be revealed in our bodies.
11For we who are living are constantly being delivered to death for Jesus'

---

[10]The presence of Jesus in spirit is equated with the holy spirit (also v. 18). This is the spirit of Jesus (Acts 16:7) and Jesus is also equated with the paraclete, comforter, in 1 John 2:1. There is no third Person in the NT.

[11]The word of God is the Gospel about the Kingdom, the foundation of saving faith, first announced by Jesus (Heb. 2:3; Mk. 1:14-15; Acts 8:4, 5, 12; Lk. 4:43; 5:1).

[12]Satan, the supernatural enemy of God who is deceiving the whole world (Rev. 12:9) and is thus the god of this present evil world-system (Gal. 1:4).

[13]Jesus is the "lord Messiah" who was born in Bethlehem (Lk. 2:11) and certainly not God Himself. God can never be born nor can He die. He is immortal (1 Tim. 6:16).

[14]Jesus referred to the treasure as the pearl of great price (Mt. 13:46), the knowledge of the Kingdom of God. Isa. 53:11 is seldom quoted, but it contains the huge truth that the Messiah makes people right by his knowledge, as well as by his sacrificial death.

sake, so that the life of Jesus may also be revealed in our mortal bodies.[15]
12So then death is at work in us, but life is at work in you.
13Since we have the same spirit of the faith as in what is written, "I
believed and for that reason I spoke," we believe and for that reason we
speak. 14We do this knowing that the One who resurrected the lord Jesus
will resurrect us also,[16] with Jesus,[17] and will present us with you. 15For
all this is for your sake, so that the grace which is spreading to more and
more people may cause thanksgiving to multiply to the glory of God.
16So we do not lose heart. Even though our outer selves are decaying,
our inner selves are being renewed day by day. 17These light afflictions
last for a little while, but they are producing for us an incomparable
weight of glory for the age to come. 18We do not focus on the things
which are seen now but at the things which are not seen, because the
things which are seen are temporary, but the things which are not seen
belong to the age to come.

5 1For we know that if the earthly "tent" which is our house is torn
down, we have[18] a building from God, a house not made by human
hands. It is a body fit for the coming age[19] and is being prepared now in
heaven. 2We certainly groan in this house, longing to be clothed with our
house which will come to us from heaven. 3When in the future we put it
on, we will not be found naked. 4For while we are in this present "tent"
we groan because of our burdens. It is not that we want to be unclothed,
but we want to be clothed, so that what is mortal will be swallowed up
by life. 5The One who prepared us for this very purpose is God, who
gave us the spirit as a down-payment.
6So we are always full of courage, knowing that while we are at
home in this body, we are absent from the lord, 7for we are living by
faith, not by sight. 8As I say, we are full of courage, and would prefer to

---

[15]Our mortal selves, certainly not a mortal body as distinct from an immortal soul, about which the Bible says nothing.

[16]The great central Christian hope is the future resurrection (1 Cor. 15:23), not a post-mortem hope of "heaven" as a disembodied soul!

[17]That is, when Jesus comes back (1 Cor. 15:23; 1 Thess. 4:13-17; Dan. 12:2).

[18]Just as the reward given to Jesus was a glory which he "had with" God in promise and prospect from before the foundation of the world (Jn. 17:5).

[19]Of the future Kingdom of God on earth at the return of Jesus (Rev. 5:10, etc).

be absent from this body and then to be at home with the lord.[20] 9So we
make it our aim, whether at home or absent, to be well-pleasing to him.
10For we must all appear before the judgment seat of the Messiah, so that
each person will be repaid for what we have done while in this body,
whether good or bad.

11So then, knowing what it means to fear the lord, we try to persuade
people. We are well-known to God, and I hope that we are well-known
also to your consciences. 12We are not trying to commend ourselves to
you again, but giving you an opportunity to take pride in us, so that you
can answer those who take pride in outward appearances rather than
what is in the heart. 13For if we are out of our minds, it is for God; if we
are of sound mind, it is for you. 14For the love of the Messiah compels us,
because we are convinced that one died for all, and so all died. 15And he
died for all so that those who live should no longer live for themselves,
but for him who died and was raised for them.

16So then, from now on we acknowledge no one from a worldly point
of view. Even though we have known Messiah from such a worldly point
of view, now we know him in that way no longer. 17So if anyone is in
Messiah he is a new creation. The old has passed away. Look: the new
has come! 18And all this is from God who reconciled us to Himself
through Messiah, and gave us the ministry of reconciliation; 19namely
that God was in Messiah reconciling the world to Himself, not counting
people's sins against them, and He has committed to us the Gospel-word
of reconciliation.

20So then we are ambassadors representing Messiah, as though God
were making His appeal through us: We appeal to you on behalf of the
Messiah, be reconciled to God. 21The one who knew no sin, God made to
be sin on our behalf, so that in him we could become[21] God's right way
of thinking and doing.

---

[20]That is, at the future arrival of Jesus — not at the moment of death, but when Jesus resurrects the faithful dead (1 Cor. 15:23). There is only one way to be "with the lord" and that is by resurrection at his future coming. The event is beautifully described in 1 Thess. 4:13-17: "In this way [and no other] we shall come to be with the lord." That event will follow the future Great Tribulation, not precede it.

[21]Salvation is a process culminating in immortality to be achieved in the first resurrection when Jesus returns (1 Cor. 15:23; Rev. 20:1-6).

6 1Working together with the Messiah, we also appeal to you not to
receive the grace of God and do nothing with it. 2For He says, “At the
acceptable time I listened to you; on the day of salvation I helped you.”
Listen, now is “the acceptable time”! Now is “the day of salvation”! 3We
give no one cause for offense in anything, so that our ministry may not
be blamed. 4But we have commended ourselves as servants of God in
everything: in great endurance, in tribulations, in hardships, in distresses,
5in beatings, in imprisonments, in riots, in troubles, in sleepless nights, in
hunger, 6by purity, by knowledge, by patience, by kindness, by holy
spirit, by genuine love, 7by the Gospel-word of truth, by the power of
God, by the weapons of uprightness in the right hand and the left, 8by
glory and dishonor, by slander and praise, considered to be deceivers and
yet genuine; 9as unknown and yet well-known, as dying and in fact we
still live, as punished but not killed; 10as sad but always rejoicing, as poor
yet making many rich, as having nothing, and yet possessing everything!

11We have spoken freely to you, Corinthians; our heart is open wide.
12Our affection for you is not restrained, but you are restrained in your
affection for us. 13Now open your hearts to us in return. I speak as to my
children.

14Do not be bound together with unbelievers.[22] For what partnership
does right have with wrong? What fellowship does light have with
darkness? 15Or what agreement does Messiah have with Belial? What
does a believer have in common with an unbeliever? 16And what
agreement does a temple of God have with idols? For we are a temple[23]
of the living God, just as God said, “I will live in them and walk with
them. I will be their God, and they will be My people.” 17So “Come out
from among them, and be separate,” says the Lord. “Do not touch
anything unclean, and I will welcome you. 18And I will be a Father to

---

[22]Christians are exhorted to marry within the biblical, New Testament faith.

[23]When Paul introduces either an individual believer or the church as “**a** temple” of God, note the absence of the definite article. When he speaks of “**the** temple of God” in 2 Thess. 2:4 he should most naturally be understood as speaking of a literal building, as does Jesus in Rev. 11:1-2. The earliest pre-millennial church fathers believed in a rebuilt Temple and an antichrist to appear shortly before the Second Coming.

you, and you will be sons and daughters to Me," says the Lord Almighty.[24]

7 1So then, since we have these promises, beloved, let us purify ourselves from all defilement of flesh and spirit, perfecting holiness in the fear of God.

2Make room in your hearts for us. We have treated no one unjustly; we have ruined no one; we have taken advantage of no one. 3I do not say this to condemn you, as I have already said that you are in our hearts to die together and to live together. 4My confidence in you is great, as is my pride in you. I am filled with encouragement. I am overflowing with joy even in all our affliction. 5For even when we came into Macedonia we had no relief, but we were afflicted on every side — by external conflicts and internal fears. 6But God, who encourages the discouraged, encouraged us by the arrival of Titus, 7and not only by his arrival, but also by the encouragement he received among you. When he told us about your longing, your sorrow, and your concern for me, I rejoiced even more. 8For although I caused you sorrow with my letter, I do not regret writing it — though I did regret it because I see that my letter made you sad, but only for a while. 9Now I am rejoicing, not that you were made sad, but that you were made sad leading to repentance. For you were made sad as God intended, so that you were not harmed in any way by us. 10For godly sorrow produces a repentance without regret, leading to salvation, but worldly sorrow produces death. 11And see what earnest concern this very thing, this godly sorrow, has produced in you — your defense of yourselves, indignation at the wrongdoer, alarm, longing, zeal, and punishment of wrong! In everything you have demonstrated yourselves to be innocent in the matter. 12So when I wrote to you, it was not because of the one who did the wrong, nor because of the one who suffered the wrong, but to reveal to you your earnest concern on our behalf before God.

---

[24]Jesus is never called "the Almighty" in the Bible. The Hebrew *El Shaddai*, Greek *pantokrator*, is always the title of God and never of Jesus. Rev. 1:8 is no exception. In Isa. 9:6 Jesus is called "mighty god," defined by the Hebrew lexicon correctly as "divine hero, reflecting the divine majesty." The divine hero of Isa. 9:6 was brought into existence, begotten, and God cannot possibly be born (or die)! "Unto us a Son has been begotten [by God, divine passive]."

13And so we have been encouraged. In addition to our own
encouragement, we rejoiced even more to see the joy of Titus, because
his spirit has been refreshed by you all. 14For if I have boasted to him at
all about you, you have not let me down. Just as we spoke nothing but
the truth to you, our boasting to Titus about you was also proven to be
true. 15His affection for you increases even more, as he remembers how
you all obeyed, and how you received him with fear and trembling. 16I
am rejoicing because in everything I have confidence in you.

8 1I must tell you, brothers and sisters, about the grace of God which
has been given to the churches of Macedonia. 2In a period of severe
trial, the abundance of their joy and their deep poverty have overflowed
in the riches of their generosity. 3For I testify that, as they were able, and
even more than they were able, they gave of their own accord, 4begging
us insistently for the privilege of sharing in the support of the saints.
5They even did more than we had expected. They gave themselves first
to the lord, and then to us, through the will of God. 6So we urged Titus
that as he had made a start before, he would also complete for you this
gracious ministry.

7But as you excel in everything — faith, speech, knowledge,
earnestness, and the love we inspired in you — see that you also excel in
this gracious gift. 8I am not saying this as a command, but I am testing
against the earnestness of others the sincerity of your love. 9For you
know the gracious generosity of our lord Jesus Messiah.[25] Even though
he was rich, he became poor for your sake,[26] so that you through his
poverty might become rich. 10I give my opinion on this matter: this
would be good for you, who made a start a year ago, not only in giving
but also in your desire to give. 11Now follow through with your desire to
complete it, according to your ability. 12If the willingness is there, it is
acceptable to give according to what you have, not according to what

---

[25]The lord Messiah is so defined in Luke 2:11; Rom. 16:18; Col. 3:24. He was born in Bethlehem after being supernaturally begotten by the Father in the womb of Mary.

[26]Parallel to Phil. 2 where the human Jesus, although invested with unique authority as the perfect image of God, did not exploit his position, but acted as a servant. There is no doctrine of the Incarnation of an imagined second member of a triune God. The human Jesus was fully endowed with divine authority and privilege. Though enjoying this astonishing status as the Son of God, Jesus adopted the role of servant.

you do not have. 13I do not say this so that others may be eased and you
suffer, but as a matter of equality. 14Your abundance at this present time
will provide for their need, so that their abundance may one day supply
your need, and there may be equality. 15As it is written, "The one who
gathered much had nothing left over, and the one who gathered little had
no lack."

16But thanks be to God, who put the same earnest care I have for you
into the heart of Titus. 17He not only welcomed our request, but because
he was so eager, he is going to see you of his own accord. 18We are
sending with him a brother whom all the churches praise for his work in
preaching the Gospel. 19And not only that, but this brother was appointed
by the churches to travel with us to administer this generous gift, to the
glory of the Lord and to show our eagerness to help. 20We did this so that
no one would discredit us in regard to this generous gift which we are
administering, 21because we are concerned about what is honorable, not
only in the sight of the Lord, but also in the sight of people. 22And we are
sending with them our brother who has often proven himself diligent in
many things, and who is now even more diligent because of the great
confidence he has in you. 23If there is any question about Titus, he is my
partner and fellow worker for you. If there is any question about our
brothers, they are messengers of the churches and an honor to the
Messiah. 24So show them openly before the churches the proof of your
love and our pride in you.

9 1For it is unnecessary for me to write to you about this offering for the
saints, 2because I know your eagerness to help, which I boast about to
those in Macedonia. I tell them that you in Achaia have been prepared to
give since last year, and your zeal has stirred up most of them. 3But I am
sending these brothers so that our boasting about you may not prove
empty, and that you are prepared, just as I said you would be. 4Otherwise
if any Macedonians should come with me and find you not ready to send
your gift, we (to say nothing of you) would be embarrassed by my
confident boasting! 5So I thought it necessary to ask these brothers to
visit you in advance, and arrange ahead of time the gift that you
promised earlier, so that it would be ready as a generous gift, not
grudgingly given.

6Remember this: the person who sows a little will reap a little; the person who sows a lot will reap a lot. 7Let each person give as he has determined in his mind, not grudgingly or under compulsion, because God loves a cheerful giver. 8And God is able to make all grace overflow to you, so that you, always having enough in everything, may overflow in every good work. 9As it is written, "The upright person scatters generously; he gives to the poor; his uprightness remains forever."

10Now the One who provides seed to the sower and bread for food will provide and multiply your seed for sowing and enlarge the harvest of your uprightness. 11You will grow rich in every way so that you can always be generous, and your generosity is producing through us thanksgiving to God. 12For this service which you are giving not only fully supplies the needs of the saints, but overflows in much giving of thanks to God. 13Because of this offering, they will glorify God for your obedient confession of the Gospel of the Messiah[27] and for the generosity of your sharing with them and with all. 14They will pray for you with great affection because of the exceeding grace of God given to you. 15Thanks be to God for His gift which is beyond description!

10 1I myself, Paul, entreat you by the meekness and gentleness of the Messiah, I who in your presence am meek among you, but in absence am bold. 2I beg you that I may not, when I am present, need to be bold with the confidence which I may have to show against some, who consider us to be conducting ourselves according to human standards. 3For even though we are human beings, we do not wage war according to human standards. 4For the weapons of our war are not physical weapons, but weapons made mighty by God for tearing down strongholds. We are tearing down false arguments 5and all arrogance which is exalted against the knowledge of God. We are taking every thought captive to make it obedient to the Messiah. 6We are also ready to punish every act of disobedience, when your obedience as a church is complete.

7You are focusing on outward appearances. If anyone is confident that he belongs to Messiah, let him think again — just as he belongs to Messiah, so we also belong to Messiah! 8For even if I boast some more

[27]The Gospel as preached by Jesus (Mk. 1:14-15), and about him.

about our authority, which the Lord gave us for building you up and not
for tearing you down, I will not be ashamed to do so. 9I do not want you
to think that I am trying to terrify you by my letters. 10For some say, "His
letters are weighty and strong, but his personal presence is not
impressive, and as a speaker he amounts to nothing." 11Those who say
that should consider this: what we are in words when we are absent, we
will also be in actions when we are present.

12For we are not so bold as to number or compare ourselves with
some of those who recommend themselves. When they measure
themselves by themselves, and compare themselves with themselves,
they show that they know nothing. 13But we will not boast beyond proper
limits, but only within the boundaries of the work to which God
appointed us, which reaches to you. 14For we were not over-extending
ourselves, as if we did not reach as far as you, because we were the first
to reach as far as you with the Gospel of the Messiah. 15And we are not
boasting beyond proper limits in others' work. But we hope that as your
faith grows, our work will be expanded among you within our appointed
limits. 16Then we can proclaim the Gospel in regions beyond you, and
not boast about what has already been done in another person's area.
17But "The one who boasts must boast in the Lord." 18For it is not the
person who commends himself who is approved, but the person whom
the Lord commends.

11 1I want you to put up with me in a little foolishness, and indeed
you are putting up with me! 2For I am jealous over you with a
godly jealousy, because I promised you in marriage to one husband, so
that I might present you as a pure virgin to the Messiah.[28] 3But I am
nervous that, just as the serpent[29] deceived Eve by his craftiness, your
minds might be corrupted from a sincere and pure commitment to the
Messiah. 4For if one comes and preaches another Jesus, different from
the one we proclaimed, or if you receive a different spirit from the one
you received, or a different Gospel from the one you believed,[30] you are

---

[28]Proving of course that the international church of true believers is the bride of Messiah, getting ready for the marriage ceremony when the Kingdom comes (Ps. 45).

[29]"Who is the Devil and the Satan" (Rev. 20:2; 12:9). Also in 2 Cor. 6:15 Belial.

[30]The Gospel of the Kingdom, the one NT Gospel, originally preached by Jesus (cp. Heb. 2:3). Paul preached the same Gospel in Acts 19:8; 20:24-25; 28:23, 31.

putting up with it beautifully! 5For I consider myself not at all inferior to those very superior "apostles" of yours! 6Even if I am unskilled in speaking, I am not unskilled in knowledge. In fact, in every way we have made this clear to you in all things.

7Or was it wrong to humble myself with manual labor so that you might be exalted, because I preached God's Gospel[31] to you at no charge? 8I "robbed" other churches by taking wages from them so that I might serve you free of charge! 9When I was present with you and I was in need, I was not a burden to anyone, because the brothers, when they came from Macedonia, supplied my needs fully. In everything I kept myself from being a burden to you, and I will continue to do so. 10As the truth of Messiah is in me, no one will keep me from this boast in all of Achaia! 11Why? Because I do not love you? God knows I do!

12And I will continue to do what I am doing, so that I may cut off any opportunity from those who desire to boast that they are our equals. 13For such people are in fact false apostles, deceitful workers, masquerading as apostles of Messiah. 14This is hardly surprising, as even Satan camouflages himself as an angel of light. 15So it is no surprise that his servants also camouflage themselves as servants of what is right. But their end will fit their actions.[32]

16I will say again, let no one think that I am foolish; but if you do, at least receive me as foolish so that I may boast a little. 17What I am saying I am not saying as the lord would, but as in foolishness, in this boastful state. 18Since many boast according to human standards, I will also boast. 19For you, being so wise, put up with fools gladly! 20For you put up with anyone who puts you into bondage, preys on you, takes advantage of you, exalts himself, or slaps you in the face.

21I admit to my disgrace that we have been "weak" by comparison! Yet in whatever way anyone is bold (I speak in foolishness of course), I am just as bold. 22Are they Hebrews? So am I. Are they Israelites? So am I. Are they descendants of Abraham? So am I. 23Are they servants of the Messiah? (I am speaking like a crazy person!) I am more so: with greater labors, in prisons more often, with beatings beyond number, often in danger of death. 24Five times I received the forty lashes minus one from

---

[31]"God's Gospel" is found 8 times in the NT (Mk. 1:14; Rom. 1:1; 15:16; 2 Cor. 11:7; 1 Thess. 2:2, 8, 9; 1 Pet. 4:17), and is defined as the Gospel of the Kingdom (Mk. 1:14).

[32]Every believer is judged by what he does (Rev. 22:12).

the Jews. 25Three times I was beaten with rods; once I was stoned; three
times I was shipwrecked. I have spent a night and day in the ocean. 26In
my many journeys I have been in danger from rivers, from robbers, from
my countrymen, from the Gentiles; dangers in the city, in the desert, on
the sea, from false brothers. 27I have faced labor and struggles, often
without sleep, in hunger and thirst, often without food, in cold and
without enough clothing to keep me warm. 28Besides all these outward
things, there is the daily pressure on me of concern for all the churches.
29Who is weak without me being weak? Who is caused to stumble
without me burning with indignation?

30If I must boast I will boast in my weakness. 31The God and Father of
the lord Jesus, the One who is blessed for all ages,[33] knows that I am not
lying. 32While I was in Damascus, the governor under King Aretas had
the city guarded in order to arrest me. 33But I was let down in a basket
from a window in the city wall, and so I escaped.

12 1Boasting is not profitable, but necessary. I will now come to
visions and revelations from the Lord. 2I know a man in Messiah
who fourteen years ago — whether in the body or out of the body I do
not know, but God knows — was caught up to the third heaven. 3And I
know that this man — whether in the body or apart from the body I do
not know, but God knows — 4was caught up into paradise,[34] and heard
unspeakable things which a human being is not allowed to utter. 5On
behalf of such a man I will boast, but on my own behalf I will not boast,
except in my weaknesses. 6For even if I desire to boast, I would not be a
fool, because I would be speaking the truth. But I hold back, so that no
one will think more of me than what he sees in me or hears from me.

7Because of the extreme greatness of these revelations, so that I
would not exalt myself, a "thorn in the flesh" was given to me, a
messenger of Satan to torment me — to keep me from exalting myself. 8I

---

[33]See Rom. 9:5 for the same definition of God, who is the Father.

[34]This was not a post-death experience! It tells us nothing at all about what happens at death. Paul did not die. He was given a vision of the future paradise (Rev. 2:7). Jesus promised the thief that he would be with him in the future paradise of the Kingdom of God on earth: "Truly I tell you today: you will be with me in paradise" (Lk. 23:43). The promise to the thief was given "today," the Friday of the crucifixion, and the position in paradise was to be in the future Kingdom (Rev. 2:7).

begged the lord three times that it would depart from me. 9He said to me,
“My grace is sufficient for you, because my power is made strong in
weakness.” That is why I will very gladly boast about my weaknesses, so
that the Messiah’s power may live in me. 10So I am very content with
weaknesses, insults, troubles, persecutions, and difficulties for the
Messiah’s sake, because when I am weak, then I am strong.

11I have become foolish, but you made me do this! For you ought to
have commended me, as I am in no way inferior to those superior
“apostles,” even though I am nothing. 12In fact, the signs of a true
Apostle were worked among you with all perseverance — signs,
wonders, and miracles. 13For in what way were you treated as inferior to
the other churches, except that I myself was not any burden to you?
Forgive me this wrong!

14Now for the third time I am preparing to come to you, and I will not
be a burden to you. For I am not after your possessions, but you! After
all, children should not have to save up for their parents, but parents for
their children. 15I will gladly spend and be spent — for you. If I love you
more, am I to be loved less? 16Even so, I have not been a burden to you.
But being crafty, I caught you by deception! 17I did not take advantage of
you through anyone I have sent to you, did I? 18I urged Titus to visit you,
and I sent another brother with him. Titus did not take any advantage of
you, did he? Did we not act in the same spirit? Did we not conduct
ourselves in the same way?

19Have you been thinking all this time that we have been trying to
defend ourselves to you? No, but in the sight of God we have been
speaking in Messiah, and it is all to build you up, beloved. 20For I am
afraid that somehow when I come I might find you not the way I want
you to be, and you might find me not the way you want me to be. I am
afraid that perhaps there will be factions, jealousy, outbursts of anger,
hostility, slander, gossip, arrogance, and disorder. 21I am afraid that when
I come again, my God may humiliate me before you, and I will mourn
over many of those who have sinned previously and have not repented of
their impurity, sexual immorality, and indecent acts they committed.

13 1This is the third time I am coming to you. “By the testimony of
two or three witnesses every fact will be established.” 2As I said
before when I was present with you the second time, now, though absent,

I write in advance to those who previously sinned and to all the others: If
I come again I will not spare anyone, 3since you are seeking proof that
the Messiah is speaking through me. And he is not weak in dealing with
you, but is powerful among you. 4For he was crucified in weakness, but
he lives because of the power of God. For we also are weak in him, but
we will live with him because of the power of God toward you.

5Examine yourselves to see if you are in the faith; test yourselves. Or
do you not recognize this about yourselves, that Jesus Messiah is in you
— unless you fail the test? 6And I hope that you will realize that we have
not failed the test! 7We pray to God that you will do no wrong — not so
that we may appear to have passed the test, but so you do what is right,
even though we may appear to have failed the test. 8For we can do
nothing against the truth, but only for the truth. 9For we rejoice when we
are weak but you are strong. We also pray for this: that you become fully
qualified. 10That is why I write these things while absent, so that when
present I will not have to treat you severely, using the authority which
the lord gave me for building up, not for tearing down.

11Finally, brothers and sisters, rejoice! Put things right. Be
encouraged. Be of the same mind. Live in peace, and the God of love
and peace will be with you. 12Greet one another with a holy kiss. 13All the
saints send their greetings. 14The grace of the lord Jesus Messiah, the
love of God, and the fellowship of the holy spirit[35] be with all of you.

---

[35]This is one of several "triadic" statements which do not in any way speak of a triune God. "Our lord Jesus Messiah" cannot possibly be the equivalent of YHVH in the Old Testament, since "our YHVH" is a linguistic impossibility and appears nowhere. There is only one Lord GOD, YHVH, and to propose that "Jesus is God" immediately posits two who are God, and thus two GODS. This is not biblical monotheism as defined by Jesus himself in Mark 12:29, John 17:3 and over and over again. The spirit is never a third Person in the NT. The spirit is the spirit of GOD or of Jesus (Acts 16:7), the operational, personal presence of either God or Jesus. The effects are the same. In Scripture the holy spirit never sends greetings and is never worshiped. The Paraclete, Mediator, Comforter, Counselor promised by Jesus in John 14-16 is identified with Jesus himself in 1 John 2:1. Thus Jesus left the earth but returned in spiritual presence. The triadic statement in Matt. 28:19-20 was not meant to be a fixed verbal formula, but a description of what is to occur at baptism. The Apostles baptized as representing Jesus, that is, in his name, teaching all that he taught.

Galatians

1 1 From Paul, an Apostle, not appointed by a group or individual, but
through Jesus Messiah and God who is the Father,[1] the One who
raised him from the dead; 2 and from all the brothers and sisters who are
with me, to the churches in Galatia: 3 Grace and peace to you from God
who is the Father and from our lord[2] Jesus Messiah, 4 who gave himself[3]
for our sins to rescue us from this present evil age, [4] according to the will
of our God and Father. 5 To Him be the glory to the ages of the ages.
Amen.

---

[1]This easy and fundamental unitarian creed appears at the beginning of Paul's letters. 1300 times the word "God" in the NT means the Father and "God" never in the Bible means a triune God.

[2]In order to remind readers of the critical difference between the lord Messiah (Lk. 2:11) and the one Lord God of biblical unitary monotheism, I have chosen to write "lord" (with lower-case "l") to emphasize constantly that the title "lord" for Jesus is derived from the all-important defining verse in Ps. 110:1, where the second lord is *adoni* in Hebrew and not the Lord God (*Adonai*). The crucial difference comes in to the Greek of the LXX and the NT Scripture as *kurios mou*, "my lord." This is the important Messianic title for royal (and other) superiors and for Jesus as Messiah. *Adoni* (my lord) is in all of its 195 occurrences never a title of Deity. When YHVH is found in a single verse contrasted with *adoni* (my lord), the distinction is invariably clear in the Greek also, i.e. *kurios* (YHVH) and *kurios mou* (my lord, *adoni*). The evidence can be investigated throughout the Hebrew Bible where *Adonai* (about 450 times) is the Lord God (very occasionally an angel representing Him, Gen. 18:3) and *adoni* is a non-Deity superior human person, occasionally an angel.

[3]No one in Scripture imagined that God could die, since He is immortal (1 Tim. 6:16). The fact that the Son of God gave up his life, died (cp. v. 1, where he came back from death) proves that he was a human being. In his first paragraph Paul has called the Father God three times (there are 1300 occurrences of the word God to mean the Father in the NT). This is the obvious and pervasive evidence of a unitary monotheistic, not Trinitarian definition of God. Of 11,500 of the words for "God," none of them can be shown to mean a Triune God. Jesus affirmed the unitary monotheism of Scripture in Mk. 12:29-34.

[4]The present evil system dominated by Satan who is "the god of this age" (2 Cor. 4:4) will continue until the future arrival of Jesus to replace it by the Kingdom of God on earth. The present evil system, the present "heaven and earth" (Mt. 24:35) will pass away and be replaced by the new world order of the Kingdom of God on earth at Christ's future coming.

6I am astonished and appalled at how quickly you are deserting the
One who called you in the grace of Messiah, for another Gospel.[5] 7Not
that there really is another Gospel — but some people are agitating you
and aiming to distort the Gospel of Messiah.[6] 8But even if we or an angel
from heaven were to preach a different Gospel from the one we preached
to you, let him be cursed.[7] 9As we have said before, I now repeat: if
anyone preaches to you a different Gospel from the one you accepted, let
him be cursed![8]

10Am I now trying to win the approval of people, or of God? Am I
trying to please people? If I were still pleasing people, I would not be a
servant of Messiah. 11I want you to know, brothers and sisters, that the
Gospel I preached is not a human idea. 12I did not receive it from people,
nor did they teach it to me, but it came through a revelation from Jesus
Messiah.[9]

13For you have heard of my previous lifestyle in Judaism, how I
fanatically persecuted God's church and tried to destroy it. 14I was
advancing in Judaism beyond many other Jews my age, as I was so
zealous for the traditions of my ancestors. 15But when the One who had
set me apart even before I was born and called me through His grace was
pleased 16to reveal His Son to me and in me, so that I could announce his

---

[5]That is, a "gospel" other than the one and only Gospel about the Kingdom as first preached by Jesus in Mark 1:14-15; cp. Heb. 2:3, and then by Paul and other evangelists (Acts 8:12; 19:8; 20:24-25; 28:23, 30, 31).

[6]This means not only the Gospel about Jesus, that he died and rose, but also the Gospel Jesus *preached*! It is necessary in our time to make this clear every time the Gospel is mentioned, since in current thinking it has lost a great portion of its biblical content as the Gospel about the Kingdom.

[7]"Let him be anathema."

[8]If Paul had preached a Gospel different from the Kingdom of God Gospel announced by Jesus he would have put himself under his own curse for falsifying the Gospel! He always preached the Kingdom as Gospel (Acts 19:8; 20:24-25; 28:23, 30, 31).

[9]Paul's creedal statement in 1 Tim. 2:5 is simple and clear: "There is one God and one mediator between God and man, the man Messiah Jesus." Paul's point in Galatians is that the Gospel is a message from God mediated by His unique agent and mediator, Jesus the Messiah. Paul's powerful warning against ultimate error is expressed in 1 Tim. 6:3. Loss of the words/teaching of Jesus means loss of the Christian faith (cp. 2 John 7-9).

Gospel[10] to the Gentiles, I did not immediately consult with any people.
17Nor did I go to Jerusalem to those who were Apostles before me, but I
first went away to Arabia, and then I returned to Damascus.
18It was only after three years that I went to Jerusalem to visit Peter,
and I stayed with him for fifteen days. 19I saw no other Apostles except
James, the lord's brother. 20With God as my witness, what I am writing
to you is not a lie. 21I then went to the regions of Syria and Cilicia. 22I was
still not personally known to the churches of Judea in Messiah. 23They
had only heard that the person who had been persecuting them was now
proclaiming the Gospel of the faith which earlier he had tried to destroy.
24And they praised God because of[11] me.

2 1After fourteen years I returned to Jerusalem with Barnabas, taking
Titus along also. 2I went as a result of a revelation, and I laid out
before them the Gospel which I proclaim among the Gentiles.[12] I did this
in private to those in authority, to make sure that I was not running, or
had not run, this race for nothing. 3Yet none of these leaders insisted that
Titus, who was with me, should be circumcised, though he was a Greek.
4That issue came up because some false brothers with false motives
secretly came in to spy on our freedom in Messiah Jesus, trying to bring
us into bondage. 5Yet we did not submit to them, even for a moment, so
that the truth of the Gospel would remain with you.[13] 6But those
influential people — whatever they were is all the same to me, since God
shows no favoritism — they added nothing to what I was preaching. 7On
the contrary, they recognized that I had been entrusted with the Gospel to

---

[10]I.e. preach his Gospel, the one Gospel of the Kingdom of God (Mk. 1:14-15; Lk. 4:43; Acts 8:12; 19:8; 20:24-25; 28:23, 30, 31).

[11]A *causal* sense ("because of") for the preposition *en* is appropriate here.

[12]The Gospel was not different from the Gospel of the Kingdom of God. There is only one Gospel and Acts 28:23-31 shows that Paul took the same salvation message, after Jews refused it, to Gentiles. "The Gospel of the grace of God" is identical with the Gospel of the Kingdom (Acts 20:24-25; cp. Lk. 9:11).

[13]"With you" in the Greek is *pros umas*. This preposition *pros* ("with") is found in John 1:1 ("the word was **with** God"), showing that a "word" can be "with" a person, i.e. in their mind. God's word or wisdom was "with [*pros*] God" as His plan from the beginning.

the Gentiles just as Peter was to the Jews.[14] 8For the One who worked
through Peter as an Apostle to the Jews also worked through me as an
Apostle to the Gentiles. 9Realizing the grace given to me, the recognized
pillars of authority, James, Peter, and John, extended to Barnabas and me
the right hand of fellowship. 10We were to go to the Gentiles and they to
the Jews. They only asked us to remember the poor, the very thing I was
eager to do.

11But when Peter came to Antioch I opposed him to his face because
he clearly was wrong: 12previously he had been eating regularly with
Gentiles until some associates of James came. Then, fearing the pro-
circumcision group, he began drawing back and separating himself from
the Gentiles. 13The rest of the Jewish Christians joined him in this
hypocrisy, so that even Barnabas was drawn into their hypocrisy. 14But
when I saw that they were not behaving according to the truth of the
Gospel, I said to Peter in the presence of all of them, "You are a Jew who
lives like a Gentile and not like a Jew. How then can you pressure the
Gentiles to live like Jews?"[15]

15We are Jews by birth and not Gentile sinners, 16yet we know that
nobody is made right by the works of the Law,[16] but through the faith of
Messiah Jesus.[17] And we have believed in Messiah Jesus so that we
might be made right by the faith of Messiah and not by the works of the
Law, because no one will be made right by the works of the Law. 17Now
if while trying to be made right in Messiah, we are found to be sinners, is
Messiah then a promoter of sin? Absolutely not! 18But if I rebuild what I

---

[14]There are not of course two different Gospels, but one Gospel for all without distinction and one Christian hope.

[15]By living a Jewish lifestyle which you know is not required under the New Covenant.

[16]Those parts of the Law like Sabbath observance or holy day observance or observing food laws, insisting on circumcision in the flesh for all males, wearing prayer tassels, etc. Paul referred to this as "circumcision" and "the whole Law" (5:3) which are not required in the New Covenant. Salvation is of course by "the obedience of faith" (Jn. 3:36; 12:44ff; Rom. 1:5; 16:26; Heb. 5:9). Gal. 3:19-29 explains that the period of Law in the letter ended with the arrival of Jesus, i.e. "when faith came" (3:24-25; Mk. 1:1, 14, 15; Lk. 16:16; Jn. 1:17).

[17]This means the same faith as Jesus had, the faith he taught, including the Shema in Mark 12:29, John 17:3. See "the faith of Jesus" in v. 20; 3:22; Rom. 3:22, 26; Eph. 3:12; Phil. 3:9; Rev. 14:12. Believing without obedience is not true belief. So Jesus warned in Matt. 7:21-27, and see Heb. 5:9.

already tore down, then I prove myself to be a sinner. 19For through the
Law I died to the Law,[18] so that I may live to God. 20I have been crucified
with Messiah, so it is no longer I who live, but Messiah lives in me. I
now live this fleshly life by the faith of the Son of God,[19] who loved me
and gave himself up for me. 21I do not nullify the grace of God,[20] because
if being made right comes through the Law, then Messiah died for
nothing.

3 1You foolish Galatians, who has deceived you? Before your eyes
Jesus Messiah was publicly shown to be crucified.[21] 2I only want to
learn one thing from you: Did you receive the spirit by the works of the
Law, or by hearing and believing the Gospel?[22] 3Are you so foolish that

---

[18]Dying to the Law would mean being unresponsive to those parts of it not required in the New Covenant, i.e. those parts of it which were only shadows of the full meaning of the law brought to light in the New Covenant, of which Paul was a minister (2 Cor. 3:6).

[19]The Greek has "the belief of the Son of God." To understand the full meaning we must think of this as the same faith as Jesus had, i.e. believing what Jesus believed as well as trusting him. The parallel "faith of Abraham" (Rom. 4:16) means of course the model of believing obedience demonstrated by Abraham who is our spiritual father. We are to copy the faith which Jesus had and taught.

[20]"The Gospel of the grace of God" is exactly the same as "the Gospel of the Kingdom of God" (Acts 20:24-25).

[21]The cross ratified the whole new system of the New Covenant, making the "works of the Law," which created a barrier between Jew and foreigner, unnecessary. The barrier was pulled down in Christ (Eph. 2:14-15).

[22]This is one of the most instructive verses in the whole NT. The spirit is received by the "hearing of faith," i.e. accepting and obeying the Gospel message (see Rom. 10:17; Eph. 1:13). This is NT shorthand for the Gospel about the Kingdom of God as preached by Jesus and Paul (Mk. 1:14-15; Acts 19:8; 20:24-25; 28:23, 31; cp. Acts 8:12, etc). Abraham is the model, who believed the promises of God and acted on them, obeyed them (v. 6). So the Christian is commanded to obey Jesus at the point of accepting and believing the *first* command of Jesus to "repent and believe the Gospel of the Kingdom" (Mk. 1:14-15). The principle that the spirit is received in the spiritual words of God or His Son is beautifully illustrated by Zech. 7:12 and by Jesus in John 6:63. God sent His spirit through the words of the prophets, and words are the expression of spirit (Job 26:4; Prov. 1:23). The spirits or minds of speakers are to be tested by the word they utter to see if they are true or false (1 Jn. 4:1-6). The words of God are put into the lips of all the prophets and ultimately the words of the final prophet and Son of God, Jesus. Believing what is true and having a love for truth is the basis of salvation (2 Thess. 2:10, 12, 13). Belief is also expressed, of course, in obedience to the command

you began in the spirit and are now trying to finish in the flesh? 4Did you
suffer so much for nothing — if it was for nothing? 5So does He who
provides you the spirit and works miracles among you do it by the works
of the Law or by your hearing and believing the Gospel?

6"Abraham believed God, and it was credited to him as making him
right."[23] 7So know this: people who believe God are children of
Abraham. 8As it is foretold in Scripture that God would make right the
Gentiles by believing, so the Gospel was preached beforehand to
Abraham: "All the nations will be blessed in you." 9So those who believe
God[24] are blessed along with Abraham, the believer.

10For all those who depend on the works of the Law are under a
curse, because it is written, "Cursed is everyone who does not continue
doing everything that has been written in the book of the Law." 11Clearly,
no one is made right before God by the Law, because "The righteous will
live by believing." 12But the Law does not depend on believing; on the
contrary, "Whoever does the works of the Law will live by them."
13Messiah redeemed us from that curse of the Law by becoming a curse
for us, because it is written, "Cursed is everyone who hangs on a cross."
14This happened so that in Messiah Jesus the blessing promised to
Abraham[25] would come to the Gentiles, so that we could receive the
promise of the spirit through belief.

15Brothers and sisters, I am speaking from human experience: even a
human contract, once ratified, is not canceled or added to. 16Now the

---

to be baptized in water (Acts 8:12; Mt. 28:19-20). The Great Commission is to relay all the commands given by Jesus until the end of the age (Mt. 28:20). This is the only way a disciple is made.

[23]It is essential to remember that belief without obedience is not faith at all. Hence we read that the Lord told Isaac, the son of Abraham, "I will increase your descendants until they are as many as the stars of the sky, and I will give your descendants all these lands, and all the nations of the earth will be blessed through your descendants, because Abraham obeyed Me, and he kept My charge, My commandments, My regulations, and My law" (Gen. 26:4-5).

[24]This statement makes clear the fact that the basis of Christian faith is believing the land/kingdom promise made to Abraham and to Jesus who preached it as the Gospel about the Kingdom (Mk. 1:14-15).

[25]The blessing of Abraham is property (the land), prosperity and progeny (Gen. 28:4, 13; 35:12; 50:24; Ex. 6:4). The land promise to Abraham is repeated in the New Covenant as the blessing of inheriting the land and the world, and the Kingdom of God (Mt. 5:5; Rev. 5:10, etc).

promises were made to Abraham and to his seed. It does not say, "seeds" in the plural, but singular "seed," that is the Messiah. 17What I mean is this: the Law which came 430 years later does not make void the previous covenant ratified by God, and so cancel the promise. 18For if the inheritance[26] is based on the Law, it is no longer based on the promise. But God in His grace gave it to Abraham through the promise.

19What was the point of the Law then? It was added because of sins, but only until the seed came to whom the promise had been made.[27] The Law was put in place through angels by a mediator. 20Now a mediator is not for just one party, while a promise depends on one person, and God is only one Person.[28] 21Does this mean that the Law is against the promises of God? Absolutely not! For if a law had been given that was able to give life, being right with God would have been based on that law. 22But the Scriptures confined everything under sin, so that the promise by the faith of Jesus Messiah[29] might be given to those who believe.

23Before faith came we were kept in custody under the Law, imprisoned until the faith which was to come would be revealed. 24The Law was our tutor and guardian until Messiah, so that we could then be made right by faith. 25But now that faith has come, we are no longer under a guardian. 26For in Messiah Jesus you are all children of God,

---

[26]That is, of the Kingdom, the basis of the Christian hope and Gospel, so completely alien to the popular notion of "going to heaven" disembodied at death.

[27]God is the creator of all seeds, but His supreme creation was the Son of God, virginally begotten, the seed of the Creator Himself, the head of the new creation, the second and final Adam. The whole point of the new creation is lost if the Son of God was not originally human. To add a previous eternal existence to the Son makes him essentially not human and thus not the second Adam. The warning against a non-human Messiah is clear in 1 John 4:1-6. But did the Church listen?

[28]Paul had never heard of a triune God who is three Persons. Or if he knew of such a concept he rejected it. Jesus never authorized belief in a triune God.

[29]All this is implied in having "the faith of Jesus": we must believe what he believed, including Mark 12:29 and John 17:3! Acts 5:32 says that "God gives His spirit to those who obey Him." The words of Jesus are life-imparting words (Jn. 6:63). Any "spirit" which does not conform to the words of Jesus and the Apostles is highly suspect (1 Tim. 6:3; 2 John 9). See "the faith of Jesus" in 2:16, 20: Rom. 3:22, 26; Eph. 3:12; Phil. 3:9; Rev. 14:12.

through faith.[30] 27For all of you who were baptized into Messiah have
clothed yourselves with Messiah. 28There is no longer Jew or Gentile,
slave or free, male or female; you are all one in Messiah Jesus. 29And if
you belong to Messiah, then you are Abraham's children, and heirs of
the promise.[31]

4 1Let me explain. As long as an heir is under age, he is not different
from a slave even though he is destined to be master of everything.
2He remains under guardians and managers until the date set by his
father. 3So we also were formerly under age, held in bondage under the
elemental principles of the world. 4But when the time was right, God sent
forth His Son, who came into existence[32] from a woman and under the
Law, 5to redeem those under the Law and give us the status of sons and
daughters. 6Because you are children, God sent the spirit of His Son into
our hearts, calling, "Abba![33] Dear Father!" 7So you are no longer a slave
but a child, and since you are a child, you are an heir through God.

8Before you knew God, you were enslaved to beings which by nature
are not gods. 9But now that you have come to know God, or rather to be
known by God, how can you turn back to the weak and worthless
elemental principles? Do you really want to be enslaved to them again?

---

[30]Compare Isa. 53:11, where Jesus saves by his knowledge, not only his death. "The Son of God came to give us an understanding in order to know God" (1 Jn. 5:20).

[31]Paul ends his argument on a triumphant high point. The true seed of Abraham are no longer people who are of the stock of natural Israel, but they are drawn from all nations and have in common the belief in the God of Abraham and in the Gospel of the Kingdom preached by Jesus. This is the new Israel of the spirit (Gal. 6:16; Phil. 3:3, contrasted with the Israel of the flesh of 1 Cor. 10:18). The promises for the international Church are those made to Abraham: "the promise to Abraham and his descendants that he would be heir of the world" (Rom. 4:13; Gen. 28:4).

[32]Paul does not use the ordinary word for being born or begotten (*gennao*) but the word *ginomai*, "to come into existence." This is a reference to the virginal begetting of Jesus in Mary. Cp. Rom. 1:3 and note the parallel with Gen. 2:7 (*egeneto*, came into existence), where Adam came into existence. Jesus is the second Adam, the head of a new race of human persons. His existence began in Mary, not in eternity, which would make the parallel with Adam impossible. Jesus came into existence as the seed of David (Rom. 1:3; 2 Tim. 2:8; Mk. 10:47-52; 11:10). See Mt. 1:18, 20; Lk. 1:35; Isa. 9:6 ("begotten [by God]"); Ps. 2:7; 1 John 5:18, not KJV. John 1:13 is most likely a reference to the virginal begetting of Jesus (see Jerusalem Bible).

[33]The Aramaic, Jesus' native tongue, for father.

10You are observing special days, months, seasons, and years.[34] 11I am fearful for you that I have somehow labored over you for nothing.

12I beg of you, brothers and sisters: become like me because I became like you. You have done me no harm. 13You remember that it was because of a physical sickness that I first announced the Gospel to you. 14And you did not treat me with contempt or reject me even though my bodily condition was a trial to you. Instead you received me as though I were an angel of God or even Messiah Jesus himself. 15So what has happened to that sense of blessing you had? For I can vouch for the fact that, if possible, you would have pulled out your eyes and given them to me. 16Have I now become your enemy because I am telling you the truth? 17These people eagerly seek you, but not for any good reasons. On the contrary, they want to isolate you from us so that you will eagerly seek them. 18But it is good always to be eagerly sought for the right reasons, and not just when I am present with you. 19My children, I am again suffering birth pains until Messiah is formed in you. 20I wish I could be present with you now and change my tone, because I am perplexed about you.

21Tell me, you who want to be under the Law, do you not listen to what the Law says? 22For it is written that Abraham had two sons, one from the slave woman and one from the free woman. 23The son from the slave woman was born of the flesh, while the son from the free woman was born through the promise. 24These two women are an allegory for two covenants. Hagar represents the covenant from Mount Sinai, bearing children into slavery. 25She is a symbol of Mount Sinai in Arabia, and corresponds to the present Jerusalem, because the city is in slavery with her children. 26But Sarah represents the heavenly Jerusalem — free and the mother of us all.[35] 27For it is written, "Rejoice, childless and barren one! Burst out in shouting, the one not suffering birth pains — because

[34]The whole context is about an unwanted *Jewish* influence. In the same context Paul is about to say that Mount Sinai is obsolete. The Gentiles were being misled into an obligation to observe sabbaths, feast days, and special times prescribed under the Old Covenant system. A strong statement about Paul's point here is found in *The Letters of Paul* by Ronald Knox. He observes on this verse: "The reference is to the Hebrew sabbaths and other observances which are here represented as a bondage not lighter than that which was imposed by heathen worship."

[35]Paul has in mind Ps. 87:5 which speaks of being born in Zion. Rebirth is caused by belief in the Kingdom of God Gospel of Jesus (Mk. 1:14-15).

the deserted woman will have many more children than the woman with a husband."

28Brothers and sisters, you are children of the promise, like Isaac. 29And just as it was then, so it is now: the one born of the flesh persecutes the one born of the spirit.[36] 30But what does the Scripture say? "Cast out the slave woman and her son, because the son of the slave woman will not inherit along with the son of the free woman." 31So then, brothers and sisters, we are not children of the slave woman but of the free woman.

5 1The Messiah has set us free to live in freedom, so stand firm and do not be subject again to the burden of slavery. 2Listen to me, Paul. I say to you that if you get circumcised, Messiah will be of no use to you. 3I solemnly emphasize again that every man who gets circumcised is obligated to keep the whole Law. 4You who are trying to be made right by the Law[37] have cut yourselves off from Messiah; you have fallen from grace. 5For we through the spirit, by faith, are expectantly waiting for the hope of righteousness. 6For in Messiah Jesus neither circumcision nor uncircumcision means anything,[38] but only faith working through love.

7You were running the race so well! Who blocked you from obeying the truth? 8This persuasion is not coming from the One who calls you. 9A little bit of yeast makes the whole lump of dough rise. 10I am persuaded in the lord that you will adopt no other view, and that whoever is troubling you will bear his judgment. 11As for me, brothers and sisters, if I were still preaching circumcision,[39] why am I still being persecuted? If I were still preaching circumcision, the stumbling block of the cross would have been removed. 12I wish that those agitating you would cut theirs right off!

13For you were called to freedom, brothers and sisters. Only do not use this freedom as an excuse to do what the flesh wants, but through love serve one another. 14For the whole Law is fulfilled in one statement:

---

[36]Paul refers as did Jesus to being "born of the spirit" (cp. Jn. 3:3, 5, 6).

[37]That is, the Law of Moses in the letter, as distinct from the Law of Messiah — the teaching of Jesus which must always be the foundation of the Christian faith.

[38]Whereas in Gen. 17 physical circumcision was the basis for membership in the covenant, for Jew and Gentile. The contrast is enormous!

[39]With circumcision in the flesh goes "the whole Law" (v. 3).

"Love your neighbor as yourself." 15But if you attack and devour one
another, watch out that you are not destroyed by one another.
16I say this: follow the spirit and you will not carry out the desires of
the flesh. 17For what the flesh desires is against the spirit, and what the
spirit desires is against the flesh. These are opposed to each other, so that
you may not do what you want. 18But if you are led by the spirit, you are
not under the Law. 19The actions of the flesh are obvious: sexual
immorality, impurity, sensuality, 20idolatry, sorcery, enmity, strife,
jealousy, outbursts of anger, rivalries, dissensions, factions, 21envy,
drunkenness, carousing, and similar things. I warn you, just as I warned
you before, that those who practice such things will not inherit the
Kingdom of God.[40] 22But the fruit the spirit produces is love, joy, peace,
patience, kindness, goodness, faithfulness, 23gentleness, and self-control.
There is no law against these things! 24Those who belong to Messiah
Jesus have crucified their flesh with its lusts and desires.
25Since we live by the spirit we should also be guided by the spirit.
26Let us not become conceited, provoking and envying each other.

6 1Brothers and sisters, if anyone is caught in any sin, you who are
spiritual should restore that person with a gentle spirit, while being
watchful of yourselves so that you are not also tempted. 2Bear one
another's burdens, and in this way you will fulfill the Law of Messiah.[41]
3For if anyone thinks more of himself than he really is, he is self-
deceived. 4Let each person examine his own work and then take pride in
himself, rather than comparing himself to another. 5For each person will
bear his own load.
6Those who are taught the Gospel-word[42] should share all good things
with their teacher. 7Do not be deceived; God will not be mocked, and
you will reap what you sow. 8If you sow to your own flesh you will from

---

[40]That is, "be saved." Note that the NT Christian goal is nothing to do with going to heaven at death, but inheriting the earth and Kingdom of God when Jesus comes back at his Parousia (second coming).

[41]The Torah of Messiah, strongly contrasted with the Torah of Moses. In 1 Cor. 9:21 Paul makes the same striking distinction between the Law (Torah) of Moses and the Law (Torah) of Messiah. Failure to see this difference remains a cause for unnecessary division and contention amongst those claiming to follow Jesus. Jesus came not to abolish Torah, but to bring it to its higher spiritual meaning (Mt. 5:17).

[42]The Gospel of the Kingdom (cp. Acts 8:12).

the flesh reap destruction, but if you sow to the spirit[43] you will from the spirit reap the Life of the Age to Come.[44] 9So let us not get discouraged in doing what is good, because at harvest time we will reap if we do not give up. 10So then, whenever we have an opportunity we should do good to all, especially to those of the family of the faith.

11Notice the large letters I am writing with my own hand. 12It is those who want to make a good outward showing who are pressuring you to be circumcised. They are only doing this so that they may not be persecuted for the cross of Messiah. 13For even those who are circumcised do not themselves really keep the Law, but they want you to be circumcised so that they can boast about your flesh. 14But may I never boast about anything except the cross of our lord Jesus Messiah, through which the world has been crucified to me, and I to the world. 15For neither circumcision nor uncircumcision means anything;[45] what matters is that we are a new creation. 16Peace and mercy be on all those who follow this rule, that is on the Israel of God.[46]

17Let no one trouble me any more, because I bear the marks of Jesus on my body.

18The grace of our lord Jesus Messiah be with your spirit, brothers and sisters. Amen.

---

[43]The essential clear difference between the two covenants is expressed by Rom. 7:6: the spirit vs. the letter of the law.

[44]As in the great, classic and definitive resurrection verse, Dan. 12:2. This verse tells us what the dead are doing and where they are doing it. The dead are currently sleeping in the dust of the ground, inactive and unconscious. They will return to life only at the future return of Jesus to resurrect the dead (1 Cor. 15:23; 1 Thess. 4:13ff; Lk. 14:14).

[45]This is precisely and deliberately contrary to the divine command in Gen. 17 that no Jew or Gentile could be part of the covenant apart from physical circumcision.

[46]The Israel of God is in this context obviously the international body of believers. Paul knows, of course, also of a future for now blinded natural, national Israel, "Israelites" (Rom. 9-11), but here he intentionally uses the word "Israel" to mean the Church. The Church is to be governed by the canon of love. Paul contrasts the Israel of the spirit here with the "Israel of the flesh" in 1 Cor. 10:18. In Phil. 3:3 Paul designates the international believers, the Church, as spiritual Jews or circumcision (cp. Rom. 2:28-29).

Ephesians

1 1 From Paul, an Apostle of Messiah Jesus by the will of God, to the
saints, the faithful in Messiah Jesus who are in Ephesus: 2 Grace and
peace to you from God who is our Father and from the lord Jesus
Messiah.

3 Blessed be the God and Father of our lord Jesus Messiah. He is the
One who has blessed us with every spiritual blessing in the heavenly
places in Messiah. 4 For He chose us[1] in him before the foundation of the
world, to be holy and unblemished before Him. In love, 5 He marked us
out beforehand to be His sons and daughters through Jesus Messiah,
according to the good purpose of His will, 6 to the praise of the glory of
His grace, which He freely gave us in the Beloved. 7 In him we have
redemption through his blood,[2] the forgiveness of our sins, according to
the riches of His grace, 8 which He kindly lavished on us. In all wisdom
and understanding 9 He made known to us the revealed secret of His will,[3]
according to His purpose which He designed in him, 10 as His plan for the
time of fulfillment — to make the Messiah head of everything in heaven
and on earth. 11 In him we were also made heirs, having been marked out
beforehand according to the plan of the One who accomplishes all things
according to the purpose of His will, 12 so that we who were the first to
hope in Messiah would live for the praise of His glory. 13 In him, when
you heard the word of the truth — the Gospel of your salvation — you
believed it and were sealed in him with the holy spirit of the promise,[4]
14 which is a down-payment on our inheritance, until we acquire
possession of that inheritance, to the praise of His glory.

15 That is why, since I heard of your faith in the lord Jesus and your
love for all the saints, 16 I always give thanks for you and remember you

---

[1] This means that all believers were included in the divine plan from the beginning. This of course is one side of the coin and does not mean that we do not have to cooperate with God's design for us. Similarly Jesus was planned from the beginning and came into existence some 2000 years ago.

[2] That is, of course, through his sacrificial death in our place and on our behalf (Mk. 10:45). Salvation is also through obeying Jesus (Heb. 5:9).

[3] The unfolding knowledge of God's Kingdom plan as announced first by Jesus (Lk. 4:43; Heb. 2:3; Mk. 1:1, 14, 15).

[4] The promise of the Gospel goes back to the promise made to Abraham, to whom the Gospel was preached in advance (Gal. 3:8). Jesus' first command was that we "repent and believe the Gospel of the Kingdom" (Mk. 1:14-15).

when I pray. 17This is my prayer: that the God of our lord Jesus Messiah,
the Father of glory, will give you a spirit of wisdom and of revelation in
your knowledge of Him. 18With the understanding of your hearts
enlightened, you will know the hope[5] to which He has called you, the
riches of the glory of His inheritance in the saints, 19and the
overwhelming greatness of His power to us who believe, according to
the energy of His mighty strength. 20He energized this same power in the
Messiah when He raised him from the dead and seated him at His right
hand[6] in the heavenly places, 21far above every ruler, authority, power,
dominion, and every name that is named, not only in this age but also in
the age to come. 22He put all things under his feet,[7] and gave him as head
over all things to the church, 23which is his body, the fullness of him who
fills all in all.

2 1And you were dead in your transgressions and sins, 2in which you
once lived following this world's present age,[8] following the ruler of
the kingdom of the air, the spirit who now energizes the children of
disobedience. 3Among them we all once lived in the lusts of our flesh,
following the desires of the flesh and of the mind, and we were by nature
children of fury,[9] just like everyone else. 4But God, who is rich in mercy,
because of His great love with which He loved us, 5even though we were
dead in our sins, made us alive together with Messiah. It is by grace that
you have been saved and are being saved. 6He raised us up with him and
seated us with him in heavenly places in Messiah Jesus.[10] 7This is so that
in the ages to come He might show the exceeding riches of His grace in

---

[5]The hope of the return of Messiah to this earth and the promise that all the holy people (the saints) will reign with him on the renewed earth (Rev. 5:10; Mt. 5:5; Dan. 7:27).

[6]As predicted by Ps. 110:1, the key text defining the position of Messiah as *adoni*, "my lord," which is in all 195 occurrences never a title of Deity, but of a human superior. Jesus is the man Messiah Jesus at the right hand of God (1 Tim 2:5).

[7]That is, God has promised to do this. At present we do not yet see everything subject to Jesus, and he is waiting till this final subjecting comes to pass (Heb. 2:8).

[8]Lit. "the age of this world": the present evil age of Gal. 1:4. Satan is currently deceiving the whole world (Rev. 12:9).

[9]Cp. John 3:36 where Jesus spoke of the fury of God resting on those who do not obey the Son.

[10]Christians as part of the body of Christ are figuratively with him in heaven where he is.

kindness to us in Messiah Jesus. 8For by grace you have been saved and
are being saved through faith, and this is not from you; it is the gift of
God, 9not from works,[11] so that no one can boast. 10For we are His
handiwork, created in Messiah Jesus for good works, which God
prepared ahead of time so that we would conduct our lives in them.

11So then, remember that at one time you Gentiles by birth, who are
called "uncircumcision" by those called "circumcision" — which is
physical and done by human hands — 12at that time you were separate
from Messiah, aliens from the community of Israel and strangers to the
covenants of the promise, without hope and without God[12] in the world.
13But now in Messiah Jesus you who were once far off have been brought
near by the blood of the Messiah. 14For he himself is our peace, the one
who made both groups into one and broke down the middle wall of
separation, the hostility between us, 15by making void in his flesh the
Law of commandments contained in decrees. He did this in order to
create in himself one new person in place of the two, so making peace,
16and to reconcile them both in one body to God through the cross, by it
killing that hostility. 17So he came and proclaimed the Gospel of peace[13]
to you who were far off and also to those who were near, 18because
through him both of us have access in one spirit to the Father. 19So then
you are no longer strangers and foreigners, but you are citizens along
with all the saints and you are members of God's household, 20built on
the foundation of the Apostles and prophets, Messiah Jesus himself
being the chief cornerstone. 21In him the entire structure is closely joined
together and is growing into a holy temple in the lord. 22In him you too
are being built together into a place where God lives in the spirit.

3 1For that reason, I, Paul, am the prisoner of the Messiah Jesus for you
Gentiles. 2Surely you have heard of the commission of the grace of

---

[11]Nevertheless the Gospel must be accepted by "a good and honest heart" (Lk. 8:15). We must "strive to enter" the Kingdom of God (Lk. 13:24), "work out our own salvation" (Phil. 2:11-12), and "he who endures to the end will be saved" (Mt. 24:13).

[12]Paul says that they were *atheoi*, practical atheists.

[13]Note that Peter says that the Gospel of peace was preached by Jesus (Acts 10:36).

God[14] given to me for you — 3that by revelation the divine secret[15] was
made known to me, as I have briefly written already. 4When you read
this, you will be able to perceive my understanding of the revealed secret
of the Messiah. 5This was not made known to people in previous
generations, as it has now been revealed to His holy Apostles[16] and
prophets in the spirit: 6it is that the Gentiles are fellow heirs and fellow
members of the same body, and share equally in the promise[17] in Messiah
Jesus through the Gospel. 7Of this Gospel I became a servant according
to the gift of God's grace which was given to me by the energy of His
power. 8To me, the very least of all the saints, this grace was given, in
order to proclaim to the Gentiles the boundless riches of the Messiah,
9and to enlighten everyone about God's plan — the now-revealed secret
which from ages past has been hidden in God, the One who created all
things.[18] 10This enlightening is so that the multifaceted wisdom of God
should now be made known through the church to the rulers and
authorities in the heavenly places, 11according to the plan for the ages
which He has realized in Messiah Jesus our lord. 12In him we have access
to God with boldness and confidence through his faith.[19] 13So I ask you
not to be discouraged by my trials for you, which are your glory.

14This is the reason that I bow my knees before the Father, 15from
whom every family in heaven and on earth is named, 16and ask that He
would grant you, according to the riches of His glory, to be strengthened

---

[14]It is important always to recall Acts 20:24-25 which equates the Gospel of the Kingdom with the Gospel of grace. There is only one saving Gospel for all.

[15]Not a mystery meaning a mystification that no one understands, but the secret now revealed about God's plan for salvation for all races equally.

[16]Paul does not claim some special Gospel revealed to him only, but he states that God's Gospel was revealed to all the Apostles.

[17]The promise is the promise made to Abraham that he would inherit the world/Kingdom of God (Rom. 4:13). It is not just a promise to be "in the Kingdom," but to *be* the Kingdom and supervise the Kingdom with Jesus when he comes to establish it on earth (Rev. 5:10; 1 Cor. 6:2; Dan. 7:18, 22, 27; Mt. 19:28).

[18]One of some 50 statements that the Father was the Creator in Genesis. Isa. 44:24 states that God created all things alone, and no one was with Him. The KJV is based on a corrupted text in this verse adding "by Jesus Christ," leading readers to think that Jesus was GOD and creator!

[19]The same faith as Jesus had, not just faith in him, but copying his faith and teaching. Anyone who denies the teaching of Jesus is anti-Christian (1 Tim. 6:3; 2 John 7-9). See "the faith of Jesus" in Rom. 3:22, 26; Gal. 2:16, 20; 3:22; Phil. 3:9; Rev. 14:12.

with power through His spirit in your inner person, 17and that the
Messiah may live in your hearts through faith, as you are being rooted
and grounded in love. 18I pray that you will be able to comprehend with
all the saints what is the width and length and height and depth, 19and to
know the love of the Messiah which surpasses knowledge, so that you
will be filled with all the fullness of God.[20]

20Now to the One who is able to do far more abundantly above all we
ask or think, according to the power that energizes us, 21to Him be the
glory in the church and in Messiah Jesus through all generations for all
the ages. Amen.

4 1So then I, the prisoner in the lord, implore you to conduct yourselves
in a way that is worthy of the calling to which you have been called,
2with all humility and meekness, with patience, bearing with one another
in love, 3making every effort to maintain the unity of the spirit in the
bond of peace. 4There is one body and one spirit, just as you were called
to the one hope of your calling, 5one lord,[21] one faith, one baptism,[22] 6one
God and Father of all, who is over all and through all and in all.

7But to each of us grace was given according to the measure of the
Messiah's gift. 8That is why it says, "When he ascended on high, he
captured a group of captives and gave gifts to people." 9Now what does
"he ascended" mean except that he had also descended into the lower
parts of the earth? 10He who descended is the same one who also
ascended far above all the heavens, so that he might fill all things. 11It
was he who gave some to be Apostles, and some to be prophets, and
some to be evangelists, and some to be pastor-teachers, 12to equip the
saints for the work of ministry, to build up the body of the Messiah,
13until we all attain to the unity of the faith and of the knowledge of the
Son of God, to a full-grown person, to the height of the Messiah's full

---

[20]Col. 2:9, "all the fullness of Deity dwells" in Jesus, is parallel to the idea expressed by Paul here that Christians are also to be filled with the fullness of God.

[21]lord Messiah (Lk. 2:11; Ps. 110:1: "my lord," not "Lord"). Jesus is the Messiah lord, not God.

[22]The water baptism for the reception of the spirit ordained and commanded by Jesus for all believers until the end of the age (Mt. 28:19-20). The noun "baptism" always refers to water baptism. 1 Cor. 12:13 is the starting point for believers who are all baptized into one body, through the one spirit.

stature. 14So we are no longer to be children, tossed back and forth by
waves and swayed by every wind of teaching, by the trickery of people
with their sleight of hand and deceitful scheming. 15Instead, speaking the
truth in love, we must grow up in all things into him who is the head, the
Messiah. 16From him the whole body, fitted and held together by every
supporting joint, with the proper working of each individual part, grows
and builds itself up in love.

17So I tell you this and testify in the lord: you must no longer conduct
yourselves as the Gentiles do, in the futility of their minds. 18They are
darkened in their understanding, alienated from the life of God because
of their ignorance[23] which is due to their hardness of heart. 19They have
become callous and have given themselves up to lust, to practice all sorts
of impurity, desiring more and more of it. 20But you did not learn that
from Messiah — 21if indeed you have heard him and have been taught by
him, as the truth is in Jesus. 22About your former way of life, you were
taught to put away the old person who is corrupted by deceitful lusts,
23and be renewed in the spirit of your minds. 24You must put on the new
person, who in the image of God[24] has been created in uprightness and in
holiness that is based on the truth.

25So then, having put away everything false, "Each one of you speak
the truth with your neighbor," because we are members of one another.
26Be angry, yet do not sin. Do not let the sun set on your anger, 27and do
not give the Devil an opportunity. 28Let the one who stole steal no longer;
instead let him work, doing with his own hands what is good, so that he
will have something to share with those who are in need. 29Let no corrupt
speech come out of your mouths, but only what is good for building
others up as the need may be, so that your words will give grace to those
who hear. 30And do not grieve God's holy spirit, with which you were
sealed for the Day of redemption. 31Let all bitterness, rage, anger,
quarreling, and slander be put away from you, with all malice. 32And be

---

[23]Reminding us of the prophets who complained that "My people are destroyed for lack of knowledge" (Hos. 4:6) and indeed "go into exile for lack of knowledge" (Isa. 5:13). Isa. 53:11 is seldom if ever preached, but it should be: "By his knowledge my upright servant will cause many to be right." Jesus "came to give us an understanding that we might come to know God" (1 Jn. 5:20).

[24]The restoration of the true image of God in man, the image lost in Adam.

kind to one another, tender-hearted, forgiving each other, just as God in
Messiah has forgiven you.

5 1So imitate God, as dearly loved children imitate their Father.
2Conduct yourselves in love, just as the Messiah loved us and gave
himself up for us, as a sweet-smelling offering and sacrifice to God.

3But sexual immorality or any impurity or coveting should not even
be mentioned among you, as is right for saints. 4And there should be no
vulgar speech, foolish talking, or crude joking, which are inappropriate,
but rather giving thanks. 5For you can be sure of this: no sexually
immoral or impure or covetous person, who is an idolater, will have any
inheritance in the Kingdom of the Messiah and God.[25]

6Let no one deceive you with empty words, for it is because of these
things that the righteous anger of God is coming on the disobedient.[26] 7So
do not participate with them, 8because you were once darkness, but now
you are light in the Lord. Conduct yourselves as children of light, 9for the
fruit of the light is in all that is good and right and true, 10as you discern
what is pleasing to the Lord. 11Do not participate in the fruitless works of
darkness, but instead expose them, 12as it is shameful even to speak of the
things which are done by them in secret. 13But everything that is exposed
by the light becomes visible, and everything that is made visible can
become light. 14That is why it says, "Wake up, you who are asleep, and
arise from the dead, and the Messiah will shine on you."

15So watch carefully how you conduct yourselves, not as unwise but
as wise, 16making the most of your time, because the days are evil. 17So
then do not be foolish, but become wise by understanding what the will
of the Lord is. 18Do not get drunk on wine,[27] which leads to ruin, but go
on being filled with spirit. 19Speak to one another in psalms, hymns and
spiritual songs, singing and making music with your hearts to the Lord;
20giving thanks always for everything in the name of our lord Jesus
Messiah to God, who is the Father; 21being subject to one another in the
fear of Messiah.

---

[25]I.e., will not be saved.

[26]Recalling the telling words of Jesus in John 3:36.

[27]Wine, *oinos* in Greek, is of course alcohol and not grape juice. It is permitted for celebration in moderation. Paul could not have written "Do not get drunk on grape juice"!

22Wives, be subject to your own husbands, as to the lord. 23For the
husband is the head of the wife, just as the Messiah is the head of the
church, his body, and is himself its savior. 24Just as the church is subject
to the Messiah, so wives should be to their husbands in everything.

25Husbands, love your wives, just as the Messiah loved the church
and gave himself up for her 26to make her holy, having cleansed her by
the washing of water with the Gospel-word, 27so that he may present the
church to himself in glory, without spot or wrinkle or any blemish, but
holy and blameless. 28In this way husbands should love their own wives
as they do their own bodies. He who loves his wife loves himself. 29For
no one ever hated his own body, but nourishes and takes care of it, just
as the Messiah also does for the church, 30because we are members of his
body. 31"For this reason a man will leave his father and mother and be
joined to his wife, and the two will become one flesh." 32This mystery is
great, but I am speaking about the Messiah and the church.
33Nevertheless each of you must also love his own wife as himself, and
the wife must respect her husband.

6 1Children, obey your parents in the Lord, because this is right.
2"Honor your father and mother," which is the first commandment
with a promise: 3"so that it may go well for you, and you may live long
on the earth."[28]

4Parents, do not provoke your children to anger, but raise them in the
discipline and instruction of the Lord.

5Servants, be obedient to your masters on earth with fear and
trembling. Do this in sincerity of heart as to the Messiah, 6not only when
you are being watched, just to please people, but as servants of the
Messiah, doing God's will from the heart. 7Serve enthusiastically, as for
the Lord and not for people, 8because you know that whatever good thing
each person does, whether slave or free, we will receive good back from
the Lord.

9Masters, treat your servants the same way, and give up making
threats, because you know that you and they have the same Master in
heaven, and there is no favoritism with Him.

---

[28]And ultimately permanent residence in the land as an immortal person when Jesus comes back. This is the Christian hope throughout the NT. See Matt. 5:5; Rev. 5:10 and Ps. 37: five references to "inheriting the earth" and "living in it forever."

10Finally, be empowered in the Lord and in the strength of His
power. 11Put on the complete armor of God, so that you will be able to
stand firm against the Devil's tactics. 12For we are essentially not fighting
against human forces,[29] but against the authorities, against the powers,
against the cosmic rulers[30] of this darkness, who are the spirit forces of
evil in the heavenly places. 13That is why you need to put on the
complete armor of God, so that you may be able to stand your ground on
the evil day, and having done everything, to still stand strong. 14So then
stand firm, buckling the belt of truth around your waist, and putting on
the breastplate of uprightness, 15and wearing on your feet the preparation
of the Gospel of peace. 16In addition, pick up the shield of the faith, so
that with it you can put out all the flaming arrows of the Evil One. 17And
put on the helmet of salvation, and take the sword of the spirit, which is
the Gospel-word of God.[31]

18With every prayer and request, pray at all times in the spirit. To do
this be alert and always persevere in making requests for all the saints.
19And pray for me, that the right words may be given to me when I begin
to speak,[32] to make known confidently the revealed secret of the Gospel.
20I am an ambassador in chains for the Gospel, so pray that I may speak it
boldly, as I should.

21So that you may know my circumstances and how I am doing,
Tychicus, the beloved brother and faithful servant in the Lord, will let
you know everything. 22I have sent him to you for this very purpose, so
that you may know about us and that he may encourage your hearts.

23Peace be to the brothers and sisters, and love with faith, from God
who is the Father and from the lord Jesus Messiah. 24Grace be with all
those who love our lord Jesus Messiah with love that will never die.

---

[29]Christadelphianism is much mistaken when it eliminates the whole dimension of spiritual evil and thinks of the Devil as the evil of human nature. Paul contradicts this idea here and makes the ultimate battle a struggle with supernatural evil forces.

[30]The Greek is *kosmokratores* — "kosmocrats." These are the evil demonic forces headed by the prince of the power of the air, the Devil.

[31]The Gospel of the Kingdom of God as announced first by Jesus (Mk. 1:14-15; Acts 10:36). The failure to define the Gospel is undoubtedly the greatest failure of contemporary evangelicalism.

[32]Lit. "in the opening of my mouth," an idiom for speaking in a somewhat formal way, by a teacher or one in authority (see Matt. 5:2; 13:35; Acts 8:35; 10:34; Rev. 13:5-6).

Philippians

1 1From Paul and Timothy, servants of Messiah Jesus, to all the saints
in Messiah Jesus who are in Philippi, including the elders[1] and
deacons: 2Grace and peace to you from God who is our Father[2] and from
the lord Jesus Messiah.[3]
3I give thanks to my God every time I remember you, 4praying
always with joy for all of you, 5because of your partnership in the Gospel
from the day you first heard it until now. 6And I am certain of this: that
the One who began a good work in you will carry it to completion at the
Day of Messiah Jesus.[4] 7It is right for me to think this way about all of
you, since I hold you in my heart, and you are all partners with me in
grace, both in my imprisonment and in the defense and establishment of
the Gospel. 8For God is my witness, how deeply I miss all of you with
the affection of Messiah Jesus. 9And I pray that your love will keep on
growing in knowledge and every kind of discernment, 10so that you can
determine what matters ultimately, and thus be pure and blameless on the
Day of Messiah.[5] 11I pray that you may be filled with the fruit of
uprightness[6] which comes through Jesus Messiah, to the glory and praise
of God.

---

[1]Elders, pastors and bishops are all the same rank — different names for the same office. The current single pastor and group of elders does not fit the NT pattern.

[2]One of over 1300 references in the NT to God as the Father. This unitarian view of God is confirmed by Jesus in Mark 12:29 and by Mal. 2:10. There was never any doubt in NT times that the Father is "the only one who is true God" (Jn. 17:3).

[3]The "my lord," *adoni* of Ps. 110:1. *Adoni* (all 195 times) is never a title for Deity.

[4]His future, single, visible Second Coming in power and glory. There is no prior secret rapture/resurrection in the NT.

[5]The single, future Second Coming of Jesus to bring the faithful dead back to life and inaugurate the coming Age of the Kingdom of God on earth (1 Cor. 15:23; Dan. 12:2, etc). There is no PRE-Tribulation resurrection/rapture in the NT. Jesus will come back once, after the Great Tribulation (Mt. 24:29).

[6]Being right with God, which is achieved by obedience to Jesus, "the obedience of faith" (Rom 1:5; 16:26; Jn. 3:36; Heb. 5:9). This includes of course belief in the atoning substitutionary death of Jesus. The commands of Jesus begin with Mark 1:14-15, belief in the Gospel of the Kingdom, and are based on the command to believe that "the Lord our God is one Lord" (Mk. 12:29, definitely a non-Trinitarian creed). Water baptism is a basic part of the commanded Great Commission (Mt. 28:19-20), until the end of the age, which is the Second Coming of Jesus to inaugurate the Kingdom worldwide.

12Now I want you to know, brothers and sisters, that what has
happened to me has actually resulted in the advancement of the Gospel:[7]
13it has become known to the whole imperial guard and to everyone else
that my imprisonment is for the cause of Messiah. 14And most of the
brothers and sisters have gained confidence in the lord[8] from my
imprisonment and have even more courage to speak the Gospel-word
fearlessly. 15Some, to be sure, preach Messiah out of envy and rivalry,
but others with good motives. 16These do so out of love, knowing that I
am here for the defense of the Gospel. 17The others proclaim Messiah out
of selfish ambition and the wrong motives, seeking to cause me trouble
in my imprisonment.

18So what is the outcome? Just that in every way, whether from false
motives or true, Messiah is being proclaimed.[9] And in this I rejoice. Yes,
and I will continue to rejoice 19because I know I will be delivered
through your prayers and the supply of the spirit of Jesus Messiah.[10] 20My
eager expectation and hope is that I will not be ashamed[11] in any way, but

---

[7]The Gospel of the Kingdom of God as originally preached by Jesus (Heb. 2:3; Mk. 1:14-15; Lk. 4:43; Mt. 13:19: "word of the Kingdom" = "word." Mk. 4:14 = "word of God," Lk. 8:11) and preached always by Paul (Acts 19:8; 20:24-25; 28:23, 31).

[8]lord Messiah.

[9]Most readers need to be reminded of what "preaching/proclaiming the Messiah" means, and for this Acts 8:4, 5, 12 provides a marvelous key. "Preaching the word" = "proclaiming the Messiah" = "preaching the Gospel about the Kingdom of God and the things concerning the name and agenda of Jesus Christ" (Acts 8:4, 5, 12). This is the full definition of all the references to "preaching the word" or "proclaiming Christ." In NT times this was clear, but today "tracts" offering salvation through Christ fail to mention the Kingdom Gospel. Thus the dictum of the Billy Graham Association is proved to be flawed when he states that "Jesus came to do three days work." This is obviously untrue since Jesus preached the Gospel of the Kingdom for a long time before mentioning his death and resurrection for the first time in Matt. 16:21.

[10]The spirit of Jesus is mentioned as active in Acts 16:7 and of course "the lord is the spirit" (2 Cor. 3:17). Jesus promised to return in spirit after departing from the disciples. He did this as the "Comforter" mentioned 4 times in the Gospel of John and a fifth time in 1 John 2:1, where the Comforter is Jesus the Mediator. Christ returned in spirit and thus did not leave the disciples as orphans (Jn. 14:18).

[11]Paul always had in mind the warning of Jesus that "he who is ashamed of me and my words" will be disqualified at the future coming of Jesus (Mk. 8:38). A half-hearted stance on the teachings of Jesus is severely condemned by Jesus in Rev. 3:16 ("spit you out of my mouth"). See also 1 Tim. 6:3; 2 John 7-9.

that now as always, with all boldness, the Messiah will be highly
honored in me, whether by my life or my death.
21For me, living is Messiah and dying is gain. 22If I live on in the
flesh, this will mean fruitful work for me, and I do not know which one
is preferable. 23I am drawn to both: I have a desire to depart and be with
Messiah[12] — which is far better — 24but to remain in the flesh is more
essential for your sake. 25Since I am persuaded of this, I know that I will
remain and continue with all of you for your development and joy in the
faith, 26so that, because of me, your pride in Messiah Jesus may increase
when I come to you again.
27Only live your lives in a manner worthy of the Messiah's Gospel.[13]
Then, whether I come and see you or stay absent, I will hear that you are
standing firm in one spirit, with one mind, contending alongside each
other for the faith of the Gospel, 28and not being frightened in any way by
those opposing you. For them this is evidence of their destruction, but of
your salvation — and all this is from God. 29For it has been granted to
you not only to believe in Messiah but also to suffer for him, 30having the
same struggle which you saw I had, and now hear that I am
experiencing.

2 1If then there is any encouragement in the Messiah, if any comfort
from love, if any fellowship in the spirit, if any sympathy or mercy,
2make my joy complete by all thinking the same way, having the same
love, being of one mind, and focusing on the one goal. 3Do nothing out
of rivalry or arrogance, but in humility consider others to be more
significant than yourselves. 4Everyone should think about not only his
own interests, but also the interests of other people. 5Think the same way
Messiah Jesus[14] thought: 6having the status of God[15] as His unique

---

[12]At the resurrection — the next second of my consciousness after falling asleep in death and remaining asleep until Jesus comes back. One can be "with Jesus" only via resurrection at the Second Coming: "In this way [via resurrection] we will be with the lord" (1 Thess. 4:17). There is no conscious existence at the moment of death, since "the dead know nothing at all" (Ecc. 9:5, 10; cp. Jn. 11:11, 14).

[13]The Gospel as preached by the Messiah — the Gospel of the Kingdom of God (Mk. 1:14-15; Luke 4:43; Acts 8:12, etc).

[14]When Paul speaks of "Messiah Jesus" he means "the *man* Messiah Jesus" in his fundamental and easy creedal statement in 1 Tim. 2:5. The man, the historical Messiah Jesus, was indeed in the image of God, and was the visible image of the invisible God

representative, he did not consider this representative equality with God as something to be used for his own advantage.[16] 7Rather he constantly emptied himself[17] by assuming the status of a servant,[18] looking like other men. 8And appearing to be just an ordinary man, he humbled himself by becoming obedient to the point of death — even to death on a cross. 9For

---

(Col. 1:15). Paul knew of no second Person of the Trinity who was alive before coming into existence in the womb of his mother Mary (Lk. 1:35). Mary is "the mother of my lord" (Lk. 1:43; cp. *adoni*, my lord, Ps. 110:1), certainly not "the mother of God." "Mother of God" is a blasphemous title suggesting that the mother is somehow superior to GOD!

[15]"in the form of God." *Morphe* (form) is the status of the human, historical Jesus who reflected God his Father. *Morphe* has to do with visible, outward appearance (cp. Ex. 24:17; Num. 12:8: "form," LXX "glory"). It carries in this passage the notion of position and status as in Tobit 1:13 ("status"). The NIV translation "being in very nature God" is false to the Greek and simply reads the much later post-biblical philosophical definition of "God the Son" into Paul. In the form of God is equivalent to being in the image of God, having the position of God, reflecting the character and glory of God. The comparison with the "form of a servant" (v. 7) enables us to understand "form" here as more like status, position, or rank. In British English we happen to use "form" as "rank" in the school terminology: "first, second, etc. form." We speak about a person being in good "form" or "shape." Jesus as the sinless Son of God was the closest reflection of his Father, God. But he was not a preexisting "God the Son," a title which appears nowhere in the Bible and belongs to a theology worked out after Bible times. Dr. Colin Brown at Fuller Seminary observed that "Phil. 2 is not about pre-existence and post-existence, but about the contrast between Christ and Adam…Adam, the original image, vainly sought to be like God" ("Ernst Lohmeyer's Kyrios Jesus Revisited"). So also Dr. James Dunn, *Christology in the Making*. F.F. Bruce expressed to me in correspondence in 1981 that he did not think that Paul believed in a preexisting Son.

[16]Much discussion surrounds Paul's meaning here. Either Jesus did not take advantage of or exploit his unique position as the Son of God; or it may be that Jesus did not grasp at a position wrongly as did Adam. The error of Adam was reversed in Jesus.

[17]The portrait of the Messiah is drawn from Isa. 53:12; the servant poured himself out in service to others. Note also 52:14; 53:2: "form," "appearance."

[18]One commentator notes: "Let us suppose *morphe* of a servant tells us that Paul is referring to the activity or function of a servant, not Jesus' intrinsic being. This would mean, as you know, that *morphe* of *theos* [form of God] tells us that Paul is referring to the activity or function of God. In John 14:10, 'It is the Father abiding in me who does the works.' Similarly for the Philippians: 'It is God at work in you' (2:13). They too are in the *morphe* of *theos* but are not to get on their high horses and attempt to seize upon equality with God, but to take rather the *morphe*, status, of a servant as Jesus did and serve others as Jesus did."

this reason God exalted him to the highest position and gave him authority above every authority, 10so that in the name of Jesus every knee will bow, in heaven and on earth and under the earth, 11and every tongue will confess that Jesus Messiah is lord, to the glory of God who is the Father.

12So then, my dear friends, just as you have always obeyed, not only when I am present, but now even more when I am absent, work out your own salvation with reverence and fear. 13For God is the One who is at work in you, energizing you both to desire and to work for His good purpose.[19]

14Do everything without complaining and disputing, 15so that you may be blameless and pure, children of God who are faultless in the midst of a crooked and perverted society, in which you shine like stars in the world. 16Hold firmly to the Gospel-word of life.[20] Then I may be proud on the Day of Messiah[21] that I did not run the race or labor for nothing. 17But even if I am being poured out[22] like a drink offering over the sacrificial service of your faith, I am happy and share my joy with all of you. 18In the same way you should rejoice and share your joy with me.

19I hope in the lord Jesus to send Timothy to you soon, so that I also may be encouraged when I hear news about you. 20For I have no one else like-minded who will genuinely care about your interests. 21All the others are seeking their own interests, not those of Messiah Jesus. 22But you know Timothy's proven character, that he has served with me in the Gospel like a son working with his father.[23] 23So I hope to send him as soon as I see how things go with me. 24And I am convinced in the lord that I myself will also come to you soon. 25But now I think it necessary to

---

[19]His great immortality program through the word of the Kingdom Gospel and through Messiah Jesus.

[20]I.e. immortality which is revealed in the Gospel (1 Tim. 1:10) and will be received when Jesus comes back to the earth to establish the Kingdom of God on a renewed earth.

[21]At his second coming.

[22]Paul was being poured out, just as Jesus emptied himself. The reference is to Isa. 53:12: "poured himself out," the selfless devotion of the suffering servant. Paul saw himself in the same category as the suffering servant, who is primarily the Messiah Jesus. Paul applied Isa. 42:6; 49:6 to himself and Barnabas in Acts 13:47.

[23]Just as Jesus served with his Father in the ministry of the Gospel of the Kingdom (Lk. 4:43).

send you Epaphroditus — my brother, coworker, and fellow soldier, as
well as your messenger and minister to my needs — 26since he has been
longing for you all and was distressed because you heard that he was
sick. 27Indeed, he was so sick that he nearly died. But God had mercy on
him, and not only on him but also on me, so that I would not have one
grief piled on another. 28Now I am very eager to send him so that you
may rejoice when you see him again, and I may be less concerned. 29So
welcome him in the lord with all joy, and hold people like him in great
honor, 30because he came close to death for the work of the Messiah,
risking his life to serve me when you could not.

3 1Finally my brothers and sisters, rejoice in the lord. Writing the same
things to you again is no trouble for me, and it is protection for you:
2Watch out for the "dogs"; watch out for the evil workers; watch out for
the mutilators of bodies. 3For we are the true, spiritual circumcision,[24] the
ones who serve in the spirit of God, take pride in Messiah Jesus, and do
not put any confidence at all in the flesh[25] — 4although I myself might
have confidence in the flesh. If anyone thinks they have good reasons for
confidence in the flesh, I have more: 5I was circumcised on the eighth
day; I am of the nation of Israel, of the tribe of Benjamin, a Hebrew born
of Hebrews; as far as the Law is concerned, I was a Pharisee; 6as for zeal,
I persecuted the church severely; as for uprightness in the Law, I was
blameless.

7But whatever advantages I had, I now think of them as
disadvantages because of the Messiah. 8More than that, I consider
everything to be a disadvantage in comparison with the supreme value of
knowing Messiah Jesus my lord.[26] For him I have suffered the loss of all
things and think of them as so much filth, so that I may gain the Messiah

---

[24]Just as in Gal. 6:16 the Galatian church, as one in Christ, and the wider church, is the Israel of God. Paul refers to national, natural Israel as Israelites and "the Israel according to the flesh" (1 Cor. 10:18). His use of "Israel of the flesh" implies of course an "Israel of the spirit." He says that Gentiles have become grafted into the commonwealth of Israel (Eph. 2:12).

[25]That is, physical circumcision which was required of Jews and Gentiles in the Old Covenant (Gen. 17), but replaced, like the sabbath day and food laws, by their spiritual equivalent in the New Covenant, the Torah of Messiah (1 Cor. 9:21; Gal. 6:2). The spiritual equivalent is rest in Messiah and avoiding all forms of unclean living.

[26]Ps. 110:1, *adoni,* all 195 times the title of non-Deity. Cp. 1 Tim. 2:5.

9and be found in him, not having my own uprightness from the Law, but
uprightness through the faith of Messiah[27] — the uprightness from God
based on faith.[28] 10My goal is to know him and the power of his
resurrection, to share in his sufferings, becoming like him in his death,
11and so somehow to attain to the advance resurrection[29] out from among
the dead persons.

12It is not that I have already obtained it — I have not yet reached that
goal — but I make every effort to take hold of it, since that is why I have
been taken hold of by Messiah Jesus. 13Brothers and sisters, I do not
think that I myself have taken hold of it yet. But one thing I do:
forgetting what is behind and stretching forward to what is ahead, 14I
keep running toward the goal in order to win the prize promised by
God's high calling in Messiah Jesus.[30] 15All who are mature should think
this way. If you think differently, God will reveal that to you. 16But let us
hold on to what we have already attained.

17Join in imitating me, brothers and sisters, and observe those who
follow our example. 18For I often told you, and now tell you again with
tears, that many are conducting themselves as enemies of the cross of the
Messiah. 19Their final end is destruction; their god is their appetites; they
take pride in their shame. They are focused on worldly things, 20but our
citizenship is in heaven; from there we eagerly await a Savior, the lord
Jesus Messiah. 21He is going to transform our humble bodies to be like

---

[27]The faith expressed in Jesus' obedience to his Father, God. This is not only faith in Jesus but the same faith as Jesus had. Christians are to preach what Jesus preached as Gospel, the Gospel about the Kingdom of God (Mk. 1:14-15; Lk. 4:43). See "the faith of Jesus" in Rom. 3:22, 26; Gal. 2:16, 20: 3:22; Eph. 3:12; Rev. 14:12.

[28]The obedience of faith (Rom. 1:5; 16:26; Heb. 5:9) which is the basis of true Christianity.

[29]The *exanastasis*: "out-resurrection," advance-guard resurrection, the first resurrection of Rev. 20:4. See also 1 Cor. 15:24. Rotherham has "the earlier resurrection, which is from among the dead."

[30]In 1 Thess. 4:13-17 Paul described the catching up to meet the descending lord Messiah in the air in order to accompany him, as many texts imply, to his position on earth as King of the coming Kingdom of God. Jesus is coming back to the earth, not going away again! The first resurrection will bring all the faithful back to life from their unconscious sleep of death (Ps. 13:3, etc). Christ is the first fruits of the resurrection program and "those who belong to Christ" will be raised to immortality at his future Coming, *Parousia* (1 Cor. 15:23).

his body of glory, by the power that enables him to subject all things to
himself.

4 1So then, my beloved brothers and sisters whom I long to see, my joy
and crown, in this way stand firm in the lord, dear friends.
2I urge Euodia and I urge Syntyche to agree in the lord. 3Yes, I also
ask you, genuine friend, to help these women who have contended for
the Gospel at my side, along with Clement and the rest of my coworkers,
whose names are in the book of life.
4Always rejoice in the lord. I will say it again: rejoice! 5Let your
gentleness be known to everyone. The lord is near. 6Do not worry about
anything, but in everything through prayer and petition, with
thanksgiving, make your requests known to God. 7And the peace of God,
which is beyond our understanding, will protect your hearts and minds in
Messiah Jesus.
8Finally, brothers and sisters, whatever is true, whatever is honorable,
whatever is right, whatever is pure, whatever is lovely, whatever is
admirable, if there is anything excellent and anything worthy of praise,
think about these things. 9Live out what you learned and received and
heard and saw in me, and the God of peace will be with you.
10I rejoice in the lord greatly because now at last you have revived
your concern for me. You were, in fact, concerned about me, but lacked
the opportunity to help. 11I do not say this out of need, because I have
learned to be content with whatever circumstances I find myself in. 12I
know both how to live with a little and how to have a lot. In any and all
circumstances I have learned the secret of being content — whether
well-fed or hungry, whether in prosperity or in need. 13I am able to do all
things through the one who empowers me. 14Still, you did well by
sharing with me in my difficulties.
15And you Philippians know that in the early days of my preaching
the Gospel, when I left Macedonia, no church shared with me in giving
and receiving, except you only. 16Even while I was in Thessalonica you
sent gifts to supply my needs several times. 17It is not that I seek the gift,
but I seek the fruit that is increasing to your account. 18I have received
everything, and have plenty. I am fully provided for, having received
from Epaphroditus what you sent — a sweet-smelling offering, an
acceptable sacrifice which pleases God. 19And my God will satisfy every

need of yours according to His riches in glory in Messiah Jesus. 20To
God who is our Father be the glory to the ages of the ages. Amen.

21Greet every saint in Messiah Jesus. These brothers who are with me
greet you. 22All the saints greet you, especially those from Caesar's
household.

23May the grace of the lord Jesus Messiah be with your spirit.

Colossians

1 1From Paul, an Apostle of Messiah Jesus by God's will, and Timothy
our brother, 2to the saints, the faithful brothers and sisters in Messiah
who live in Colossae: Grace and peace to you from God,[1] who is our
Father.

3We are always thankful to God, the Father of our lord Jesus
Messiah, when we pray for you, 4since we heard about your faith in
Messiah Jesus and your love for all the saints. 5This faith and love are

---

[1]The one God (*o theos*: transliteration reflects modern Greek pronunciation), the only true God, the God of Abraham, Isaac and Jacob and of Jesus. "The only one who has immortality whom no one can see or has ever seen" (1 Tim. 6:16). The God of the NT is certainly not the triune God of later church councils. "God" (often "*the* God") means the Father over 1300 times in the NT, echoing the summary statement of the Hebrew Bible in Mal. 2:10, where the one Creator God is defined as the one Father. Thousands of singular personal pronouns define God as a single divine Self/Person (cp. "I am YHVH," and "I YHVH" some 215 times, plus thousands of other singular personal pronouns defining God). This concept is very uncomplex. It has been passionately held by Jews during the whole of their history and is the heart of Jewish belief today. Jews are rightly aghast that a triune God should be imported into their sacred Scripture. The unitarian view of God was held by Jesus and is thus binding on his followers (Mk. 12:29; Jn. 17:3; 5:44). The simple concept of One God, the Father became hopelessly confused when later "church fathers" tried to explain God in terms of Greek philosophical concepts unknown to Jesus and the NT. Ps. 110:1 provides the key to the relationship between the One God, Yahweh, and "my lord" (*adoni*). *Adoni* is always a non-Deity title, every one of the 195 times it appears in the OT. The false capital on the second lord of Ps. 110:1 misleads many readers. Many commentators have even misreported the second lord as "Lord" and misled the public by saying the second lord is *Adonai*, which it is not! Jesus is the lord Messiah (Lk. 2:11), not the Lord God, which would make two who are God and thus two Gods. In about every 6th verse in the NT (17% of the verses) you are going to encounter the word GOD or equivalent. This is very often in the Greek "**the** God," i.e. the One God of Israel, not any God of our invention. Bishop N.T. Wright says that with the expression "**the** God" (not just "God") the writers of the NT were providing "an essentially **Jewish monotheistic concept of God**" (*Jesus and the People of God*, 1992, pp. xiv-xv). That truth is explicitly stated by Jesus in Mk. 12:29: "The Lord our God is one Lord." That is not a Trinitarian creed and the founder of our faith was a unitarian. Jesus never authorized worship of a triune God. There is no verse in the Bible where "God" means a triune God. In the Bible when people said "GOD" (YHVH, *Elohim*, *Adonai*, *theos*, about 11,000 times) none of those statements about GOD means a triune God. For an intelligent devotional life and relation to God in spirit and truth, this is the *first* truth which needs to be taught. It must not be withheld from seekers after God and Jesus.

based on the hope[2] stored up for you in heaven.[3] You heard about this
hope in the word of the truth, that is, the Gospel, 6 which has come to
you. That Gospel is producing fruit[4] and growing all over the world, just
as it has among you, since the day you heard it and understood God's
grace in truth.[5] 7 You learned the Gospel from Epaphras, our much-loved
fellow servant. He is a faithful minister of the Messiah on our behalf,
8 and he has told us about your love in the spirit.

---

[2]Of the future Kingdom on earth (Mt. 5:5; Rev. 5:10; Ps. 37, etc.). The fact is that love, the cardinal virtue of Christians, is *based on*, i.e. is dependent on a grasp of the hope of the future Kingdom on earth, the promised inheritance. Any confusion over the future hope will result in a diminishing of love and a distortion of the Gospel. It will result in a loss of vital life through the spirit.

[3]It is essential not to misunderstand here. The reward is now promised and stored up in heaven, waiting to be conferred on true believers by Christ when he returns to the earth in order that the saints can rule with him on that future renewed earth (Rev. 2:26; 3:21; 5:10; 20:1-6; 1 Cor. 6:2; 2 Tim. 2:12; Dan. 7:18, 22, 27; Lk. 19:11ff). Note the parallel with John 17:5 where Jesus asked for the glory which he "had with God," i.e. prepared and promised from the beginning. In God's great plan, and in biblical idiom, you can "have" things now which are guaranteed for the future (see also Mt. 6:1). In John 17:22, 24 believers who were not even yet born "have been given" (i.e. in promise) the same glory. On no account is the NT to be read with alien English thought forms in mind. Jesus and the early church leaders (with the exception of Luke) were Jews! And Jesus never said, despite mistranslation in some versions like NIV, that he was going *back* to the Father! He was in fact going to the Father, with Whom he now is, at God's right hand, until his future Second Coming (Acts 1:11; 3:21, etc).

[4]An obvious reference to the parable of the sower, where fruit is born by those who *first* accept and understand the Gospel of the Kingdom — "the word of the Kingdom" (Mt. 13:19). All true Gospel preaching goes back to the Gospel as preached by Jesus (Heb. 2:3). Without the life-giving seed, which is the word of the Kingdom (Lk. 8:11; Mt. 13:19), there can be no fruit. There can be no true repentance and forgiveness in the absence of an understanding of the word of the Kingdom (Mk. 4:11-12). The Devil works at destroying the faith at its root which is the Gospel of the Kingdom. Luke 8:11-12 are dramatically significant on this point. The Devil knows that an intelligent and obedient reception of the Gospel of the Kingdom leads to the acquiring of immortality (2 Tim. 1:10).

[5]Grace and truth are not opposing values. They are bound up with each other. There is no grace apart from truth and no truth apart from grace. Grace in the NT never means a weakening of the importance of the truth (2 Thess. 2:10). Jesus "came to give us an *understanding* in order to know God" (1 Jn. 5:20), and it is by Messiah's *knowledge* that he makes us right with God (Isa. 53:11), as well as by his atoning, substitutionary death.

9And so, since the day we heard this, we have not stopped praying for
you. We are asking that you may be filled with the knowledge of His
will in all spiritual wisdom and understanding, 10so that you may conduct
yourselves in a way worthy of the lord, fully pleasing to him, producing
fruit in every good work and growing in the knowledge of God. 11Our
prayer is that you may be strengthened with all power, according to His
glorious might, leading to a steady endurance and patience, with joy,
12giving thanks to the Father, the One who has made you fit to have a
share in the saints' inheritance in the light.[6]

13He rescued us from the domain of darkness and transferred[7] us to
the Kingdom of the Son whom He loves, 14in whom we have redemption,
the forgiveness of our sins.

15He is the visible image[8] of the invisible God, the firstborn[9] over all
creation, 16because in him[10] in intention everything was originally

---

[6] In the Age to Come. The power of the spirit must be experienced now as a downpayment of the future inheritance of the Kingdom at the return of Jesus (2 Cor. 1:22; 5:5; Eph. 1:14).

[7] The Kingdom of God has not yet begun worldwide. This happens at the future 7th trumpet (Rev. 11:15-18). But Christians in preparation for that Kingdom have been removed from the evil of the present world-systems by being radically separate and different. In that sense the international body of believers, God's Israel (Gal. 6:16; Phil. 3:13), the church, is the Kingdom of God, the royal family in training for the coming worldwide empire of God and Jesus, when Jesus returns at his spectacular, visible return. Until that future arrival of Jesus in power and glory, Christians must be prepared to suffer affliction. This will be alleviated and brought to an end when believers receive "release and relief" at the future coming of Jesus following the Great Tribulation (Mt. 24:29ff; 2 Thes. 2:4-9). On no account should believers fall for the colossal falsehood that the teachings of Jesus, including of course in Matt. 24, Mark 13 and Luke 21, are not for them! See also 1 Tim. 6:3; 2 John 7-9.

[8] Jesus as the image of God is of course the second Adam, not God (which would make two Gods, which is not monotheism) or a created angel. The subject of discourse here is the Messiah supernaturally begotten in Mary (Mt. 1:18, 20; Lk. 1:35). He is the fulfillment of the wisdom of God planned from the beginning. Jesus is here, as always, the man Messiah as in 1 Tim 2:5.

[9] Israel was also God's firstborn (Ex. 4:22). The sense is that of the preeminent one. Jesus is now, under God, the head of all creation and also the preeminent one from the dead, as being the first human to be raised from death to immortality. Only God has immortality inherently (1 Tim. 6:16). Jesus the Son of God was given immortality when he was resurrected on the Sunday following his crucifixion on Friday (Lk. 24:21, etc). All things will ultimately be subjected to the One God, the Father (1 Cor. 15:28).

created[11] by God in heaven and on earth — the visible and invisible,
whether thrones or dominions, rulers or authorities — all these things are
now created[12] by God through him and for him. 17He is superior to all
things and in him everything coheres. 18He is also the head of the body,
the church; he is the beginning, the firstborn from the dead,[13] so that he
himself might be promoted to become first in everything.[14] 19For God

---

[10]"In him." This is certainly not "by him." "*en auto*. This does not mean 'by him'" (*Expositors Greek Testament*, Vol. 3, p. 504). I take *en* here as causal, i.e., because of him, for his sake, with him in view, with him in intention. "We must render [*en*] 'because of' in Col. 1:16" (Turner, *A Grammar of NT Greek*, Vol. 3, p. 253). James Dunn translates "in him in intention" (*Christology in the Making*, p. 190). Christians were also "*en*" Christ before the world began (Eph. 1:4). This is existence in the divine plan, not actual existence (cp. 2 Tim 1:9; 1 Pet. 1:2, 20). F.F. Bruce was supportive of this understanding of Paul when he wrote to me in June, 1981: "But whether any New Testament writer believed in the Son's separate conscious existence as a second Divine Person' before his incarnation is not so clear. On balance, I think the Fourth Evangelist did so believe; I am not nearly so sure about Paul."

[11]Aorist of "create." The passive is a divine passive. "Everything was created," i.e., *by God*, as is stated some 50 times in Scripture. God was entirely unaccompanied at the original creation. Isa. 44:24 is the decisive and definitive verse on this point. Cp. Rev. 4:11. "The passive 'were created' indicates, in a typically Jewish fashion, the activity of God the Father, working *in* the Son. To say 'by,' here and at the end of verse 16, could imply, not that Christ is the Father's agent, but that he was alone responsible for creation" (N.T. Wright, *The Epistles of Paul to the Colossians and to Philemon*, p. 71). To say that Jesus was involved in the original creation as active agent destroys the witness of Matthew and Luke in the birth narratives. It also destroys the unitarian creed of Jesus and the NT (Mk. 12:29; Jn. 17:3).

[12]Perfect passive tense of "create" with continuing results. The change of verb tense is striking and deliberate (see Turner, *Grammatical Insights into the NT*, p. 125: "They have been and are being created."). The new creation is through Jesus and the earlier creation of authorities was "because of" of Jesus, "in him in intention," certainly not "by him." God the Father created by Himself (Isa. 44:24) and God, not Jesus (who did not yet exist!) rested on the 7th day (Heb. 4:4). Jesus the Son of God is actively involved in the New Creation and Jesus is the one now sanctifying his brothers and sisters (Heb. 2:11). Jesus knew that God, not he himself, "created them male and female at the beginning" (Mk. 10:6).

[13]The first human being to gain immortality by being raised by the Father from death.

[14]Jesus was *promoted* to this position of superiority, by resurrection. It is obvious, then, that he is not God, since God cannot be promoted! Jesus gained that supreme position when God exalted him to His right hand in accordance with Ps. 110:1 (equal to the celebration of man in Ps. 8:4-6), which is the key theological and Christological verse governing the NT. The second lord (*adoni*) is never a title of Deity. One cannot gain

was pleased to have all His fullness live in him,[15] 20and through him to
reconcile all things to Himself by making peace through the blood of his
cross — through him, whether things on earth or in heaven.
21And you were once alienated and hostile in your minds,
participating in evil activities. 22But now He has reconciled you through
the death of the historical person[16] of His Son, to present you before Him
holy, faultless, and blameless — 23if, that is, you remain in the faith,
grounded and steadfast,[17] without shifting away from the hope promised
in the Gospel which you heard. This Gospel has been heralded in all
creation under heaven, and I, Paul, have become a minister of that
Gospel.
24Now I rejoice in my sufferings for your sake, and I am completing
in my present human life[18] what still remains of Messiah's afflictions for
the sake of his body, that is, the church. 25I became the church's servant,
according to God's commission which was given to me for you, to

---

first position, if one always had it! The same confusion of thought is exposed by Bishop Wright's "life after life after death." You cannot become alive if you are already alive. It is likewise impossible to "begin to exist" (Mt. 1:18, 20; Lk. 1:35; 1 Jn. 5:18) if one already exists! The idea of a literally preexisting Son of God throws the entirety of Scripture into incoherence. There is no "God the Son" in the NT. This was an invention of the very confused philosophical theology of post-biblical "fathers." The Son was "foreknown" by God (1 Pet. 1:20), and this is very different concept from "preexistence." The Greek word for preexistence, *prouparchein* (found in the NT), is never used of Jesus. The whole point of the Bible is lost if Jesus is not fully a man. "Orthodoxy" declares him to be "*man*, but not *a* man." Scripture is the story of the reconciliation of God and *man*, and how *man* can fulfill his destiny (Ps. 8; 110). God does not need to be reconciled to God! And Jesus, if his "ego" *is* God, is an inappropriate model for us as human beings.

[15]Note that the same language about "the fullness of God" is applicable to believers also in Eph. 3:19. Having the fullness of God, via His spirit, thus does not mean that a person *is* God!

[16]Note the use of "flesh" to mean human person, as in 2:1.

[17]An obvious rejection of the false popular teaching of "once saved, always saved." Christianity in its pristine form constantly urges us to continue in the process of salvation. And "salvation is now nearer to us [not further behind us!] than when we first believed" (Rom. 13:11). Some people "believe for a while," Jesus said, but they give up the Christian life when others things interfere (Lk. 8:13).

[18]Literally "my flesh."

complete the preaching of the Gospel-word of God,[19] 26that is, the divine
secret hidden for ages and generations which has now been revealed to
His saints. 27God chose to make known among the Gentiles the riches of
the glory of this revealed mystery, which is Messiah in you, the hope for
glory.[20] 28We proclaim him, warning and teaching everyone in all
wisdom, so that we may present everyone mature in Messiah. 29I work
hard for this, striving with his energy[21] which works powerfully in me.

2 1For I want you to know how great my struggle is for you, for those in
Laodicea, and for all who have not seen me in person. 2I want their
hearts to be encouraged and joined together in love, and I want them to
have all of the riches which come from a conviction in the understanding
of the knowledge of God's revealed mystery[22] — summed up as
Messiah. 3In him all the treasures of wisdom and knowledge are hidden.[23]
4I am writing this so that no one will deceive you with persuasive
arguments. 5For although I am absent in person I am with you in spirit,
and I am rejoicing to see your good discipline and the strength of your
faith in Messiah.
6So then, as you received Messiah Jesus, the lord,[24] continue to
conduct yourselves in harmony with him, 7having been rooted in him and

---

[19]The word of God/Gospel is always to be defined as "the Gospel about the Kingdom and the name of Jesus Christ" (Acts 8:12; Lk. 4:43; 8:12; Mt. 13:19; Heb. 2:3, etc).

[20]Glory and future Kingdom of God convey the same idea. James and John asked for positions of authority in the future "Kingdom" or "glory" (Mk. 10:37; Mt. 20:21).

[21]Heb. 2:11: Jesus is the one making the members of the church holy, sanctifying them.

[22]The mystery of the Kingdom, God's unfolding Kingdom plan, is the primary content of the Gospel and was first preached by Jesus (Heb. 2:3). The Kingdom had existed in a preliminary form in OT times (1 Chron. 14:2; 18:14; 28:5; 2 Chron. 13:8; 17:5; 20:30).

[23]The beginning of that wisdom is found in the creed of Jesus in Mark 12:29, the long-neglected definition of Jesus, declaring who the only true God is. Repentance involves giving up false ideas about God and embracing Jesus by embracing Jesus' words, his Gospel and beliefs. Jesus, without his words, is a false Jesus (see Jn. 12:44ff).

[24]The lower case "lord" is deliberate to reinforce the vitally important distinction between the Lord God (Yahweh) and the Messianic lord Jesus, the *adoni*, "my lord," of Ps. 110:1. This verse is an umbrella and controlling verse for the NT view of the relationship of God and Jesus. It is cited many more times by far than any other verse from the Hebrew Bible. Jesus used it to stump all his adversaries and to put an end to all dispute (Mk. 12:35ff). Jesus is "the lord Messiah" who was born (Lk. 2:11) and thus

now being built up in him and established in the faith just as you were taught it, and overflowing with gratitude.

8Be careful that no one takes you captive with empty and deceptive philosophy based on human tradition and on the elemental spirit forces[25] of the world and not based on Messiah. 9For in him the entire fullness of God's character and mind lives bodily, 10and you share this fullness in him who is the head over every ruler and authority. 11In him also you were circumcised with a non-physical, non-literal circumcision, one not done with hands, that is, by putting off the sinful self[26] in the spiritual circumcision done by the Messiah. 12You were buried with him when you were baptized in water, and with him you were also raised from death, so to speak, through belief in the creative energy of God, the One who raised him from the dead. 13Although you were dead in your sins and in the uncircumcision of your sinful self, He made you alive with him, having forgiven us all our sins. 14God erased the certificate of debt which was against us[27] with all of its decrees[28] which were opposed to us, and took it out of the way by nailing it to the cross. 15He disarmed the rulers and authorities and shamed them publicly; He triumphed over them in Jesus at the cross.

16Therefore,[29] do not let anyone, whoever he is, try to exercise authority over you[30] in regard to food and drink or in the matter of annual

---

the Lord's (Yahweh's) Messiah (Lk. 2:26). The blind men understood the meaning of "lord, son of David" (Mt. 20:30).

[25]Demonic forces and teachings promoted by demons, lying spirits.

[26]Literally, "the body of flesh," meaning unregenerate human nature.

[27]Peter in Acts 15:10 admitted that the detailed regulations of Torah had been a burden which the forefathers had been unable to bear.

[28]The parallel in Eph. 2:14-15 clarifies what this is: It is those regulations which put up a barrier between Jew and Gentile, "the Torah (law) of commandments expressed in dogmas." These were "the enmity" which divided Jew and Gentile. They are no more, now that Christ has come and inaugurated the New Covenant. Christ has "abolished" those elements of the law (Eph. 2:15). This in no way affects the obligation of all believers to obey Jesus. The "obedience of faith" summarizes the Christian view and frames the book of Romans (1:5; 16:26; cp. Heb. 5:9 which is decisive).

[29]That is, in view of the cancellation of these Old Covenant, temporary obligations.

[30]That is, criticize you and try to regulate you with commands which take you back to the shadow instead of keeping you in harmony with Messiah who has come and has replaced the shadow calendar.

holy days, monthly new moons,[31] and the weekly Sabbath.[32] 17This whole calendar is a single shadow of what was to come, but by contrast the reality is the Messiah.[33] 18Let no one disqualify you from the prize by

---

[31]Paul writes "holy day" and "new moon" but he includes obviously the various annual holy days and the regular monthly new moons.

[32]On no account should the reader be misled into thinking that Paul excludes the weekly Sabbath here. Sabbath appears often in a plural form where the meaning is the singular weekly Sabbath (even in the ten commandments, see Exod. 20:10, LXX). The translations are correct here to write "Sabbath day" or "Sabbath," meaning the weekly Sabbath. When holy days, new moons and Sabbath are listed together the weekly Sabbath is *always* meant. The weekly Sabbath has no more status in the New Covenant than "new moons" or "holy days." They are all equally a shadow replaced by the Christ who has come. Obligatory Sabbath keeping thus pulls a believer back under the Old Covenant. See Lk. 16:16 and Jn. 1:17 for the difference between the Law of Moses in the letter and the New Covenant Law of Messiah in the spirit.

[33]The substance or reality, of which the calendar was a shadow only, is very clearly the body of Christ. The same comparison of shadow and body appears in Heb. 8:5 and 10:1: the body or person of Christ takes the place of the shadow of the law. In Heb. 10:5-10, the body, i.e. person, of Christ has come, making a reversion to the shadows of the law a serious mistake, denying the benefits of the risen, supernatural Messiah and his presence with us in the truth of the Gospel. Paul is adamantly against a mixing of the letter and the spirit (Rom. 7:6). Jesus is the one who has come. Note that Adam "**is** the type of the one who **is** to come" (Rom. 5:14), but that does not mean that Adam or Christ have not come! The OT calendar is not an obligatory shadow of things still to come, still required as obedience. This would destroy the whole context here. Messiah has come. He is the body, the reality of which the law is a sketch or outline. Our new life is in him, not in the shadows of calendar observance. Sabbath and holy day keeping are irrelevant and actually detrimental when enforced as obligatory in the New Covenant in Messiah. The shadow is in itself the shadow of the Christ who *has* come, and the calendar has no value now that Christ has come and effected a non-literal circumcision (v. 11). Circumcision includes "the whole law" (Gal. 5:2-3) which goes with it, i.e. those regulations which separated Jews from Gentiles. Paul referred to this as "the works of Torah." Christians, since Christ has come, are now celebrating a continuous rest in Christ. They are to be celebrating the feast continuously (1 Cor. 5:8). The spirit of the law replaces the letter of the law and to insist on the letter simply causes believers to retrogress to Moses. Paul worked hard against this fatal mixing of Moses and Jesus. After all Jesus had come to fulfill, i.e. fill with its fullest meaning, the Torah. Mark 7:19 is a striking testimony to Jesus' abolition of food laws, repeated with even greater clarity in Rom. 14:14, 20, where the issue is clean and unclean foods (i.e. Lev. 11). The message is that Christians are to live in the clear light of Christ and not go backwards into the temporary shadow of the Old Covenant which is now superseded. Note too that in 2 Cor. 3 the Sinai event is no longer what matters. And in

insisting on ascetic practices[34] and the worship of angels, going on about
so-called visions he has seen, inflated for no reason by his unconverted
mind. 19Such a person has not held firmly to the head, from whom the
whole body, supported and held together by the ligaments and tendons,
grows with the growth which comes from God.

20If you have died with Messiah to the elemental spirit forces of the
world, why, as if you were alive in the world, do you submit to decrees
— 21do not handle, do not taste, do not touch? 22All these regulations
refer to things that will perish with use; they are just human commands
and doctrines. 23These rules may seem to be wise with their invented
religion, ascetic practices, and severe treatment of the body, but they are
in reality of no value in stopping sinful indulgence.[35]

3 1If then you have been raised with the Messiah, keep seeking what is
above, where the Messiah is seated at the right hand of God.[36] 2Focus
your minds on what is above, not on what is on the earth, 3because you
have died, and your life is now hidden with the Messiah in God. 4When

---

Gal. 4 Paul makes his point as strongly as he can by saying that a desire to revert to the *letter* of the ten commandments is bondage and Hagar!

[34]A banning of all alcohol is not the teaching of the Bible. Jesus performed an extraordinary miracle by turning 120 gallons of water into wine. The Baptists and others, not to be outdone, performed a similar miracle by turning that wine into grape juice! It was the "temperance" movement which rejected all use of alcohol, being actually a "prohibition" movement. Paul did not say, "Do not get drunk on grape juice"! (Eph. 5:18). The word is *oinos* which is alcohol, not grape juice. The use of alcohol for celebration (Deut. 14:26) is not forbidden by the Bible, but excess use, drunkenness is, it goes without saying, always condemned. Jesus recognized the use of wine in the Lord's supper and no one would have questioned this. On no account should churches advocate policies which make their members more righteous than Jesus and weaken their testimony to the world we seek to convert! Such misunderstanding makes church members appear foolish even to outsiders, and involves a strange pharisaical tendency. The biblical model is always the right one.

[35]Obligatory vegetarianism would be an example of such teaching. Or total abstinence from alcohol which goes beyond the standard set by God and Jesus.

[36]Ps.110:1: "my lord," *adoni. Adoni* is never a title of Deity but of a human superior, occasionally an angel.

the Messiah, your life, is revealed, then you also will be revealed with
him in glory.[37]
5So then, put to death whatever in you is worldly: sexual immorality,
impurity, lust, evil desire, and greed which is idolatry. 6Because of these
things God's righteous fury will come on the disobedient,[38] 7and you
once conducted yourselves in this way when you were living that life.
8But now you must put away all of these: anger, rage, malice, slander,
and filthy language from your mouth. 9Do not lie to one another since
you have put off the old self with its practices, 10and you have put on the
new self, who is being renewed in knowledge in the image of the One
who created you. 11Now there is no Gentile or Jew, circumcised or
uncircumcised, barbarian, Scythian, slave or free, but Messiah is all and
in all.
12So as God's chosen ones, holy and loved, put on heartfelt
compassion, kindness, humility, gentleness and patience, 13bearing with
one another and forgiving one another, if anyone has a complaint against
another; just as the Lord has forgiven you, so also you must forgive each
other. 14In addition to all this, put on love, which ties everything together
in perfect unity. 15And let the peace of the Messiah, to which you were
called as one body, control your hearts, and be thankful. 16Let the
Messiah's Gospel-word live richly in you, as you teach and admonish
one another in all wisdom, singing psalms, hymns and spiritual songs
with gratitude in your hearts to God. 17And whatever you do in word or
action, do everything in the name of the lord Jesus,[39] giving thanks
through him to God, who is the Father.[40]

---

[37]i.e. the glory of the future Kingdom on earth. Christians will be glorified by being given spiritual bodies in the resurrection (1 Cor. 15:23, 44). Our present natural bodies will be replaced by "spirit-animated" bodies.

[38]Jesus expressed exactly this idea in John 3:36, and Heb. 5:9 informs us that there is no salvation apart from obedience to Jesus.

[39]By his authority and as representing him and his teachings.

[40]The One God is the Father no less than 1300 times in the NT, and God is never defined as Father, Son and Holy Spirit anywhere in the Bible — that is to say no text ever speaks of "one God, consisting of Father, Son and Holy Spirit." Note that the faith statements of most churches are foreign in this respect to Jesus and the Bible. Jesus rejected all worship, except as directed to the One God of Israel, the God of Jesus.

18Wives, be in submission to your husbands, as is appropriate in the
Lord.[41] 19Husbands, love your wives and never become bitter against
them. 20Children, obey your parents in everything, because this pleases
the Lord. 21Parents, do not aggravate or irritate your children so they will
not become discouraged.

22Servants, obey your masters on earth in everything, not just when
they are looking, in order to please people, but from sincere hearts, out of
reverence for the lord. 23Whatever work you do, do it wholeheartedly, as
for the lord and not for people, 24since you know that you are going to
receive from the lord the reward, which is the inheritance.[42] You are
serving the lord Messiah.[43] 25For the one who does wrong will be paid
back for the wrong he has done, and there is no favoritism.

4 1Masters, do what is right and fair for your servants, since you know
that you also have a master in heaven.

2Persevere in prayer, with alertness and thanksgiving. 3At the same
time pray also for us that God may open to us a door for the Gospel-
word — to speak the revealed mystery[44] of the Messiah, for which I am
in prison. 4Pray that I may explain it clearly, as I should.

---

[41]Some occurrences of "Lord" may refer either to the Lord God, the Father or to Jesus, the lord Messiah. God and Jesus are at work, of course, in perfect harmony (Jn. 10:30).

[42]The inheritance of the Kingdom. Refer always to the words of Jesus in Matt. 19:28-29 and of Paul in 1 Cor. 6:2: "Don't you understand that the saints are going to govern the world?" Luke 19:11ff is the ideal parable for establishing the NT sense of the Kingdom as primarily the Messianic Kingdom to be inaugurated at the Second Coming of Jesus (Rev. 11:15-18; Mk. 15:43; Lk. 21:31). This is of course based on the promises and prophecies of Dan. 7:18, 22, 27 and all OT prophecy (Acts 3:21). Paul warned them that they were not *now* ruling as kings (1 Cor. 4:8).

[43]The lord Messiah who was born in Bethlehem (Lk. 2:11). This is the second lord (*adoni*, "my lord") of Ps. 110:1, cited and alluded to more by far than any other verse from the Hebrew Bible. This verse provides the umbrella, stellar witness to the crucial difference between the One Lord God, the Father (Jesus is not once called the Lord God) and *the man* Messiah Jesus (1 Tim. 2:5). *Adoni* ("my lord") appears 195 times in the OT and never means the Lord God. The Son is not only "the lord Messiah" (Lk. 2:11) but also the LORD's (Yahweh's) Messiah (Lk. 2:26).

[44]This is of course not a mystification! It is the unfolding immortality, Kingdom program of God and the Messiah summed up as the Gospel of the Kingdom of God announced by Jesus (Mk. 1:14-15; Lk. 4:43; Acts 19:8; 20:24-25; 28:23, 31, etc).

5Conduct yourselves in wisdom towards outsiders, making full use of each opportunity. 6Your speech should always be gracious, as if flavored with salt, so that you may know how you should respond to each person.

7Tychicus, a dear brother and faithful minister and fellow servant in the Lord, will give you all my news. 8I have sent him to you for this very purpose, so that you may know about us and so that he may encourage your hearts. 9With him is Onesimus, a faithful and much loved brother, who is one of you. They will tell you about everything going on here.

10Aristarchus, my fellow prisoner, greets you, and so does Mark, Barnabas' cousin, about whom you have received instructions: if he comes to you, welcome him. 11Jesus who is called Justus greets you too. These are the only ones of the circumcision, the Jews, who are my co-workers for the Kingdom of God, and they have been a comfort to me. 12Epaphras, who is one of you and a servant of Messiah Jesus, greets you. He is always contending for you in his prayers, so that you may stand mature, fully assured of everything God wills. 13For I can testify about him that he works very hard for you, for those in Laodicea, and for those in Hierapolis. 14Luke,[45] the much-loved physician, and Demas greet you. 15Pass on my greetings to the brothers and sisters in Laodicea, and to Nympha and the church which meets in her house. 16And when this letter has been read among you, see that it is read also in the church of the Laodiceans; and make sure you also read the letter from Laodicea. 17Tell Archippus, "Pay attention to the ministry you received in the lord, so that you carry it out fully."

18This greeting is in my own handwriting — Paul. Do remember my imprisonment. Grace be with you.

---

[45]Luke wrote more of the NT than any other writer (if we assume Paul did not write Hebrews) and he had the unique privilege and responsibility of recording the life of Christ and the history of the church after the ascension. Luke strove to show us that the saving Gospel of the Kingdom was preached by Jesus, and that exactly the same Kingdom of God Gospel was preached by Paul and the other NT writers after Jesus had gone to heaven (Lk. 4:43; Acts 8:12; 14:22; 19:8; **20:24-25**; 28:23, 31).

1 Thessalonians

1 1From Paul, Silvanus, and Timothy to the church of the Thessalonians
in God who is the Father and in the lord Jesus Messiah: Grace and
peace to you.
2We give thanks to God always for you all, mentioning you in our
prayers. 3We constantly remember your work based on faith, your labor
based on love, and your perseverance based on your hope[1] in our lord
Jesus Messiah in the presence of our God and Father. 4We know,
brothers and sisters loved by God, that He has chosen you. 5For our
Gospel came to you not only in words, but also in power and holy spirit
producing strong conviction. You know what kind of people we proved
to be among you for your sake. 6You became imitators of us and of the
lord, after you received the Gospel-word with the joy of holy spirit,
despite much persecution. 7As a result you became a model to all the
believers in Macedonia and Achaia. 8For from you the Gospel-word of
the lord rang out, not only in Macedonia and Achaia, but also
everywhere the faith you have in God has become known, so that we do
not need to say anything. 9For people report how you received us, and
how you turned to God from idols, to serve the living and true God,[2]
10and to wait for His Son from heaven, whom He raised from the dead —
Jesus, who will rescue us from the coming wrath.

2 1For you yourselves know, brothers and sisters, that our visit to you
was not for nothing. 2Although we had previously suffered and been
mistreated in Philippi, as you are aware, we had the boldness in our God
to preach God's Gospel[3] to you, despite much opposition. 3For our
exhortation does not proceed from error, impure motives, or deception,

---

[1]Hope is directed to the Second Coming, and hope is the solid basis on which love and faith are to be built (Col. 1:4-5). The Gospel of the coming Kingdom defines the Christian hope.

[2]Paul demonstrates the same strict unitary monotheism as Jesus in John 17:3, where the Father is the "only one who is true God," and the Messiah is His agent whom He commissioned.

[3]"God's Gospel," the one and only true Gospel (also v. 8-9), is found 8 times in the NT: Mk. 1:14; Rom. 1:1; 15:16 (framing the book of Romans); 2 Cor. 11:7; 1 Thess. 2:2, 8, 9; 1 Pet. 4:17. This shows the complete unity of the NT based on the one Gospel of the Kingdom as Jesus preached it (Mk. 1:14-15; Lk. 4:43; 8:11). Paul also preached the Kingdom of God as Gospel always (Acts 19:8; 20:24-25; 28:23, 30, 31).

4but just as we have been approved by God to be entrusted with the Gospel, so we speak it, not to be pleasing to people but to God, who examines our hearts. 5For we never came with flattering words, as you are aware, nor did we act in greed — as God is our witness — 6nor did we seek glory from people, either you or others, even though we could have imposed our authority as Apostles of Messiah. 7Instead we came to you in gentleness, as a nursing mother takes care of her own children. 8Having this affection for you, we took delight in sharing with you not only God's Gospel, but also our very selves, because you have become so dear to us.

9For you remember, brothers and sisters, our toil and labor. Working night and day so that we would not be a burden to any of you, we preached to you God's Gospel. 10You are witnesses, as is God, of how holy and uprightly and blamelessly we conducted ourselves toward you who believe. 11You know how, like a father with his children, 12we were exhorting and encouraging and imploring each one of you to behave in a way worthy of the God who is calling you into His own Kingdom and glory.[4]

13We also thank God constantly that when you received the word of God[5] you heard from us, you accepted it not as the word of humans, but what it truly is, the Gospel-word of God which transmits its energy to you who believe it.[6] 14For you, brothers and sisters, became imitators of the churches of God in Messiah Jesus in Judea, because you suffered the same things from your own countrymen as they did from the Jews, 15who killed both the lord Jesus and the prophets, and persecuted us. They do not please God and oppose all people, 16preventing us from speaking to the Gentiles so that they may be saved. So they always fill up the measure of their sins, but wrath has begun to come on them.[7]

---

[4]The object and hope of the Christian life and faith is to govern and reign in the future Kingdom of God to be introduced by Jesus at his return (Dan. 7:18, 22, 27; Mt. 19:28; 1 Cor. 6:2; Rev. 5:9-10; 20:1-6; Lk. 19:17).

[5]The Gospel of the Kingdom (Mk. 1:14-15).

[6]The Kingdom Gospel is the very creative energy of God and so any depletion or reduction of the Gospel weakens the entire Christian enterprise. A "washed out" Gospel bears no fruit. The Gospel of the Kingdom imparts the seed of immortality by which Christians are born again (Jn. 3:3; 1 Pet. 1:23).

[7]This is precisely what Jesus had said in John 3:36. In Jn. 12:48 failure to accept Jesus' *words*, not just his death and resurrection, is the same as rejecting Jesus.

17But we, brothers and sisters, having been apart from you for a short
time — in person but not in spirit — we desired even more to see your
faces. 18We wanted to come to you — I, Paul, tried several times — but
Satan prevented us. 19For who is our hope or joy or crown of pride? Is it
not you, in the presence of our lord Jesus at his coming?[8] 20For you are
our glory and our joy.

3 1So when we could not stand it any longer, we thought it good to be
left behind in Athens. 2We sent Timothy, our brother and fellow
worker for God in the Gospel of Messiah, to strengthen and encourage
you in your faith, 3so that no one would be upset by the current
afflictions. For you know that we are destined for this. 4Certainly, when
we were with you, we kept telling you in advance that we would suffer
affliction, and as you know that is what happened. 5That is why, when I
could not stand it any longer, I sent to find out about your faith, in fear
that the Tempter had somehow tempted you, and our labor would have
been in vain.

6But now Timothy has returned from his visit to you and has brought
us good news of your faith and love. He said that you have good
memories of us always and long to see us, just as we long to see you.
7So, brothers and sisters, in all our distress and affliction we were
comforted about you through your faith. 8Now we live, if you stand firm
in the lord. 9How can we thank God enough for all the joy we have
because of you before our God? 10Night and day we pray earnestly that
we may see your faces, and complete what is lacking in your faith.

11Now may God Himself, who is our Father, and Jesus our lord direct
our way to you. 12May the lord make you increase and abound in love for
one another and for everyone, as we do for you, 13so that he may
establish your hearts blameless in holiness before our God and Father at
the coming[9] of our lord Jesus with all his saints.

---

[8]"At his Parousia," Second Coming.

[9]Paul's and the NT Christian hope is invariably directed to the one future, visible Parousia, Second Coming of Jesus. He never anticipated being with Christ apart from this tremendous event (4:17). This is so different from the current, popular view of the Christian future.

4 1Finally then, brothers and sisters, we request and exhort you in the
lord Jesus that as you received from us instruction about how to
behave and please God — just as you do behave — that you excel even
more. 2For you know the commands we gave you through the lord Jesus.
3This is the will of God: that you become holy, that you abstain from
sexual immorality, 4that each of you knows how to control your own
body in holiness and honor, 5not in the passion of lust, like the Gentiles
who do not know God. 6No one should take advantage of or wrong his
brother or sister in these matters, because the Lord is the avenger in all
these things, as we told you before and warned solemnly. 7For God has
not called us to impurity, but in holiness. 8So anyone who rejects this is
not rejecting human beings but God, who gives His holy spirit to you.

9About brotherly love, you do not need anyone to write to you,
because you yourselves have been taught by God to love one another.
10And you are showing this love to all the brothers and sisters throughout
Macedonia. But we urge you, brothers and sisters, to do so even more,
11aiming to lead a quiet life and attend to your own business, working
with your own hands, as we commanded you. 12In this way you will
behave properly before outsiders and not be in need.

13We do not want you to be ignorant, brothers and sisters, about those
who have fallen asleep,[10] so that you will not grieve like others who have
no hope. 14Since we believe that Jesus died and rose again, in the same
way God will bring with Jesus, escorting him,[11] those who have fallen
asleep in Jesus. 15For we tell you this by the word of the lord: We who
are alive, who remain until the coming of the lord, will not go ahead of
those who have fallen asleep. 16For the lord himself will come down from
heaven with a shout of command, accompanied by the voice of the
archangel and the trumpet of God, and the dead in Messiah will rise first.

---

[10]Death is called "the sleep of death" in Ps. 13:3. It is a state of complete unconsciousness which will end only when the dead are "woken up" from the sleep of death at the future resurrection when Jesus comes back. Dan. 12:2 and John 11:11, 14 are simple and decisive verses on this important topic.

[11]How this happens is explained in the next sentence. The dead in Christ will be raised from death and the believers who survive, without dying, until the return of Jesus will be caught up in one company to meet Jesus as he descends in order that all may escort the royal personage to the earth to which he is returning to rule in Jerusalem. "To be brought with Jesus presupposes rising from the dead as part of the process, v. 16" (*Expositor's Bible Commentary*, p. 276).

17Then we who are alive and remain will be caught up[12] together with
them in the clouds to meet the lord in the air.[13] In this way we will be
with the lord always. 18So comfort one another with these words.

5 1About the times and seasons, brothers and sisters, you have no need
that anything be written to you. 2For you know well that the Day of
the Lord will come like a thief in the night. 3When people are saying,
"We have peace and safety," then sudden destruction will come on them,
like birth pains on a pregnant woman, and they will not escape. 4But you,
brothers and sisters, are not in darkness, so that the day would surprise
you like a thief, 5because you are all children of light and children of
day.[14] We do not belong to the night, nor to darkness, 6so let us not sleep
as others do, but let us be wide awake and sober. 7For those who sleep,
sleep at night, and those who get drunk do it at night. 8But since we
belong to the day let us be sober, putting on the breastplate of faith and
love, and the helmet of the hope of salvation. 9For God has not destined
us for His anger, but for obtaining salvation through our lord Jesus
Messiah. 10He died for us, so that whether we are awake or asleep in
death,[15] we will come to life together with him. 11So encourage one
another and build each other up, just as you are doing.

---

[12]The Greek verb here, *harpazo*, means to snatch away, catch up. It has been misused to promote a so-called pre-Tribulation "rapture," an illusory event 7 years before the Second Coming of Jesus in power. There is only one Second Coming and not two. There is no noun "rapture" in the NT. The snatching up here is part of the complex of events which will occur at the one single, visible return of Jesus to establish his Kingdom on earth. Jesus is coming back to the earth in order to rule on the earth (Rev. 5:10; Dan. 7:27). He is not going away again. His coming is not a "drive through." He has a "one-way" ticket to the earth. The seventh trumpet of Rev. 11:15-18 is of course the same event as the last trumpet of 1 Cor. 15:52.

[13]This is of course a catching up of the Christians to meet the royal personage who is on his way back to the earth. "Hence the lord will meet his church. She will not need to wait until he sets foot on earth; but those who are ready, 'looking for their lord when he shall return' (Lk. 22:35-40) will hear his trumpet call and 'go forth to *meet* the bridegroom' (Mt. 25: 1, 6)" (*Cambridge Bible for Schools and Colleges*, p. 106).

[14]Enlightened by the saving truth of the Gospel. Salvation is impossible without "a *passion* for truth in order to be saved" (2 Thess. 2:10).

[15]This is proof of the state of the dead up to the moment of resurrection. They are unconscious in sleep, not already being rewarded or punished, which would throw the whole NT scheme and program into confusion.

12We ask you, brothers and sisters, to respect those who labor among
you and are over you in the lord and admonish you. 13Honor them in love
because of their work. Be at peace among yourselves. 14We urge you,
brothers and sisters, to admonish the undisciplined, encourage the
discouraged, support the weak, and be patient with everyone. 15See that
no one returns evil for evil to anyone, but always seek what is good for
one another and for all. 16Always rejoice. 17Pray without ceasing. 18In
everything give thanks, because this is the will of God in Messiah Jesus
for you. 19Do not quench the spirit; 20do not treat prophecies with
contempt, 21but examine everything, and hold firmly to what is good.
22Avoid every form of evil.

23Now may the God of peace Himself make you completely holy, and
may your whole spirit, soul, and body[16] be kept blameless at the coming
of our lord Jesus Messiah. 24He who calls you is faithful, and He will do
this.

25Brothers and sisters, pray for us.

26Greet all the brothers and sisters with a holy kiss. 27I solemnly
command you in the lord to have this letter read to all the brothers and
sisters.

28The grace of our lord Jesus Messiah be with you.

---

[16]This one verse is not meant to be a "scientific" analysis. "Soul" usually refers to the whole personality, "spirit" more to the mind and intellect. "Body" often also refers to the whole person (Rom. 12:1). There is no significant difference between soul and spirit (Lk. 1:46-47). Each word has a range of meanings. "Soul" never means an immortal soul, which is a pagan idea (see our booklet *What Happens When We Die?* At focusonthekingdom.org).

2 Thessalonians

1 1From Paul, Silvanus, and Timothy to the church of the Thessalonians in God who is our Father and in the lord Jesus Messiah: 2Grace and peace to you from God who is the Father and from the lord Jesus Messiah.

3We should always give thanks to God for you, brothers and sisters, as is appropriate, because your faith is thriving, and the love of each one of you towards one another is growing. 4So we speak proudly about you in the churches of God because of your perseverance and faith in all the persecutions and afflictions which you are enduring. 5This is evidence of the righteous judgment of God, so that you may be made worthy of the Kingdom of God, for which you are now suffering. 6For it is justice for God to repay with affliction those who are afflicting you, 7and to give relief to you who are afflicted, together with us. He will do this when the lord Jesus will be revealed from heaven with his mighty angels,[1] 8in flaming fire dealing out punishment[2] to those who do not know God and do not obey the Gospel of our lord Jesus. 9They will pay the penalty of the destruction of the age to come, dismissed from the presence of the lord and from the glory of his might, 10when he comes on that Day to be glorified among his saints[3] and admired among all those who have believed — and you did believe our Gospel-testimony. 11With this in view we pray for you always, that our God will make you worthy of His call, and powerfully fulfill your every desire for goodness and every work of faith, 12so that the name of our lord Jesus will be glorified in you, and you in him, according to the grace of our God and the lord Jesus Messiah.

---

[1]It is obvious that Paul believed in a single future coming (Parousia, arrival) of Jesus. There is no hint of a "secret" coming 7 years earlier. In Paul's mind the point of time until which Christians must endure affliction is the public arrival of Jesus in power and glory to punish his enemies. This absolutely excludes a double second coming. Paul's churches would expect affliction to be their lot right up to the glorious arrival of Jesus to punish his enemies and reward the faithful.

[2]This is the well-known (in both Testaments) awful Day of the Lord (Zeph. 1:14-18, etc.), in which He will pour His just fury on an evil world that has not submitted to the teaching of Jesus. Luke 21:22 speaks of this time as the "days of vengeance in which everything will be fulfilled."

[3]The saints will be glorified rulers and governors in the Kingdom, with Jesus (Lk. 19:17; Rev. 2:26-27; Dan. 7:18, 22, 27: all nations "will obey them," RSV).

2 1In connection with the coming of our lord Jesus Messiah and our
being gathered together to him, we ask you, brothers and sisters: 2Do
not be quickly shaken out of your senses or disturbed by any "spiritual"
utterance, any message or letter pretending to come from us, which
suggests that the day of the Lord is immediately at hand or has already
come.[4] 3Do not let anyone deceive you by any means, because before that
day comes there must first be the great rebellion, and the lawless man
must appear, the one destined for destruction. 4He elevates himself over
everything that is called God and all that people hold in reverence. He
finally even installs himself[5] in the temple[6] of God, claiming to be God.[7]
5Do you not remember that I used to tell you about all this while I was

---

[4]The error is to say either that the promised Day has happened or will happen with no events preceding it. The popular "pre-tribulation" rapture theory is condemned by Paul's words here. There is only one future Second Coming of Jesus.

[5]"Intrudes into, and sits down in...He in person sits down enthroned in the temple...The temple which Christ had cleansed, and in which the first Christians prayed, and likewise Paul himself, that house of prayer for all people was an object of interest to every Christian church" (Lange, *Commentary*, 2 Thessalonians, p. 128).

[6]Most naturally understood as a real building, and a vital piece of information about the future in Jerusalem. Note F.F. Bruce: "the picture here is of a material shrine." And *TDNT* on Rev. 11:1: "In this case we are fairly obviously to think in terms of the earthly temple in Jerusalem" (Vol. 4, p. 887). A temple is to be expected in Israel, since the Abomination of Desolation will stand there (Mt. 24:15; Mk. 13:14), and Dan. 9:27, 11:31 and 12:11 speak of the sacrificial system being interrupted. Rev. 11:1-2 likewise refers to the final 3 ½ year period of tribulation connected with trampling down (see Zech. 12:3, LXX) cited by Jesus also in Luke 21:24. Rev. 11:2 is a reference to Dan. 8:11-13 where the sanctuary is cast down. Cp. Isa. 63:18, Ps. 79:1 for the final period of violence before the arrival of the Kingdom. When Paul first introduces the church or an individual believer as "a temple," he does not use the definite article. The church is "*a* temple of God" (1 Cor. 3:16).

[7]Paul here alludes to Dan. 11:36 where the final wicked King of the North is described. Jesus referred to the Abomination of Desolation standing where *he* ought not to (Mk. 13:14), that is, installing himself in a holy place (Mt. 24:15). Dan. 12:11, the important key to defining the Abomination of Desolation, informs us that from the appearing of the Abomination of Desolation about 3 ½ years will elapse until the end of the vision which is marked by the resurrection of the dead who are currently sleeping in the dust of the ground and will awake to receive their inheritance in the Kingdom and "the Life of the Age" (Dan. 12:2). This Life of the Age to Come appears some 49 times in the NT, the life to be gained by resurrection (or being transformed while still alive if a person is still living when Jesus returns).

still with you?[8] 6So you know that at present there is a power which holds
him back, so that he will not be revealed before his appointed time.
7Meanwhile the secret energy of lawlessness is already at work; however,
he who now restrains will continue to do so until he is taken out of the
way. 8Then that lawless one will be revealed, the one whom the lord
Jesus will destroy by the breath of his mouth and obliterate by the
brilliance of his coming.[9] 9That lawless one will stage his own "coming"

---

[8]Paul spent perhaps only a few weeks founding the Thessalonian church, but his teaching on the "time of the end" and the important sequence of events leading to the return of Jesus was of utmost importance to him and discussed often. The vital importance of this information, which is similar to Jesus' famous Olivet discourse in Matt. 24, Mark 13 and Luke 21, needs to be properly understood by believers and passed on to subsequent generations until the supreme event of the Second Coming happens. Repeated false and failed date-setting has not only sold millions of books but tends to throw the whole subject into disrepute. It is quite clear that Jesus will come back *once* only in the future. A so-called "PRE-tribulation" rapture is imaginary and not found anywhere in the NT. Especially striking is its complete absence from the careful sequence of events given by Jesus in Matt. 24 (and parallels). Remember that the mistaken theory posits both a rapture and resurrection of dead saints, before the onset of the Great Tribulation. That huge event, a *pre*-tribulation rapture-resurrection, is not mentioned ever by Jesus. The only coming he recognizes happens *after* the Great Tribulation (Mt. 24:29-31). When some say that Jesus was speaking to Jews in Matt. 24 they imply that none of the words of Jesus are for us! We all know that the disciples of Jesus were Jews, but we ought to know that the words of Jesus are for all believers until the end of the age (cp. Jn. 12:44ff; 2 Jn. 7-9 for a solemn warning). If Matt. 24 is not addressed to us, then is the sermon on the mount, also delivered to the Jewish disciples of Jesus, not for us?

[9]Paul gives us a crucial piece of understanding in reference to prophecy. He quotes from Isa. 11:4, and the context of all Paul's quotations must be studied in detail. There is to be an Assyrian enemy of God and God's people, including the nation of Israel. He is called "the Assyrian," pointing to his origin in the Middle East, not Europe! (Europe is not the subject of biblical prophecy.) The Messiah in Mic. 5:5-6 is the one who at his coming will deliver Israel from the invading Assyrian. That term might include geographical areas such as ancient Assyria, Babylon, Persia (see Ezra 6:22 where the Persian king is called the king of Assyria), and Syria. Zech. 5 speaks of a future commercial venture in the area of the land of Nimrod (see Gen. 10:9-11). Zech. 12:3 in the LXX speaks of a terrible invasion of Israel, a trampling down of Jerusalem and the nations mocking Jerusalem (a further ref. is in Zech. 13:8-9; 14:1-2). Luke 21:24 is cited by Jesus from Zech. 12:3, LXX and Jesus refers again to this verse in Rev. 11:2-3. When the Messiah comes he will rescue Israel from the Assyrian antichrist (the King of the North of Dan. 11). The Assyrian will be destroyed in the lake of fire and brimstone (Isa. 30:33).

with Satan's power to aid him. It will be accompanied by all kinds of
miracles, signs, and amazing but deceptive displays of Satanic power.
10His wicked deceptions will completely fool those who are on the way
to destruction, as a punishment for their refusal to develop a passion for
the truth in order to be saved.[10] 11Because of this God will let loose on
them an energy of delusion so that they will believe what is false. 12As a
result, judgment will fall on those who decided not to believe the truth
but took pleasure in wickedness.

13But we should always give thanks to God for you, brothers and
sisters loved by the lord, because God has chosen you from the
beginning to be saved by becoming holy through the spirit and believing
the truth. 14To this He called you through our Gospel, so that you may
participate in the glory[11] of our lord Jesus Messiah. 15So then, brothers
and sisters, stand firm and hold on to the traditions we taught you,
whether by spoken message or by letter from us.

16Now may our lord Jesus Messiah himself and God who is our
Father,[12] who loved us and through grace gave us the comfort of the Age
to Come and good hope, 17encourage and strengthen your hearts in every
good work and word.

3 1Finally, brothers and sisters, pray for us that the Gospel-word of the
Lord will speed on and be honored, just as it was with you, 2and that
we will be delivered from perverse and wicked people, as not everyone
has the faith. 3But the Lord is faithful, who will strengthen you and guard
you from the Evil One. 4And we have confidence in the Lord about you,
that you are doing and will do what we command. 5May the Lord direct
your hearts to the love of God and to the perseverance of the Messiah.

6We command you, brothers and sisters, in the name of our lord Jesus
Messiah, to avoid any brother or sister who leads an undisciplined life

---

[10]The indispensable quality required for salvation is a "love for the truth" of all that Jesus and the Apostles taught as the faith. Not to love that truth is the equivalent of wickedness (v. 12). This is more than ethics; it entails believing all of Jesus' teachings.

[11]"Glory" is a synonym for the future Kingdom to be revealed at the Second Coming of Jesus.

[12]This is one of 1300 references in the NT to God as the Father. This is massive evidence for a unitary, non-Trinitarian understanding of monotheism, shared by all Bible writers.

and not according to the tradition you learned from us. 7For you know
that you ought to imitate us, because we did not behave in an
undisciplined way among you, 8nor did we eat anyone's food without
paying. Instead with labor and toil we worked night and day in order not
to be a burden to any of you. 9This is not because we do not have that
right, but to offer ourselves as an example for you to imitate. 10Even
when we were with you we used to give you this command: anyone who
is not willing to work should not eat. 11For we hear that some among you
are leading an undisciplined life, not working but interfering in others'
business. 12Those people we command and exhort in the lord Jesus
Messiah to work quietly and earn their own living. 13And you, brothers
and sisters, do not grow weary doing what is right.

14If anyone does not obey what we write in this letter, note that
person and do not associate with him, so that he may be ashamed. 15Yet
do not count him as an enemy, but keep admonishing him as a brother.

16May the Lord of peace Himself give you peace at all times and in
all ways. The Lord be with you all.

17I write this greeting with my own hand — Paul, which is my
genuine signature in every letter. This is my handwriting. 18The grace of
our lord Jesus Messiah be with you all.

1 Timothy

1 1From Paul, an Apostle of Messiah Jesus by the command of God our
Savior and of Messiah Jesus our hope, 2to Timothy, my genuine child
in the faith: Grace, mercy and peace from God who is the Father and
from Messiah Jesus our lord.[1]

3As I urged you when I was departing for Macedonia, remain in
Ephesus to command certain people not to teach false doctrines, 4nor to
embrace myths and endless genealogies. These merely promote empty
speculations rather than God's immortality plan, which operates by faith.
5But the object of our teaching is love produced by a pure heart, a good
conscience and a genuine faith. 6Some have veered away from these and
have turned aside to pointless discussions. 7They want to be teachers of
the Law, but they do not understand either what they are saying or the
subject they are confidently insisting on.

8Now we know that the Law is good provided one uses it
legitimately, 9which means realizing that the Law is not meant for an
upright person, but for the lawless and rebellious, for the godless and
sinners, for the unholy and irreverent, for those who kill their father or
mother, for murderers, 10for the sexually immoral, homosexuals,
kidnappers, liars, perjurers, and whatever else contradicts the health-
giving teaching. 11This teaching is based on the Gospel of the glory of the
blessed God, which was entrusted to me.

12I give thanks to Messiah Jesus our lord[2] who has given me strength,
because he considered me faithful and put me in ministry — 13although I
was previously a blasphemer, a persecutor, and a violent man. Yet I
received mercy because I had acted from ignorance and unbelief, 14and
the grace of our lord overflowed, with the faith and love which are in
Messiah Jesus.[3] 15This saying is trustworthy and deserves to be fully

---

[1]Paul's unitarian faith is repeated at the outset of his letters. God is the Father (as about 1300 times in the NT) and Jesus is the my/our lord of Ps. 110:1 where *adoni* (195 times in the OT) is never a title of Deity. Jesus is the lord Messiah (Lk. 2:11), not the Lord God — which would make two Gods!

[2]Paul certainly prayed to Jesus sometimes, thanksgiving being a form of prayer. This was authorized by Jesus in John 14:14 (not KJV).

[3]The faith Paul describes is the same faith as was found in Jesus. We not only have faith in Jesus; we must have the same faith as he, implying obedience to him and his words/Gospel of the Kingdom. See the warning in 1 Tim. 6:3; 2 John 7-9.

accepted: "Messiah Jesus came into the world to save sinners" — and I
am the worst of them. 16But this is why I received mercy, so that in me as
the worst of sinners Messiah Jesus would demonstrate his enormous
patience, as an example for those who will believe in him for the Life of
the Age to Come.[4] 17Now to the King of the ages, who is immortal and
invisible, the only one who is God,[5] be honor and glory to the ages of the
ages! Amen.

18Timothy, my child, I am giving you this instruction in keeping with
the prophecies which were previously made about you, so that through
these prophecies you fight the good fight. 19In order to do this, you must
maintain the faith and a good conscience. Some have rejected these and
have shipwrecked the faith. 20Hymenaeus and Alexander are among
them, and I have delivered them over to Satan, so that they may be
disciplined not to blaspheme.

2 1First of all, then, I urge that requests, prayers, intercessions, and
thanksgivings be made for everyone, 2including kings and all who are
in authority, so that we may lead a tranquil and peaceful life in all
godliness and dignity. 3These prayers are good and pleasing to God our
Savior, 4as He desires all people to be saved and come to the knowledge
of the truth[6] — 5namely that there is one God and one mediator between
that one God and humanity, Messiah Jesus, who is himself human. 6He
gave himself as a ransom for all, a testimony at the appointed time. 7To
this I was appointed a herald and Apostle — I am telling the truth; I am
not lying — and a teacher of the Gentiles in faith and truth.

---

[4]The Age to Come is the future age of the Kingdom of God to be inaugurated worldwide when Jesus returns to sit on the throne of David in Jerusalem. It will replace "the present evil age" (Gal. 1:4) which is under the control of Satan who is "the god of this world-system" (2 Cor. 4:4).

[5]A typical unitarian, non-Trinitarian statement about who the one God is. It reflects exactly the Jewish heritage of Paul and all NT writers. Mal. 2:10 summarized this simple creed: "Do we not all have one Father? Has not one God created us?" God and Father are equivalent, as is true of 1300 occurrences in the NT. In Dan. 3:17, LXX the young men appealed to "our one LORD" and Jesus affirmed the unitarian creed of Israel in Mark 12:29 in complete agreement with a first-century Jewish scholar.

[6]The knowledge of the truth has as its framework the unitarian statement which follows in which the definition of the One God and Jesus are made crystal clear, following the pattern established by the umbrella text Ps. 110:1 which governs the NT.

8So then I want the men in every place to pray, lifting up holy hands
without anger or argument. 9Also the women should dress in proper
clothing, with modesty and decency. Their beauty should not be
elaborate hairstyles, gold, pearls, or expensive clothes, 10but good works,
as is proper for women claiming reverence for God. 11A woman should
learn quietly[7] with full submission. 12But I do not allow a woman to teach
or domineer over a man; instead she is to be quiet. 13For Adam was
formed first, then Eve. 14And Adam was not deceived, but the woman,
because she was completely deceived, fell into sin. 15But she will be
preserved through childbearing, if she continues in faith, love and
holiness with self-restraint.

3 1This saying is trustworthy: "If any man aspires to the office of elder[8]
he desires a noble work." 2An elder, then, must be above reproach,
the husband[9] of one wife, temperate, self-controlled, respectable,
hospitable, an able teacher, 3not a drunkard, not violent, but gentle,
peaceable, free from the love of money. 4He should manage his own
household competently, keeping his children under control with all
dignity. 5But if someone does not know how to manage his own
household, how will he take care of God's church? 6He must not be a
new convert, or he might become arrogant and fall into the same
condemnation as the Devil did.[10] 7He also must have a good reputation
with outsiders, so that he may not fall into disgrace and the Devil's trap.

8Similarly, deacons should be honorable, not hypocritical, not given
to excessive drinking,[11] not greedy, 9holding the revealed truths of the

---

[7]This text must not be allowed to contradict the earlier instruction in 1 Cor. 11:5 that women may "pray and prophesy" (i.e. encourage and edify), provided it is done appropriately.

[8]Bishops, pastors and elders have the same rank in the NT. They are different ways of describing the leaders and teachers of the church.

[9]Paul did not burden women with being in charge of the church groups. The leadership role he confines to persons who are husbands of one wife. This of course means *if* they are married, which would normally be the case. Paul recognized a celibate man to be perfectly valid for ministry, and Paul himself was apparently not married.

[10]Showing that the Devil exercised free will to rebel against God. He was condemned for his rebellion (Gen. 3:14-15; Rom. 16:20; Rev. 20:2-3).

[11]Excess of alcohol is condemned in Scripture, but not alcohol (wine and strong drink) in itself. There is a huge difference between drunkenness and the appropriate use of

faith with a clear conscience. 10And they must first be tested, and if they
prove themselves blameless then let them serve as deacons. 11Their
wives, too, must be honorable, not slanderers, but temperate and faithful
in everything. 12Deacons must be husbands of one wife, and competently
manage their children and their own household. 13For those who have
served well as deacons acquire a good standing for themselves and great
confidence in the faith which is in Messiah Jesus.

14I am hoping to come to you soon, but I am writing these
instructions to you so that, 15if I am delayed, you will know how people
ought to behave in God's household which is the church of the living
God, the support and foundation of the truth. 16And most certainly the
revealed truth of our faith is great: he who[12] was manifested as a human
person, vindicated in the spirit, seen by angels, preached among the
Gentiles, believed in the world, taken up in glory.

4 1Now the spirit says explicitly that in the later times some will depart
from the faith and occupy themselves with lying spirits and teachings
propagated by demons,[13] 2through the hypocrisy of liars whose
consciences are seared. 3These people forbid marriage and demand
abstinence from foods which God created to be eaten with thanksgiving
by those who believe and know the truth. 4For everything created by God
is good, and no food should be rejected[14] if it is received with
thanksgiving, 5because it is made holy by God's word and by prayer.

6By pointing these things out to the brothers and sisters, you will be a
good servant of Messiah Jesus, nourished by the words of the faith and
of the sound teaching which you followed. 7But refuse to have anything

---

alcohol for celebration and for the lord's supper. Jesus turned 120 gallons of water into wine, for purposes of celebration at a wedding. The so-called "temperance" movement was actually a prohibition movement, going beyond Scripture.

[12]The KJV is based on a corrupted manuscript here, reading "God was manifested…" The Greek has "he who was manifested…" referring to Jesus as the Son of God, defined by Luke 1:35.

[13]I.e. teachings proceeding from the mind of demons, supernatural personalities.

[14]Jesus had spiritualized the food laws, "cleansing all foods" as the Markan comment in Mark 7:19 shows: "Thus Jesus spoke, cleansing all foods." Paul likewise, speaking as a Jew and a Christian, viewed the food laws of Lev. 11 as obsolete (see Rom. 14:14, 20; 1 Cor. 9:20-21). To reintroduce them would mean erecting the barrier between Jew and Gentile which has been removed in Christ (Eph. 2:14; Col. 2:16-17; Gal. 4:10).

to do with godless and foolish myths. Rather, train yourself in godliness,
8because: Physical training has limited value, but godliness is valuable in
every way as it holds promise for the present life and for the Life to
come. 9This saying is trustworthy and deserves to be fully accepted.
10That Life is what we are laboring and striving for, because we have set
our hope on the living God, who is the Savior of all people, especially of
believers.

11Command and teach these things. 12Do not let anyone look down on
you because you are young, but be an example for the believers in
speech, conduct, love, faith and purity. 13Until I arrive, give attention to
the public reading of Scripture, exhortation, and teaching. 14Do not
neglect your spiritual gift, which was given to you accompanied by
prophetic words when the elders laid hands on you. 15Work hard at these
things; devote yourself to them, so that your progress may be visible to
everyone. 16Be conscientious about your life and your teaching.
Persevere in this, as by doing so you will save both yourself and those
who listen to you.

5 1Do not speak harshly to an older man, but appeal to him as a father.
Speak to younger men as brothers, 2older women as mothers, and
younger women as sisters, with absolute purity.

3Honor and support widows who are genuinely in need. 4But if a
widow has children or grandchildren, they should first learn to do their
duty toward their own family and repay their parents, because this is
pleasing to God. 5The widow who is really in need, left all alone, has set
her hope on God and continues night and day in requests and prayers.
6But the widow who lives for pleasure is dead even while she lives.
7Keep commanding these things, so that no one may be blamed. 8But if
someone does not provide for his own relatives, especially his immediate
family, he has denied the faith and is worse than an unbeliever.

9A widow may be placed on the support list if she is at least sixty
years old and has been the wife of one husband.[15] 10She must be known
for good works — that is, if she has brought up her children well, shown
hospitality, washed the feet of the saints,[16] helped those in distress — if

[15]I.e. she had been faithfully married.
[16]A reference to acts of service rendered to Christians.

she has devoted herself to doing good in every way. 11But do not put younger widows on the list; for if they are drawn away from Messiah by sensual desire, they want to get married 12and will receive condemnation for breaking their previous pledge.[17] 13At the same time they also learn to be lazy, going around from house to house. They become not only lazy, but also gossips and busybodies, discussing things they should not. 14So I want younger women to get married, raise children, and manage their households, and give the Adversary no reason to accuse us. 15For some have already wandered away to follow Satan. 16If any believing woman has relatives who are widows she should help them, and the church should not be burdened, so that it may help the widows who are genuinely in need.

17The elders who lead well should be considered worthy of double honor and financial compensation, especially those who work hard at preaching and teaching. 18For the Scripture says, “Do not muzzle an ox when it is treading out the grain,” and “The worker deserves his wages.” 19Do not accept an accusation against an elder unless two or three witnesses support it. 20Publicly rebuke those elders who continue in sin so that the rest will be afraid. 21I solemnly charge you in the presence of God and Messiah Jesus and the chosen angels to obey these instructions without prejudice or any favoritism. 22Do not be too hasty to appoint someone an elder and so share in the sins of others. Keep yourself pure.

23Stop drinking only water, but drink a little wine because of your stomach and your frequent illnesses.

24Some people’s sins are obvious, going ahead of them leading to judgment. Other people’s sins appear later. 25So also good works are obvious, and even those which are not obvious cannot remain hidden.

6 1All who are under the yoke as servants are to regard their own masters as worthy of all respect, so that God’s name and the teaching may not be spoken against. 2And those who have masters who are believers should show them no less respect because they are brothers, but should serve them even more conscientiously, because those who benefit from their service are believers and beloved. Teach and urge these things.

---

[17]Possible meanings are original Christian faith, or promise not to get married.

3If anyone teaches other doctrines and does not agree with the health-
giving words, namely the teachings given by our lord Jesus Messiah,[18]
and thus with the teaching that promotes godliness, 4he is conceited,
understanding nothing, but has an unhealthy craving for disputes and
arguments over words. This leads to envy, dissension, slander, evil
suspicions 5and constant quarrels among people whose minds are
corrupted, who are deprived of the truth, and who imagine that godliness
is a way to financial gain. 6Now godliness along with contentment is a
great gain. 7For we brought nothing into the world, so we can take
nothing out either. 8If we have food and clothes we are to be content with
that. 9But those who want to get rich fall into temptation and are trapped
by foolish and harmful desires, which plunge people into ruin and
destruction. 10For the love of money is a root of all kinds of evil, and by
craving it some have strayed from the faith and pierced themselves with
a world of pain.

11But you, man of God, run from all those things; instead pursue
righteousness, godliness, faith, love, perseverance and gentleness. 12Fight
the good fight of the faith. Take hold of the Life of the Age to Come to
which you were invited and for which you made a good public
confession in front of many witnesses. 13In the presence of God who
gives life to all things, and Messiah Jesus, who gave his good confession
before Pontius Pilate, I charge you 14to obey this command without fault
or blame until the appearing of our lord Jesus Messiah, 15which God will
bring at the right time. He is the blessed and only Sovereign, the King of
kings and Lord of lords. 16He is the only one who has immortality[19] and
lives in unapproachable light, and no human has seen or can see Him. To
Him be the honor and dominion of the coming age! Amen.

17Command those who are rich in this present age not to be arrogant
or to set their hope on the uncertainty of riches, but to set their hope on

---

[18]Everything in the NT, salvation itself, depends on our adherence to Jesus by believing and practicing his *teaching* (Jn. 7:16), summarized as the Gospel of the Kingdom (Mk. 1:14-15; Matt. 13:19). The Devil's main objective is to stop people believing in the word of the Gospel of the Kingdom (Lk. 8:11-12; Mk. 4:11-12).

[19]The Father is the One God 1300 times in the NT. He alone has immortality inherently. God cannot be born or die. God conferred immortality on Jesus and promises immortality to the faithful in the resurrection to come at the return of Jesus (1 Cor. 15:23).

God who richly provides us with all things to enjoy. 18Instruct them to do
good, to be rich in good works and to be generous, sharing with others.
19In this way they are storing up treasure for themselves as a good
foundation for the Age to Come, so that they may take hold of the life
that really is life.

20Timothy, guard what has been entrusted to you, avoiding the
profane chatter and contradictions of that system of “knowledge” which
is falsely named. 21By professing it, some people have veered away from
the faith. Grace be with you all.

2 Timothy

1 1From Paul, an Apostle of Messiah Jesus by the will of God, for the
promise of Life in Messiah Jesus, 2to Timothy, my beloved spiritual
child: Grace, mercy and peace from God who is the Father[1] and from
Messiah Jesus our lord.[2]

3I am giving thanks to God, whom I serve with a clear conscience as
did my ancestors, as I constantly remember you in my prayers night and
day. 4Remembering your tears, I am longing to see you again so that I
may be filled with joy. 5I remember too your genuine faith which was
first living in your grandmother Lois, then in your mother Eunice, and I
am convinced that it is in you. 6That is why I remind you to keep burning
strongly the gift of God that is in you through the laying on of my hands.
7For God did not give us a spirit of timidity, but one of power, love and
self-discipline.

8So then never be ashamed of the Gospel-testimony of our lord nor of
me his prisoner. Instead share with me in suffering for the Gospel, by the
power of God. 9He is the One who saved us, inviting us with a holy
calling, not because of our works but because of His own purpose and
grace,[3] which was given to us in Messiah Jesus before the ages of time,[4]
10but has now been revealed by the appearing of our savior Messiah
Jesus. He abolished death and brought life and immortality to light by

---

[1]The Greek literally is "God Father," or Father God. The word "God" refers 1300 times in the NT to the Father who is "the only one who is true God" (Jn. 17:3). Jesus is called "god" once in Heb. 1:8 (Ps. 45:6), and Thomas in John 20:28 recognizes finally that in seeing the Messiah one is seeing God, who is perfectly expressed in His unique Son (Jn. 14:9).

[2]Jesus is the lord Messiah (Lk. 2:11), definitely not the Lord God, which would make two Gods and thus break the first commandment. The title "our lord" is derived from the centrally important and definitive Ps. 110:1 where the Messiah is "my lord," *adoni*, which in all of its 195 occurrences never means God. *Adoni*, my lord, gives us the expression "our lord Jesus Messiah," repeatedly used of Jesus. The blind men recognized the Messianic title "lord" when they appealed to Jesus as "lord, son of David" (Mt. 20:30; cp. 15:22). It has been observed that the title "lord" is applicable to God, other superiors, and even a gardener (Jn. 20:15).

[3]The Gospel of the grace of God is defined as the Gospel about the Kingdom in Acts 20:24-25. God's great plan and purpose is to grant immortality to human beings who obey Jesus (Heb. 5:9).

[4]Heb. 1:2 says that God made "the ages" with Messiah in mind, and even before those ages began the divine plan had been conceived.

means of the Gospel.[5] 11God appointed me a herald and Apostle and
teacher of this Gospel, 12and that is why I am now suffering these things.
But I am not ashamed, because I know the one I have believed and I am
convinced that he is able to guard what has been entrusted to me until
that Day. 13Hold on tightly to that pattern of sound words which you have
heard from me, in the faith and love which are in Messiah Jesus.[6] 14Guard
that good treasure entrusted to you, through holy spirit which lives in us.

15You know that everyone in the province of Asia abandoned me,
including Phygelus and Hermogenes. 16May the lord grant mercy to the
household of Onesiphorus because he often refreshed me and was not
ashamed of my chains. 17When he was in Rome he diligently sought me
out and found me. 18May the lord grant that he will find mercy from the
Lord on that Day. You know very well all the ways he served in
Ephesus.

2 1And so you, my child, be strong in the grace which is found in
Messiah Jesus. 2What you have heard from me in the presence of
many witnesses, entrust to faithful people who will be competent to
teach others as well. 3Share with me in suffering as a good soldier of
Messiah Jesus. 4No one serving as a soldier entangles himself in the
concerns of everyday life. His object is to please his recruiter. 5And an
athlete wins no medal unless he competes according to the rules. 6The
hardworking farmer deserves to be the first to get a share of the crops.
7Think about what I am saying and the lord will give you a complete
understanding.

8Remember Jesus Messiah, resurrected from the dead, a biological
descendant of David according to my Gospel. 9For this Gospel I am
suffering to the point of being a criminal in chains, but the Gospel-word
of God[7] is not chained up! 10So I am enduring everything for the sake of

---

[5]The one Gospel of the Kingdom as first preached by Jesus (Mk. 1:14-15; Lk. 4:43; Heb. 2:3) and by all the NT writers (Paul in Acts 19:8; 20:24-25; 28:23; 30, 31; cp Acts 8:12).

[6]The same faith and preaching of the Gospel of the Kingdom as modeled by Jesus himself (Lk. 4:43; Mk. 1:14-15). Faith in Jesus must never be divorced from belief in and obedience to the words of Jesus, beginning in Mark 1 and not forgetting Jesus' foundational definition of God in Mark 12:29.

[7]The shorthand phrase for the Gospel of the Kingdom, not a synonym for the Bible. See Matt. 13:19; Mark 4; Luke 8; 4:43; 5:1 and often in Acts.

the chosen ones, that they too may gain salvation in Messiah Jesus with its glory of the Coming Age. 11This saying is trustworthy: If we died with him, we will live with him. 12If we endure, we will reign as kings with him.[8] If we renounce him, he will renounce us. 13If we are unfaithful he remains faithful, because he cannot deny himself.

14Remind the believers of these things, and solemnly charge them before God not to fight about words, which is in no way beneficial but only ruins the listeners. 15Be diligent to present yourself approved to God, a worker who has no need to be ashamed, soundly expounding the Gospel-word of the truth. 16But avoid profane chatter, because it will lead people to even greater godlessness. 17Their message will spread like gangrene. Among these are Hymenaeus and Philetus, 18who veered from the truth by saying that the resurrection has already happened, and they are overthrowing some people's faith. 19Nevertheless God's solid foundation remains firm, engraved with this inscription: "The Lord knows those who belong to Him," and "Everyone who professes the name of the Lord must turn away from evil."

20Now in a large house there are not only gold and silver bowls but also wooden and clay ones, some for special use and others for ordinary use. 21If anyone cleanses himself,[9] he will become a special instrument, set apart as holy, useful to the master, ready for every good work. 22So flee from youth's evil desires and pursue uprightness, faith, love and peace, in fellowship with those who call on the lord from a pure heart. 23But reject foolish and ignorant disputes, because you know that they generate only conflict. 24And the lord's servant must not be engaged in conflict, but kind to everyone, competent to teach, and patient, 25with gentleness correcting opponents. Perhaps God will grant them repentance leading to the knowledge of the truth, 26and they may come to their senses and escape the Devil's trap, after being captured by him to do his will.

3 1But understand this: Terrible times will come in the last days. 2People will be lovers of themselves, lovers of money, boastful, arrogant, blasphemers, disobedient to parents, ungrateful, unholy,

---

[8]Rev. 5:9-10; Dan 7:18, 22, 27 (RSV); Mt. 19:28; Rev. 20:1-6.

[9]This is certainly not Calvinism! Paul exhorts the believer to take responsibility for being a pure vessel.

3unloving, irreconcilable, slanderers, lacking self-control, brutal, hating
what is good, 4treacherous, reckless, conceited, lovers of pleasure rather
than lovers of God. 5They will have an outward form of religion but deny
its power. So avoid these people. 6For some of them worm their way into
households and capture weak women burdened down with sins and
driven by a variety of passions. 7Such women are always learning but
never able to arrive at a knowledge of the truth.[10] 8Just as Jannes and
Jambres opposed Moses, these people oppose the truth. Their minds are
corrupted, and they are disqualified in the faith. 9They will not make
further progress, as their stupidity will be clear to everyone, just as it was
with Jannes and Jambres.

10But you have followed my teaching, conduct, goal, faith, patience,
love and endurance, 11and the persecutions and sufferings which I
experienced in Antioch, Iconium, and Lystra. What persecutions I
endured, and the lord rescued me from all of them. 12In fact, all who
desire to live in a godly way in Messiah Jesus are bound to suffer
persecution. 13But evil people and charlatans will get worse and worse,
deceiving and being deceived.[11] 14You, however, continue in the things
you have learned and been convinced of. You know who you learned
them from, 15and from your childhood you have known the holy
Scriptures,[12] which are able to provide you with the wisdom which leads
to salvation, through the faith which is in Messiah Jesus. 16All Scripture
is inspired by God and is profitable for teaching, for exposing error, for
correcting, and for training in uprightness, 17so that the man of God may
be a master of his craft, equipped for every good work.

---

[10]Defined in 1 Tim. 2:4-5 as the right understanding of the true God in relation to the man Messiah Jesus.

[11]Note that it is wicked to be deceived!

[12]This is the Bible's own word for "the Bible." Paul does not, as is commonly done today, refer to the whole Bible as "the word of God." "The word of God" in the NT is almost always the "code-word" for the Gospel of the Kingdom, the Christian Gospel (Mt. 13:19; Lk. 8:12; Acts 8, 4, 5, 12). The loss of the phrase "word of God" to mean the Kingdom of God Gospel is today's most catastrophic suppression of vital information. Some even write whole books about the Church's purpose, without bothering to note that Jesus' purpose was expressly to preach the Gospel about the Kingdom (Lk. 4:43).

4 1Before God and the Messiah Jesus, who is going to judge the living
and the dead, I solemnly testify to his appearing and his Kingdom.[13]
2Herald that Gospel-word. Persist with this, whether it is convenient or
inconvenient. Correct, rebuke and exhort with all patience in teaching.
3For the time is approaching when people will not tolerate sound
teachings. Instead, following their own desires they will amass for
themselves teachers to satisfy their itching ears. 4They will turn away
from listening to the truth and wander off to myths. 5But you keep a clear
head about everything, endure hardship, do the work of an evangelist,
fully carry out your ministry.

6For I am already being poured out like a drink offering, and the time
of my departure[14] is close. 7I have fought the good fight; I have
completed the race; I have kept the faith. 8There is reserved for me for
the future the crown of uprightness which the lord, the upright judge,
will award to me on that Day — and not only to me, but also to all who
have longed for his appearing.

9Make every effort to come to me soon. 10For Demas has deserted me
because of his love for the present age.[15] He went off to Thessalonica.
Crescens has gone to Galatia and Titus to Dalmatia. 11Only Luke is with
me. Pick up Mark and bring him with you because he is very useful to
me in ministry. 12I have sent Tychicus to Ephesus. 13When you come
bring the cloak I left in Troas with Carpus, as well as the scrolls,
particularly the parchments. 14Alexander the coppersmith did me a lot of
harm. The Lord will repay him for what he did. 15Be careful of him
yourself, because he strongly opposed our words.

16At my first trial no one stood in my defense; they all deserted me.
May it not be counted against them. 17But the lord stood with me and
gave me strength so that through me the proclamation of the Gospel
might be accomplished for all the Gentiles to hear. And so I was rescued
from the jaws of the lion. 18The lord will rescue me from every evil

---

[13]This is a final and definitive proclamation by solemn testimony to the Gospel of the Kingdom which Jesus and Paul had always preached as the saving Gospel. It is called God's Gospel (Mk. 1:14-15; Lk. 4:43; Acts 19:8; 20:24-25; 28:23, 31; cp. Acts 8:12).

[14]Departure from this life, in death.

[15]The present evil age is the ongoing age until the Second Coming of Jesus, when he will introduce his revolutionary world government, the Kingdom of God on a renewed earth.

action and will save me by bringing me into his heavenly Kingdom.[16] To
him be the glory to the ages of the ages. Amen.
19Give my greetings to Prisca and Aquila and to the household of
Onesiphorus. 20Erastus remained in Corinth, and Trophimus I left sick in
Miletus. 21Make every effort to come before winter. Eubulus sends
greetings, as do Pudens, Linus, Claudia, and all the brothers and sisters.
22The lord be with your spirit. Grace be with you.

[16]As throughout the Bible this is the Kingdom which originates in heaven and will appear on a renewed earth when Jesus comes back. Nothing in Scripture teaches that "heaven" is the destination of the dying.

Titus

1 1From Paul, a servant of God and Apostle of Jesus Messiah, for the faith of God's chosen ones and the knowledge of the truth which leads to godliness, 2in the hope of the Life of the Age to Come, which God, who cannot lie, promised before the ages began.[1] 3Now at the right time He has revealed this hope in His Gospel-word, in the proclamation I was entrusted with by the command of God our Savior. 4To Titus, my genuine child in our common faith: Grace and peace from God who is the Father and from Messiah Jesus our Savior.

5The reason I left you in Crete was to put in order what was left undone and, as I directed you, to appoint elders in every town: 6An elder must be blameless, the husband of one wife, with believing children who cannot be accused of wild behavior or rebellion. 7As God's manager, the elder must be blameless, not arrogant, not quick-tempered, not a drunkard, not violent, not greedy for money, 8but hospitable, loving what is good, sensible, upright, holy, and self-controlled. 9He must hold to the faithful Gospel-word as it has been taught, so that he will be able to encourage people with that sound teaching and also refute those who contradict it.

10For there are many rebellious people, idle talkers and deceivers, especially those of the circumcision.[2] 11It is necessary to silence them, because they are disturbing whole households by teaching for dishonest gain what they should not teach. 12One of their very own, a prophet, said, "Cretans are always liars, evil beasts, lazy gluttons." 13This testimony is true. So you must rebuke them sharply, so that they may become sound in the faith 14and not pay attention to Jewish myths and the commands of people who reject the truth. 15To the pure everything is pure, but to the corrupt and unbelieving nothing is pure; in fact both their minds and consciences have been corrupted. 16They claim to know God, but they deny Him with their actions. They are detestable, disobedient and unqualified to do anything good.

---

[1]This is the equivalent of the "word" which was in the beginning with God (Jn. 1:1). For the "word" which can be "with" someone see Jer. 27:18.

[2]Wrongly promoting circumcision in the flesh and a return to the Law of Moses. See the strong warnings against returning to the letter of the law in Galatians, that is to those laws which separated Jews from Gentiles.

2 1But you must speak what is consistent with sound teaching: 2Older
men are to be self-controlled, serious, sensible, and sound in faith,
love and endurance. 3Similarly, older women[3] are to be reverent in
behavior, not slanderers, not excessive drinkers, but teaching what is
good. 4That way they may train the younger women to love their
husbands and children, 5to be self-controlled, pure, workers at home,
kind, and subject to their own husbands, so that the Gospel-word of God
may not be spoken against.

6Similarly, urge younger men to be self-controlled. 7In everything set
an example of good works yourself, showing in your teaching doctrinal
integrity and dignity. 8Your message should be sound beyond criticism,
so that opponents may be ashamed because they have nothing evil to say
about us.

9Servants are to be in submission to their masters in everything and to
aim to please them, not talking back, 10not stealing, but demonstrating
complete good faith, so that they may make the teaching of God our
Savior attractive in every way.

11For the grace of God has appeared, bringing salvation to all people,
12training us to reject godlessness and worldly desires and to live in a
self-controlled, upright and godly way in the present age,[4] 13while we
wait expectantly for the blessed hope — the appearing of the glory of our
great God and of our Savior, Jesus the Messiah. 14He gave himself for us
to redeem us from all iniquity and to purify for himself a people of his
own, who are eager to do what is good. 15Teach these things; exhort and
correct with full authority. Do not let anyone look down on you.

---

[3]Not "women elders," but elderly women.

[4]"The present evil age" of Gal. 1:4. "Satan is currently deceiving the whole world" (Rev. 12:9). In the coming millennium, that activity will cease entirely (Rev. 20:3). This makes the doctrines of amillennialism and post-millennialism impossible! The protest of Henry Alford needs to be repeated: "If, in a passage where two resurrections are mentioned, where certain 'souls' lived at the first, and the rest of the dead 'lived' only at the end of a specified period after the first — if in such a passage the first resurrection may be understood to mean 'spiritual' rising with Christ, while the second means literal rising from the grave — then there is an end of all significance in language, and Scripture is wiped out as a definite testimony to anything" (*Greek Testament*, Vol. 4, p. 726).

3 1Remind the believers to be subject to rulers and authorities, to obey
them, to be ready for every good work, 2to speak evil of no one, to be
peaceable, gentle, and always considerate to all people. 3For we too were
once foolish, disobedient, deceived, captive to various passions and
desires, living in malice and envy, hated by and hating one another.

4But when God our Savior's kindness and love for mankind
appeared, 5He saved us not because of upright works which we had done
but because of His mercy, through the washing of rebirth and renewal of
holy spirit. 6This spirit He poured out on us abundantly through Jesus
Messiah our Savior, 7so that being made right by his grace, we become
heirs with the hope of the Life of the Age to Come. 8This saying is
trustworthy. And I want you to emphasize these things, so that those who
have believed God[5] may be careful to devote themselves to good works.
These things are excellent and profitable for everyone. 9But avoid stupid
controversies, genealogies, quarrels and disputes about the Law, because
they are unprofitable and worthless. 10Reject a divisive person after a first
and second warning, 11knowing that such a person is corrupted and
sinning, and stands self-condemned.

12When I send Artemas or Tychicus to you, make every effort to
come to me in Nicopolis, because I decided to spend the winter there.
13Do whatever you can to help Zenas the lawyer and Apollos on their
journey, so they have everything they need. 14Let our people learn to
engage in good work[6] in order to provide for urgent need, so that they
will not be unfruitful.

15All those who are with me send their greetings. Greet those who
love us in the faith. Grace be with all of you.

---

[5]"Believing God" begins in the New Testament with believing the Gospel message about the Kingdom preached by Jesus. God's unique Son (Lk. 1:35) and agent Jesus gave his first command to us all with the words, "Repent and believe the Gospel about the Kingdom" (Mk. 1:14-15; cp. Acts 8:12; 19:8; 28:23, 30, 31). The Gospel had its beginning with the preaching of John the Baptist and Jesus (Lk. 16:16; Jn. 1:17). See Heb. 2:3 for the foundational truth that Jesus preached the saving Gospel.

[6]Probably implying earning an honest living by hard work.

Philemon

1From Paul, a prisoner for Messiah Jesus, and Timothy our brother,
to Philemon, our dear friend and coworker, 2to our dear sister Appia, to
our fellow soldier Archippus, and to the church which meets in your
house: 3Grace and peace to you from God who is our Father and from the
lord Jesus Messiah.

4I always thank my God, mentioning you in my prayers, 5because I
hear of your faith and love toward the lord Jesus and for all the saints. 6I
pray that your participation in the faith may become even more effective
through the knowledge of everything good that is in you in Messiah. 7For
I have received great joy and encouragement from your love, because the
hearts of the saints have been refreshed through you, brother.

8So, although I have enough boldness in Messiah to command you to
do what is right, 9I prefer to appeal to you instead, on the basis of love —
I, Paul, an elderly man and now also a prisoner for Messiah Jesus. 10I am
appealing to you for my child whom I fathered in the faith during my
imprisonment, Onesimus. 11He was once useless to you, but he is now
useful to both you and me. 12I am sending him — who is my own heart
— back to you. 13I wanted to keep him with me, so that during my
imprisonment for the Gospel he could serve me in your place. 14But I did
not want to do anything without your consent, so that the good you do
might not be forced, but from your free will. 15For perhaps he was
separated from you for a short time for this reason, so that you might get
him back forever, 16no longer as a slave, but better than a slave — as a
dear brother. He is especially so to me, but now will be even more to
you, both in humanity and in the lord.

17So if you consider me a partner, receive him as though he were me.
18If he has wronged you at all or owes you anything, charge that to me.
19I, Paul, am writing this with my own hand: I will repay — not to
mention that you owe me your own self! 20Yes, brother, may I benefit
from you in the lord. Refresh my heart in Messiah.

21Confident in your obedience, I am writing to you, knowing that you
will even go beyond what I say.

22Meanwhile, also prepare a place for me to stay, because I hope that
through your prayers I will be restored to you.

23Epaphras, my fellow prisoner in Messiah Jesus, sends his greetings
to you, 24as do Mark, Aristarchus, Demas, and Luke, my coworkers.
25The grace of the lord Jesus Messiah be with your spirit.

Hebrews

1 1 God,[1] after He in the past spoke to our ancestors through the
prophets at many times and in many ways, 2 has in these last days
spoken to us in a Son,[2] whom He appointed heir of all things, through
whom also He made the ages. 3 His Son is the radiance of His glory, the
exact image[3] of His person, and upholds all things by the word of his
power. After he had purified us of our sins, he sat down at the right hand
of the Majesty on high,[4] 4 having become so much better than the angels[5]
as he has inherited a name[6] far superior to theirs.

---

[1]In Greek, "*the* God" (as very often with the definite article), the only God known to the NT community, the God of Abraham, Isaac and Jacob, and the God of Jesus, the Son. The significance of the article "*the* God" is to ensure that no other than the God of Israel is to be imagined.

[2]There is a deliberate, clear contrast here between how God spoke in OT times and how he later spoke for the first time in one who was uniquely His Son. The obvious implication is of course that there was no Son during the OT times. The Son is the great new personality coming into existence by divine begetting in Mary (Lk. 1:35; Mt. 1:18: *genesis* of the Son; 1:20: "that which is begotten, brought into existence, in her").

[3]The exact expression of any person or thing, marked likeness, precise reproduction in every respect. Cp. "We beheld his glory as of a uniquely begotten Son" (Jn. 1:14). The image of God is a human being, not God! Man is also said to be the image and glory of God (1 Cor. 11:7). Image implies visibility and so Jesus is the visible image of the invisible God. No one has seen God at any time (Jn. 1:18), which would be false if the Son was actually God and had appeared and spoken as an angel in OT times!

[4]Fulfilling the key decisive, explanatory text in Ps. 110:1 where the second lord, *adoni* in the Hebrew, is not *Adonai*! *Adoni* is, in all of its 195 occurrences, the title of non-Deity, never of Deity. No one in biblical times thought that there was more than one God! The One God is called the Father 1300 times in the NT Scriptures. Jesus as the *adoni*, my lord, of Ps. 110:1 is alongside the One God but certainly not a second God. Jesus is the man Messiah (1 Tim 2:5) and the second Adam.

[5]Obviously then, the Son of God was never an angel! And thus he was certainly not Michael, the archangel. Michael is "*one* of the chief angels" (Dan. 10:13). Jesus is unique. Hebrews 1 is a sustained argument against the false notion that Jesus was or is an angel. The *whole* point of the second Adam is that he is a human being, now immortalized.

[6]"Name" in the NT indicates everything a person is and stands for, in this case authority and agenda, etc. "Name" does not mean how to pronounce the name in Hebrew. The Greek NT makes no issue at all about God's name in Hebrew, but it could have, since it records the Aramaic word used by Jesus, "Abba."

5For to which of the angels did God ever say at any time,[7] "You are
My Son; today I have fathered you"?[8] And again, "I will be to him a
Father, and he will be to Me a Son"? 6And again, when He brings the
firstborn into the world[9] He says, "Let all the angels of God worship
him."[10]

---

[7]It is an amazing miracle of misunderstanding to claim as Jehovah's Witnesses that Jesus was and is Michael, an archangel, which mean a high-ranking angel!

[8]"Begotten you." To beget is to cause to come into existence. This shows that Jesus did not always exist and cannot be God (making two Gods!). He was begotten of course in the womb of Mary as Matt. 1:18, 20 and Luke 1:35 describe expressly. The prophecy of Deut. 18:15-18 affirmed in Acts 3:22 and 7:37 would be completely misleading if the promised Messiah were to be either an angel or GOD Himself as a second member of a Trinity.

[9]To be "brought into the world" points to the beginning of the Son's existence. This verse does not refer to the later resurrection of the firstborn from the dead, but in fulfillment of Ps. 2:7 to his beginning of Jesus' life at conception.

[10]All three quotations are chosen to make the same point. They refer to the beginning of existence, the begetting of the Son, i.e. in the womb of Mary. This begetting of the Son is described in Luke 1:35: "the one to be begotten"; Matt. 1:1, 18, 20: "what is begotten in her." The first quotation, Ps. 2:7, says of the Son, "You are My Son. Today I have become your Father [=begotten you]." This statement is repeated in Ps. 110:3 in the LXX version of the OT and many Heb. manuscripts. In all probability the Hebrew Masoretic text was muddled and corrupted there by a false pointing of the vowels. That is to say that the original was probably "yeliditicha" ("I have begotten you," as found correctly in the LXX and some Heb. manuscripts of Ps. 110:3) and not "yaldutecha" (the rather meaningless "your youth"). "This was probably in the original, but owing to corruption of the Hebrew text, *not perhaps unintentional*, these words had no influence in Judaism" (*TDNT*, Vol. 1, p. 668, emphasis mine). The second quotation is from 2 Sam. 7:14 and 1 Chron. 17:13, which drops the reference to Solomon in 2 Sam. 7, and predicts, 1000 years before Jesus the Son was begotten, brought into existence, in Mary, that God would become the Father of a genealogical descendant of David. Rom. 1:3 repeats this information perfectly, describing the Son of God as *coming into existence* as a descendant of David. He is at the same moment God's Son and David's son. This is an exact fulfillment, too, of "a child will be begotten [i.e. by God, a divine passive] to us [Israel]" (Isa. 9:6). The child to be begotten is described in that text synonymously as the "Son who will be given [by God]." Hence "God loved the world in this way: that He gave His uniquely begotten Son" (Jn. 3:16). 1 John 5:18 describes the Son as "the one begotten," i.e. brought into existence at a point in time. The idea of the "eternal [timeless] generation" (a nonsensical "beginningless beginning") of the Son made havoc of all these texts. It transformed the real Jesus of the Bible into a timeless figure, "God the Son," with no beginning in history. This false idea eventually perverted the strict monotheism of the Bible as confirmed by Jesus in Mark 12:29 as

7Of the angels He says, "He makes His angels winds, and His
servants a flame of fire."

8But of the Son He says, "Your throne, O god,[11] is forever and ever.
The scepter of uprightness is the scepter of your Kingdom. 9You have
loved uprightness and hated iniquity; therefore God, your God,[12] has
anointed you with the oil of gladness above your fellows." 10And, "You,
lord,[13] in the beginning laid the foundation of the earth, and the heavens
are the works of your hands.[14] 11They will perish,[15] but you continue.

"the most important" truth of all, defining the "only one who is true God," i.e. the Father (see Jn. 17:3 for Jesus' unitary monotheistic confession which is the great key to life in the coming age, the Life of the [future] age of Dan. 12:2, mentioned some 40 times in the NT). For confirmation, see *TDNT* which states that "it is correctly observed that Ps. 2:7, 2 Sam. 7:14 and the 'firstborn' from Ps. 89:27 stand in exact exegetical connection" (Vol. 6, p. 880).

[11]The word "god" here is one of only two (for certain) uses of the word *theos* (God) for Jesus. The quotation is from Ps. 45:6 where the NAB translation correctly translates as "god" (not God), explaining that the king is "representing God to the people."

[12]Someone who has a God cannot be God! To be Son of God means that you are *not* God! No one in biblical times thought that God could be born! (Lk. 2:11), much less that God could die. The Son of God died (Rom. 5:10).

[13]This passage needs very careful study since it quotes the LXX (Greek Septuagint) and *not* the version found in standard OT translations from the Hebrew. In the LXX, not the Hebrew text, God addresses someone *else* and calls him "lord." This is obviously the lord Messiah who is in charge of the *new* creation. The psalm quoted here, Ps. 102, is all about the new world order coming, the Kingdom of God on earth, when the nations will be united and at peace, in the new society (generation) of the future. For a full explanation of Heb. 1:10, please see my *Jesus Was Not a Trinitarian*, appendix 3. Here it suffices to say that the LXX introduced the words "He [God] answered" the supplicant. The difference occurred when the Hebrew homonym (a word spelled the same but with a different meaning) *anah*, to answer *or* to afflict, was thought by the LXX to mean "answer" rather than "afflict or weaken." This changed entirely the sense of the text, and our writer to the Hebrews was reading the LXX and not the Hebrew. None of this is problematic, but a little technical for those not familiar with the Bible's original languages. The LXX here has become Scripture as written in the NT book of Hebrews.

[14]It should be carefully noted that the whole discussion concerns not the Genesis creation but the new creation of "the society/ inhabited earth to come" about which we are speaking (as the writer says in 2:5). In Ps. 102 in the LXX God addresses another who is "lord" — obviously the lord Messiah, whom God is using to build the new creation. That agent of the New Creation is Jesus and his role is beautifully described in Isa. 51:16, where God puts His words into the mouth of His chosen agent, the Messiah, for the purpose of creating the new heavens and earth, the new society on earth. This is

They will all grow old as clothes do. 12You will roll them up like a robe,
and they will be changed like clothes; but you are the same. Your years
will never end."
13But to which of the angels did God ever say at any time,[16] "Sit at
My right hand until I make your enemies a footstool for your feet"?
14Are they not all spirits in service, sent out to serve those who are going
to inherit salvation?

2 1Therefore we ought to pay closer attention to what we have heard, so
that we do not drift away. 2For if the word spoken through angels[17]
proved firm, and every violation of it and act of disobedience to it
received its just penalty, 3how will we escape if we neglect so great a
salvation? This salvation had its beginning when spoken through the
lord, and was confirmed to us by those who heard him. 4God
corroborated their witness by signs, wonders, various miracles, and gifts
of holy spirit distributed according to His own will.
5For He did not subject the world order to come,[18] about which we
are speaking, to angels. 6But one has somewhere testified, "What is man,
that You take note of him? Or the son of man, that You are concerned

---

expected at the future Second Coming of Jesus (2 Pet. 3:12-13), linking us to the "new heavens and earth" of Isa. 65:17, where peace and prosperity will prevail worldwide and the surviving human population will live very long lives. Dying at the age of 100 will be considered a life cut off prematurely (65:20).

[15]There will be a shaking of heaven and earth at the end of this age and a further change at the end of the millennium. A new heaven and earth will appear at the Parousia and a further renewal after the millennium. During that thousand years the saints will reign with Messiah in that renewed world (2:5; Mt. 19:28; Rev. 2:26-27; 1 Cor. 6:2).

[16]Repeating the important fact that Jesus could not possibly be an angel! This point frames the whole chapter. The Jehovah's Witnesses ignored that important scriptural truth. They also created an amazing two-class theory which (unless a JW thinks he is one of the 144,000 special class) results in the average JW confessing that he/she is *not* born again, not a saint (holy one) and not part of the body of the Messiah — i.e. not a Christian, not having the spirit. By an amazing feat of misunderstanding that same "second class" group is at your door to teach you the NT faith!

[17]In Old Testament times, when the Son of God did not yet exist.

[18]This has been a discussion of the glorified second Adam to whom God has assigned the control of the inhabited earth of the future, in the future Kingdom. Jesus was promoted to his present position of supremacy under the One God. You cannot be promoted to that position if you are already God!

about him? 7You made him for a little while lower than the angels. You
have crowned him with glory and honor, 8and You have put all things in
subjection under his feet." For in subjecting all things to him, He left
nothing that is not subject to him. But at present we do not yet see all
things subjected to him.

9But we do see him who was made for a little while lower than the
angels, Jesus, because of his suffering of death crowned with glory and
honor, so that by the grace of God he would taste death for everyone.
10For it was fitting for Him, for whom are all things and through whom
are all things, in bringing many children to glory,[19] to make the pioneer
of their salvation perfect through sufferings. 11For both he who makes
holy and those being made holy are all from one Person. That is why he
is not ashamed to call them brothers: 12"I will declare Your name[20] to my
brothers. Among the congregation I will sing Your praise." 13Again, "I
will put my trust in Him." Again, "Look, here I am with the children[21]
God has given me."

14Since then the children share in flesh and blood, he himself shared
in the same, so that through death he would bring to nothing the one who
had the power of death, that is, the Devil, 15and free all those who were
slaves all their lives to the fear of death. 16For most certainly his concern
is not for angels, but he is concerned about the descendants of Abraham.
17Therefore he was obligated to be made like his brothers in all things,
so that he could become a merciful and faithful high priest in things
pertaining to God, to make atonement for the sins of the people. 18Since

---

[19]The same destiny of rulership in the future Kingdom is promised for Jesus and his true followers.

[20]"Name" is everything that God stands for, His character, His attributes, His amazing immortality program being worked out in Messiah.

[21]Jesus' children would be those created, begotten, by Jesus' Gospel preaching. The Gospel of the Kingdom is the *seed* of regeneration (Lk. 8:11-12). It is the indispensable basis for salvation. The Devil knows of this seed of salvation and immortality and exerts maximum energy to prevent the Gospel of the Kingdom from lodging in the mind of the potential convert. Paul in the same way became the father of Timothy using the Gospel of the Kingdom as the agent of the new birth. Alternatively, "children" might be a reference to the Father's sons and daughters.

he himself suffered being tempted,[22] he is able to help those who are
tempted.

3 1Therefore, holy brothers and sisters, partners in a heavenly calling,[23]
consider the Apostle and High Priest[24] of our confession: Jesus, 2who
was faithful to Him who appointed him, as Moses was in all His house.
3For he has been counted worthy of more glory than Moses, just as the
builder of a house has more honor than the house. 4For every house is
built by someone, but the builder of all things is God. 5Moses was
faithful in all His house as a servant, as a testimony to those things which
were to be spoken afterwards, 6but Messiah is faithful as a son over
God's house. And we are His house, if we hold fast our confidence and
the hope in which we glory firm to the end.[25]

7Therefore, as the holy spirit says, "Today if you hear His voice, 8do
not harden your hearts, as when they rebelled in the day of testing in the
wilderness, 9where your ancestors tested Me and tried Me, and saw My
actions for forty years. 10Therefore I was angry with that generation, and
said, 'Their hearts are always going astray, and they did not know My
ways.' 11As I swore in My anger, 'They will not enter My rest.'"

12Take care, brothers and sisters, that there is not in any of you an evil
heart of unbelief that rebels against the living God. 13But encourage one
another day by day, as long as it is called "Today," so that none of you
will be hardened by the deceptiveness of sin. 14For we have become

---

[22]It should be evident that GOD cannot be tempted! The proposition that Jesus *is* God and that Jesus was tempted is incoherent. "God cannot be tempted" (James 1:13). Nor can God die (1 Tim. 6:16). Jesus the Son of God died. The inference that Jesus is not GOD is obvious.

[23]This calling is heavenly in the sense that it comes from God and is a supernatural calling. It is a calling to reign on the renewed earth with Jesus when he comes (Rev. 5:9-10; 2:26; 3:21; 20:1-6). Paul had a heavenly vision in Acts 26:19, but that does not mean that Paul was *in* heaven!

[24]The High Priest and Apostle is obviously not God Himself. The Son of God was a unitarian Jew (Mk. 12:29) who never imagined himself to be absolute Deity, making two Gods. Jesus was certainly the unique agent of the One God, and his origin in his mother's womb was supernatural (Lk. 1:35; Mt. 1:20: "begotten in her"). The Father and Son work in perfect harmony (Jn. 10:30) and the same unity is given to God and the believers (Jn. 17:11, 22).

[25]In direct contradiction to the popular doctrine of "once saved, always saved" (see Rom. 11:22; Lk. 8:13, etc.).

partners with the Messiah, if we hold our initial assurance firm to the
end.[26] 15As it says, "Today if you hear His voice, do not harden your
hearts, as when they rebelled against Me." 16For who was it who, when
they heard, rebelled? Was it not all those who came out of Egypt led by
Moses? 17And with whom was He angry for forty years? Was it not with
those who sinned, whose bodies fell in the wilderness? 18And to whom
did He swear that they would not enter His rest, except to those who
disobeyed?[27] 19We see then that they could not enter because of unbelief.

4 1Therefore let us fear, that while the promise of entering His rest
remains open, any one of you may come short of it. 2For indeed we
have had the Gospel preached to us, just as they did, but the Gospel-
word they heard did them no good, because it was not united with faith
in those who heard. 3But we who have believed are destined to enter that
rest, while He said about others, "As I swore in My anger, they will not
enter My rest," although His works were finished from the foundation of
the world. 4For He has said somewhere about the seventh day, "God
rested on the seventh day from all His works,"[28] 5and to repeat the words
quoted earlier, "They will not enter My rest." 6Therefore it remains for
some to enter it, yet those to whom the Gospel was preached before
failed to enter because of disobedience.[29] 7So He again sets a certain day,
"Today," speaking through David a long time afterwards, as was quoted
before, "Today if you hear His voice, do not harden your hearts."

---

[26]Again, as in v. 6, the popular doctrine of "once saved always saved" is clearly false. See my "The 'If's' of Christianity" at www.restorationfellowship.org

[27]Obedience to God and Jesus is the key to NT salvation. Hence Paul's good phrase which frames Romans (1:5; 16:26): "the obedience of faith," and Jesus' black and white warning in John 3:36 and 12:44ff. Obedience is to the words of Jesus under the New Covenant, and anyone who departs from those words is a threat to salvation (see 1 Tim. 6:3; 2 Jn. 7-9; Heb. 5:9). Faith in Jesus is false unless it is based on obedience to the words and teachings of Jesus as well as the words of Jesus-in-Paul. Matt. 7:21-27 is a severe warning in this regard. The popular notion that "Jesus came to do three days' work" (Billy Graham) or that "the Gospel is not in the Gospels" (C.S Lewis) is dangerously misleading. It leads us away from the essential saving words and teachings of Jesus (Jn. 12:44ff).

[28]It would be completely at variance with this verse to say that Jesus the Son was active in the Genesis creation!

[29]Another of many clear texts which make obedience to God and Jesus the absolute criterion of true faith (cp. 5:9).

8For if Joshua had given them rest, He would not have spoken
afterward of another day. 9So there remains a future time of rest[30] for the
people of God. 10For the one who enters His rest has himself also rested
from his works, as God did from His. 11Let us therefore work hard[31] to
enter that rest, so that no one falls by following the same example of
disobedience. 12For the Gospel-word of God is living and active and
sharper than any two-edged sword, piercing even to the dividing of soul
and spirit, of joints and marrow, and able to discern the thoughts and
intentions of the heart.[32] 13And there is no creature hidden from God's
sight, but all things are naked and exposed to the eyes of Him to whom
we must give an account.

14So since we have a great high priest who has passed through the
heavens, Jesus, the Son of God, let us hold tightly to our confession.
15For we do not have a high priest who cannot sympathize with our
weaknesses, but one who has been in all points tempted as we are,[33] yet
without sin. 16Let us therefore draw near with boldness to the throne of
grace, so that we may receive mercy and find grace to help us in time of
need.

5 1For every high priest is chosen from among men[34] and is appointed
to represent men in things pertaining to God, to offer both gifts and

---

[30]"A rest" or "a Sabbath rest," but this is certainly not a reference to weekly Sabbath observance, since the whole of the OT calendar is now a "shadow" replaced by the substance which is the person of the risen Messiah (10:1-10; Gal. 4:10; Eph. 2:14; Col. 2:16-17). Paul contrasts the shadow calendar negatively (*to de soma*) with the body which is Christ's.

[31]Compare the words of Jesus: "Agonize to enter [the Kingdom of God] through the narrow gate" (Lk. 13:24).

[32]In the New Covenant it is Jesus who is able to search the minds and hearts (Rev. 2:23).

[33]A decisive text against the so-called Deity of Jesus. God cannot be tempted (James 1:13), but Jesus was. Jesus remained sinless.

[34]A High Priest is by definition chosen from among human beings. This makes obvious the falsehood that Jesus was both God and a High Priest! A priest by definition mediates between God and man and is himself a man. 1 Tim. 2:5 is the creedal statement which solidifies this idea with complete clarity and without the alarming complexities of later conciliar theology. Those councils produced a confusing maze of "hypostases" and "essence," and a mass of incomprehensible definitions and distinctions, showing how much of "orthodoxy" is alien to the Bible.

sacrifices for sins. 2A high priest can deal gently with those who are
ignorant and in error, because he himself is also subject to weakness.
3Because of this, he must offer sacrifices for sins for both the people and
for himself. 4And nobody takes this honor on himself, but he is called by
God, just as Aaron was.

5So also it was not Messiah who glorified himself to become a high
priest, but it was the One who said to him, "You are My Son; today I
have fathered you." 6And God says also in another place, "You are a
priest forever in the order of Melchizedek."

7In his earthly life he offered up prayers[35] and requests, with loud
crying and tears, to the One who was able to save him from death, and he
was heard because of his godly fear. 8Although he was a Son,[36] he
learned obedience through the things which he suffered. 9Having been
perfected, he became to all of those who obey him[37] the source of the

---

[35]It is obvious that Deity does not pray to Deity. It will not help to try to cut Jesus into two halves, and have him do some things as man and others as God! Jesus was a single self, a single personality, the man Messiah. He was not two selves, operating in two different spheres. He cannot by definition be 100% plus 100%, which would turn him into two persons. One commentator burdened by the impossible struggle of having to produce a Jesus with "two natures" admits that "Deity has no need to make supplication. The fact that Jesus prayed for himself demonstrates his real humanity" (Montefiore). But if Jesus prayed for him*self* and that was his humanity, it is clear that commentator has to admit that Jesus had another self which was not "his humanity," but another divine self. The resultant Jesus is obviously two selves. The doctrine of "two natures" is utterly foreign to the Bible as well as being impossibly confusing.

[36]Some Trinitarians say that "Son of God" means an eternal Son, Deity. This and many texts make such an idea impossible. The Son of God was born, the Son of God died, and the Son of God learned obedience. The Son also prayed to God. All this shows that the Son of God was the human Messiah begotten in Mary (Mt. 1:18, 20; Lk. 1:35). The idea of an "eternal Son" or "eternally begotten" Son is an imaginative fiction imposed on the NT with no scriptural authority whatsoever. It does not appear until the 3rd century in the writings of the philosophically minded Origen. Isa. 9:6 proves that the child/Son begotten by God and given by God is not God Himself. God cannot be begotten. The Son of God was begotten and for that very reason is entitled to be called the Son of God (Lk. 1:35).

[37]Obedience to Jesus is invariably the condition of salvation. Faith without obedience is false faith and cannot save. John 3:36 and 12:44ff and 1 Tim. 6:3, 2 John 7-9 repeat the same point. Paul wisely called the true faith "the obedience of faith" (Rom. 1:5; 16:26, framing the whole book of Romans).

salvation of the age to come,[38] 10having been designated by God a high
priest in the order of Melchizedek.

11About this we have much to say, and it is hard to explain, because
you have become dull in hearing. 12For although by this time you should
be teachers, you again need someone to teach you the first principles of
the oracles of God. You have gone back to needing milk, and not solid
food. 13Everyone who lives on milk is not experienced in the word of
righteousness, because he is a baby. 14But solid food is for those who are
full grown, who through practice have exercised their senses to discern
good and evil.

6 1Therefore leaving the elementary teaching about the Messiah, let us
press on to maturity — not re-laying a foundation of repentance from
dead works, of faith toward God, 2of the teaching of baptisms and laying
on of hands, the resurrection of the dead, and the judgment of the age to
come. 3This we will do, if God permits. 4For concerning those who have
once been enlightened and have tasted the heavenly gift, and have been
made sharers in holy spirit, 5and have tasted the goodness of the Gospel-
word of God and the miraculous powers of the age to come, 6and then
have fallen away, it is impossible to renew them again to repentance,
since they crucify the Son of God for themselves all over again, putting
him to open shame. 7For soil which drinks the rain that falls often on it
and produces useful plants for those who garden, receives a blessing
from God; 8but if it produces thorns and thistles, it is useless and about
to be cursed, and its end is to be burned up.

9But, beloved, we are convinced of better things for you, things
leading to salvation, even though we are speaking like this. 10For God is
not unjust, to forget your work and the love you have shown for His
name, in having served and continuing to serve the saints. 11We desire
that each one of you shows the same diligence for the fulfillment of your
hope until the end, 12so that you will not be sluggish, but imitators of
those who through faith and perseverance inherit the promises.

13For when God made the promise to Abraham, since He could swear
by no one greater, He swore by Himself 14with these words, "Surely I
will bless you, and surely I will multiply you." 15And so having

---

[38]Of the future Kingdom of God on earth.

persevered, he obtained the promise.[39] 16For people swear by someone
greater than themselves, and with them an oath is a confirmation to end
all dispute. 17In the same way God, determined to show more clearly to
the heirs of the promise that His purpose was unchangeable, intervened
with an oath, 18so that by two unchangeable things, since it is impossible
for God to lie,[40] we who have taken refuge would have strong
encouragement to hold tightly to the hope set before us. 19This hope we
have as an anchor of the soul, a hope both sure and steadfast which
enters within the veil; 20where Jesus has entered as a pioneer for us,
having become a high priest forever in the order of Melchizedek.

7 1This Melchizedek, king of Salem, priest of the Most High God, met
Abraham as he was returning from the slaughter of the kings and
blessed him. 2Abraham allocated a tenth part of the plunder to him. He
was, by the meaning of his name, first "king of justice,"[41] and then also
"king of Salem," which means "king of peace." 3Without father, without
mother, without a recorded genealogy, beginning of days or end of life,[42]
he is like the Son of God[43] and remains a priest continually.

4Now consider how great this man was, because even Abraham, the
patriarch, gave him a tenth of the best plunder. 5Those of the sons of
Levi who receive the priest's office have a command in the Law to
collect tithes from the people, that is, from their brothers, although they
too are descendants of Abraham. 6But Melchizedek, whose genealogy is
not traced from the sons of Levi, collected a tithe from Abraham, and

---

[39]Not of course the ultimate promise of the life of the age to come in the future Kingdom, which depends on Abraham's resurrection, but the historical promises already fulfilled, particularly the birth of a son when Abraham and Sarah were old. Israel of course entered the land under Joshua, but there will be a final, future entry into the land/Kingdom for all the saints, with Jesus at his return.

[40]It is impossible for God to lie or die. Jesus the Son of God died (Rom. 5:10) and cannot therefore be God!

[41]Pointing to the future Kingdom, a world order in which social justice will prevail for the first time in human history. The Christian calling is to prepare now to assist Jesus in that coming new world order.

[42]It is a very great misunderstanding of the text to suppose that Melchizedek was an uncreated person with no parents! Jews said of Sarah that she had no parents, meaning that their names were not recorded.

[43]As a "type" or model.

blessed him who possessed the promises. 7But without dispute the lesser
is blessed by the greater. 8In one case tithes are received by mortal men,
but in that case by one of whom it is testified that he lives on. 9And, so
to speak, through Abraham even Levi, who receives tithes, paid tithes,
10because Levi was still in his ancestor Abraham's body when
Melchizedek met him.

11So if perfection was through the Levitical priesthood (for based on
it the people received the Law), what further need would there have been
for another priest to arise in the order of Melchizedek, and not in the
order of Aaron? 12For when the priesthood is changed, a change in the
Law must take place also.[44] 13For the one these things are spoken about
belongs to another tribe, and no one from that tribe has ever officiated at
the altar. 14It is clear that our lord was a descendant of Judah, and Moses
said nothing about priests in that tribe. 15This becomes clearer still when
there arises another priest like Melchizedek, 16who becomes a priest not
by a law of physical descent but by the power of an indestructible life,
17for it is testified, "You are a priest forever in the order of
Melchizedek."

18On the one hand a former commandment is set aside because of its
weakness and uselessness, 19because the Law made nothing perfect. On
the other hand a better hope is brought in, and through this hope we draw
near to God. 20Since he was not made priest without the taking of an
oath — 21the others became priests without an oath, but he was made
priest with an oath by Him who said to him, "The Lord has sworn and
will not change His mind, 'You are a priest forever'" — 22because of
this, Jesus has become the guarantee of a better covenant.

23Many have been made priests, because they were prevented from
continuing by death. 24But Jesus, because he lives forever, holds his
priesthood permanently. 25He is therefore able to save completely those
who draw near to God through him, because he always lives to intercede
for them.[45]

---

[44]Showing the all-important difference between the new and old covenants. Galatians is an impassioned warning against reverting to the OT practices, including calendar observance, which lead us away from the spiritual freedom available in Christ. A muddling of the two covenants is dangerous to our spiritual life.

[45] To insist on the annual observance of the Day of Atonement or the Holy Days demonstrates a misunderstanding of the supreme significance of the once and for all,

26For such a high priest is fitting for us: holy, guiltless, undefiled,
separated from sinners, and exalted above the heavens. 27He does not
need, like those high priests, to offer up sacrifices daily, first for their
own sins, and then for the sins of the people, because he did this once for
all when he offered up himself. 28For the Law appoints men as high
priests who are subject to weakness, but the word of the oath, which
came after the Law, appoints a Son made perfect forever.

8 1Now the main point of what has been said is this: We have such a
high priest, who has taken his seat at the right hand[46] of the throne of
the Majesty[47] in the heavens, 2a servant in the sanctuary and in the true
tabernacle, which the Lord set up, not man. 3For every high priest is
appointed to offer both gifts and sacrifices, so it is necessary that this
high priest also have something to offer. 4If he were on earth, he would
not be a priest at all, because there are priests who offer the gifts
according to the Law. 5They do their service in a copy and shadow of the
heavenly things, just as Moses was warned by God when he was about to
make the tabernacle: "See that you make everything according to the
pattern shown to you on the mountain." 6But now Jesus has obtained a
superior ministry, since he is also the mediator of a better covenant,
which has been given as Law[48] based on better promises.

---

permanent effects of the New Covenant inaugurated by the sacrificial, substitutionary death of Jesus, Son of God. Col. 2:16-17 contrasts the Mosaic calendar negatively with the substance — Christ, who replaces it. See our booklet *The Law, the Sabbath and New Covenant Christianity* at focusonthekingdom.org

[46]The *adoni*, my lord (not Lord) of Ps. 110:1 which is the golden text from the Hebrew Bible, more often quoted in the NT than any other verse. *Adoni* in all of its 195 occurrences means a non-Deity superior, i.e. a man, occasionally an angel, but never God. The idea of GOD speaking to GOD is profoundly contrary to biblical unitary monotheism. In Ps. 45:6 the Messiah is addressed as "god," where *elohim* is used in a Messianic sense. Moses was also called "god" (*elohim*) as representing the one true Lord God (Ex. 7:1). Jesus is never called "the Lord God," nor "the Almighty" — *El Shaddai* in Hebrew and *pantokrator* in Greek.

[47]God, the Father's throne (Rev. 3:21). Jesus will sit on his own throne in Jerusalem in the millennium.

[48]"en-Torahed" on better promises. This shows that the New Covenant Torah of Messiah (Gal. 6:2; 1 Cor. 9:21) supersedes the Old Torah in the letter. The New Covenant was introduced and ratified by Jesus (Lk. 22:28-30) and Paul was "a minister of the New Covenant" (2 Cor. 3:6). At the Parousia it will be made with Jews who

7For if that first covenant had been faultless, then there would have
been no need for a second. 8But finding fault with them, He says, “Look,
the days are coming, says the Lord, when I will make a new covenant
with the house of Israel and with the house of Judah; 9it will not be like
the covenant that I made with their fathers, on the day when I took them
by the hand to lead them out of the land of Egypt; because they did not
continue in My covenant, and I had no regard for them, says the Lord.
10For this is the covenant that I will make with the house of Israel after
those days, says the Lord: I will put My laws into their minds, and I will
write them on their hearts. I will be their God, and they will be My
people. 11And each one will not teach his fellow citizen or his brother,
saying, ‘Know the Lord,’ because all will know Me, from their least to
their greatest. 12For I will be merciful toward their evil actions, and I will
remember their sins no more.”

13When He said, “A new covenant,” He has made the first obsolete.
And what has become obsolete and has grown old is near to
disappearing.

9 1Now the first covenant had rules for divine service and the earthly
sanctuary. 2A tabernacle was prepared. In the outer part, which is
called the Holy Place, were the lampstand, the table, and the sacred
bread. 3Behind the second veil there was a tabernacle which is called the
Holy of Holies, 4which had a golden altar of incense, and the ark of the
covenant overlaid on all sides with gold. In the ark were a golden jar
holding the manna, Aaron’s rod that budded, and the stone tablets of the
covenant. 5Above the ark were the cherubim of glory overshadowing the
mercy seat. But of these things we cannot now speak in detail.

6So when these things had been prepared in this way, the priests
continually go into the outer tabernacle, performing the services, 7but
into the second the high priest goes alone once a year, and not without
blood, which he offers for himself and for the sins of the people done in
ignorance. 8The holy spirit is showing that the way into the Holy Place
had not yet been revealed while the outer tabernacle is still standing.
9This is a symbol of that time when gifts and sacrifices were offered

---

accept the Messiah at that time (Rom. 11:26). Meanwhile any Jew or Gentile is urged to believe and obey the Messiah Jesus.

which could not make the worshiper perfect in conscience, 10being only
food and drink and various washings, physical rules imposed until a time
of reformation.

11But now Messiah has appeared as the high priest of the good things
to come. He entered through the greater and more perfect tabernacle, not
made with hands, that is to say, not of this present creation, 12and he
entered once for all into the Holy Place, not through the blood of goats
and calves, but through his own blood, and so he secured the redemption
of the age to come. 13For if the blood of goats and bulls, and the ashes of
a heifer sprinkling those who have been defiled, consecrate for the purity
of the body, 14how much more will the blood of Messiah, who through
the spirit of the age to come offered himself without defect to God,
purify our consciences from dead works to serve the living God!

15For this reason he is the mediator of a new covenant, so that those
who have been called may receive the promise of the inheritance of the
age to come, since a death has taken place for the redemption of the
violations committed under the first covenant. 16For where there is a
will,[49] there must be proven the death of the one who made it. 17For a will
is valid at death, and it is never in force while the one who made it lives.
18So even the first covenant was ratified with blood. 19For when every
commandment had been spoken by Moses to all the people according to
the Law, he took the blood of calves and goats, with water and scarlet
wool and hyssop, and sprinkled both the book itself and all the people,
20saying, "This is the blood of the covenant which God commanded
you." 21And in the same way he sprinkled both the tabernacle and all the
vessels of ministry with the blood. 22According to the Law, nearly
everything is purified with blood, and without the shedding of blood
there is no forgiveness.

23It was necessary therefore for the sketches of the things in the
heavens to be purified with these sacrifices, but the heavenly things[50]
themselves required better sacrifices than these. 24For Messiah did not
enter a holy place made with hands, which is a copy of the true one, but
into heaven itself, now to appear in the presence of God for us. 25And he

---

[49]The writer uses a second meaning here for the same word "covenant," i.e. "will" rather than covenant.

[50]Relating to future things, the future Kingdom of God to be inaugurated worldwide when Jesus returns.

did not need to offer himself often, the way the high priest enters the
holy place year after year with blood not his own, 26for then he would
have had to suffer often since the foundation of the world. But now once
at the consummation of the ages, he has been revealed to put away sin by
the sacrifice of himself.[51] 27Just as it is appointed for people to die once,
and after this comes judgment, 28so Messiah also, having been offered
once to bear the sins of many, will appear a second time, not to bear sin,
but to bring salvation to those who are eagerly waiting for him.

10 1For the Law, having a shadow[52] of the good things to come, but
not the reality itself,[53] can never with the same sacrifices offered
continually, year by year, make perfect those who draw near. 2Otherwise
would they not have ceased to be offered, because the worshipers,
having been once purified, would have no more consciousness of sin?
3But in those sacrifices there is a reminder of sins year after year. 4For it
is impossible for the blood of bulls and goats to take away sins. 5So
when he comes into the world[54] he says, "You did not desire sacrifice and
offering, but You prepared a body[55] for me. 6You have no pleasure in
whole burnt offerings and sacrifices for sin. 7Then I said, 'Look, I[56] have
come (in the scroll of the book it is written of me) to do Your will, O
God.'"

---

[51]I.e. as a sacrificial person, or body. God had determined this role for the Messiah as predicted in the Psalms. Many of the psalms predict the activity of the Messiah.

[52]A sketch, a rough outline.

[53]Just as in Col. 2:16-17 the Messiah, who has come, is the reality of which the calendar of "holy days, new moons and weekly sabbath" are a single shadow. In Rom. 5:14 "Adam *is* a type" of the one who is to come. The sense is of course that Adam *was* a type of the one who *was* to come. In the same way the calendar was a shadow of Messiah whose body is the reality of the shadow. The person is the body of Messiah who sacrificed himself (9:26).

[54]To "come into the world" means to be born. Every human being comes into the world. Jesus did too, but by a miraculous biological miracle wrought in Mary (Lk. 1:35; Mt. 1:18, 20). God begat His Son, brought him into existence.

[55]The sense is a sacrificial person, not just a body as a shell into which a person entered! 9:26 speaks of the offering of the Messiah himself, the whole person. Rom. 12:1 in the same way speaks of Christians as "bodies," i.e. whole persons.

[56]The "I" here is the sacrificial body or person of the Messiah predicted in God's plan in Ps. 40. The person/body of Messiah replaces the shadow of the Torah sacrifices and calendar (see Col. 2:16-17; Eph. 2:14; Gal. 4:10, 3:19-29).

8After saying above, "Sacrifices and offerings and whole burnt
offerings and sacrifices for sin You did not desire, and had no pleasure
in" — which are offered according to the Law — 9then he said, "Behold,
I have come to do Your will." He abolishes the first in order to establish
the second. 10By His will we have been made holy through the offering
of the body of Jesus Messiah once for all.

11Every priest stands day after day serving and offering time and
again the same sacrifices which can never take away sins. 12But he,
when he had offered one sacrifice for sins for all time, sat down at the
right hand of God, 13where he is now waiting until his enemies are made
a footstool for his feet.[57] 14For by one offering he has perfected for all
time those who are being made holy. 15The holy spirit also witnesses to
us, for after saying, 16"This is the covenant that I will make with them
after those days, says the Lord: I will put my laws on their hearts, and I
will write them on their minds," then He says, 17"I will remember their
sins and their iniquities no more." 18Now where there is forgiveness of
these, there is no longer any offering for sin.

19Therefore, brothers and sisters, since we have boldness to enter the
holy place by the blood of Jesus, 20by a new and living way that he
inaugurated for us through the curtain, that is, his flesh, 21and since we
have a great priest over God's house, 22let us draw near with a sincere
heart in full assurance of faith, because we have had our hearts sprinkled
clean from an evil conscience, and our bodies washed with pure water.
23Let us hold fast the hope that we confess without wavering, because He
who made the promise is faithful. 24And let us consider how to stimulate
one another to love and good works, 25not abandoning our own
assembling together, as is the habit of some, but encouraging one
another, and even more as you see the Day[58] approaching.

---

[57]Another reference to the key Ps. 110:1 which defines the Messianic program and differentiates between the one YHVH, the God of the Bible, and the non-Deity Messiah who is *adoni* (my lord). This is exactly Paul's creed in 1 Tim. 2:5. Note that Jesus is still *waiting* for his enemies to be subject to him. Jesus is not yet sitting on his Davidic throne in Zion. This throne is promised to him in Lk. 1:32 and Ps. 2:6. Joseph of Arimathea was still waiting for the appearance of the Kingdom of God, after the resurrection of Jesus (Mk. 15:43).

[58]Of Messiah's future coming to inaugurate the Kingdom of God on earth, worldwide.

26For if we deliberately keep on sinning after we have received the
knowledge of the truth, there remains no longer a sacrifice for sins, 27but
a terrifying expectation of judgment, and the fury of a fire which will
destroy God's enemies.[59] 28Anyone who disregarded Moses' Law was put
to death without mercy on the testimony of two or three witnesses.
29How much greater punishment do you think a person deserves who has
trodden under foot the Son of God, and has profaned the blood of the
covenant by which he was made holy, and has insulted the spirit of
grace? 30For we know Him who said, "Vengeance belongs to Me; I will
repay," and again, "The Lord will judge His people." 31It is a terrifying
thing to fall into the hands of the living God.

32But remember the former days when, after you were enlightened,
you endured a great struggle with suffering, 33partly by being publicly
exposed to abuse and afflictions, and partly by sharing with those who
were treated that way. 34For you shared the suffering of those in prison,
and joyfully accepted the seizing of your possessions, knowing that you
have for yourselves a better and lasting possession. 35So do not throw
away your confidence, because it has a great reward. 36For you need
endurance so that, when you have done the will of God, you will receive
the promise. 37"In a very little while, he who is coming will come, and
will not delay.[60] 38But My righteous one will live by faith. If he shrinks
back, My soul takes no pleasure in him." 39But we are not of those who
shrink back to destruction, but of those who have faith leading to
obtaining life.

---

[59]The biblical hell-fire is a consuming destruction, the lake of fire which annihilates human persons. It is not the blasphemous, eternal, conscious torture of the wicked taught popularly. See Jude 7 for "everlasting fire," that is, the fire of the age to come.

[60]These words written in BC times by Haggai (2:6; cp. Isa. 26:20; Hab. 2:3) show that the Second Coming is always "shortly," even though chronologically it may be far off. The prophets lived by inspiration and vision in the climactic times just before the return of Jesus in glory, that is, on the brink of the coming Kingdom, when the world will come under new management. The kingdoms of this present system will be replaced by the Kingdom of God (Rev. 11:15). The coming of YHVH in the prophets is revealed to be the future coming of Jesus in the NT. Jesus, the Son of God, is the perfect agent of the One God, and is given YHVH activities to perform, without actually *being* YHVH, which would make two YHVHs!

11 1Now faith is the assurance of what we hope for, the conviction of
what we do not see. 2By faith, the people of old gained approval.
3By faith, we understand that the ages were set in order by the word
of God,[61] so that what is visible was made out of things which are
invisible. 4By faith, Abel offered to God a greater sacrifice than Cain,
and God showed that he was righteous by receiving his gifts; and
through faith he, though he is dead, still speaks. 5By faith, Enoch was
taken up so that he would not see death,[62] and he was not found because
God took him up. Before being taken up he had been commended as
pleasing to God. 6And without faith it is impossible to please God,
because the one who comes to God must believe that He exists and that
He rewards those who seek Him.[63] 7By faith, Noah, when he was warned
about things not yet seen, with a godly fear prepared an ark for the
salvation of his family. Through this he condemned the world and
became an heir of the righteousness which comes by faith.
8By faith, Abraham, when he was called, obeyed[64] by going out to a
place which he was to receive as an inheritance. He went out, not
knowing where he was going. 9By faith, he lived as a foreigner[65] in the
land of the promise,[66] as in a foreign country, living in tents with Isaac
and Jacob, fellow heirs of the same promise. 10For he was looking
forward to the city[67] with firm foundations, whose architect and builder is
God. 11By faith, even Sarah herself received power to conceive, even past
child-bearing age, since she considered Him faithful who had promised.

---

[61]The creative word (not Word) of God which was in the beginning with God and through which all came into existence (Jn. 1:1-3, commented and clarified by 1 Jn. 1:1-3: the "eternal life" which was promised and which was "with the Father," in His plan and purpose as His wisdom).

[62]This must have been a removal to a safe location, since all these listed here eventually died (v. 13).

[63]This entails, in view of the massive confusion displayed by all the differing denominations, a persistent search for the truth required for the true worship of the one true God (Jn. 4:24; 2 Thess. 2:10; Jude 3).

[64]This is exactly "the obedience of faith" taught throughout the NT (Rom. 1:5; 16:26: Heb. 5:9; Jn. 3:36).

[65]A resident alien.

[66]That is, the land of the promise made to Abraham, the basis of the Christian Gospel (Gal. 3:8). The promised land is therefore on this planet earth, which will be renewed and purged by the Messiah at his return.

[67]"The city *to come*," when Jesus comes back (13:14), on the renewed earth.

12So there were fathered by one man, and him as good as dead, as many
descendants as the stars of heaven, and as uncountable as the grains of
sand on the seashore.

13These all died[68] in faith, without receiving the promises, but they
saw them and welcomed them from a distance, and confessed that they
were strangers and foreigners in the land.[69] 14For those who speak in
such a way make it clear that they are seeking a country of their own. 15If
they had been thinking of that land which they had left, they would have
had opportunity to return. 16But they desire a better land, that is, a
heavenly one.[70] So God is not ashamed to be called their God, because
He has prepared a city for them.[71]

17By faith, Abraham, when he was tested, offered up Isaac. He was
ready to offer up his only son, the one who had been promised to him.
18God had said, "Through Isaac your descendants will come." 19And he
reasoned that God is able even to raise someone from the dead. As a
type, he did receive Isaac back from the dead. 20By faith, Isaac blessed
Jacob and Esau concerning the future. 21By faith, Jacob, when he was
dying, blessed each of the sons of Joseph, and worshiped, leaning on his
staff. 22By faith, Joseph, at the end of his life, mentioned the exodus of
the children of Israel, and gave instructions about his bones.

23By faith, Moses, when he was born, was hidden for three months by
his parents, because they saw that he was a beautiful child, and they were
not afraid of the king's command. 24By faith, Moses, when he had grown
up, refused to be called the son of Pharaoh's daughter, 25choosing rather

---

[68]This verse is exceedingly important since it proves false that popular idea that the dead are currently alive in heaven or being tormented in hell, or even purgatory. This verse has the power to collapse the whole structure of much religion inherited uncritically as tradition.

[69]Resident aliens, "green card" people, whose citizenship was not in any of the current nation-states. These present nations and kingdoms will become the Kingdom of God only at the seventh trumpet of Rev. 11:15-18

[70]Not a country *in* heaven, of course, but a heavenly Kingdom, originating in heaven and coming in the future with Jesus from heaven, the promised Kingdom of God on earth of the Christian Gospel (Mt. 5:5; Rev. 5:9-10). Messiah is coming back to the earth; we are not going to him, except to meet him in the air, to escort him to his destination in Jerusalem to sit on the throne of David.

[71]"The city to come" of 13:14 — not somewhere else to which we go away from the earth!

to share ill treatment with God's people than to enjoy the fleeting pleasures of sin. 26He considered the reproach of the Messiah greater riches than the treasures of Egypt, because he was looking forward to the reward.[72] 27By faith, he left Egypt, not fearing the anger of the king; for he endured, as if seeing Him who is unseen. 28By faith, he kept the Passover and the sprinkling of the blood, so that the destroyer of the firstborn would not touch them. 29By faith, they passed through the Red Sea as if on dry land, and when the Egyptians tried it, they were swallowed up.

30By faith, the walls of Jericho fell down after the people marched around them for seven days. 31By faith, Rahab the prostitute did not die with those who were disobedient, after she had welcomed the spies in peace.

32What more shall I say? Time would fail me if I tell of Gideon, Barak, Samson, Jephthah, David, Samuel, and the prophets. 33By faith they conquered kingdoms, ruled in justice, obtained promises, shut the mouths of lions, 34quenched the power of fire, escaped the edge of the sword, from weakness were made strong, grew mighty in war, and caused foreign armies to flee. 35Women received back their dead by resurrection, and others were tortured, not accepting release, to obtain a better resurrection. 36Others were mocked and flogged, chained and imprisoned. 37They were stoned, sawn apart, tempted, killed with the sword. They went around in sheep skins and goat skins; they were destitute, afflicted, ill-treated — 38the world was not worthy of them — wandering in deserts, mountains, caves, and holes in the ground.

39All these, having gained approval for their faith, did not receive the promise,[73] 40because God had provided something better for us, so that they would not be made perfect without us.[74]

---

[72]That is, he was focused on the Kingdom and immortality.

[73]They all died as in v. 13 and they remain dead, unconscious, until the 7th trumpet which will signal the resurrection of the dead at Messiah's return (1 Cor. 15:23; Lk. 14:14). For clear confirmation, see Ecc. 9:5, 10; Dan. 12:2 and our booklet *What Happens When We Die?* at focusonthekingdom.org

[74]We will all be granted immortality at the same moment, at the future resurrection when Jesus returns (1 Cor. 15:23).

12 1Therefore, since we are surrounded by such a great cloud of
witnesses, let us lay aside every weight and the sin which so easily
entangles us, and let us run with perseverance the race set before us,
2fixing our eyes on Jesus, the pioneer and perfecter of the faith.[75]
Because of the joy set before him[76] he endured the cross, disregarding its
shame, and has taken his seat at the right hand of the throne of God.[77]
3Consider him who has endured such hostility from sinners against
himself, so that you do not grow weary and give up.

4You have not yet resisted to the point of bloodshed in your striving
against sin, 5and you have forgotten the exhortation addressed to you as
children: "My son, do not take lightly the Lord's discipline, or give up
when you are corrected by Him, 6because those whom the Lord loves He
disciplines, and He chastises every son He accepts." 7For the sake of
discipline you have to endure. God is dealing with you as with children,
and what child is there whom his father does not discipline? 8But if you
do not experience discipline, which all children share in, then you are
illegitimate and not true children. 9Besides, we had earthly fathers to
discipline us, and we respected them. Shall we not much more be subject
to the Father of spirits, and receive life?[78] 10For they disciplined us for a
short time as seemed good to them, but He disciplines us for our benefit,
so that we may share His holiness. 11All discipline at the time seems not
joyful but painful, yet afterward it produces the peaceful fruit of
righteousness for those trained by it.

12Therefore strengthen your weak hands and your feeble knees, 13and
make straight paths for your feet, so that what is lame may not be put out
of joint, but rather healed.

14Pursue peace with all people, and holiness, because without it no
one will see the Lord. 15Take care that no one comes short of the grace of
God, that no one like a shoot of bitterness springs up and causes trouble,

---

[75]Jesus is the "A to Z," the first and the last (Rev. 1:17) of God's salvation program.

[76]This shows how vitally important it is to define the Christian hope (on which faith and love are built, Col. 1:4-5). The hope is to assist Jesus in managing the coming society of the Kingdom of God. The Devil achieved an enormous victory when he reduced Christian hope to vague and vacuous promises of "heaven when you die."

[77]Assuming at his exaltation the position of *adoni,* my lord (Ps. 110:1), a title in the Hebrew which never applies to Deity. To make that verse mean that God speaks to God violates biblical monotheism.

[78]The Life of the Age to Come, that is, immortality.

and many are defiled by it. 16Let no one be an immoral or godless person
like Esau, who sold his own birthright for a single meal. 17For you know
that later when he wanted to inherit the blessing, he was rejected,
because he found no opportunity for repentance although he sought the
blessing with tears.

18For you have not come to something that can be touched, to a
blazing fire, darkness, gloom and whirlwind, 19the blast of a trumpet, and
a voice speaking words that those who heard begged to hear no more.
20For they could not bear what was commanded: "If even an animal
touches the mountain, it must be stoned." 21So fearful was the sight that
Moses said, "I am terrified and trembling." 22But you have come to
Mount Zion, the city of the living God, the heavenly Jerusalem, and to
multitudes of angels, 23to the church and assembly of the firstborn who
are enrolled in heaven, and to God, the Judge of all, and to the spirits of
the righteous made perfect, 24and to Jesus, the mediator of a new
covenant, and to the sprinkled blood that speaks of something better than
the blood of Abel.

25See that you do not refuse Him who is speaking. For if they did not
escape when they refused him who warned them on the earth, how much
less will we if we reject Him who warns from heaven? 26His voice shook
the earth then, but now He has promised, "Once more I will shake not
only the earth, but also the heavens." 27This phrase "Once more"
indicates the removing of those things that can be shaken, of created
things, so that those things which cannot be shaken may remain.
28Therefore, since we are destined to receive a Kingdom[79] which cannot
be shaken, let us show gratitude and offer service pleasing to God, with
reverence and awe, 29because our God is a consuming fire.

13 1Let love of the brothers and sisters continue. 2Do not neglect to
show hospitality to strangers, because in doing so some have
entertained angels without knowing it. 3Remember those in prison as
though you were in prison with them, and those who are ill-treated since
you are suffering with them. 4Let marriage be held in honor among all,
and let the marriage bed be undefiled, because God will judge the

---

[79]As described in Dan. 7:14, 18, 22, 27 and in many passages as the heart of the Christian Gospel of the Kingdom as preached by Jesus and Paul and all NT writers.

sexually immoral and adulterers. 5Be free from the love of money,
content with what you have, because He has said, “I will never leave
you, nor will I abandon you.” 6So we can confidently say, “The Lord is
my helper, and I will not fear. What can people do to me?”

7Remember your leaders, who spoke to you the Gospel-word of God;
consider the outcome of their way of life and imitate their faith. 8Jesus
Messiah is the same yesterday, today, and forever. 9Do not be carried
away by different and strange teachings, for it is good that the heart be
strengthened by grace, not by eating ceremonial food, which did not
benefit those who did so. 10We have an altar from which those who serve
the tabernacle have no right to eat. 11For the bodies of those animals,
whose blood the high priest brings into the holy place as an offering for
sin, are burned outside the camp. 12Therefore Jesus also, so that he would
make the people holy by his own blood, suffered outside the gate. 13So
let us go out to him outside the camp, bearing the abuse he suffered.
14For we do not have here a lasting city, but we seek the city to come.[80]

15Through him, then, let us continually offer up a sacrifice of praise
to God, that is, the fruit of our lips giving thanks to His name. 16And do
not neglect to do good and to share, because with such sacrifices God is
pleased.

17Obey your leaders and submit to them, because they keep watch
over you and will give an account. Let them do this with joy and not with
grief, because that would not be good for you.

18Pray for us, for we are sure that we have a good conscience and
desire to conduct ourselves honorably in all things. 19And I urge you to
pray that I may be restored to you very soon.

20Now may the God of peace, who brought back from the dead the
great shepherd of the sheep, our lord Jesus, through the blood of the
covenant of the age to come, 21equip you with every good thing to do His
will, working in us what is pleasing in His sight, through Jesus Messiah,
to whom be the glory to the ages of the ages. Amen.

22Now I urge you, brothers and sisters, to bear with my word of
exhortation, because I have written to you briefly. 23Know that our
brother Timothy has been freed, and with him, if he comes soon, I will

[80]The city to come is the Jerusalem of the Kingdom of God which will come into existence when Jesus returns to inaugurate his millennial Kingdom on a renewed earth. The saints of all the ages will govern and reign with Jesus in that future Kingdom.

see you. 24Greet all of your leaders and all the saints. Those from Italy
send their greetings.
25Grace be with you all.

James

1 1From James, a servant of God and of the lord Jesus Messiah,[1] to the
twelve tribes in the Dispersion,[2] scattered in various parts of the
world:[3] Greetings.
2Count it all joy, my brothers and sisters, when you face various
trials, 3as you know that the testing of your faith produces endurance.
4And let endurance perfect its work, so that you may be perfect and
complete, lacking in nothing.
5If any of you lacks wisdom, you should ask God, who gives to all
freely and ungrudgingly, and it will be given to you. 6But ask in faith
without doubting, because a doubter is like a wave of the sea, blown and
tossed about by the wind. 7Such a person should not expect to receive
anything from the Lord, 8being of two minds and unstable in everything.
9Let the brothers and sisters in humble circumstances take pride in
their high standing. 10And the rich should take pride in their low
standing, because they will fade away like wildflowers. 11When the heat
of the sun burns the wildflowers, they dry up and their beauty perishes.
In the same way, rich people will wither away in the midst of their
activities.
12Blessed are those who endure testing, because when they have
passed the test they will receive the crown of Life which God has
promised to those who love Him.[4] 13No one facing temptation should say,

---

[1]The lord Messiah was born in Bethlehem (Lk. 2:11). God cannot be born. The lord Messiah is so named based on the all-important Ps. 110:1 where the second lord is *adoni*, "my lord," a title which in all of its 195 occurrences never refers to GOD, who is *Adonai*, the Lord God. The "my lord" of Ps. 110:1 becomes the "our lord Jesus Messiah" of the NT. God the Father is the God of Abraham, Isaac and Jacob, the God of David and the God of Jesus. The one God is "the God and Father of our lord Jesus Messiah." Jesus is Son of God as defined and described by Luke 1:35. The notion held by some that the Son *is* the Father (Oneness or Modalism) fails because the Father and Son speak to each other (note particularly Ps. 110:1).

[2]Paul of course considered, as did Peter, the whole church to be the spiritual "Israel of God" (Gal. 6:16; Phil. 3:3) without losing sight of a future for now blinded, national Israel of the flesh (1 Cor. 10:18; see Rom. 9-11). Paul calls these "Israelites" (Rom. 9:4; 11:1; 2 Cor. 11:22).

[3]The diaspora, scattered descendants of Israel.

[4]This is the Christian reward, as everywhere in the NT. The gift is the Life of the Age to Come in the future Kingdom on earth, and rulership with Jesus in that coming Kingdom. The true believers are the royal family of the coming Kingdom in training to

"I am being tempted by God," because God cannot be tempted by evil,
nor does He Himself tempt anyone. 14But everyone is tempted by the lure
and trap of their own desires. 15Those desires conceive and give birth to
sin, which then grows up and gives birth to death. 16Do not be deceived,
my beloved brothers and sisters. 17Every good act of giving and every
perfect gift is from above, and comes down from the Father of lights,[5]
who is without change or turning shadow. 18He gave birth to us by the
Gospel-word of truth,[6] according to His own plan, so that we would be
the first fruits of His new creation.

19So then, my beloved brothers and sisters, understand this: let
everyone be quick to listen, slow to speak, and slow to get angry,
20because God's righteousness does not work through human anger. 21So
put away all filthiness and wickedness, and with humility allow the
Gospel-word planted in you to save you. 22But be doers of that word, and
not only hearers, so deceiving yourselves. 23Someone who hears the
Gospel-word but does not obey it is like a person who examines his face
in a mirror 24and walks away, immediately forgetting what he looked
like. 25But one who examines the perfect law of freedom and perserveres
in it — who does not become a forgetful listener but one who obeys it —
that person will be blessed in what he does.[7]

---

supervise and administer the coming age of the Kingdom on earth (see Rev. 2:26; 3:21; 5:10; 20:1-6; Dan. 7:18, 22, 27). There will be surviving mortal nations in the Kingdom who form the subjects of that future Kingdom. Zech. 14 and Isa. 65:17ff are some of many passages describing the new society of the future Kingdom. The world will be under new management.

[5]The very Jewish idiom "coming down from heaven" simply means that something is a gift from God. In John 6:51 Jesus spoke of his *flesh* coming down from heaven. This is automatically read by some as teaching that Jesus was alive in heaven before coming into existence in Mary. However, once it is seen that "coming down from heaven" means that something is God's gift, then no proof at all is offered for preexistence in the phrase "coming from heaven" or "coming down from heaven" (see also 3:15-17).

[6]Rebirth as described by all the NT writers is initiated by belief in the seed message of Jesus' Gospel of the Kingdom, as demonstrated by him in the parable of the sower (Mt. 13:19; Lk. 8:11-12; cp. 1 Pet. 1:23-25). The Gospel about the Kingdom as preached first by Jesus according to Heb. 2:3 is the essential basis of all true Christian faith (cp. Acts 8:12).

[7]This is exactly the lesson of all Scripture, summarized brilliantly in Ps. 1:3: "Everything he does succeeds."

26If any consider themselves to be religious and do not control their
tongues but deceive themselves, their religion is useless. 27Pure and
undefiled religion before the God and Father is this: to take care of
orphans and widows in their suffering, and to keep oneself
uncontaminated by the world-system.

2 1My brothers and sisters, do not show any favoritism as you hold the
faith of our lord Jesus Messiah[8] of glory. 2Suppose a well-dressed
person wearing fine jewelry comes into your gathering, and a shabbily-
dressed person also comes in. 3If you show special attention to the one
wearing the fine clothes and say to him, "Take the seat of honor," but to
the poor person you say, "Stand over there or sit on the floor," 4have you
not made distinctions among yourselves and become judges with wrong
standards? 5Listen, my beloved brothers and sisters: Did not God choose
the world's poor to be rich in faith and heirs of the Kingdom[9] which He
promised to those who love Him? 6But you have insulted the poor
person. Is it not the rich who oppress you, who drag you into court? 7Are
they not the ones who besmirch the honorable name to whom you
belong?

8You will do well to fulfill the royal law of Scripture: "Love your
neighbor as yourself." 9But you sin if you show favoritism, and you are
convicted by the law as sinners. 10For someone who keeps the whole law
but fails in one point has become guilty of it all. 11For the One who said,
"Do not commit adultery" also said, "Do not murder." So if you do not
commit adultery but do commit murder, you have become a law breaker.
12So speak and act as those to be judged by the law of freedom. 13For

---

[8]The faith of the Messiah is not just faith in him but the same faith as he had. Christians are to have the faith of Jesus, that is faith in and obedience to all that he taught and modeled.

[9]The biblical promise is always that Christians will inherit the Kingdom on earth. The popular language about "going to heaven," or "heaven at death," or "pie in the sky when you die" is a constantly deceiving feature and hides the biblical truth of an important part of the saving Gospel. The Christian believer is invited to train now for the coming Kingdom and to rule the world with Jesus when he comes back (see Rev. 2:26; 3:21; 5:10; 20:1-6; Dan. 7:18, 22, 27; 1 Cor. 6:2; 2 Tim. 2:12; Mt. 19:28; Lk. 19:17). This is the heart of the New Covenant (see Lk. 22:28-30, where the Greek reads, "Just as my Father **covenanted** to me a Kingdom, I **covenant** to give you a Kingdom, and you will sit on thrones to administer the tribes of Israel").

judgment will be without mercy to the one who has shown no mercy.
Mercy triumphs over judgment.
14What is the use, my brothers and sisters, if you claim to have faith
but you do not have works? Can that faith save you? 15If a brother or
sister is without clothing and lacks daily food, 16and one of you just says
to them, "Go in peace; keep warm and eat enough food," but you do not
meet their physical needs, what good is that? 17So faith, if it has no
works, is dead by itself.
18But someone might say, "One person has faith, and another has
works." I say: Show me your faith without works, and I will show you
my faith from my works. 19You believe that God is one Person;[10] that is
right! Even the demons believe that and tremble. 20But do you not see,
you foolish person, that faith without works is useless? 21Was not
Abraham our father made right by works when he offered Isaac his son
on the altar? 22You see that faith was acting together with his works,[11]
and by works his faith was perfected. 23The Scripture was fulfilled:
"Abraham believed God, and this was credited to him as making him
right," and he was called "God's friend." 24You see then that by works a
person is made right, and not by faith alone. 25In the same way, was not
Rahab the prostitute also made right by works when she welcomed the
messengers and sent them out by a different route? 26For just as the body
without spirit is dead, so faith without works is dead.

3 1Not many of you should become teachers, my brothers and sisters, as
you know that we teachers will receive a stricter judgment. 2For we
all stumble in many ways. If someone does not stumble in what he says,
he is a perfect person, able to control the whole body as well. 3When we
put bits into horses' mouths so that they obey us, we guide the whole

---

[10]James speaks for the whole of NT Christianity, including Jesus in Mark 12:29. The NT church did not believe in the Trinity but in the one-Person GOD, the Father, so named as God 1300 times in the NT. The Father is named as God about every 6th verse in the NT. This is massive evidence for unitary monotheism. Jesus affirmed the unitary monotheistic Shema (Hear, O Israel) of Mark 12, which was the oath of allegiance for all Jews including Jesus, whose faith and belief is our model. Our definition of God must be the definition of God which Jesus taught. 1 Tim. 6:3 and 2 John 7-9 warn strongly against failure to adhere to the teachings of Jesus.

[11]Summed up beautifully as "the obedience of faith" (Rom. 1:5; 16:26; cp. Heb. 5:9; Jn. 3:36), which ought to feature prominently in all Christian discussion.

animal. 4And huge ships are driven by strong winds, but are steered by a
very small rudder wherever the pilot chooses. 5In the same way, the
tongue, though a small part of the body, boasts of great things. Think
about what a large forest a small fire can set ablaze. 6And the tongue is
like a fire; it is a world of evil among the parts of our bodies. It corrupts
the whole body, setting on fire the course of our life, and it is set on fire
by Gehenna.

7All kinds of creatures, animals or birds, reptiles or fish, have been
tamed by human beings, 8but no human being can tame the tongue. It is
an uncontrollable, venomous evil. 9With our tongues we bless the Lord
and Father, and with our tongues we curse our fellow human beings who
are made in the image of God. 10Out of the same mouth come both
blessing and cursing. It ought not to be this way, my brothers and sisters.
11Do both sweet and bitter water flow from the same spring? 12Can a fig
tree produce olives, my brothers and sisters, or a grapevine produce figs?
No, neither can salt water make fresh water.

13Who among you is wise and understanding? Show your works from
your good conduct in the humility of wisdom. 14But if you have bitter
jealousy and selfishness in your hearts, do not boast and lie against the
truth. 15This is not the wisdom that comes down from above, but is
earthly, unspiritual and demonic. 16For wherever there is jealousy and
selfishness, there will be disorder and every kind of evil. 17But the
wisdom which comes from above is first pure, then peace-loving, gentle,
cooperative, full of mercy and good fruits, without favoritism and
hypocrisy. 18And the fruit of uprightness is planted in peace by those who
make peace.[12]

4 1What is the source of fighting and conflict among you? Is it not your
passions at war within you? 2You desire, but do not have. You murder
and envy but cannot obtain, so you fight and quarrel. You do not have
because you do not ask. 3When you do ask you do not receive because
you ask wrongly, to use it on your passions. 4You adulteresses, do you
not know that friendship with the world means hostility towards God? So
whoever chooses to be a friend of the world makes himself an enemy of

---

[12]In Acts 10:34-37 the Gospel of the Kingdom preached by Jesus (Lk. 4:43) is called "the Gospel of peace preached through Jesus."

God. 5Do you think that for no reason the Scripture says: “God jealously
desires the spirit that He has put in us”? 6But He gives more grace. As it
says, “God is against the proud but gives grace to the humble.” 7So
submit yourselves to God. Resist the Devil[13] and he will flee from you.
8Draw close to God, and He will draw close to you. Cleanse your hands,
you sinners, and purify your hearts, you of two minds. 9Be sorrowful and
grieve and weep. Let your laughing be turned into crying and your joy
into dismay. 10Humble yourselves before the Lord and He will exalt you.

11Do not speak evil against each other, brothers and sisters. The one
who speaks against or judges a brother or sister speaks evil against and
judges the law. But if you judge the law, you are not a doer of the law
but its judge. 12There is only one Lawgiver and Judge, the One who is
able to save and to destroy. So who are you to judge your neighbor?

13Come now, you who say, “Today or tomorrow we will go to such
and such a town and stay there for a year, doing business and making a
profit.” 14But you do not even know about tomorrow, much less the rest
of your life. You are like a puff of steam that appears for a little while
and then vanishes. 15You should say instead, “If the Lord is willing, we
will live and do this or that.” 16But as it is you are boasting in your
arrogance, and all such boasting is evil. 17So anyone who knows the right
thing to do and does not do it is guilty of sin.

5 1Come now, you rich, weep and wail loudly over the miseries that are
coming to you. 2Your riches have rotted away and your clothes have
been eaten by moths. 3Your gold and silver have rusted, and their rust
will testify against you and consume your flesh like fire. It is in the last
days that you have chosen to hoard treasure. 4Listen! The pay you
withheld from the workers who mowed your fields cries out against you,
and the cries of those who harvested have reached the ears of the Lord of

---

[13]The Devil is of course the fallen angel of Scripture (1 Tim. 3:6). He fell into condemnation. He was not created evil. Satan is certainly never a synonym for the human tendency to sin. The Devil “came up to” Jesus in Matt. 4:3, i.e. approached from the outside, and the temptation was thus external to him. It would be a serious assault on Scripture to say that Jesus, internally, produced twisted versions of Scripture. The serpent in Genesis, who is identified as the Devil and the Satan (Rev. 12:9; 20:2), was utterly guilty for his lies. The Christadelphian system which attributes no moral responsibility to the Serpent/Devil, thus implying that God was the source of lie, should be exposed as an unfortunate twisting of Scripture.

Hosts. 5You have lived in earthly luxury and indulgence. You have
fattened yourselves for the day of slaughter. 6You have condemned and
murdered the upright person; he did not resist you.

7So then, brothers and sisters, be patient until the lord's coming.[14]
See how a farmer patiently waits for the precious produce of the earth
until it receives the early and late rains. 8So you too be patient and make
your hearts strong, because the lord's coming is near. 9Brothers and
sisters, do not complain against one another so that you may not be
judged. Look, the judge is standing at the door! 10You have the prophets
who spoke in the name of the Lord as an example of patience in
suffering, brothers and sisters. 11See how we regard as blessed those who
have patiently persevered. You have heard of the perseverance of Job
and you know the outcome for him from the Lord, because the Lord is
very kind and merciful.

12Above all, my brothers and sisters, do not swear, either by heaven
or by earth or with any other oath. But your "yes" should mean yes and
your "no" should mean no, so that you may not fall under judgment.

13Are any among you suffering? They should pray. Are any happy?
They should sing praises. 14Are any among you sick? They should call
the elders of the church to pray over them and anoint them with oil in the
name of the Lord. 15The prayer of faith will restore the sick, and the Lord
will raise them up. If they have committed sins they will be forgiven.
16So confess your sins to one another and pray for one another so that
you may be healed. The energized prayer of the upright is very powerful.
17Elijah was human like us, and when he prayed earnestly for no rain, it
did not rain on the land for three and a half years. 18Then he prayed again
and it rained and the land grew its crops.

19My brothers and sisters, if anyone among you goes astray from the
truth and someone turns him back, 20know that whoever turns a sinner
back from going astray into error will save that person from death and
cover a great number of sins.

---

[14]The one future, visible Parousia of Jesus when he comes to rule the world from Jerusalem. There will be no prior, invisible "secret rapture."

1 Peter

1 1From Peter, an Apostle of Jesus Messiah, to the spiritual resident
aliens of the Dispersion who are living in the provinces of Pontus,
Galatia, Cappadocia, Asia, and Bithynia, who are chosen 2in the
foreknowledge of God who is the Father, through being made holy in the
spirit, for the purpose of obedience to Jesus Messiah[1] and sprinkling with
his blood: Grace and peace be multiplied to you.

3Blessed be the God and Father of our lord Jesus Messiah,[2] who in
His great mercy has caused us to be born again[3] into a living hope
through the resurrection of Jesus Messiah from the dead. 4That hope is an
imperishable and undefiled inheritance[4] which will never fade away, now
stored up for you[5] in heaven, 5you who by the power of God are now
being safeguarded through faith for the salvation ready to be revealed in
the last time. 6This hope brings you joy, even though now for a little
while, if necessary, you have to suffer various trials. 7The point of the

---

[1]This is a central and essential foundation for biblical faith. "The obedience of faith" is Paul's phrase framing the book of Romans (Rom. 1:5; 16:26). See also John 3:36; 12:44ff; Heb. 5:9. There is no true faith without obedience. Jesus' first command is found in Mark 1:14-15.

[2]It is evident that someone who *has* a God cannot be coequally God! Jesus has God as his Father and the explicit reason for this relationship is definitively laid out for us in the opening chapters of the NT. Luke reports the angel as announcing that "for precisely that reason" (the miracle in Mary) Jesus is the Son of God. Had that easy definition been maintained, centuries of quarreling followed by an entrenched Trinitarian tradition, contrary to Luke 1:35 and Matt. 1:18, 20 (the Son "begotten in her"), could have been avoided.

[3]This is the rebirth taught by Jesus in John 3:3, 5. Rebirth occurs in the NT when people respond to the Gospel of the Kingdom as preached by Jesus — the seed/word of the Kingdom (Mt. 13:19; Lk. 8:11) sown in the mind. The Gospel includes of course an understanding of the substitutionary death of Jesus and his resurrection.

[4]Of the future Kingdom of God on earth at the return of Jesus. "Messiahans" (Christians) are nowhere said to have *inherited* the Kingdom already. They will inherit the Kingdom and rule in it when Jesus returns (Dan. 7:14, 18, 22, 27; Rev. 5:10; 2:26; 3:21; 20:1-6; Mt. 19:28; 1 Cor. 6:2).

[5]As your promised future reward, to be manifested when Jesus returns. In the same way Jesus prayed to have bestowed on him the glory as his reward, which he "had," i.e. in promise before the world began (Jn. 17:5). That same glory had been given (past tense of promise) to disciples not yet born when Jesus spoke those words in John 17 (17:22, 24; Mt. 6:1: "reward with your Father").

trials is the testing of your faith,[6] which is more precious than gold that
perishes even though it is tested by fire. The object is that your faith may
result in praise, glory, and honor for you at the revelation[7] of Jesus
Messiah. 8You have not seen him, but you love him. Although you do
not see him now, yet you believe in him and rejoice greatly with an
unspeakable joy which is full of glory, 9because you will receive the
ultimate goal of your faith — the salvation of yourselves.

10About this salvation, the prophets who prophesied the grace that
would come to you searched and investigated diligently. 11They were
seeking to know what person or time the Messianic spirit[8] in them was
pointing to when predicting the sufferings destined for Messiah, and the
glories to come after. 12To them it was revealed that they were serving
not themselves but you in these things, which have now been announced
to you through those who preached the Gospel to you by the holy spirit
sent from heaven — things angels long to peer into.

13So then, preparing your minds for action and being self-disciplined,
focus all your hope on the grace which is going to be brought to you at
the revelation[9] of Jesus Messiah. 14As obedient children, do not follow
the previous lusts which you had when you were in ignorance, 15but like
the Holy One who called you, become holy yourselves in all of your
behavior. 16For it is written, "You are to be holy, because I am holy."

17If you call on Him as Father, the One who impartially judges each
person's work, live your time as "resident aliens"[10] in reverent fear.
18You know that you were redeemed from the useless way of life handed
down from your ancestors, not with perishable things like silver or gold,
19but with precious blood like that of a spotless and pure lamb, the blood
of Messiah. 20He was foreknown[11] before the foundation of the world;

---

[6]Christians are being trained for positions of royal office in the coming Kingdom.

[7]Second Coming, *Parousia*.

[8]The Messianic spirit is the spirit of everything to do with God's Messianic program in His Son. The patriarchs were "messiahs" also (Ps. 105:15), sharing the same anointing of the spirit.

[9]Second Coming.

[10]Spiritual foreigners, "green card" people, kept apart from the politics of the present system.

[11]Just as all true believers are foreknown (v. 2) in God's plan, not literally preexisting! Foreknowledge is entirely different and contradictory to and incompatible with "preexistence." Jeremiah was likewise foreknown (Jer. 1:5).

however, he was revealed in these final times for your sake. 21Through
him you are believers in God, who resurrected him from the dead and
gave him glory, so that your faith and hope are in God.

22Seeing that you have purified yourselves by your obedience to the
truth[12] for genuine brotherly love, so love one another from the heart
fervently. 23You have been born again,[13] not from perishable seed, but
from an imperishable seed — the Gospel-word of God,[14] which is living
and lasting. 24For "All humanity is like grass, and all of their glory like
wildflowers. Grass withers and flowers fall, 25but the word of the Lord
endures forever." And this is the word which was preached as Gospel to
you.

2 1So then, ridding yourselves of all wickedness, all deceit, hypocrisy,
envy, and all slander, 2like newborn babies[15] long for the
unadulterated Gospel milk,[16] so that by it you may grow up to salvation,
3since you have experienced the kindness of the lord.

4Coming to him, a living stone rejected by people, but chosen by God
and valuable to Him, 5you yourselves, like living stones, are being built
up as a spiritual house to be a holy priesthood,[17] to offer up spiritual

---

[12]Equivalent to obedience to Jesus Christ (v. 2) and to the Gospel which he commanded as the basis of true belief (Mk. 1:14-15).

[13]Rebirth and conversion must of course happen now. Immortality is to be gained fully at the return of Jesus (Lk. 14:14).

[14]The word/Gospel of the Kingdom (Mt. 13:19) as preached by Jesus is the essential seed of rebirth, containing the seed of immortality (Lk. 8:11). The essential saving content of the Gospel is the Kingdom of God as preached as gospel by Jesus (Heb. 2:3) and Paul and all NT writers. This includes of course, but is not limited to, the fact of Jesus' death and resurrection (see Acts 8:12 for a brilliant shorthand definition of the saving Gospel).

[15]It would be a glaring falsehood to maintain that Christians can now only be in the "begotten," i.e. fetal stage. We are now born again (1:3, 23; James 1:18) and are newborn babes in need of spiritual milk.

[16]"The milk of the word," and "the word" is shorthand for the Gospel of the Kingdom (Lk. 4:43; 5:1, etc).

[17]Thus taking the royal priestly role assigned to Israel in Ex. 19:6. The international Church becomes the new Israel of God (Gal. 6:16; cp. 1 Cor. 10:18: "Israel of the flesh"; Phil. 3:3: true circumcision) There is also in prophecy a future for a national collective conversion of now blinded, natural, national Israel , all 12 tribes. This will guarantee the vision of Matt 19:28; Isa. 19:25.

sacrifices that are acceptable to God through Jesus Messiah. 6For it
stands written in Scripture, "Look, I am laying in Zion a chosen stone, a
valued cornerstone; the one who believes in him will never be shamed."
7This supreme honor is for you who believe, but for those who do not
believe, "The stone which the builders rejected has become the
cornerstone," 8and "a stone they stumble over, and a rock which offends
them." They stumble by disobeying[18] the Gospel-word,[19] as they were
appointed.

9But you are a chosen race, a royal priesthood, a holy nation, a people
who are God's own possession,[20] so that you may announce the
excellence of Him who called you out of darkness into His wonderful
light. 10In time past you were not a people, but now you are the people of
God. You had not received mercy, but now you have received mercy.

11Dear friends, I urge you as foreigners and spiritual resident aliens to
abstain from the lusts of human nature which battle against you.
12Conduct yourselves honorably among the non-believers, so that
although they now malign you as evildoers, they may see the good things
you do and glorify God in the coming day of visitation.

13Subject yourselves for the lord's sake to all human government[21] —
to a king as the supreme authority, 14and to governors who are sent by the
king to punish evildoers and approve those who do what is right. 15For
this is the will of God: that you by doing what is good may silence the
ignorance of foolish people. 16Live as free people, not using your
freedom as an excuse for evil, but living as servants of God. 17Honor all
people; love the brothers and sisters; fear God; honor the king.

---

[18]John 3:36 states the two polar opposites — faith or disobedience. There is no genuine faith without obedience and no obedience which is not based on faith in Messiah and his Gospel of the Kingdom, the subject of Jesus' first and fundamental command (Mk. 1:14-15).

[19]That is the Gospel message as commanded by Jesus as the first element of the Gospel, for belief, in Mark 1:14-15.

[20]These are OT descriptions of the status and position of Israel, now referred to the New Covenant international believers as the Israel of God (Gal. 6:16) and the true circumcision (Phil. 3:3).

[21]The word in Greek, *ktisis*, is important. It is literally a creation but means an institution or government. The important notion that Jesus is head of all authority in the new creation, the new order of things, is prominent in Col. 1:15 where he is "the firstborn over all creation," meaning "the highest of the kings of the earth" (Ps. 89:27).

18Servants, be in subjection to your masters with all respect, not only to the good and gentle, but also to the unjust. 19For it is commendable if someone endures hardship, suffering unjustly because of conscience toward God. 20What credit is it if you sin and are harshly treated, and you patiently endure it? But if you do what is right and suffer and patiently endure it, this finds approval with God.

21For you were called to this, since Messiah also suffered for you, leaving you an example to follow in his steps. 22"He never sinned, and no deceit was ever found in his mouth." 23When he was slandered, he did not slander back. When he suffered, he did not threaten, but committed himself to the One who judges justly. 24He himself bore our sins in his body on the cross,[22] so that we might die to sin and live to uprightness. By his wounds you have been healed. 25For you were going astray like sheep, but now you have come back to the pastor and overseer of your selves.

3 1In the same way, wives, submit yourselves to your own husbands, so that even if any do not obey the Gospel-word they may be won over by the behavior of their wives, without a word, 2as they see your pure, respectful behavior. 3Let your beauty not be just on the outside — elaborate hairstyles, gold jewelry, or fine clothes — 4but in the inner person of the heart, the unfading beauty of a gentle and quiet spirit, which is of the highest value in the sight of God. 5For this is how the holy women of the past who hoped in God adorned themselves, by being subject to their husbands, 6as Sarah obeyed Abraham, calling him "my lord." You become her spiritual children when you do what is right and do not fear.

7Husbands, similarly, live with your wives with understanding of her as the weaker vessel, and show her honor as a fellow heir of the grace of life, so that your prayers will not be hindered.

8In summary, all of you must be of one mind, sympathetic, loving, kind, and humble in spirit. 9Do not pay back evil for evil or insult for insult, but bless others instead, because you were called to inherit a blessing. 10For "Those who desire to love life and see good days must

---

[22]This is the substitutionary death of Christ in our place (Mk. 10:45). He died for us and in place of us (see Isa. 53:10-12).

keep their tongues from evil and their lips from speaking deceit. 11They
must turn away from evil and do good; they must seek peace and pursue
it. 12For the eyes of the Lord are on the upright, and His ears are open to
their prayers, but the face of the Lord is against those who do evil."
13Who is going to harm you if you are zealous for what is good? 14But
if you do suffer for doing what is right, you are blessed. "Do not be
afraid of them, and do not be troubled." 15But honor the lord Messiah as
holy in your hearts, and always be ready to give an answer to anyone
who asks you to explain the hope you have. Do it with gentleness and
respect, 16keeping a clear conscience so that people who slander your
good conduct in Messiah may be put to shame when they speak against
you. 17For it is better that you suffer for doing what is right, if it is God's
will, than for doing what is wrong. 18For Messiah also suffered for sins
once for all, the just for the unjust, to bring you to God. He was put to
death, a mortal human being;[23] however he was made alive again by
resurrection in the spirit.[24] 19In this resurrected condition he went and
made a proclamation to the spirits[25] in prison, 20who in the past were
disobedient, at the time when God waited patiently in the days of Noah
while the ark was being built. In the ark, a few, that is, eight human
persons, were saved through water. 21That is a symbol of water baptism,

---

[23]There is no trace here or elsewhere in the NT of a "dual nature" of Jesus. The Messiah, the person, was mortal and was put to death. The appalling complications of later theology, in which the "man Jesus" but not Jesus as Deity died, are unknown to Scripture. They belong to the distortion of the faith introduced from the second century, under the perverting influence of Hellenistic philosophy. For further information see Martin Werner, *The Formation of Christian Dogma*.

[24]In a new spiritual condition, as resurrected, with a spiritual body. Jesus did nothing while he was dead. It was after he was "made alive," which in other passages means resurrection from death (1 Sam. 2:6; 2 Kings 5:7; 1 Cor. 15:22), that he announced his triumph over death to fallen spirits, that is, angels who were disobedient in the days of Noah when eight human beings were rescued in the ark. Thus in his resurrected state, after being dead for three days, from Friday to Sunday, Jesus made this announcement of his triumph to the angels who had sinned in the time of Noah (Gen. 6:1-5).

[25]"Spirits," used absolutely without qualification, and referring to a collective group of personalities, invariably means demons or angels, never human beings. Humans *have* spirit, but are not collectively "spirits." Heb. 12:9, 23 speak of the "spirits" of human beings. 1 Jn. 4:1 describes the spiritual utterances of human beings; and 1 Cor. 12:10 likewise refers to the spirits of human beings.

which now saves you[26] — not the removal of dirt from the body, but the
pledge of a good conscience to God — through the resurrection of Jesus
Messiah, 22who is now at the right hand of God.[27] He has gone into
heaven, with angels and authorities and powers having been subjected to
him.

4 1So then, since Messiah suffered in his body, arm yourselves with the
same mindset, because the one who has suffered in his body has
finished with sin; 2so that you live the rest of your time in this life not
pursuing human desires, but the will of God. 3For you have already spent
enough of your past time doing what non-believers desire, in
debauchery, lusts, drunkenness, carousing, drinking binges, and
abominable idolatries. 4They are shocked that you no longer rush with
them into the same flood of evil, and they malign you. 5They will have to
give an account to Him who stands ready to judge the living and the
dead. 6For this purpose the Gospel has been preached to those who are
now dead, so that although they were judged in the flesh by human
standards, they may live to God in the spirit.

7The end of all things is approaching, so be clear-headed and self-
controlled for prayer. 8Most importantly, be earnest in your love for one
another, because love covers a multitude of sins. 9Be hospitable to one
another without grumbling. 10As each one has received a gift, use it to
serve one another, as good managers of the grace of God in its various
forms. 11Whoever speaks, speak the words of God; whoever serves, serve
with the strength which God supplies, so that in everything God may be
glorified through Jesus Messiah. To Him belong the glory and the
dominion to the ages of the ages. Amen.

12Dear friends, do not be shocked at the trial by fire which has come
on you to test you, as though some strange thing were happening to you.

---

[26]Water baptism is an essential part of NT obedience to Jesus. Jesus was baptized and baptized others (Jn. 3:26; 4:1), and the Apostles always baptized new converts. Jesus commanded water baptism till the end of the age (Mt. 28:19-20). To explain away the repeated NT command to be baptized in water as an intelligent believer, is to court disaster. Obedience to Jesus and his teachings is the fundamental condition of salvation (Jn. 3:36; 12:44ff; Heb. 5:9; 1 Tim. 6:3). Jesus rebuked the Pharisees who "rejected God's purpose for themselves" by refusing to be baptized by John (Lk. 7:30).

[27]The *adoni*, my lord, of Ps. 110:1. *Adoni* is never a reference to Deity.

13But rejoice to the extent that you share in Messiah's sufferings, so that
at the revelation of his glory[28] you may also rejoice with the greatest joy.
14If you are insulted for the name and agenda of Messiah, you are
blessed, because the spirit of glory and of God rests on you. 15Let none of
you suffer as a murderer, thief, criminal, or meddler in others' affairs.
16But if you suffer for being a Christian, do not be ashamed, but glorify
God by bearing that identity. 17For the time has arrived for judgment to
begin with the household of God, and if it starts with us, what will be the
end for those who refuse to obey God's Gospel?[29] 18"If it is with
difficulty that the upright are saved, what will become of the ungodly
and sinners?" 19So then those who suffer in accord with the will of God
should entrust themselves to the faithful Creator, as they continue to do
what is right.

5 1I urge the elders among you, as a fellow elder and a witness of the
sufferings of Messiah, and also as one who will share in the glory[30]
which will be revealed: 2Shepherd[31] God's flock among you, overseeing
not under compulsion but voluntarily under God, not for dishonest profit
but eagerly, 3and not lording it over those entrusted to your care, but
being examples to the flock. 4Then when the chief Pastor is revealed, you
will win the crown of glory[32] which will never fade away. 5Likewise, you
younger ones, be subject to the elders. And all of you clothe yourselves

---

[28]At his Second Coming, *Parousia,* to raise the faithful of all the ages and catch up the surviving believers (1 Thess. 4:13-17). This is a future visible event, a single arrival. There is no such thing as a PRE-tribulation secret rapture. Jesus will return once and his glory will be revealed in full splendor.

[29]Obedience to God's Gospel is the subject of Jesus' first and foundational command that we are to "Repent and believe the Gospel of the Kingdom," God's Gospel (Mk. 1:1, 14-15). "God's Gospel" appears 8 times in the NT: Mk. 1:14; Rom. 1:1; 15:16 (framing the book of Romans); 2 Cor. 11:7; 1 Thess. 2:2, 8, 9; 1 Pet. 4:17.

[30]Of the future Kingdom of God to be inaugurated on earth at the return (*parousia*) of Jesus.

[31]I.e. pastor the people of God. Elders, pastors, bishops and overseers are the same rank in the NT. This changed in post-biblical times.

[32]The Christian reward throughout Scripture is to co-administer the future Kingdom with Jesus. Dan. 7:14, 18, 22, 27 (RSV) lays this out and the theme is repeated often in the NT. The idea of disappearing to heaven is foreign to the Bible. "'Heaven' is never in fact used in the Bible for the destination of the dying" (Dr. J.A.T. Robinson, *In the End God,* p. 105).

with humility towards one another, because "God sets Himself against
the proud, but He gives grace to the humble."

6So humble yourselves under the mighty hand of God, that He may
exalt you when the time comes, 7casting all your cares on Him, because
He cares about you. 8Be clear-minded and alert. Your adversary, the
Devil, is prowling around like a roaring lion, searching for someone to
devour.[33] 9Resist him, firm in the faith, knowing that your brothers and
sisters throughout the world are faithfully enduring the same kinds of
sufferings. 10And after you have suffered a little while, the God of all
grace, who invited you to His glory in the Age to Come through
Messiah, will Himself perfect, confirm, strengthen, and establish you.
11To Him belongs the dominion to the ages of the ages. Amen.

12Through Silvanus, whom I consider a faithful brother, I have
written this short letter to encourage you and to testify that this is the true
grace of God. Stand firm in it. 13She who is in Babylon,[34] chosen together
with you, greets you, as does Mark, my son.[35] 14Greet one another with a
kiss of love. Peace to all of you who are in Messiah.

---

[33]The Devil here is the same as the Satan (his Hebrew title) and is of course a supernatural evil personality, who "fell into condemnation" (1 Tim. 3:6). "The Devil" is never in the Bible a synonym for the internal sinful tendency of human beings. Demons in the narrative accounts of the ministry of Jesus are supernatural evil personalities (certainly not the spirits of dead human beings!), and they are carefully distinguished from the demonized human beings whom they oppress. In Luke 4:41 the demons cry out and recognize Jesus as Messiah. These are evidently not "mental diseases" or disturbed human beings, who, as we all know, do not know that Jesus is Messiah!

[34]A reference to the church living probably in geographical Babylon.

[35]That is, spiritual son. Paul, too, considered his converts to be "begotten" by him as their teacher (1 Tim. 1:18).

2 Peter

1 1From Simon Peter, a servant and Apostle of Jesus Messiah, to those who have been given the same valuable faith as ours, through the righteousness of our God and of our Savior, Jesus Messiah: 2Grace and peace be multiplied to you in the knowledge of God and of Jesus our lord,[1] 3since His divine power has granted us all things for life and godliness, through the knowledge of Him who called us to His own glory and excellence. 4By these He has granted us His valuable and exceedingly great promises, so that through these promises you may share in the divine nature, you who have escaped from the worldly corruption which is produced by lust. 5Because of all this, be very diligent to add to your faith moral excellence; to moral excellence, add knowledge; 6to knowledge, self-control; to self-control, perseverance; to perseverance, godliness; 7to godliness, mutual affection; and to mutual affection, love. 8For if these things are yours and are continually increasing, they will ensure that you are not unproductive or unfruitful in the true knowledge of our lord Jesus Messiah. 9But the person who lacks these things is blind, near-sighted, as he has forgotten the cleansing from his former sins. 10So then, brothers and sisters, be even more diligent to make your calling and choosing firm.[2] For as long as you practice these things, you will never fall, 11and in this way there will be richly provided to you the entry into the Kingdom in the Age to Come[3] of our lord and savior, Jesus Messiah.

12So then I intend to keep on reminding you of these things, even though you know them and are well established in the truth which has come to you. 13I think it is right, as long as I am in this tent, to stimulate your minds by reminding you, 14knowing that the laying down of my tent

---

[1]"Our lord" takes us back to the all-important Ps. 110:1 (cited massively in the NT) where the Messiah is "my lord" (*adoni*). "Our lord" cannot be a reference to YHVH because "our YHVH" or "my YHVH" is impossible as language, since YHVH is a proper name. The falsehood that because Jesus is called "lord" he must be YHVH (making two Gods!) needs to be exposed. *Adoni*, "my lord," refers to non-Deity in each of its 195 occurrences.

[2]The popular doctrine of "once saved always saved" does not harmonize with Peter's understanding of conversion and salvation.

[3]The Kingdom which will begin at the future arrival of Jesus (Lk. 21:31), the period of future history called by Jesus the new birth of the world (Mt. 19:28; cp. Isa. 65:17; 66:22; 2 Pet. 3:13).

is approaching, as our lord Jesus Messiah made clear to me. 15And I will
be diligent to ensure that, any time after my departure,[4] you will always
be able to call these things to mind.[5]

16For we were not telling cleverly fabricated stories when we
informed you of the power and coming[6] of our lord Jesus Messiah;
instead we had been eyewitnesses of his majesty. 17For he received honor
and glory from God who is the Father, when the voice came to him from
the Majestic Glory with these words: "This is My beloved Son; I am
delighted with him."[7] 18We ourselves heard this voice from heaven when
we were with him on the holy mountain.[8]

19So we all have the word of prophecy strongly confirmed, and you
will do well to pay careful attention to it in your hearts, as you would to
a lamp shining in a dark place, until the Day[9] dawns and the morning star
arises.[10] 20Above all, know this: no prophecy of Scripture comes from the

---

[4]His death, which is not a departure to another world as a disembodied spirit, but to Hades, the world of all the dead, where he would sleep the sleep of death (Ps. 13:3; Ecc. 9:5, 10) until his wakening at the future resurrection (Dan. 12:2, 13; Rev. 20:4-6, first resurrection).

[5]This is a strong indication that Peter was collecting the writings which belong to the NT canon of authoritative Scripture. This was complete with the book of Revelation written later, about 96 AD. Jesus had affirmed the canon of the Hebrew Bible (quoted often from the Greek, LXX version in the NT) as "the Law, Prophets and Psalms [Writings]" (Lk. 24:44). It is false to say that the Roman Catholics settled on the canon of Scripture. The authority to do this was apostolic. Revelation naturally closes the New Covenant Scripture which was inspired in Greek, as is all the NT Scripture.

[6]The Second Coming. The word here, *Parousia,* is the technical word for the future arrival of Jesus in glory to inaugurate his Kingdom on earth. It occurs 24 times in the NT.

[7]This was a confirmation that Jesus was indeed the unique Son of God. He did not *become* Son first at his baptism, much less at his resurrection or ascension. He was procreated supernaturally as Son, and Luke 1:35 defines with precision the basis of Jesus being Son of God. Jesus was further "declared to be Son of God **with power**" at the resurrection (Rom. 1:4).

[8]The event was of course the Transfiguration recorded in Matt. 17, Mark 9 and Luke 9. Peter here clarifies that it was a vision of the Second Coming. Matthew calls it a vision (*orama*) (Mt. 17:9).

[9]Of the Second Coming, *Parousia.*

[10]I am grateful to Robert Shank for the translation of this verse (*Until*, p. 307). Cp. Eph. 3:17.

prophet's own imagination, 21because no prophecy ever came from
human will; instead men led by holy spirit spoke from God.

2 1But false prophets also arose among the people, just as there will be
false teachers among you. They will surreptitiously introduce
destructive heretical teachings, and even deny the Master who bought
them. In this way they will bring on themselves swift destruction. 2Many
will follow their indecent lifestyles, and because of these false teachers
the way of the truth will be spoken against. 3In their greed they will take
advantage of you with invented[11] words. Their judgment announced long
ago will not lie idle; their destruction will not sleep.

4For if God did not spare the angels[12] who sinned, but cast them into
Tartarus, chained up in complete darkness to be kept until the judgment;
5and if He did not spare the ancient world but protected Noah, a
proclaimer of uprightness, as the eighth with seven others, when He
brought a flood on the godless world; 6and if by reducing the cities of
Sodom and Gomorrah to ashes He condemned them to destruction,
making them an example of what is coming to the godless; 7and if He
rescued upright Lot, who was anguished over the debauched lives of the
wicked — 8for that upright man living among them was tortured in
himself day after day by their lawless activities he saw and heard —
9since these things are so, then the Lord knows how to rescue the godly
from trials, and to keep the unrighteous for punishment on the day of
judgment, 10especially those who indulge the corrupt desires of the flesh
and show contempt for authority. Brazen and arrogant, they are not
afraid to speak evil of angelic beings. 11But even angels, who are stronger
and more powerful, do not bring an accusatory judgment against them
before the Lord.

---

[11]The Greek word is *plastos*, from which we get "plastic." These are artificial and thus deceptive words. Many churchgoers are victims of a massive "group-think."

[12]It is quite mistaken to challenge all translations and common sense by trying to avoid the word "angels" here. In NT Greek *aggelos* means non-humans 98% of the time, and a very occasional exception, to mean a human messenger, is made very clear. The reference here is obviously to angels. The allusion is of course to the extraordinary wickedness described in Gen. 6, a cohabitation between evil angels and some human females, producing giants.

12But these men, like irrational animals born as creatures of instinct to
be captured and killed, slander ones they do not understand, and they
will like animals be destroyed, 13suffering harm as the wages of doing
harm. They think it is a pleasure to revel in broad daylight, and are stains
and blemishes, reveling in their deceit while they feast together with you.
14Their eyes are full of adultery and never stop sinning; they entice
unstable persons. They have trained their hearts to be greedy, these
cursed children. 15They have left the right way and have gone astray,
following the way of Balaam the son of Beor, who loved the wages of
wrongdoing. 16But he was rebuked for his own sin. A donkey, which
cannot talk, spoke with a human voice and restrained the prophet's
madness.

17These men are springs without water and mists driven along by a
storm, and the deepest darkness has been reserved for them. 18For by
speaking high-sounding nonsense they entice, by fleshly passions and
debauchery, people who are barely escaping from those who live in
error. 19They promise these people liberty, but they themselves are slaves
of depravity, for people are slaves of whatever masters them. 20For if,
after they have escaped the contamination of the world by the knowledge
of our lord and savior Jesus Messiah, they are again entangled in it and
overcome, then their last state is worse for them than their first. 21For it
would be better for them not to have known the right way than, having
known it, to turn back from the holy command delivered to them. 22This
true proverb describes them: "A dog returns to its own vomit, and a sow,
after washing, returns to rolling in the mud."

3 1Dear friends, this is now the second letter I am writing to you, and in
both of them I stimulate your sincere minds by reminding you:
2remember the words prophesied by the holy prophets as well as the lord
and savior's command through your Apostles.

3Above all, know this: in the last days blatant mockers will come,
following their own sinful lusts 4and saying, "Where is his promised
coming?[13] For ever since the patriarchs fell asleep in death, everything
continues just as it has from the beginning of the creation." 5But this is
what they willfully ignore: that the heavens existed long ago and the

---

[13]That is "Second Coming," *Parousia.*

earth was formed out of water and by water by God's word. 6And by
being flooded with water, the world at that time was destroyed. 7But by
His word the present heavens and earth are reserved for fire, kept for the
day of judgment and destruction of godless people.[14]
8But do not ignore this one thing, my dear friends: that with the Lord
one day is like a thousand years, and a thousand years are like one day.[15]
9The Lord is not slow to keep His promise, as some think of slowness,
but He is patient with you, because He does not want anyone to perish,
but for all to come to repentance.
10But the Day of the Lord will come like a thief. On that Day the
heavens will pass away[16] with a terrific noise, the heavenly bodies will
melt with intense fire, and the earth and everything done on it will be

---

[14]Peter states that the first ordering of the world for Adam (*kosmos*, the world as made for man) in Gen. 1 was replaced by a different order, "heavens and earth," at the flood. There will be a future "new [renewed] heavens and earth" at the return of Jesus (Isa. 65:17; 66:22; 51:16). "Heaven and earth" does not mean, as popularly, the whole vast universe, but rather the ordered world as seen by man, and in which man dwells, more like the concept of "society," the "theater" made for man. Gen. 1 describes the ordered world of sky and land or earth as Adam experienced it. Peter here equates "heaven and earth" with the society or "world that then was." He contrasts that past society with the society after the flood and still existing now. Peter gives us vital commentary on Gen. 1. Genesis is about the created world made for man. The birds fly in the sky (heaven) and the sun is placed in the sky (heaven). The whole system was built with water above and below. It was later deluged and changed by water (Gen. 7:11). It is wrong to make the innocent text in Gen. 1 deal with issues of the origin of the ultimate Universe in which God dwells. The sun is millions of miles away, we know, but in the simple Bible cosmogony it is in the firmament, where (literally "on the face of," Gen. 1:20) also the birds fly! In Mt. 24:34-35 this present system (*genea*) is defined as "heaven and earth," meaning the present world system, not the entire universe.

[15]Giving a basis for the idea that God allows a 7,000 year period with the millennium as the last 1000 years.

[16]This would not mean the destruction of the whole universe. The earth will be renewed and is the promised inheritance of the faithful. Peter means by "heavens and earth" not the universe but our earth and sky, atmosphere. According to Peter that pre-flood "heavens and earth" was deluged (v. 5-6). This demonstrates Peter's meaning of "heavens and earth" (exactly, too, as Gen. 1, which is usually misunderstood). The "world that then was" came to an end at the flood, through water. The present "heavens and earth," i.e. society, will be replaced by the new Creation at the return of Jesus (see Mt. 19:28; Isa. 65:17ff; 66:22). Thus for Peter, history is seen in three distinct blocks.

laid bare.[17] 11Since all these things are to be dissolved in this way, what
sort of people should you be in holy and godly living, 12as you look out
for and hasten the coming of the Day of God? That Day will cause the
burning heavens to be dissolved, and the heavenly bodies to melt with
intense fire. 13But, according to His promise, we are expectantly waiting
for new heavens and a new earth, where uprightness will live.[18]

14So then, dear friends, in view of the fact that you are expecting
these things, be diligent to be found spotless and blameless before Him,
and at peace. 15Count the patience of our lord as salvation, just as our
dear brother Paul also wrote to you, according to the wisdom given to
him. 16In all of his letters he speaks of these things. In those letters there
are some things which are difficult to understand, which the ignorant and
unstable twist to their own destruction, as they also twist the rest of the
Scriptures.[19] 17So you, my dear friends, since you have been told in
advance, beware that you are not led astray by the error of these wicked
men and fall from your own stability. 18But grow in the grace and
knowledge of our lord and savior Jesus Messiah. To him be glory both
now and in the future age-long day.[20] Amen.

---

[17]Planet earth will not be destroyed. If it were, the promise made to the faithful of all the ages could not be fulfilled. Abraham has been promised the earth as his inheritance and Jesus assured the meek that they will inherit the earth (Mt. 5:5; Ps. 37). There will occur a great depopulation of the world, with "few people left" (Isa 24:6). A mortal population surviving will provide the renewed society of the future (Heb. 2:5). The notion that there will be no human beings left on earth after Jesus' return is a complete falsehood, rendering vast amounts of prophecy of the coming Kingdom age pointless.

[18]The renewed society of the future will be characterized by international disarmament: The nations will converge on Jerusalem to learn how to live uprightly and they will beat their swords into plowshares, their tanks into tractors (see Isa. 2:1-4). Isa. 65:17-25 gives us an extended description of the renewal to begin at the Second Coming of Jesus. There will be mortals ruled over by the then immortalized saints (Rev. 2:26-27, etc). See also Isa. 19:19-25 and many passages in the prophets which describe the future Kingdom on a renewed earth.

[19]It is important to note that Paul's writings are here reckoned as Holy Scripture. Jesus had defined the limits of the OT canon in Luke 24:44: The Law, the Prophets and the Psalms (Psalms being the leading book of the third section of Hebrew Scripture, i.e. the Writings).

[20]Probably a reference to the millennium as the first stage of the future Kingdom of God. Peter had earlier spoken of a day as equal to 1000 years in God's plan. The Greek speaks of "the day which is an age," "the age-long day."

1 John

1 1What was from the beginning, what we have heard, what we have
seen with our own eyes, what we have observed and touched with our
hands, concerning the word of life — 2and the life was revealed, and we
have seen and testify and proclaim to you that life of the age to come
which was with the Father,[1] and which was revealed to us. 3What we
have seen and heard we proclaim to you too, so that you may have
fellowship with us. And our fellowship is with the Father and with His
Son Jesus Messiah. 4So we are writing these things to you so that our joy
may be complete.

5This is the message we have heard from him and announce to you:
God is light, and in Him there is no darkness at all. 6If we say that we
have fellowship with Him but keep on walking in darkness, we are lying
and not practicing the truth. 7But if we walk in the light as He is in the
light, we have fellowship with one another, and the blood of Jesus, His
Son,[2] purifies us from all sin. 8If we say that we have no sin, we are
deceiving ourselves and the truth is not in us. 9But if we confess our sins,
He is faithful and righteous, forgiving our sins and purifying us from all
unrighteousness. 10If we say that we have not sinned, we make Him a
liar, and His Gospel-word is not in us.

---

[1]This provides exactly the necessary commentary of John on his own gospel in John 1:1. It was the promise of life in the age to come, immortality and thus the immortality Plan which was "with God" (*pros ton theon* and here *pros ton patera*, "with the Father," defining God as the Father, as 1300 times in the NT). *Pros* means "with" in John 1:1, but not "with" meaning two *persons* next to each other. John in his gospel uses *meta* and *para* for one person with another. Gal. 2:5 is an example of the Gospel truth "with [*pros*] you." The meaning of *pros* there is "in your thinking," "in the mind of." In Heb. 2:17 (NJB) Jesus is a high priest "for their relationship to [*pros*] God." John 1:1 does not say that "the word" was the Son. There is no justification for writing "Word" instead of, correctly, "word." "It is a common but patent misreading of the opening of John's gospel to read it as 'In the beginning was the Son, and the Son was with God, and the Son was God'" (Colin Brown, *Ex Auditu*, Vol. 7, p. 89). All English translations before the KJV in 1611 read "all things were made by it," (Jn. 1:3) and many did not capitalize "word."

[2]The blood of Jesus, the Son, proves of course that the Son of God was mortal and thus not the One God, who alone has immortality, and thus cannot die (1 Tim. 6:16).

2 1My little children, I am writing these things to you so that you may
not sin. And if anyone sins, we have an advocate[3] with the Father —
Jesus Messiah the righteous. 2He himself is the atoning sacrifice[4] for our
sins, and not only ours, but for the whole world.[5]

3This is how we know that we have come to know Him: if we keep
His commands.[6] 4A person who says, "I have come to know Him," but

---

[3]The word in Greek is *parakletos,* and it appears only in the writings of John. In the gospel of John, four times, it denotes the operational presence and power of Jesus which he promised would be with the disciples after his ascension to the right hand of the Father. Here the *parakletos* is identified precisely with the risen Jesus. NET Bible says, "Here…it is Jesus, not the Spirit, who is described as *parakletos*. The reader should have been prepared for this interchangeability of terminology, however, by John 14:16, where Jesus told the disciples that he would ask the Father to send them 'another' paraclete (*allos*, 'another of the same kind'). This implies that *Jesus himself had been a paraclete* in his earthly ministry to the disciples. This does not answer all the questions about the meaning of the word here, though, since it is not Jesus' role now as an advocate during his earthly ministry which is in view, but his role as an advocate in heaven before the Father. The context suggests intercession in the sense of legal advocacy, as stress is placed upon the righteousness of Jesus. The concept of Jesus' intercession on behalf of believers does occur elsewhere in the NT, notably in Rom. 8:34 and Heb. 7:25. Something similar is taking place here, and is the best explanation of 1 John 2:1. An English translation like 'advocate' or 'intercessor' conveys this." There is no need to posit two different *parakletos*, nor any need to speak of a third Person in Scripture. The spirit of God and also in the NT "the spirit of Jesus" or "spirit of Christ" (Acts 16:7; Phil. 1:19; Rom. 8:9; 1 Pet. 1:11) is the operational, personal presence of God or Jesus acting in various ways. It is certainly not just an impersonal "force." In 2 Cor. 3:17, Paul says that "the lord is the spirit and wherever that spirit of the lord is, there is freedom." The holy spirit is never worshiped or prayed to in Scripture and never sends greetings. The "spirit of Elijah" (Lk. 1:17) is not a different person from Elijah, and logically neither is the spirit of God or of Jesus a distinct person.

[4]John says that the Messiah died, proving that he cannot be God, who cannot die (1 Tim. 6:16).

[5]This text makes the "limited atonement" of Calvinism false. So does 1 Tim. 2:4: "God desires that **all** men be saved." The death of Jesus is for every human person, but each must repent and obey Jesus and his Gospel of the Kingdom and saving death, including all the saving knowledge taught by Jesus (Isa. 53:11; 1 John 5:20, etc.). Lk. 8:11-12 makes believing the Gospel of the Kingdom (Mt. 13:19) a necessary condition for true repentance and forgiveness from God (see also Mk. 4:11-12).

[6]Another fine statement about the pervading NT insistence on the "obedience of faith" for salvation (Rom. 1:5; 16:26; Heb. 5:9; 1 Pet. 1:2; Jn. 12:44ff). Faith without obedience is failed faith (see Mt. 7:21ff for a solemn warning). We must choose to obey

does not keep His commands, is a liar, and the truth is not in him.[7] 5But
in whoever obeys His Gospel-word,[8] the love of God has most certainly
been perfected. This is how we know that we are in Him. 6The person
who says he remains in God should conduct himself just as Jesus did.

7Beloved, it is not a new commandment I am writing to you, but an
old commandment which you have had from the beginning. The old
commandment is the Gospel-word you have already heard. 8On the other
hand, it is a new commandment I am writing to you, which is true in him
and in you, because the darkness is passing away and the true light is
already shining. 9The person who says he is in the light but hates his
brother or sister is still in the darkness. 10The person who loves his
brother or sister lives in the light, and there is nothing in him to make
him stumble. 11But the person who hates his brother or sister[9] is in the
darkness, and walks in the darkness, and does not know where he is
going, because the darkness has blinded his eyes.

12I am writing to you, little children, because your sins have been
forgiven through the name[10] of Jesus. 13I am writing to you, fathers,
because you know Him who has been from the beginning. I am writing
to you, young people, because you have overcome the Evil One. I have

---

God and Jesus (Jn. 7:17; Rev. 22:12). We are to be rewarded for what we have done, the obedience of faith (Heb. 5:9; Jn. 3:36).

[7]This is yet another of many strong NT assertions that faith without obedience is futile and will not save. Hence the important phrase "obedience of faith" which frames Romans (1:5; 16:26). Heb. 5:9 is explicit that salvation is for those who obey Jesus. Jesus said this often in the gospels, notably John 3:36, where belief and disobedience are opposites. Note too Jesus' final cry to us all in John 12:44ff. Baptism in water, as explicit, necessary obedience, is an important command of Jesus until the end of the age (Mt. 28:19-20; Acts 10:47-48).

[8]The "word" is not vaguely the Bible as a whole, but specifically the Gospel of the Kingdom message proclaimed first by Jesus and then by all the Apostles (Heb. 2:3; Lk. 4:43; 8:11; Mk. 1:14-15, etc.).

[9]This puts an enormous strain upon international wars and civil wars in which Christians have opposed and killed other Christians. The obvious solution is that believers should remain politically neutral as "resident aliens." See for this discussion our "Towards the Cessation of Church Suicide" at our website restorationfellowship.org

[10]"Name" means everything which Jesus stands for, beginning with his Gospel of the Kingdom, which is the primary content of the saving Gospel, as well as his death and resurrection, and the object of belief commanded by Jesus' first order to us in Mark 1:14-15: "Repent and believe the Gospel of the Kingdom."

written to you, children, because you know the Father. 14I have written to
you, fathers, because you know Him who has been from the beginning. I
have written to you, young people, because you are strong, and the
Gospel-word of God[11] lives in you, and you have overcome the Evil One.
15Do not love the world or the things in the world. If anyone loves the
world, the love of the Father is not in him, 16because all that is in the
world — the lust of the flesh, the lust of the eyes, and the pride in
material possessions — is not from the Father but from the world. 17And
the world is passing away with its lusts, but the person who does the will
of God will live in the age to come.
18Children, it is a last hour. Just as you heard that the Antichrist[12] is
coming, even now many antichrists have arisen. That is how we know
that it is a last hour. 19They went out from us, but they did not belong to
us, because if they had belonged to us they would have continued with
us. By their leaving it was shown that none of them really belonged to
us. 20But you have an anointing from the Holy One, and you all have
knowledge. 21I have not written to you because you do not know the
truth, but because you do know it, and no lie is of the truth. 22Who is the
liar but the person who denies that Jesus is the Messiah?[13] This one is the

---

[11]The Gospel as Jesus preached it.

[12]Antichrist here is the title of a single individual, parallel to the Abomination of Desolation "standing where **he** ought not to" (Mk. 13:14), the final King of the North of Dan. 11 who comes to "his end" (Dan. 9:26; 11:45) in the holy land. This would be the Man of Sin of 2 Thess. 2, the final individual Beast of Revelation, and the Assyrian of Isa. 10 and Mic. 5:6. John does not deny that the single Antichrist will appear but adds that the spirit of antichrist manifested in many antichrists is already at work to deceive and seduce believers into error. The fundamental deceit lies in denying that Jesus was a fully historical and fully human person, a man. "Someone might assume that 'many antichrists' implies there is no personal, individual Antichrist. But this was not John's thought…He looks at the plurality of antichrists — those who deny that Jesus is the Messiah and put themselves unequivocally against Christ — as proof of the emergence of one supreme foe of Christ" (A. Berkeley Mickelsen, *Interpreting the Bible*, p. 373).

[13]This is the quintessential litmus test for true belief throughout the NT. The true confession is not "Jesus is God," but "Jesus is the Messiah" = the Son of God (Lk. 1:35). On that confession Jesus promised to build his one Church (Mt. 16:16). It is possible to mouth the words "Jesus is the Messiah," but by misunderstanding the meaning of Messiah, one can in fact deny the Messiahship of Jesus. In "theology" some give with one hand and inconsistently take away with the other. This results in confusing, contradictory and false definitions of "Christ" and "Son of God," and false definitions of God (contrary to Mk. 12:29; Ps. 110:1; Jn. 17:3).

antichrist[14] — the person who denies the Father and the Son. 23Whoever
denies the Son[15] does not have the Father; whoever confesses the Son has
the Father also.[16] 24As for you, let that remain in you which you heard
from the beginning. If what you heard from the beginning remains in
you, you will remain in the Son and in the Father. 25This is the promise
which he himself promised us: the life of the age to come.

26I have written these things to you about those who are trying to
deceive you. 27As for you, the anointing which you received from him
lives in you, and you do not need anyone to teach you. But as his
anointing teaches you about all things, it is true and is no lie. Just as it
has taught you, you live in him.

28Now, little children, remain in him, so that when he appears[17] we
may have confidence and not be ashamed before him at his coming. 29If
you know that he is righteous, you also know that everyone who does
what is right has been fathered by him.[18]

3 1See what love the Father has given to us, so that we may be called
children of God[19] — and that is what we are. That is why the world

---

[14]The Antichrist is both a future final evil individual, the Abomination of Desolation who, Jesus said, would stand in a holy place (Mt. 24:15) or "standing where *he* ought not" (Mk. 13:14; the Greek masculine participle tells us that this is an individual person), and one of his many forerunners. These latter deceivers hold a false view of the person of Christ though their existence by no means denies the reality of the one supreme manifestation who is yet to come.

[15]I.e. denies the Son to be the Messiah, as just stated.

[16]Obviously a right understanding of the Father as the only God (Jn. 17:3) and of the Son as the Messiah go together. An error in regard to the identity of the one leads to a wrong understanding of the other. Luke 1:35 defines the Son of God precisely and Mark 12:29 defines the One God, Father as also 1 Cor. 8:4-6. Jesus is the lord Messiah (Lk. 2:11; Ps. 110:1), not the Lord GOD, which would lead to two GODS and polytheism. The simple distinction between two lords in Ps. 110:1 is constantly overlooked.

[17]At his future single Second Coming. There is no PRE-tribulation rapture/resurrection in the Bible.

[18]That is, born again following the instructions of Jesus in John 3. Rebirth is by the seed message of the Kingdom Gospel, as in the parable of the sower which gives us Jesus' theology of salvation (Mt. 13:19; Lk. 8:11-12; Mk. 4:11-12).

[19]Not by adoption but by rebirth as sons and daughters which brings about a "genetic" relationship with the Father who "fathered us," gave us new existence through the seed which is the Gospel of the Kingdom (Mt. 13:19; Lk. 8:11).

does not recognize us, because they did not recognize him. 2Beloved, we
are children of God now,[20] and what we will be has not yet been
revealed. We do know that when he is revealed[21] we will be like him,
because we will see him just as he is. 3Everyone who has that hope in
him purifies himself, just as he is pure.

4Everyone who practices sin also practices lawlessness; sin is
lawlessness. 5You know that he was revealed to take away sins; there is
no sin in him. 6Whoever lives in him does not continue sinning; whoever
continues in sin has not understood[22] him or known him. 7Little children,
do not let anyone deceive you. The one who does what is right is
righteous, just as he is righteous. 8The one who practices sin is of the
Devil, as the Devil has been sinning from the beginning. For this purpose
the Son of God was revealed: to destroy the Devil's works. 9Everyone
who has been fathered by God does not continue in sin, because His
seed[23] remains in him, and so he cannot continue in sin because he has
been fathered by God. 10By this the children of God and the children of
the Devil are clearly revealed: everyone who does not do what is right is
not of God, nor those who do not love their brothers and sisters.

11This is the message you have heard from the beginning: we should
love one another, 12unlike Cain, who was of the Evil One, and murdered
his brother. And why did he murder him? Because he did what is evil,
and his brother did what is right.

13So do not be surprised, brothers and sisters, if the world hates you.
14We know that we have passed over from death to life because we love
the brothers and sisters. The one who does not love remains in death.

---

[20]Certainly not just in the fetal stage, but born from God: "Having been born again…desire the milk of the word" (1 Pet. 1:23; 2:2). James says, "He brought us forth" (James 1:18).

[21]At Jesus' Second Coming, *Parousia*.

[22]Literally "has not seen him." The sense is "seeing with the mind," not literally.

[23]A fundamentally important reference to the Gospel of the Kingdom as the essential seed causing rebirth. Luke 8:11 (cp. Mt. 13:19) reports Jesus as giving that definition of seed. Peter speaks of the Gospel as seed in 1 Peter 2:23-25 and relates it as did Jesus to rebirth. Christians become part of a family destined for immortality, for which the spirit now is the downpayment guarantee of future glory and immortality.

15Whoever hates his brother or sister is a murderer,[24] and you know that
no murderer has the life of the Age to Come in him. 16By this we came to
know love: he laid down his life for us, and so we ought to lay down our
lives for the brothers and sisters. 17But whoever has the world's material
possessions and sees his brother or sister in need, and shuts off any
compassion for him, how can God's love live in such a person? 18Little
children, let us not love with words only, but in action and truth. 19By this
we will know that we are of the truth, and we persuade our conscience
before Him, 20that if our conscience condemns us, God is greater than our
conscience and knows all things. 21Beloved, if our conscience does not
condemn us, we have boldness before God, 22and whatever we ask we
receive from Him, because we keep His commands and do the things
that are pleasing in His sight.

23This is His command: that we believe in the name[25] of His Son
Jesus Messiah, and love one another, just as he gave us the
commandment. 24The person who keeps His commands lives in Him, and
He in him. By this we know that He lives in us: by the spirit He has
given us.

4 1Beloved, do not believe every spirit, but test the spirits to see if they
are from God, because many false prophets have gone out into the
world. 2By this you know the spirit of God: every spirit which confesses
Jesus Messiah as having come[26] as a fully human being[27] is from God,

---

[24]The brutal, unrepented murder of the unitarian scholar Michael Servetus in 1553 by religious reformer John Calvin ought to give pause to all who align themselves with Calvin.

[25]The "name" of the Son of God stands for his whole character, teaching and Gospel agenda.

[26]This does not mean arriving from a previous life somewhere else! It means making his appearance from birth from his mother, in the case of Jesus uniquely by virginal begetting (Lk. 1:35; Mt. 1:18, 20: "begotten in her"; cp. 2 Sam. 7:14; Ps. 2:7; Isa. 9:6: the "child will be begotten [by God]").

[27]Dr. Geoffrey Lampe at Cambridge rightly charged "orthodoxy" with the failure to embrace a fully human Jesus. He complained that a preexisting Jesus could not be a genuine human person: "The Christological concept of the pre-existent divine Son...reduces the real, socially and culturally conditioned personality of Jesus to the metaphysical abstraction 'human nature.' It is this universal humanity which the Son assumed and made his own...According to this Christology, 'the eternal Son' [according to orthodoxy] assumes a timeless human nature, or makes it timeless by

3while every spirit which does not confess that Jesus, the one so
identified, is not from God. It is the spirit of the Antichrist, which you
have heard is coming, and now that spirit is in the world already. 4You
are from God, little children, and you have overcome them, because the
One who is in you is greater than the one who is in the world. 5They are
from the world, so they speak as from the world, and the world listens to
them. 6We are from God; the person who knows God listens to us, while
the person who is not from God does not listen to us. This is how we
recognize the spirit of the truth[28] and the spirit of falsehood.

7Beloved, let us love one another, because love is from God.
Everyone who loves has been fathered by God and knows God. 8The
person who does not love does not know God, because God is love. 9By
this the love of God was revealed in us: God has sent His unique Son
into the world[29] so that we may live through him. 10In this is love: not that
we have loved God, but that He loved us and sent His Son as the atoning
sacrifice[30] for our sins. 11Beloved, since God loved us in this way, then
we ought to love one another. 12No one has seen God at any time. If we
love one another God lives in us, and His love is perfected in us. 13By
this we know that we live in Him and He in us: He has given us a portion
of His spirit. 14And we have seen and testify that the Father has sent the
Son to be the Savior of the world.

15Whoever confesses that Jesus is the Son of God,[31] God lives in him,
and he in God. 16And we have come to know and have believed the love

---

making it his own; it is a human nature which owes nothing essential to geographical circumstances; it corresponds to nothing in the actual concrete world; Jesus Christ has not, after all, really 'come in the flesh'" (*God as Spirit*, p. 144). Dr. Lampe wrote also of the dangerous threat to monotheism once Jesus was declared to *be* God. This would make two Gods. Luther mistranslated this verse and thus altered John's meaning by rendering, "into the flesh." This has been corrected in all modern German versions.

[28]John's favorite definition of the holy spirit is "the spirit of the truth." Spirit must be defined and it is always linked with the truth. Hence Paul spoke about the need for "a passion for truth in order to be saved" (2 Thess. 2:10). John said the spirit is the truth (5:6; cp. Jn. 6:63).

[29]To be sent into the world is nothing to do with arriving from another realm literally. John the Baptist was "sent from God" (Jn. 1:6) but he did not "preexist." Jesus sent us the disciples in the same sense as God sent him! (Jn. 17:18).

[30]Since the Son died, he cannot by definition *be* God, who cannot die.

[31]Assuming that "Son of God" is understood in its original biblical, Messianic sense, not the unbiblical "God the Son."

which God has in us. God is love, and the person who lives in love lives
in God, and God lives in him. 17By this, love is perfected with us, so that
we may have confidence on the day of judgment, because as Jesus is, so
are we in this world. 18There is no fear in love, but perfect love casts out
fear, because fear has to do with punishment. The person who fears has
not been perfected in love. 19We love, because He first loved us. 20If
anyone says, "I love God," but hates his brother or sister, he is a liar. If
he does not love his brother or sister whom he has seen, how can he love
God whom he has not seen? 21And this command we have from Him: the
person who loves God should also love his brother and sister.

5 1Whoever believes that Jesus is the Messiah has been fathered by
God, and whoever loves the Father loves the Son He fathered,
brought into existence.[32] 2By this we know that we love the children of
God: when we love God and obey His commands. 3Loving God means
obeying His commands. And His commands are not a burden, 4because
everyone who has been fathered by God overcomes the world. This is
the power that has overcome the world — our faith.

5Who is the person who overcomes the world? It is the one who
believes that Jesus is the Son of God.[33] 6He is the one who came by water
and blood, Jesus the Messiah, not by the water only, but by the water and
blood. It is the spirit which testifies, because the spirit is the truth. 7For
there are three that testify: 8the spirit, the water, and the blood, and these
three agree.[34] 9If we accept the witness of people, the witness of God is
greater, because this is God's testimony which He has testified about His
Son. 10The one who believes in the Son of God has the testimony in
himself; the one who does not believe God has made Him a liar, because

---

[32]Literally, the Father is "the begetter," the one who brought His Son into existence (5:18; Lk. 1:35; Mt. 1:18). The Son explicitly had an origin in time. He began to exist.

[33]The Son of God was begotten, brought into existence, not an "eternally generated" Son, which has no recognizable meaning. Trinitarian Dr. McCleod admits: "It is far from clear what content, if any, we can impart to the concept [of eternal generation]. It is revealed but it is revealed as a mystery…The writings of the fathers abound with protestations of inevitable ignorance on the matter" (*The Person of Christ*, p. 131).

[34]The Greek manuscripts were corrupted much later by a false insertion about Father, word and spirit in 1 John 5:7. This has been properly rejected as a forgery by every modern translation, though it appeared in the King James Version of 1611. It is now universally regarded as false.

he has not believed the testimony that God has given about His Son.
11And the testimony is this: God has given us the life of the age to come,
and that life is in His Son. 12The one who has the Son has that life; the
one who does not have the Son of God does not have that life.

13I have written these things to you who believe in the name[35] of the
Son of God, so that you may know that you have the life of the age to
come. 14And this is the confidence we have before Him: that whenever
we ask anything according to His will, He listens to us. 15And if we know
that He listens to whatever we ask, we know that we have the requests
which we have asked of Him.

16If anyone sees his brother or sister committing a sin not resulting in
death, he is to ask, and God will give life to the person who commits a
sin not resulting in death. There is a sin resulting in death. I am not
saying that he should make a request for that. 17All unrighteousness is
sin, but there is sin not resulting in death.

18We know that those fathered by God do not continue in sin. Rather,
the Son of God, the one fathered and brought into existence,[36] protects
them and the Evil One does not touch them. 19We know that we are from
God and belong to God, and the whole world lies in the power of the
Evil One.[37] 20And we know that the Son of God has come and has given
us the intellectual understanding[38] to know Him who is true. We are in
Him who is true, in His Son Jesus Messiah. This One is the true God and

---

[35]That is, the agenda and teaching of Jesus, all he is and all he stands for.

[36]The one begotten (by God). *Gennetheis* points to a moment in time when the Son came into existence. This is denied in Trinitarian theology which speaks of God the Son, coequal and coeternal with the Father. Cp. Isa. 9:6 which speaks of the predicted Son to be begotten, with the same verb in the aorist tense, pointing to a moment in time. There is no “eternally generated Son” in the Bible.

[37]Satan is the god of this age (2 Cor. 4:4) and is said to be currently deceiving the whole world (Rev. 12:9). That massive power to deceive on a grand scale will last until the Devil is removed and imprisoned at the start of the future millennium, when he will be able to deceive no longer (Rev. 20:3). One cannot be deceiving the whole world and not deceiving it any longer, at the same time! This fact proves that amillennialism is false to the NT text, especially Rev. 20:1-6. Saints are not now ruling the world (1 Cor. 4:8).

[38]*Dianoia* describes the power of intellect. Cp. Isa. 53:11 where Jesus makes us right through his knowledge (cp. Dan. 12:3).

is[39] the life of the age to come.[40] 21Little children, guard yourselves against idols.

---

[39]That is, this true belief in the one true God leads to the Life of the Age to Come in the Kingdom (cp. Dan. 12:2).

[40]This is an exact repetition of the words of Jesus in John 17:3. "This is the true GOD" is a reference here, as in John 17:3, to the Father who is "the only one who is true God." The word "this" in John must sometimes be understood in context and not by the immediately preceding subject. See for example 1 John 2:22 and 2 John 7, where if we take the closest antecedent, Christ would be antichrist! It is logical nonsense to say that "the only true GOD" is the Father alone (Jn. 17:3), and then to say that Jesus is also that "only true God." "Only" excludes all others from being "the only true God"! The One God is so named, i.e. as the Father, 1300 times in NT Scripture and the Bible uses singular personal pronouns for Him thousands of times. This is the basis of the most important command of all (Mk. 12:29 = Deut. 6:4). John 17:3 is an unequivocal unitarian proposition which Augustine could avoid only by forging the text, altering the order of the words and changing the sense: "The proper order of the words is, 'That they may know You and Jesus Christ, whom you have sent, as the only true God" (*Tractates on the Gospel of John*, 105).

2 John

1From the elder to the chosen lady and her children, whom I love in
the truth, and not only I, but all those who know the truth, 2because of the
truth that lives in us and will be with us forever. 3Grace, mercy and peace
will be with us from God who is the Father and from Jesus Messiah, the
Son of the Father, in truth and love.

4I was delighted because I have found some of your children living in
the truth, just as were were commanded by the Father. 5Now, dear lady, I
ask you, not as if I am writing a new command to you, but one we have
had from the beginning: that we love one another. 6And this is love: that
we live in obedience to His commands.[1] This is the command, just as
you have heard from the beginning, that you should be following.

7For many deceivers have gone out into the world, who do not
confess Jesus Messiah as coming as a fully human being. This is a
deceiver and an antichrist. 8Watch out, so that you do not lose what we
have worked for, but will receive a full reward. 9Everyone who in the
name of "progress" does not remain in the teaching of the Messiah, does
not have God. The person who remains in his teaching has both the
Father and the Son. 10If anyone comes to you and does not bring that
teaching, do not welcome him into your house or greet him as a fellow
believer, 11because the one who does shares in his wicked work.

12I have many more things to write to you, but I do not want to do this
with paper and ink. I hope to come and talk to you face to face, so that
our joy may be complete.

13The children of your chosen sister greet you.

---

[1]The ideal of a son in the first-century Jewish environment is that the son loves and obeys his father, that he learns the father's trade or business, and thirdly that he reflects and represents his father perfectly. Jesus did all this superbly well, without sinning.

3 John

1From the elder to the beloved Gaius, whom I love in the truth: 2Dear
friend, I pray that everything may go well with you and that you may be
as physically healthy as you are spiritually healthy. 3For I was delighted
when the brothers arrived and testified about your commitment to the
truth, how you continue to live in the truth. 4I have no greater joy than to
hear that my children are living in the truth.

5Dear friend, you show faithfulness in your service to the brothers,
though they are strangers. 6They have spoken to the church about your
love. You will do well to help them on their trip in a way worthy of God,
7because they are traveling for His name,[1] and they accepted nothing
from unbelievers. 8So we ought to support such people so that we
become co-workers together for the truth.

9I wrote to the church, but Diotrephes, who loves to be in first place,
would not accept what we say. 10If I come, I will call attention to what he
is doing — falsely accusing us with wicked words. As if that is not
enough, he not only does not welcome the brothers himself, but he
prevents those who want to welcome them and throws them out of the
church.

11Dear friend, do not imitate what is evil, but imitate what is good.
The person who does what is good is of God; the person who does what
is evil has not seen God.[2] 12Demetrius has a good report from everyone,
and from the truth itself. We also testify to him, and you know that our
testimony is true.

13I had many things to write to you, but I am unwilling to do it with
pen and ink. 14I hope to see you shortly, and we will speak face to face.

15Peace be with you. The friends here greet you. Greet the friends
there by name.

---

[1]"Name" means everything God stands for, his Gospel, his character and teaching.

[2]"Not seen God" means here that they have not understood God, a mental "seeing."

Jude

1From Jude, a servant of Jesus Messiah, and brother of James,[1] to
those who are called, dear to God who is the Father, and preserved by
Jesus Messiah. 2May mercy, peace, and love be multiplied to you.

3Beloved, while I was very eager to write to you about our shared
salvation, I am now compelled to write to you, urging you to struggle[2]
earnestly in defense of the faith[3] handed down once for all time to the
saints.[4] 4For certain men have sneaked in among you, who were written
about long ago for this condemnation, godless people who twist the
grace of our God into debauchery and who deny the only Master and our
lord Jesus Messiah.

5I want to remind you, though you have already been fully informed,
that the Lord, after saving the people out of the land of Egypt, later
destroyed those who did not believe. 6And angels who did not keep their
positions of authority but deserted their own place, He has kept in
everlasting chains under complete darkness until the judgment of the
great day. 7Likewise Sodom and Gomorrah and the surrounding towns,
in the same way as these angels,[5] gave themselves over to extreme sexual

---

[1]James and Jude were half-brothers of Jesus, children born of Mary and Joseph. The ideas that Mary was a perpetual virgin and that she was sinless (the doctrine of her "immaculate conception") are utterly false to the Bible. So is the idea that Mary is now alive in heaven. The dead are in fact all dead awaiting the future resurrection at the return of Jesus (1 Cor. 15:23; Heb. 11:13, 39; Ecc. 9:5, 10; Dan. 12:2). Mary is presented by those systems of theology which say she is now alive, as a goddess and mediator. This is a very pagan concept and ought not to be believed by Christians.

[2]Cp. "Strive to enter through the narrow door" (Lk. 13:24).

[3]"The faith" refers to the doctrinal content embraced by all true believers. "Doctrine" is equivalent to all forms of teaching.

[4]If there is no such thing as original Christianity preserved in the apostolic canon of the NT, this command is pointless, and it would be impossible to define original Christianity at all. The NT canon is required if there is to be "the faith." Jesus cited the law, prophets and psalms (writings) as the limit of the OT Scripture (Lk. 24:44), and it makes perfect sense that God gives a canon for His final revelation in Jesus. The book of Revelation, as a prophecy from Jesus, closes the canon, and ends with severe warnings about adding to or taking away from the sacred writing. Paul's writings are expressly called "Scripture" (2 Pet. 3:16). Luke 10:7 is called Scripture in 1 Tim. 5:18.

[5]The reference is to the awful event of angelic-human cohabitation in Gen. 6:1ff. The sons of God (*bnay elohim*) are angels, as 2 Pet. 2:4 also says. The Hebrew *bnay elohim*, sons of God, always means angels (Job 1:6; 2:1; 38:7; Ps. 29:1; 89:6). In Dan. 3:25, 28

immorality and went after different flesh, and are shown as an example
in suffering the punishment of the fire of the Age to Come.[6]

8Similarly, these men in their dreaming defile the flesh, reject
authority, and slander angelic beings. 9But the archangel Michael, when
he argued with the Devil in a dispute over Moses' body, did not dare to
bring against him an accusatory judgment, but said, "The Lord rebuke
you!"[7] 10But these men speak evil of what they do not understand; and
the things they know by instinct, as irrational animals do, bring about
their ruin. 11Alas for them! They have followed the way of Cain. For gain
they have run headlong into Balaam's error. So they will perish as in the
rebellion of Korah. 12These men are like treacherous rocky reefs at your
love feasts when they feast with you fearlessly, caring for and feeding
only themselves. They are clouds without rain carried along by winds;
trees at harvest time without fruit — twice dead, uprooted. 13They are
wild waves of the sea, throwing out their own shame like foam;
wandering stars, for whom the deepest darkness has been reserved
forever.

14It was against these men that Enoch, the seventh in descent from
Adam, prophesied: "Look! The Lord is coming with tens of thousands of
His holy angels, 15to execute judgment against all, and to convict every
person of all their godless actions which they have done in a godless
way, and of all the harsh words that godless sinners have spoken against
Him." 16These people are grumblers and fault-finders, following their
own sinful desires. They make arrogant speeches, impressing people for
their own advantage.

"a son of the gods" is an angel (cp. Heb. 1:10 with Ps. 97:7). "Spirits," unqualified, as a class of personalities, always refers only to angels (Heb. 1:14) or demons (1 Pet. 3:19), not to humans.

[6]This is a highly instructive verse in regard to the nature of future punishment, which is not unending torture as taught by some systems. The fire which destroyed Sodom and Gomorrah is not still burning! Nevertheless it was "eternal fire." "Eternal" here as elsewhere means "to do with the Age to Come" (*aionios,* as in "eternal" life = the life of the Age to Come based on Dan. 12:2). The nature of that fire is elsewhere defined as destructive and consuming (cp. Ps. 37:20; Oba. 16; Mal. 4:3). Its effects are irreversible and the fire is inextinguishable in the sense that nothing will prevent it bringing about its totally consuming effects.

[7]The story of the Devil and Moses is found in the extra-biblical book Assumption of Moses. Cp. Zech. 3:2 where Joshua rebukes *the* Satan, the supernatural evil angel.

17But you, beloved, remember the prophecies spoken by the Apostles
of our lord[8] Jesus Messiah. 18They said to you, "In the last days there will
be mockers, following their own godless desires." 19These people cause
divisions and are worldly minded, without the spirit. 20But you, beloved,
by building yourselves up in your most holy faith and praying in holy
spirit, 21keep yourselves in the love of God, expectantly awaiting the
mercy of our lord Jesus Messiah that brings the life of the age to come.
22Have mercy on those who are doubting; 23save others by snatching them
out of the fire; and on others have mercy, but with fear,[9] hating even the
clothing contaminated by the flesh.

24Now to Him who is able to keep you from falling, and to make you
stand, with great joy, blameless in the presence of His glory, 25to the only
one who is God[10] our Savior, through Jesus Messiah our lord, be glory,
majesty, dominion and authority, before every age, now, and for all the
ages to come. Amen.

---

[8]The phrase "my lord" and "our lord" cannot refer to the Lord GOD, Yahweh, since "my YHVH" and "our YHVH" are impossible phrases in Hebrew and never appear.

[9]Being cautious not to be "infected" by the sins of others.

[10]Exactly the same words as used by Jesus when he described the Father as "the only one [*monos*] who is true God [*theos*]" in John 17:3; 5:44. This is a unitary (non-Trinitarian) monotheistic proposition and creed closely associated with the life of the Age to Come, immortality in the future Kingdom when Jesus returns to rule on a renewed earth (Rev. 5:10; Isa. 65:17ff, etc). The Bible is committed throughout to the strict monotheism described thousands of times by singular personal pronouns (14 forms) for the One God.

Revelation

1 1This is the revelation from Jesus Messiah.[1] God[2] gave it to him to show to his servants the things which must happen soon.[3] He made it clear by sending his angel to his servant John, 2who then testified about everything he saw concerning the word of God,[4] the testimony which came from Jesus Messiah. 3Blessed is the one who reads the words of this prophecy, and blessed are those who hear and obey what is written, because the time is near.

4From John to the seven churches in the province of Asia:[5] Grace and peace to you from Him who is, who was, and who is to come,[6] and from the seven spirits before His throne, 5and from Jesus Messiah, the faithful

---

[1]The Revelation is both from him and about him, i.e. everything Jesus taught as Gospel-testimony — the Gospel of the Kingdom, God's Gospel (Mk. 1:14-15).

[2]As on 1300 occasions the word "God," often "the God," means the Father of Jesus. On no occasion does "God" in the Bible mean a triune GOD, a concept entirely foreign to the Jewish heritage and environment of Jesus (see for his creed Mk. 12:29, citing and affirming the unitarian creed of Deut. 6:4). None of the thousands of the words for "God" in Scripture ever means a triune God.

[3]The Book of Revelation is the teaching of Jesus (1 Tim. 6:3) and thus vitally important for all believers claiming to follow Jesus. The book is largely a mosaic of prophecies, allusions or quotations from the Hebrew Bible. It also unpacks in greater detail the end-time teaching of Jesus in Matt. 24, Mark 13 and Luke 21. The final "week" (especially its second half) of Dan. 9:24-27 is expounded in detail, and this final period of 7 years just before the arrival of Jesus is of vital importance to believers. Some 2000 years ago Paul was insistent that his converts understand the detail of the final times of this age, and the rule of antichrist, the Man of Sin, standing in the Temple (2 Thess. 2:4). There are over 400 allusions to the OT prophets and 88 allusions to Daniel, which is the necessary basis for understanding Revelation. So Jesus emphasizes the need to understand Daniel ("let the reader understand," Matt. 24:15).

[4]"Word of God" is not just a synonym for the Bible (the Bible calls itself "Scripture"). In the NT "the word" or "the word of God" is the "in-house" "code-word" for the saving Gospel of the Kingdom as first preached by Jesus (Heb. 2:3; Mk. 1:14-15) and constantly preached by the NT community under its apostolic leadership. The Gospel begins with the Gospel as Jesus preached it (see Mk. 1:1; Lk. 4:43; 5:1; Acts 8:3, 4, 12 and many other examples of "word" = Gospel, especially Mt. 13:19; Lk. 8:11-12).

[5]What we know as Asia Minor or Turkey today.

[6]This is the equivalent in Greek of the name of God, Yahweh, based on the verb "to be" in Ex. 3:14. Note that Jesus is never the Almighty, *Pantokrator*, *El Shaddai*. The Almighty is invariably the Father.

witness, the firstborn from among the dead,[7] and the ruler over the kings
of the earth. To him who loves us and freed us from our sins by his
blood, 6and has assigned us a Kingdom, as priests to his God and Father[8]
— to him be the glory and the power to the ages of the ages. Amen.
7Look! He is coming with the clouds, and every eye will see him,[9] even
those who pierced him. All the tribes of the earth will mourn because of
him. This will certainly happen. Amen.

8"I am the Alpha and the Omega," says the Lord God,[10] "who is, who
was, and who is to come, the Almighty."

9I, John, your brother and partner with you in the persecution,
Kingdom and perseverance which are in Jesus, was on the island called
Patmos because of the word of God[11] and the testimony of Jesus. 10On the
Lord's day[12] I was in the spirit, when I heard behind me a loud voice like
a trumpet, 11which said, "Write down what you see on a scroll, and send
it to the seven churches: Ephesus, Smyrna, Pergamum, Thyatira, Sardis,
Philadelphia, and Laodicea."

---

[7]The mention of death shows that the person indicated cannot be God! God is immortal (1 Tim. 6:16); the Messiah Jesus, Son of God, died (Rom. 5:10). An immortal person cannot die!

[8]God is called the God *of* Jesus often in the NT. As we have mentioned many times, the word "God" never means a triune God in Old or New Testaments. The idea of a God in three Persons is absolutely alien to the Bible and is a much later and gradual development, representing a departure from Scripture. This is known well to many scholars, exegetes and historians.

[9]The idea of an *invisible* Second Coming is quite false to the New Testament. 1914 (or any other proposed date, now past) certainly did not mark the inauguration of the Kingdom of God, nor the coming of Jesus. Jesus will return after the future Great Tribulation (Mt. 24:29-30) and it will be a single, visible event with momentous effects for the future of the world. Satan will then be bound so that he can no longer deceive the nations (Rev. 20:2-3).

[10]This is of course a reference to the Father, not Jesus who is mentioned separately in v. 5. Jesus is nowhere called "the Lord God," and never called the Almighty, *pantokrator* in Greek or *El Shaddai* in Hebrew.

[11]The one saving Gospel of the Kingdom of God, preached first by Jesus (Heb. 2:3).

[12]Not the ordinary expression "day of the Lord," the future coming of Jesus, but the technical term "dominical day," probably a reference to Sunday as the day marking the new creation. "Dominical day" may nevertheless also refer to the future day of God's intervention at the Parousia of Jesus.

12I turned to see who was speaking to me, and I saw seven golden
lampstands, 13and among these lampstands was one like a Son of Man.[13]
He was wearing a robe that reached down to his feet, with a golden sash
across his chest. 14His head and hair were white like wool, as white as
snow, and his eyes were like a flame of fire. 15His feet were like polished
bronze refined in a furnace, and his voice was like the roar of many
waters. 16He had seven stars in his right hand, and a sharp double-edged
sword was coming out of his mouth. His face was shining like the sun at
full strength.[14]

17When I saw him I fell at his feet as though dead. He placed his right
hand on me and said, "Do not be afraid. I am the first and the last,[15] 18the
one who lives. I was dead, but look — now I am alive to the ages of the
ages. I have the keys of death and 'gravedom.'[16] 19So write what you saw,
what is and what will take place after this.[17] 20The revealed secret of the
seven stars which you saw in my right hand and the seven golden
lampstands is this: the seven stars are the angels of the seven churches,
and the seven lampstands are the seven churches."

2 1"To the angel of the church in Ephesus, write this: The one who
firmly holds the seven stars in his right hand, the one who walks
among the seven golden lampstands, says: 2I recognize your works, your
labor and perseverance, and that you cannot tolerate evil. You have

---

[13]The Son of Man is the figure revealed in Dan. 7 and this was Jesus' favorite self-designation. It means "human being" and reminds us of 1 Tim. 2:5, the creedal statement which shows that there is one God, the Father ,and one man Messiah as our mediator. This is exactly the truth given us by the prophetic utterance of Ps. 110:1 where Yahweh speaks to "my lord" not "my Lord." *Adoni*, my lord, is the title of non-Deity (all 195 times), in this case the perfect title for the supremely exalted human, Messianic figure, Jesus.

[14]Reminding us of the appearance of the future resurrection glory of the saints, as described by Jesus in Matt. 13:43, quoting Dan. 12:3.

[15]Jesus is the first and last in the category specified by the context. He is certainly not GOD, which would make two GODs! He is the first and last who died. God cannot die (1 Tim. 6:16). So Jesus cannot be GOD. He is the first and last, beginning and end of the saving process, and he is the agent of the One God, his Father. Jesus defined the Father as "the only one who is true GOD" (Jn. 17:3).

[16]Hades, the world of all the dead who are currently asleep, non-conscious, until a future resurrection (Ecc. 9:5, 10).

[17]An allusion to Dan. 2:45.

tested those who call themselves Apostles but are not, and have found
that they are false. 3I know that you have persevered and endured for the
sake of my name,[18] and have not grown weary. 4But I have this against
you: you have left your first love. 5Therefore remember the state you
have fallen from, and repent and do the works you did at first. Otherwise
I will come to you and remove your lampstand from its place — if you
do not repent. 6But you have this in your favor: you hate the practices of
the Nicolaitans, which I also hate. 7Let everyone who has ears listen to
what the spirit says to the churches. To the one who overcomes, I will
grant the privilege of eating from the tree of life, which is in the Paradise
of God.[19]

8"To the angel of the church in Smyrna, write this: The first and last,
the one who was dead but came to life, says: 9I recognize your suffering
and poverty (but you are rich). I also know the slander by those who say
they are Jews and are not, but are a synagogue of Satan. 10Do not be
afraid of what you are about to suffer. The Devil is about to throw some
of you into prison, so that you may be tested, and you will have trouble
for ten days. Prove yourself faithful until death, and I will give you the
crown of life. 11Let everyone who has ears listen to what the spirit says to
the churches. The one who overcomes will not be harmed by the second
death.

12"To the angel of the church in Pergamum, write this: The one who
has the sharp double-edged sword says: 13I know where you live, where
Satan's throne is. Yet you hold firmly to my name; my faith[20] you did not
renounce, even in the days of Antipas, my faithful witness, who was
killed among you, where Satan lives. 14But I have a few things against
you, because you have there some who hold the teaching of Balaam, who
taught Balak to throw a stumbling block before the children of Israel, to
eat food sacrificed to idols and to commit sexual immorality. 15In the
same way you also have some holding to the teaching of the Nicolaitans.
16Therefore repent, or else I am coming to you quickly and will make war

---

[18]That is, everything I stand for, my whole character, work and Kingdom-Gospel preaching.

[19]The future Kingdom of God on earth at the Second Coming (5:10; Mt. 5:5).

[20]"My faith" means not only faith in Jesus but the same faith which Jesus demonstrated, including all his teachings summed up as the Gospel of the Kingdom of God, the Christian Gospel (Mk. 1:14-15; Lk. 4:43; Acts 19:8; 20:24-25; 28:23, 31).

against those people with the sword of my mouth. 17Let everyone who
has ears listen to what the spirit says to the churches. To the one who
overcomes, I will give some of the hidden manna, and a white stone with
a new name written on it, which no one can understand except the one
who receives it.

18"To the angel of the church in Thyatira, write this: The Son of
God,[21] who has eyes like a flame of fire and feet like polished bronze,
says: 19I know your works — your love, faith, service and perseverance. I
also know that your recent works are greater than the first. 20But I have
this against you: you tolerate that woman Jezebel, who calls herself a
prophetess. With her teaching she deceives my servants to commit
sexual immorality and to eat food sacrificed to idols. 21I gave her time to
repent, but she refuses to repent of her sexual immorality. 22Look! I am
about to throw her on a bed of severe illness, and those who commit
adultery with her into great suffering, unless they repent of her practices.
23And I will kill her followers with plague, and all the churches will
know that I am he who searches minds and hearts. I will repay each of
you according to your works. 24But to the rest of you in Thyatira, who do
not hold this teaching, who have not learned the 'deep things' of Satan,
as they call them, to you I say: I am putting no additional burden on you.
25But hold on to what you have firmly until I come. 26To the one who
overcomes and continues in my works until the end, I will give authority
over the nations.[22] 27He will govern them with a rod of iron, and shatter
them like clay pots, just as I have received the right to rule from my
Father; 28and I will give him the morning star. 29Let everyone who has
ears listen to what the spirit says to the churches."

3 1"To the angel of the church in Sardis write this: The one who has the
seven spirits of God and the seven stars says: I know your works, that

[21]Son of God is defined first of all by Luke 1:35 as the miraculously generated, fathered, Son of God. Jesus was uniquely begotten in Mary (Mt. 1:18, 20) and called Son of God precisely because of (*dio kai*) the supernatural miracle worked in Mary by the operational presence and power of God, His spirit. Luke 1:35 provides an indispensable definition of Son of God. Psalm 2:7 is the OT basis of this, along with 2 Sam. 7:14.

[22]This is the Messianic promise of Ps. 2 granted to Jesus and his followers (see Dan 7:14, 18, 22, 27; 1 Cor. 6:2; Mt. 19:28; 2 Tim. 2:12; Rev. 12:5; 19:15; 5:9-10). This verse is a beautiful and concise summary of the Christian faith of the NT.

you have a reputation for being alive, but you are dead. 2Wake up, and
strengthen what remains that is about to die, because I have not found
your works complete in the sight of my God. 3So remember what you
have received and heard, obey it and repent. If you do not wake up, I will
come like a thief, and you will in no way know when I will come to you.
4But you have a few people in Sardis who have not stained their clothes,
and they will walk with me dressed in white, because they are worthy.
5The one who overcomes will be dressed like them in white, and I will in
no way erase his name from the book of life,[23] but will declare his name
before my Father and His angels. 6Let everyone who has ears listen to
what the spirit says to the churches.

7"To the angel of the church in Philadelphia, write this: The one who
is holy and true, who has the key of David, who opens and no one can
shut, and who shuts and no one can open, says: 8I recognize your works.
Look! I have put in front of you an open door which no one can shut,
because you have a little power, and have obeyed my word and have not
denied my name. 9Look! I will make some of the synagogue of Satan,
who say they are Jews and are not, but are lying — I will make them
come and worship at your feet and recognize that I have loved you.
10Because you have kept my word of perseverance, I will keep you from
the time of testing which is about to come on the whole world,[24] to test
those who live on the earth. 11I am coming quickly. Hold firmly to what
you have, so that no one will take away your crown.[25] 12The one who
overcomes, I will make a pillar in the temple of my God, and he will
never leave it. I will write on him the name of my God, and the name of
the city of my God — the new Jerusalem which will come down out of
heaven from my God — and my new name.[26] 13Let everyone who has
ears listen to what the spirit says to the churches.

---

[23]Showing that there is no such thing as "once saved always saved." Salvation can be lost (Rom. 11:22; Lk. 8:13; Heb. 6:4-8; 10:26ff).

[24]This is certainly not by an imagined pre-tribulation rapture. Jesus will come back once only, after the Great Tribulation. Safety from the time of extreme trouble will be by escaping it on earth.

[25]The authority to rule the world with Jesus when he comes back to the earth.

[26]Jesus speaks of God as "my God" four times in this verse, showing of course that he himself is not God. There is only one Lord God according to the creed of Jesus (Mk. 12:29, cited from Deut. 6:4). Jesus is the man Messiah now seated at the right hand of the One God (Ps. 110:1; Mk. 14:62; Acts 7:55-56). See also the Messianic title "lord

14“To the angel of the church in Laodicea, write this: The Amen, the
faithful and true Gospel-witness,[27] the ruler of God’s creation, says: 15I
recognize your works, that you are neither cold nor hot. I wish you were
cold or hot![28] 16So because you are lukewarm, neither hot nor cold, I am
going to vomit you out of my mouth. 17Because you say, ‘I am rich and
have acquired great wealth, and do not need anything,’ but do not
recognize that you are wretched, miserable, poor, blind and naked, 18I
advise you to buy from me gold refined by fire so that you may become
rich. Buy from me white clothing to put on so that your shameful
nakedness will not be revealed, and buy ointment to put on your eyes so
that you can see. 19All those I love, I correct and discipline. So be zealous
and repent. 20Listen! I am standing at the door and knocking. If anyone
hears my voice and opens the door, I will come to his house to eat with
him, and he with me.[29] 21The one who overcomes, I will give the
privilege of taking his seat with me on my throne, just as I overcame and
took my seat with my Father on His throne. 22Let everyone who has ears
listen to what the spirit says to the churches.”

4 1After this I looked, and saw a door opened in heaven. The first voice
I had heard, like a trumpet, said, “Come up here,[30] and I will show
you what must happen after this.” 2Immediately I was in the spirit, and I

Messiah” (Lk. 2:11) and “lord, son of David” (Matt 15:22; 20:31). The NT presents Jesus as the promised Messiah, descended from David, supernaturally brought into existence by God’s creative power (Lk. 1:35). The Trinity was a post-biblical development under the damaging influence of Greek philosophy. This development caused the creed of Jesus, Christianity’s founder, to be discarded. Mark 12:29 is the basis of all good theology and practice.

[27]Jesus was the original preacher of the saving Gospel (Mk. 1:14-15; Lk. 4:43; Heb. 2:3, etc). This proves the complete falsity of the unfortunate words of C.S. Lewis: “The gospel is not in the Gospels.”

[28]Both hot water and cold water are therapeutically beneficial, but lukewarm water is not.

[29]This text is misused when it is offered to potential converts as an invitation “to ask Jesus into their heart.” Such language is foreign to the very specific language of the NT that converts are to “repent and believe the Gospel about the Kingdom of God” (Acts 8:12; Mk. 1:14-15).

[30]The fanciful idea was advanced by some that this meant a pre-tribulation rapture of the Church, but this text says nothing at all about such an event. There is only one future, visible *Parousia* (arrival) of Jesus.

saw a throne in heaven, and one sitting on the throne. 3He looked like a
jasper stone and sardius, and there was a rainbow around the throne,
looking like an emerald. 4Around the throne there were twenty-four
thrones, and twenty-four elders were seated on those thrones, dressed in
white clothing with golden crowns on their heads.

5Out from the throne came flashes of lightning and roars of thunder.
Seven blazing lamps, which are the seven spirits of God, were burning in
front of the throne, 6and in front of the throne was something like a sea of
glass, like crystal. In the middle and around the throne were four living
creatures covered in eyes, in front and behind. 7The first being looked
like a lion, the second like a calf, the third had a face like a man, and the
fourth looked like an eagle flying. 8Each of the four living creatures had
six wings and was covered with eyes all around and inside. Day and
night they do not rest, saying, "Holy, holy, holy is the Lord God,[31] the
Almighty, who was, who is, and who is to come."[32]

9When the living creatures give glory, honor, and thanks to the One
who is seated on the throne, who lives to the ages of the ages, 10the
twenty-four elders fall down before the One who sits on the throne and
worship the One who lives to the ages of the ages. They offer their
crowns before His throne and say, 11"Worthy are You, our Lord and God,
to receive glory, honor, and power, because You created all things, and
by Your will they existed and were created."[33]

5 1Then I saw a scroll in the right hand of the One seated on the throne,
written on both sides and sealed with seven seals. 2I saw a powerful
angel proclaiming loudly, "Who is worthy to open the scroll and to break
its seals?" 3But nobody in heaven or on earth or under the earth was able
to open the scroll and look into it. 4Then I wept bitterly because no one
was found who was worthy to open the scroll or look into it. 5One of the

---

[31]The *El Shaddai* of the OT, the Almighty. Jesus is never called "the Lord God" or "the Almighty."

[32]This gives us in Greek the meaning of the divine name YHVH, derived from the verb "to be." God is the self-existent one. The actual Hebrew form of God's personal name is not found in the New Covenant scriptures. He appears, following the LXX, as the Lord, i.e. the Lord God.

[33]Perhaps indicating an existence in the plan and mind of God before they came into actual existence.

elders said to me, "Stop weeping. Look, the lion from the tribe of Judah, the descendant of David, has overcome, so he is able to open the scroll and its seven seals."

6I then saw standing in the middle of the throne area, among the four living creatures and the elders, a Lamb looking as if it had been killed. He had seven horns and seven eyes. The seven eyes represent the seven spirits of God sent out to the whole earth. 7He came and took the scroll from the right hand of the One seated on the throne. 8When he had taken the scroll, the four living creatures and the twenty-four elders fell down before the Lamb. Each of them had a harp and golden bowls full of incense, which represent the prayers of the saints. 9They sang a new song with these words: "You are worthy to take the scroll and to open its seals, because you were killed, and with your blood you purchased for God people from every tribe, language, people, and nation. 10You constituted them as a Kingdom and priests to our God, and they will reign as kings on the earth."[34]

11Then I looked and heard the voices of many angels around the throne, the living creatures and the elders. There were thousands and thousands of them 12singing loudly together, "Worthy is the Lamb who was killed to receive power and wealth, wisdom and strength, and honor, glory, and praise!"

13Then I heard every creature in heaven, on earth, under the earth, in the sea, and all that is in them, singing: "To the One seated on the throne and to the Lamb be praise, honor, glory, and ruling power to the ages of the ages!" 14The four living creatures responded, "Amen!" and the elders fell down and worshiped.

6 1I watched as the Lamb opened the first of the seven seals, and I heard one of the four living creatures saying with a voice like thunder, "Come!" 2So I looked and there came a white horse. Its rider carried a bow, and he was given a crown, and as a conqueror he rode out to conquer.

---

[34]These centrally important verses beautifully summarize the Christian faith. The words were applied first to the nation of Israel (Exod. 19:6) and are now applied, as are other OT Israel texts, to the New Covenant international "Israel of God" (Gal. 6:16; Phil. 3:3; contrast the "Israel of the flesh" of 1 Cor. 10:18).

3When the Lamb opened the second seal, I heard the second living being say, "Come!" 4So another horse came out, a fiery red one. Its rider was given permission to remove peace from the earth, so that people would murder one another, and he was given a large sword.

5When the Lamb opened the third seal, I heard the third living being say, "Come!" So I looked, and there came a black horse. Its rider had balance scales in his hand. 6I heard something like a voice coming from among the four living creatures: "A quart of wheat for a day's wages; three quarts of barley also for a day's wages. But do not damage the oil or the wine."

7When the Lamb opened the fourth seal, I heard the fourth living being say, "Come!" 8So I looked and there came a pale horse. Its rider was called Death, and Hades followed close behind. They were given authority over a quarter of the earth, to kill people with the sword, famine, disease, and wild animals of the earth.

9When the Lamb opened the fifth seal, I saw beneath the altar the persons who had been murdered because of the Gospel-word of God[35] and because of their faithful testimony. 10They cried out, "How long, O holy and true Master, before you judge those who live on the earth and avenge our blood?" 11A white robe was given to each of them, and they were told to rest[36] a little longer until the number was complete, both of their fellow servants and of their brothers and sisters who would be killed as they had been.

12I watched as the Lamb opened the sixth seal, and there was a great earthquake. The sun became as black as hairy sackcloth, and the full moon became blood-red. 13The stars of the sky fell to the earth, like a fig tree dropping unripe figs when shaken by a strong wind. 14The sky was split apart like a scroll being rolled up, and every mountain and island was moved out of its place. 15The kings of the earth, the important people, the generals, the rich, the powerful, and everyone, slave or free, hid themselves in the caves and among the rocks in the mountains.

---

[35]The Gospel of the Kingdom as preached always by Jesus and Paul and all the NT believers. Heb. 2:3 points to Jesus as the first preacher of salvation.

[36]They are to rest in the "sleep of death" (Ps. 13:3), and then they will be woken from that unconscious condition to rise in the resurrection at the return of Jesus (Dan. 12:2; 1 Cor. 15:23; 1 Thess. 4:13-18, etc). They are seen as clothed, and so the idea of a disembodied soul is foreign here as to the whole of Scripture.

16They said to the mountains and the rocks, "Fall on us, and hide us from
the face of the One seated on the throne, and from the righteous anger of
the Lamb, 17because the great day of their righteous anger has come, and
who can possibly survive it?"

7 1After this I saw four angels standing at the four corners of the earth,
holding back the four winds of the earth so that no wind would blow
on the earth, on the sea, or on any tree. 2Then I saw another angel rise up
from the east, who had the seal of the living God. He shouted out to the
four angels who had been given permission to damage the earth and the
sea, 3"Do not damage the earth, the sea or the trees until we have put a
seal on the foreheads of the servants of our God."

4I heard the number of those who were sealed: 144,000, sealed from
all the tribes of the children of Israel: 5from the tribe of Judah twelve
thousand were sealed, from the tribe of Reuben twelve thousand, from
the tribe of Gad twelve thousand, 6from the tribe of Asher twelve
thousand, from the tribe of Naphtali twelve thousand, from the tribe of
Manasseh twelve thousand, 7from the tribe of Simeon twelve thousand,
from the tribe of Levi twelve thousand, from the tribe of Issachar twelve
thousand, 8from the tribe of Zebulun twelve thousand, from the tribe of
Joseph twelve thousand, from the tribe of Benjamin twelve thousand
were sealed.

9After that I looked, and there was a huge crowd which nobody could
count, people from every nation, tribe, people and language. They were
standing before the throne and before the Lamb, dressed in white robes,
with palm branches in their hands. 10They cried out, "Salvation belongs
to our God, who is seated on the throne, and to the Lamb!" 11All the
angels stood in a circle around the throne and around the elders and the
four living creatures, and they fell on their faces before the throne and
worshiped God. 12They said, "Amen! Praise and glory, wisdom and
thanksgiving, and honor, power, and strength be to our God to the ages
of the ages. Amen!"

13One of the elders asked me, "Who are these people dressed in white
robes, and where did they come from?" 14I replied, "My lord, you know
the answer." Then he said to me, "These are the ones who have come out

of the Great Tribulation.[37] They have washed their robes and made them
white in the blood of the Lamb. 15That is why they are before the throne
of God, and they worship Him day and night in His temple, and the One
seated on the throne will shelter them. 16They will never be hungry or
thirsty again; the sun will not beat down on them, or any scorching heat,
17because the Lamb in the middle of the throne area will shepherd them
and guide them to springs of life-giving water. And God will wipe away
every tear from their eyes."

8 1When the Lamb opened the seventh seal, there was silence in heaven
for about half an hour. 2I then saw the seven angels who stand before
God, and seven trumpets[38] were given to them.

3Another angel came and stood at the altar, holding a golden censer.
He was given a large quantity of incense to add to the prayers of all the
saints on the golden altar which is before the throne. 4The smoke from
the incense, together with the prayers of the saints, rose before God from
the angel's hand. 5Then the angel took the censer, filled it with fire from
the altar, and threw it on the earth. There followed crashes of thunder,
rumbling, lightning flashes, and an earthquake.

6The seven angels holding the seven trumpets prepared to blow them.

7The first angel blew his trumpet. There followed hail and fire, mixed
with blood, and they were thrown to the earth. One third of the earth was
burned up, one third of the trees were burned up and all the green grass
was burned up.

8The second angel blew his trumpet. Something like a huge mountain
burning with fire was thrown into the sea. One third of the sea became
blood, 9one third of the creatures living in the sea died, and one third of
the ships were completely destroyed.

10The third angel blew his trumpet. A huge star fell from heaven,
blazing like a torch. It fell on one third of the rivers and on the springs of
water. 11The name of the star is "Wormwood." One third of the water

---

[37]It is easiest to understand the group listed as from the tribes of Israel as a picture of Israel coming to faith under the pressure of the Tribulation. The "great crowd" (v. 9) would then be Gentiles from all the other nations.

[38]The series of trumpets culminates in the great, final event of this age, the visible Second Coming of Jesus and the resurrection of the faithful dead of all the ages. This event is detailed in 11:15-18 (cp. 1 Cor. 15:23; 1 Thes. 4:13-17; Lk. 14:14; Dan. 12:3).

became bitter wormwood, and many people died from drinking the water
because it was made poisonous.
12The fourth angel blew his trumpet. One third of the sun was struck,
one third of the moon, and one third of the stars, so that a third of them
were darkened. So there was no light for a third of the day, and for a
third of the night.
13Then I looked, and I heard an eagle flying above, calling out loudly,
"Disaster, disaster, disaster for those who live on the earth, because of
the remaining trumpets which the three angels are about to blow!"

9 1The fifth angel blew his trumpet. I saw a star from heaven that had
fallen to the earth. He was given the key to the pit of the abyss. 2He
opened the abyss, and smoke went out of it like smoke from a huge
furnace. The sun and the air were darkened by the smoke. 3Out of the
smoke came locusts on the earth, and they were given power like that of
scorpions. 4They were told not to hurt the earth's grass or any green plant
or any tree, but only the people who did not have God's seal on their
foreheads. 5They were not given permission to kill anyone, but to torture
them for five months. The torture was like that of a scorpion when it
stings a person. 6During that time people will seek death, but will not be
able to find it; they will want to die, but death will escape them.
7The locusts looked like horses prepared for war. On their heads were
something like golden crowns, and their faces looked like men's faces.
8Their hair was like women's hair, and their teeth were like lions' teeth.
9They had breastplates looking like iron, and the noise made by their
wings sounded like many horses and chariots charging into battle. 10They
have tails and stingers like scorpions, and in their tails is their ability to
hurt people for five months. 11They have as king over them the angel of
the abyss,[39] whose name in Hebrew is Abaddon, and in Greek, Apollyon.
12The first disaster is past, but two disasters are still coming after
these things.[40]
13The sixth angel blew his trumpet. I heard a single voice coming
from the horns of the golden altar which is before God 14saying to the

---

[39]A demonic figure. Some demons are currently loose and under the prince of the power of the air (Eph. 2:2), the sublunar space; others are currently bound in Tartarus (2 Pet. 2:4).

[40]Compare Dan. 2:45: "after these things."

sixth angel who had the trumpet: "Free the four angels who are bound at
the great river Euphrates!" 15The four angels who had been kept ready for
that hour, day, month and year were freed to kill one third of humanity.
16The number of soldiers on horseback was 200 million; I heard their
number. 17This is what the horses and their riders looked like in the
vision: The riders' breastplates were fiery red, dark blue and sulfur
yellow. The horses' heads looked like lions' heads, and fire, smoke and
sulfur came from their mouths. 18One third of humanity was killed by
these three plagues — by the fire, the smoke and the sulfur which came
out of their mouths. 19The power of the horses is in their mouths and in
their tails, because their tails are like snakes with heads which inflict
harm.

20The rest of humanity, who were not killed by these plagues, did not
repent of the works of their hands. They did not stop worshiping
demons,[41] and idols of gold, silver, bronze, stone and wood, which
cannot see, hear or walk. 21And they did not repent of their murders, their
magic arts, their sexual immorality, or their thefts.

10 1Then I saw another powerful angel descending from heaven,
wrapped in a cloud, with a rainbow over his head. His face was
like the sun, and his legs were like pillars of fire. 2He had in his hand a
small scroll that was open. He put his right foot on the sea and his left
foot on the land. 3He shouted like the roaring of a lion, and when he
shouted, the seven thunders sounded. 4When the seven thunders spoke, I
was about to write, but I heard a voice from heaven say, "Seal up what
the seven thunders said, and do not write it down." 5Then the angel
whom I saw standing on the sea and on the land raised his right hand to
heaven, 6and swore by the One who lives to the ages of the ages, who

[41]Demons are supernatural evil personalities responsible for much human suffering. They are also the authors of "doctrines of demons," "seducing spirits." The Satan, or the Devil is their prince and he is allowed an extensive power as the one now "deceiving the world" (Rev. 12:9). That power will cease entirely when the Devil will be imprisoned and bound to the millennial period (Rev. 20:2). The proof that the millennium is in the future is that the Devil cannot be concurrently "deceiving the whole world" and "not deceiving the world any longer" (Rev. 20:2). Amillennialism is a very great deception, since it lures believers into thinking that the Devil is currently bound! And the coming of the spirit at Pentecost "in a few days time" was definitely not the coming of the Kingdom, to be at a time unknown (Acts 1:6-7).

created heaven and everything in it, the earth and everything in it, and the sea and everything in it,[42] "There will be no more delay![43] 7But in the days when the seventh angel is about to blow his trumpet, then the mystery of God's plan will be completed — the Gospel which He announced to His servants the prophets."

8Then the voice I had heard from heaven spoke to me again: "Go and take the open scroll from the hand of the angel standing on the sea and on the land." 9So I went to the angel and asked him to give me the small scroll. He said to me, "Take it and eat it. It will make your stomach bitter, but it will be as sweet as honey in your mouth." 10So I took the small scroll from the angel's hand and ate it. It tasted as sweet as honey in my mouth, but when I had eaten it, my stomach became bitter. 11Then I was told, "You must prophesy again about many peoples, nations, languages, and kings."

11 1Then I was given a measuring rod like a staff, and I was told: "Get up and measure the temple of God,[44] and the altar, and the ones who worship there. 2Do not measure the outer courtyard of the temple. Cast it out,[45] because it has been given[46] to the Gentile nations.

---

[42]One of some 50 clear statements that the Father is the Creator of the heavens and earth, and that He was alone at that creation (Isa. 44:24).

[43]The King James' mistranslation here, "there should be time no longer," helped to obscure the biblical future, making it impossible for readers to understand that there will be a succession of ages of time, beginning with the age of the 1000 years of Messianic rule on earth (20:1-6).

[44]"A rebuilt temple will exist during the time of the tribulation (Dan. 9:27; 12:11; Mt. 24:15; 2 Thess. 2:4)" (*MacArthur Study Bible*, NASU, p. 1976). "This certainly implies that there will be some kind of temple building in Jerusalem at this time" (*New Testament and Wycliffe Bible Commentary*, 1971, p. 1072).

[45]This is an allusion to Dan. 8:11-14 where the sanctuary (8:11) is "thrown down/away." For a description of these final days of this age, read Joel 2:15-3:15. Jesus alluded to all this in Matt. 24, Mark 13 and Luke 21, with the appearance of the Abomination and in Luke 21:24 the surrounding of Jerusalem by hostile nations. The allusion to Dan. 8 shows that that chapter was not fulfilled in BC times. For the peaceful Kingdom of God which will follow the distressing times, read Ps. 72, 89, 102, 93-99. Dan. 8:17, 19 describe the prophecy of this chapter as belonging to "the time of the end."

[46]Probably a divine passive meaning that God has allowed this or decreed it to happen.

They will trample under foot the holy city for forty-two months.[47] 3And I
will give my two witnesses authority to prophesy for a period of 1,260
days,[48] dressed in sackcloth." 4These are the two olive trees and the two
lampstands standing before the Lord of the earth. 5If anyone wants to
injure them, fire comes out of their mouths and completely burns up their
enemies. If anyone wants to harm them, they must be killed in this way.
6These two witnesses have the authority to shut up the sky so that it does
not rain during the period of their prophesying. They also have the power
to turn the waters into blood, and to strike the earth with every kind of
plague, as often as they want.

7When they have finished their Gospel-testimony, the beast[49] who
comes up from the abyss will battle with them, defeat them, and kill

---

[47]The chronological key to Revelation is introduced here by Jesus. 42 months or 3 ½ years is the second half of the final period of 7 years contained in the 70 "weeks of years" prophecy of Dan. 9:24-27. The same final period is found in Dan. 7:25; 12:7; Rev. 12:6, 14; 13:5. Much of Revelation describes that period of time. Prominent is the idea of a final trampling under foot of the holy city, found in Zech. 12:3 in the LXX and cited by Jesus in Luke 21:24, the Olivet discourse: "It will come to pass in that day that I will make Jerusalem a stone trodden by all the nations. Everyone who tramples on it shall utterly mock it. And all the nations of the earth will be gathered against it" (Zech 12:3, LXX). This is reflected in the words of Jesus in Luke 21:20-24: "When you see Jerusalem surrounded by armies, then recognize that her desolation is near...because these are the days of vengeance so that all things which are written will be fulfilled…There will be great distress on the land and wrath to this people, and they will fall by the edge of the sword and will be led captive into all nations, and Jerusalem will be trampled under foot until the times of the Gentiles are fulfilled" (cp. Zech. 13:8-14:2). The final trampling of Jerusalem will be relieved only by the arrival of Jesus to rescue his people. Jesus here alludes to this same period of final affliction and predicts the trampling of Jerusalem by hostile Gentiles (cp. Ps. 79:1; Isa. 63:18; Pss. Solomon 2:2, 19; 17:22).

[48]This period of time is based on the last half of the last period of seven years (the "heptad") of Dan. 9:27 (see Dan. 7:25; 12:7, 11). This period is mentioned several times in Revelation (11:2-3; 12:6, 14; 13:5). It certainly was not fulfilled in NT times. It clearly refers to the final few years of this present evil age (Gal. 1:4), and Paul cites the distinctive phrase "final and decisive end" in Rom. 9:28. This phrase is based on Dan. 9:27 and Isa. 10:22-23 and 28:22. The final and decisive end will occur at the return of Jesus.

[49]The final Antichristian figure, the King of the North of Dan. 11 and the Assyrian of Isaiah, a demonically inspired tool of the Devil, as was Judas. Paul referred to him as the Man of Sin standing in the Temple of God (2 Thess. 2:3-4), and John says, "You have heard that Antichrist is coming" (1 Jn. 2:18). He added that the spirit of antichrist,

them. 8Their dead bodies will lie in the street of the great city that is
symbolically called Sodom and Egypt, where their lord was also
crucified. 9For three and a half days those from among the peoples,
tribes, languages and nations will look at their dead bodies, and will not
allow them to be placed in a tomb. 10And those who live on the earth will
rejoice over them and celebrate, giving gifts to each other, because these
two prophets had tormented those who live on the earth.

11But after three and a half days a breath of life from God entered
them, and they stood on their feet.[50] Tremendous fear fell on those
watching them. 12The two witnesses heard a loud voice from heaven
saying to them, "Come up here!" So they went up to heaven in a cloud
while their enemies watched. 13At that same time there was a huge
earthquake, and a tenth of the city collapsed. Seven thousand people
were killed in the earthquake, and the rest were terrified and gave glory
to the God of heaven.

14The second disaster has passed; the third disaster is coming quickly.

15Then the seventh angel blew his trumpet, and loud voices in heaven
said, "The kingdom of the world has now become the Kingdom of our
Lord[51] and of His Messiah, and he will reign to the ages of the ages."
16The twenty-four elders seated on their thrones before God fell on their
faces and worshipped God, 17saying, "We give You thanks, Lord God,
the Almighty, the One who is and who was, because You have taken
Your great power and begun to reign.[52] 18The nations were angry, but
Your righteous fury has come, and the time has come for the dead to be
judged. The time has come to give to Your servants, the prophets, their

---

promoted by many false teachers, was already at work to deceive. But he certainly did not exclude the well-known single Antichrist of the end-times. Jesus called him "the Abomination of Desolation standing where *he* ought not to" (see Mk. 13:14).

[50]Perhaps a temporary restoration to life in full view of their enemies. The two prophets will of course gain immortality in the first resurrection at the return of Jesus (1 Cor. 15:23).

[51]The beginning of the Kingdom of God as a worldwide government occurs only at the future 7th trumpet. This is because the expected Kingdom will have Jesus as its King ruling from Jerusalem, and the saints of all the ages, resurrected, will take their royal positions with the Messiah in that Kingdom.

[52]This is a key verse for the whole Plan of God. The Kingdom in its primary sense will begin only at the Second Coming of Messiah in glory.

reward,[53] as well as the saints, and those who fear Your name, both small
and great. And the time has come to destroy those who are destroying the
earth."
19 Then the temple of God in heaven was opened, and the ark of His
covenant was seen in His temple. There were flashes of lightning,
rumblings, crashes of thunder, an earthquake, and a huge hailstorm.

12 1 Then a great sign appeared in heaven: a woman clothed with the
sun, and with the moon under her feet, and on her head a crown of
twelve stars. 2 She was pregnant, and she cried out in labor pains as she
was about to give birth.
3 Then another sign appeared in heaven: a huge red dragon with seven
heads and ten horns, and on its heads seven crowns. 4 The dragon's tail
swept away one third of the stars of heaven, and threw them to the earth.
Then the dragon stood before the woman who was about to give birth, so
that when she gave birth he might devour her child.[54]
5 The woman gave birth to a son, a male child, who is destined to rule
all the nations with a rod of iron.[55] Her child was caught up to God and to
His throne.[56] 6 The woman fled into the wilderness, where she has a place
prepared for her by God, so that she would be taken care of there for
1,260 days.[57]

---

[53] They will gain immortality along with the faithful of all the ages. This is the great objective of God's word or plan to grant believers indestructible life, tasted now in the spirit as a downpayment.

[54] This is precisely parallel to Luke 8:11-12 where the Gospel of the Kingdom (Mt. 13:19) is planted as a seed in a person's understanding (cp. Isa. 53:11). Then "the Devil comes and snatches away the word [of the Kingdom] which has been sown in the heart so that **he cannot believe it and be saved**" (cp. Acts 8:12, where belief in the Gospel of the Kingdom is the essential requisite for intelligent faith before baptism in water). The seed-word of the Kingdom (Lk. 8:11) is the non-negotiable core truth of the NT Gospel of salvation. Satan obstructs this life-giving Gospel of the Kingdom and tries to remove it so that no new children of God can be born (again).

[55] Obviously a reference to Ps. 2, where the Messiah's future victory is predicted.

[56] A reference to the ascension of Jesus, after his resurrection.

[57] The second half of the final period of seven years of Dan. 9:24-27, the period of the intense Great Tribulation (Mt. 24:21; Mk. 13:19; Lk. 21:22, all based on Dan. 12:1). The woman represents the "ideal Israel," the true people of God, from whom the Messiah came.

7Then there was war in heaven: Michael and his angels fought the
dragon, and the dragon and his angels fought back. 8But the dragon and
his angels were not strong enough, so there was no longer a place for
them in heaven. 9So the huge dragon — the original serpent, the one
called the Devil and Satan, who is deceiving the whole world[58] — was
thrown down to the earth, and his angels were thrown down with him.[59]
10Then I heard a loud voice in heaven saying, "Now the salvation, the
power, the Kingdom of our God and the ruling authority of His Messiah
have come,[60] because the accuser of our brothers and sisters, the one who
accuses them day and night before our God, has been thrown down. 11But
they overcame him by the blood of the Lamb and by the word of their
testimony. They did not love their lives even when facing death.
12Therefore rejoice, you heavens, and all who live in them. But disaster to
the earth and sea, because the Devil has gone down to you in great anger,
knowing that he has only a short time!"

13When the dragon realized that he had been thrown down to the
earth, he pursued the woman who had given birth to the male child. 14But
two wings of a huge eagle were given to the woman, so that she could fly
into the wilderness to her place, where she would be taken care of for a
time, times, and half a time,[61] away from the presence of the serpent.
15Then the serpent spewed water like a river out of his mouth after the
woman, trying to sweep her away by a flood. 16But the earth helped the
woman by opening its mouth and swallowing up the river which the
dragon had spewed out of his mouth. 17The dragon became enraged with

---

[58]But in the millennium he will no longer be able to deceive the nations (20:3). This proves that the millennium is not in progress now! Amillennialism is false to the Scripture.

[59]The reference is to a final effort of the Devil and his fallen angels. It lies in the future and coincides with the time of the Great Tribulation. See v. 12, "a short time."

[60]This is the phrase used by Luke 2:26 to define who Jesus is, the "Lord's Messiah." Jesus is of course "the lord Messiah" (Lk. 2:11) who was born as the promised seed of David, in Bethlehem.

[61]The same period of time, based on the last half of the final "week" of years of Dan. 9:24-27. It appears as 1260 days or 42 months. It is extended by a further 30 days in Dan. 12:11 and it ends with the resurrection of the dead (Dan. 12:2) which is the climax of Daniel's final vision. It was very commonly agreed, and with excellent reason, among early classical premillennial church fathers that the Antichrist's dominion would last for a period of 3 1/2 years, based on Dan. 7:25; 8:14, 9:27; 12:7, 11-12.

the woman and went off to make war on the rest of her children,[62] those
who keep God's commandments and hold Jesus' Gospel-testimony.

13 1The dragon stood on the sand by the sea. Then I saw a beast
coming up out of the sea, with ten horns and seven heads. On its
horns were ten crowns, and on its heads a blasphemous name. 2The beast
that I saw was like a leopard, and its feet were like a bear's, and its
mouth was like a lion's mouth. The dragon gave the beast his power, his
throne, and great authority to rule. 3One of the beast's heads looked as if
it had been killed, but the fatal wound had been healed. The whole world
was amazed and followed the beast. 4They worshiped the dragon because
he had given his authority to the beast, and they also worshiped the beast
and said, "Who is like the beast? Who is able to make war against him?"
5The beast was given a mouth speaking arrogant words and blasphemies,
and he was given ruling authority for forty-two months.[63] 6So he opened
his mouth in blasphemy against God, to blaspheme His name and His
dwelling place, that is, those who live in heaven.

7He was permitted to make war with the saints, and to overcome
them. Ruling authority over every tribe, people, language, and nation
was given to him. 8All who live on earth will worship him, everyone
whose name has not been written in the book of life belonging to the
Lamb who was killed from the foundation of the world.[64] 9Whoever has
ears, listen! 10If anyone has to go into captivity, into captivity he will go.

---

[62]Some of the faithful are accounted worthy of escaping the time of intense trouble; the rest remain to be persecuted by the Devil. "Because you have preserved the word of my perseverance [my Gospel], I will preserve you from the hour of testing which is about to come upon the whole world, to test those who live on the earth" (3:10). See also "the time of Jacob's trouble" in Jer. 30 and 31.

[63]The final half of the seventieth "seven" of Daniel's 70-week prophecy in Dan. 9:24-27. Revelation is largely an "unpacking" of this final seven-year period at the end of the age.

[64]Typical of many Bible statements in which things future are said to have happened already, since they are fixed in the unchanging Plan of God. John 17:5 is another good example, where the glory Jesus "had" before the world began was a glory in prospect and promise. The same glory was promised in John 17:22, 24 to believers not yet even born when Jesus prayed his final prayer. A fine modern paraphrase, *Listen to Me* by John Woodbridge, correctly translates John 17:22, "I will give them the glory that you have given to me," capturing the proper sense of the past tense. Christians "have" a reward with God which will be bestowed at the resurrection (Mt. 6:1).

If anyone is to be killed by the sword, then by the sword he must be killed. This requires perseverance and the faith of the saints.

11Then I saw another beast coming up from the earth. He had two horns like a lamb, but he spoke like a dragon. 12He exercises all the ruling authority of the first beast on his behalf. He makes the earth and those who live in it worship the first beast, the one whose fatal wound had been healed. 13He performs great signs, even making fire come down out of the sky to the earth in front of people. 14He deceives those who live on the earth by the signs he was permitted to perform on behalf of the beast. He told those who live on the earth to make an image to the beast who was wounded by the sword and yet lived. 15He was empowered to give breath to the image of the beast[65] so that it could speak and could cause all those who would not worship the image of the beast to be killed. 16He also causes everyone, small and great, rich and poor, and free and slave, to receive a mark on their right hands or on their foreheads. 17And no one would be able to buy or sell unless he has that mark, which is the name of the beast or the number of his name. 18This calls for wisdom. Let the one who has insight calculate the number of the beast, as it is a man's number, and his number is 666.

14 1Then I looked, and there was the Lamb standing on Mount Zion, and with him 144,000 who had his name[66] and the name of his Father written on their foreheads. 2I heard a sound from heaven, like the sound of many waters and like the sound of great thunder. The sound I heard was like that of harpists playing their harps, 3and they sang a new song before the throne and before the four living creatures and the elders. No one could learn the song except the 144,000 who had been redeemed from the earth. 4These are the ones who have not defiled themselves with women, for they are virgins. These are the ones who follow the Lamb wherever he goes. They were purchased from among mankind as first fruits to God and to the Lamb. 5In their mouth was found no lie, for they are blameless.

65Reminiscent of "the Abomination of Desolation standing where he ought not to" in "the holy place" (Mk. 13:14; Mt. 24:15).

66Standing for the character and agenda of Messiah, the lamb. Jesus is the "lion of the tribe of Judah" (5:5).

6Then I saw another angel flying overhead, and he had a Gospel
about the age to come[67] to proclaim to those living on earth — to every
nation, tribe, language, and people. 7He said loudly, "Fear God, and give
Him glory, because the hour of His judgment has come. Worship Him
who made heaven and earth, the sea and springs of water!"

8A second angel followed the first, saying, "Fallen, fallen is Babylon
the great! She made all the nations drink the wine of her immoral
passion."[68]

9A third angel followed the other two, saying loudly, "If anyone
worships the beast and his image, and receives the mark on his forehead
or on his hand, 10that person also will drink the wine of God's anger,
which is mixed undiluted in the cup of His wrath, and he will be
tormented with fire and sulfur in the presence of the holy angels and in
the presence of the Lamb. 11The smoke from their torment goes up
forever and ever.[69] They have no rest day and night, those who worship
the beast and his image, and anyone who receives the mark of his name."

12This requires the perseverance of the saints, those who keep the
commandments of God and the faith of Jesus.[70]

13Then I heard a voice from heaven say, "Write: Blessed are the dead
who die in the Lord from now on." "Yes," says the spirit, "so they may
rest from their labor, because their works will follow them."

14Then I looked, and there was a white cloud, and seated on the cloud
was one like a son of man. He had on his head a golden crown, and in his
hand a sharp sickle. 15Then another angel came out of the temple,
shouting to the one seated on the cloud, "Use your sickle and reap,

---

[67]The Christian Gospel of the Kingdom (Mk. 1:14-15; Lk. 4:43; Acts 8:12; 19:8; 20:24-25; 28:23, 31).

[68]Scripturally immorality can be both spiritual and literal. False religion is spiritual fornication.

[69]Lit. "to ages of ages." The image is from Isa. 34:8-10 where Edom will suffer a destruction in the Day of the Lord's vengeance and "its smoke will go up forever. From generation to generation it will be desolate. No one will pass through it forever and ever." The image tells of a permanent desolation of that land, not of permanent torture of people.

[70]"The faith of Jesus" means "the same faith as Jesus had." Christian faith means obeying Jesus' teachings and thus demonstrating not only faith in Jesus but the same faith and belief as modeled by Jesus. This includes the creed of Jesus in Mk. 12:29; Jn. 17:3.

because the time to reap has come, as the harvest of the earth is ripe!"[71] 16So the one seated on the cloud swung his sickle over the earth, and the earth was reaped.

17Then another angel came out of the temple in heaven, and he also had a sharp sickle. 18Another angel came from the altar, the one who has authority over the fire, and he called loudly to the angel who had the sharp sickle, "Use your sharp sickle, and gather the clusters from the vine of the earth, because its grapes are now ripe!" 19So the angel swung his sickle to the earth and gathered the grapes from the vine of the earth, and threw them into the great winepress of the wrath of God. 20Then the winepress was trodden outside the city, and blood came out of the winepress, up to the height of horses' bridles for a distance of 200 miles.

15 1I saw another great and astonishing sign in heaven: seven angels who have the seven last plagues. They are the last because in them God's anger is finished.

2Then I saw something like a sea of glass mixed with fire, and those who had been victorious over the beast, his image and the number of his name. They were standing on the sea of glass, holding harps of God. 3They sang the song of Moses, the servant of God, and the song of the Lamb: "Great and astonishing are Your works, Lord God, the Almighty![72] Just and true are Your ways, King over the nations. 4Who will not fear You, Lord, and praise Your name? For You alone are holy.[73] All the nations will come and worship before You because Your righteous acts have been revealed."

5After this I looked, and the temple of the tabernacle of the testimony in heaven was opened. 6The seven angels who had the seven plagues came out of the temple, dressed in clean, bright linen, and wearing wide golden belts around their chests. 7Then one of the four living creatures

---

[71]"The harvest is the end of the age," Jesus had said in Matt. 13:39 (not the end of the world, or of history, or of time!).

[72]A title exclusively used for the One God, the Father and never for Jesus, who is "a divine hero" in Isa. 9:6, certainly not *El Shaddai*, the *pantokrator*, the Almighty. Jesus stated in John 17:3 that the Father is "the only one who is true God." This is an unarguable unitarian statement. 1300 times in the NT God is said to be the Father. Cp. Mal. 2:10 which encapsulates the biblical definition of God.

[73]One of masses of unitarian descriptions of the God of the Bible, the God of Israel, and the God of Jesus.

gave to the seven angels seven golden bowls full of the anger of God,
who lives to the ages of the ages. 8The temple was filled with smoke
from the glory of God and from His power. So no one was able to enter
the temple until the seven plagues of the seven angels were finished.

16 1Then I heard a loud voice from the temple saying to the seven
angels, "Go and pour out on the earth the seven bowls of God's
anger."

2So the first angel went and poured out his bowl on the earth, and
ugly, painful sores came on the people who had the mark of the beast
and who worshiped his image.

3Then the second angel poured out his bowl into the sea, and it
became blood like that of a dead person, and every living creature in the
sea died.

4Then the third angel poured out his bowl into the rivers and springs
of water, and they became blood. 5I heard the angel of the waters saying,
"You are just, the One who is and who was,[74] O Holy One, because You
have judged these things. 6For they poured out the blood of saints and
prophets, so You have given them blood to drink. They deserve this." 7I
heard the altar respond, "Yes, Lord God, the Almighty, true and just are
Your judgments."

8Then the fourth angel poured out his bowl on the sun, and the sun
was permitted to scorch people with fire. 9So people were scorched with
burning heat, yet they blasphemed the name of God, who has the
authority over these plagues, and they did not repent and give Him glory.

10Then the fifth angel poured out his bowl on the throne of the beast,
and his kingdom became dark. People gnawed their tongues because of
the pain. 11They blasphemed the God of heaven because of their pain and
their sores, but they still did not repent of their works.

12Then the sixth angel poured out his bowl on the great river, the
Euphrates.[75] Its water was dried up, so that the way might be prepared for
the kings from the east.

13Then I saw coming out of the mouth of the dragon, and out of the
mouth of the beast, and out of the mouth of the false prophet, three

---

[74]The meaning of the word YHWH, the God of Israel, based on Exod. 3:14.

[75]Implying that Babylon is the seat of the beast's empire. Cp. the Assyrian of Isaiah and Micah 5.

unclean spirits that looked like frogs. 14For they are spirits of demons,
performing miraculous signs,[76] and they go out to the kings of the whole
earth to gather them together for the battle of the great day of God, the
Almighty. 15("Look! I will come like a thief. Blessed is the one who stays
alert and keeps his clothes, so that he will not walk around naked and
people see his shame.") 16The spirits gathered the kings and their armies
together to the place which is called in Hebrew, "Armageddon."[77]

17Then the seventh angel poured out his bowl into the air, and a loud
voice came out of the temple, from the throne, saying, "It is done!"
18There were flashes of lightning, rumblings, and crashes of thunder, and
there was a massive earthquake. No earthquake like it has occurred since
there were people on earth, so powerful was that earthquake. 19The great
city was split into three parts, and the cities of the nations collapsed. So
Babylon[78] the great was remembered in the sight of God and was given
the cup of the wine of His fierce anger. 20Every island fled away, and the
mountains could not be found. 21Huge hailstones, each one weighing
about 100 pounds, came down out of the sky on people. They
blasphemed God because of the plague of the hail, since this plague was
so terrible.

17 1Then one of the seven angels who had the seven bowls came and
spoke to me. "Come," he said. "I will show you the judgment of
the great prostitute who sits on many waters, 2with whom the kings of the
earth committed sexual immorality, and those who live on earth got

---

[76]It is often naively supposed that any miracle or sign originates with GOD. The main attraction of the beast and the false prophet, his henchman, is their power to perform miracles. Jesus warned against this in Matt. 7:21ff. Truth and love of the truth are the only criterion for recognizing "the spirit of the truth," which is closely linked to the words of Jesus (Jn. 6:63). Cp. Zech 7:12, which is a most valuable testimony. Isa. 53:11 instructs us that the Messiah's *knowledge* makes people right, not just his death and resurrection.

[77]Mount of Megiddo, in the northern part of Israel. Others think it is at Sinai where the saints will be gathered before marching to Jerusalem to confront the armies of the Antichrist (cp. "When the saints go marching in...").

[78]A revived Babylon could turn out to be the center of the antichristian power (see Zech. 5, Mic. 5 and the many references to an end-time Assyrian, from the land of Nimrod in Isa. See also my article "The Assyrian in Messianic Prophecy" at www.restorationfellowship.org).

drunk on the wine of her sexual immorality." 3So he carried me away in the spirit to a wilderness. There I saw a woman sitting on a scarlet-colored beast[79] which was full of blasphemous names and had seven heads and ten horns. 4The woman was dressed in purple and scarlet clothing and adorned with gold, precious stones and pearls. She had in her hand a golden cup full of abominable things and the unclean things of her sexual immorality. 5On her forehead was written a name, a mystery: "Babylon the Great, the mother of prostitutes[80] and of the abominations of the earth." 6I saw that the woman was drunk on the blood of the saints, and on the blood of the witnesses of Jesus.[81] When I saw her, I was greatly astonished. 7The angel said to me, "Why are you astonished? I will explain to you the mystery of the woman and of the beast that carries her, which has the seven heads and the ten horns.

8"The beast you saw was, and is not, and is about to come up out of the abyss and go to destruction. Those who live on the earth whose names have not been written in the book of life from the foundation of the world, will be astonished when they see that the beast was, and is not, and will come.[82] 9This requires a mind which has wisdom. The seven heads are seven mountains on which the woman sits, 10and they are also seven kings. Five have fallen, one is, and the other has not yet come, and when he comes, he must remain for a short time. 11The beast who was, and is not, is himself an eighth king and yet is one of the seven, and he is

---

[79]The woman, a prostitute because of her false religion, represents the final form of ecclesiastical evil. The beast is the final political ruler with whom the prostitute cooperates, until finally the beast destroys her. That spirit of false religion and of church-state alliance has been a feature of traditional Christianity for centuries. The kingdoms of this world-system cannot represent true faith until Jesus intervenes as described by the "anchor" text in 11:15-18.

[80]There is strong evidence of an original reading of "male prostitutes" (see *Word Biblical Commentary*, Vol. 52C, p. 909).

[81]This is firstly Jesus' faithful Gospel of the Kingdom preaching. His death and resurrection are of course essential elements of the Christian Gospel, but never to the exclusion of the Gospel about the Kingdom which Jesus preached (Lk. 4:43; Heb. 2:3; 2 Jn. 7-9; 1 Tim. 6:3; Jn. 3:36; 5:24; cp. Isa. 53:11; Dan. 12:3).

[82]Is this a reference to a pseudo-Parousia or coming? The verb is related to the noun *Parousia*.

going to destruction. 12The ten horns which you saw are ten kings[83] who
have not yet received a kingdom, but they will receive authority to reign
as kings with the beast for one hour. 13These kings are of one mind, and
they give their power and authority to the beast. 14They will make war
against the Lamb, but the Lamb will overcome them, because he is lord
of lords and king of kings, and those who are with him are the called,
chosen, and faithful."

15Then the angel said to me, "The waters which you saw, where the
prostitute sits, are peoples, multitudes, nations, and languages. 16The ten
horns which you saw, they and the beast will hate the prostitute and will
make her desolate and naked. They will consume her flesh and burn her
up with fire. 17For God has put in their minds to do what He has in mind,
to be of one mind,[84] and to give their kingdom to the beast, until the
words of God will be fulfilled. 18And the woman you saw is the great
city, which reigns over the kings of the earth."

18 1After this I saw another angel coming down out of heaven. He
had great authority, and the earth was lit up by his glory. 2He
shouted with a powerful voice, "Fallen, fallen is Babylon the great! She
has become a residence of demons,[85] a haunt for every unclean spirit, and
a haunt for every unclean and hated bird. 3For all the nations have drunk
the wine of her immoral passion, and the kings of the earth have
committed sexual immorality with her, and the merchants of the earth
have become rich from the power of her sensuality."[86]

4Then I heard another voice from heaven saying, "Come out of her,
My people, so that you will not take part in her sins and receive her

---

[83]Very probably the 10 nations listed in Ps. 83, headed by Assyria, who features prominently in the end-time vision of Isaiah and Micah 5. They are contemporary and together fight Jesus at his coming.

[84]Cp. Ps. 83:5: "one mind and covenant."

[85]"Demons" is a synonym for "unclean spirits."

[86]Suggesting a final, very powerful commercial center in Babylon. Jeremiah 50 and 51 are extensively quoted in Rev. 18 and seem to point to the rise and final demise of such a system. Babylon in BC times was never destroyed in the manner predicted by OT prophecy. People live in Babylon to this day. All this suggests a revival of Babylon as a commercial center (Zech. 5). The Antichrist has various titles: King of the North, the Beast, the Assyrian. Assyria may include different areas including Persia (Iran) (Ezra 6:22).

plagues, 5because her sins have piled up as high as heaven, and God has remembered her sins. 6Repay to her just as she paid others, and repay her double for everything she did. In the cup which she mixed, mix double for her. 7To the degree that she glorified herself and lived sensuously, give her the same degree of torment and mourning, because she said to herself, ‘I reign as a queen, and am no widow; I will never mourn!’ 8That is why her plagues will come in a single day: disease, mourning, and famine, and she will be burned up with fire, because the Lord God who judges her is mighty.”

9Then the kings of the earth who committed immoral acts and lived sensuously with her will weep and wail over her, when they see the smoke of the fire that burns her up. 10They will stand far away because they are afraid of her torturous end.[87] They will say, “Alas, alas, O great city, Babylon, the mighty city! For in one hour your judgment has come!”

11Then the merchants of the earth[88] will weep and mourn over her, because nobody buys their cargo any more: 12merchandise of gold, silver, precious stones, pearls, fine linen, purple cloth, silk, scarlet fabric; all kinds of things made of citron wood, all kinds of items made of ivory, all kinds of items made of expensive wood, bronze, iron, and marble, 13cinnamon, spice, incense, myrrh, frankincense, wine, olive oil, fine flour, wheat, cattle and sheep, horses and wagons, slaves and human persons. 14The fruit you desired has gone from you; all your luxurious and splendid things have gone from you, and you will never find them again! 15The merchants who sold these things, who were made rich by her, will stand far away because they are afraid of her torturous end. They will weep and mourn, 16saying, “Alas, alas, the great city, she who was dressed in fine linen, purple and scarlet clothing, and adorned with gold, precious stones and pearls! 17For in one hour such great wealth has been destroyed.” And every ship captain, passenger and sailor, and all who make their living from the sea stood far away. 18As they saw the smoke of the fire that burned her up, they shouted, “What is like the

---

[87]This seems to be the sense of the word “torment” used of the sudden final, torturous destruction of Babylon and also of the Devil in 20:10. Babylon’s torment will happen in one day on which she is suddenly and finally destroyed.

[88]Suggesting a huge and evil commercial venture at the end of the age, before Jesus arrives.

great city?" 19And they threw dust on their heads, and were crying out
with weeping and mourning, "Alas, alas, the great city, in which all who
had their ships on the sea became rich from her wealth! For in one hour
she has been destroyed!"

20Rejoice over her, O heaven, and you saints, apostles and prophets,
because God has pronounced judgment against her for you.

21Then a mighty angel picked up a stone like a huge millstone, threw
it into the sea, and said, "In this way with violence Babylon, the great
city, will be thrown down, and will not be found any more![89] 22The sound
of harpists, musicians, flute players and trumpeters will never be heard in
you any more. No craftsmen of any trade will be found in you any more.
The sound of a mill will not be heard in you any more. 23The light of a
lamp will not shine in you any more. The voices of the bridegroom and
bride will not be heard in you any more. For your merchants were the
important people of the earth, because by your sorcery all the nations
were deceived. 24In her was found the blood of prophets and of saints,
and of all who have been killed on the earth."

19 1After these things[90] I heard what sounded like the loud voice of a
great multitude in heaven, saying, "Hallelujah! Salvation, glory
and power belong to our God, 2because His judgments are true and just.
For He has judged the great prostitute, who corrupted the earth with her
sexual immorality, and He has avenged the blood of His servants at her
hand." 3A second time they shouted, "Hallelujah! Her smoke goes up to
the ages of the ages." 4The twenty-four elders and the four living
creatures fell down and worshipped God who is seated on the throne,
saying, "Amen! Hallelujah!"

5Then a voice came from the throne, saying, "Give praise to our God,
all you His servants, you who fear Him, the small and the great." 6Then I
heard what sounded like the voice of a great multitude, like the roar of
many waters and like loud crashes of thunder. They shouted,
"Hallelujah! For the Lord our God, the Almighty, has begun to reign![91]

---

[89]A reference to the fulfillment of the lengthy prophecy of Babylon in Jer. 50, 51.
[90]The same expression appears in Dan. 2:45.
[91]This is the moment for which believers are to pray "Your Kingdom come." The Kingdom of God, the center of the saving Gospel, is firstly and primarily the new world government which Jesus will supervise with the saints of all the ages on the earth, at his

7Let us rejoice and be glad and give Him glory, because the wedding of
the Lamb has come, and his bride has made herself ready."[92] 8She was
permitted to dress in bright, clean, fine linen, as the fine linen represents
the righteous acts of the saints.

9Then the angel said to me, "Write: Blessed are those who are invited
to the wedding banquet of the Lamb!" He said to me, "These are the true
words of God." 10So I fell at his feet to worship him, but he said to me,
"Do not do this! I am a fellow servant with you and your brothers and
sisters who hold Jesus' Gospel-testimony. Worship God, for Jesus'
Gospel-testimony is the spirit of prophecy."[93]

11Then I saw heaven opened, and there was a white horse. The one
riding it is called Faithful and True, and in justice he judges and makes
war. 12His eyes are like a flame of fire, and on his head are many crowns.
He has a name written which no one knows but he himself. 13He is
dressed in clothing dipped in blood, and his name is "The Word of
God."[94] 14The armies which are in heaven, clothed in white, clean, fine
linen, were following him on white horses. 15Out of his mouth proceeds a

---

Second Coming (*Parousia*). The life of that Kingdom can be experienced in the present in spirit, provided we repent and believe in God, the Messiah and their Gospel of the Kingdom. The spirit is given to us as a foretaste and downpayment of future immortality.

[92]Cp. 2 Cor. 11:1-3 where Paul is distressed that like the deception of Eve by the Satan in the garden, the virgin church might be seduced by false, counterfeit versions of the Gospel and Jesus. This would repeat the disaster in Eden.

[93]The Gospel of the Kingdom itself is a grand prophecy of God's intention to produce peace on earth worldwide when the Messiah returns to rule from Jerusalem (see Dan. 2:44; 7:14, 18, 22, 27, etc). Believing the Gospel as Jesus preached it brings the true spirit of God and Jesus.

[94]Jesus as Son of God is what the word/wisdom of God became. The word is the NT synonym for the Gospel of the Kingdom. Jesus is the preacher of that Gospel and is therefore God's word. He is uniquely expressive of his Father, God. On no account is he himself actually God (which would make two Gods). But Jesus is and was fully expressive of God, his Father, such that "If you have seen the Son you have seen the Father" (Jn. 14:9). Jesus reflects the word and character of his Father, as the perfect, sinless Son who always carried out the Father's will. Thomas finally came to this full understanding when he greeted Jesus as "my lord [Messiah] and my God" (Jn. 20:28), i.e. I now see what I did not earlier understand, that if I have seen the Son I have seen the Father, God in Christ.

sharp sword, so that with it he can strike[95] the nations. He will rule them
with an iron rod.[96] He treads the wine press of the fierce anger of God,
the Almighty. 16He has on his clothing and on his thigh a name written:
"King of kings and lord of lords."

17Then I saw an angel standing in the sun, and he shouted to all the
birds flying high in the sky, "Come! Gather together for the great
banquet of God, 18to eat the flesh of kings, the flesh of commanders, the
flesh of powerful people, the flesh of horses and those who ride them,
and the flesh of all people, both free and slave, small and great." 19Then I
saw the beast and the kings of the earth and their armies gathered
together to make war against him who rode on the horse, and against his
army.

20And the beast was seized, and with him the false prophet who had
performed the signs on his behalf, with which he deceived those who had
received the mark of the beast and those who worshiped his image.
These two were thrown alive into the lake of fire burning with sulfur.
21The rest were killed with the sword coming out of the mouth of the one
who rode the horse, and all the birds gorged themselves with their flesh.

20 1Then I saw an angel coming down out of heaven, holding in his
hand the key of the abyss and a huge chain. 2He seized the Dragon
— the original Serpent,[97] who is the Devil and Satan — and bound him
for a thousand years. 3The angel threw him into the abyss, shut it, and

---

[95]Including the supernatural destruction of the Antichrist, defined by Paul as the Assyrian, citing Isa. 11:4 in 2 Thess. 2:8.

[96]Quoting the all-important Messianic Ps. 2 which also defines the Son as one who was begotten not in eternity but in time, "today," fulfilled in Luke 1:35; Matt. 1:18, 20; 1 John 5:18; Isa. 9:6 where the promised Son is begotten (by God).

[97]"Serpent" is the vivid "code word" for the Satan/Devil who tempted the first human pair. This was certainly no "non-responsible" animal as wrongly taught by Christadelphianism. The original murderous lie came from this "serpent" (compare for a similar code name "that fox" Herod, Lk. 13:32), and he was fully responsible for the lie and punished for it by God. Satan thus fell into condemnation (1 Tim. 3:6). If the serpent was not responsible, the awful blasphemy would be implied that God was the author of the lie! John Thomas wrote that the serpent "was incapable of moral intention. It did not intend to deceive; but it did deceive; therefore it was a deceiver. It did not intend to lie; but it did lie; and therefore it was a liar and the father of a lie…It became the spiritual father of all intentional liars, deceivers, unbelievers and man-killers, who are styled 'the serpent's seed'" (*Elpis Israel*, p. 90).

sealed it, so that he could not deceive the nations any longer,[98] until the thousand years were finished. After that he must be freed for a short time.

4Then I saw thrones, and seated on them were those who had been given authority to rule. And I saw those persons who had been beheaded because of the testimony of Jesus and because of the Gospel-word of God.[99] They had not worshiped the beast or his image, and had not received the mark on their forehead or hand. They came to life and began to reign as kings with the Messiah for a thousand years.[100] 5The rest of the dead did not come to life until the thousand years were finished. This is the first resurrection.[101] 6Blessed and holy is the one who has a part in the

---

[98]In 12:9 the Devil is deceiving the entire world. Here his deceptive activity is brought to a complete end. This demonstrates clearly that the millennium is a *future* period of time to begin when Jesus comes back. It is the first stage of the future Kingdom of God on earth.

[99]This by no means teaches that only martyrs can be in the first resurrection. Such an idea would contradict the whole NT. John was not martyred and would be excluded! John singles out certain distinguished ones among all those appointed to reign with Messiah, which is the goal of the Christian life.

[100]It is a considerable nonsense to try to read this "coming to life" as other than a real resurrection from death to life. The ones who "come to life" and "begin to reign" (ingressive aorist) with Messiah for 1000 years are those who had been beheaded! This is not conversion or "spiritual" resurrection! "Come to life" in both v. 4 and 5 is a literal resurrection from literal death. There is an exact grammatical parallel with John 11:44: "the one who had died came out" (cp. the same word to describe the resurrection of Jesus in 2:8: "came to life"). All the promises in the NT of governorship as the reward of the saints are in the future. Saints are expressly *not* ruling now. To imagine otherwise is strongly condemned by Paul in 1 Cor. 4:8.

[101]This resurrection includes unarguably a resurrection of decapitated people, i.e. a literal, physical resurrection. The rest of the dead are to be resurrected only at the end of the 1000 years. The amazing nonsense which was made of this passage by Augustine involved the attempt to place the first resurrection in the first century AD. The Church was then said to be already ruling, and conversion marked a first "resurrection." *Peake's Bible Dictionary* on Augustine's fatal mishandling of the words of Rev. 20 needs to be made public everywhere: "Since the age of Augustine, however, an effort has been made to allegorize the statements of Revelation and apply them to the history of the Church. The binding of Satan refers to the binding of the strong man by the stronger, foretold by Christ. The thousand years is not to be construed literally, but represents the whole history of the Church from the Incarnation to the final conflict [the amazing theory known as amillennialism]. The reign of the saints is a prophecy of the domination of the world by the Church. The first resurrection is metaphorical, and

first resurrection. Over them the second death has no power, but they
will be priests of God and of the Messiah, and they will reign with him
for one thousand years.[102]

7When the thousand years are finished, Satan will be released from
his prison, 8and will go out to deceive the nations at the four corners of
the earth, Gog and Magog, to gather them together for the battle. In
number they are like the grains of sand of the sea. 9They went up on the
broad plain of the earth, and surrounded the camp of the saints[103] and the
beloved city. But fire came down from heaven and completely devoured
them. 10And the Devil who deceived them was thrown into the lake of
fire and sulfur, where the beast and the false prophet had been thrown
earlier.[104] They will suffer an anguished destruction lasting day and night
to the ages of the ages.[105]

11Then I saw a large white throne and the One who was seated on it,
from whose presence the earth and sky fled away, and no place was
found for them.[106] 12And I saw the dead, the great and the small, standing
before the throne. Then books were opened, and another book was
opened, which is the book of life. So the dead were judged by what was
written in the books, according to their works. 13The sea gave up the dead

---

simply refers to the spiritual resurrection of the believer in Christ. But exegesis of this kind is dishonest trifling...To put such an interpretation on the phrase 'first resurrection' is simply playing with terms. If we explain away the obvious meaning of the words, then, as Alford says, 'There is an end of all significance in language, and Scripture is wiped out as a definite testimony to anything.'" *Peake's Bible Dictionary* goes on to dismiss the whole millennial teaching as a Jewish and alien concept foisted on Christianity! So much for the teaching of Jesus! The strong warnings of Jesus in 22:18-19 should be taken with the utmost seriousness.

[102]Fulfilling the Kingdom program as described in Dan. 2:44; 7:14, 18, 22, 27; 1 Cor. 6:2; 2 Tim. 2:12; Rev. 5:9-10; 2:26; 3:21 and note especially the amazing prophecy of Jesus in Matt. 19:28. Cp. the parable of the nobleman in Luke 19:11ff.

[103]Showing that the saved believers are on the earth, having inherited it as Jesus promised (Mt. 5:5; Ps. 37:9, 11, 18, 22, 29).

[104]At the arrival of Jesus in 19:20, his *Parousia.*

[105]I take the word "torment" here to mean a sudden, disastrous destruction which is irreversible. In 18:7-8 Babylon is tormented but this is described as destruction "in one day," and being consumed by fire. Holy angels have immortality (Lk. 20:36), but evil, sinning angels (2 Pet. 2:4; Jude 6) can have their life removed at any point God chooses. Cp. the destruction from which there is no recovery in Ps. 92:7; Job 20:7.

[106]Suggesting a new system.

in it, and death and Hades gave up the dead in them, and each person
was judged according to his works. 14Then death and Hades were thrown
into the lake of fire. The lake of fire is the second death. 15If anyone was
not found in the book of life, that person was thrown into the lake of
fire.[107]

21 1Then I saw a new heaven and a new earth,[108] for the first heaven
and the first earth have disappeared, and the sea existed no more.
2I saw the holy city, new Jerusalem, coming down out of heaven from
God, prepared like a bride dressed for her husband. 3And I heard a loud
voice from the throne saying, "Look! God's residence is now among
human beings. He will live with them, and they will be His people, and
God Himself will be with them. 4He will wipe away every tear from their
eyes. Death will not exist any more, or mourning, or crying, or pain,
because the first things have disappeared."[109]

---

[107] There is no reprieve or recovery or resurrection from the second death, which is final extinction, annihilation. In the second resurrection, not everyone is destroyed. This implies a first opportunity of salvation for some persons rising in the second resurrection. Rom. 2:14-16 speaks of "Gentiles who did not have the law doing some of the things of the law by nature," or instinct, operating under the constraints of their conscience. Since God wants "all people to be saved and come to the knowledge of the truth" (1 Tim. 2:4), it follows that those living before the time of Christ who had no opportunity of obeying Jesus will have this at some time in the future. In John 15:22, 24; 16:9 Jesus implied that judgment is on a "sliding scale" and responsibility is based on what could reasonably be known. The final revelation through Jesus, which we now have, and with modern technology and the availability of Bibles on a scale hitherto unheard of, renders the whole human race more responsible for heeding the words of Jesus.

[108] This is a further renewal, since a new heaven and earth appeared after the flood (2 Pet. 3:6-7) and will occur at the second coming of Jesus to establish the millennial Kingdom (2 Pet. 3:10-13). The millennial scene in Isa. 65:17ff describes a new system, a new society on earth, a "new heaven and earth," not a new universe. At that time peace will prevail on earth (Isa. 65:25), but some will be considered cursed if they die at the age of a hundred (Isa. 65:20). Isa. 51:16 and Ps. 102 (LXX) show that God has appointed Jesus as the executive of the new system where the Messiah will "establish the heavens and found the earth, and say to Zion, 'You are my people,'" a situation certainly not true of today.

[109] This is an appropriate use of the verb "pass away." Its popular use to describe "dying" is misleading by Bible standards since when people come to the end of their lives they die or sleep the sleep of death, or "sleep with their fathers." Resurrection at

5And the One seated on the throne said, "Look! I am making
everything new." Then He said, "Write this down, because these words
are faithful and true." 6He also said to me, "It is done! I am the Alpha
and the Omega, the beginning and the end. I will give freely to anyone
who is thirsty from the spring of the water of life. 7The one who
overcomes will inherit these things, and I will be his God, and he will be
My son. 8But the cowards, unbelievers, abominable, murderers, sexually
immoral, sorcerers, idolaters and all liars, their part will be in the lake
that burns with fire and sulfur, which is the second death."

9Then one of the seven angels who had the seven bowls full of the
seven last plagues came and said to me, "Come, I will show you the
bride, the Lamb's wife." 10So he carried me away in the spirit to a great
and high mountain, and showed me the holy city, Jerusalem, coming
down out of heaven from God. 11The city had the glory of God. Its
brightness was like a precious jewel, like a crystal-clear jasper stone. 12It
had a huge, high wall with twelve gates, and at the gates twelve angels,
and the names of the twelve tribes of Israel were written on the gates.
13On the east were three gates, and on the north three gates, and on the
south three gates, and on the west three gates. 14The wall of the city had
twelve foundations, and on them were the twelve names of the twelve
Apostles of the Lamb.

15The angel who spoke to me had a golden measuring rod to measure
the city, its gates, and its wall. 16The city is square; its length is the same
as its width. He measured the city with the rod: 1400 miles. Its length,
width, and height are equal. 17He also measured its wall: 144 cubits or
about 200 feet, according to human measurements, which are also
angelic. 18The wall was jasper, and the city was pure gold, like clear
glass. 19The foundations of the city's wall were decorated with every
kind of precious stone. The first foundation was jasper, the second
sapphire, the third chalcedony, the fourth emerald, 20the fifth sardonyx,
the sixth carnelian, the seventh chrysolite, the eighth beryl, the ninth
topaz, the tenth chrysoprase, the eleventh jacinth, and the twelfth

---

the return of Jesus to reign in his Kingdom is the only biblical way out of death. The idea of a surviving immortal soul is disastrous for a clear understanding of Scripture, since if man is immortal then part of him must continue to live. If man is immortal then the whole point of the Bible is derailed since it is the epic story of how mortal man, including Jesus, the Son of Man, may attain immortality by resurrection from death.

amethyst. 21The twelve gates were twelve pearls. Each one of the gates was made from one pearl. The main street of the city was pure gold, like transparent glass.

22I saw no temple in the city because the Lord God — the Almighty — and the Lamb are its temple. 23The city does not need the sun or moon to shine on it because the glory of God lights it, and its lamp is the Lamb. 24The nations[110] will walk by its light, and the kings of the earth will bring their glory into it. 25Its gates will never be shut during the day, and there will be no night there. 26They will bring the glory and the wealth of the nations into it, 27but nothing impure will enter it, nor anyone who practices abominable things or lying, but only those who are written in the Lamb's book of life.

22 1Then the angel showed me the river of the water of life, as clear as crystal, coming from the throne of God and of the Lamb, 2and flowing in the center of the city's main street. On each side of the river was the tree of life, producing twelve crops of fruit, yielding its fruit every month. The leaves of the tree were for the healing of the nations.[111] 3There will be no longer be any curse. The throne of God and of the Lamb will be in the city, and His servants will serve Him. 4They will see His face, and His name will be on their foreheads. 5There will be no night, and they will not need lamplight or sunlight, because the Lord God will illuminate them. They will reign as kings to the ages of the ages.[112]

6Then the angel said to me, "These words are faithful and true. The Lord, the God of the spirits of the prophets, sent His angel to show to His servants the things which must happen soon."

---

[110]Some manuscripts speak here of "the nations being saved." The process of restoration is ongoing.

[111]There is evidently still a process of healing and restoration even at this time period. The book of Revelation closes the curtain, with a restorative process still ongoing. Healing leaves are not needed for those who have been made immortal. Some are still in process of gaining immortality. There are still nations in this time period, as there were in the earlier millennial period (see Isa. 19:23-25 for Israel, Egypt and Assyria as converted nations).

[112]The promise of rulership with Jesus in 5:9-10; 2:26; 3:21; Dan. 9:27 continues forever and ever as a permanent appointment to royal office, which is the heart of the New Covenant: kingship being covenanted to King Messiah Jesus and this is shared with his followers (see Lk. 22:28-30, where "grant" is "covenant").

7"Look! I am coming soon. Blessed is the one who keeps the words
of the prophecy of this book."

8I, John, am the one who heard and saw these things. When I heard
and saw, I fell down to worship before the feet of the angel who showed
me these things. 9But he said to me, "Do not do this! I am a fellow
servant with you and with your brothers the prophets, and with those
who obey the words of this book. Worship God."

10Then he said to me, "Do not seal up the words of the prophecy in
this book, because the time is near. 11The one who does evil, let him do
evil still. The one who is morally filthy, let him be filthy still. The one
who is upright, let him do right still. The one who is holy, let him be
holy still."[113]

12"Look! I am coming soon, and my reward is with me, to pay each
person according to what he has done. 13I am the Alpha and the
Omega,[114] the first and the last, the beginning and the end."

14Blessed are those who wash their robes so that they may have the
right to the tree of life, and may enter the city by the gates. 15Excluded
are the dogs, sorcerers, sexually immoral, murderers, idolaters, and
everyone who loves and practices lying.

16"I, Jesus, have sent my angel to testify these things to you for the
churches. I am the shoot[115] and the offspring of David, the bright
morning star."

17The spirit and the bride say, "Come!" And let the one who hears
say, "Come!" Let the one who is thirsty come. Let the one who wants
it[116] take the water of life free of charge.

---

[113]There is no fatalism here. The sense is echoed by Dan. 12:10: "The wicked will act wickedly, and none of the wicked will understand." The opportunity for repentance and true faith is always open.

[114]Jesus is the Alpha and Omega (=the first and the last) *who died* (1:17-18). God cannot die. A title shared with God does not make Jesus God.

[115]The Hebrew idea of "root" of David may be misleading in English. Root and shoot are used with the same meaning and point to David, the ancestor of the Messiah. Isa. 53:2 speaks of a shoot and a root coming *up* out of the ground (see the standard commentaries).

[116]The NT concludes with a plainly anti-Calvinist text! Each human person who desires or is willing to come, let him come. The choice is ours. We are not robots, but responsible for our relationship with God. Human choice is clear from John 7:17: "If

18 I testify to everyone who hears the words of the prophecy in this
book: If anyone adds to them, God will add to him the plagues described
in this book.[117] 19 And if anyone takes away[118] from the words of this book
of prophecy, God will take away that person's share in the tree of life
and in the holy city, which are described in this book.

20 The one who testifies to these things says, "Yes, I am coming
soon." Amen! Come, lord Jesus.

21 The grace of the lord Jesus be with all. Amen.

---

anyone will do his will, he will know whether the teaching is from God, or whether I speak from myself."

[117]Jesus spoke of the canon of Hebrew Scripture in Luke 24:44 and said of Scripture that "it cannot be broken" (Jn. 10:35).

[118]It is possible to take away words by twisting their meaning so badly that the prophecy is defaced and altered. The value and energizing power of Scripture is then eliminated.